KaMiKaZe 3

士貴智志
SHIKI SATOSHI

Kami-Kaze Vol. 3
Created by Satoshi Shiki

Translation - Ray Yoshimoto
English Adaptation - Luis Reyes
Copy Editor - Sarah Morgan
Retouch and Lettering - Hugo Bordes
Production Artist - Mike Estacio
Cover Design - James Lee

Editor - Tim Beedle
Digital Imaging Manager - Chris Buford
Pre-Production Supervisor - Erika Terriquez
Art Director - Anne Marie Horne
Production Manager - Elisabeth Brizzi
Managing Editor - Vy Nguyen
VP of Production - Ron Klamert
Editor-in-Chief - Rob Tokar
Publisher - Mike Kiley
President and C.O.O. - John Parker
C.E.O. and Chief Creative Officer - Stuart Levy

A 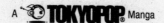 Manga

TOKYOPOP Inc.
5900 Wilshire Blvd. Suite 2000
Los Angeles, CA 90036

E-mail: info@TOKYOPOP.com
Come visit us online at www.TOKYOPOP.com

ISBN: 1-59532-926-9

First TOKYOPOP printing: October 2006
10 9 8 7 6 5 4 3 2 1
Printed in the USA

KAMI·KAZE™

Volume 3

By Satoshi Shiki

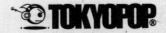

HAMBURG // LONDON // LOS ANGELES // TOKYO

Story so far

KAMI·KAZE™

Imprisoned for a thousand years, the Eighty-Eight beasts seek resurrection from their world so that they can unleash their wrath upon present-day Japan. And a band of young warriors would love nothing more than to let loose these beasts so that they can feast upon the human world. Mikogami Misao, a high school student with no awareness of her past or importance to the world, is the Girl of Mizu (or Water). Misao, like the warriors who seek her, is part of an ancient collective of super-powered humans called the Matsurowanu Kegai no Tami—a group made up of five separate warriors representing the five elements. It is their blood that is necessary to free the Eighty-Eight beasts from their captivity. Three of the Matsurowanu Kegai no Tami seek to aid the beasts, while one stands alongside Misao in hope of preventing their return: the Man of Hani (Earth), Ishigami Kamuro. Unfortunately, both have been overcome and now are prisoners of their enemies. And even worse, Kamuro's blood has been spilled, setting in motion events that may lead our world to Armageddon.

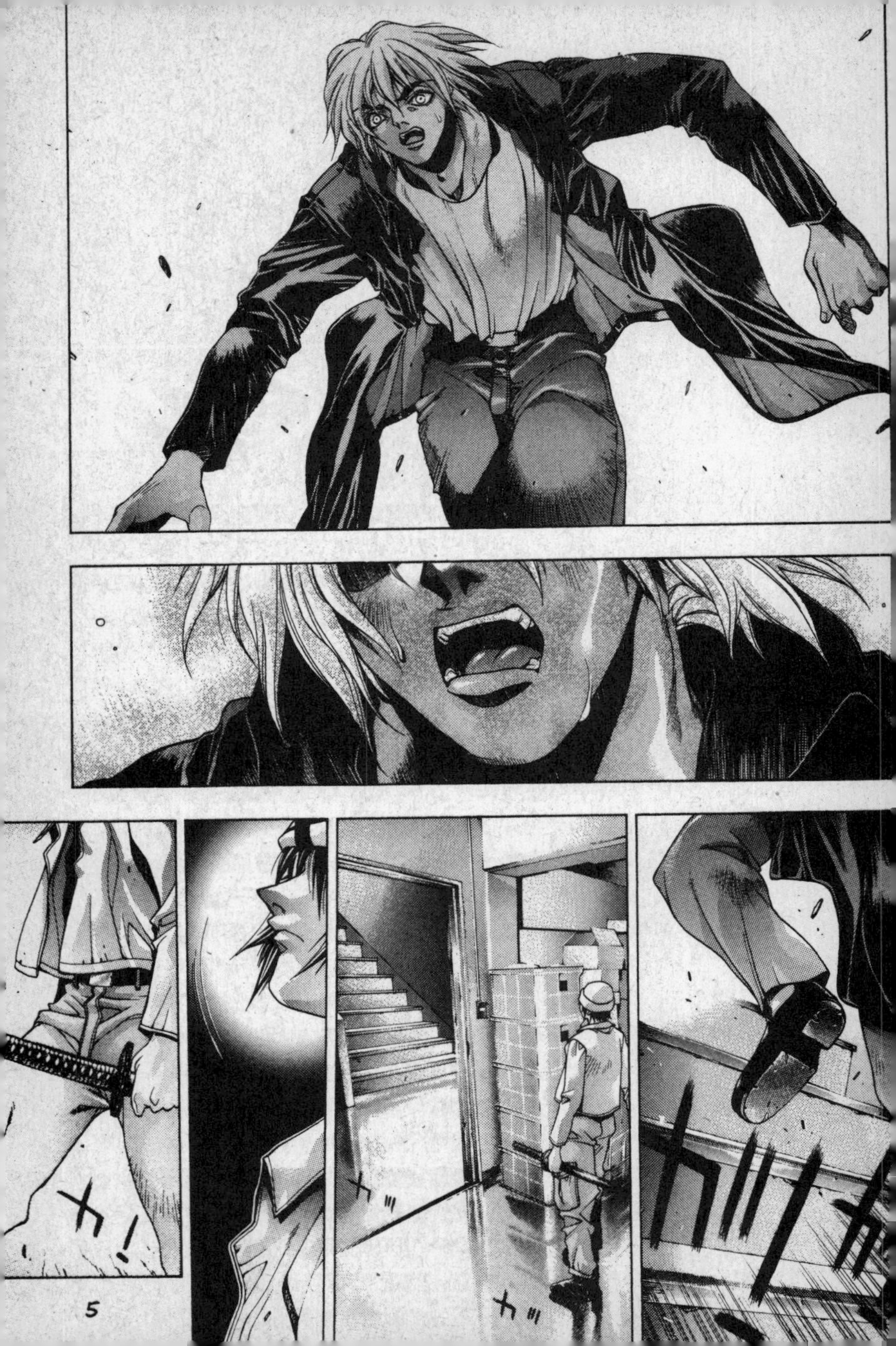
カッカッ
カッ
カッ
カ!

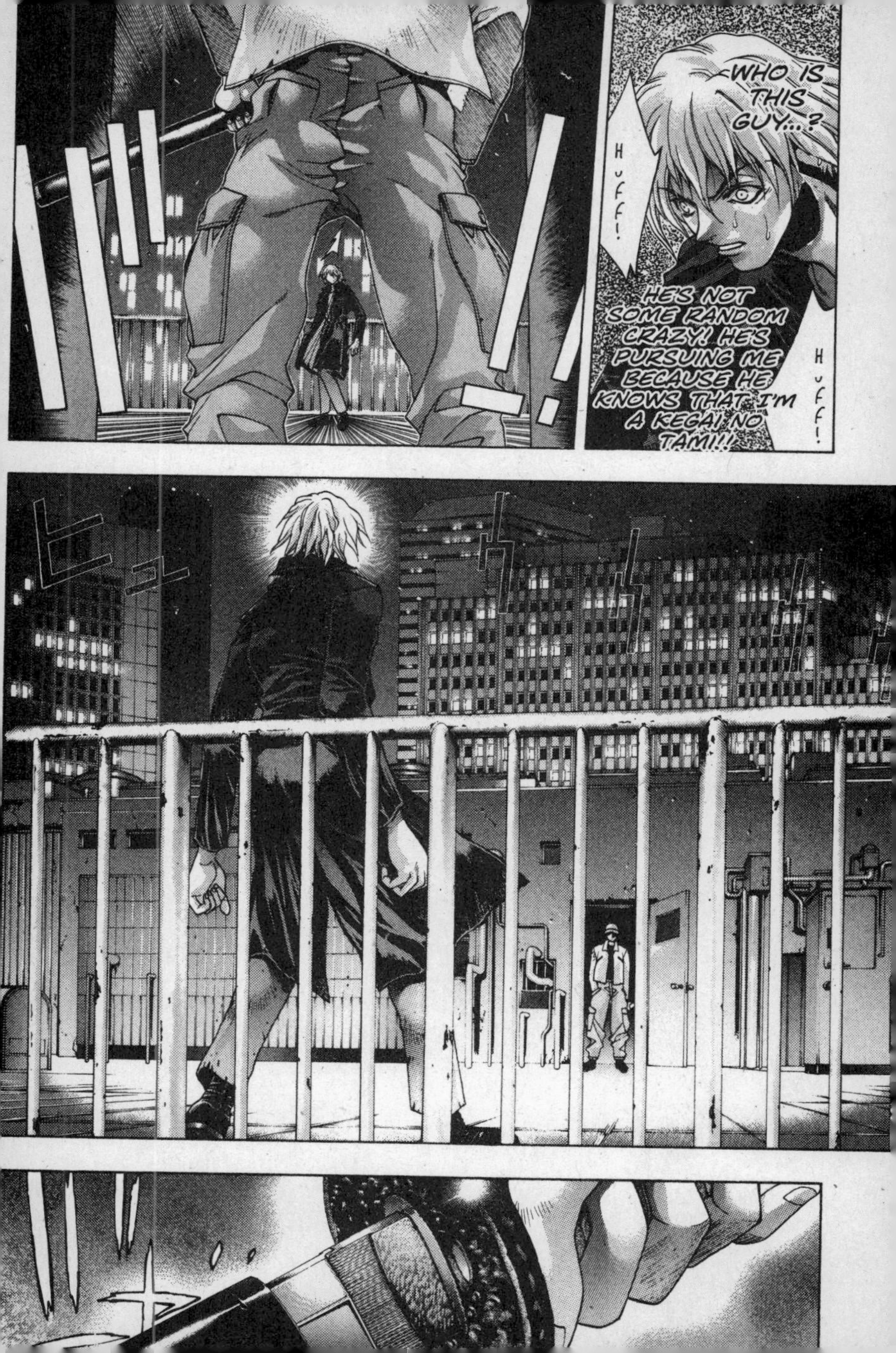
WHO IS THIS GUY...?
HUFF!
HE'S NOT SOME RANDOM CRAZY! HE'S PURSUING ME BECAUSE HE KNOWS THAT I'M A KEGAI NO TAMI!!
HUFF!

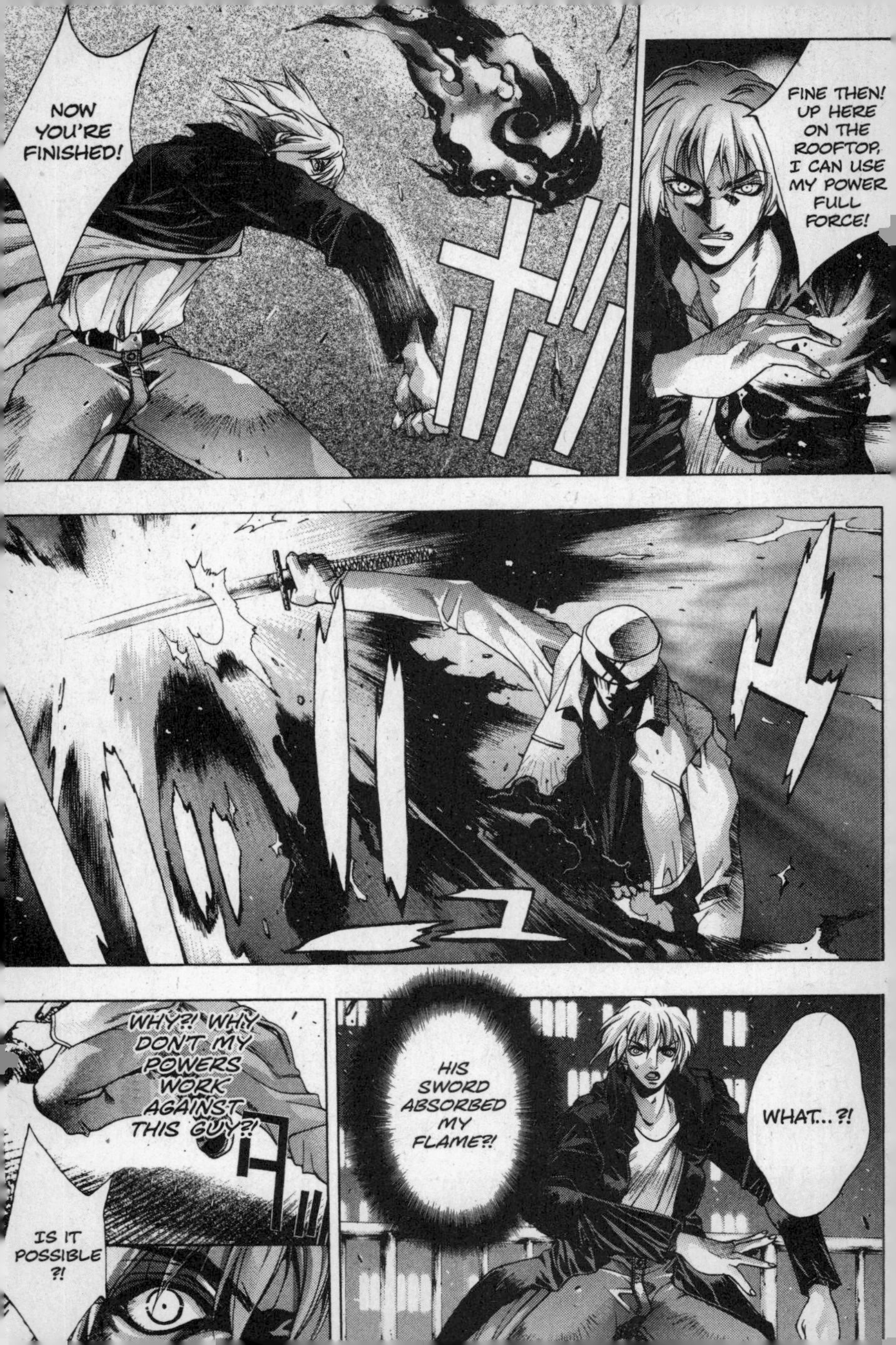

FINE THEN! UP HERE ON THE ROOFTOP, I CAN USE MY POWER FULL FORCE!
NOW YOU'RE FINISHED!
WHAT...?!
HIS SWORD ABSORBED MY FLAME?!
WHY?! WHY DON'T MY POWERS WORK AGAINST THIS GUY?!
IS IT POSSIBLE ?!

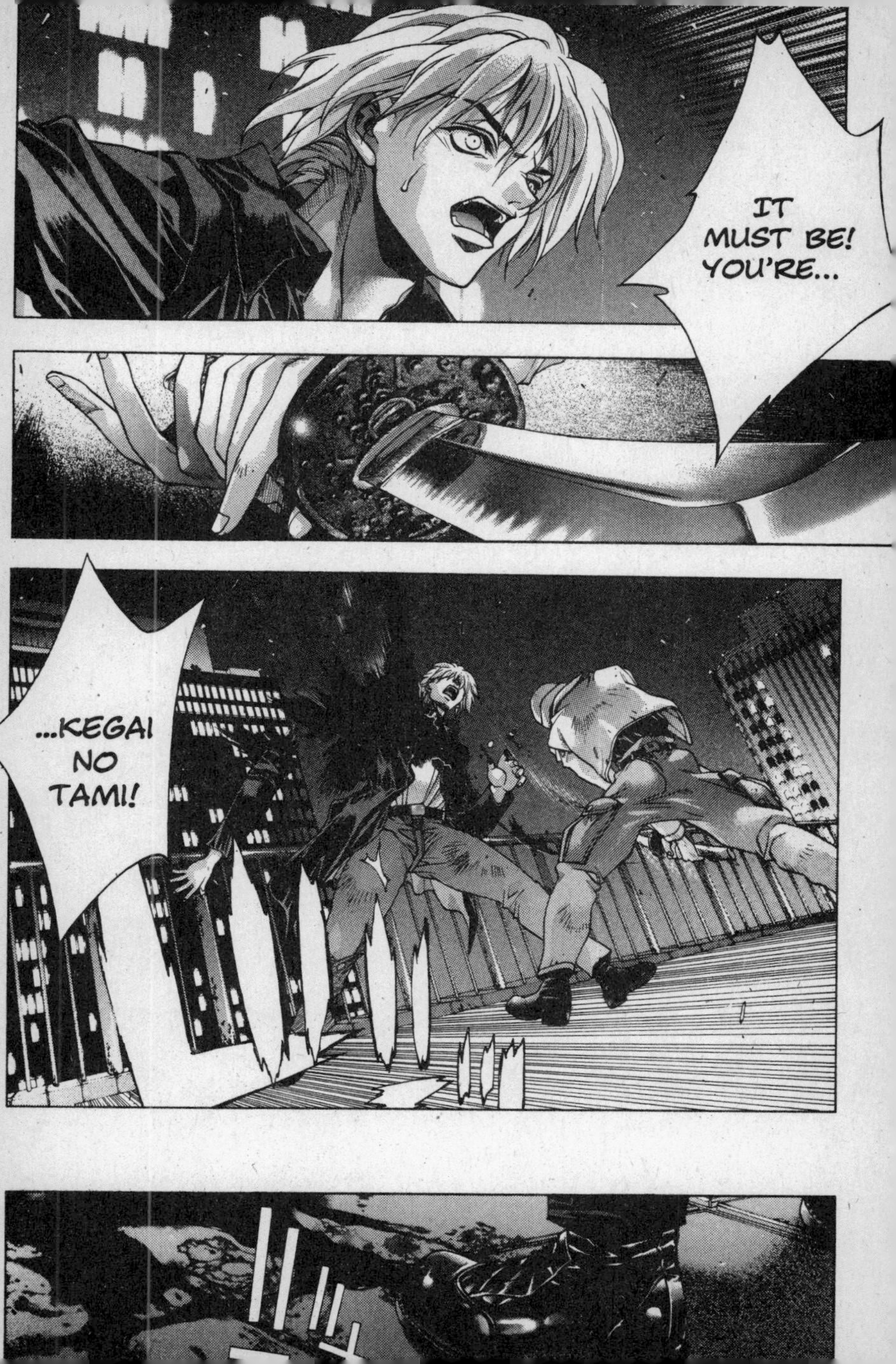
IT MUST BE! YOU'RE...
...KEGAI NO TAMI!

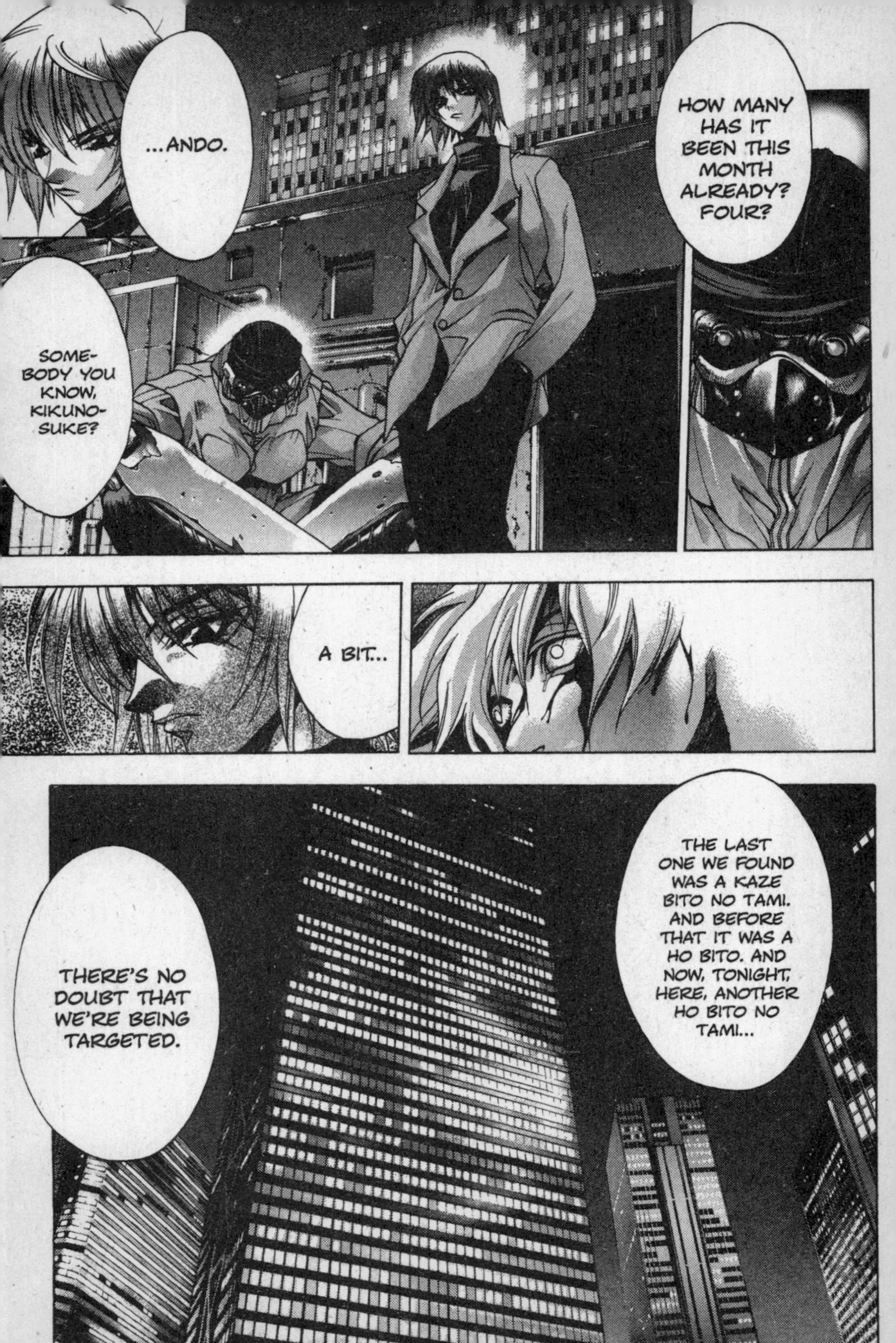
HOW MANY HAS IT BEEN THIS MONTH ALREADY? FOUR?
...ANDO.
SOME-BODY YOU KNOW, KIKUNO-SUKE?
A BIT...
THE LAST ONE WE FOUND WAS A KAZE BITO NO TAMI. AND BEFORE THAT IT WAS A HO BITO. AND NOW, TONIGHT, HERE, ANOTHER HO BITO NO TAMI...
THERE'S NO DOUBT THAT WE'RE BEING TARGETED.

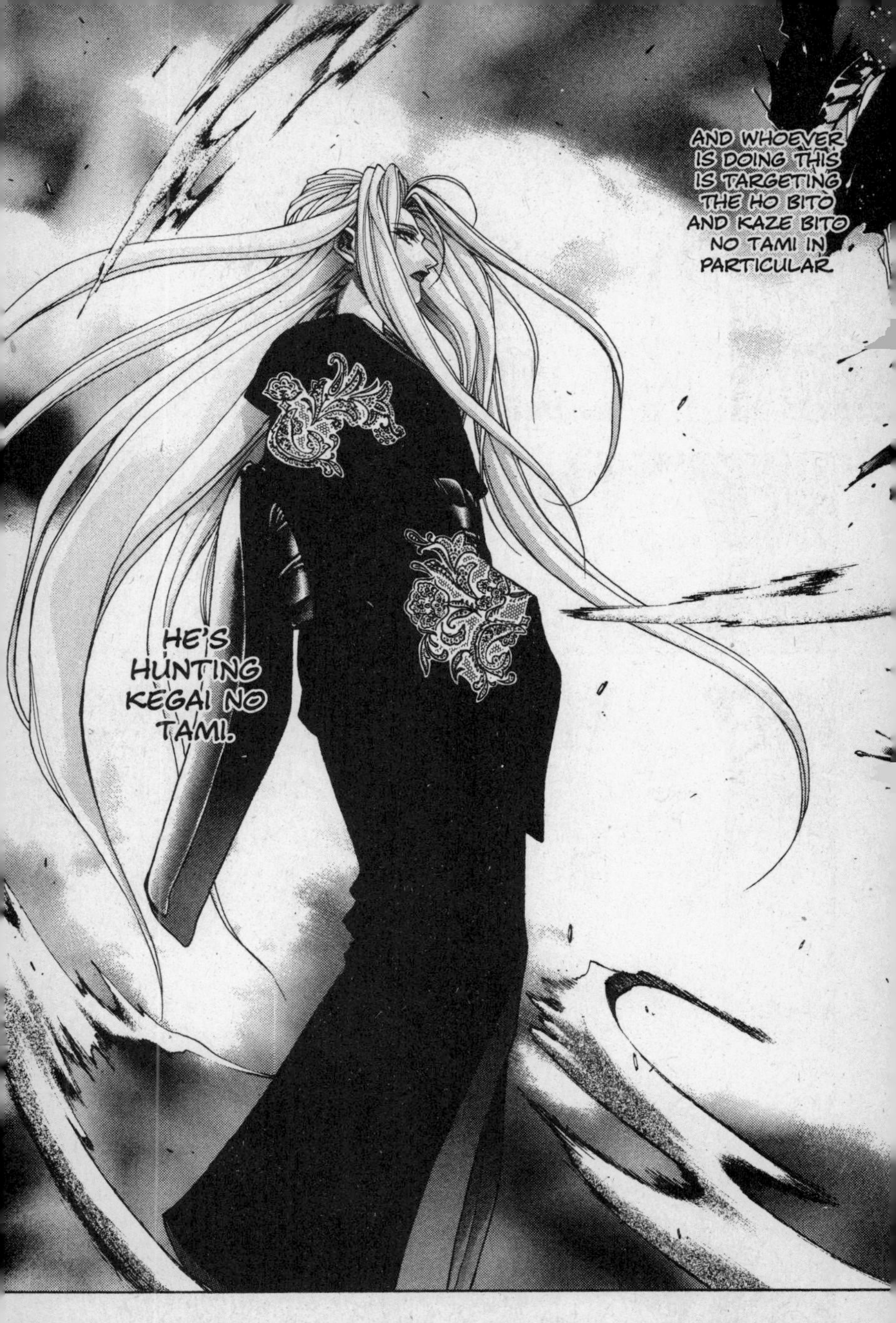
AND WHOEVER IS DOING THIS IS TARGETING THE HO BITO AND KAZE BITO NO TAMI IN PARTICULAR
HE'S HUNTING KEGAI NO TAMI.

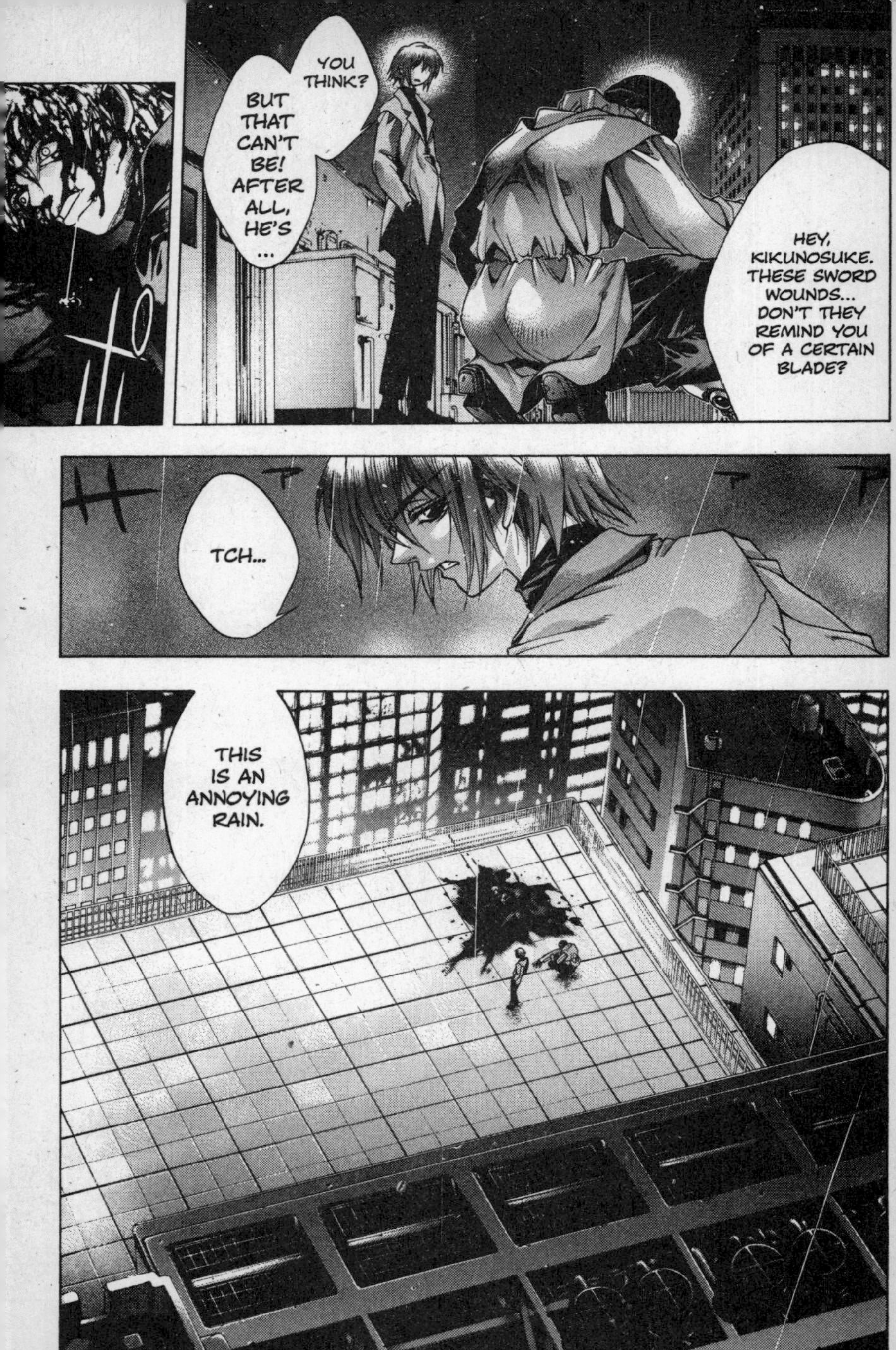
HEY, KIKUNOSUKE. THESE SWORD WOUNDS... DON'T THEY REMIND YOU OF A CERTAIN BLADE?
YOU THINK?
BUT THAT CAN'T BE! AFTER ALL, HE'S ...
TCH...
THIS IS AN ANNOYING RAIN.

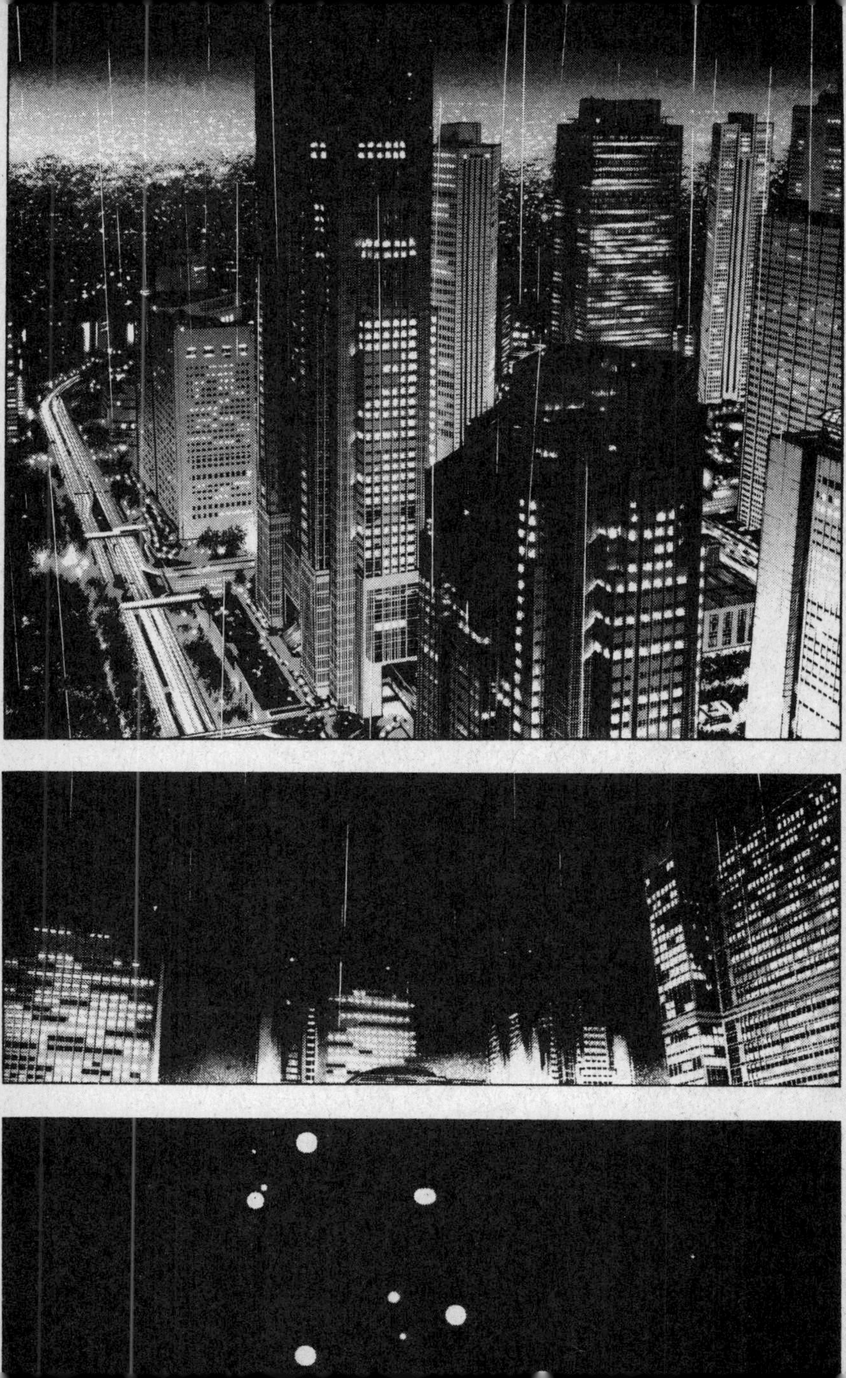

Six months later...

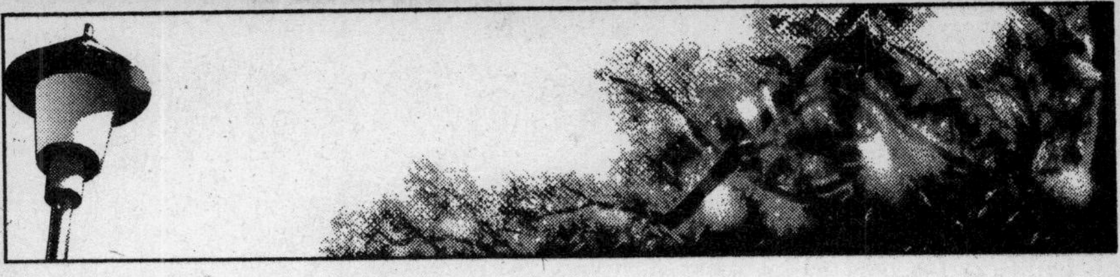

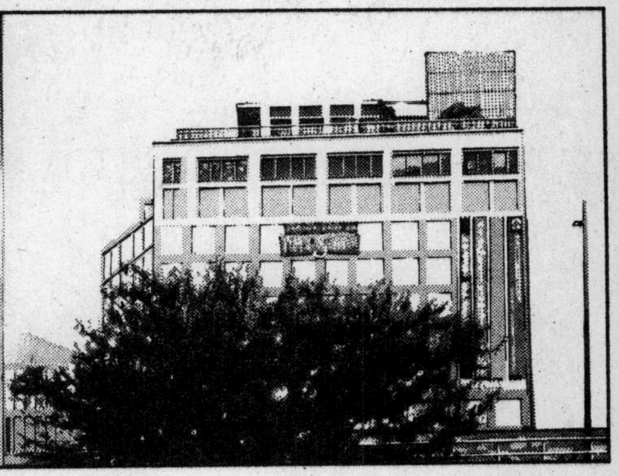

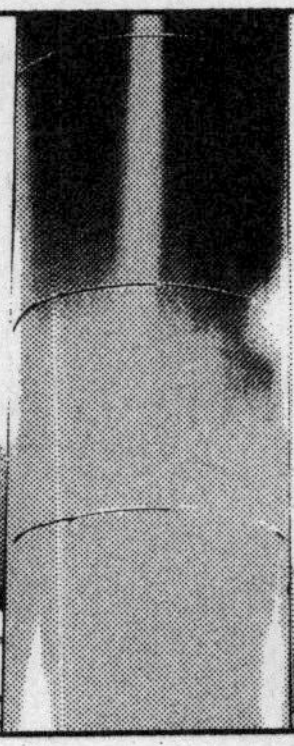

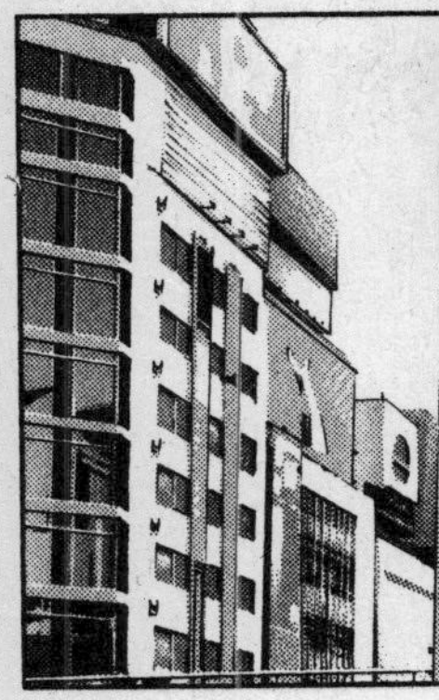

Chapter 20: Another Sacred Sword

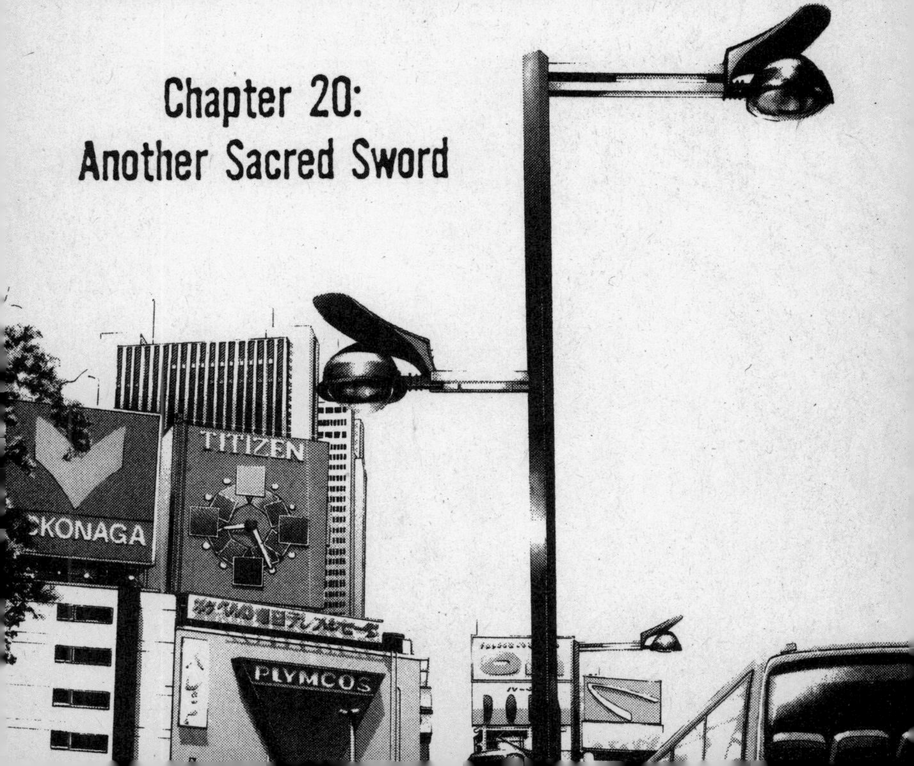
TITIZEN
CKONAGA
PLYMCOS

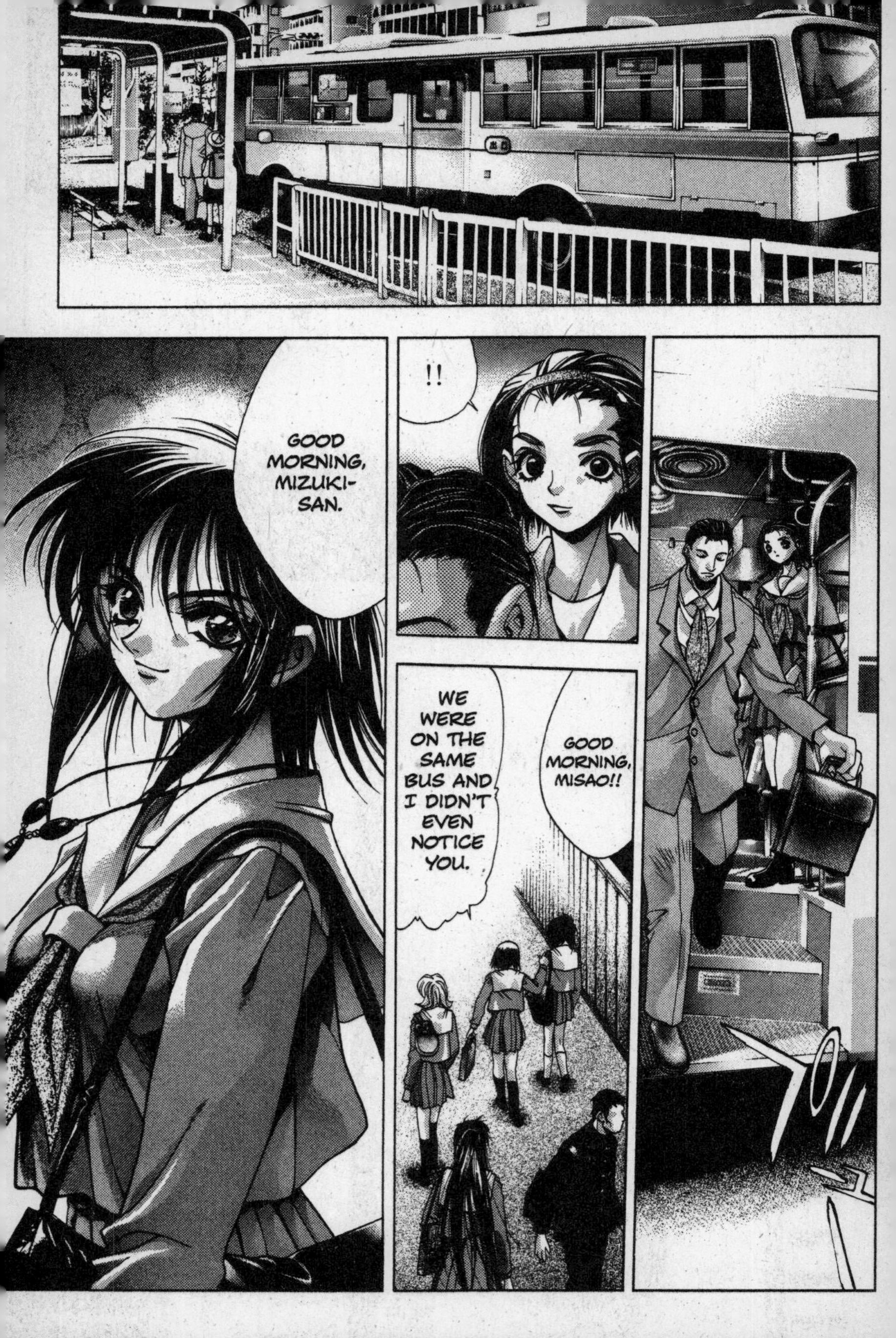
!!
GOOD MORNING, MISAO!!
WE WERE ON THE SAME BUS AND I DIDN'T EVEN NOTICE YOU.
GOOD MORNING, MIZUKI-SAN.

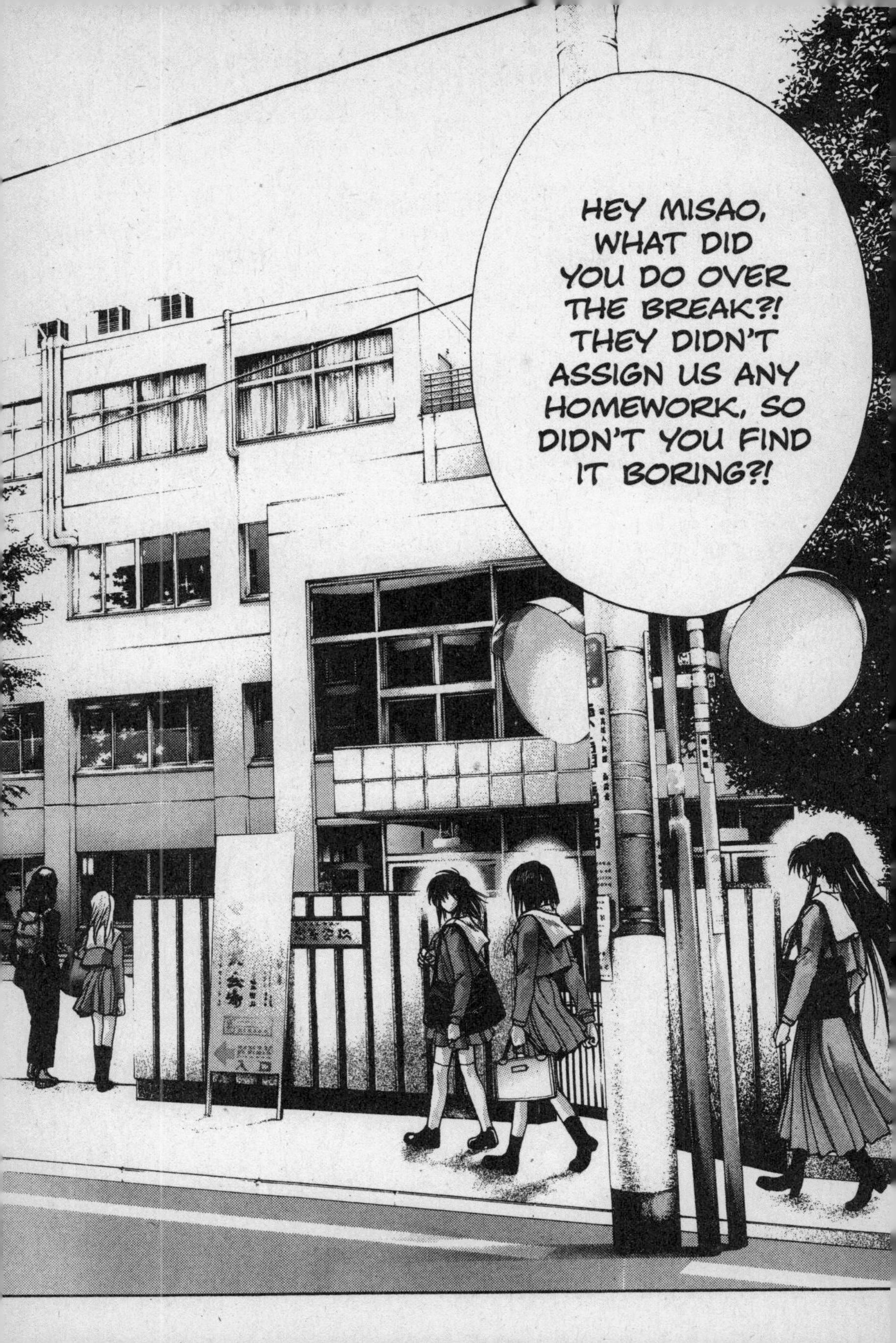
HEY MISAO, WHAT DID YOU DO OVER THE BREAK?! THEY DIDN'T ASSIGN US ANY HOMEWORK, SO DIDN'T YOU FIND IT BORING?!

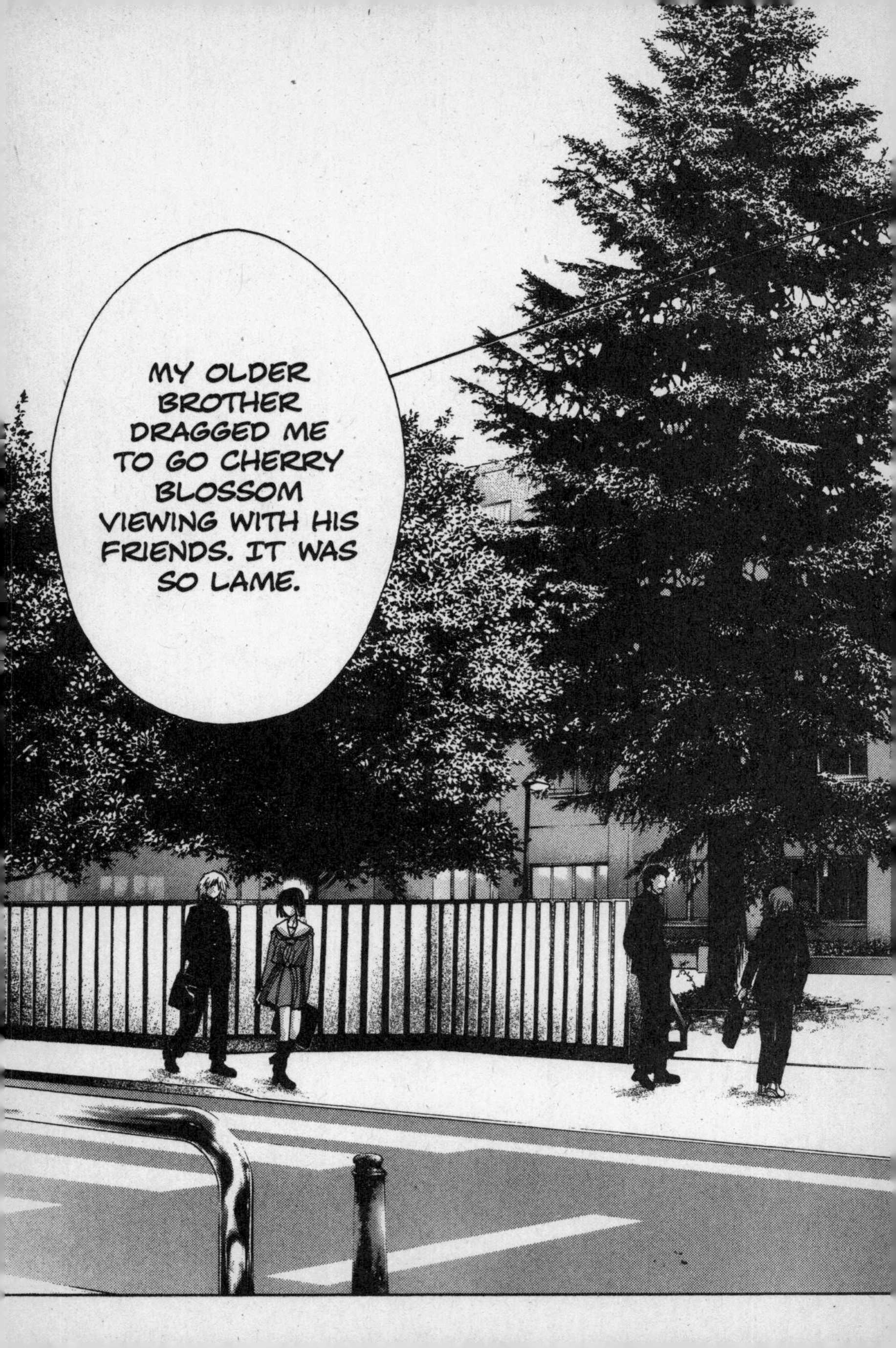
MY OLDER BROTHER DRAGGED ME TO GO CHERRY BLOSSOM VIEWING WITH HIS FRIENDS. IT WAS SO LAME.

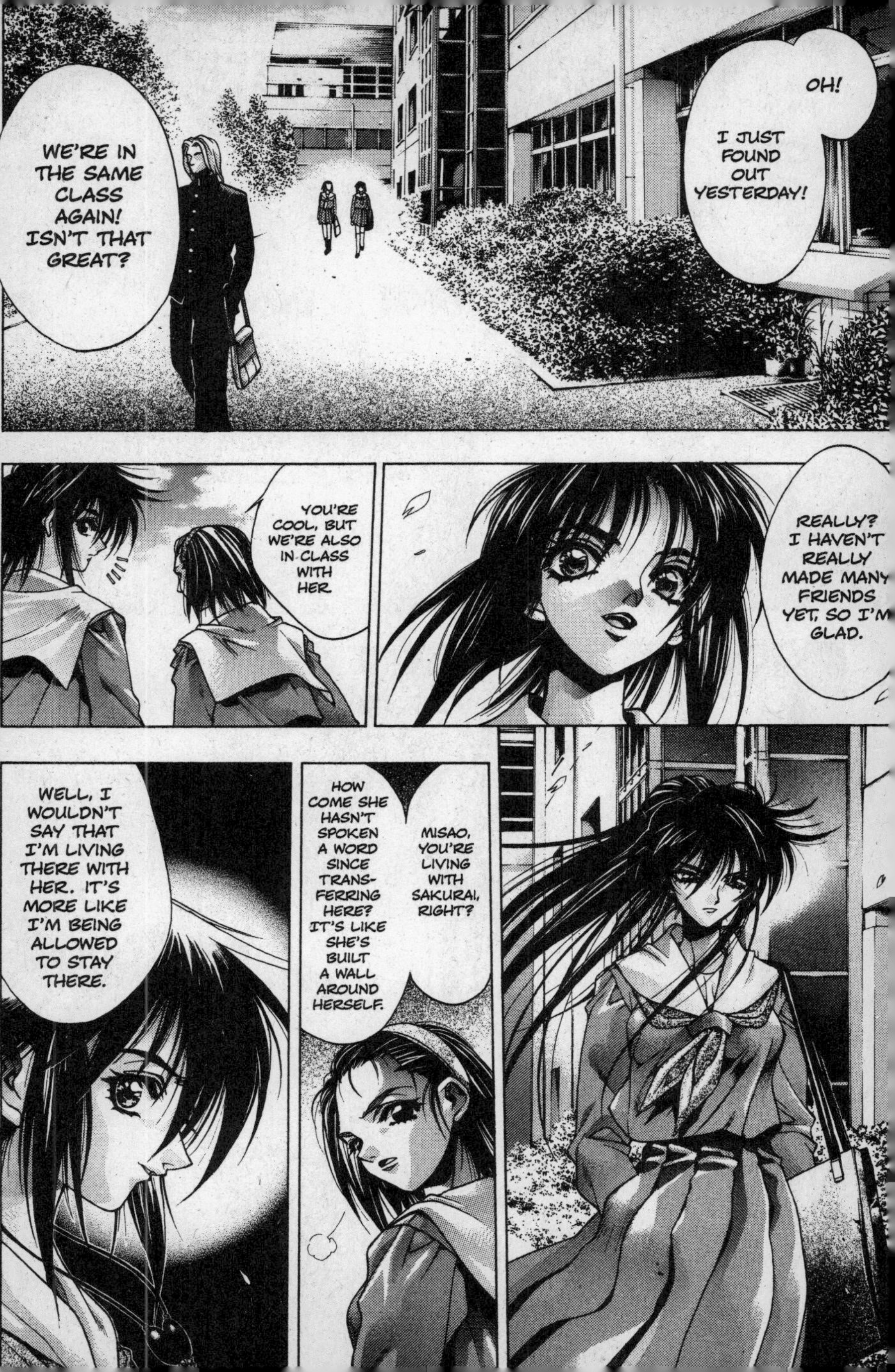
OH!
I JUST FOUND OUT YESTERDAY!
WE'RE IN THE SAME CLASS AGAIN! ISN'T THAT GREAT?
REALLY? I HAVEN'T REALLY MADE MANY FRIENDS YET, SO I'M GLAD.
YOU'RE COOL, BUT WE'RE ALSO IN CLASS WITH HER
MISAO, YOU'RE LIVING WITH SAKURAI, RIGHT?
HOW COME SHE HASN'T SPOKEN A WORD SINCE TRANSFERRING HERE? IT'S LIKE SHE'S BUILT A WALL AROUND HERSELF.
WELL, I WOULDN'T SAY THAT I'M LIVING THERE WITH HER. IT'S MORE LIKE I'M BEING ALLOWED TO STAY THERE.

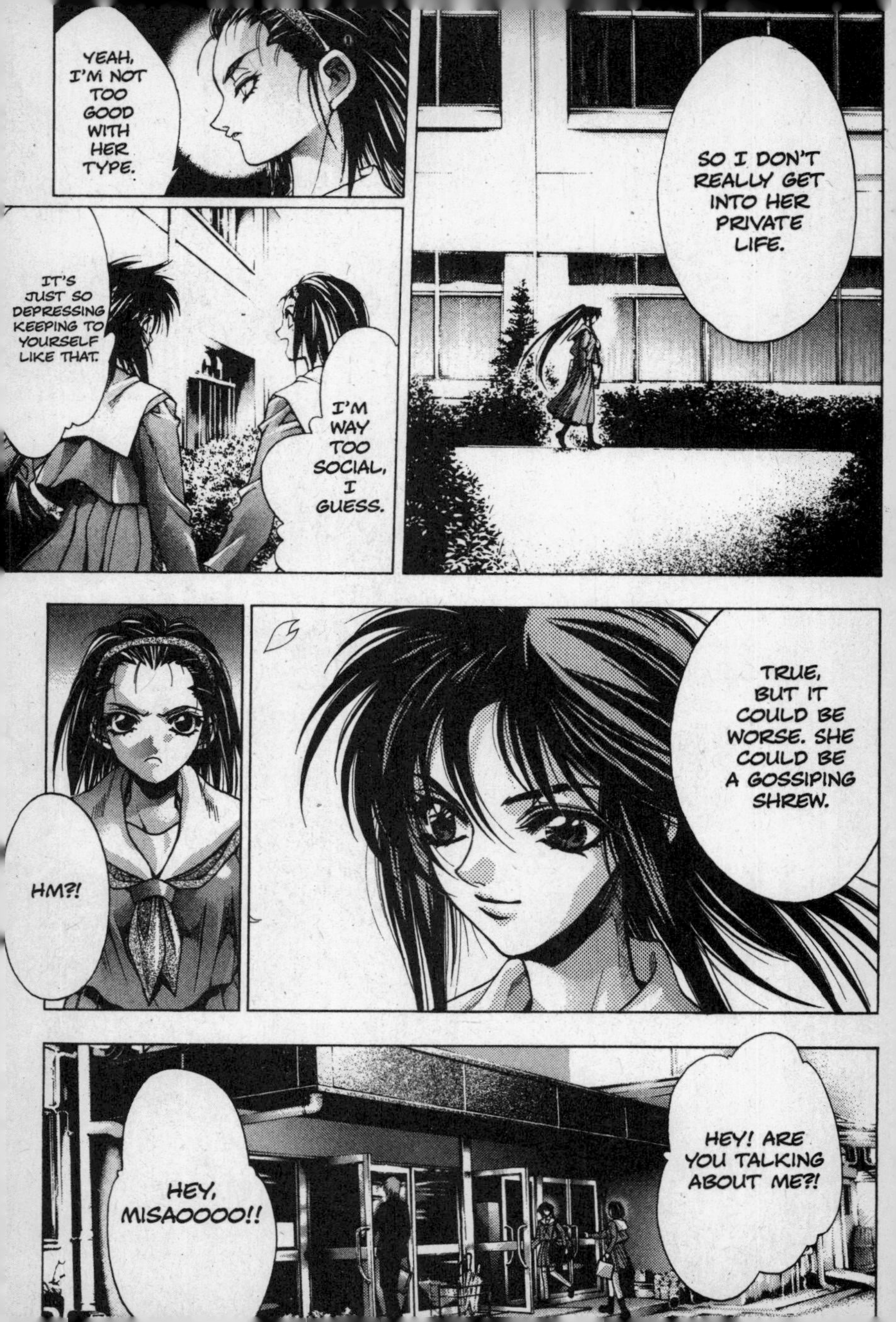
SO I DON'T REALLY GET INTO HER PRIVATE LIFE.
YEAH, I'M NOT TOO GOOD WITH HER TYPE.
I'M WAY TOO SOCIAL, I GUESS.
IT'S JUST SO DEPRESSING KEEPING TO YOURSELF LIKE THAT.
TRUE, BUT IT COULD BE WORSE. SHE COULD BE A GOSSIPING SHREW.
HM?!
HEY! ARE YOU TALKING ABOUT ME?!
HEY, MISAOOOO!!

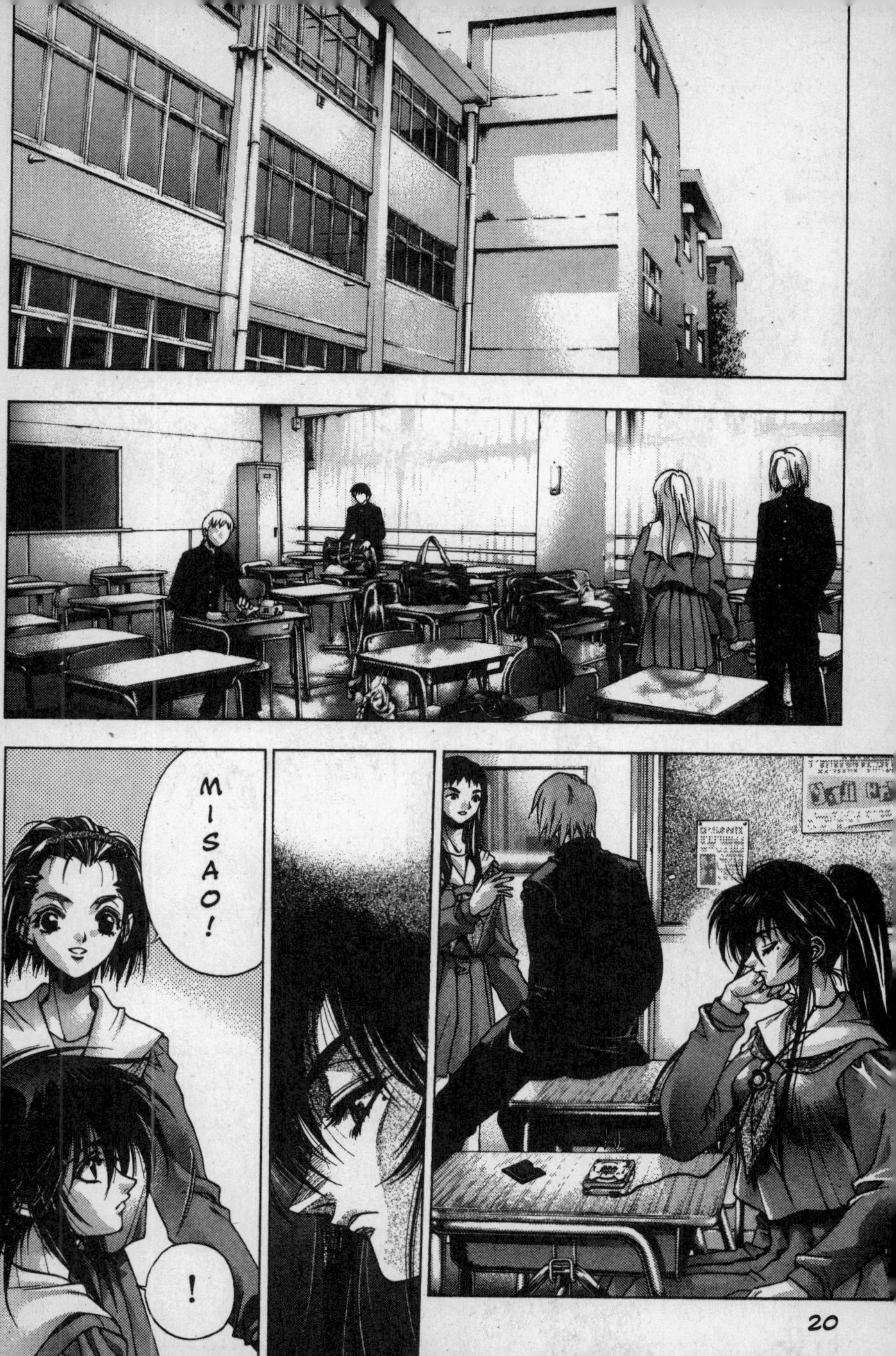

MISAO!
!

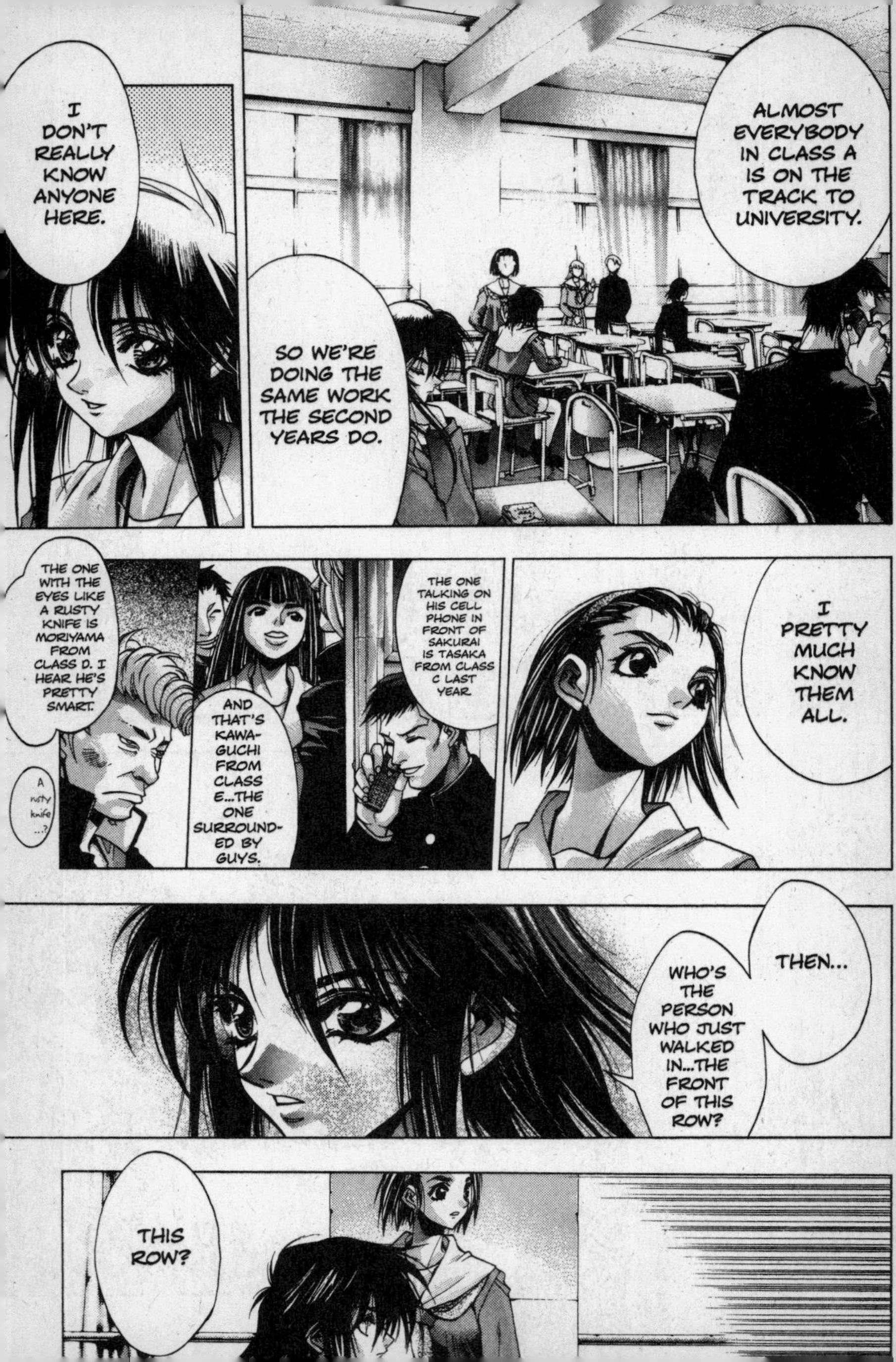
ALMOST EVERYBODY IN CLASS A IS ON THE TRACK TO UNIVERSITY.
SO WE'RE DOING THE SAME WORK THE SECOND YEARS DO.
I DON'T REALLY KNOW ANYONE HERE.
I PRETTY MUCH KNOW THEM ALL.
THE ONE TALKING ON HIS CELL PHONE IN FRONT OF SAKURAI IS TASAKA FROM CLASS C LAST YEAR.
AND THAT'S KAWAGUCHI FROM CLASS E...THE ONE SURROUNDED BY GUYS.
THE ONE WITH THE EYES LIKE A RUSTY KNIFE IS MORIYAMA FROM CLASS D. I HEAR HE'S PRETTY SMART.
A rusty knife...?
THEN...
WHO'S THE PERSON WHO JUST WALKED IN...THE FRONT OF THIS ROW?
THIS ROW?

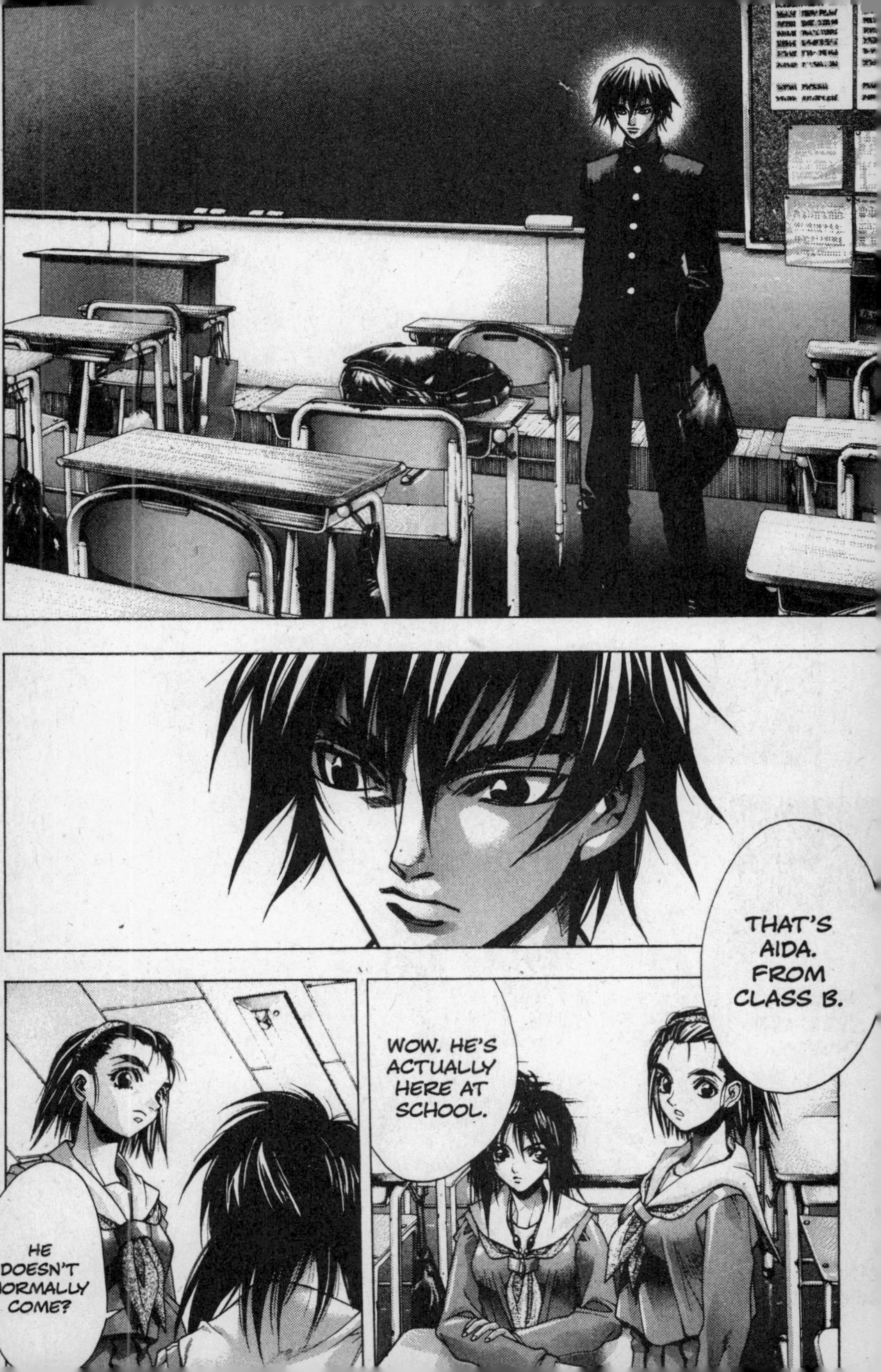
THAT'S AIDA. FROM CLASS B.
WOW. HE'S ACTUALLY HERE AT SCHOOL.
HE DOESN'T NORMALLY COME?

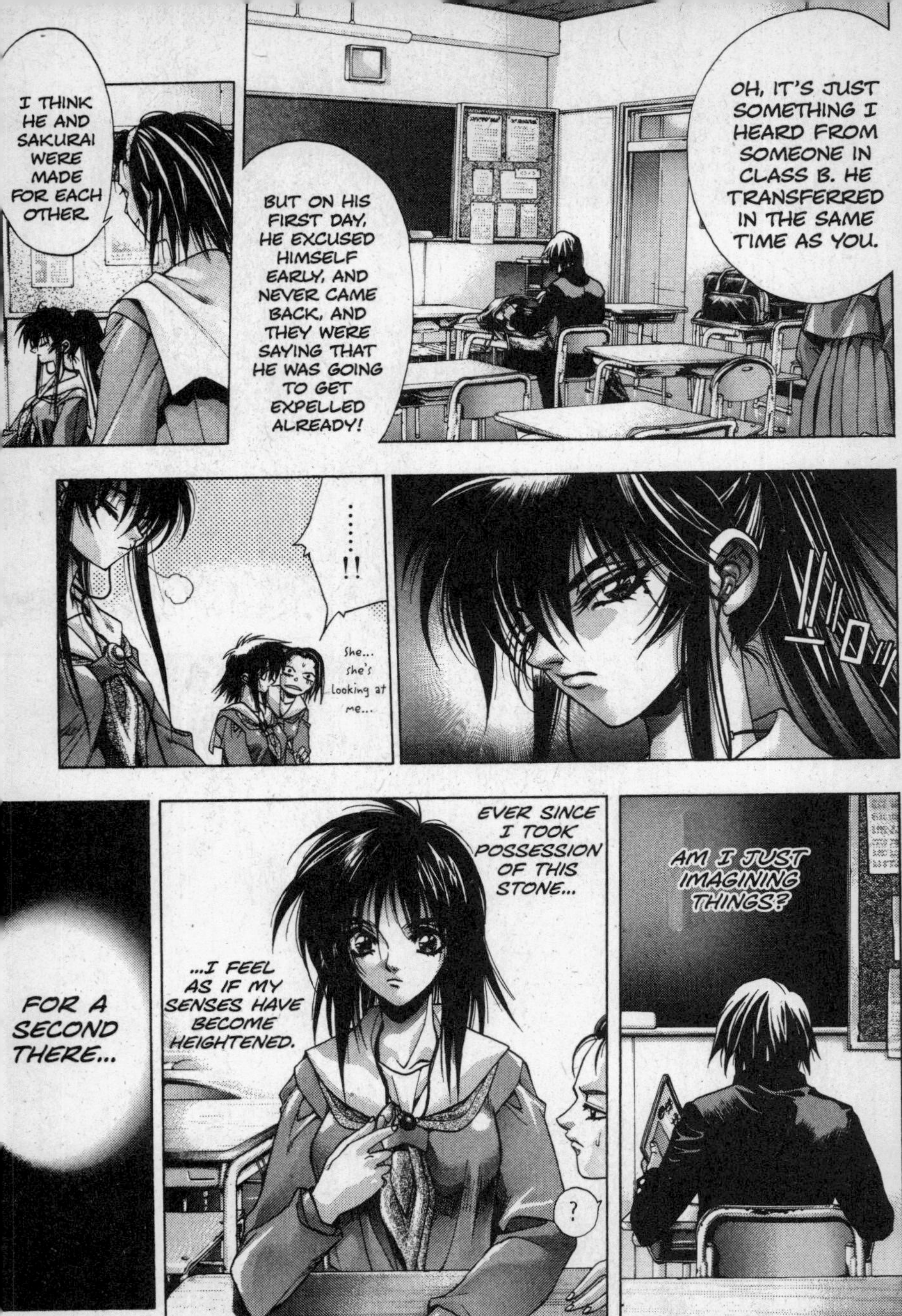
OH, IT'S JUST SOMETHING I HEARD FROM SOMEONE IN CLASS B. HE TRANSFERRED IN THE SAME TIME AS YOU.
BUT ON HIS FIRST DAY, HE EXCUSED HIMSELF EARLY, AND NEVER CAME BACK, AND THEY WERE SAYING THAT HE WAS GOING TO GET EXPELLED ALREADY!
I THINK HE AND SAKURAI WERE MADE FOR EACH OTHER.
......!!
She... she's looking at me...
AM I JUST IMAGINING THINGS?
EVER SINCE I TOOK POSSESSION OF THIS STONE...
...I FEEL AS IF MY SENSES HAVE BECOME HEIGHTENED.
?
FOR A SECOND THERE...

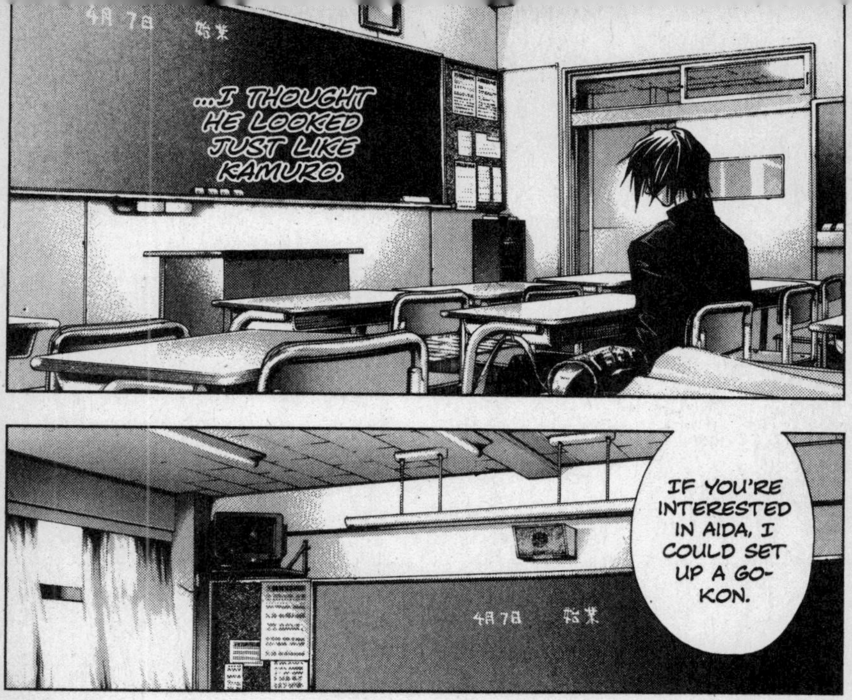
4月7日 始業
...I THOUGHT HE LOOKED JUST LIKE KAMURO.
IF YOU'RE INTERESTED IN AIDA, I COULD SET UP A GO-KON.

Go-kon: a meeting party held by young people.

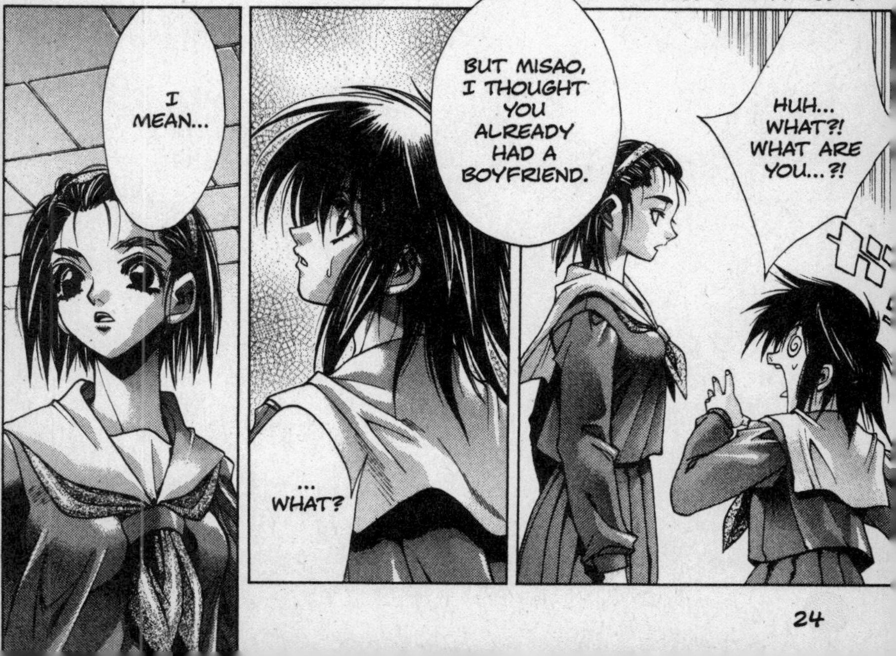
HUH... WHAT?! WHAT ARE YOU...?!
BUT MISAO, I THOUGHT YOU ALREADY HAD A BOYFRIEND.
... WHAT?
I MEAN...

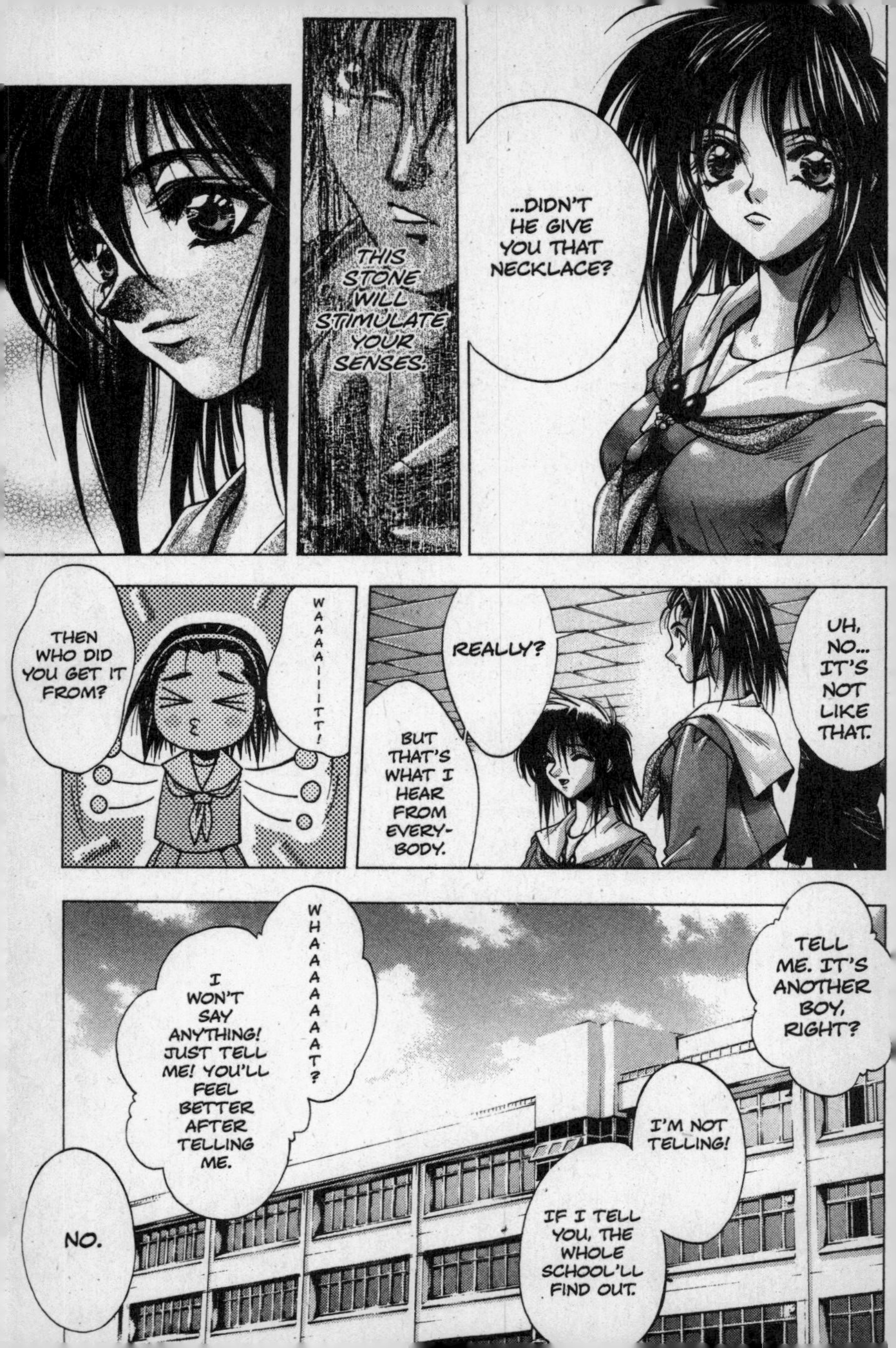
...DIDN'T HE GIVE YOU THAT NECKLACE?
THIS STONE WILL STIMULATE YOUR SENSES.
UH, NO... IT'S NOT LIKE THAT.
REALLY?
BUT THAT'S WHAT I HEAR FROM EVERYBODY.
WAAAAIIITT!
THEN WHO DID YOU GET IT FROM?
TELL ME. IT'S ANOTHER BOY, RIGHT?
I'M NOT TELLING!
IF I TELL YOU, THE WHOLE SCHOOL'LL FIND OUT.
WHAAAAAAAAAT?
I WON'T SAY ANYTHING! JUST TELL ME! YOU'LL FEEL BETTER AFTER TELLING ME.
NO.

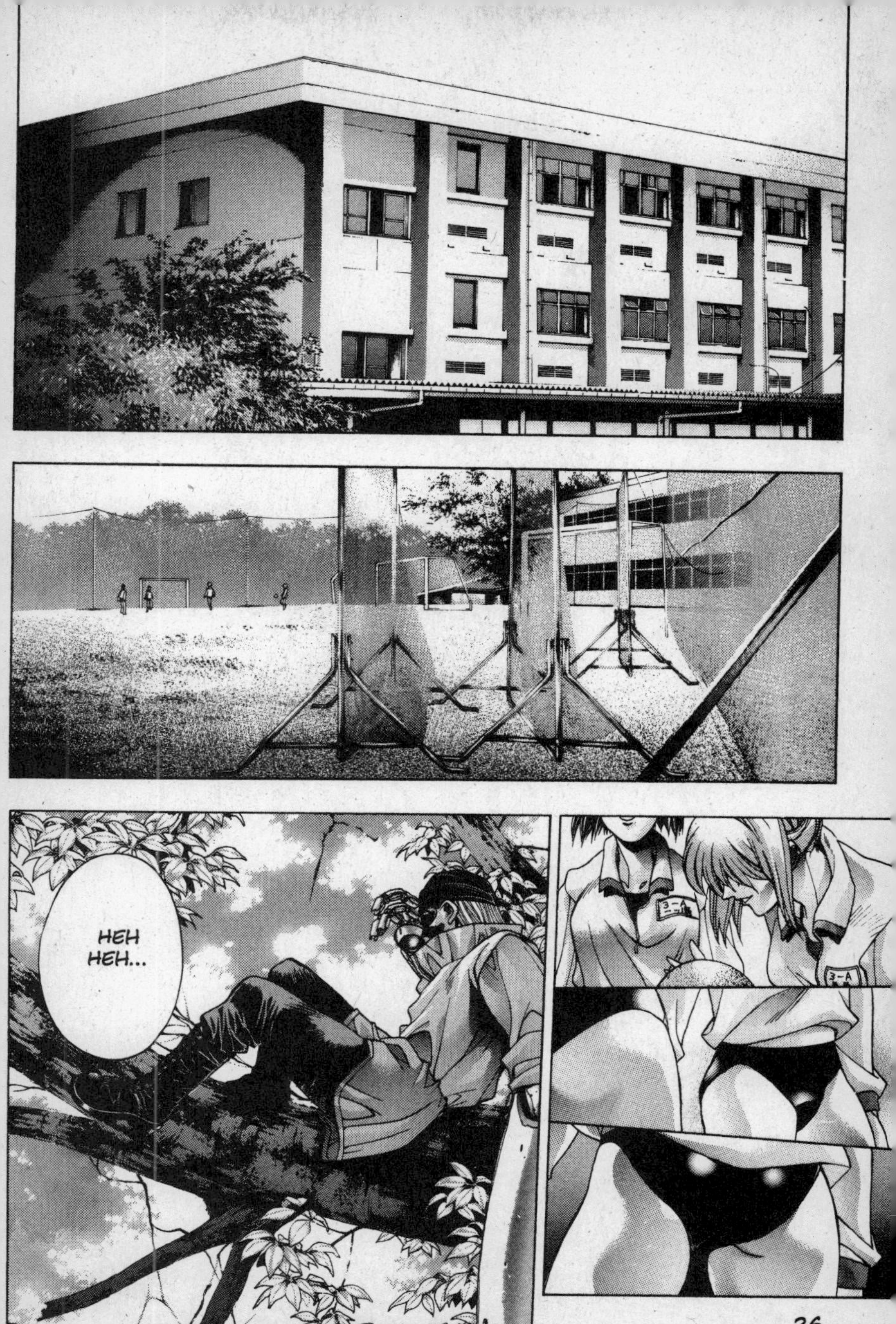
HEH HEH...
3-A
3-A

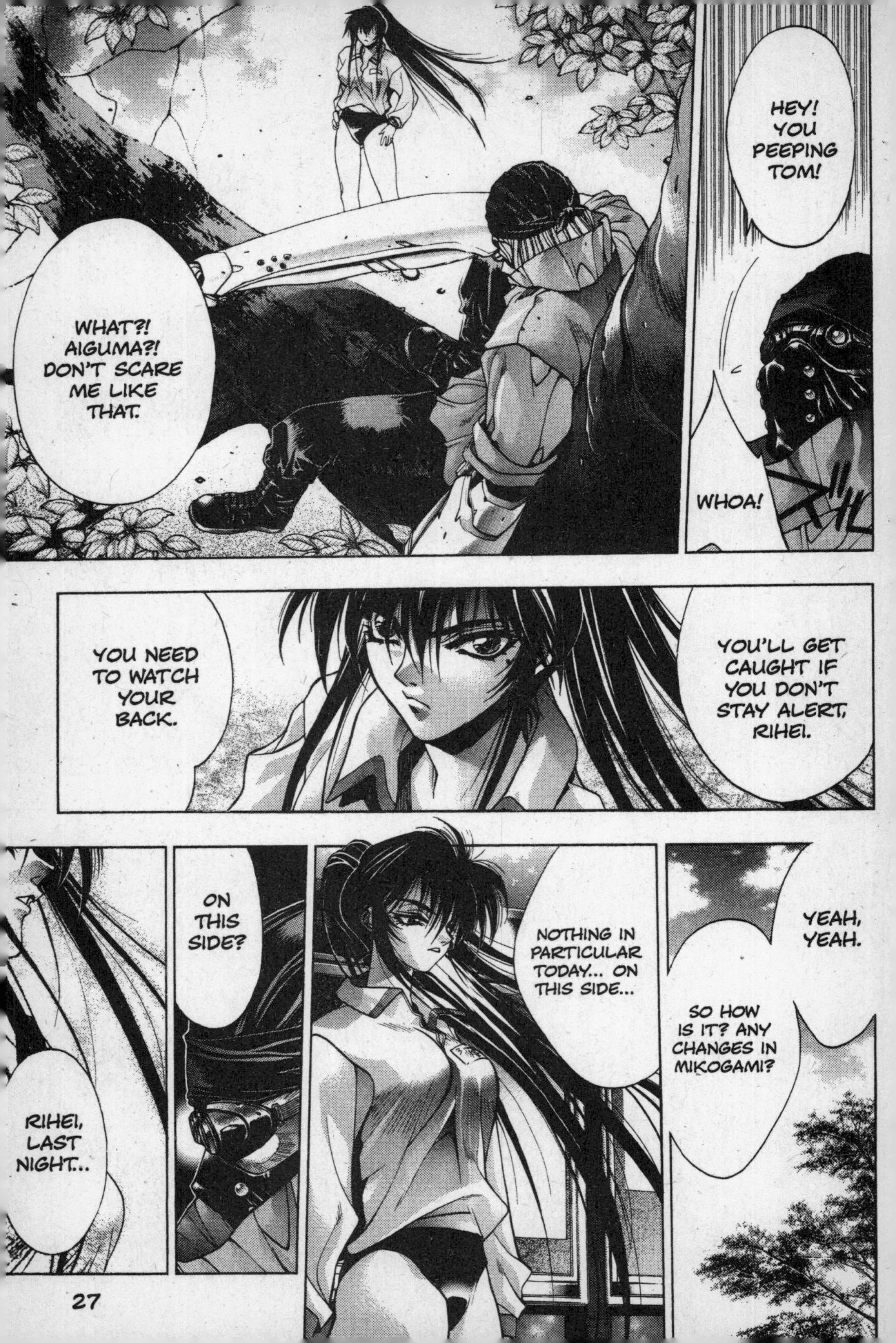
HEY! YOU PEEPING TOM!
WHOA!
WHAT?! AIGUMA?! DON'T SCARE ME LIKE THAT.
YOU'LL GET CAUGHT IF YOU DON'T STAY ALERT, RIHEI.
YOU NEED TO WATCH YOUR BACK.
YEAH, YEAH.
SO HOW IS IT? ANY CHANGES IN MIKOGAMI?
NOTHING IN PARTICULAR TODAY... ON THIS SIDE...
ON THIS SIDE?
RIHEI, LAST NIGHT...

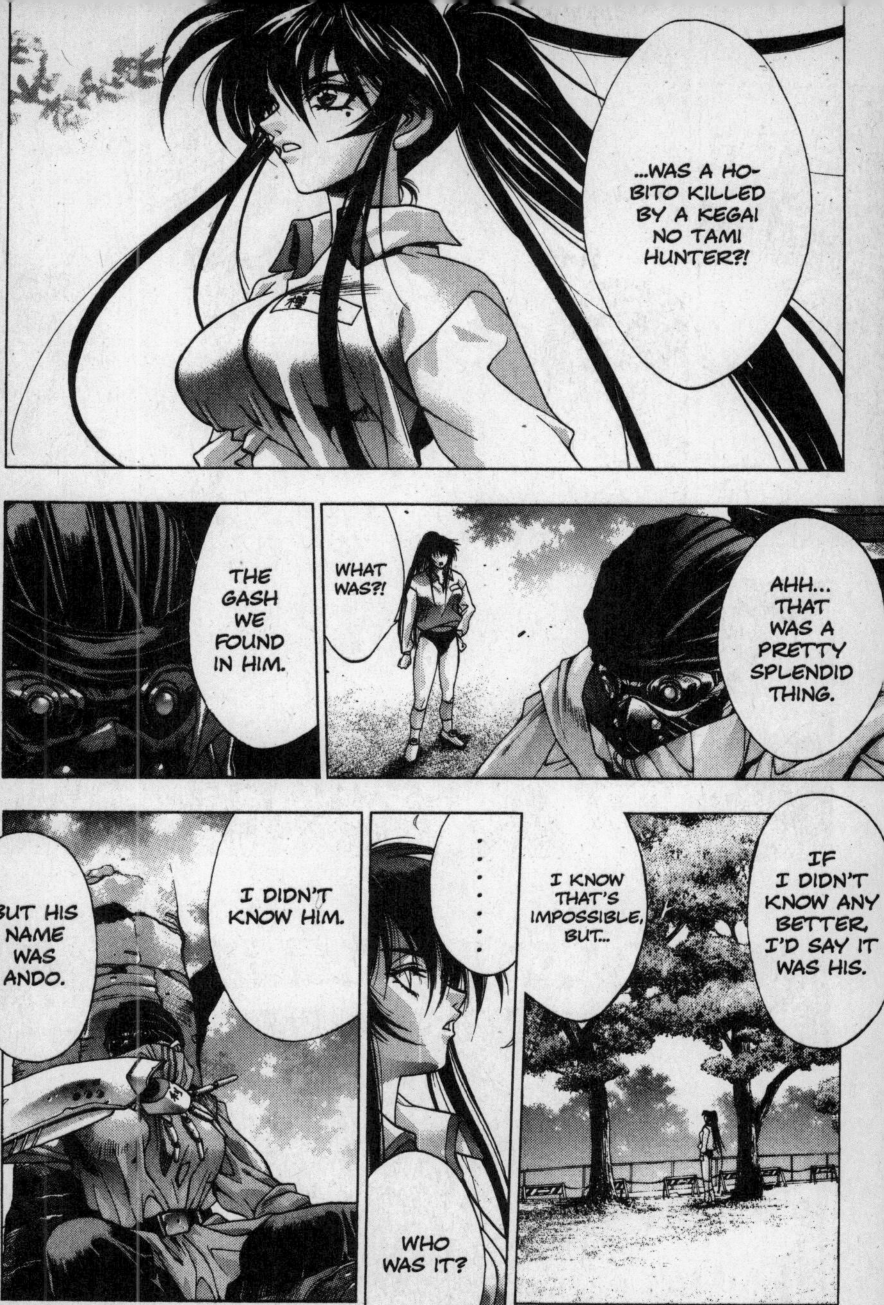
...WAS A HO-BITO KILLED BY A KEGAI NO TAMI HUNTER?!
AHH... THAT WAS A PRETTY SPLENDID THING.
WHAT WAS?!
THE GASH WE FOUND IN HIM.
IF I DIDN'T KNOW ANY BETTER, I'D SAY IT WAS HIS.
I KNOW THAT'S IMPOSSIBLE, BUT...
....
WHO WAS IT?
I DIDN'T KNOW HIM.
BUT HIS NAME WAS ANDO.

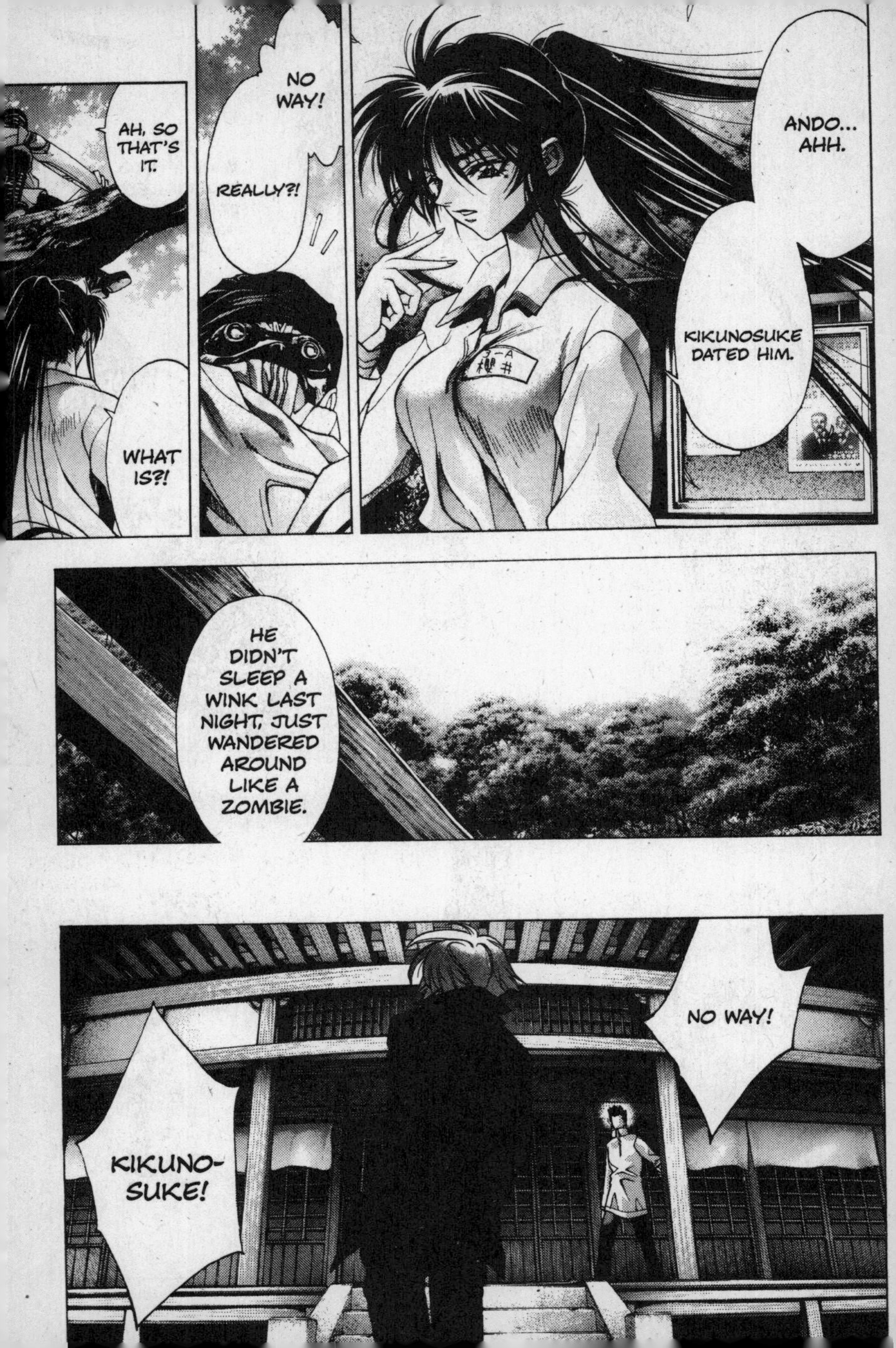
ANDO... AHH.
KIKUNOSUKE DATED HIM.
NO WAY!
REALLY?!
AH, SO THAT'S IT.
WHAT IS?!
HE DIDN'T SLEEP A WINK LAST NIGHT, JUST WANDERED AROUND LIKE A ZOMBIE.
NO WAY!
KIKUNO-SUKE!

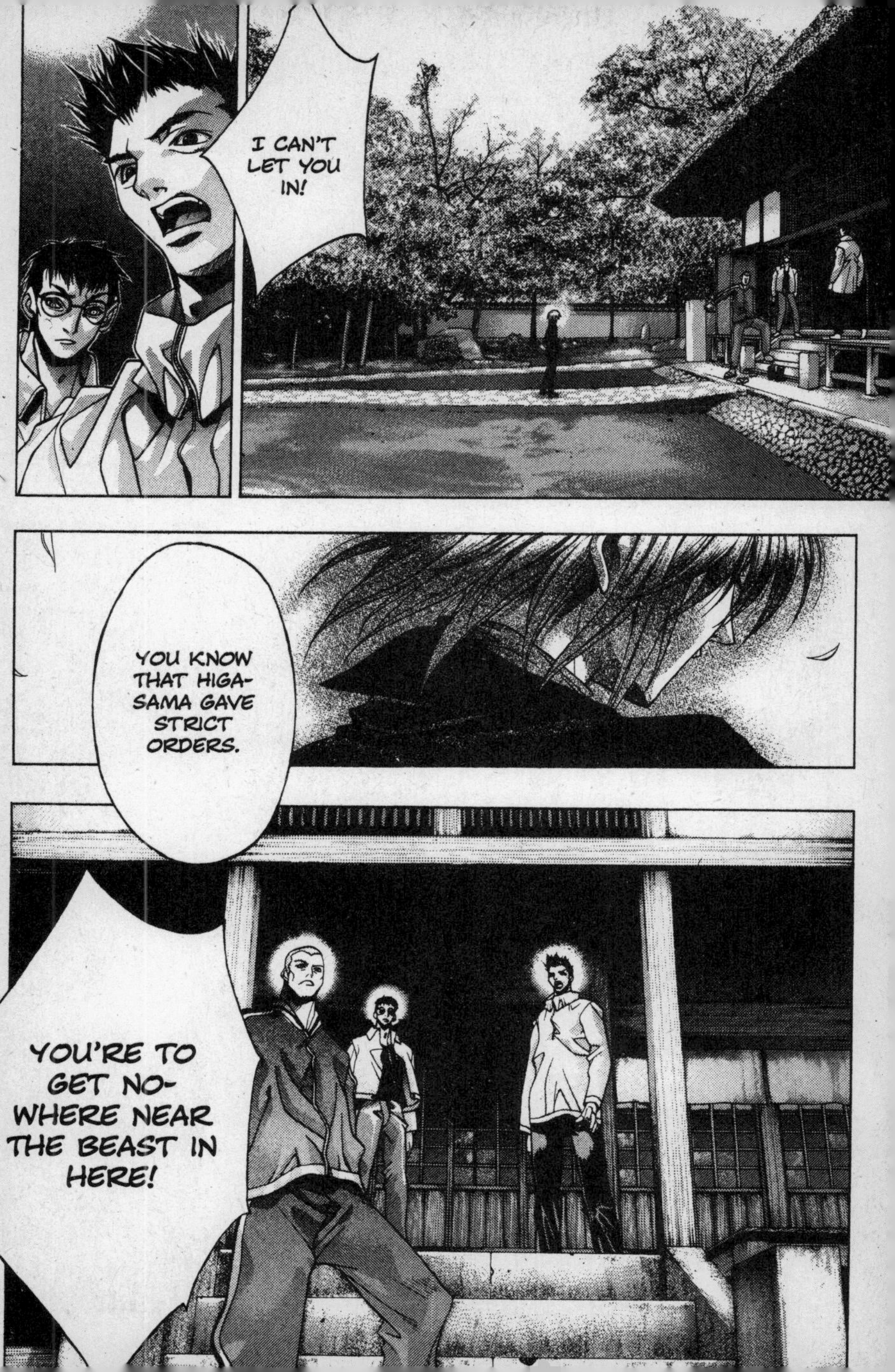
I CAN'T LET YOU IN!
YOU KNOW THAT HIGA-SAMA GAVE STRICT ORDERS.
YOU'RE TO GET NO-WHERE NEAR THE BEAST IN HERE!

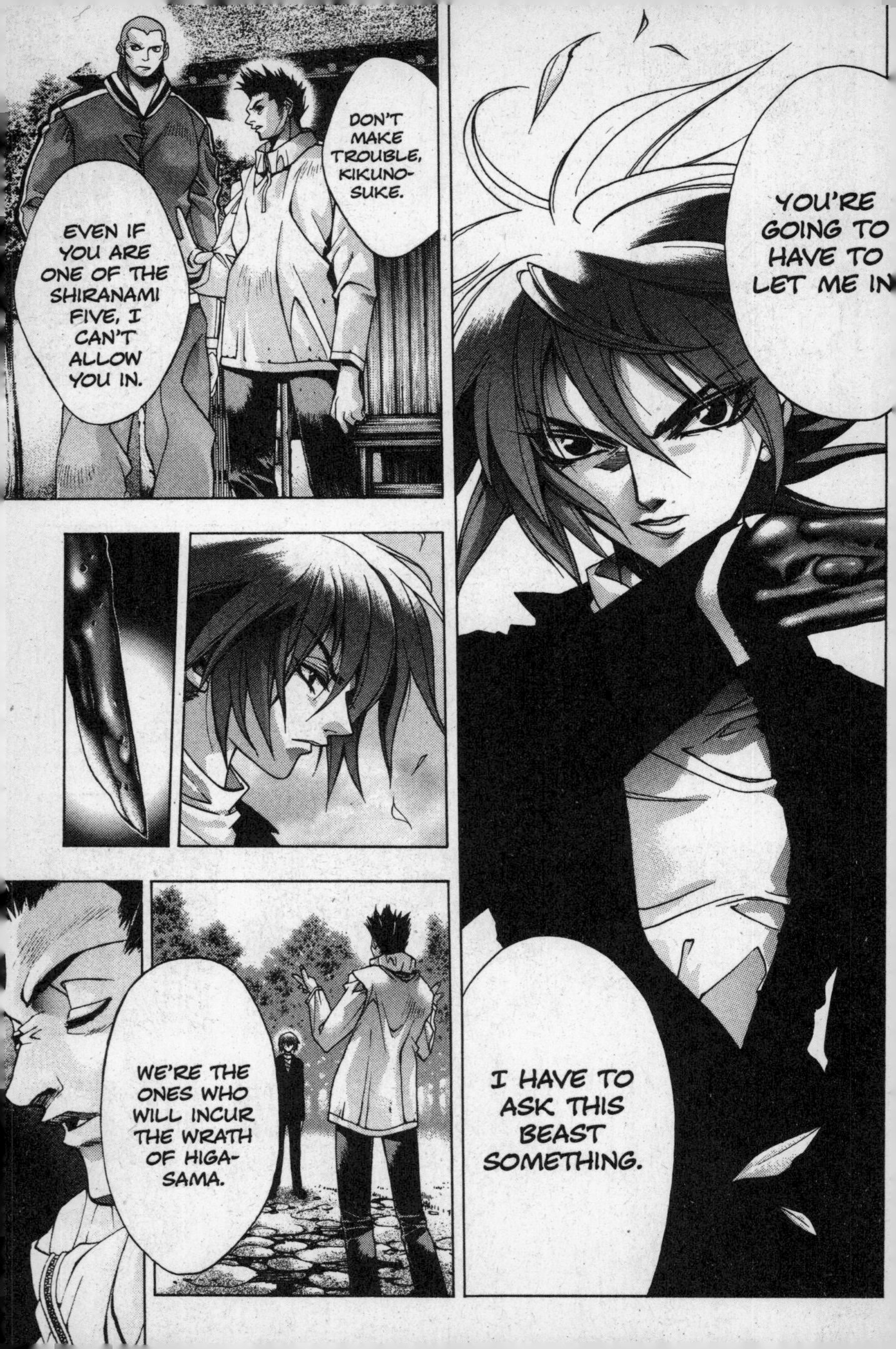
YOU'RE GOING TO HAVE TO LET ME IN
I HAVE TO ASK THIS BEAST SOMETHING.
DON'T MAKE TROUBLE, KIKUNO-SUKE.
EVEN IF YOU ARE ONE OF THE SHIRANAMI FIVE, I CAN'T ALLOW YOU IN.
WE'RE THE ONES WHO WILL INCUR THE WRATH OF HIGA-SAMA.

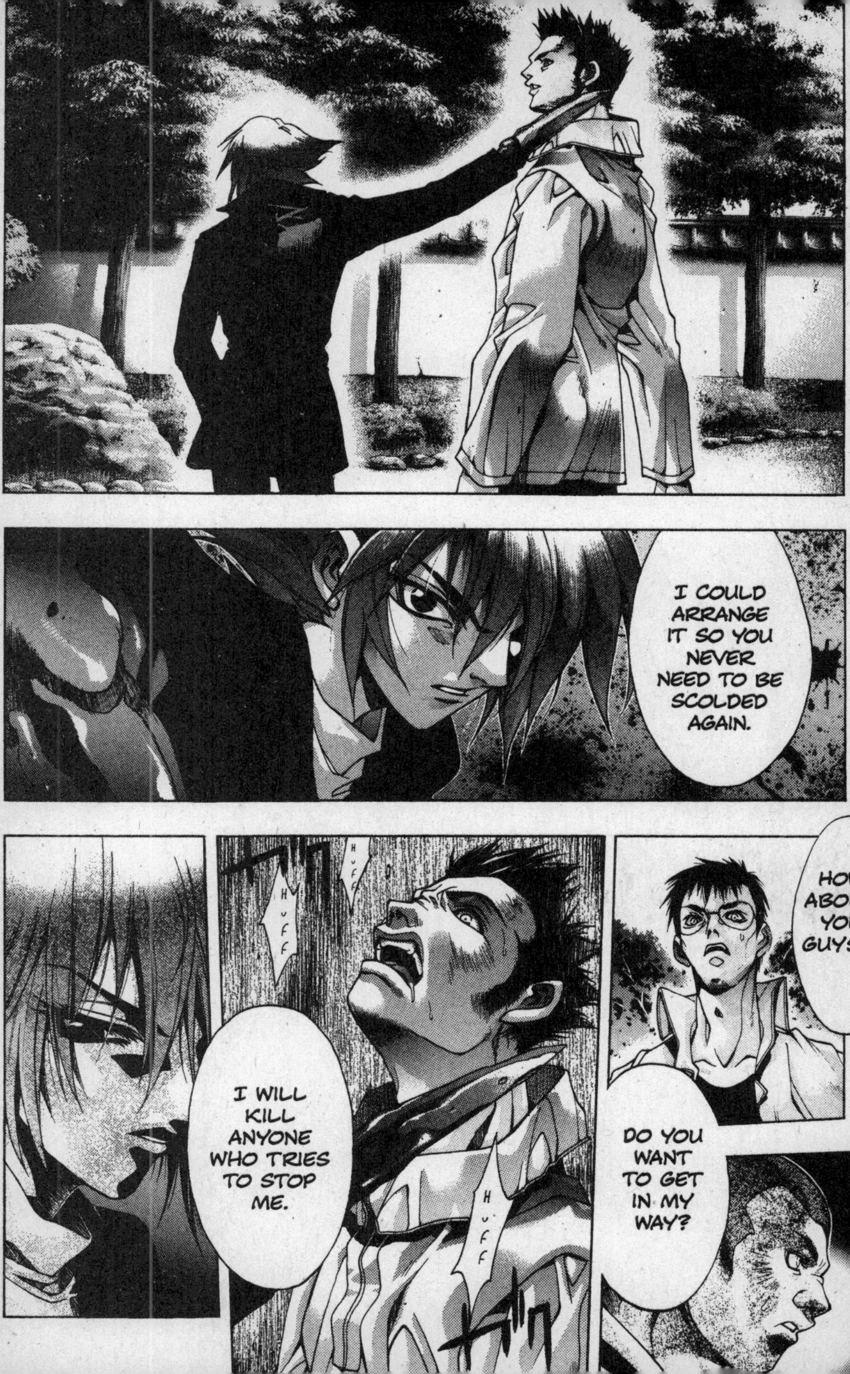
I COULD ARRANGE IT SO YOU NEVER NEED TO BE SCOLDED AGAIN.
HOW ABOUT YOU GUYS...
DO YOU WANT TO GET IN MY WAY?
HUFF
HUFF
I WILL KILL ANYONE WHO TRIES TO STOP ME.
HUFF

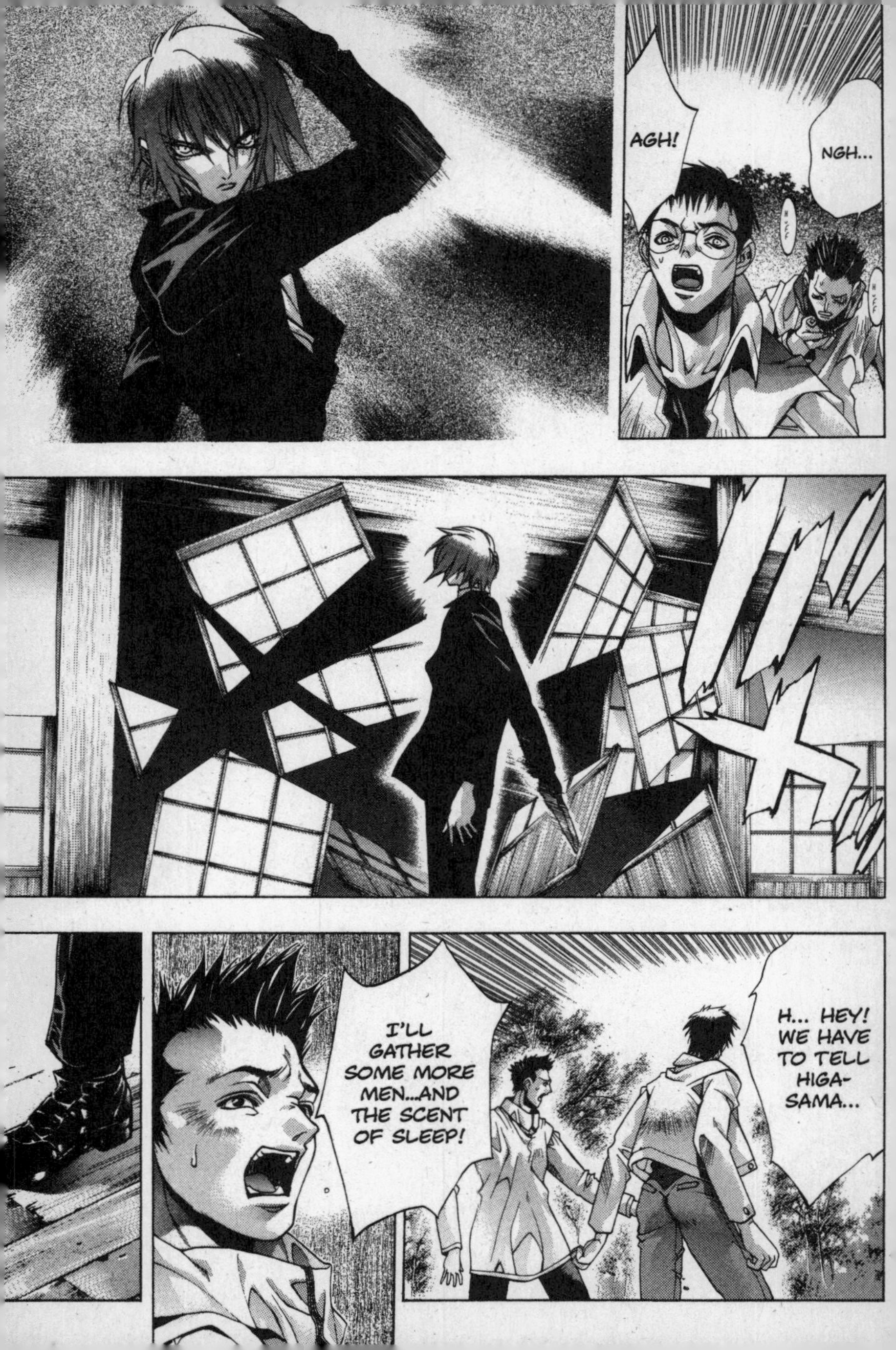
NGH...
AGH!
H... HEY! WE HAVE TO TELL HIGA-SAMA...
I'LL GATHER SOME MORE MEN...AND THE SCENT OF SLEEP!

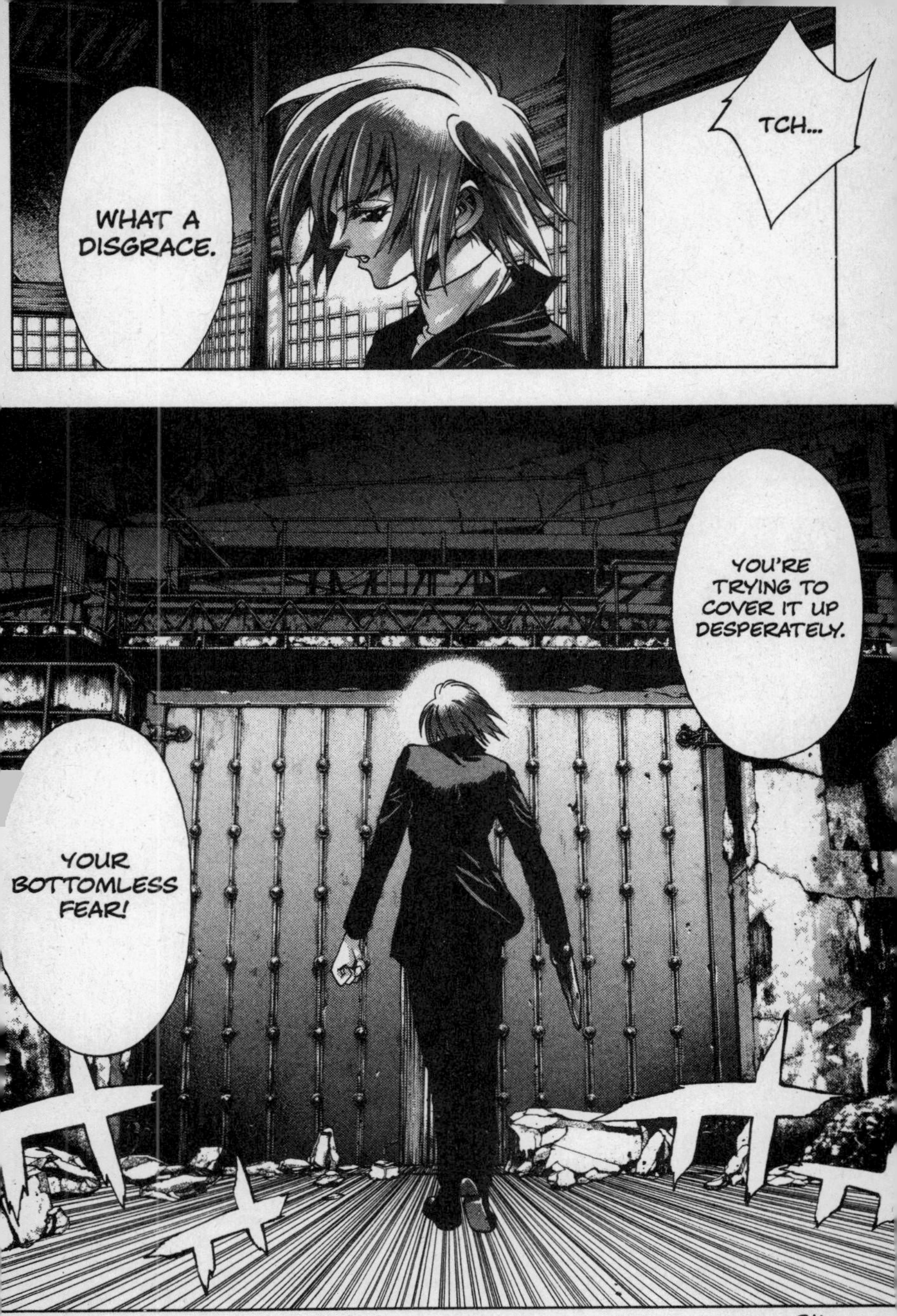
TCH...
WHAT A DISGRACE.
YOU'RE TRYING TO COVER IT UP DESPERATELY.
YOUR BOTTOMLESS FEAR!

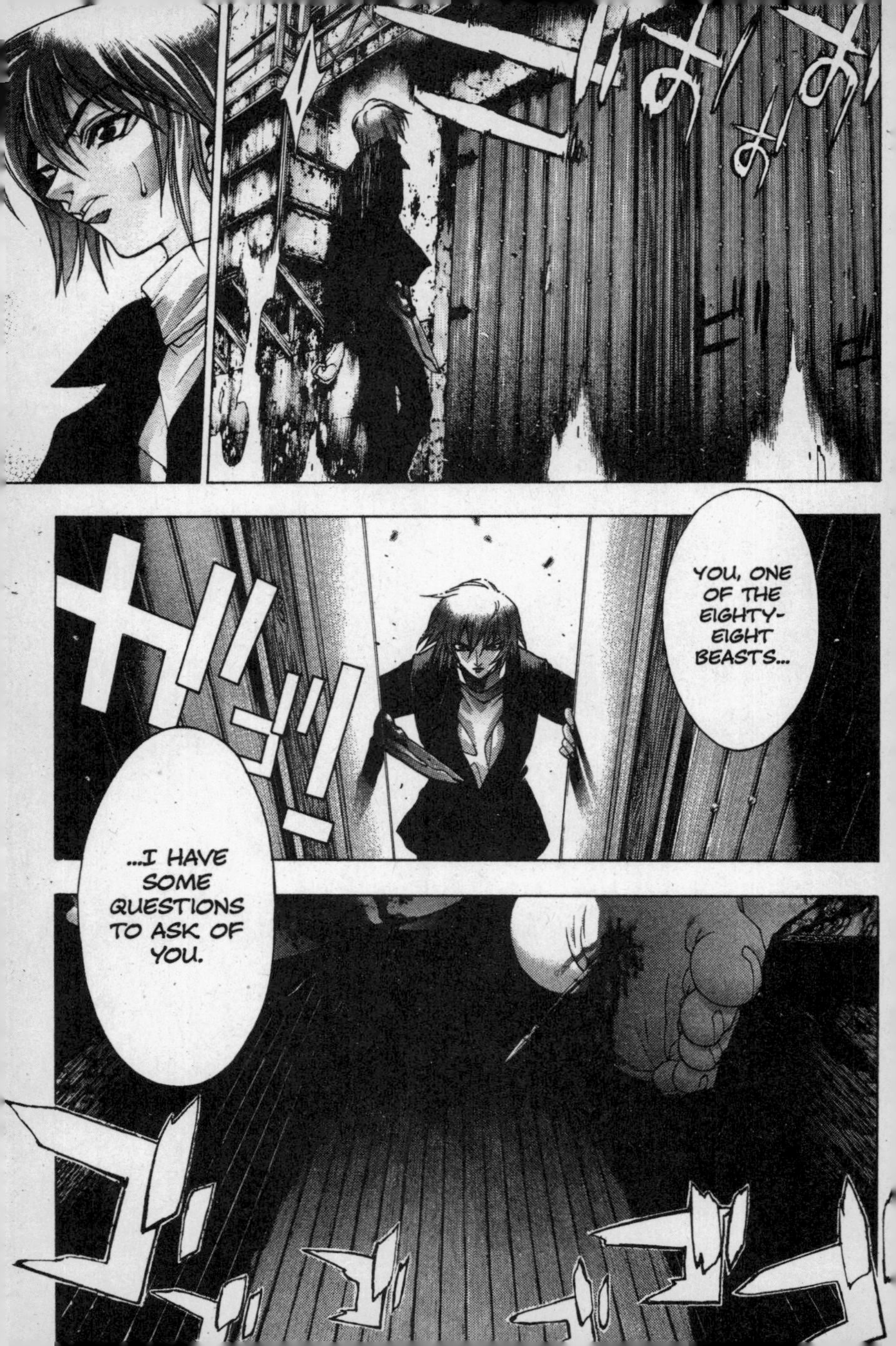
YOU, ONE OF THE EIGHTY-EIGHT BEASTS...
...I HAVE SOME QUESTIONS TO ASK OF YOU.

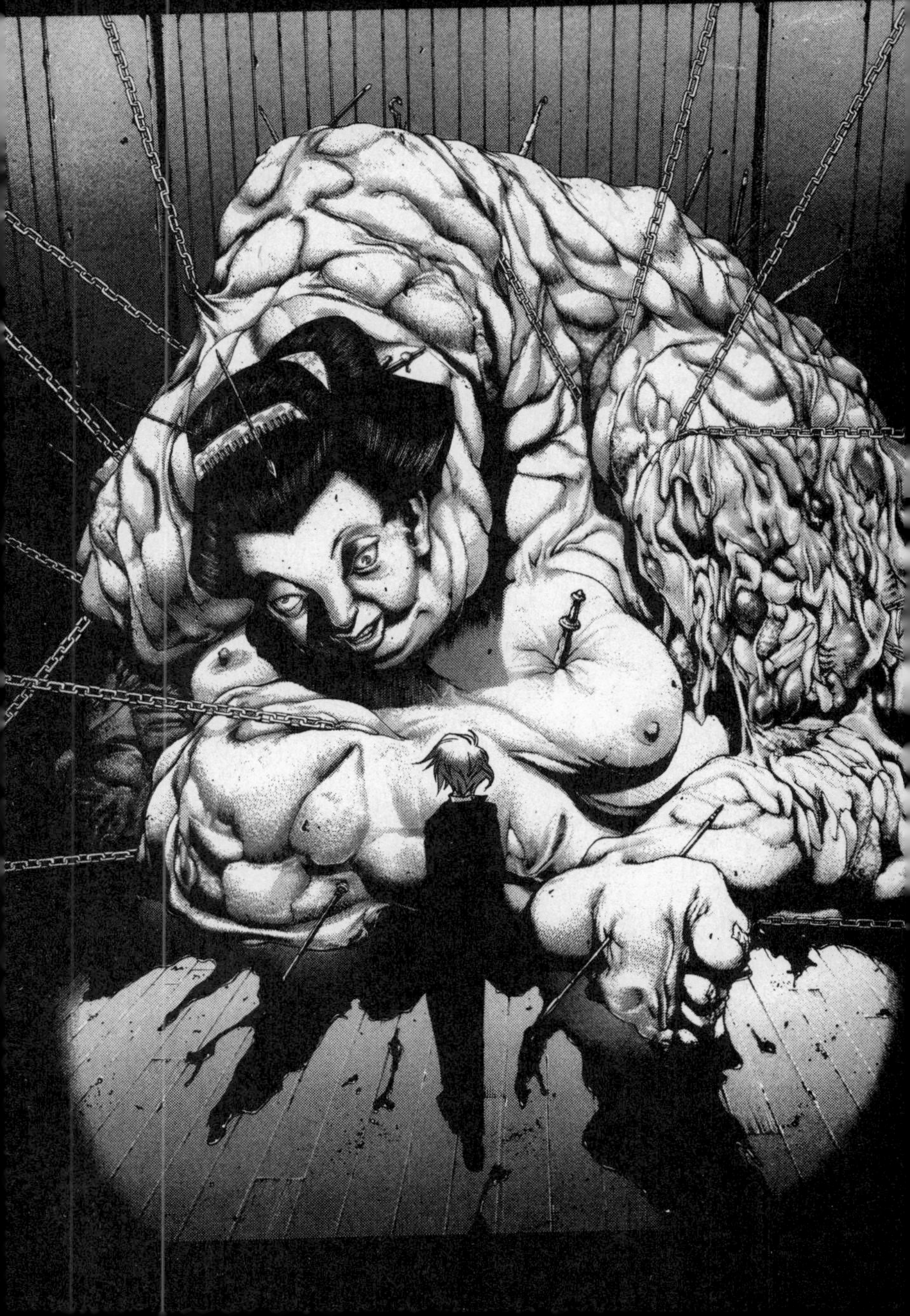

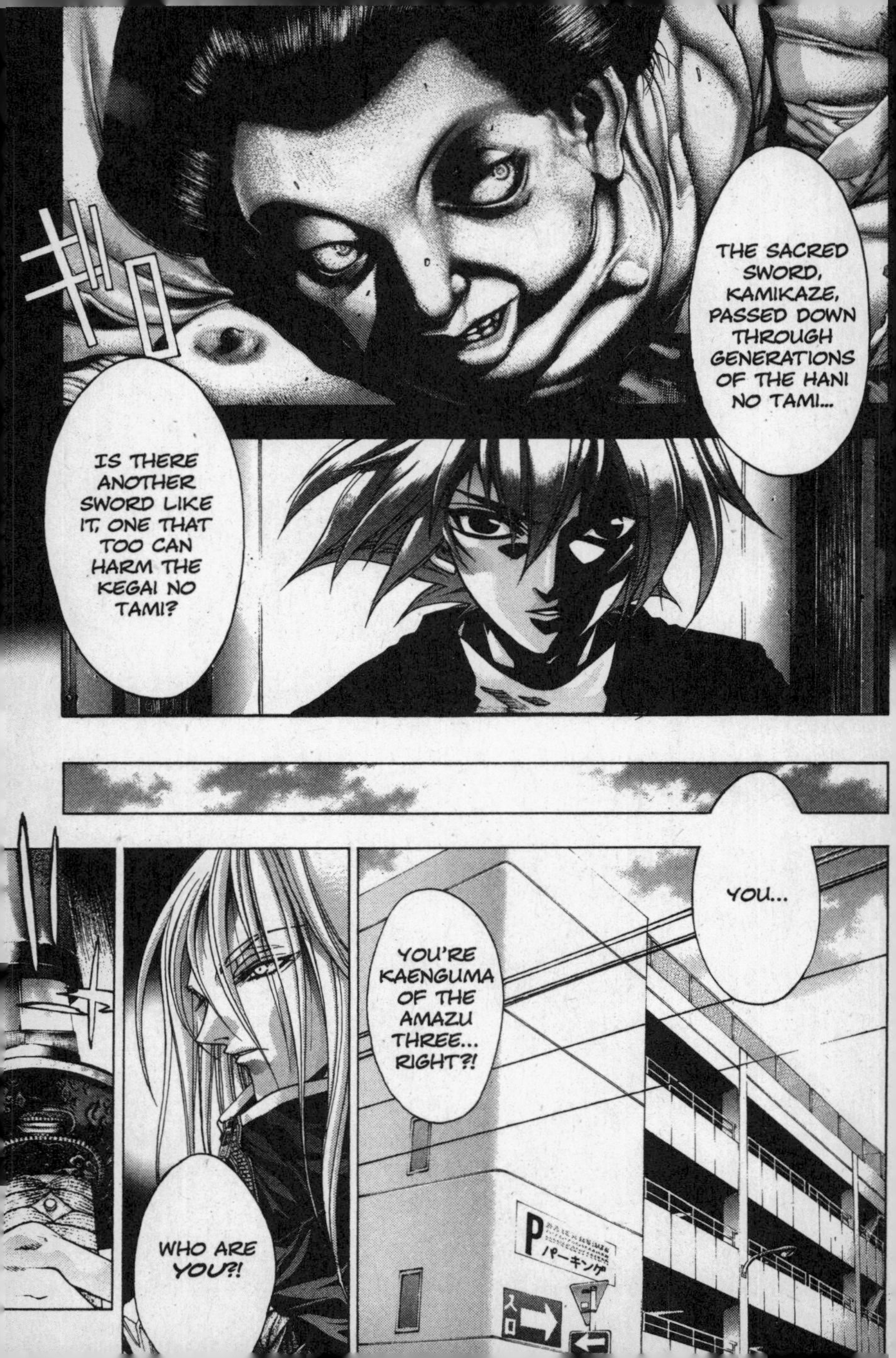
THE SACRED SWORD, KAMIKAZE, PASSED DOWN THROUGH GENERATIONS OF THE HANI NO TAMI...
IS THERE ANOTHER SWORD LIKE IT, ONE THAT TOO CAN HARM THE KEGAI NO TAMI?
YOU...
YOU'RE KAENGUMA OF THE AMAZU THREE... RIGHT?!
WHO ARE YOU?!

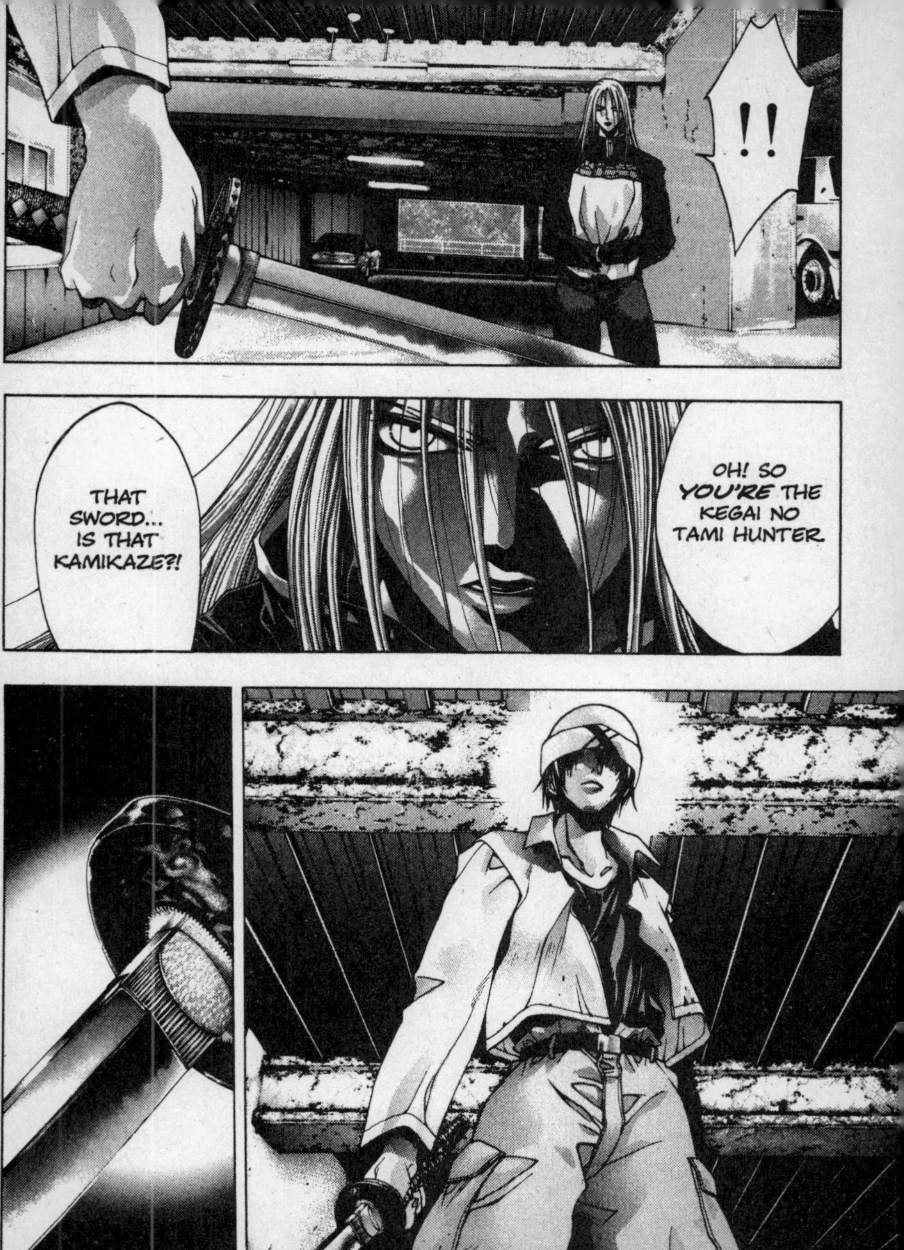
!!
OH! SO *YOU'RE* THE KEGAI NO TAMI HUNTER
THAT SWORD... IS THAT KAMIKAZE?!

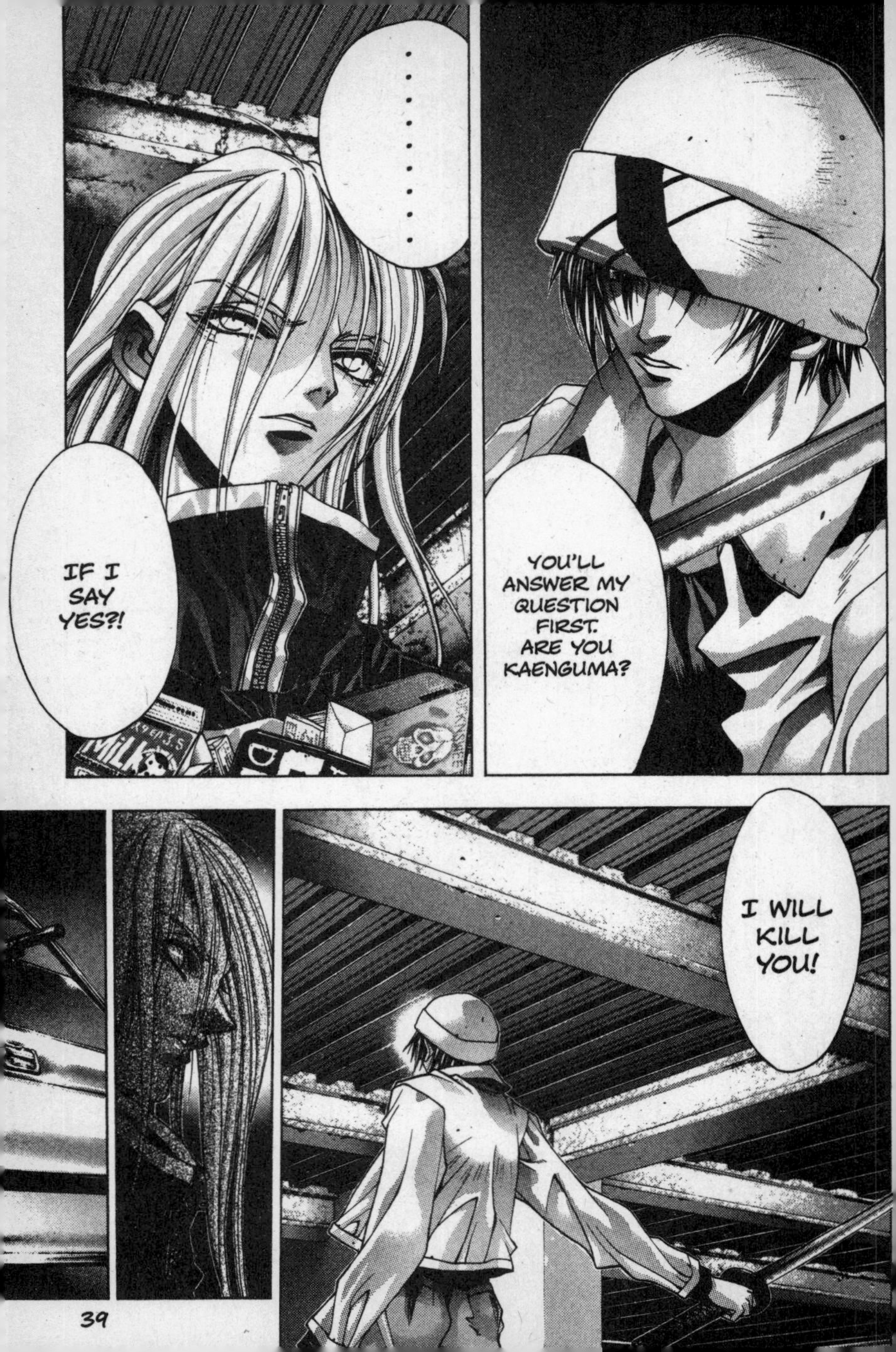

YOU'LL ANSWER MY QUESTION FIRST. ARE YOU KAENGUMA?
......
IF I SAY YES?!
I WILL KILL YOU!

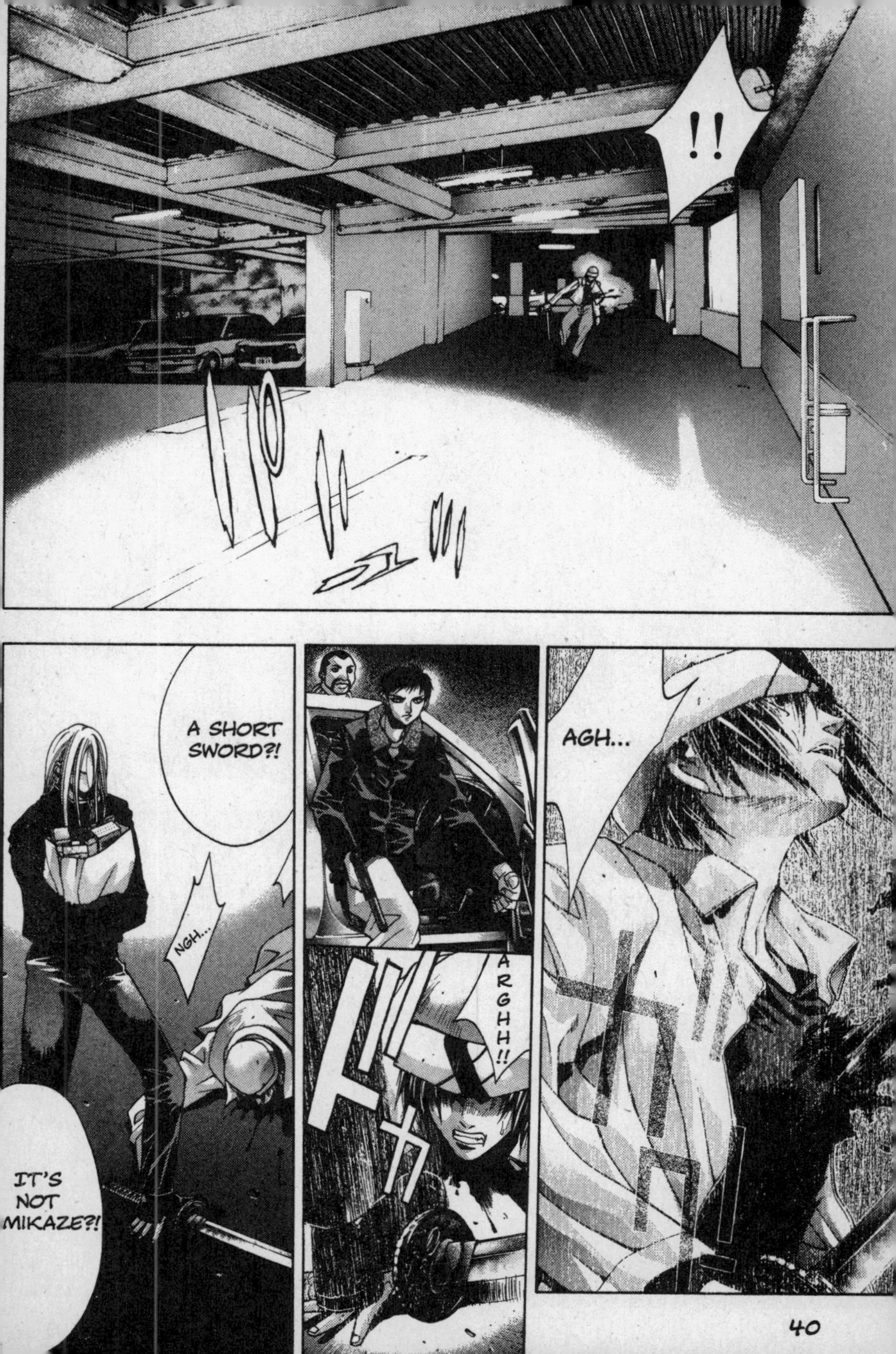
!!
AGH...
ARGHH!!
A SHORT SWORD?!
NGH...
IT'S NOT MIKAZE?!

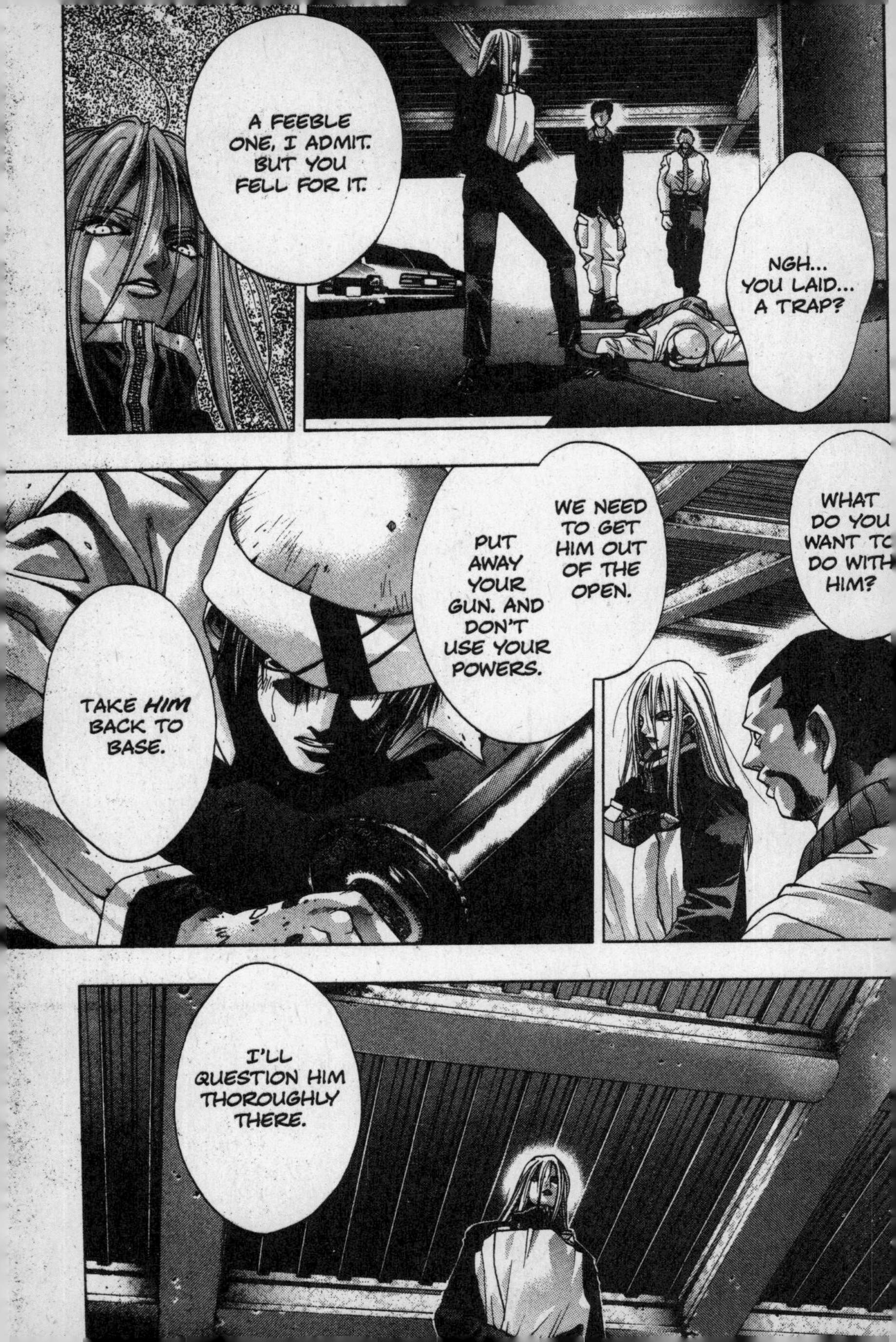
NGH... YOU LAID... A TRAP?
A FEEBLE ONE, I ADMIT. BUT YOU FELL FOR IT.
WHAT DO YOU WANT TO DO WITH HIM?
WE NEED TO GET HIM OUT OF THE OPEN.
PUT AWAY YOUR GUN. AND DON'T USE YOUR POWERS.
TAKE *HIM* BACK TO BASE.
I'LL QUESTION HIM THOROUGHLY THERE.

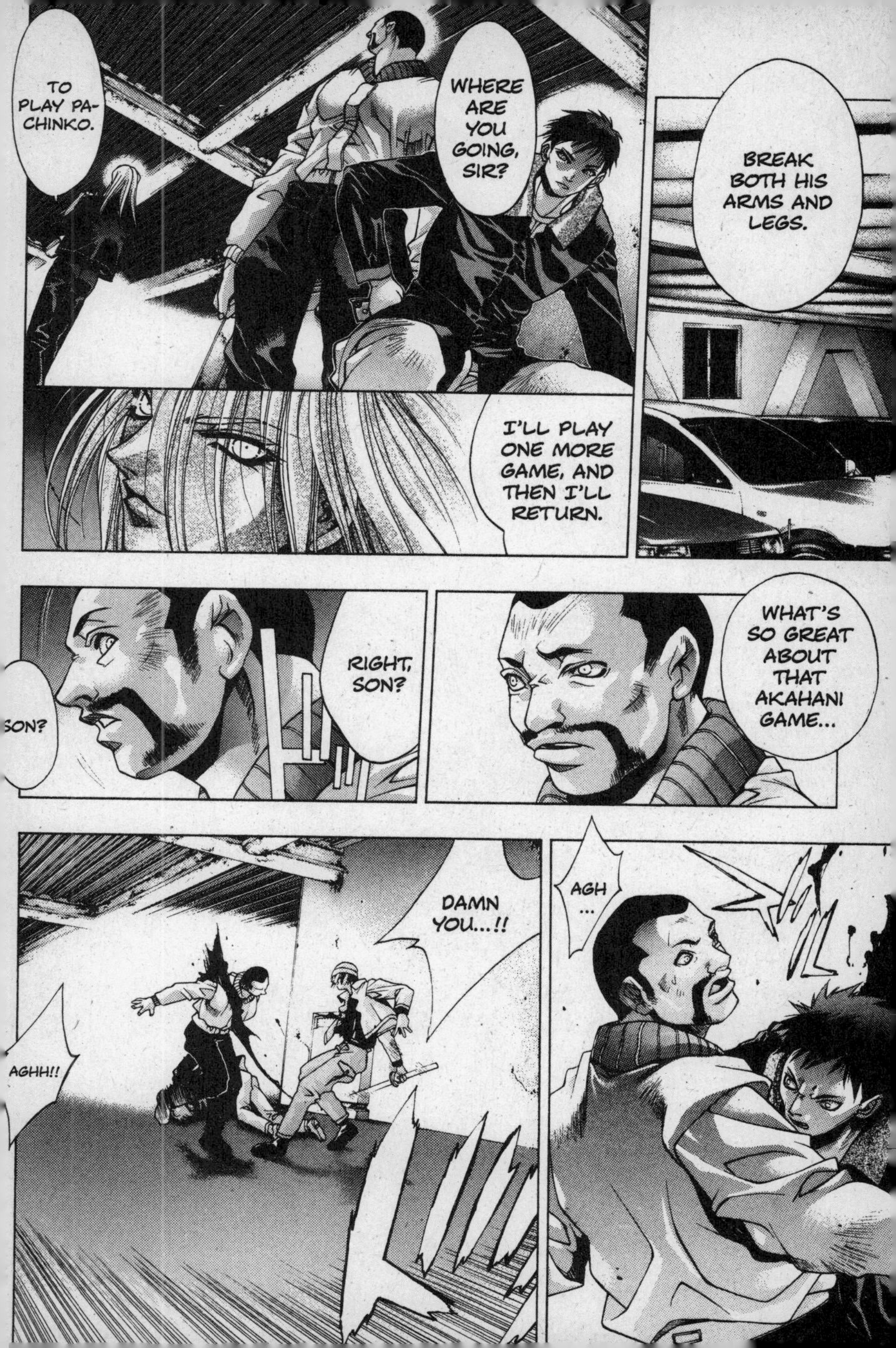
BREAK BOTH HIS ARMS AND LEGS.
WHERE ARE YOU GOING, SIR?
TO PLAY PA-CHINKO.
I'LL PLAY ONE MORE GAME, AND THEN I'LL RETURN.
WHAT'S SO GREAT ABOUT THAT AKAHANI GAME...
RIGHT, SON?
SON?
AGH ...
DAMN YOU...!!
AGHH!!

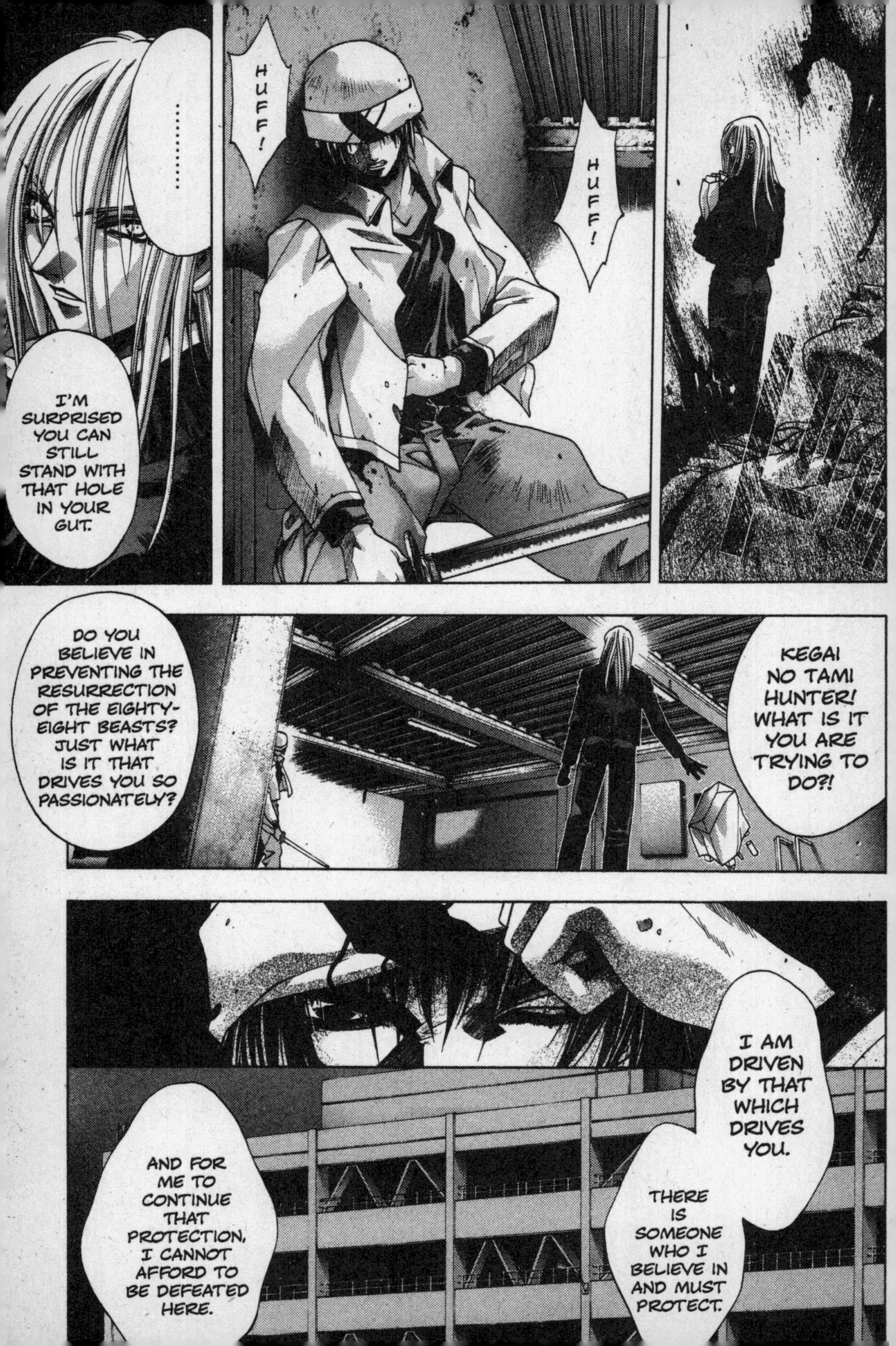

HUFF!
HUFF!
......
I'M SURPRISED YOU CAN STILL STAND WITH THAT HOLE IN YOUR GUT.
KEGAI NO TAMI HUNTER! WHAT IS IT YOU ARE TRYING TO DO?!
DO YOU BELIEVE IN PREVENTING THE RESURRECTION OF THE EIGHTY-EIGHT BEASTS? JUST WHAT IS IT THAT DRIVES YOU SO PASSIONATELY?
I AM DRIVEN BY THAT WHICH DRIVES YOU.
THERE IS SOMEONE WHO I BELIEVE IN AND MUST PROTECT.
AND FOR ME TO CONTINUE THAT PROTECTION, I CANNOT AFFORD TO BE DEFEATED HERE.

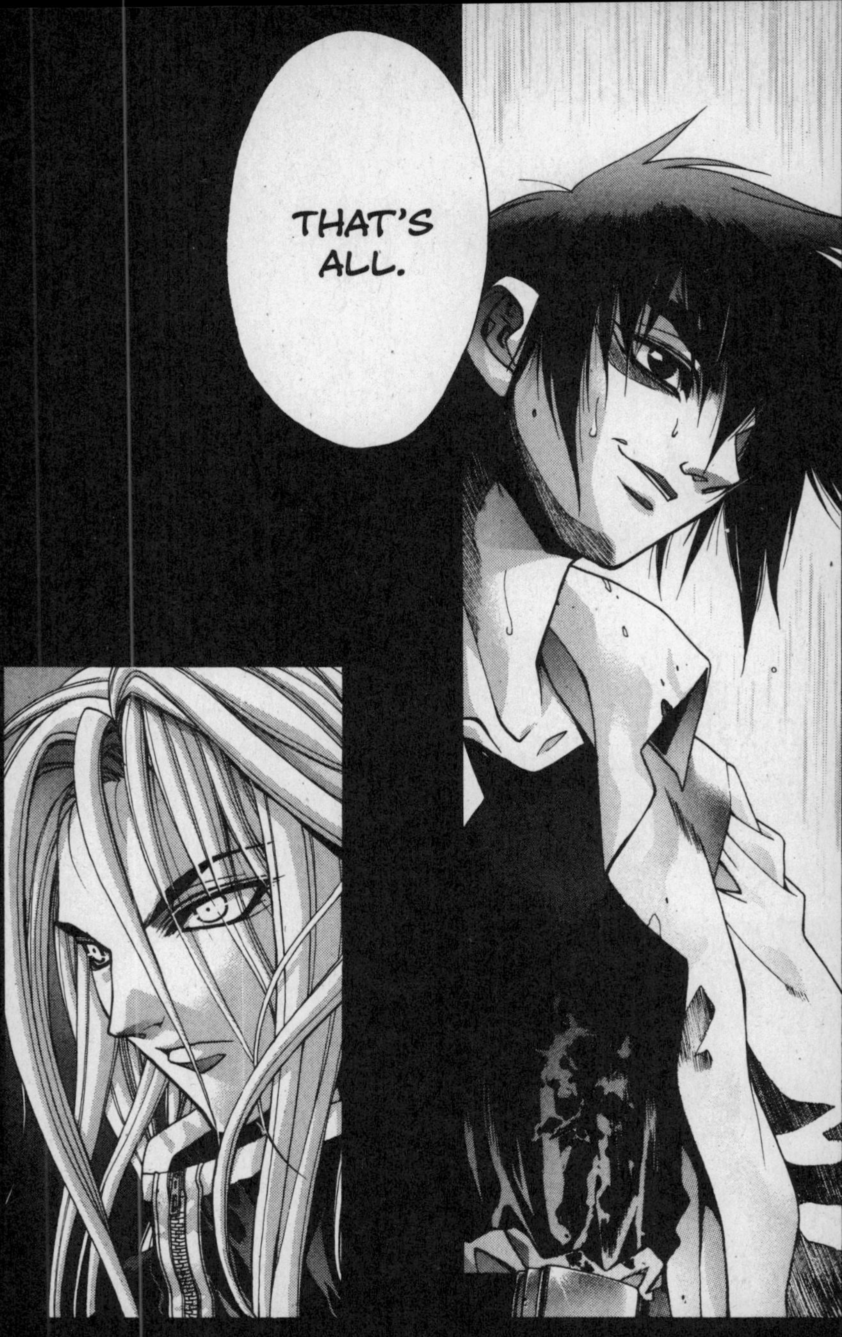
THAT'S ALL.

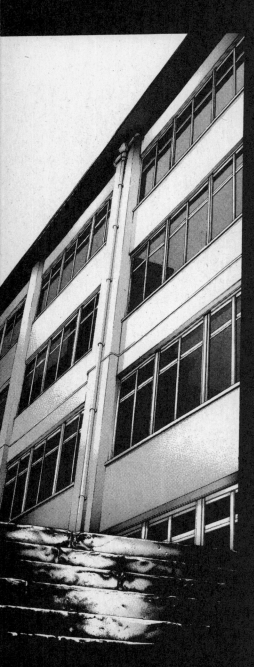

Chapter 21: Distrust

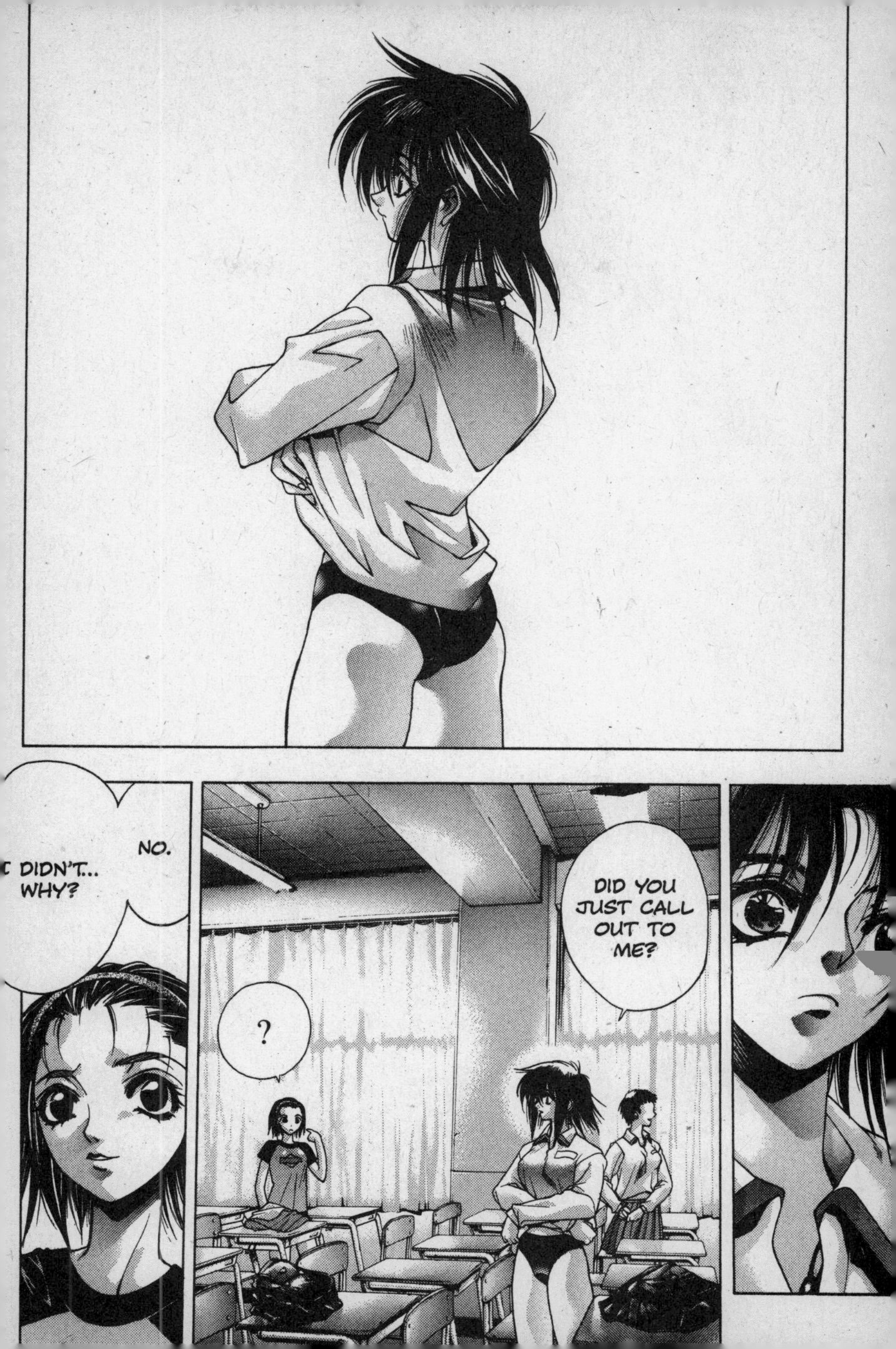
DID YOU JUST CALL OUT TO ME?
?
NO.
DIDN'T... WHY?

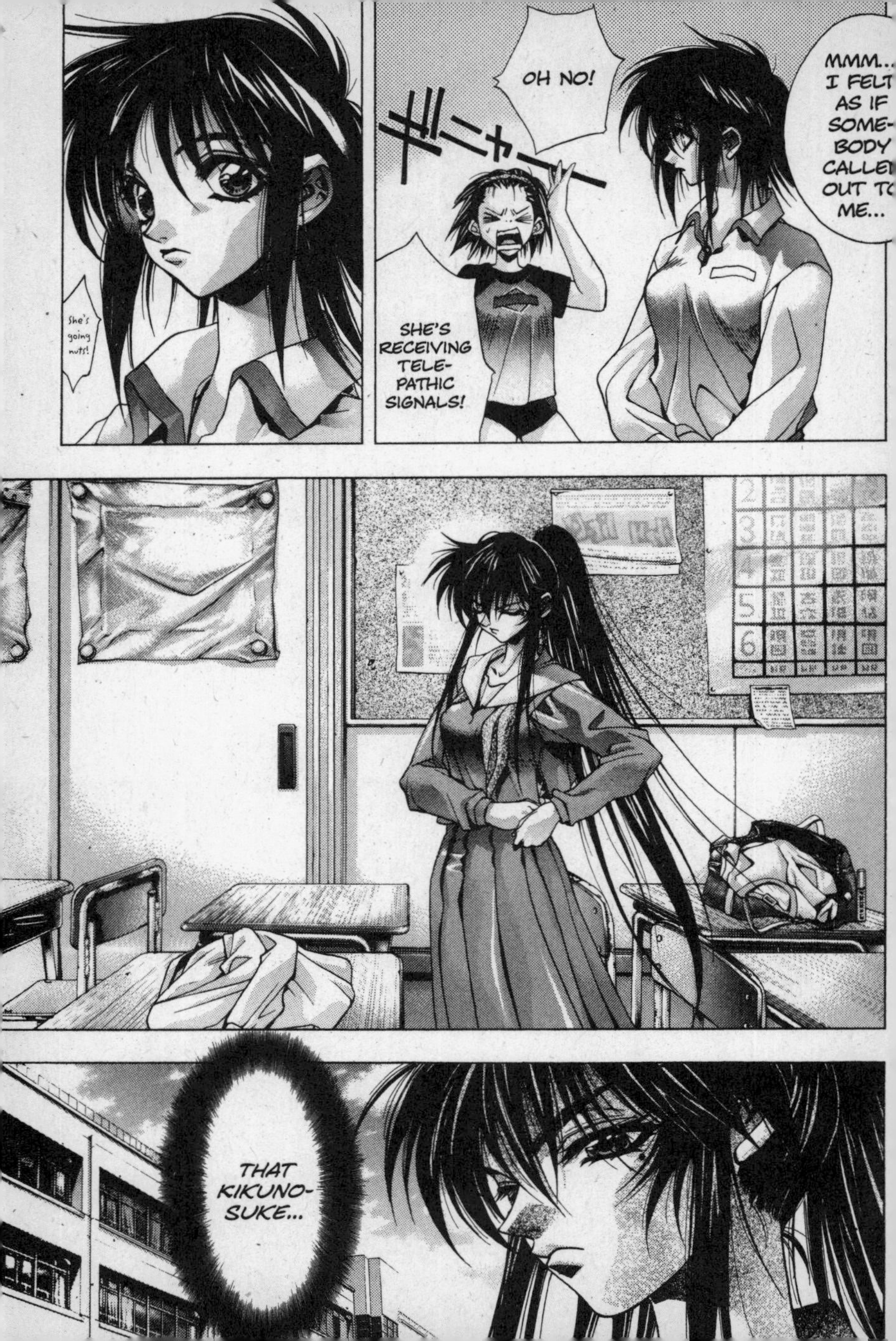
MMM... I FELT AS IF SOME-BODY CALLED OUT TO ME...
OH NO!
SHE'S RECEIVING TELE-PATHIC SIGNALS!
She's going nuts!
THAT KIKUNO-SUKE...

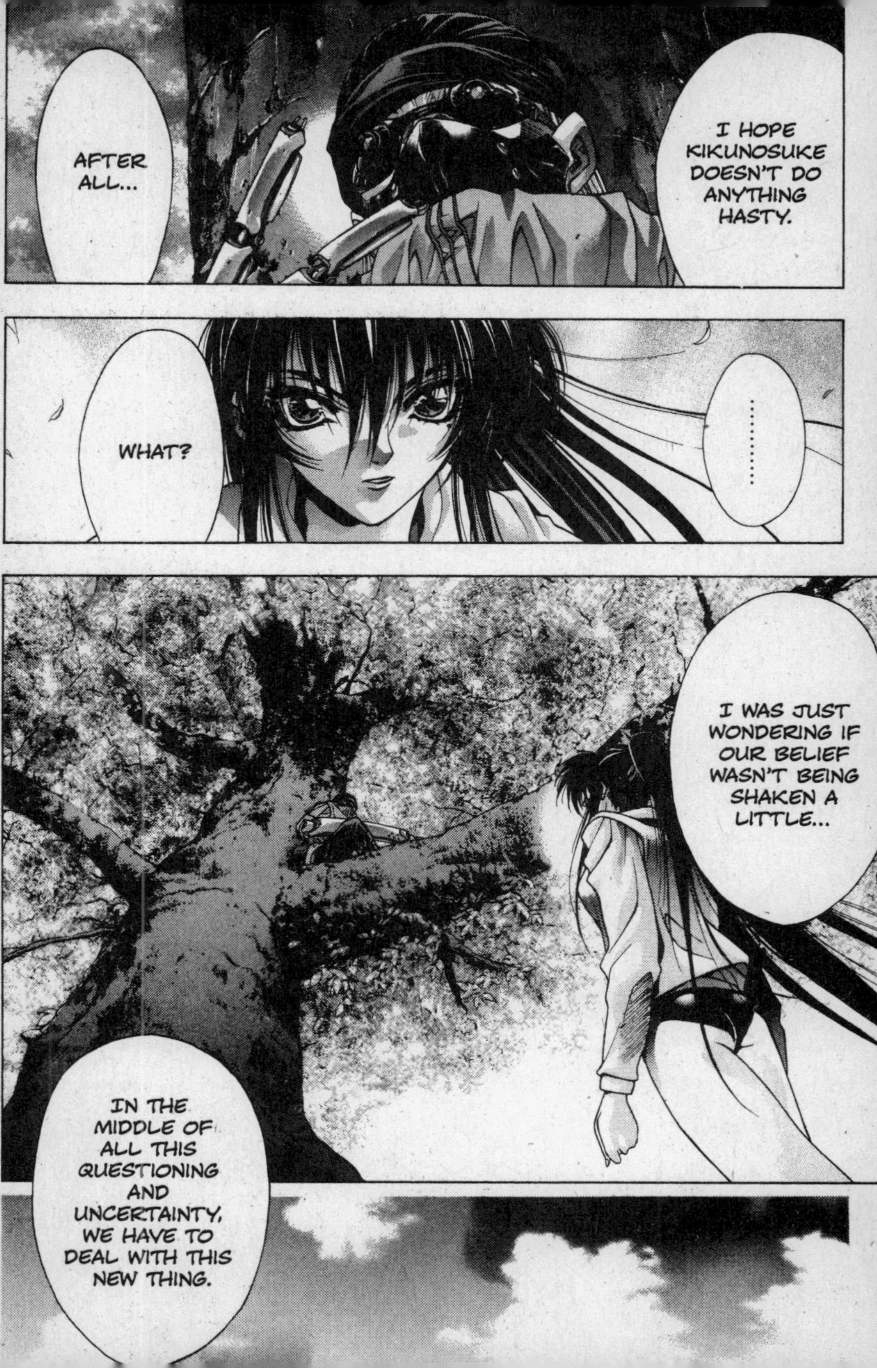
I HOPE KIKUNOSUKE DOESN'T DO ANYTHING HASTY.
AFTER ALL...
......
WHAT?
I WAS JUST WONDERING IF OUR BELIEF WASN'T BEING SHAKEN A LITTLE...
IN THE MIDDLE OF ALL THIS QUESTIONING AND UNCERTAINTY, WE HAVE TO DEAL WITH THIS NEW THING.

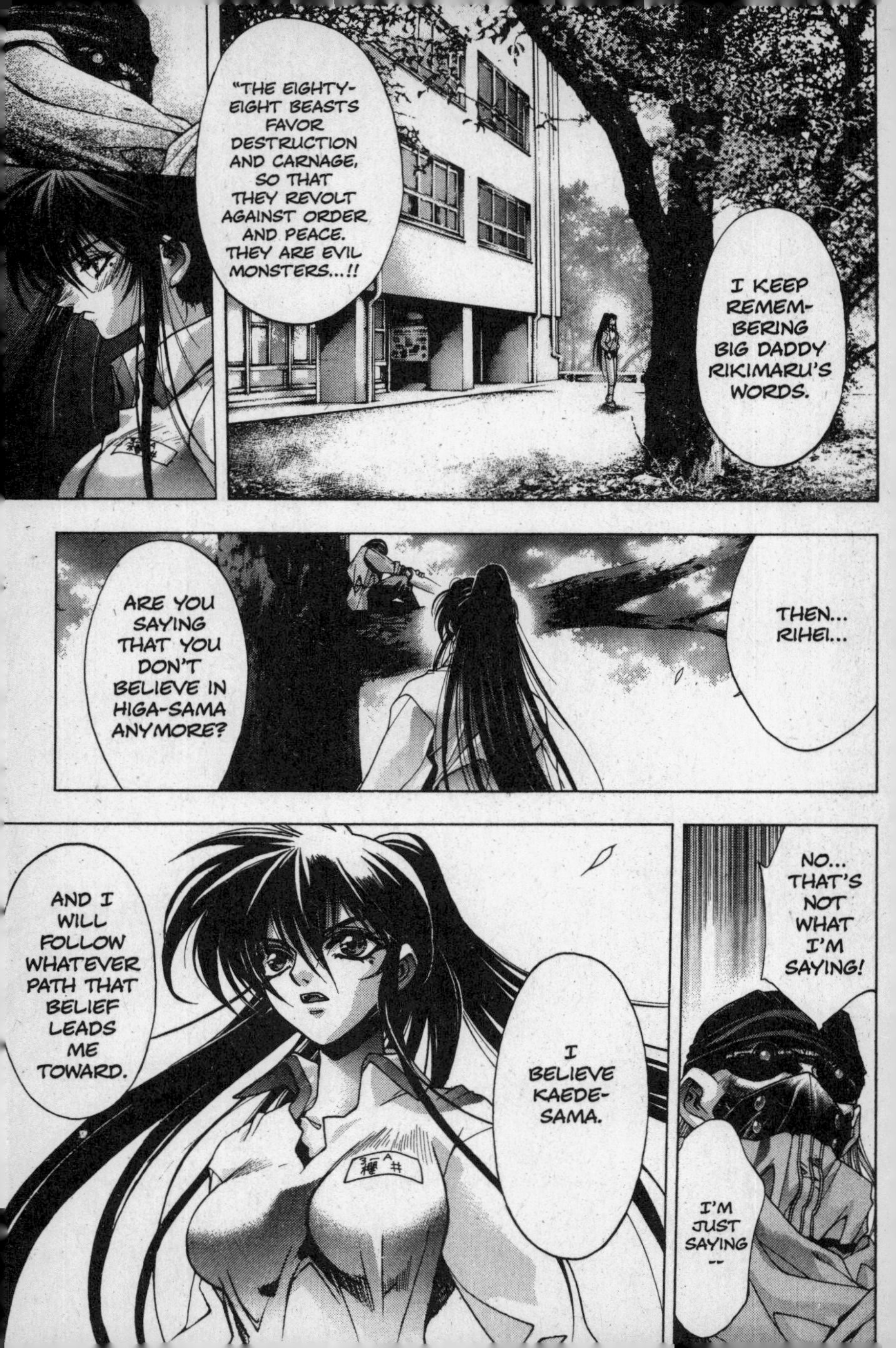
I KEEP REMEMBERING BIG DADDY RIKIMARU'S WORDS.
"THE EIGHTY-EIGHT BEASTS FAVOR DESTRUCTION AND CARNAGE, SO THAT THEY REVOLT AGAINST ORDER AND PEACE. THEY ARE EVIL MONSTERS...!!
THEN... RIHEI...
ARE YOU SAYING THAT YOU DON'T BELIEVE IN HIGA-SAMA ANYMORE?
NO... THAT'S NOT WHAT I'M SAYING!
I'M JUST SAYING --
I BELIEVE KAEDE-SAMA.
AND I WILL FOLLOW WHATEVER PATH THAT BELIEF LEADS ME TOWARD.

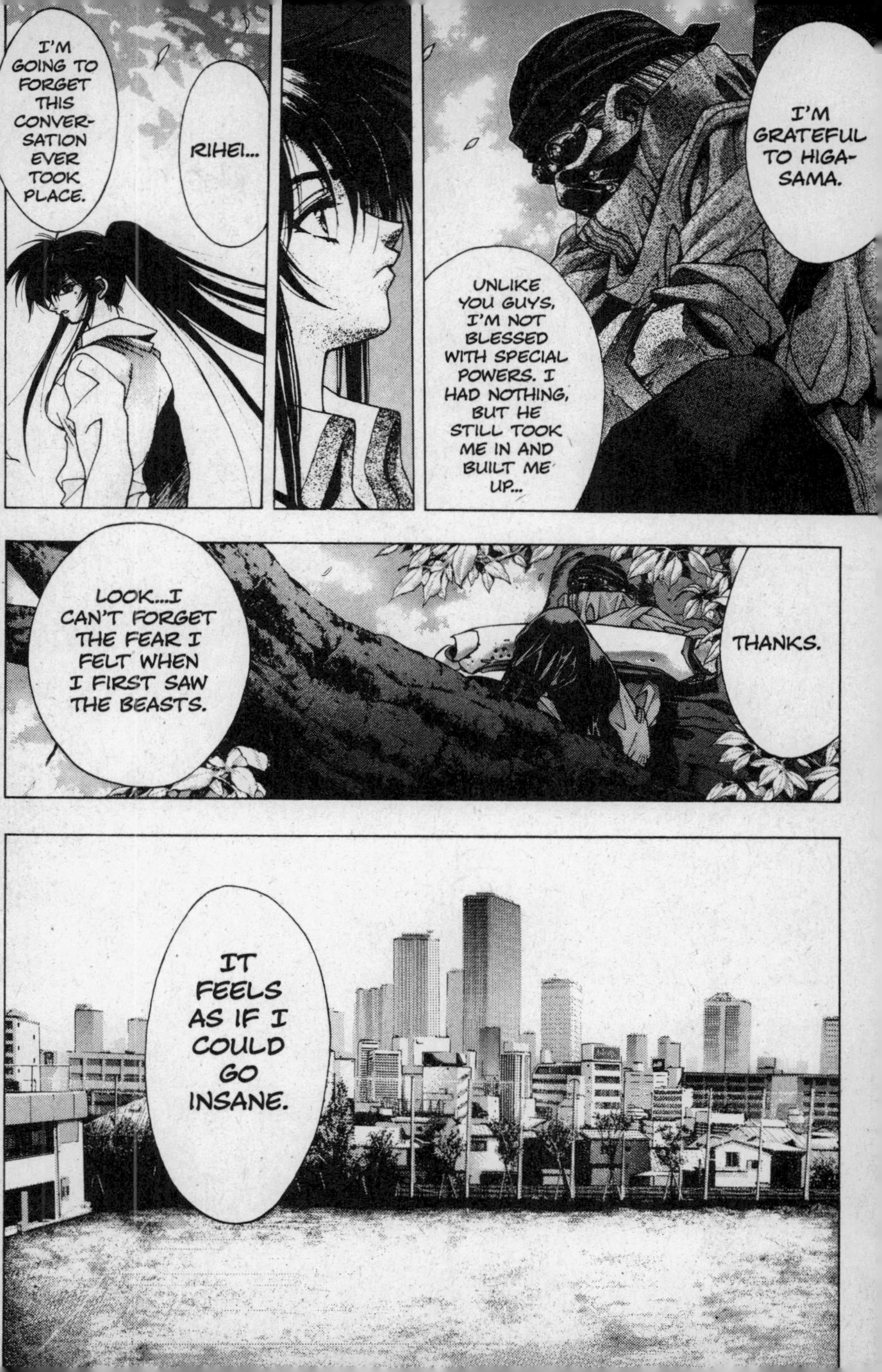
I'M GRATEFUL TO HIGA-SAMA.
UNLIKE YOU GUYS, I'M NOT BLESSED WITH SPECIAL POWERS. I HAD NOTHING, BUT HE STILL TOOK ME IN AND BUILT ME UP...
RIHEI...
I'M GOING TO FORGET THIS CONVER-SATION EVER TOOK PLACE.
THANKS.
LOOK...I CAN'T FORGET THE FEAR I FELT WHEN I FIRST SAW THE BEASTS.
IT FEELS AS IF I COULD GO INSANE.

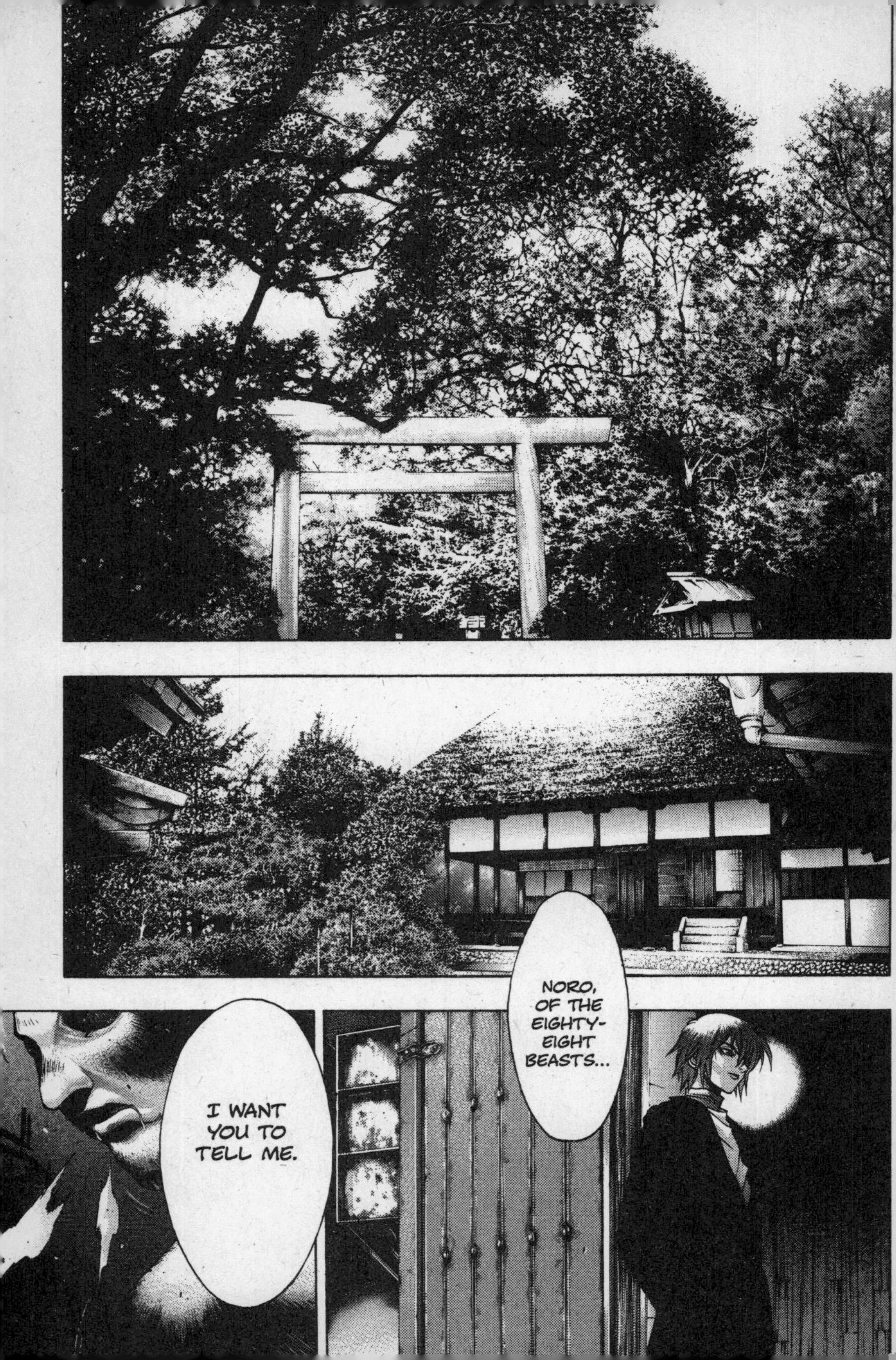
NORO, OF THE EIGHTY-EIGHT BEASTS...
I WANT YOU TO TELL ME.

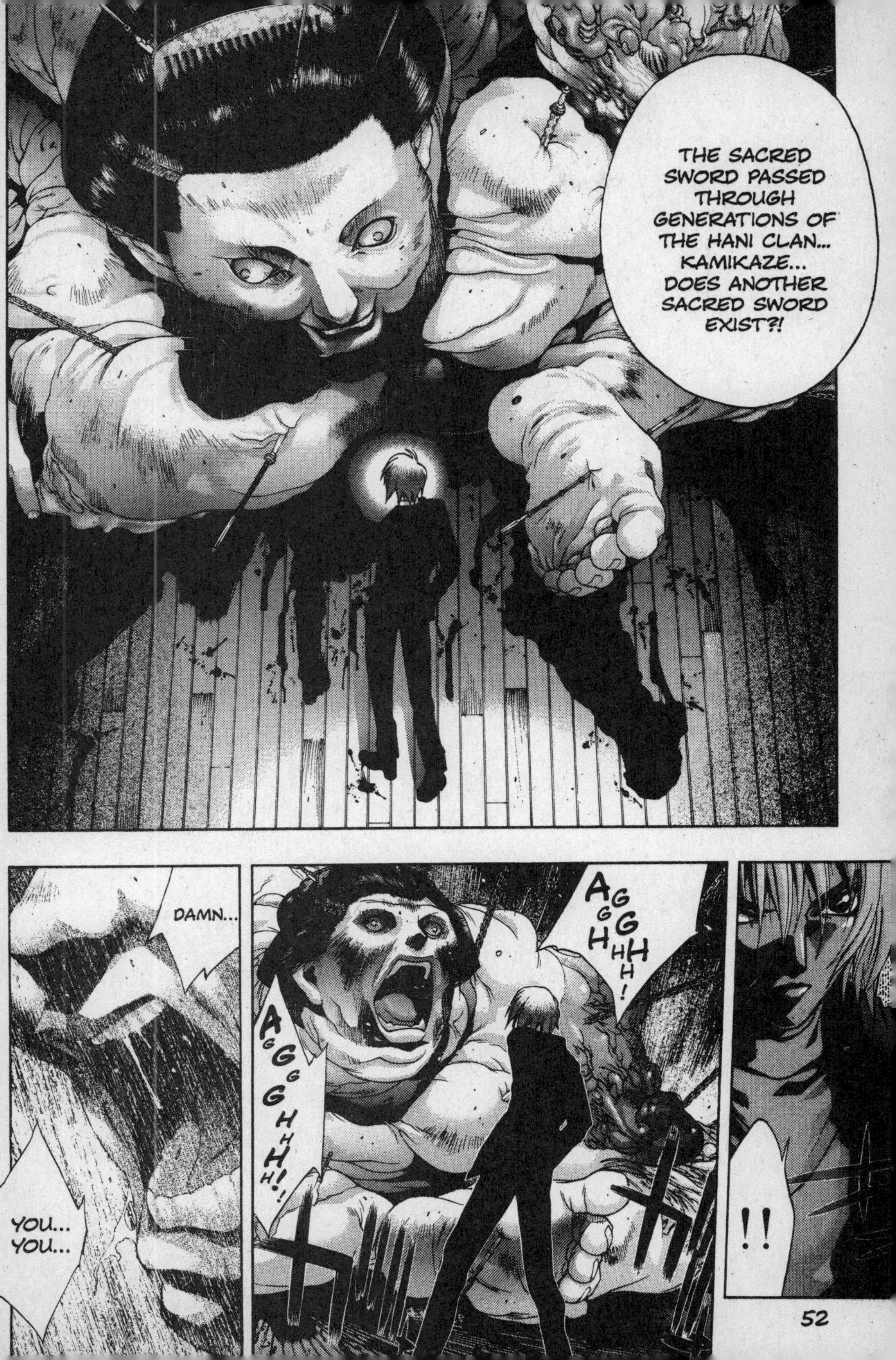

THE SACRED SWORD PASSED THROUGH GENERATIONS OF THE HANI CLAN... KAMIKAZE... DOES ANOTHER SACRED SWORD EXIST?!
!!
AGGGHHHH!
AGGGGHHHH!!
DAMN...
YOU... YOU...

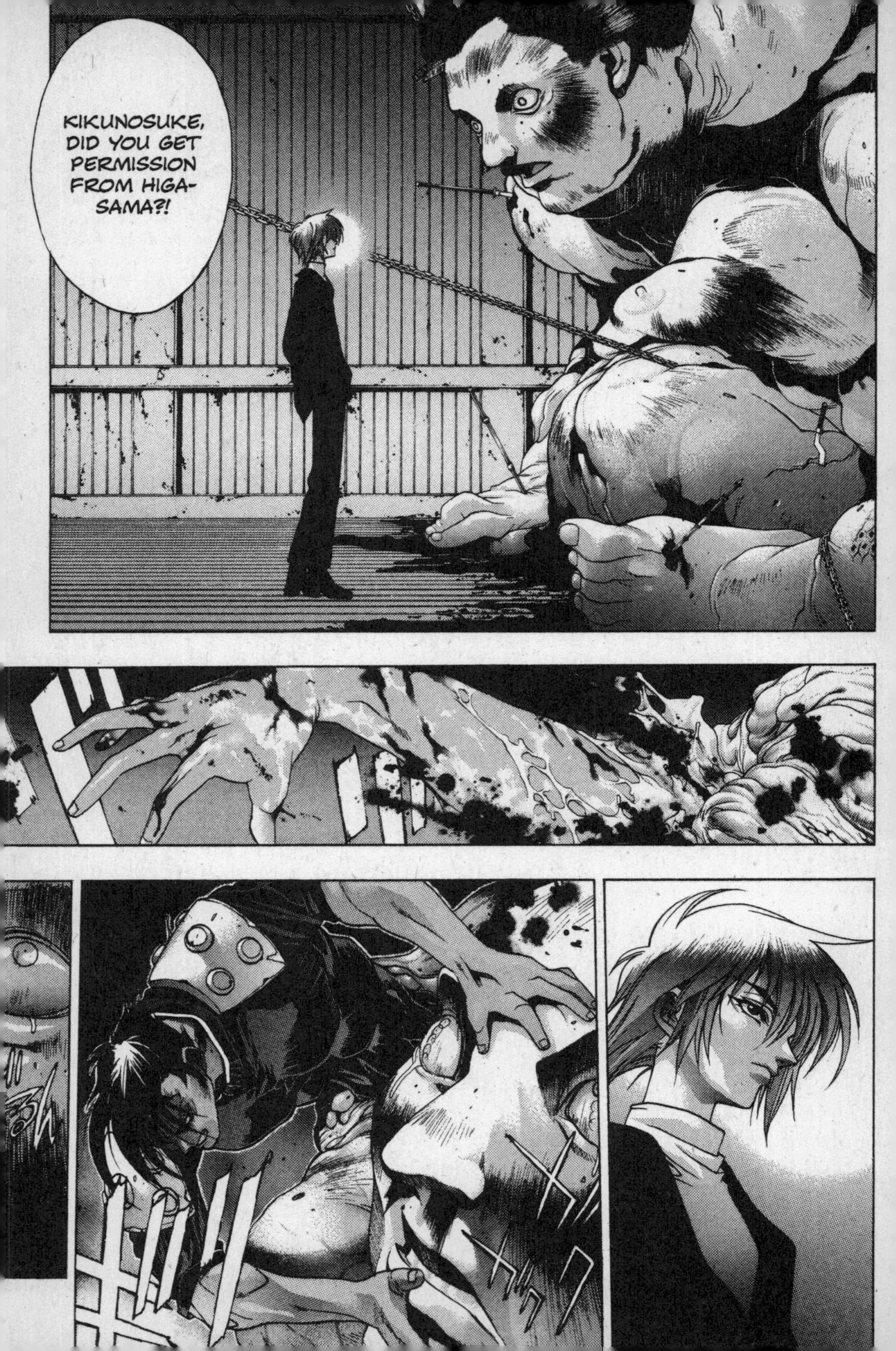
KIKUNOSUKE, DID YOU GET PERMISSION FROM HIGA-SAMA?!

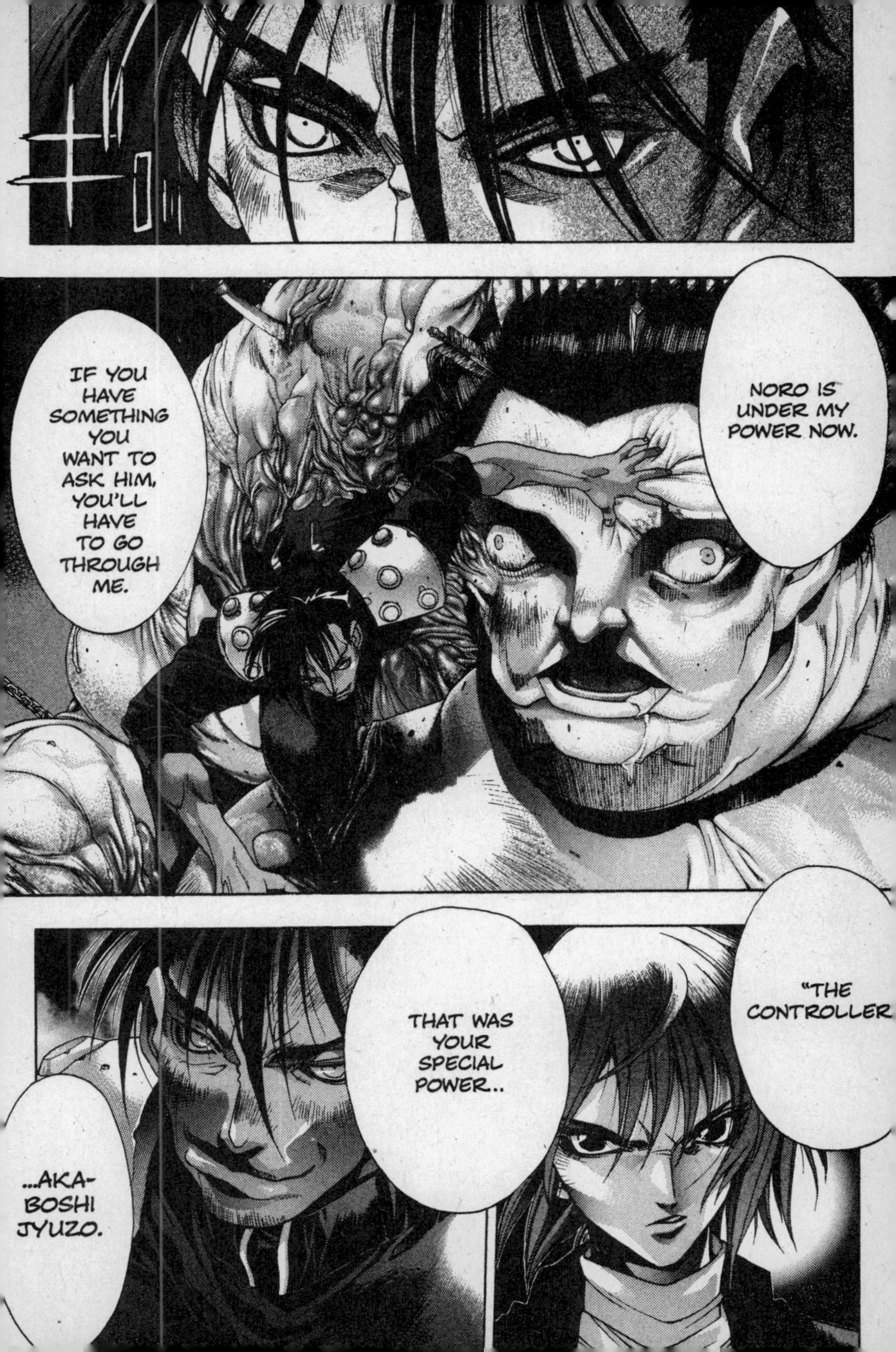
NORO IS UNDER MY POWER NOW.
IF YOU HAVE SOMETHING YOU WANT TO ASK HIM, YOU'LL HAVE TO GO THROUGH ME.
"THE CONTROLLER
THAT WAS YOUR SPECIAL POWER...
...AKA-BOSHI JYUZO.

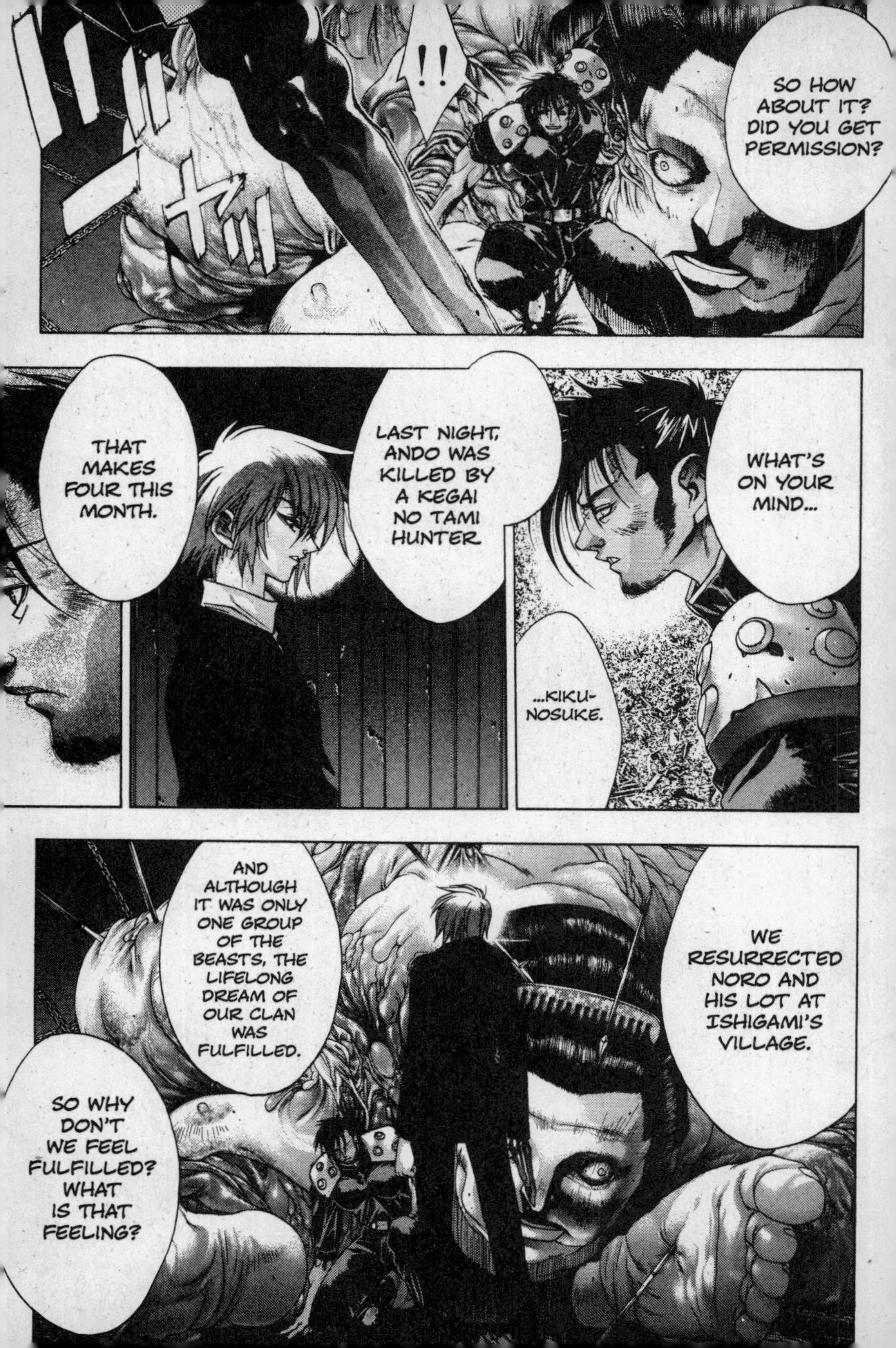
SO HOW ABOUT IT? DID YOU GET PERMISSION?
!!
WHAT'S ON YOUR MIND...
...KIKU-NOSUKE.
LAST NIGHT, ANDO WAS KILLED BY A KEGAI NO TAMI HUNTER
THAT MAKES FOUR THIS MONTH.
WE RESURRECTED NORO AND HIS LOT AT ISHIGAMI'S VILLAGE.
AND ALTHOUGH IT WAS ONLY ONE GROUP OF THE BEASTS, THE LIFELONG DREAM OF OUR CLAN WAS FULFILLED.
SO WHY DON'T WE FEEL FULFILLED? WHAT IS THAT FEELING?

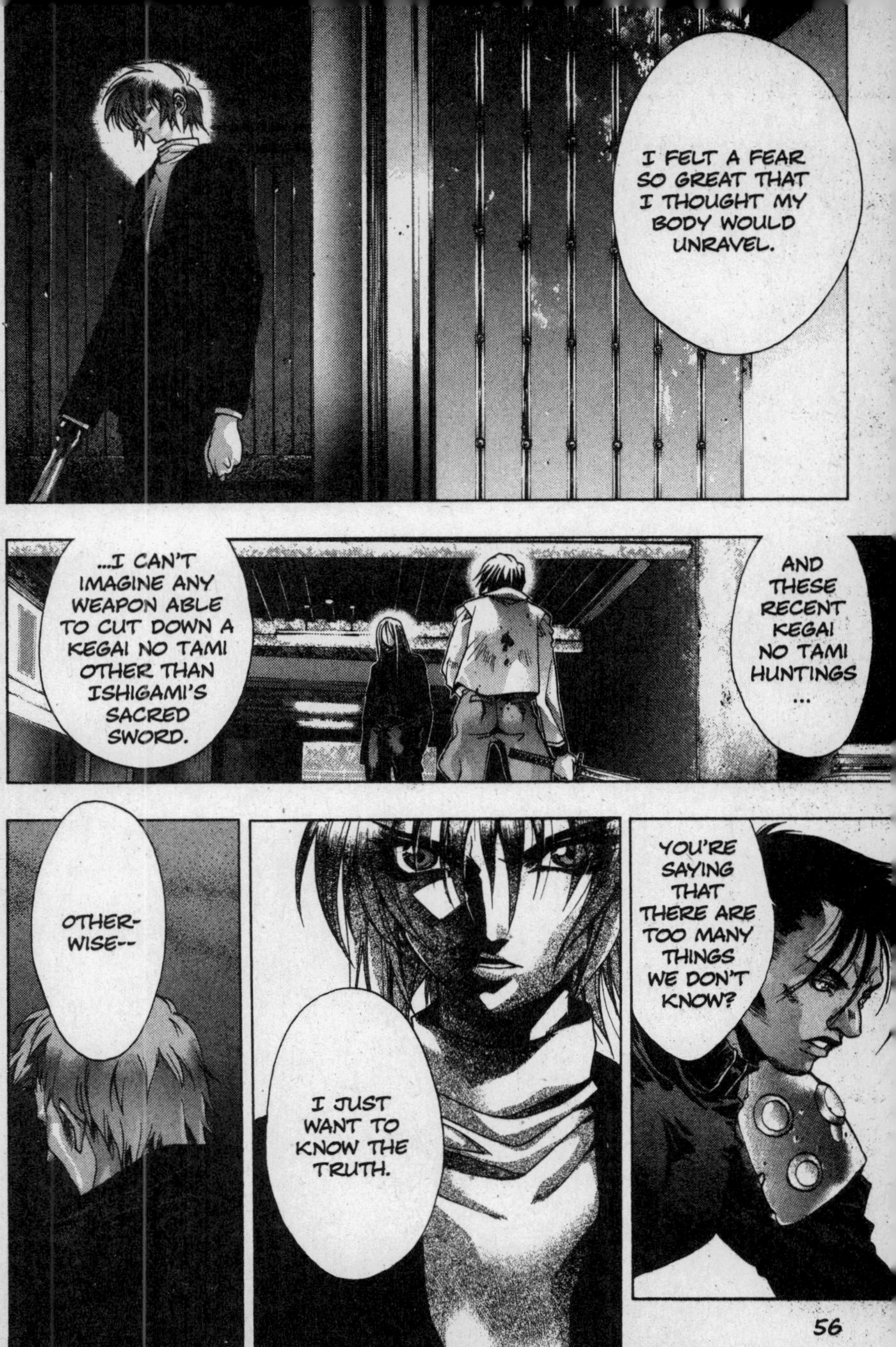
I FELT A FEAR SO GREAT THAT I THOUGHT MY BODY WOULD UNRAVEL.
AND THESE RECENT KEGAI NO TAMI HUNTINGS...
...I CAN'T IMAGINE ANY WEAPON ABLE TO CUT DOWN A KEGAI NO TAMI OTHER THAN ISHIGAMI'S SACRED SWORD.
YOU'RE SAYING THAT THERE ARE TOO MANY THINGS WE DON'T KNOW?
I JUST WANT TO KNOW THE TRUTH.
OTHER-WISE--

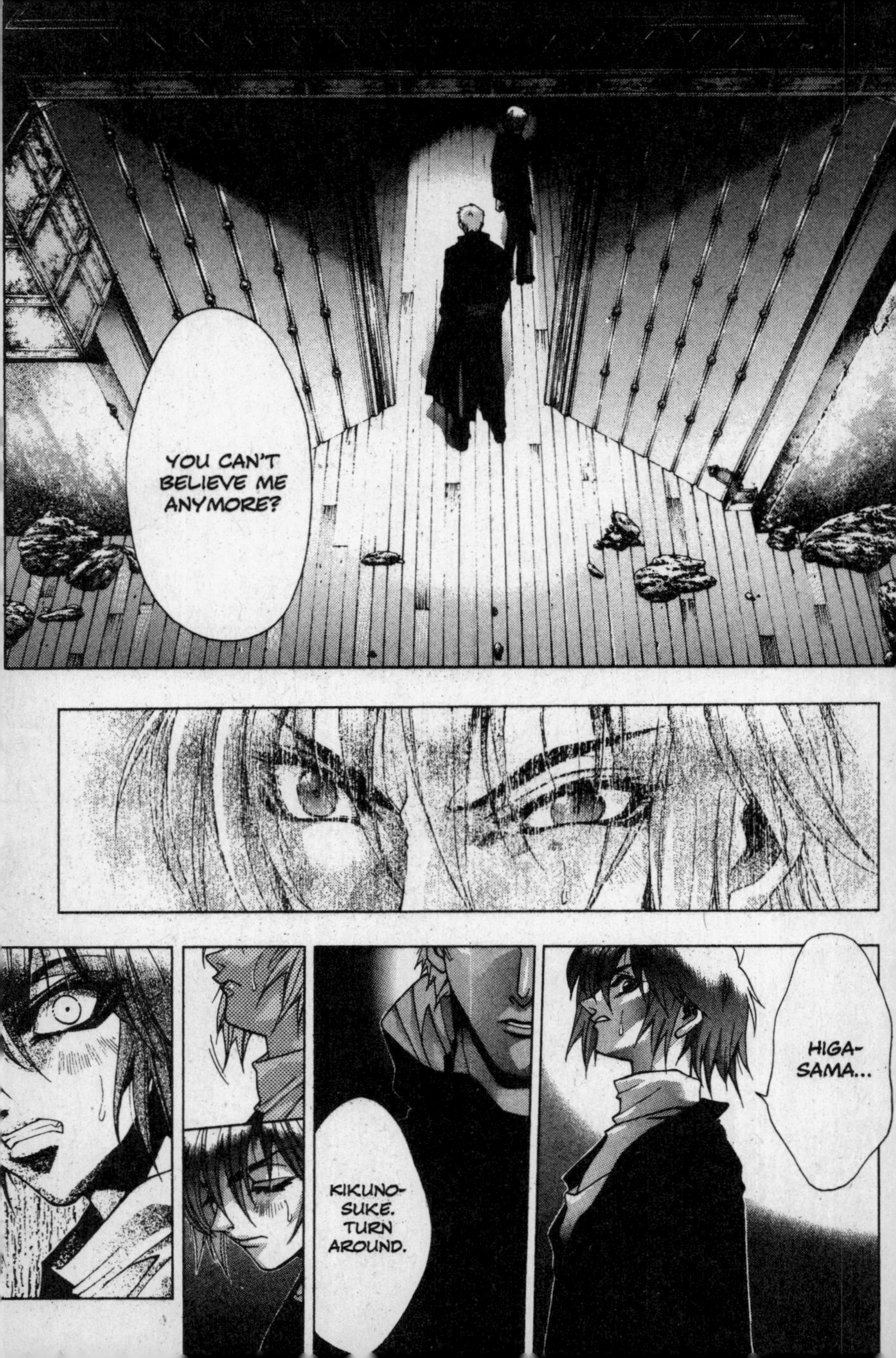
YOU CAN'T BELIEVE ME ANYMORE?
HIGA-SAMA...
KIKUNO-SUKE. TURN AROUND.

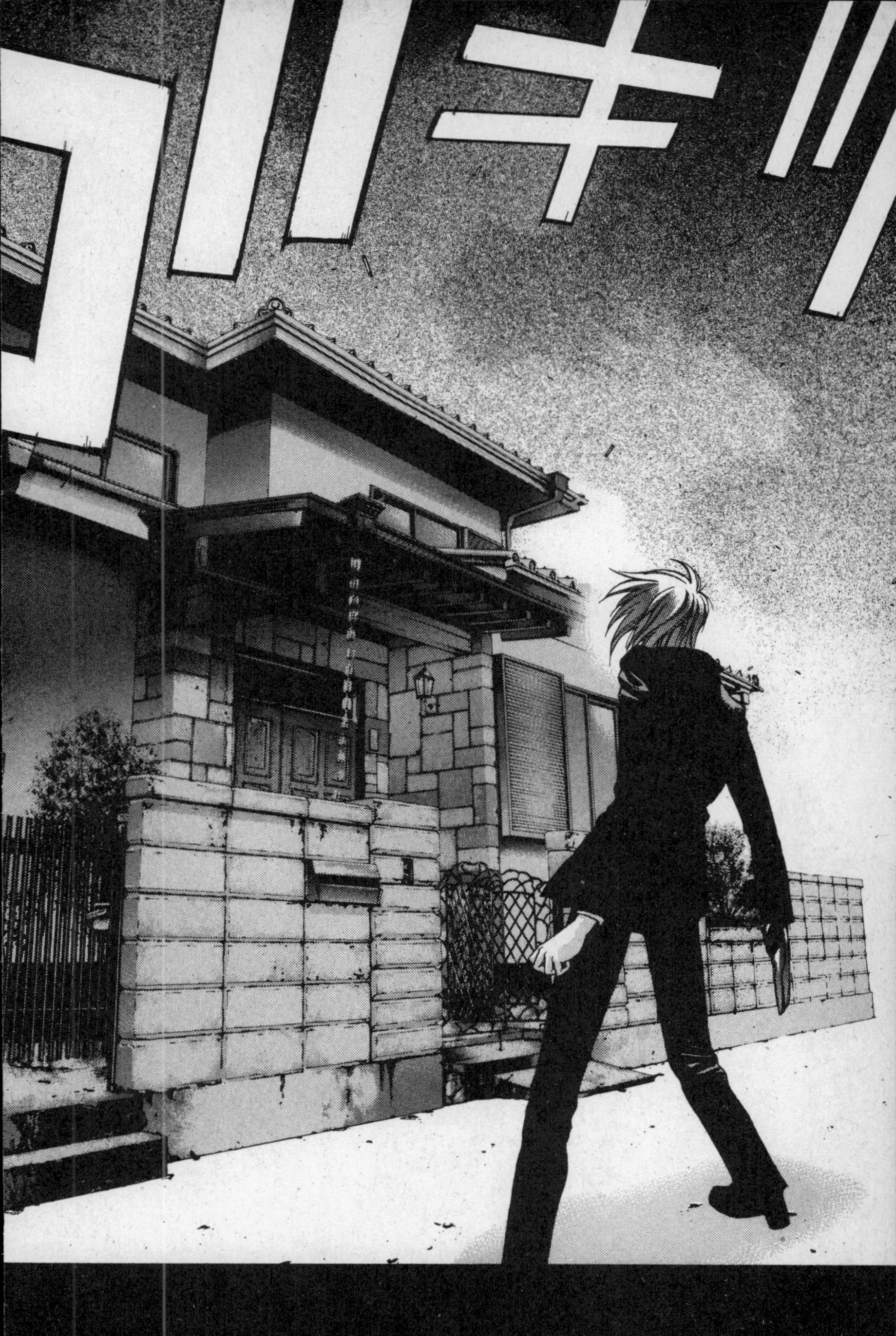

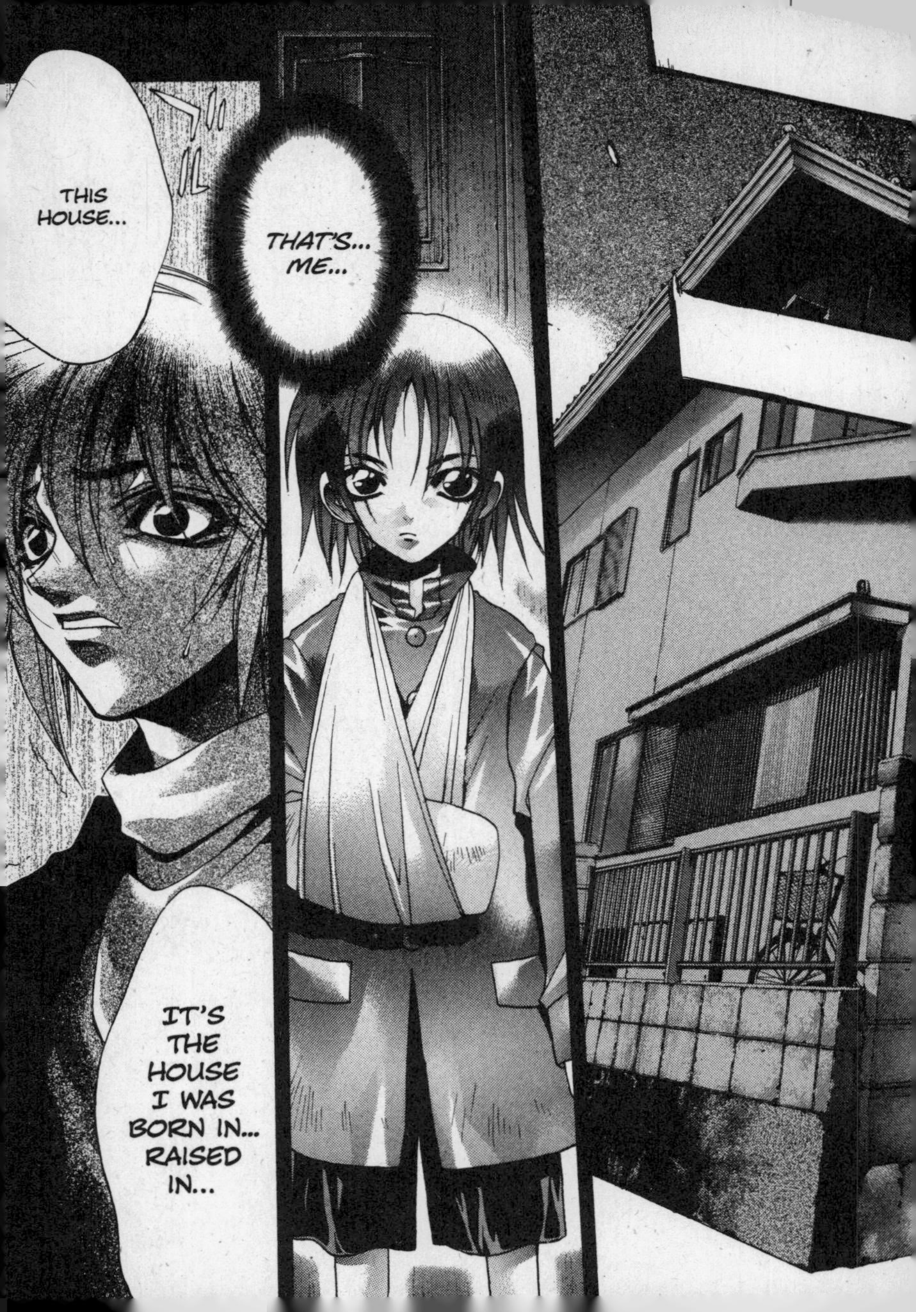
THAT'S... ME...
THIS HOUSE...
IT'S THE HOUSE I WAS BORN IN... RAISED IN...

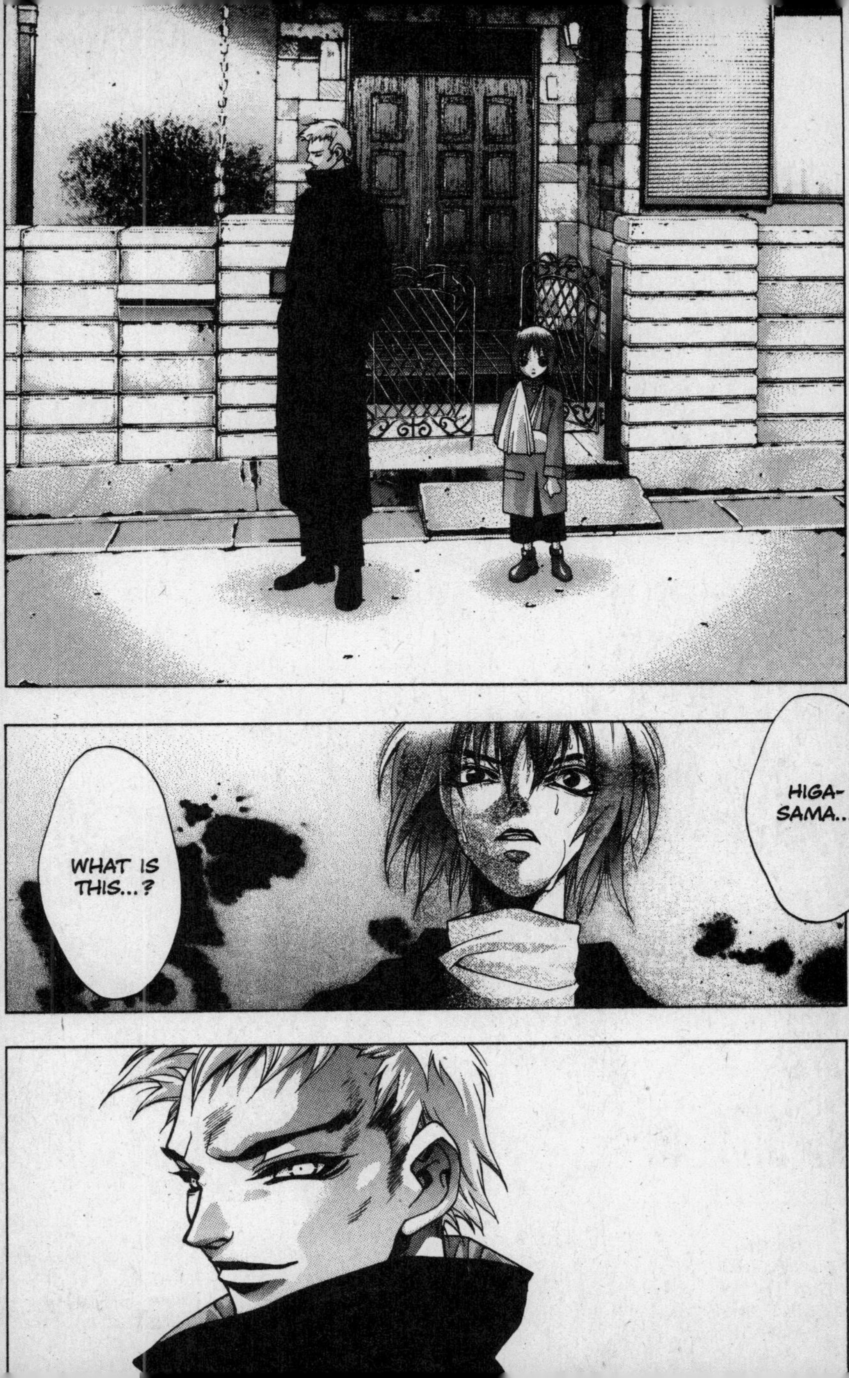
HIGA-SAMA...
WHAT IS THIS...?

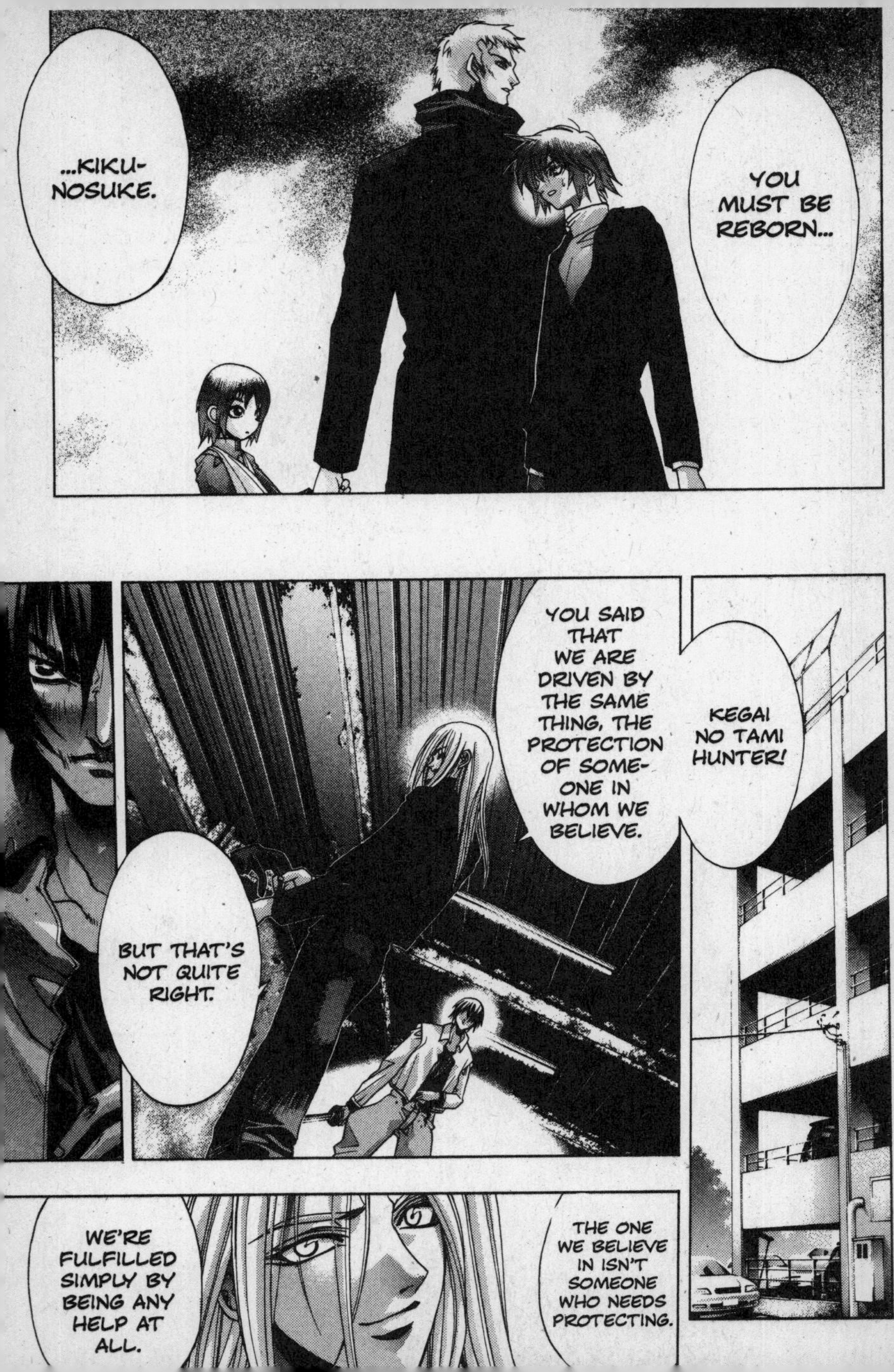
YOU MUST BE REBORN...
...KIKU-NOSUKE.
KEGAI NO TAMI HUNTER!
YOU SAID THAT WE ARE DRIVEN BY THE SAME THING, THE PROTECTION OF SOME-ONE IN WHOM WE BELIEVE.
BUT THAT'S NOT QUITE RIGHT.
THE ONE WE BELIEVE IN ISN'T SOMEONE WHO NEEDS PROTECTING.
WE'RE FULFILLED SIMPLY BY BEING ANY HELP AT ALL.

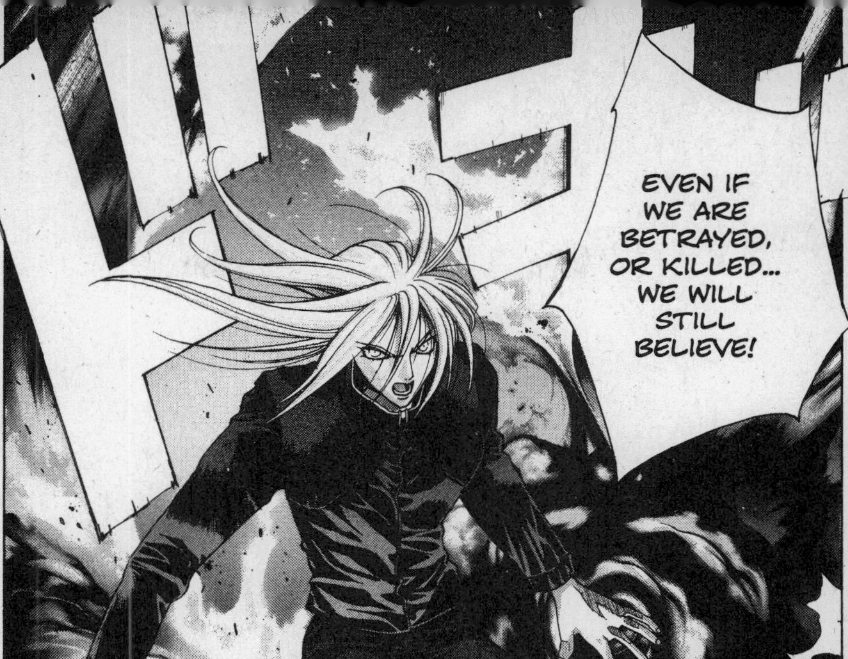
EVEN IF WE ARE BETRAYED, OR KILLED... WE WILL STILL BELIEVE!
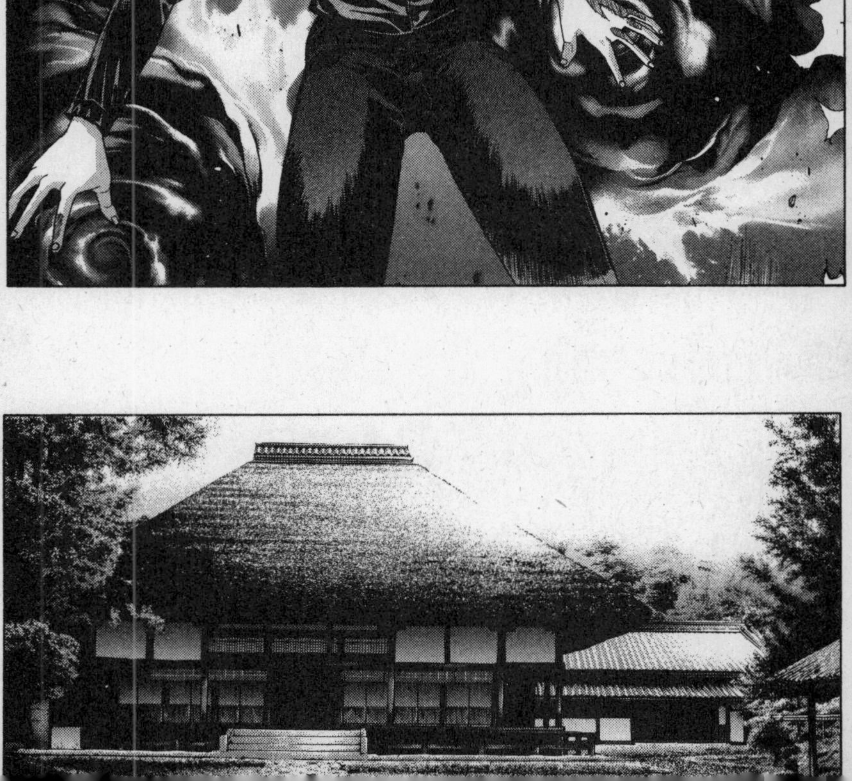

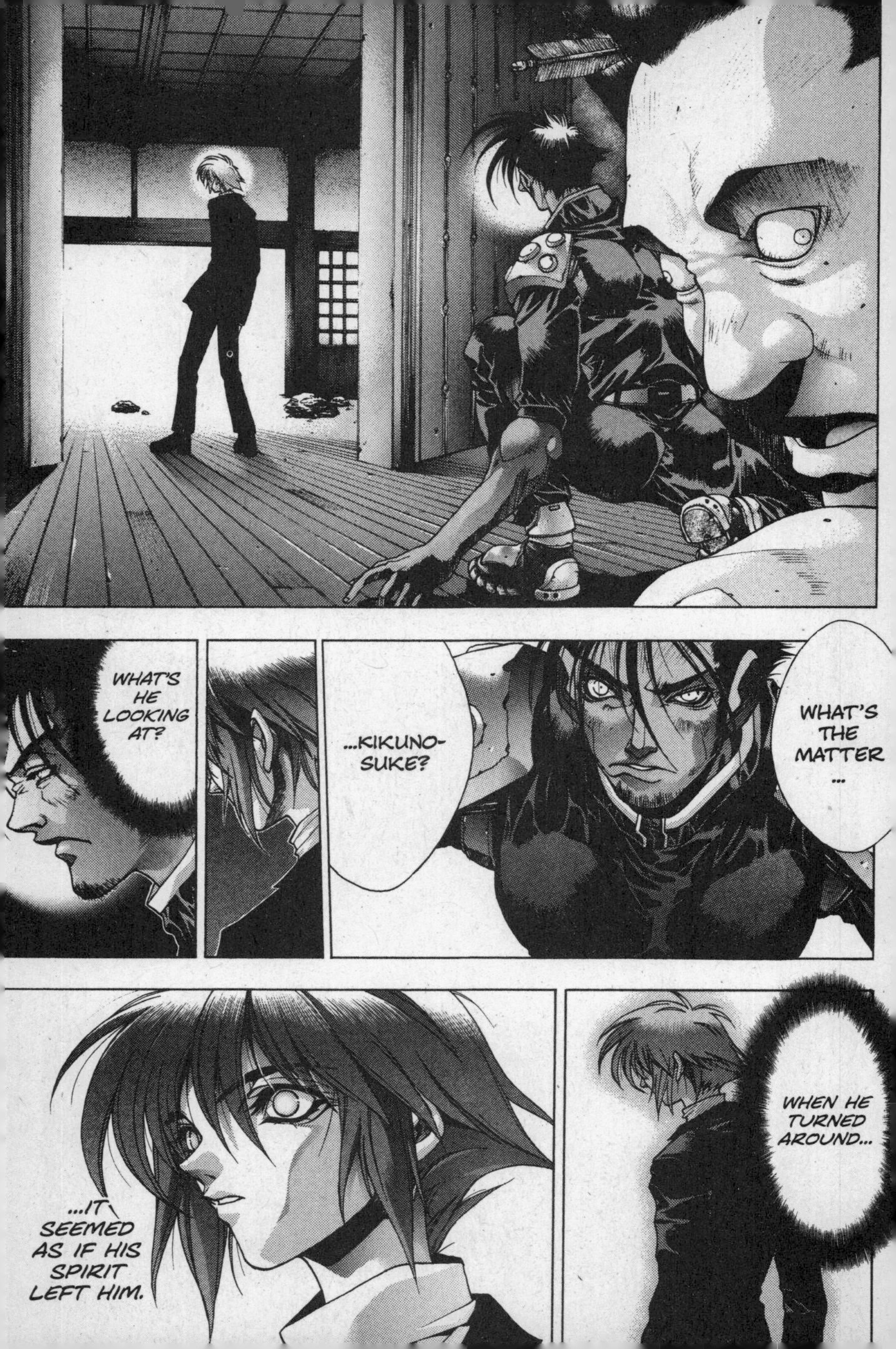
WHAT'S THE MATTER ...
...KIKUNO-SUKE?
WHAT'S HE LOOKING AT?
WHEN HE TURNED AROUND...
...IT SEEMED AS IF HIS SPIRIT LEFT HIM.

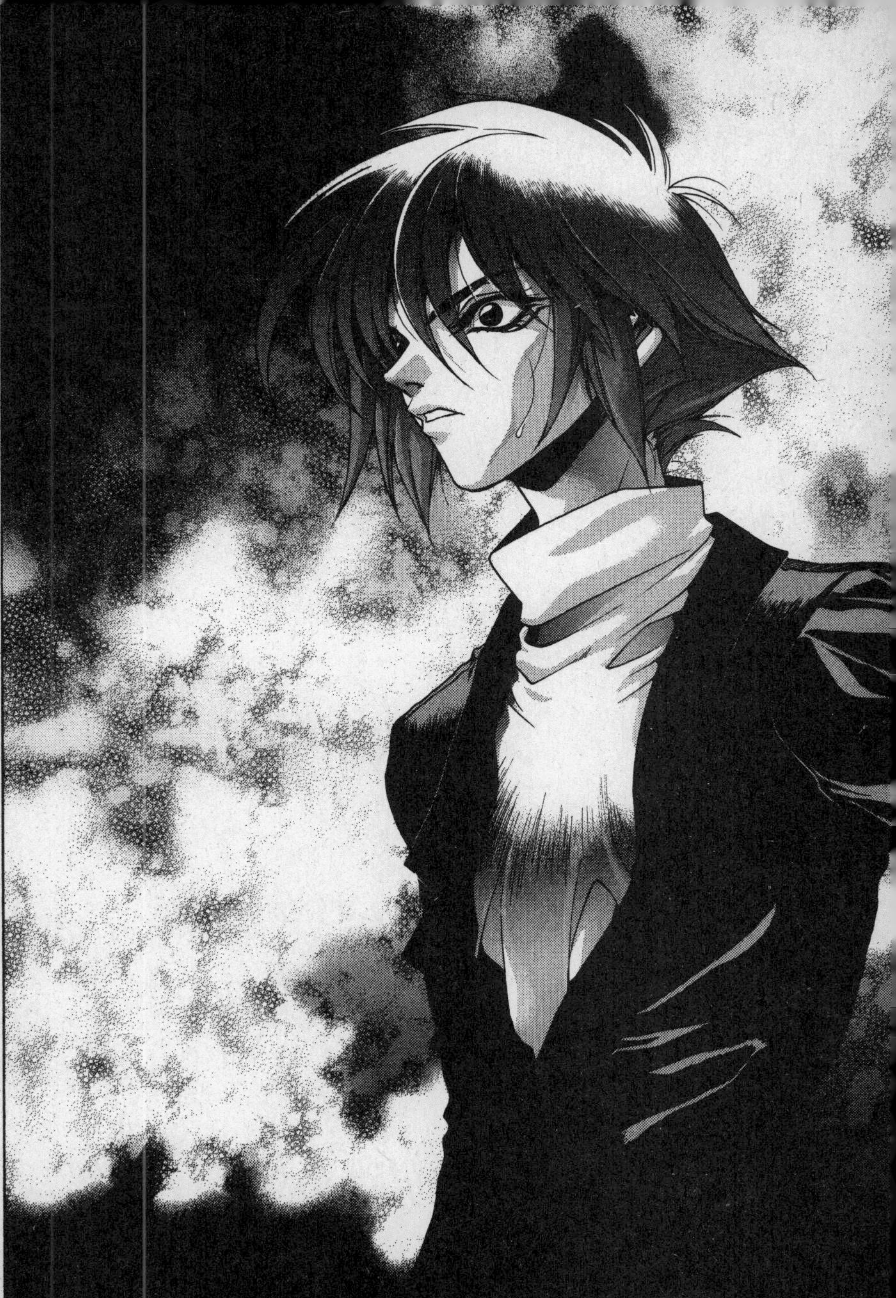

Chapter 22: Breaking with the Past

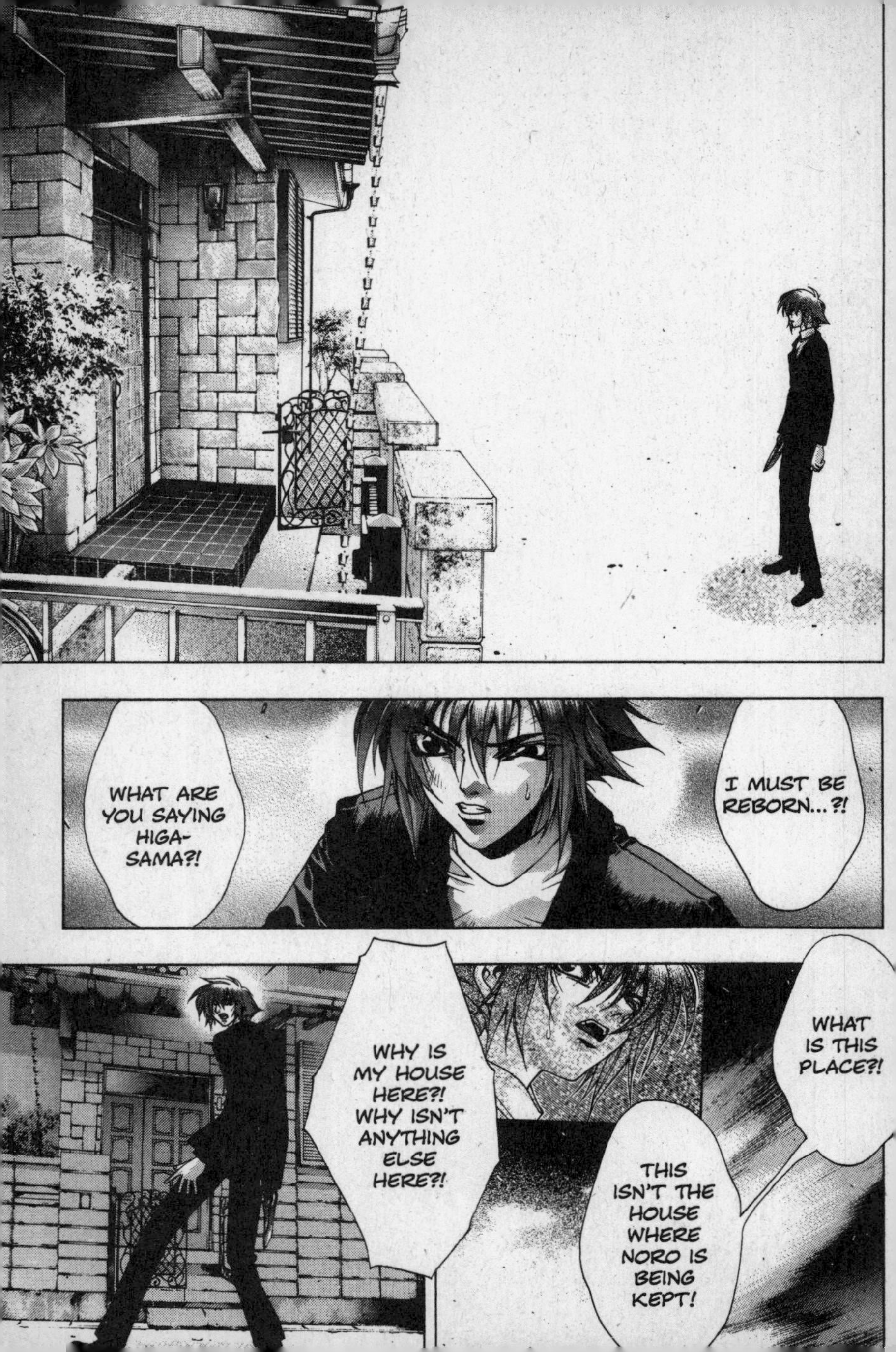
I MUST BE REBORN...?!
WHAT ARE YOU SAYING HIGA-SAMA?!
WHAT IS THIS PLACE?!
THIS ISN'T THE HOUSE WHERE NORO IS BEING KEPT!
WHY IS MY HOUSE HERE?! WHY ISN'T ANYTHING ELSE HERE?!

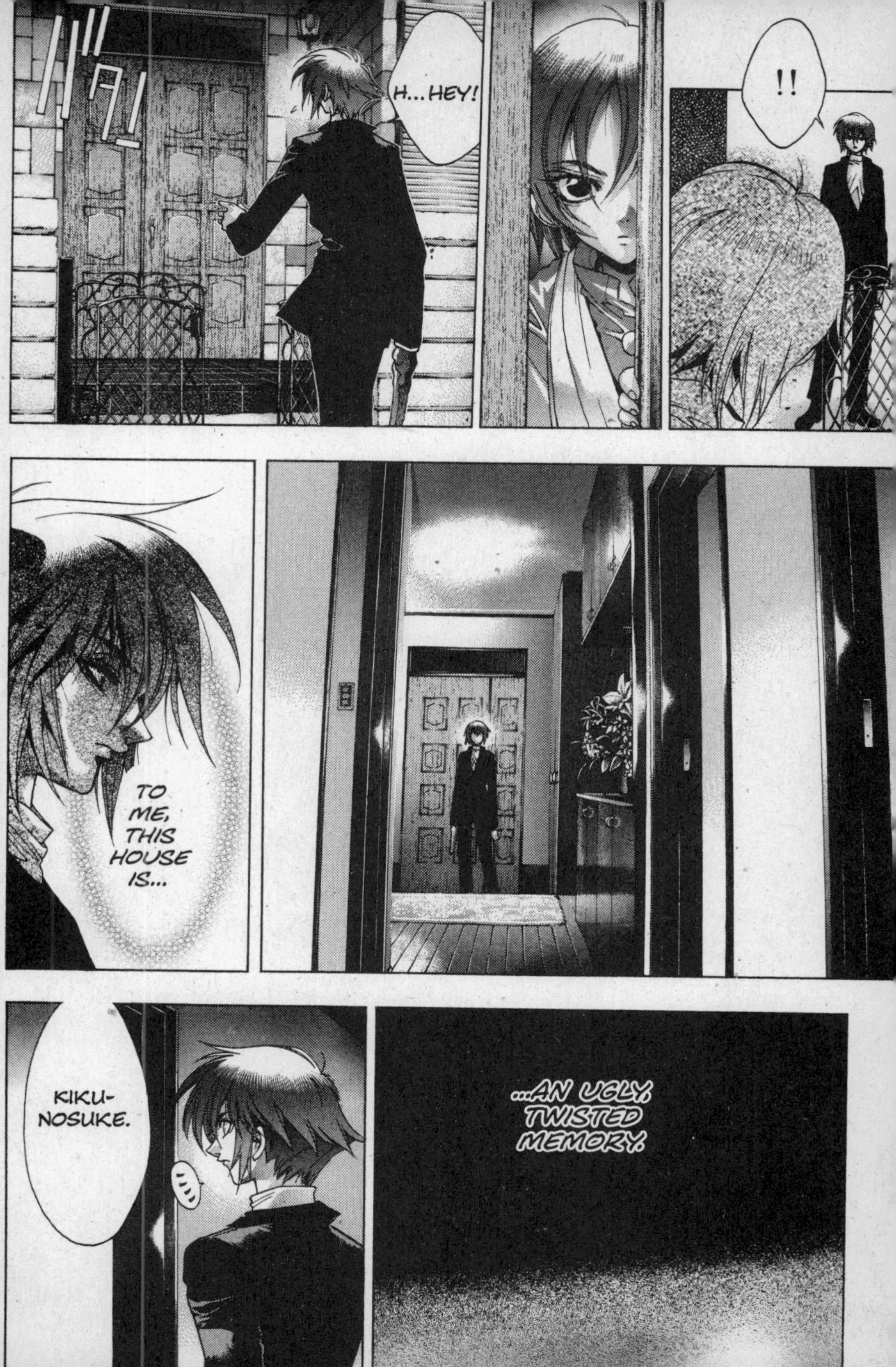
!!
H...HEY!
TO ME, THIS HOUSE IS...
...AN UGLY, TWISTED MEMORY.
KIKU-NOSUKE.
...

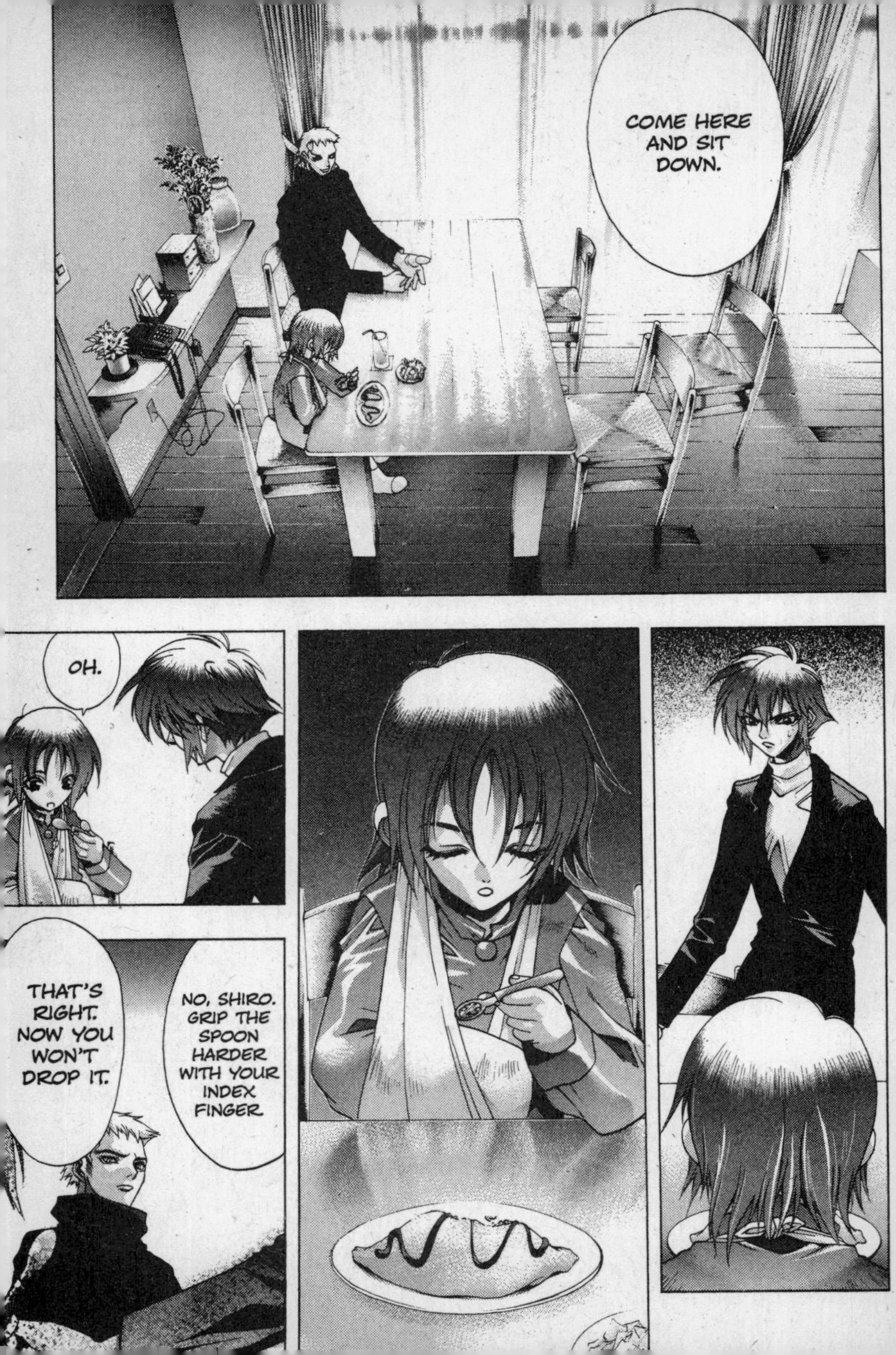
COME HERE AND SIT DOWN.
OH.
NO, SHIRO. GRIP THE SPOON HARDER WITH YOUR INDEX FINGER
THAT'S RIGHT. NOW YOU WON'T DROP IT.

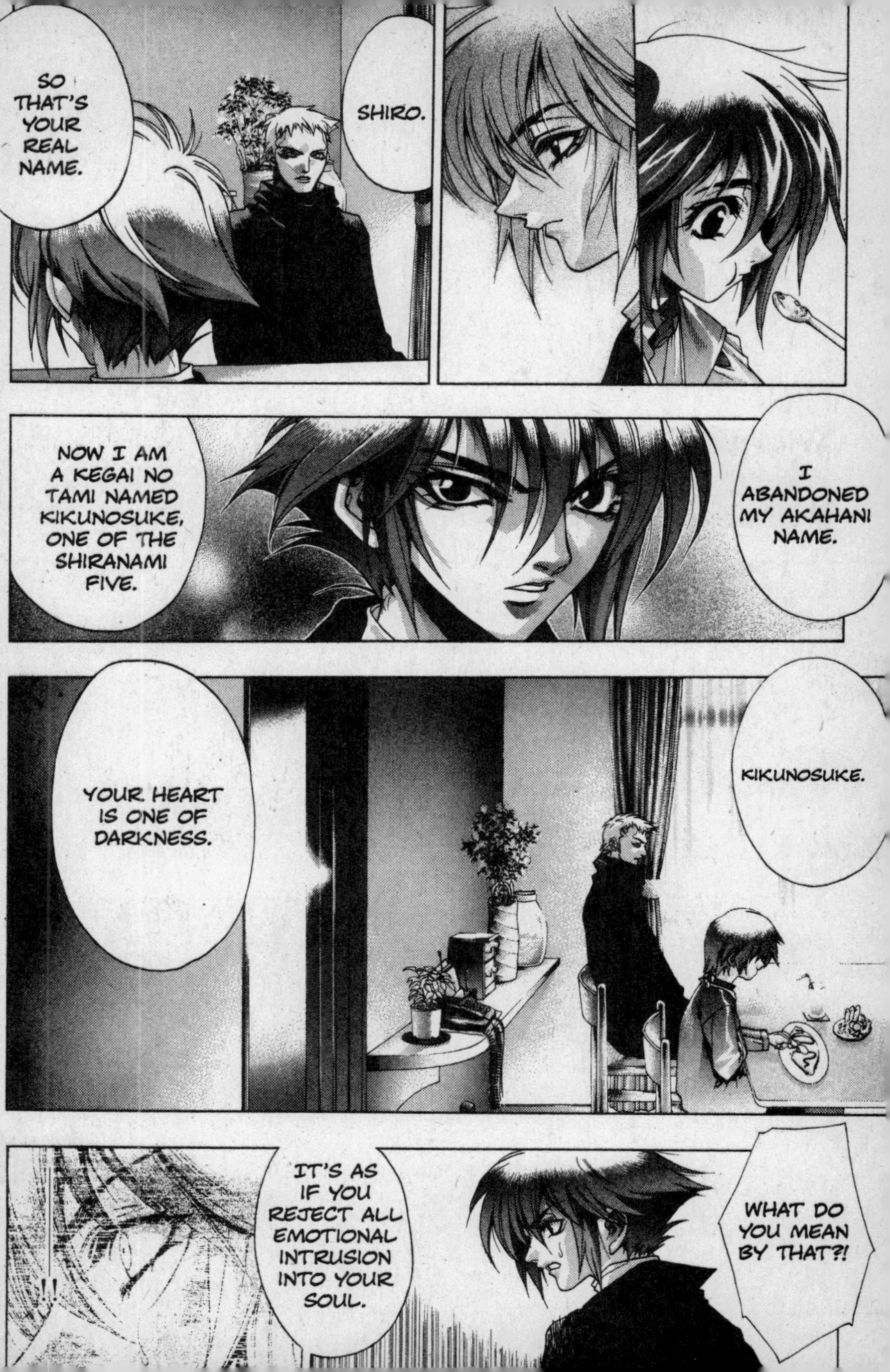
SHIRO.
SO THAT'S YOUR REAL NAME.
I ABANDONED MY AKAHANI NAME.
NOW I AM A KEGAI NO TAMI NAMED KIKUNOSUKE, ONE OF THE SHIRANAMI FIVE.
KIKUNOSUKE.
YOUR HEART IS ONE OF DARKNESS.
WHAT DO YOU MEAN BY THAT?!
IT'S AS IF YOU REJECT ALL EMOTIONAL INTRUSION INTO YOUR SOUL.
!!

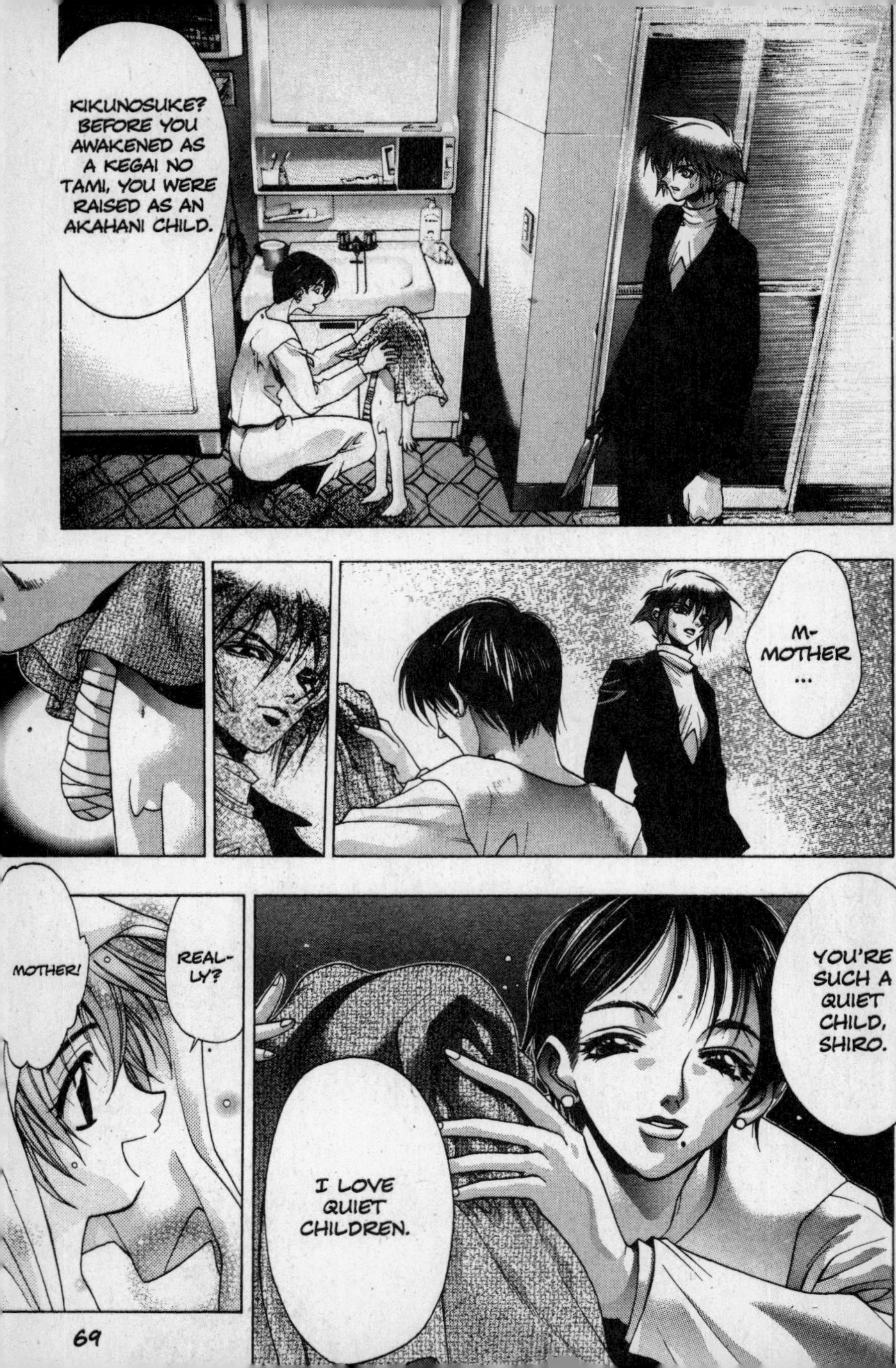
KIKUNOSUKE? BEFORE YOU AWAKENED AS A KEGAI NO TAMI, YOU WERE RAISED AS AN AKAHANI CHILD.
M-MOTHER ...
YOU'RE SUCH A QUIET CHILD, SHIRO.
I LOVE QUIET CHILDREN.
REAL-LY?
MOTHER!

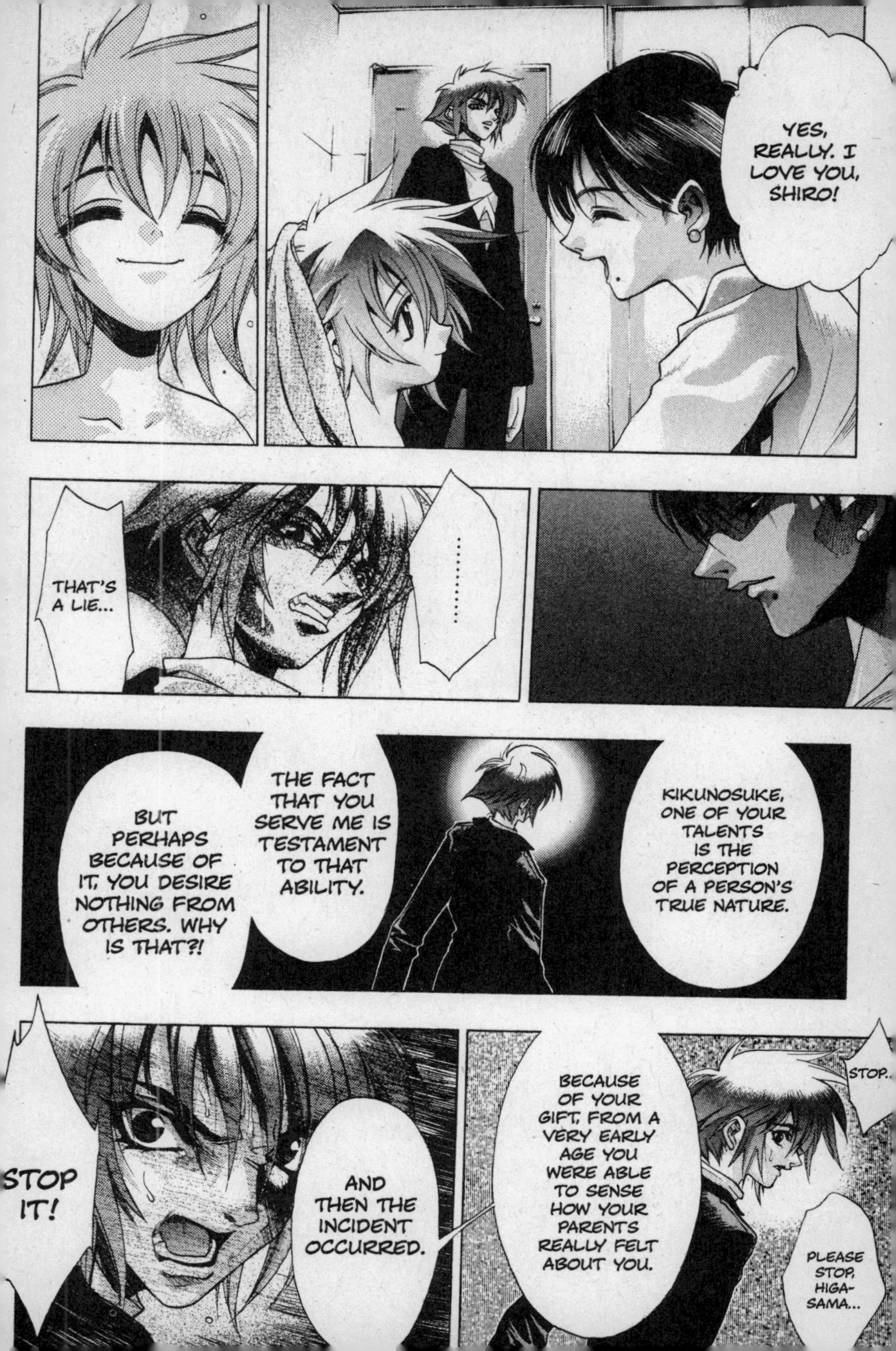
YES, REALLY. I LOVE YOU, SHIRO!
......
THAT'S A LIE...
KIKUNOSUKE, ONE OF YOUR TALENTS IS THE PERCEPTION OF A PERSON'S TRUE NATURE.
THE FACT THAT YOU SERVE ME IS TESTAMENT TO THAT ABILITY.
BUT PERHAPS BECAUSE OF IT, YOU DESIRE NOTHING FROM OTHERS. WHY IS THAT?!
STOP...
BECAUSE OF YOUR GIFT, FROM A VERY EARLY AGE YOU WERE ABLE TO SENSE HOW YOUR PARENTS REALLY FELT ABOUT YOU.
PLEASE STOP, HIGA-SAMA...
AND THEN THE INCIDENT OCCURRED.
STOP IT!

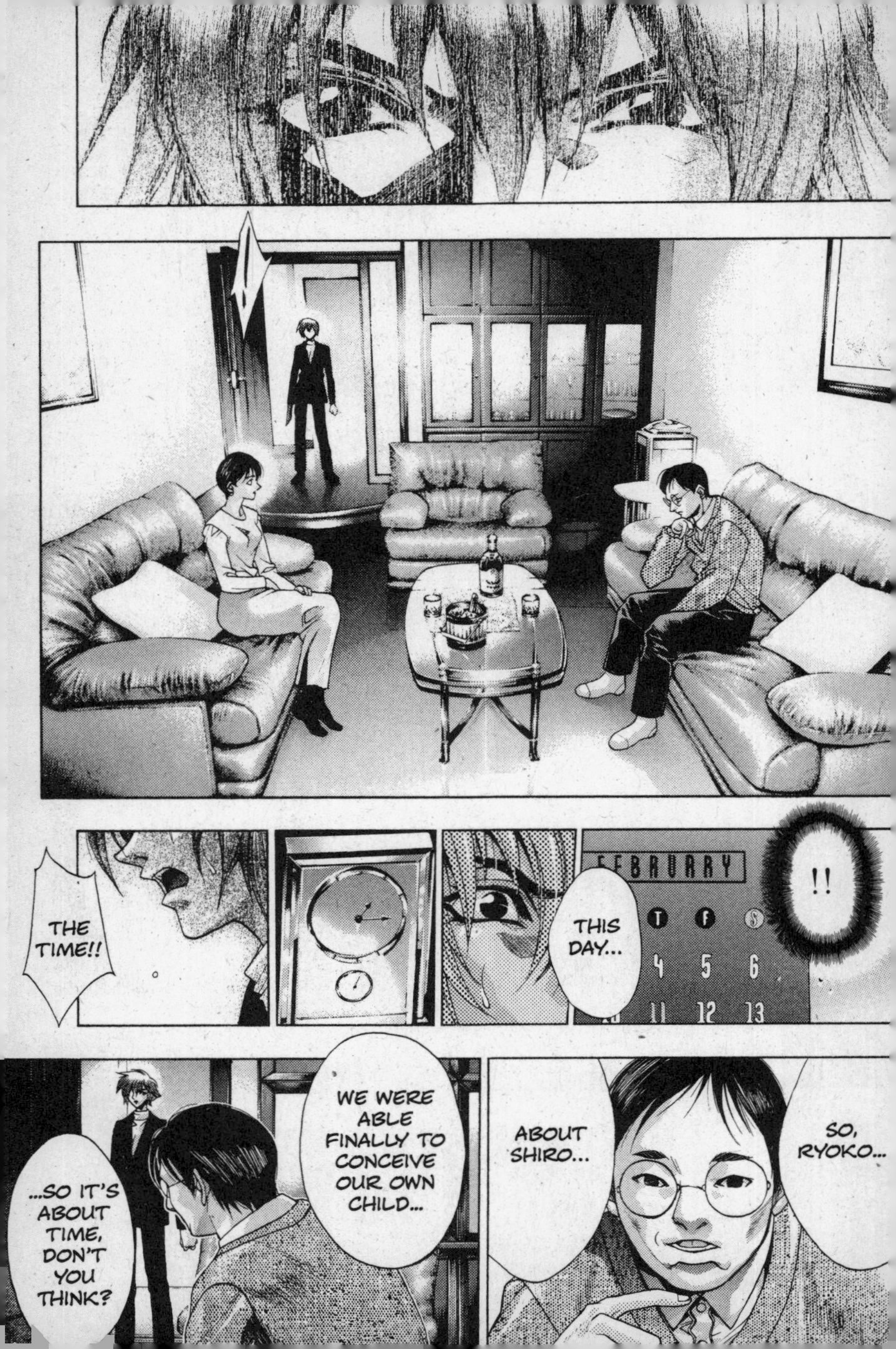
!!
THIS DAY...
THE TIME!!
SO, RYOKO...
ABOUT SHIRO...
WE WERE ABLE FINALLY TO CONCEIVE OUR OWN CHILD...
...SO IT'S ABOUT TIME, DON'T YOU THINK?

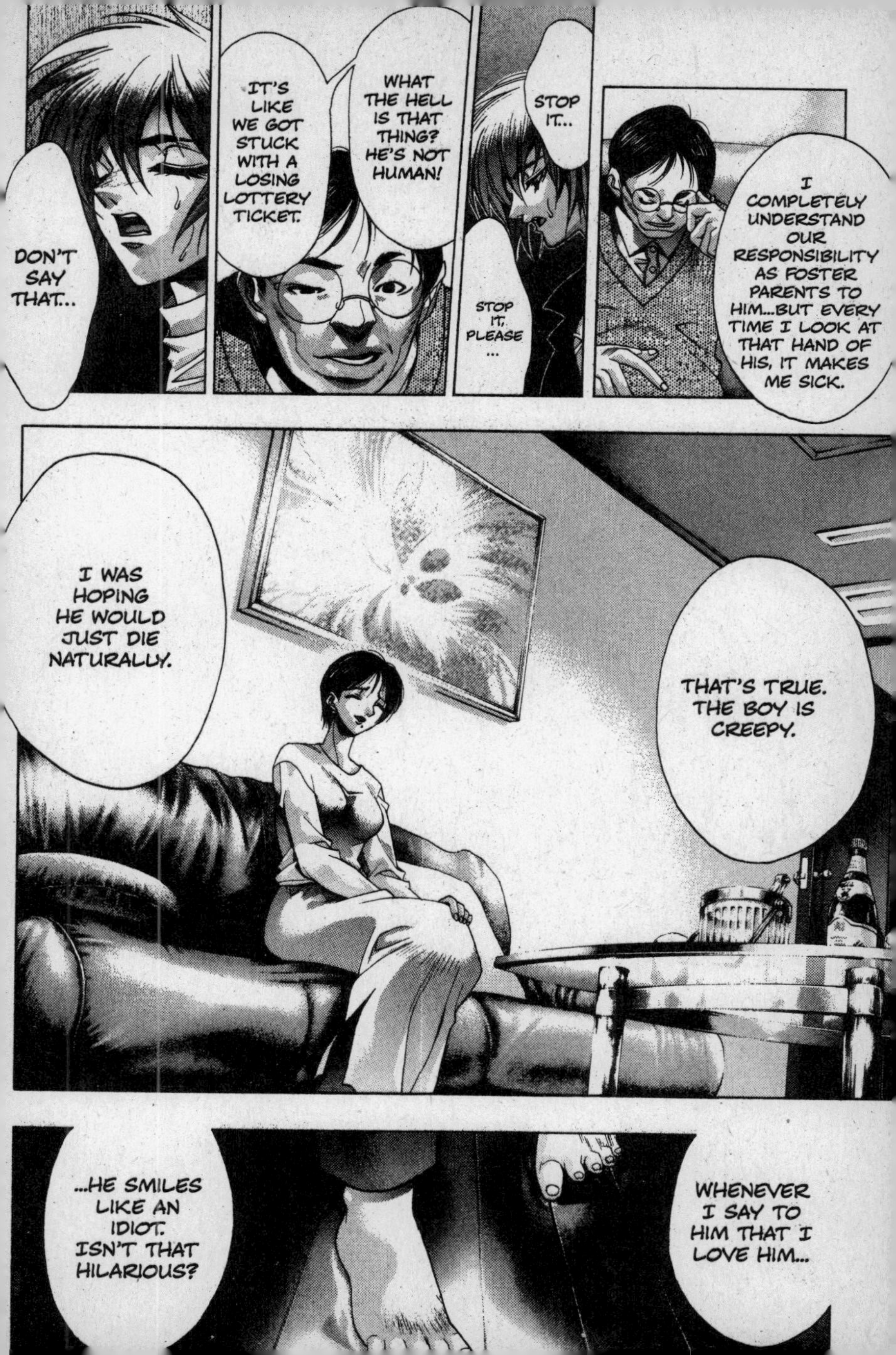
I COMPLETELY UNDERSTAND OUR RESPONSIBILITY AS FOSTER PARENTS TO HIM...BUT EVERY TIME I LOOK AT THAT HAND OF HIS, IT MAKES ME SICK.
STOP IT...
STOP IT, PLEASE...
WHAT THE HELL IS THAT THING? HE'S NOT HUMAN!
IT'S LIKE WE GOT STUCK WITH A LOSING LOTTERY TICKET.
DON'T SAY THAT...
THAT'S TRUE. THE BOY IS CREEPY.
I WAS HOPING HE WOULD JUST DIE NATURALLY.
WHENEVER I SAY TO HIM THAT I LOVE HIM...
...HE SMILES LIKE AN IDIOT. ISN'T THAT HILARIOUS?

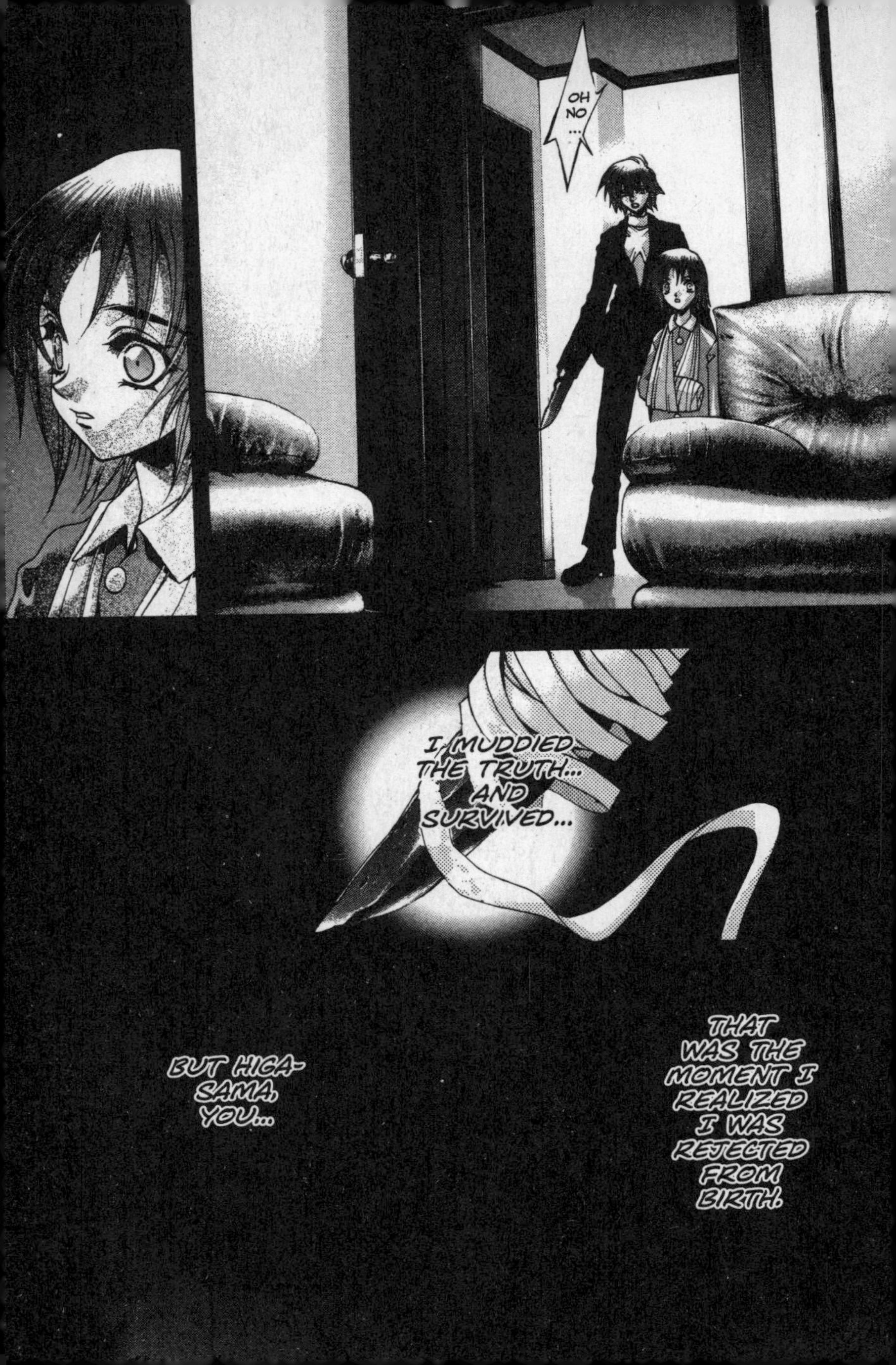
OH NO ...
I MUDDIED THE TRUTH... AND SURVIVED...
THAT WAS THE MOMENT I REALIZED I WAS REJECTED FROM BIRTH.
BUT HIGA-SAMA, YOU...

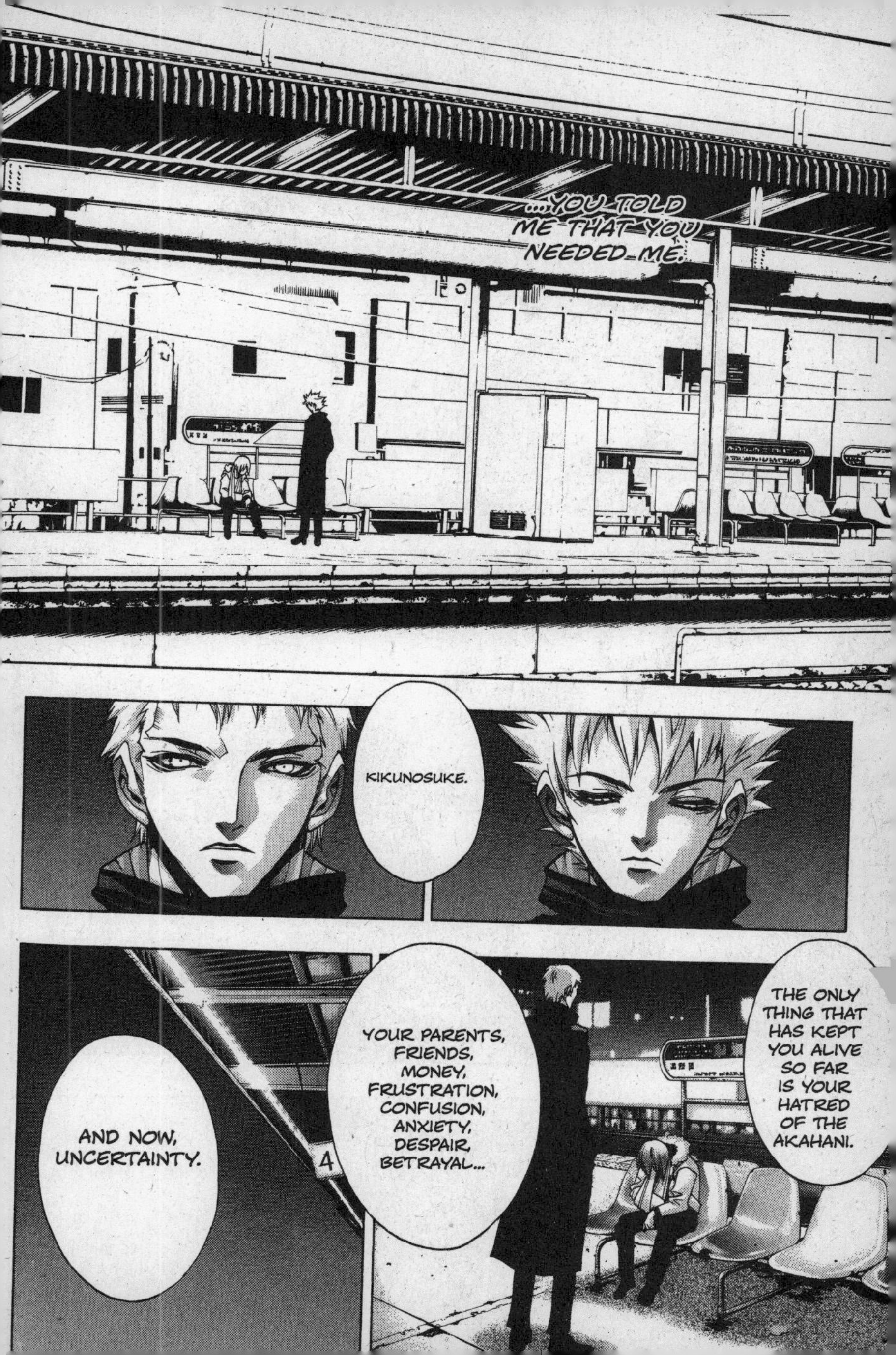
...YOU TOLD ME THAT YOU NEEDED ME.
KIKUNOSUKE.
THE ONLY THING THAT HAS KEPT YOU ALIVE SO FAR IS YOUR HATRED OF THE AKAHANI.
YOUR PARENTS, FRIENDS, MONEY, FRUSTRATION, CONFUSION, ANXIETY, DESPAIR BETRAYAL...
AND NOW, UNCERTAINTY.
4

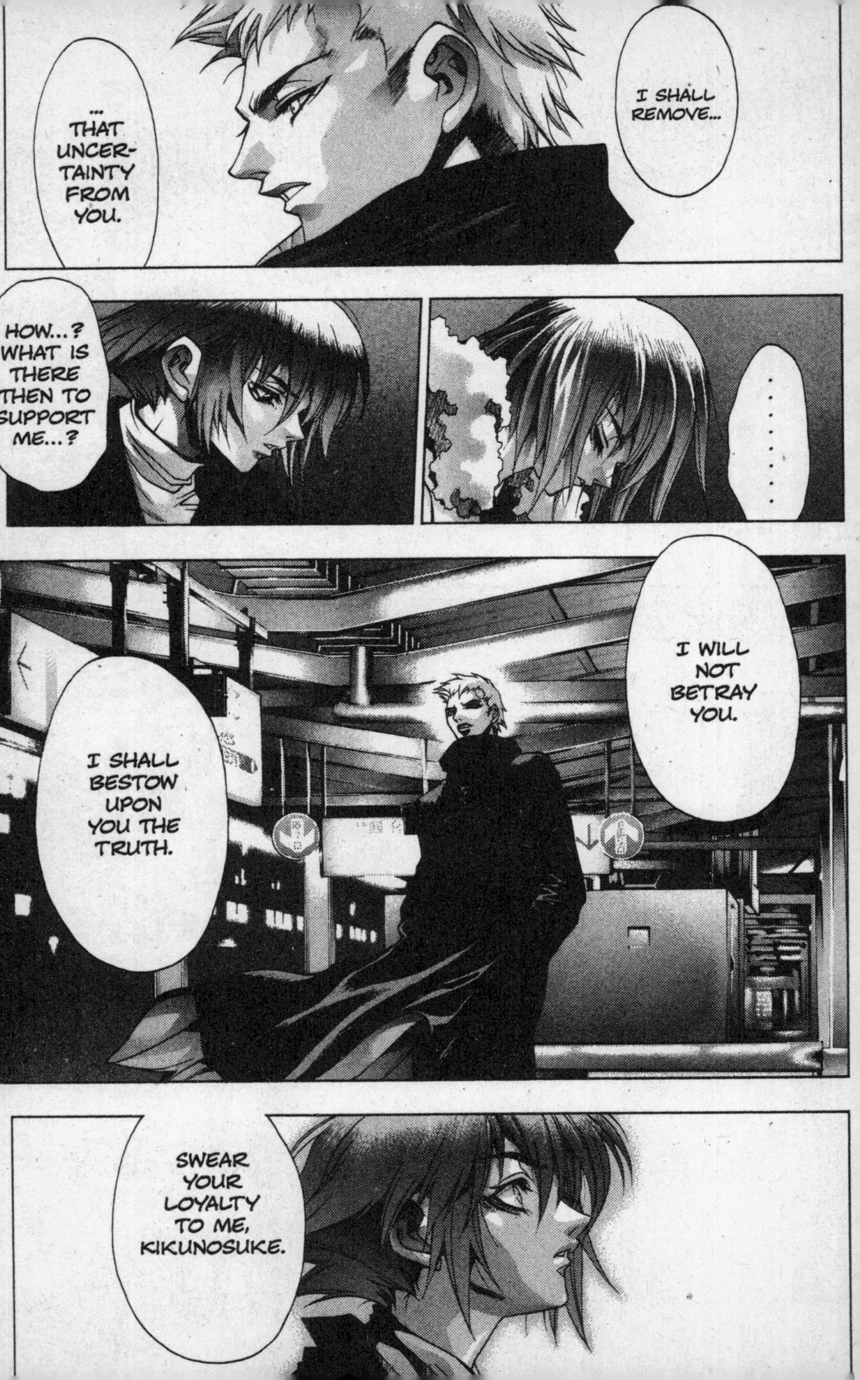
I SHALL REMOVE...
...THAT UNCERTAINTY FROM YOU.
......
HOW...? WHAT IS THERE THEN TO SUPPORT ME...?
I WILL NOT BETRAY YOU.
I SHALL BESTOW UPON YOU THE TRUTH.
SWEAR YOUR LOYALTY TO ME, KIKUNOSUKE.

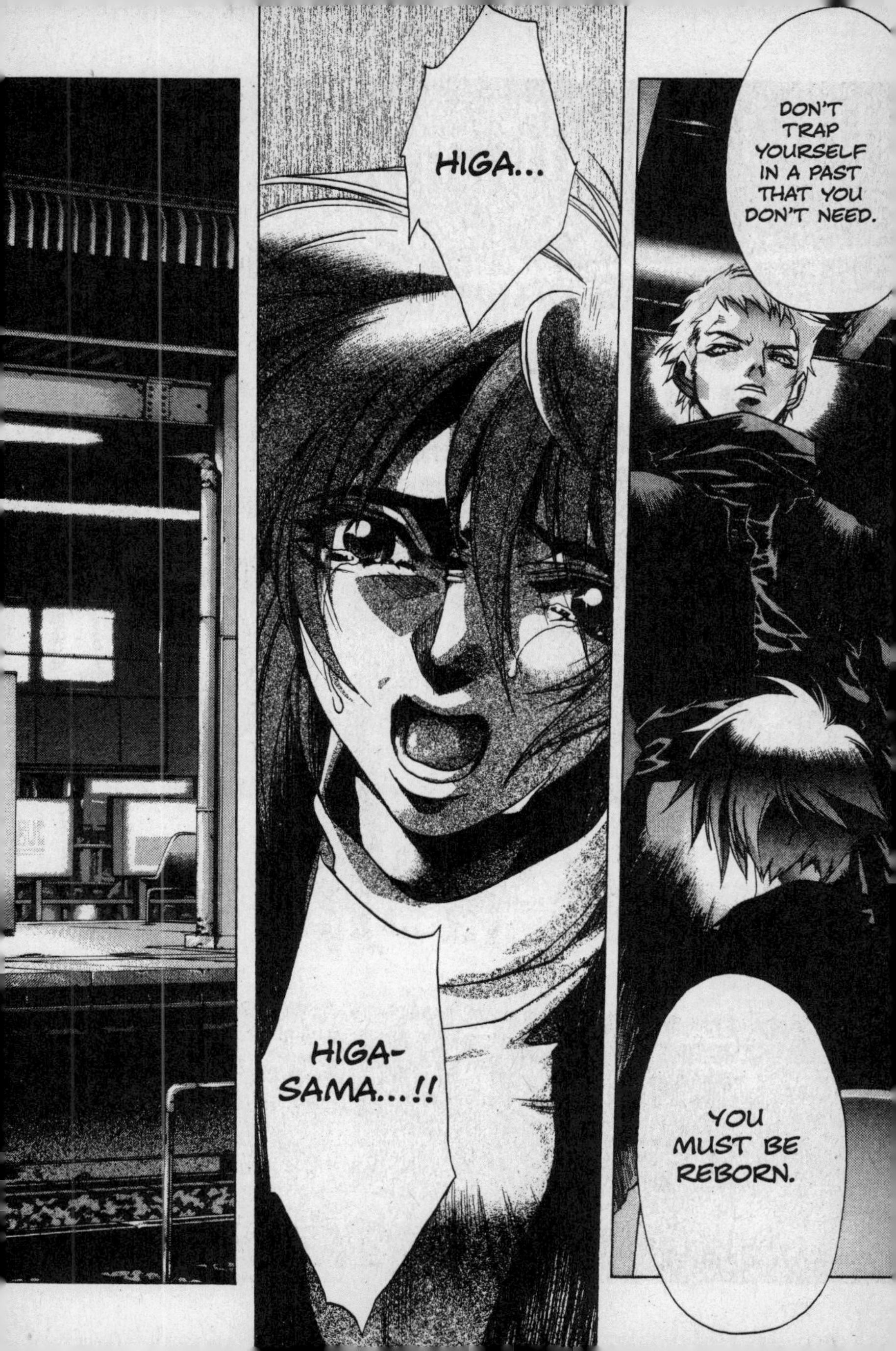
DON'T TRAP YOURSELF IN A PAST THAT YOU DON'T NEED.
YOU MUST BE REBORN.
HIGA...
HIGA-SAMA...!!

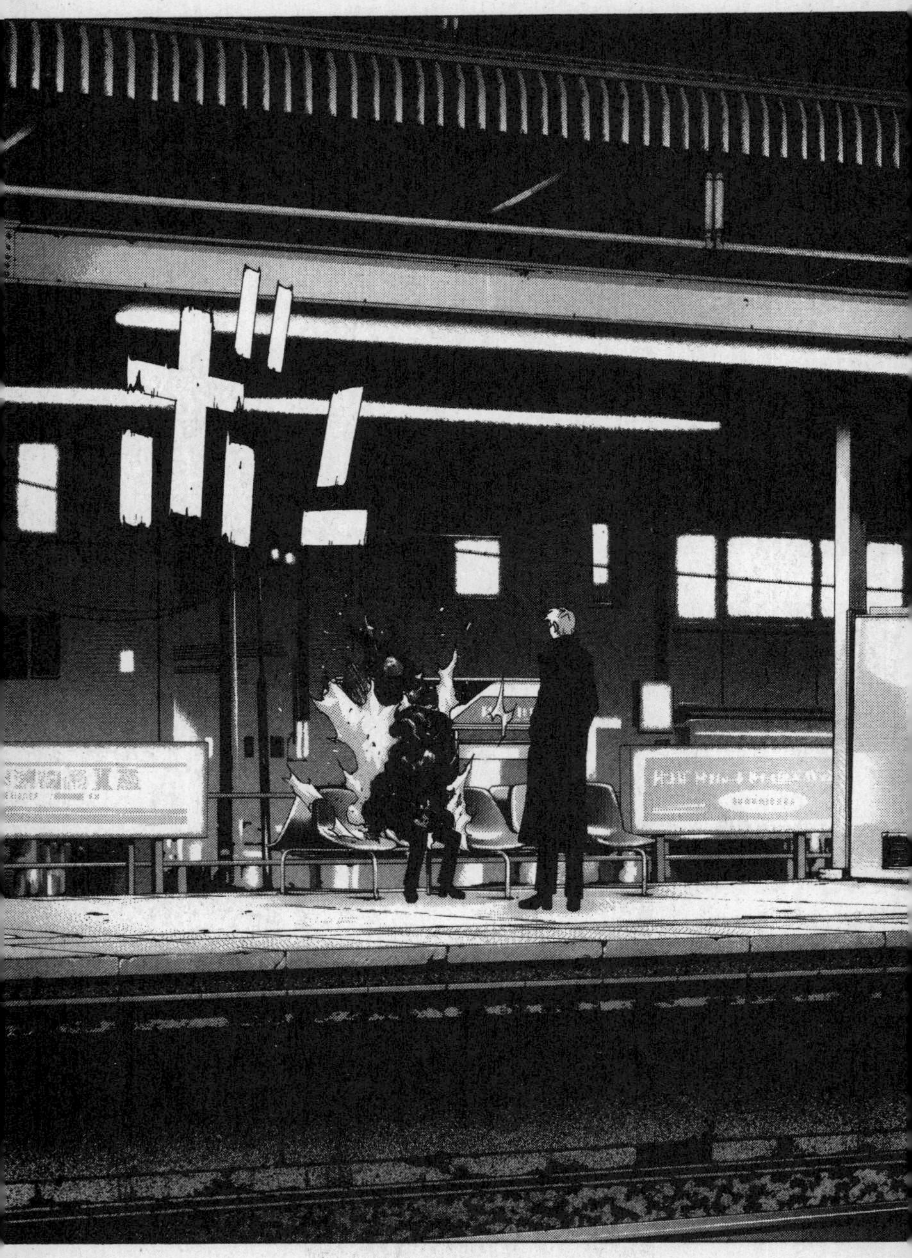
ボ!

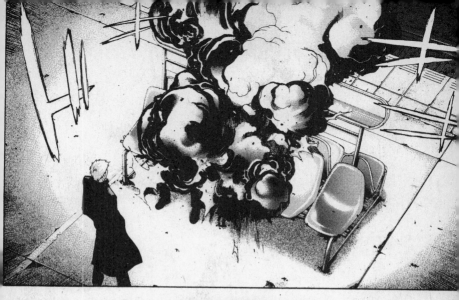

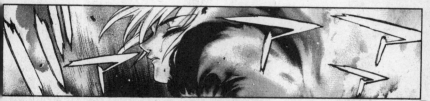

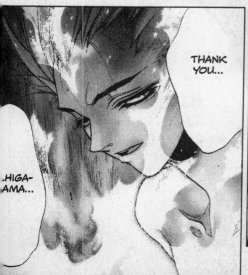

THANK
YOU...

.HIGA-
AMA...

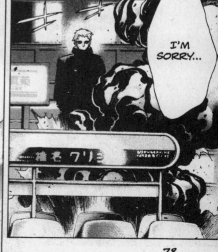

I'M
SORRY...

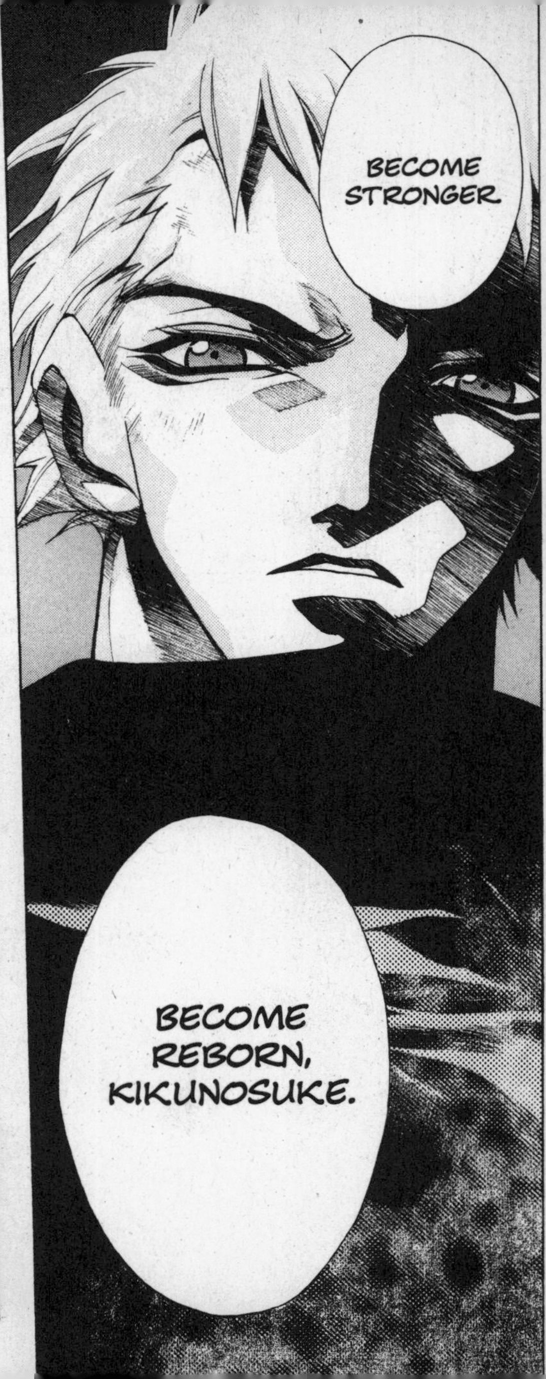
BECOME STRONGER
BECOME REBORN, KIKUNOSUKE.

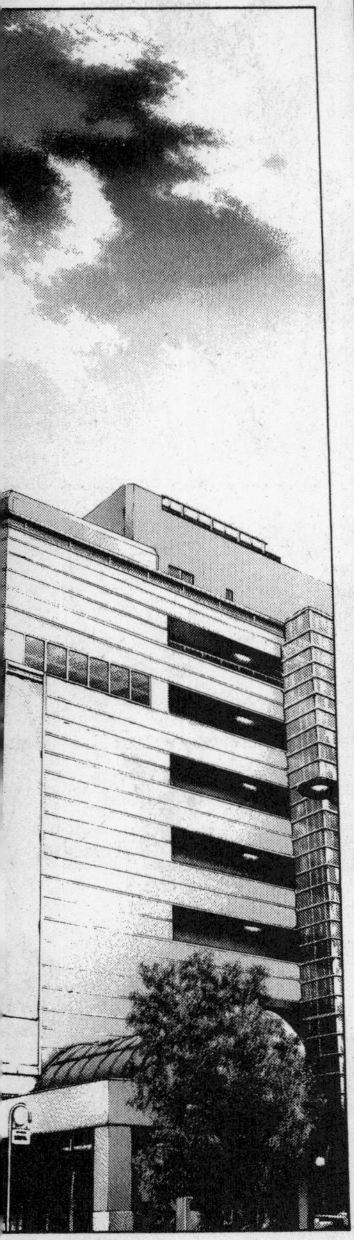

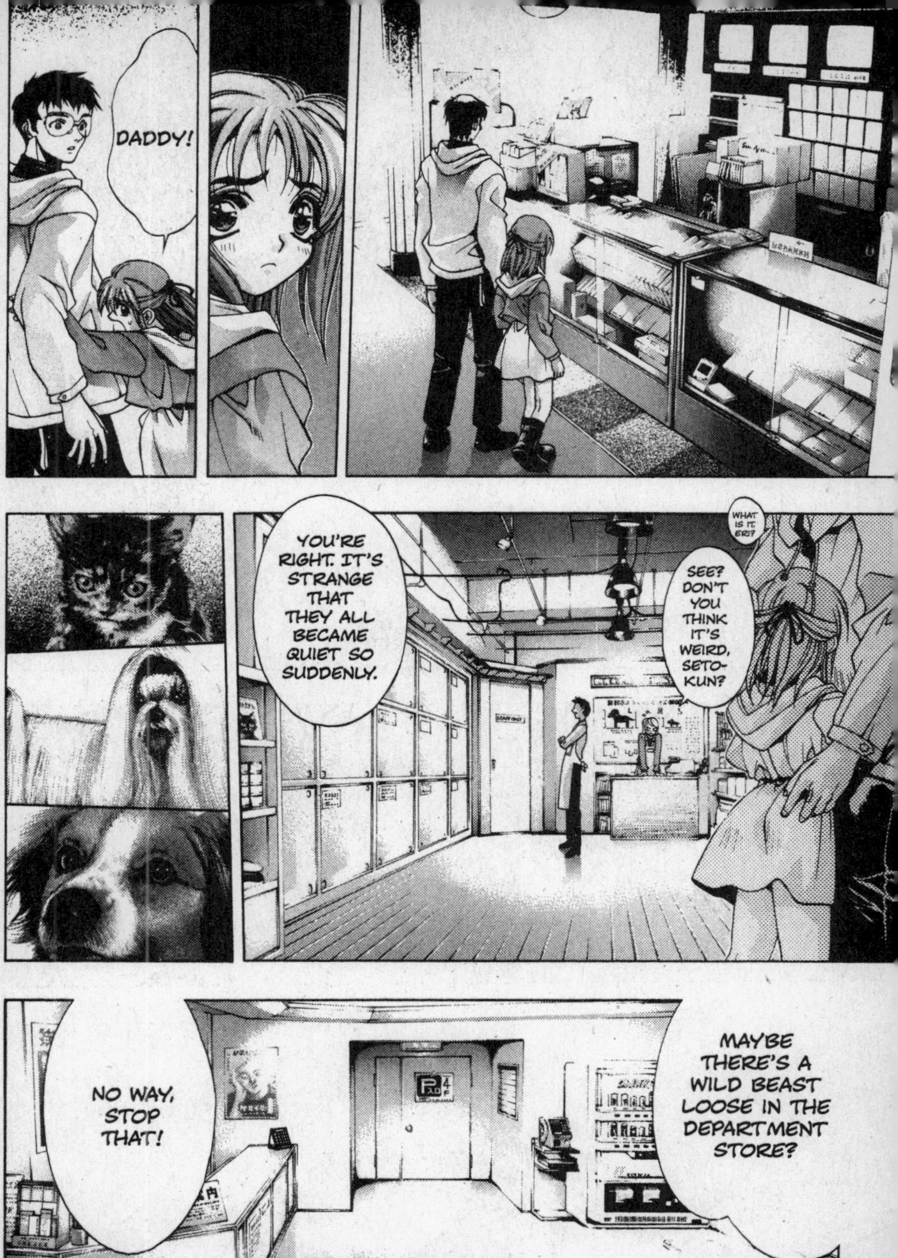
DADDY!
WHAT IS IT, ERI?
SEE? DON'T YOU THINK IT'S WEIRD, SETO-KUN?
YOU'RE RIGHT. IT'S STRANGE THAT THEY ALL BECAME QUIET SO SUDDENLY.
MAYBE THERE'S A WILD BEAST LOOSE IN THE DEPARTMENT STORE?
NO WAY, STOP THAT!

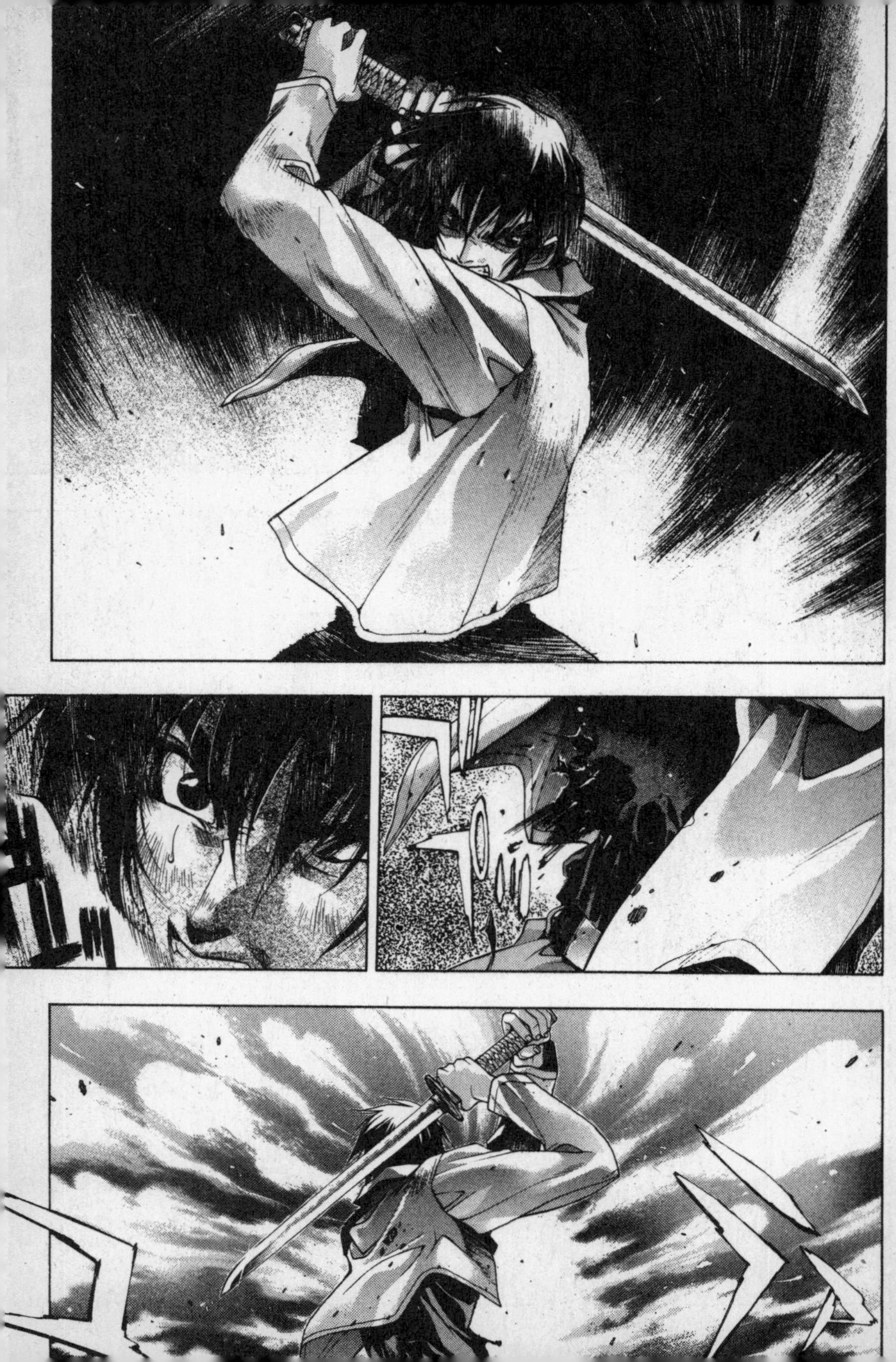

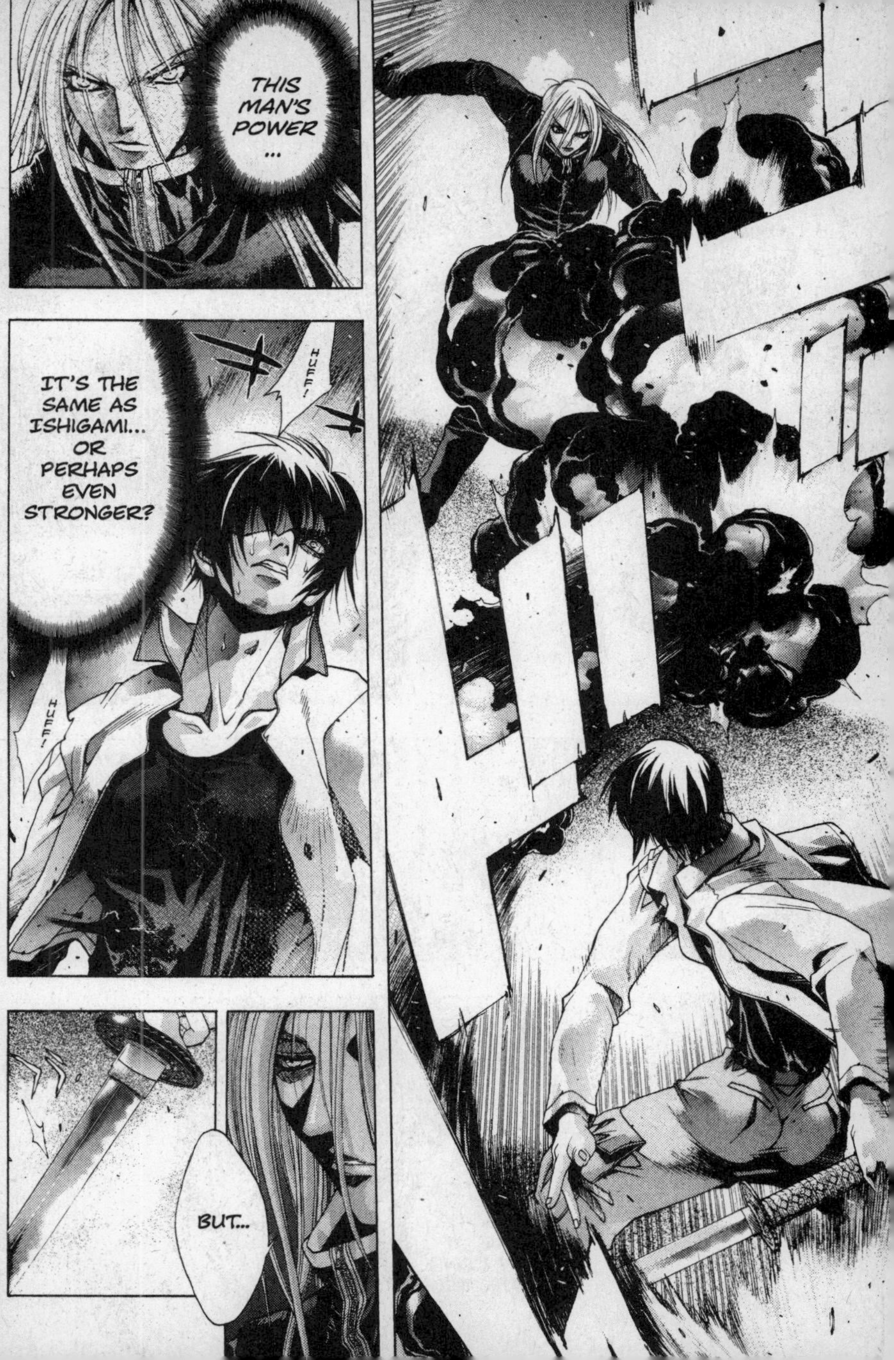
THIS MAN'S POWER ...
HUFF!
IT'S THE SAME AS ISHIGAMI... OR PERHAPS EVEN STRONGER?
HUFF!
BUT...

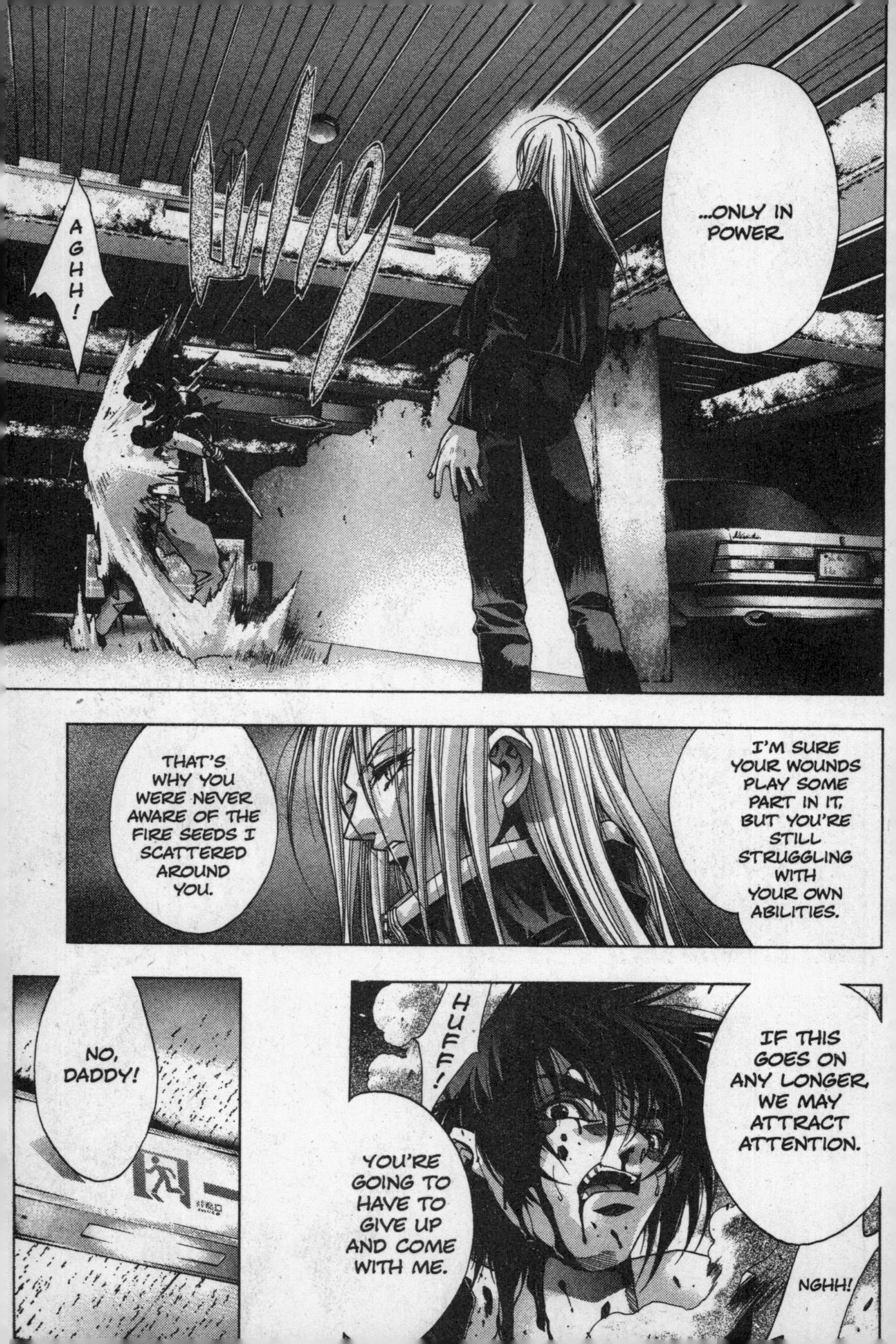
...ONLY IN POWER
AGHH!
I'M SURE YOUR WOUNDS PLAY SOME PART IN IT, BUT YOU'RE STILL STRUGGLING WITH YOUR OWN ABILITIES.
THAT'S WHY YOU WERE NEVER AWARE OF THE FIRE SEEDS I SCATTERED AROUND YOU.
IF THIS GOES ON ANY LONGER, WE MAY ATTRACT ATTENTION.
HUFF!
YOU'RE GOING TO HAVE TO GIVE UP AND COME WITH ME.
NGHH!
NO, DADDY!

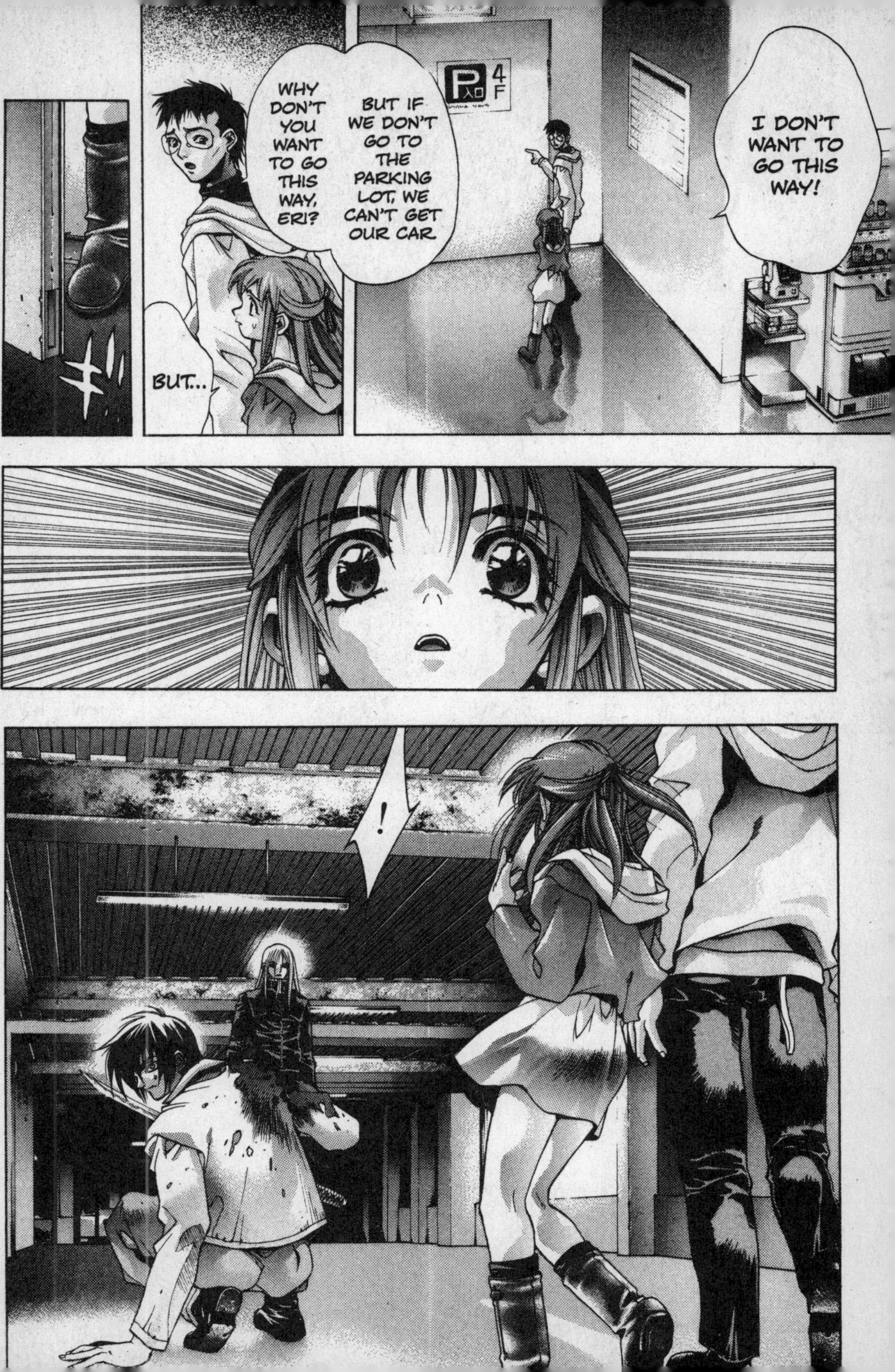
I DON'T WANT TO GO THIS WAY!
P 入口 4F
BUT IF WE DON'T GO TO THE PARKING LOT, WE CAN'T GET OUR CAR
WHY DON'T YOU WANT TO GO THIS WAY, ERI?
BUT...
!

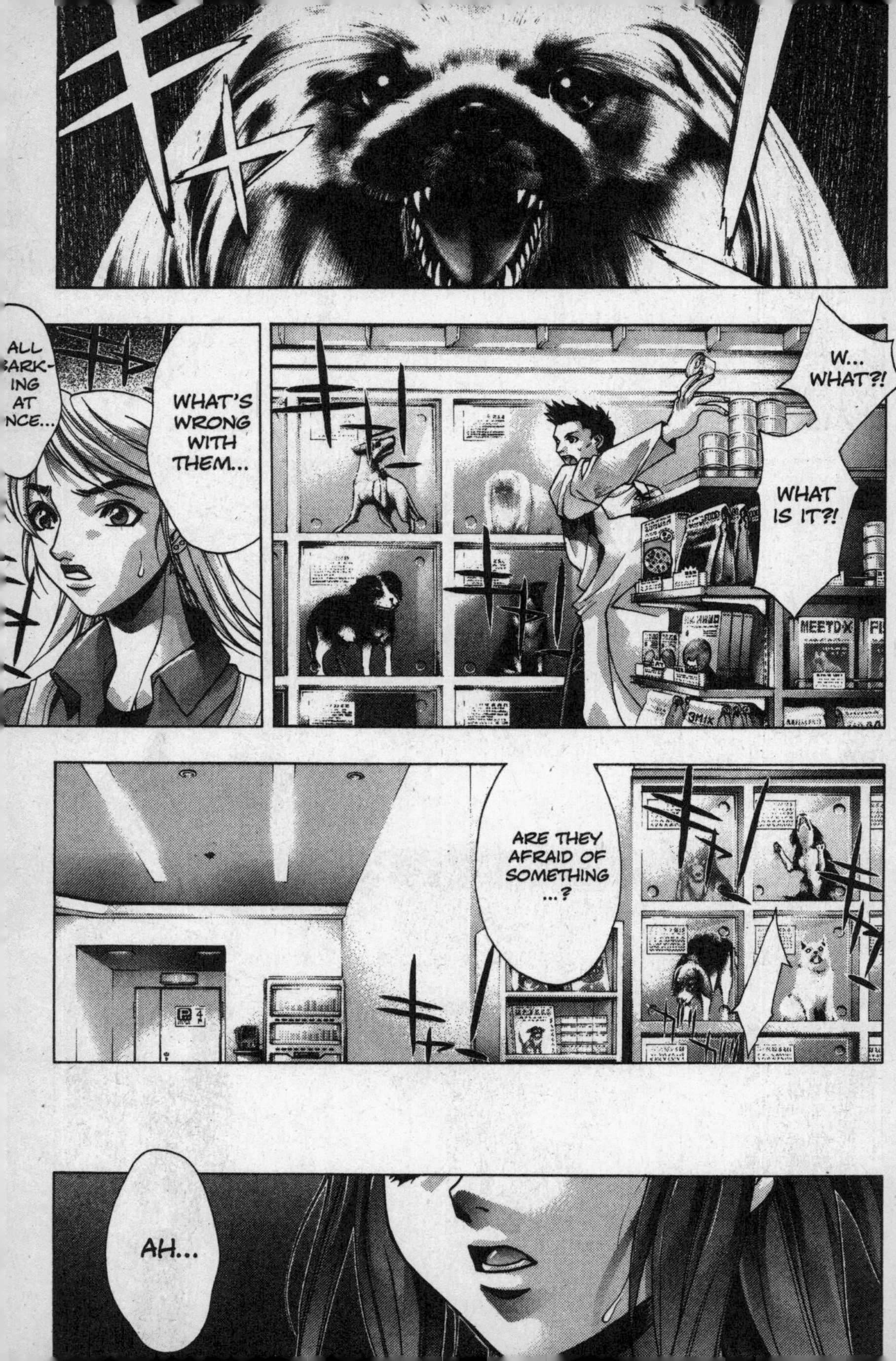
W... WHAT?!
WHAT IS IT?!
WHAT'S WRONG WITH THEM...
ALL ARK-ING AT NCE...
ARE THEY AFRAID OF SOMETHING ...?
AH...

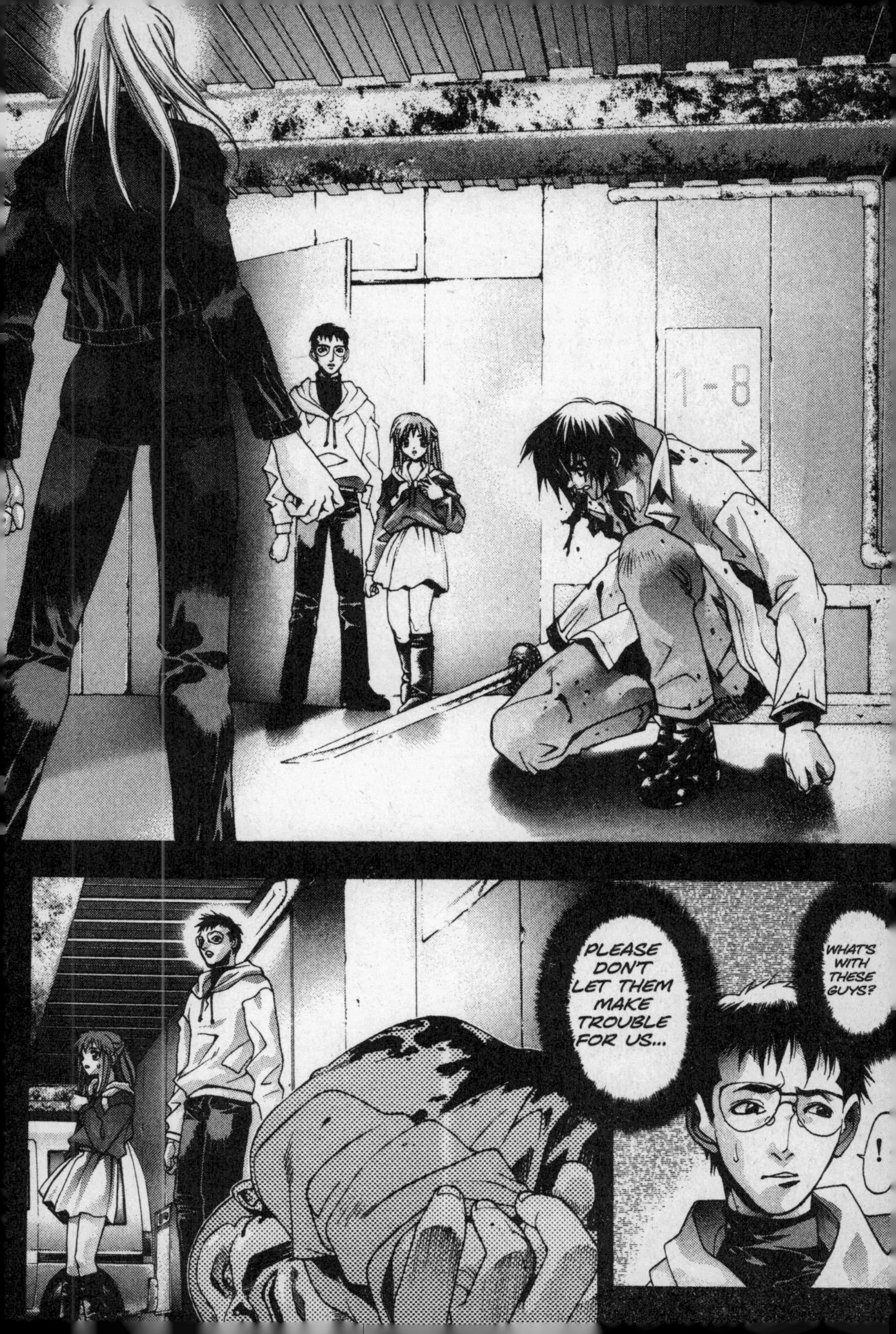
1-8
WHAT'S WITH THESE GUYS?
!
PLEASE DON'T LET THEM MAKE TROUBLE FOR US...

Chapter 23: To the Homeland

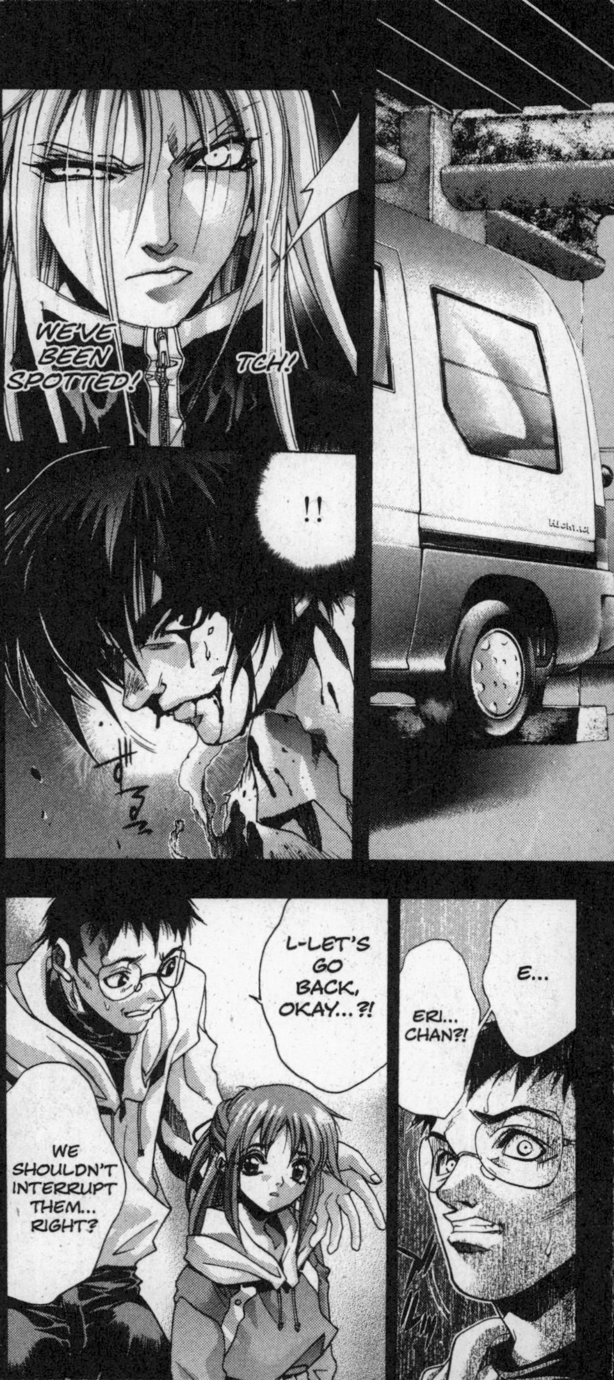
TCH!
WE'VE BEEN SPOTTED!
!!
E...
ERI... CHAN?!
L-LET'S GO BACK, OKAY...?!
WE SHOULDN'T INTERRUPT THEM... RIGHT?

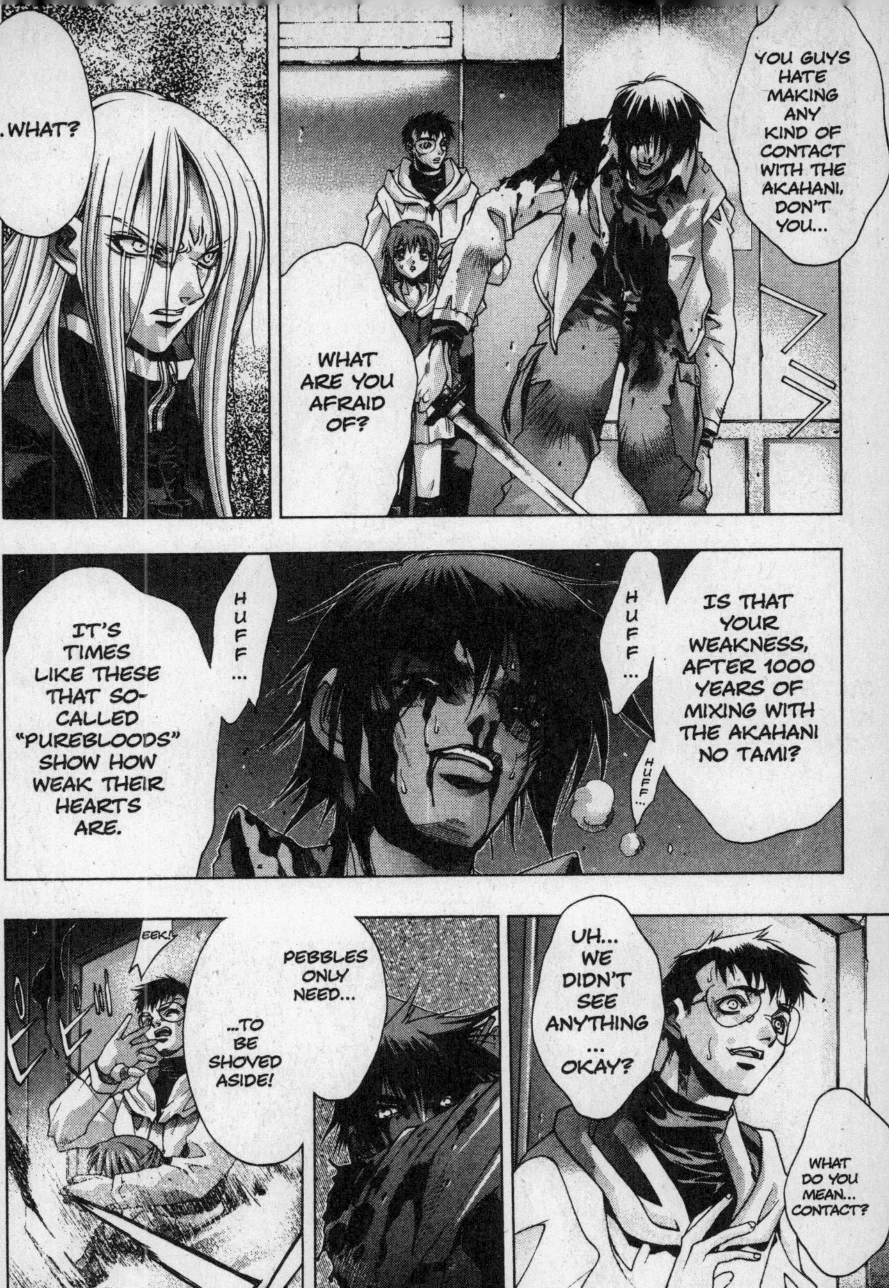
YOU GUYS HATE MAKING ANY KIND OF CONTACT WITH THE AKAHANI, DON'T YOU...
WHAT ARE YOU AFRAID OF?
...WHAT?
IS THAT YOUR WEAKNESS, AFTER 1000 YEARS OF MIXING WITH THE AKAHANI NO TAMI?
HUFF...
HUFF...
HUFF...
IT'S TIMES LIKE THESE THAT SO-CALLED "PUREBLOODS" SHOW HOW WEAK THEIR HEARTS ARE.
UH... WE DIDN'T SEE ANYTHING ...OKAY?
WHAT DO YOU MEAN... CONTACT?
PEBBLES ONLY NEED...
...TO BE SHOVED ASIDE!
EEK!

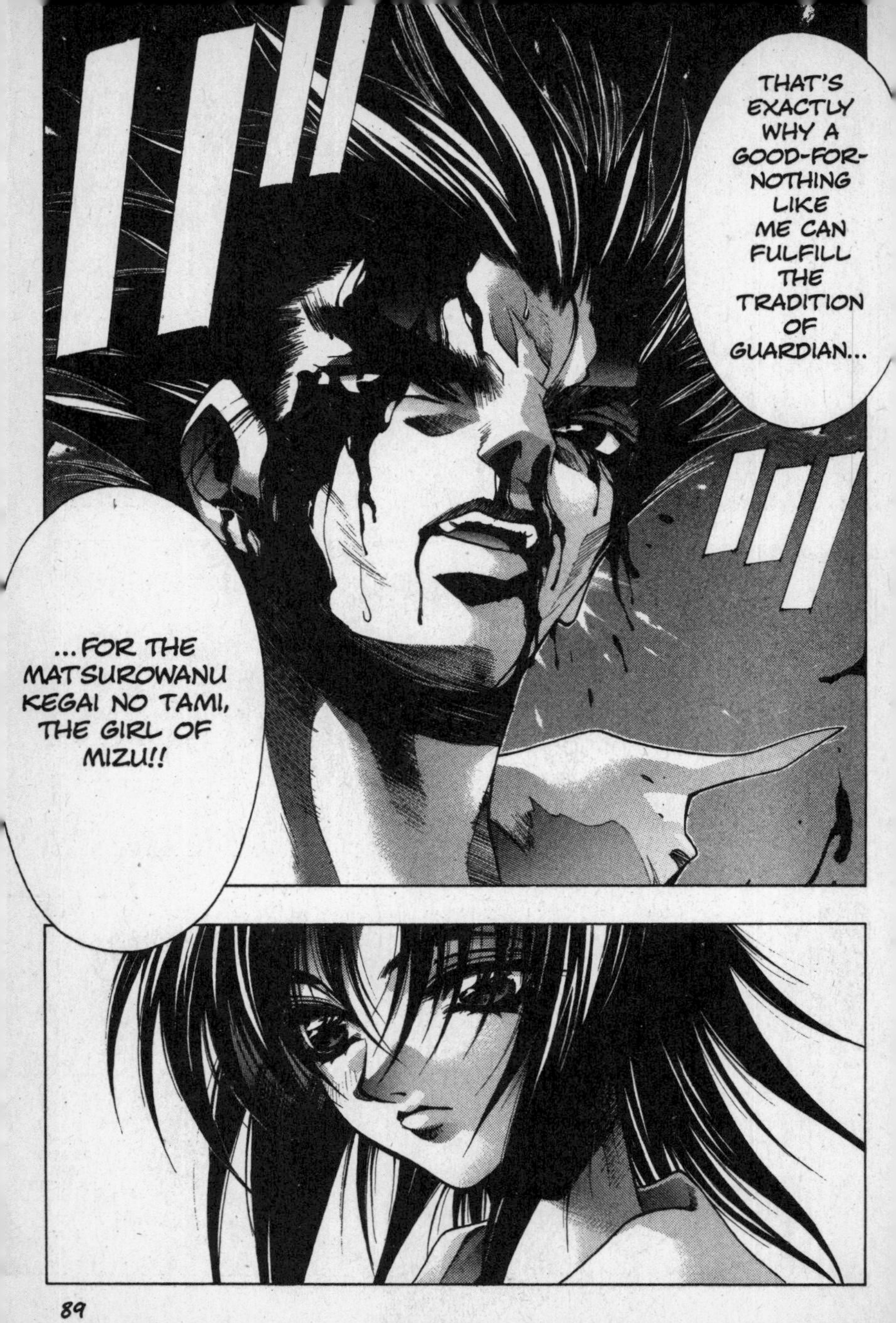
THAT'S EXACTLY WHY A GOOD-FOR-NOTHING LIKE ME CAN FULFILL THE TRADITION OF GUARDIAN...
...FOR THE MATSUROWANU KEGAI NO TAMI, THE GIRL OF MIZU!!

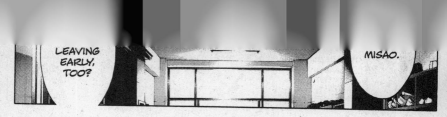

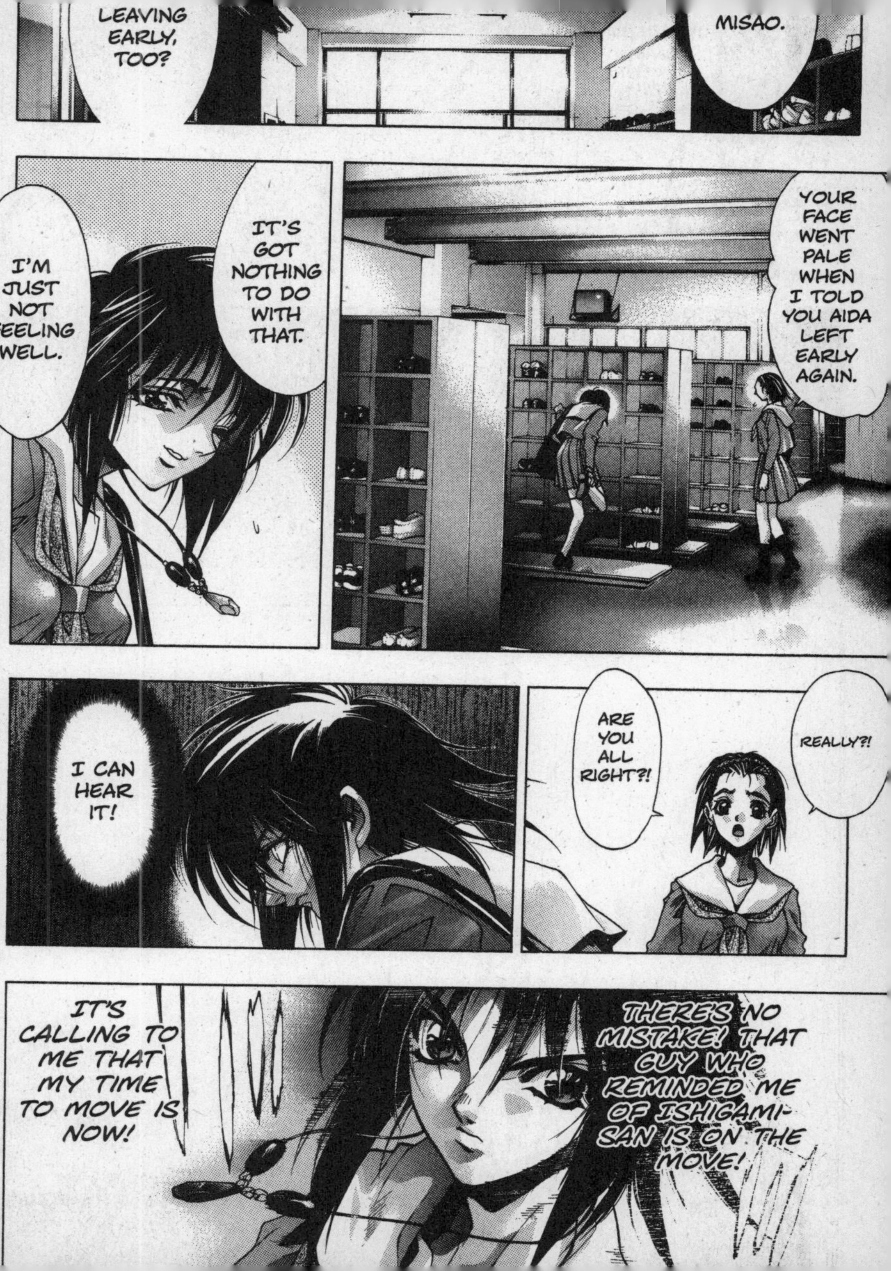
MISAO.
LEAVING EARLY, TOO?
YOUR FACE WENT PALE WHEN I TOLD YOU AIDA LEFT EARLY AGAIN.
IT'S GOT NOTHING TO DO WITH THAT.
I'M JUST NOT FEELING WELL.
REALLY?!
ARE YOU ALL RIGHT?!
I CAN HEAR IT!
THERE'S NO MISTAKE! THAT GUY WHO REMINDED ME OF ISHIGAMI-SAN IS ON THE MOVE!
IT'S CALLING TO ME THAT MY TIME TO MOVE IS NOW!

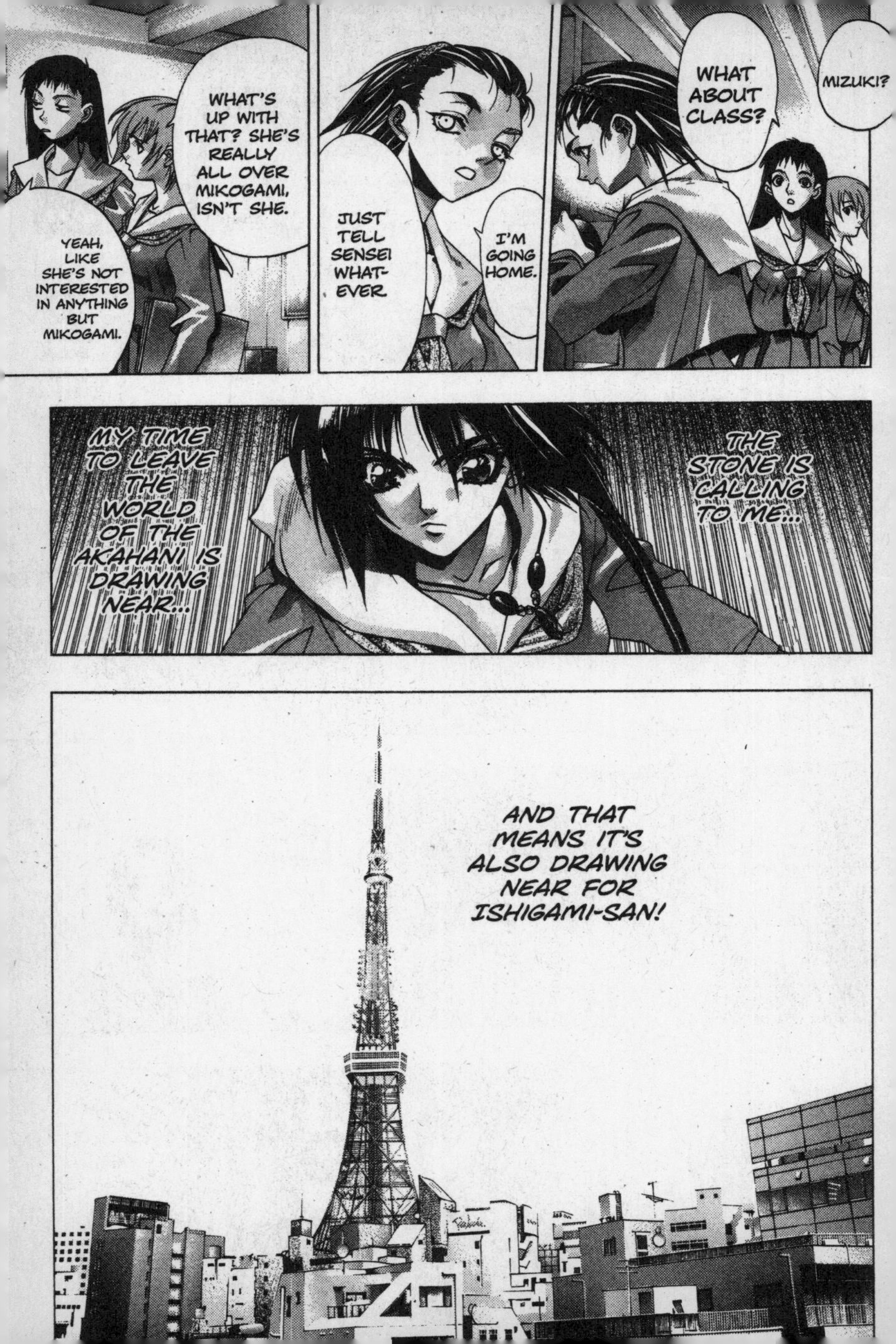
MIZUKI?
WHAT ABOUT CLASS?
I'M GOING HOME.
JUST TELL SENSEI WHATEVER.
WHAT'S UP WITH THAT? SHE'S REALLY ALL OVER MIKOGAMI, ISN'T SHE.
YEAH, LIKE SHE'S NOT INTERESTED IN ANYTHING BUT MIKOGAMI.
THE STONE IS CALLING TO ME...
MY TIME TO LEAVE THE WORLD OF THE AKAHANI IS DRAWING NEAR...
AND THAT MEANS IT'S ALSO DRAWING NEAR FOR ISHIGAMI-SAN!

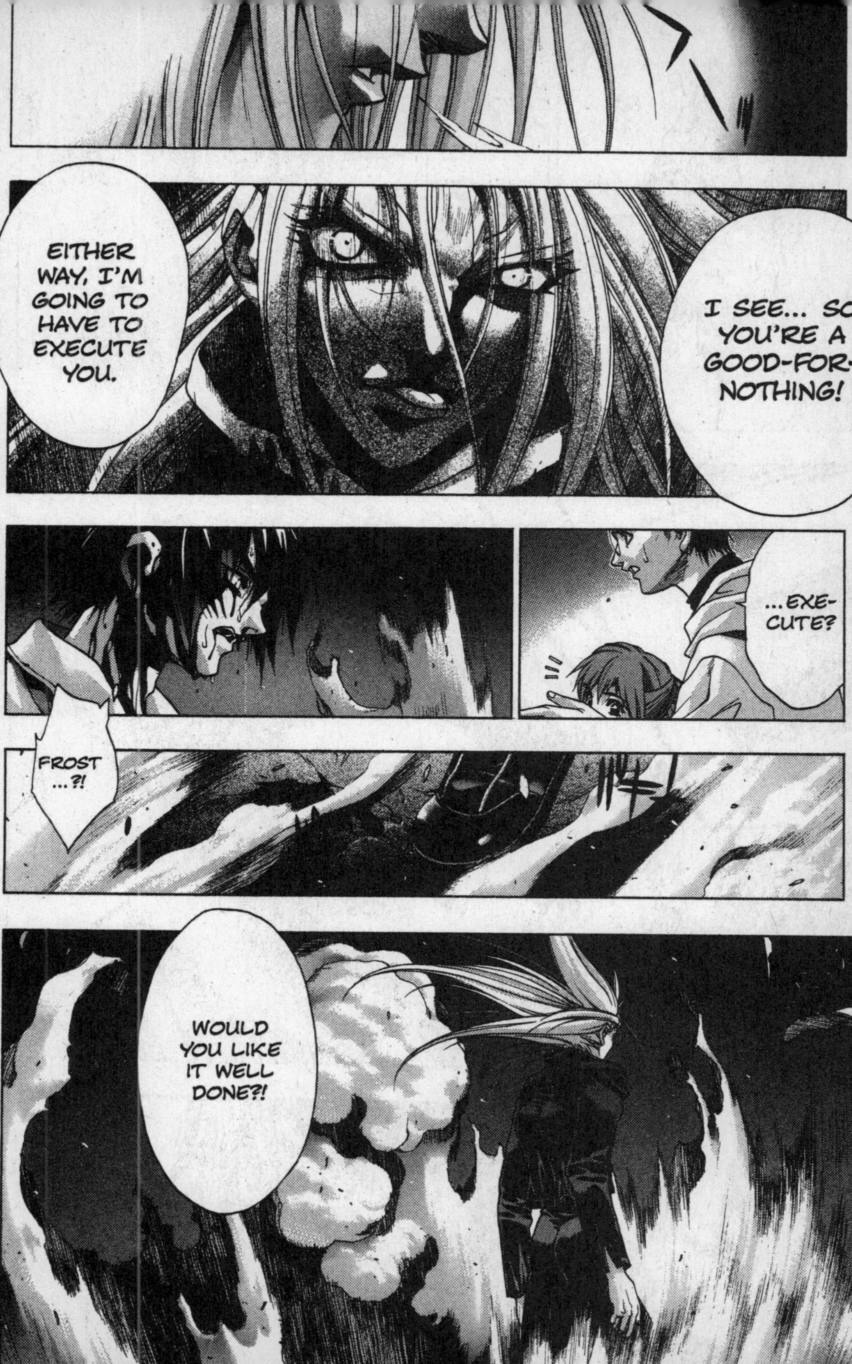
I SEE... SO YOU'RE A GOOD-FOR-NOTHING!
EITHER WAY, I'M GOING TO HAVE TO EXECUTE YOU.
...EXE-CUTE?
FROST ...?!
WOULD YOU LIKE IT WELL DONE?!

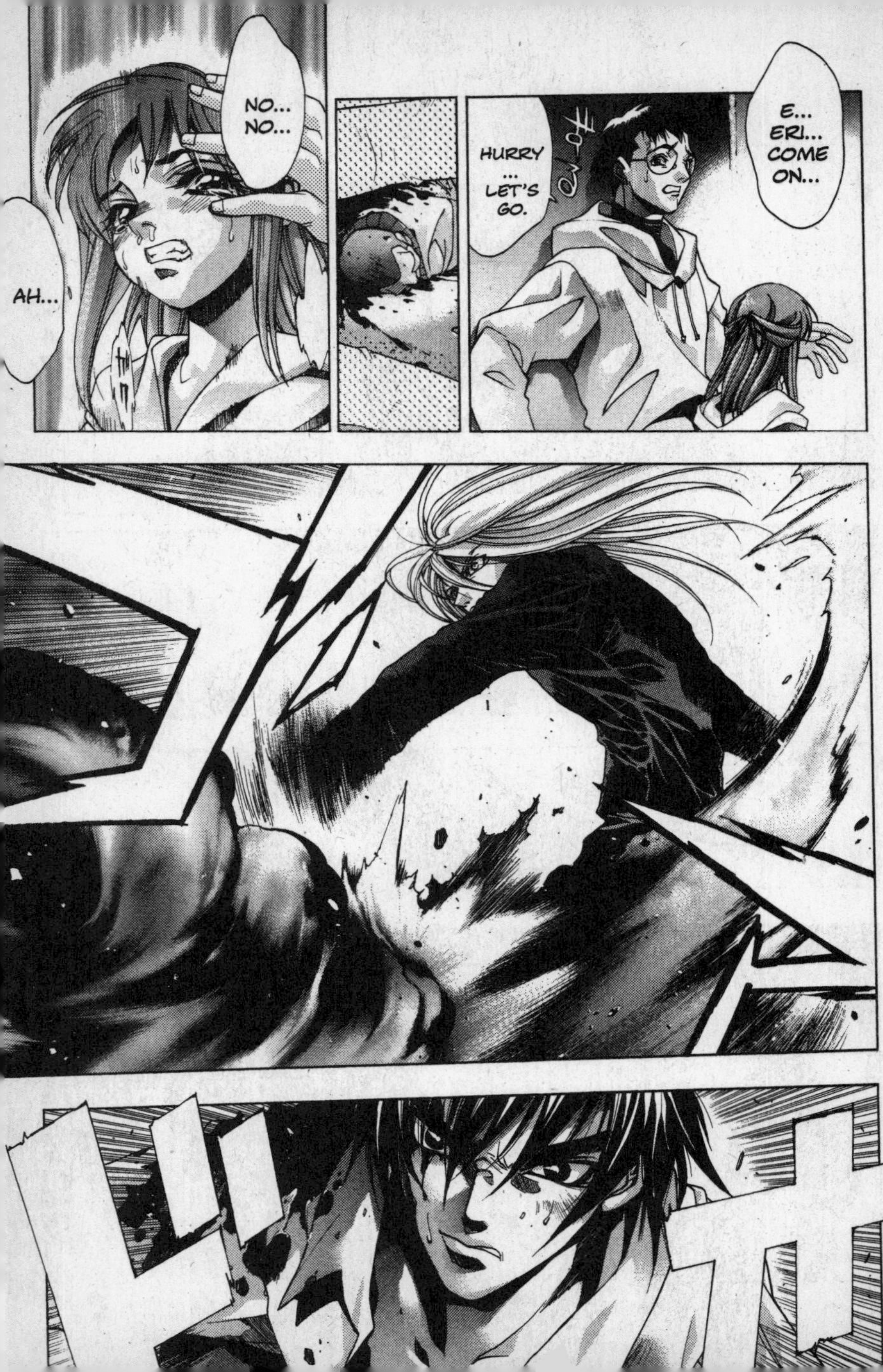
E... ERI... COME ON...
HURRY ... LET'S GO.
NO... NO...
AH...

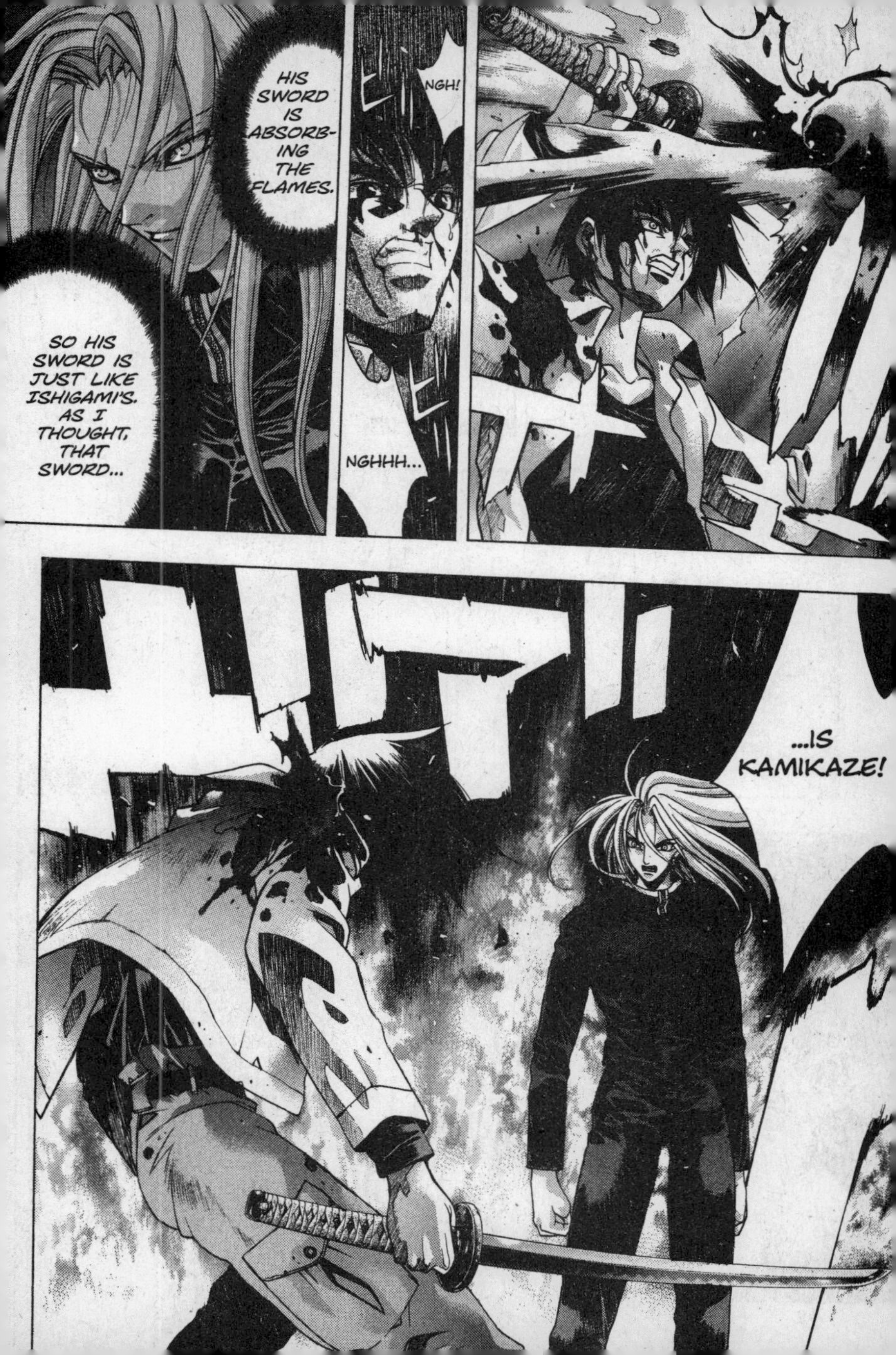
NGH!
NGHHH...
HIS SWORD IS ABSORBING THE FLAMES.
SO HIS SWORD IS JUST LIKE ISHIGAMI'S. AS I THOUGHT, THAT SWORD...
...IS KAMIKAZE!

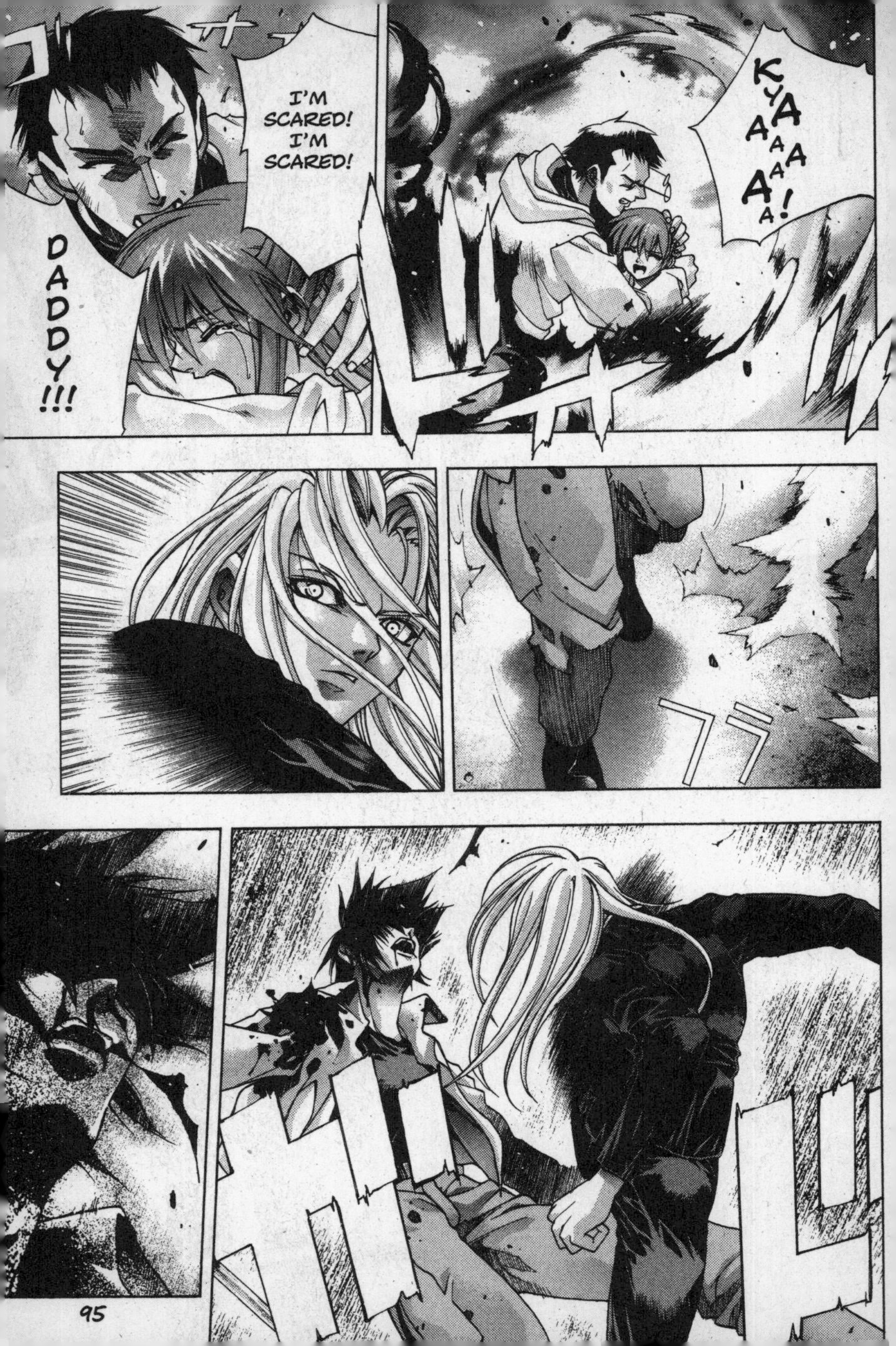
KYAAAAAAA!
I'M SCARED! I'M SCARED!
DADDY!!!

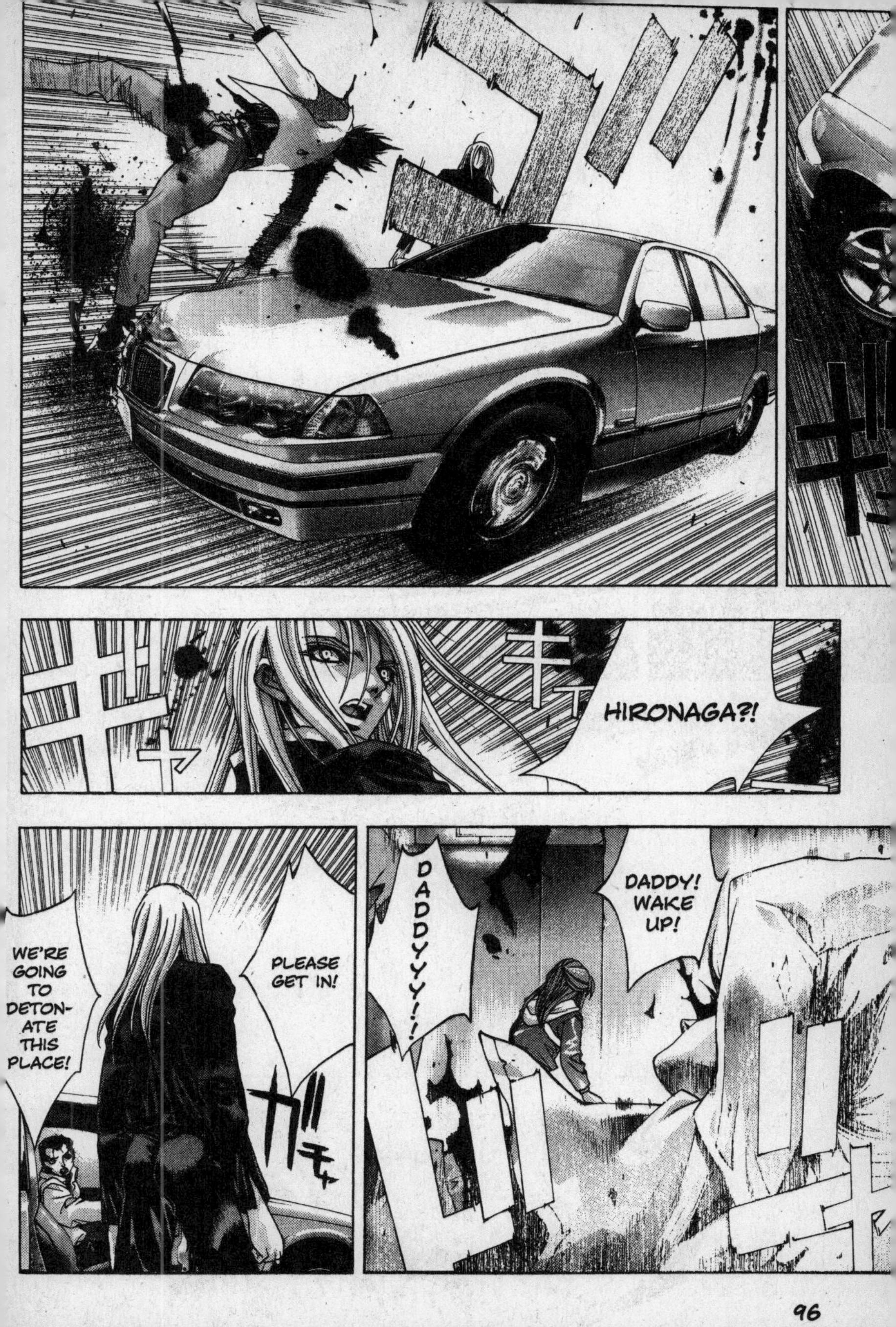
HIRONAGA?!
DADDY! WAKE UP!
DADDYYY!!
PLEASE GET IN!
WE'RE GOING TO DETON-ATE THIS PLACE!

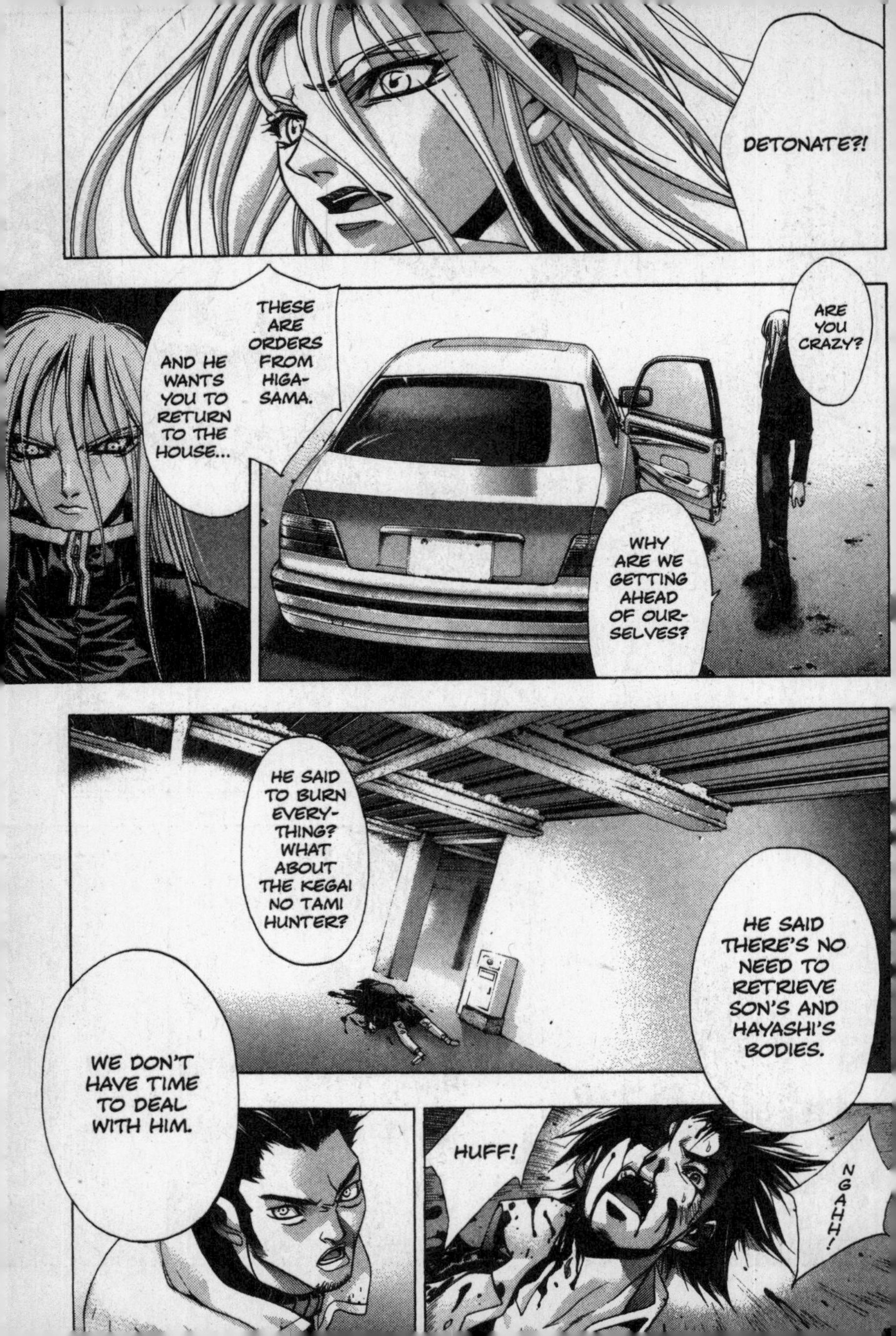
DETONATE?!
ARE YOU CRAZY?
WHY ARE WE GETTING AHEAD OF OUR-SELVES?
THESE ARE ORDERS FROM HIGA-SAMA.
AND HE WANTS YOU TO RETURN TO THE HOUSE...
HE SAID TO BURN EVERY-THING? WHAT ABOUT THE KEGAI NO TAMI HUNTER?
HE SAID THERE'S NO NEED TO RETRIEVE SON'S AND HAYASHI'S BODIES.
WE DON'T HAVE TIME TO DEAL WITH HIM.
HUFF!
NGAHH!

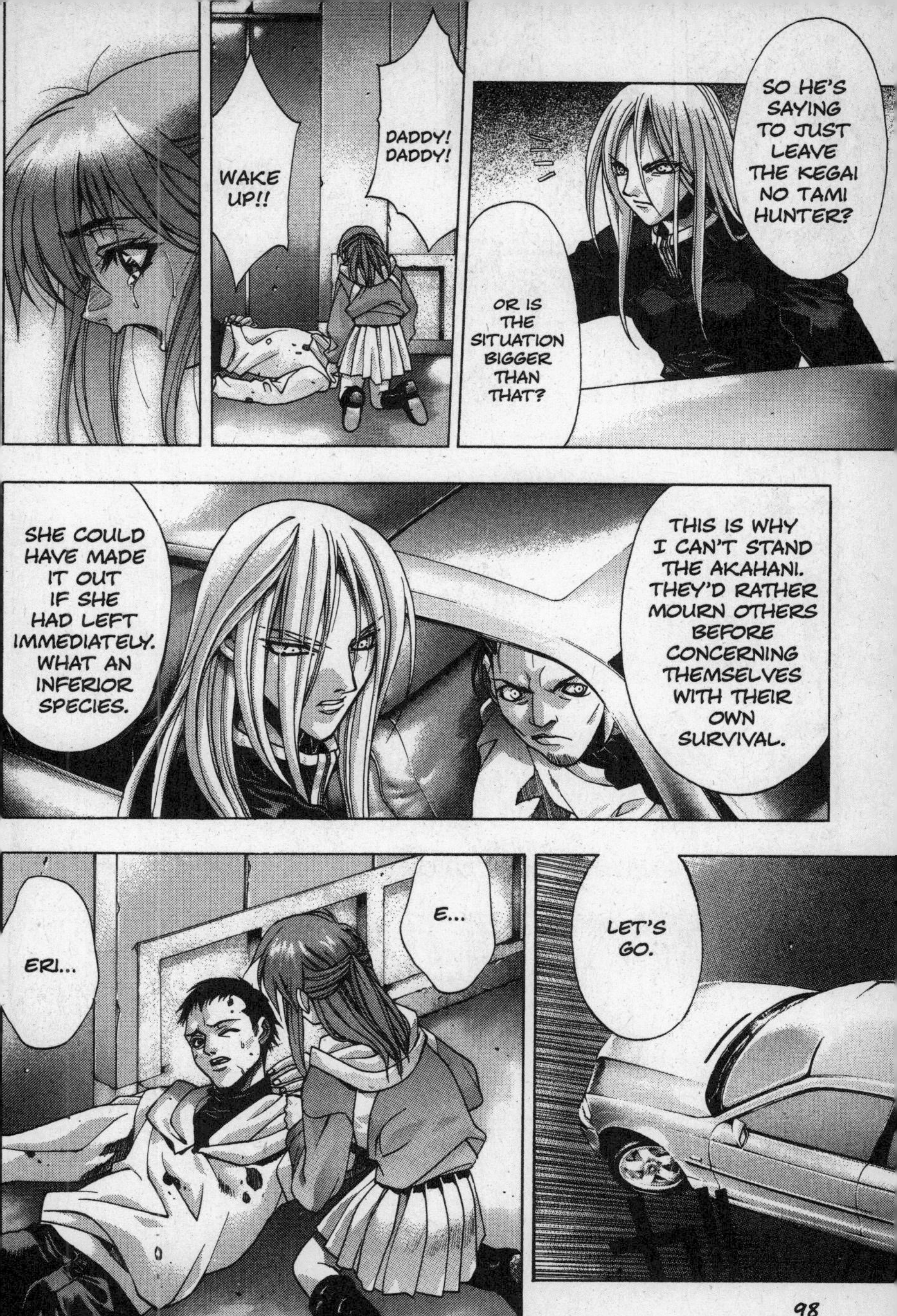
SO HE'S SAYING TO JUST LEAVE THE KEGAI NO TAMI HUNTER?
OR IS THE SITUATION BIGGER THAN THAT?
DADDY! DADDY!
WAKE UP!!
THIS IS WHY I CAN'T STAND THE AKAHANI. THEY'D RATHER MOURN OTHERS BEFORE CONCERNING THEMSELVES WITH THEIR OWN SURVIVAL.
SHE COULD HAVE MADE IT OUT IF SHE HAD LEFT IMMEDIATELY. WHAT AN INFERIOR SPECIES.
LET'S GO.
E...
ERI...

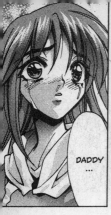

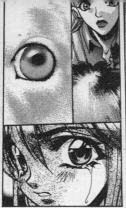

DADDY
...

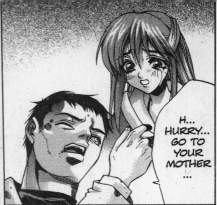

H...
HURRY...
GO TO
YOUR
MOTHER
...

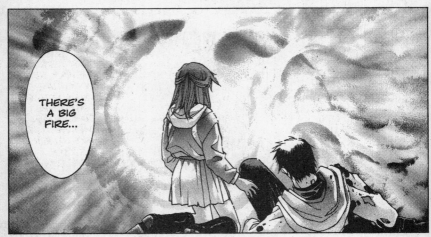

THERE'S
A BIG
FIRE...

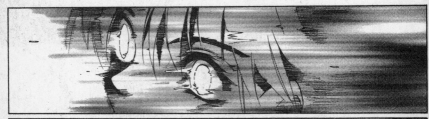

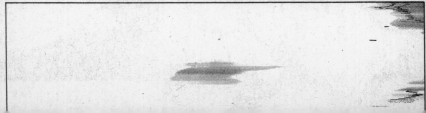

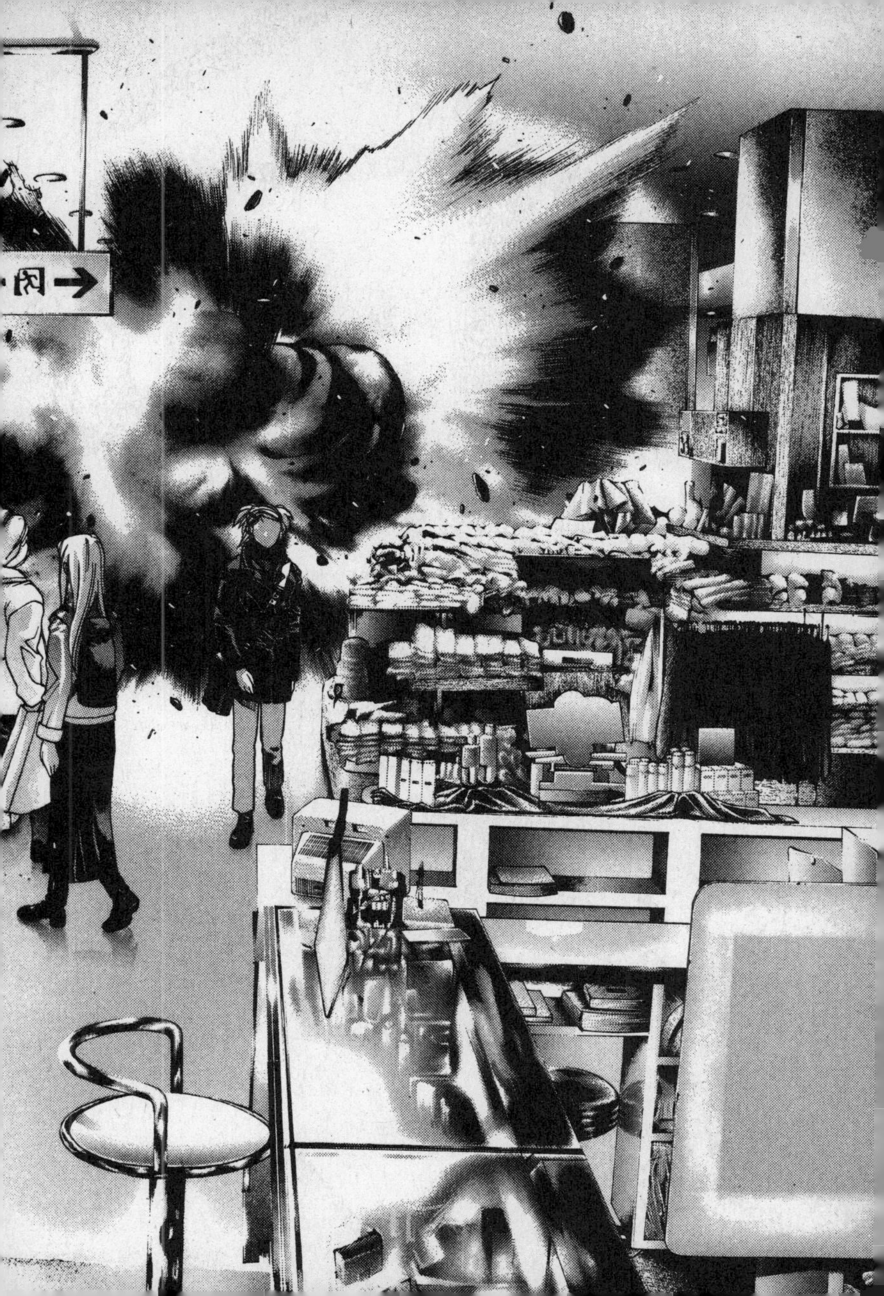
肉

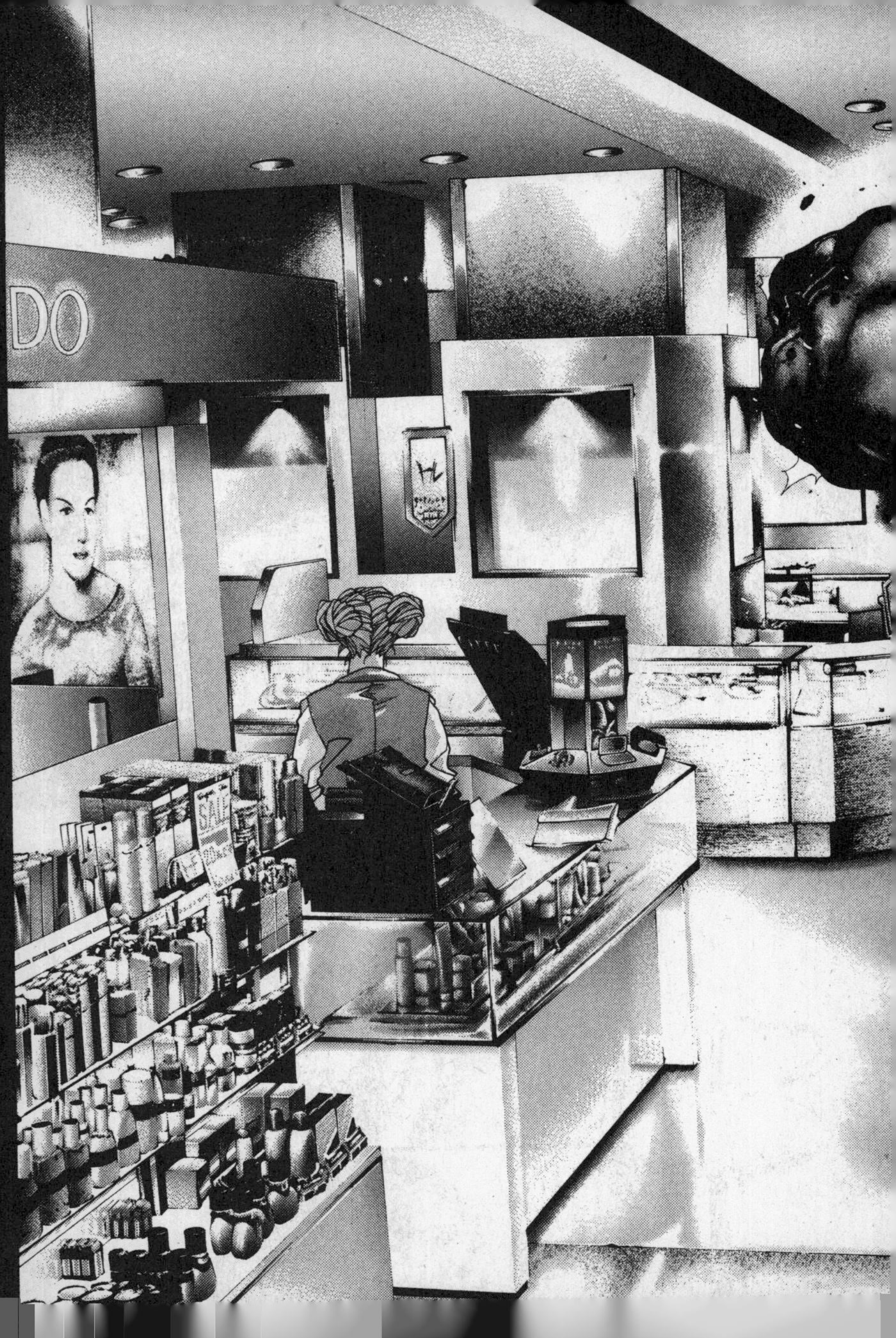
DO
SALE

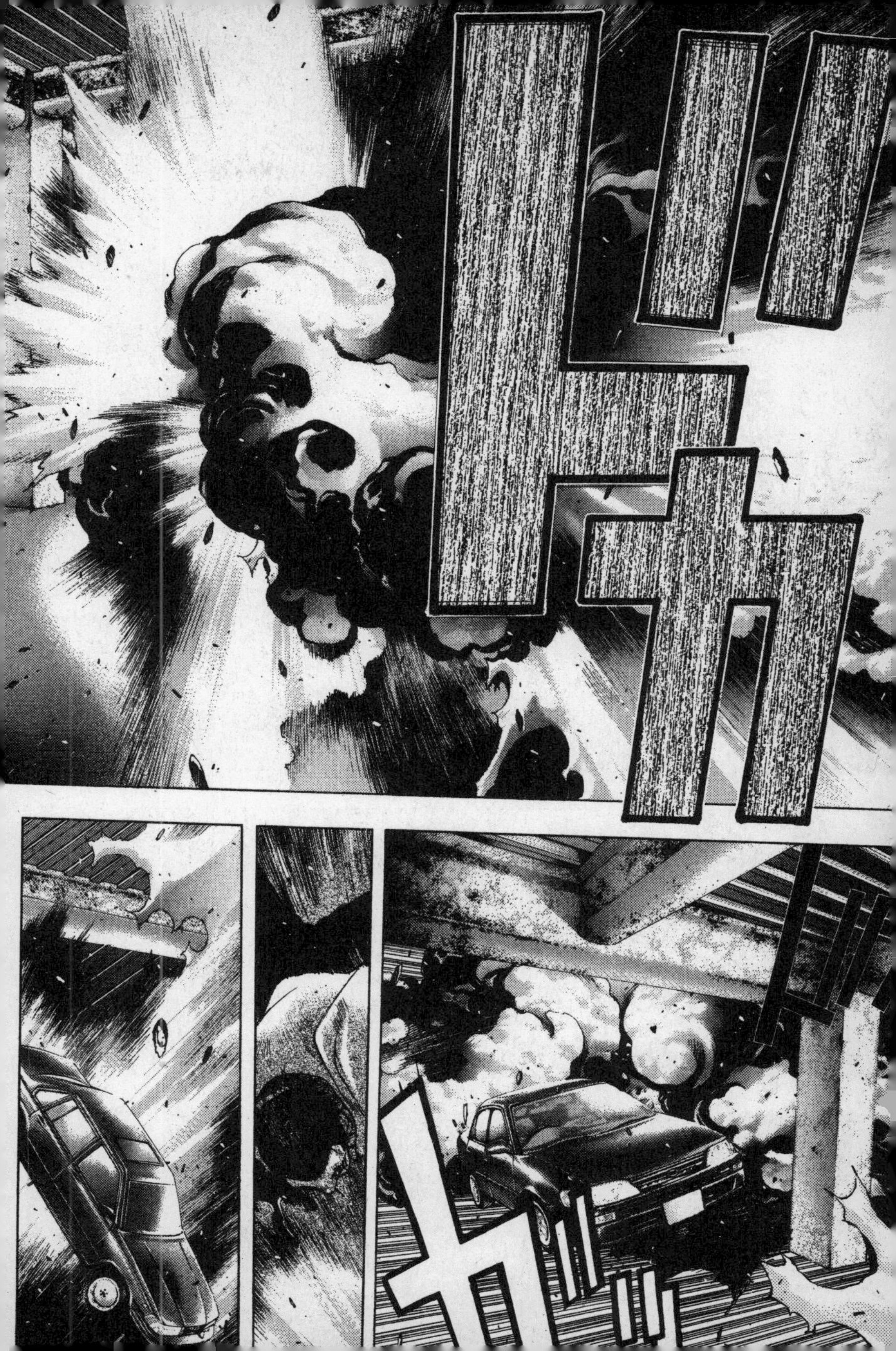
ドカ

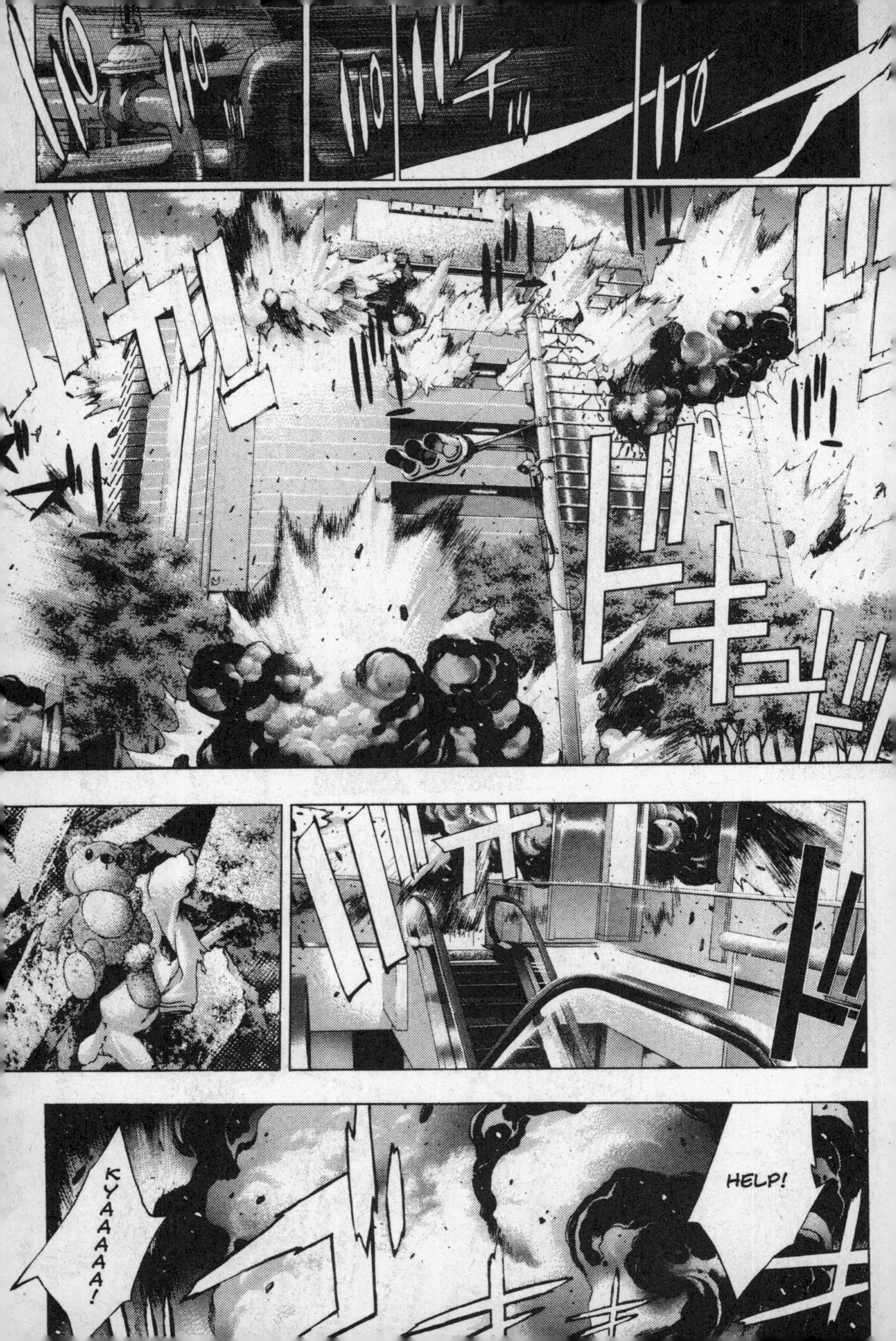
HELP!
KYAAAAAA!

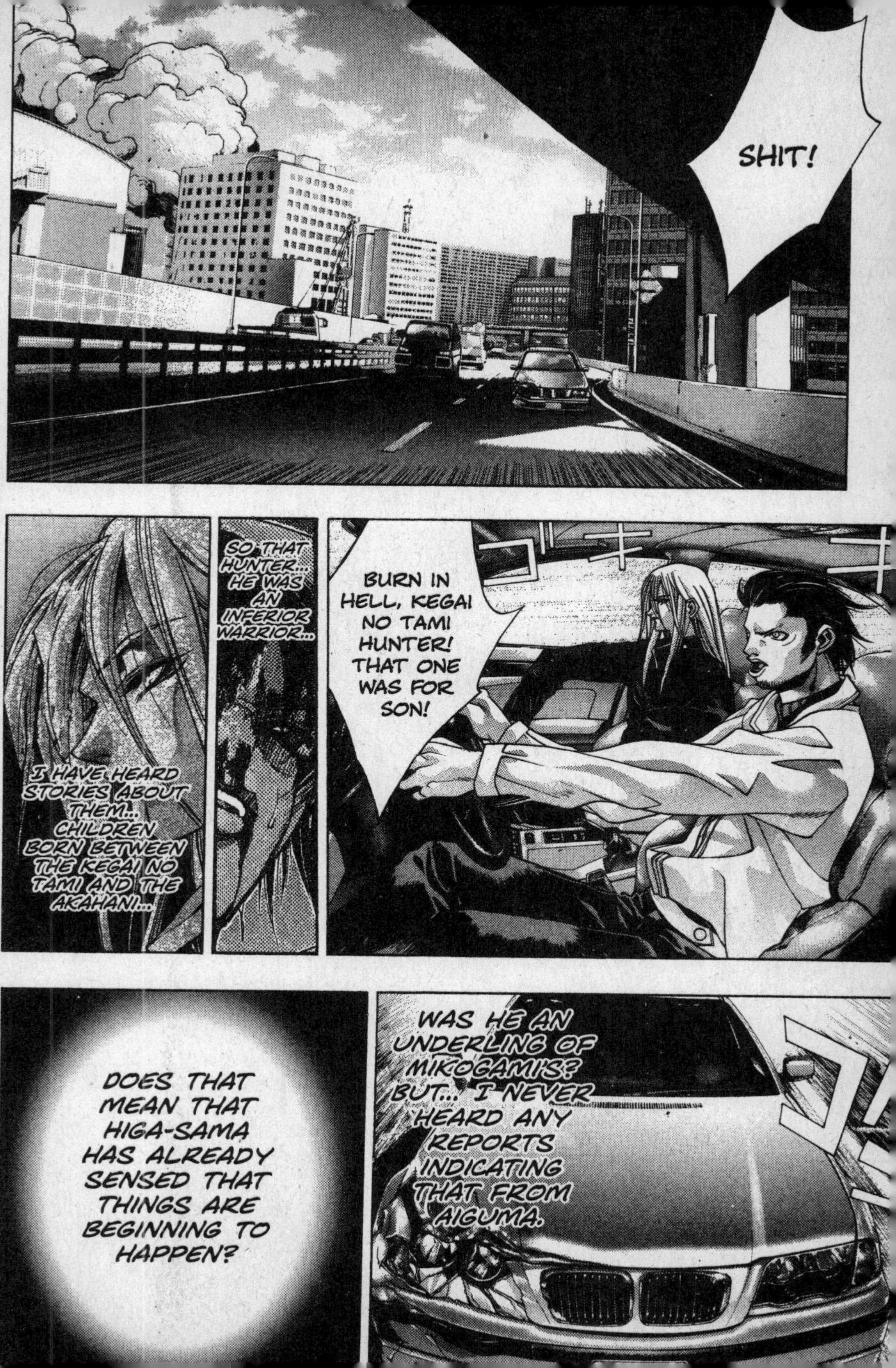
SHIT!
BURN IN HELL, KEGAI NO TAMI HUNTER! THAT ONE WAS FOR SON!
SO THAT HUNTER... HE WAS AN INFERIOR WARRIOR...
I HAVE HEARD STORIES ABOUT THEM... CHILDREN BORN BETWEEN THE KEGAI NO TAMI AND THE AKAHANI...
WAS HE AN UNDERLING OF MIKOGAMI'S? BUT... I NEVER HEARD ANY REPORTS INDICATING THAT FROM AIGUMA.
DOES THAT MEAN THAT HIGA-SAMA HAS ALREADY SENSED THAT THINGS ARE BEGINNING TO HAPPEN?

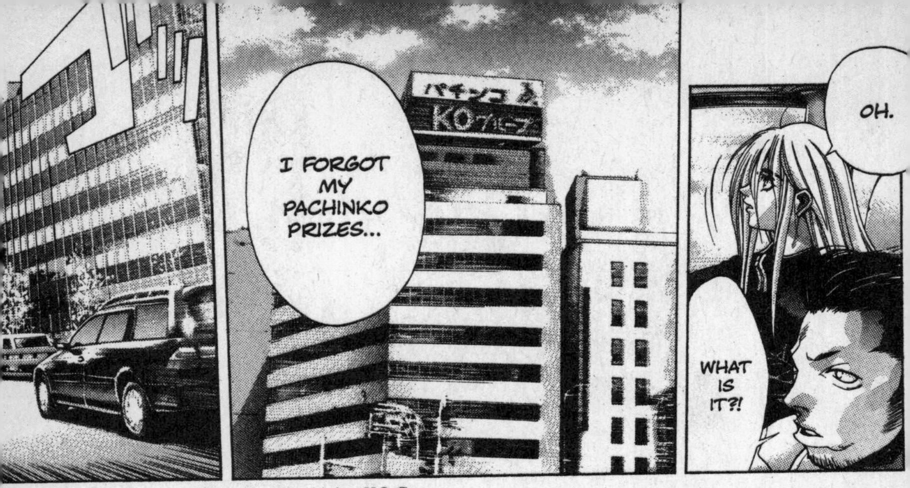
OH.
WHAT IS IT?!
I FORGOT MY PACHINKO PRIZES...
Sign: Pachinko; KO Group

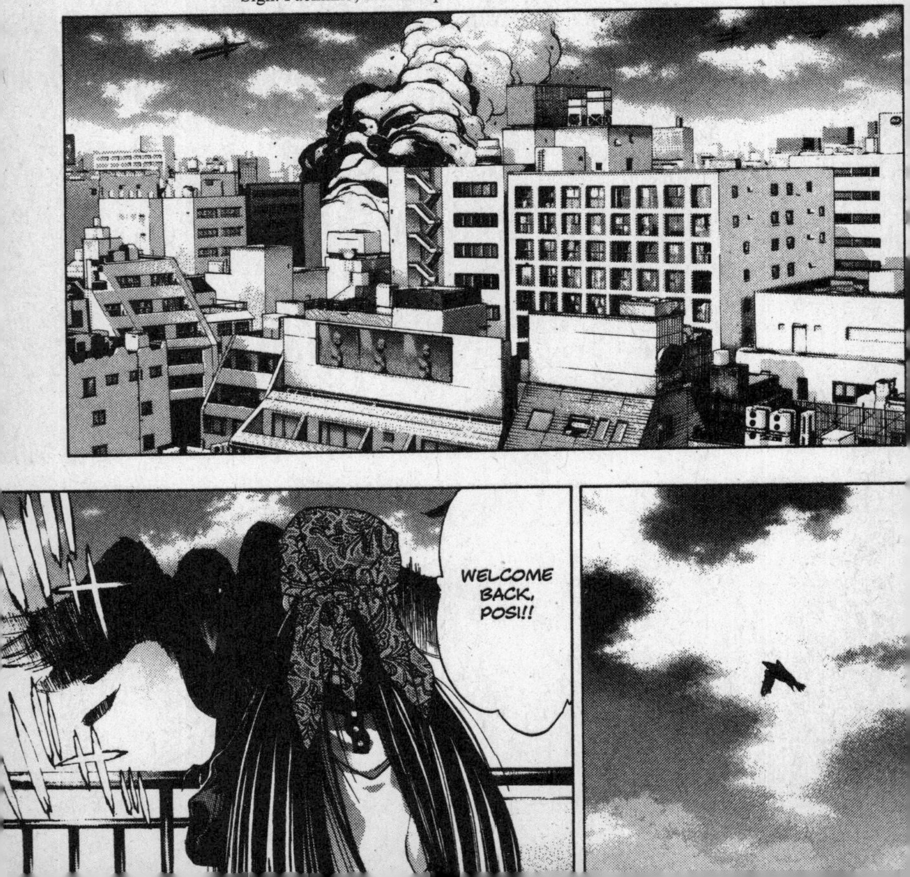
WELCOME BACK, POSI!!

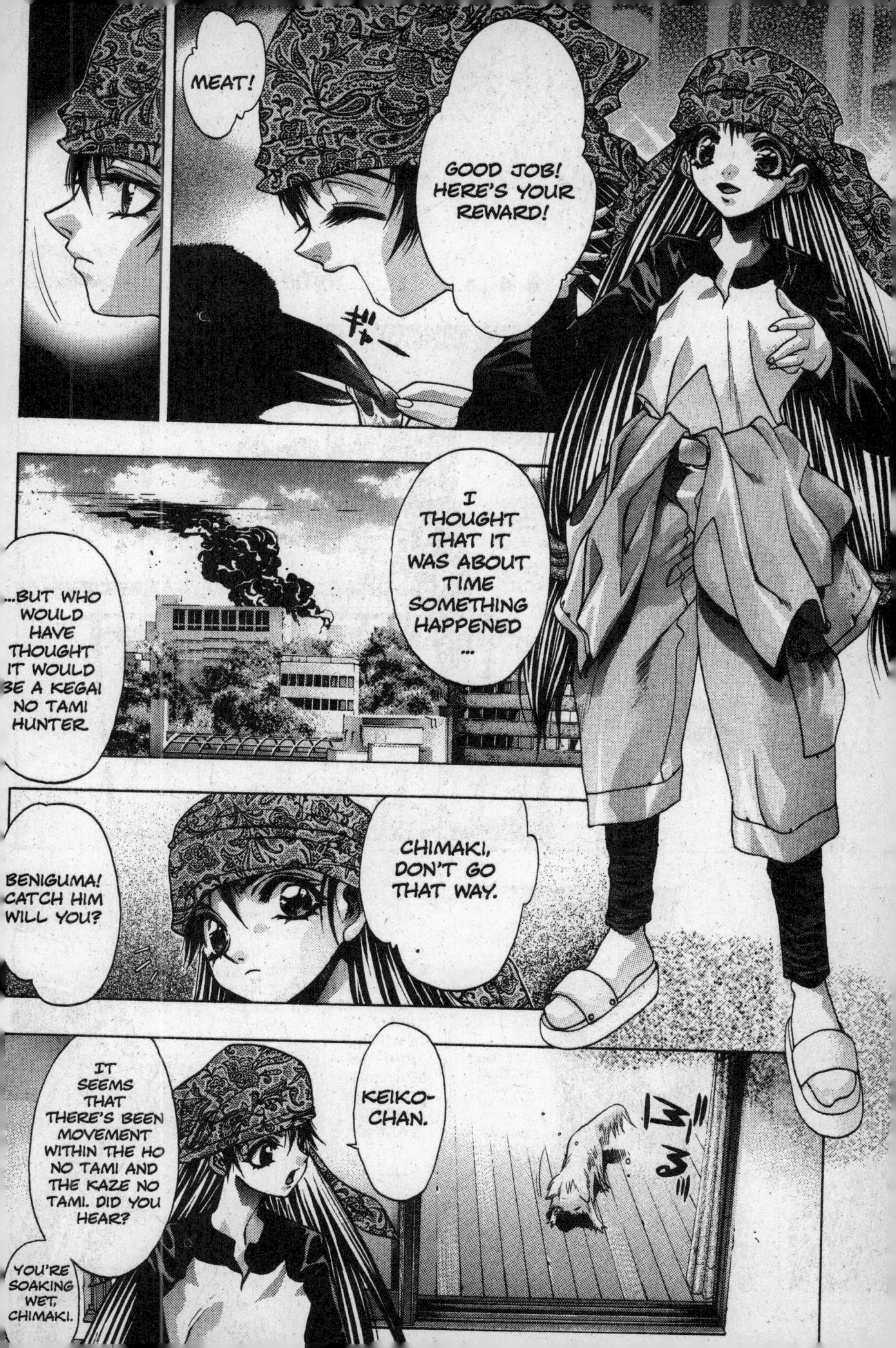
GOOD JOB! HERE'S YOUR REWARD!
MEAT!
ギャー
I THOUGHT THAT IT WAS ABOUT TIME SOMETHING HAPPENED ...
...BUT WHO WOULD HAVE THOUGHT IT WOULD BE A KEGAI NO TAMI HUNTER
CHIMAKI, DON'T GO THAT WAY.
BENIGUMA! CATCH HIM WILL YOU?
KEIKO-CHAN.
IT SEEMS THAT THERE'S BEEN MOVEMENT WITHIN THE HO NO TAMI AND THE KAZE NO TAMI. DID YOU HEAR?
YOU'RE SOAKING WET, CHIMAKI.

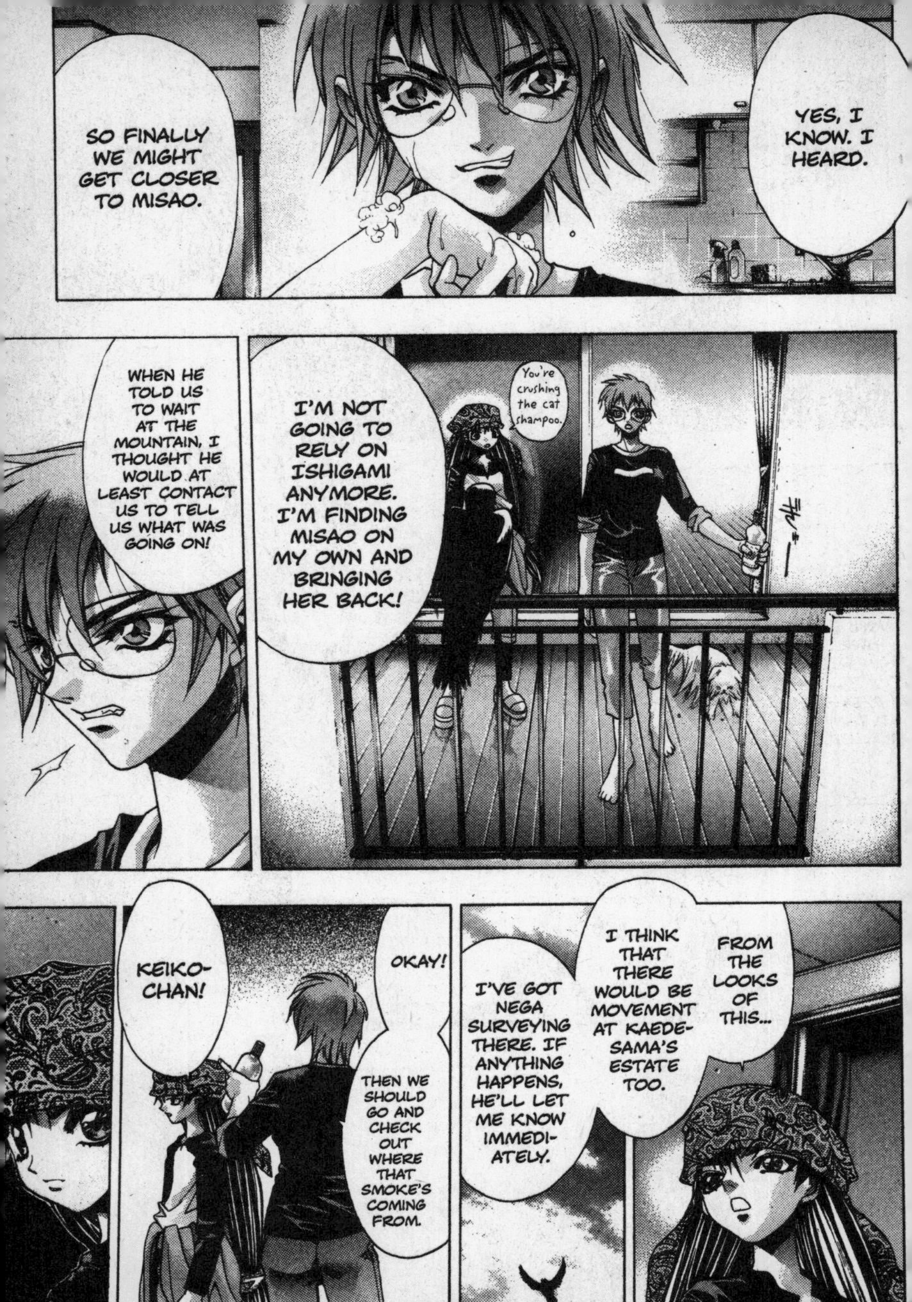
YES, I KNOW. I HEARD.
SO FINALLY WE MIGHT GET CLOSER TO MISAO.
I'M NOT GOING TO RELY ON ISHIGAMI ANYMORE. I'M FINDING MISAO ON MY OWN AND BRINGING HER BACK!
You're crushing the cat shampoo.
WHEN HE TOLD US TO WAIT AT THE MOUNTAIN, I THOUGHT HE WOULD AT LEAST CONTACT US TO TELL US WHAT WAS GOING ON!
FROM THE LOOKS OF THIS...
I THINK THAT THERE WOULD BE MOVEMENT AT KAEDE-SAMA'S ESTATE TOO.
I'VE GOT NEGA SURVEYING THERE. IF ANYTHING HAPPENS, HE'LL LET ME KNOW IMMEDI-ATELY.
OKAY!
THEN WE SHOULD GO AND CHECK OUT WHERE THAT SMOKE'S COMING FROM.
KEIKO-CHAN!

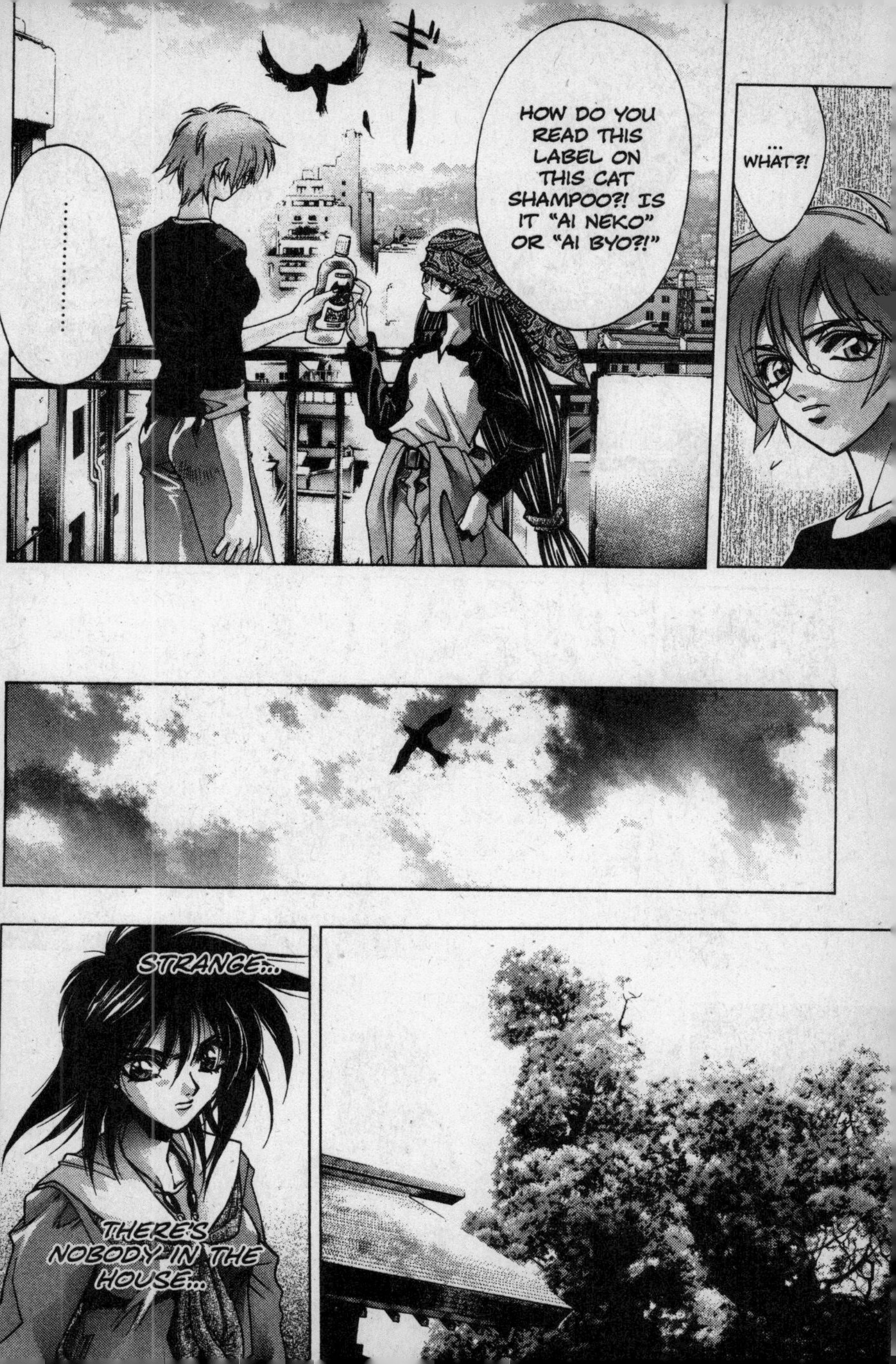

... WHAT?!
HOW DO YOU READ THIS LABEL ON THIS CAT SHAMPOO?! IS IT "AI NEKO" OR "AI BYO?!"
ギャー
......
STRANGE...
THERE'S NOBODY IN THE HOUSE...

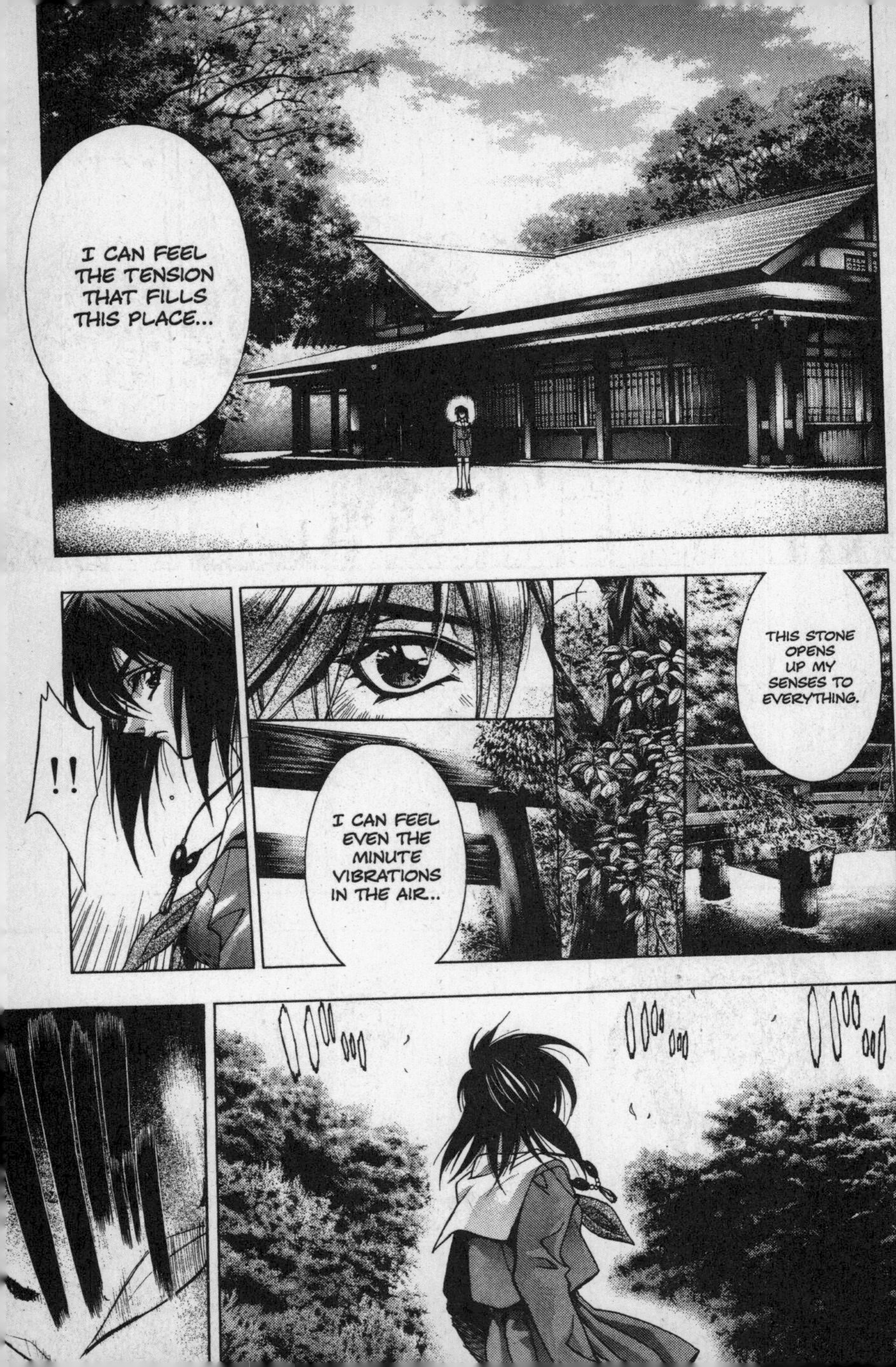
I CAN FEEL THE TENSION THAT FILLS THIS PLACE...
THIS STONE OPENS UP MY SENSES TO EVERYTHING.
I CAN FEEL EVEN THE MINUTE VIBRATIONS IN THE AIR..
!!

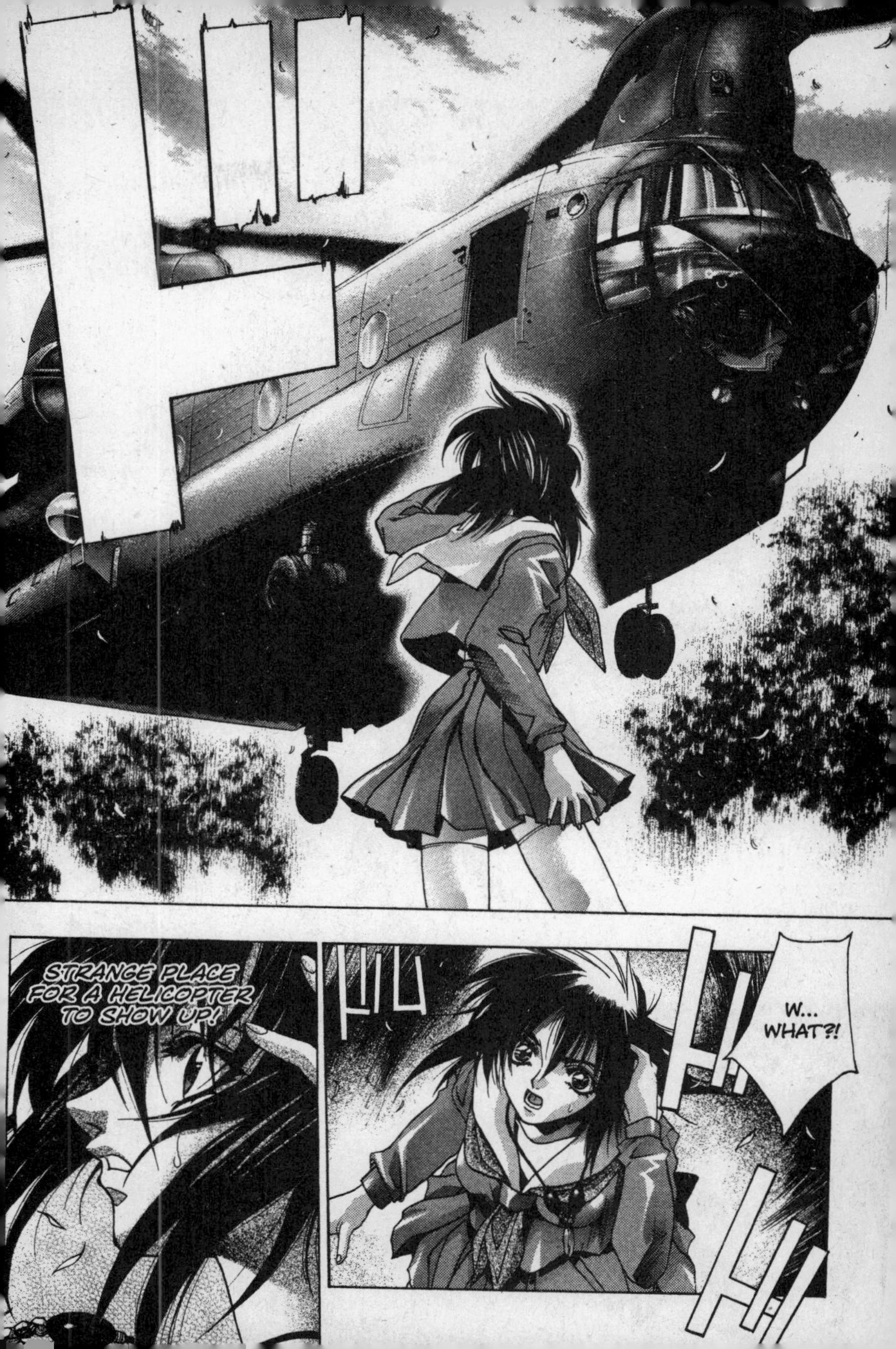
W... WHAT?!
STRANGE PLACE FOR A HELICOPTER TO SHOW UP!

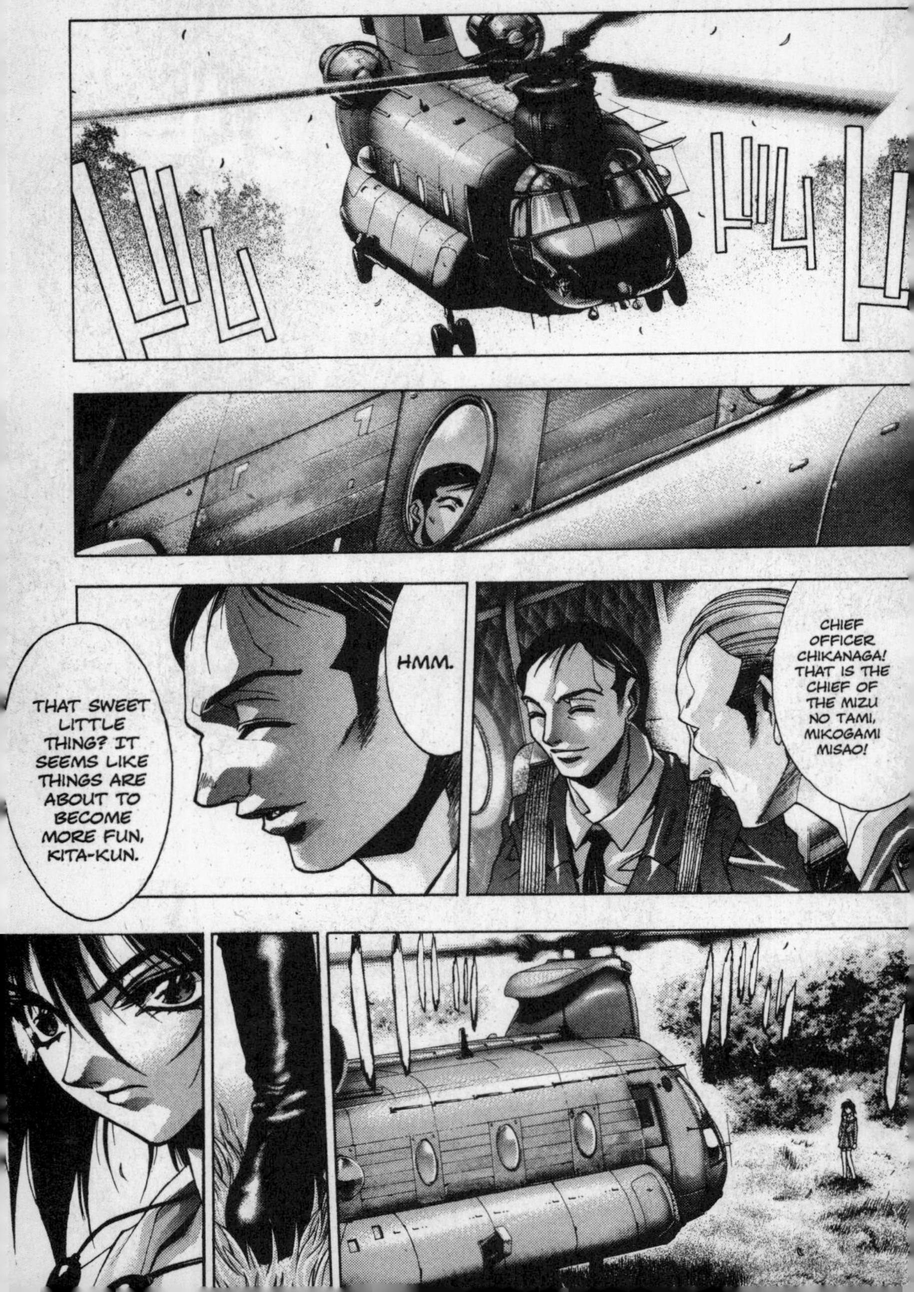
CHIEF OFFICER CHIKANAGA! THAT IS THE CHIEF OF THE MIZU NO TAMI, MIKOGAMI MISAO!
HMM.
THAT SWEET LITTLE THING? IT SEEMS LIKE THINGS ARE ABOUT TO BECOME MORE FUN, KITA-KUN.

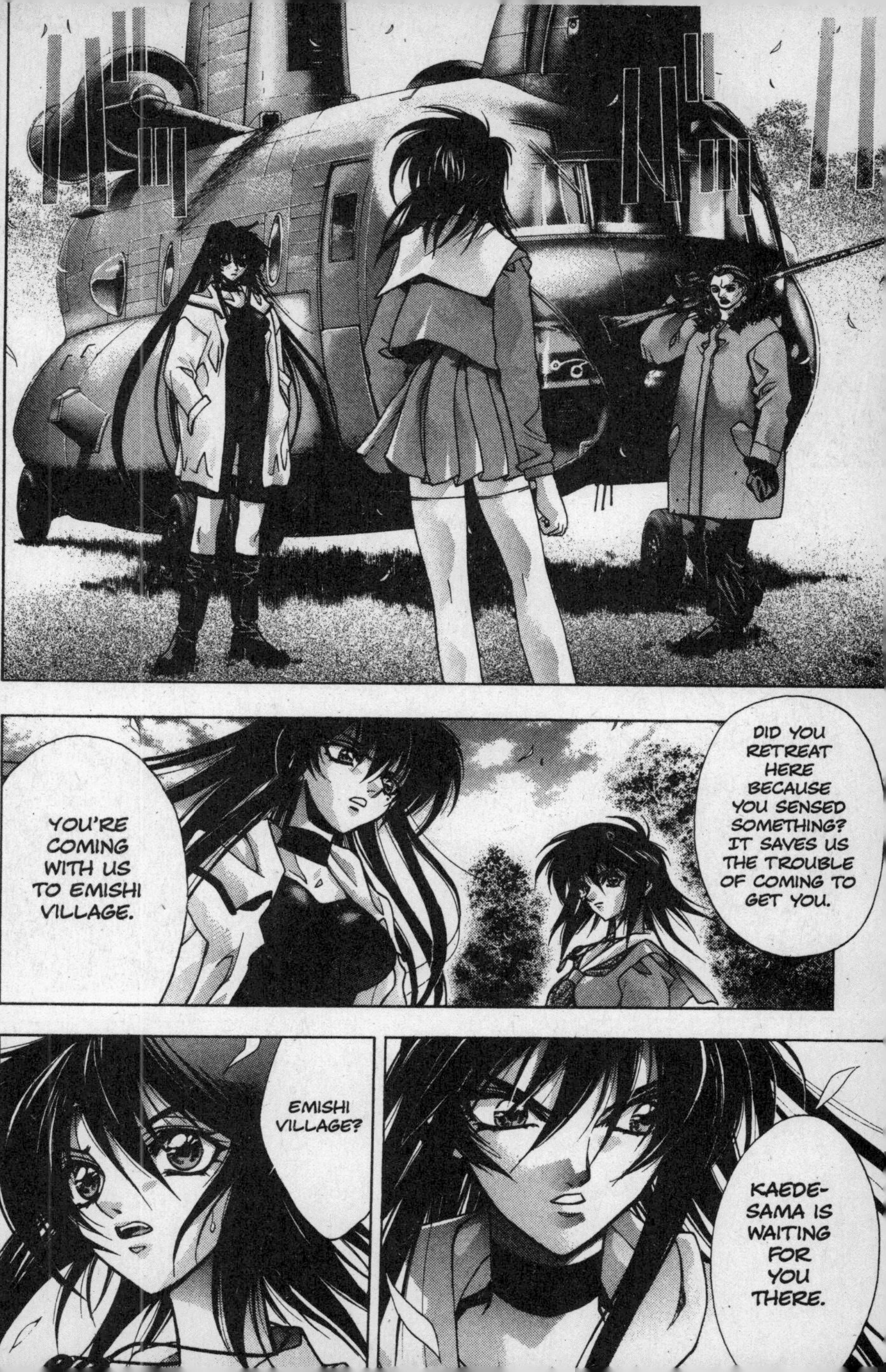
DID YOU RETREAT HERE BECAUSE YOU SENSED SOMETHING? IT SAVES US THE TROUBLE OF COMING TO GET YOU.
YOU'RE COMING WITH US TO EMISHI VILLAGE.
EMISHI VILLAGE?
KAEDE-SAMA IS WAITING FOR YOU THERE.

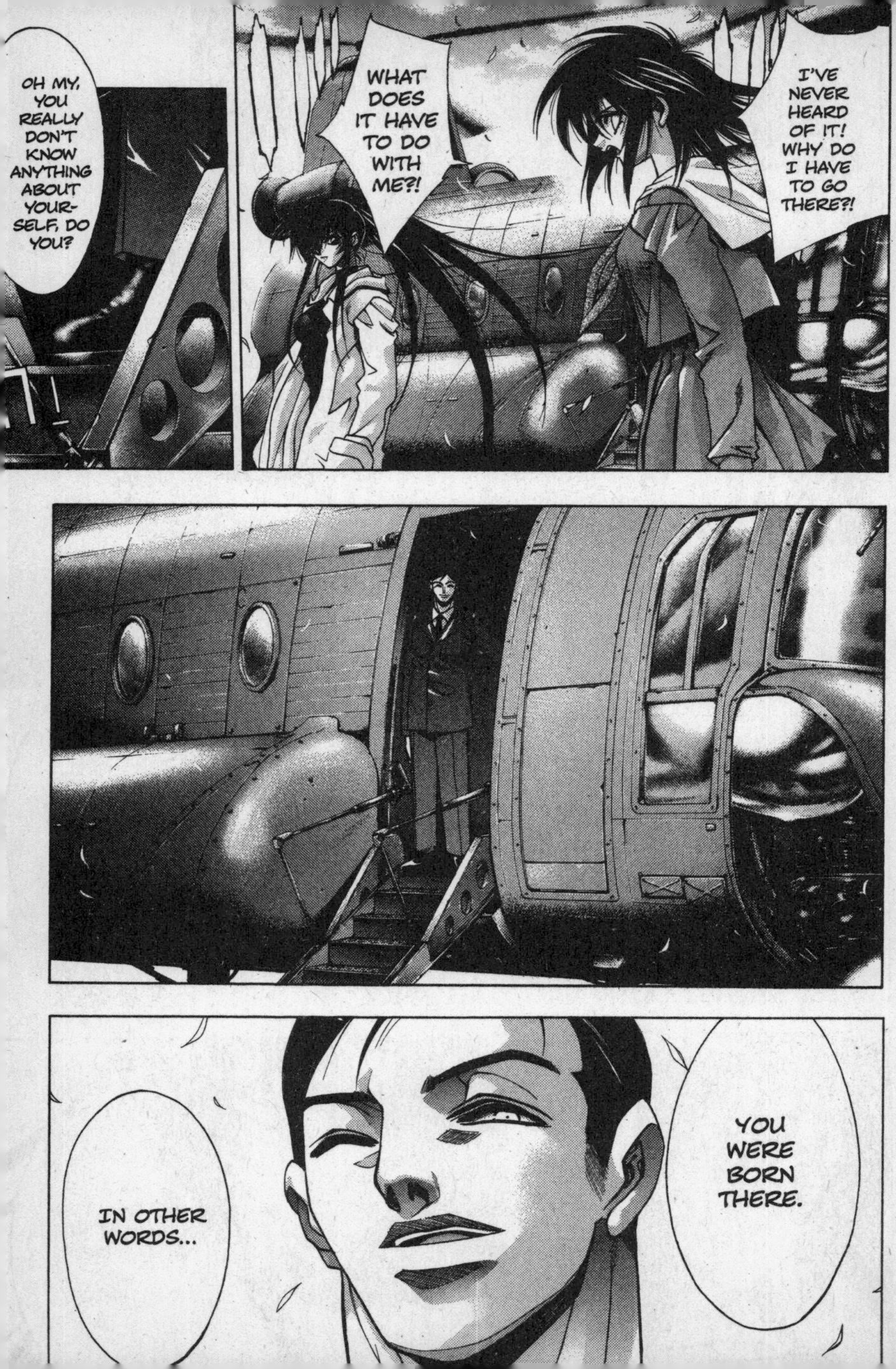
I'VE NEVER HEARD OF IT! WHY DO I HAVE TO GO THERE?!
WHAT DOES IT HAVE TO DO WITH ME?!
OH MY, YOU REALLY DON'T KNOW ANYTHING ABOUT YOURSELF, DO YOU?
YOU WERE BORN THERE.
IN OTHER WORDS...

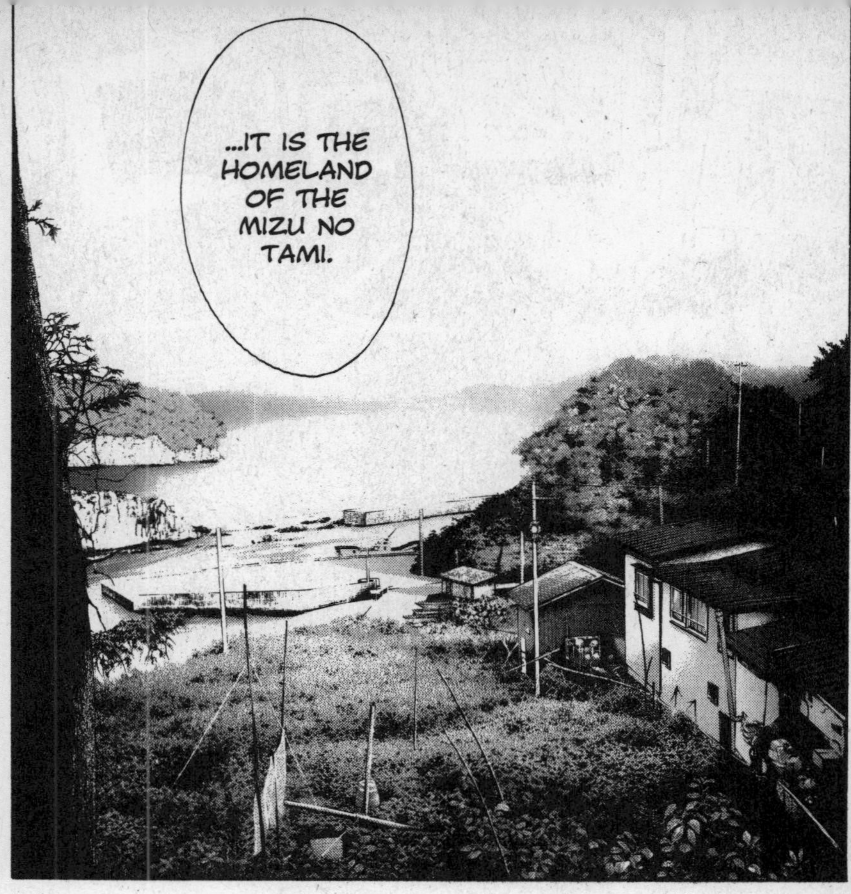
...IT IS THE HOMELAND OF THE MIZU NO TAMI.

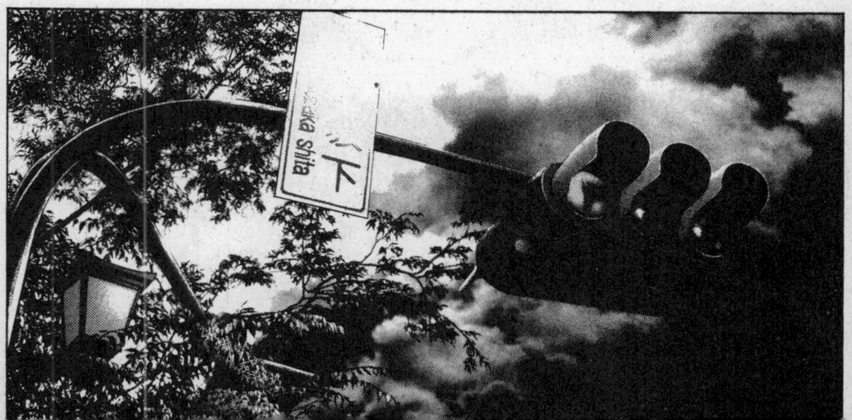
ka Shita
下

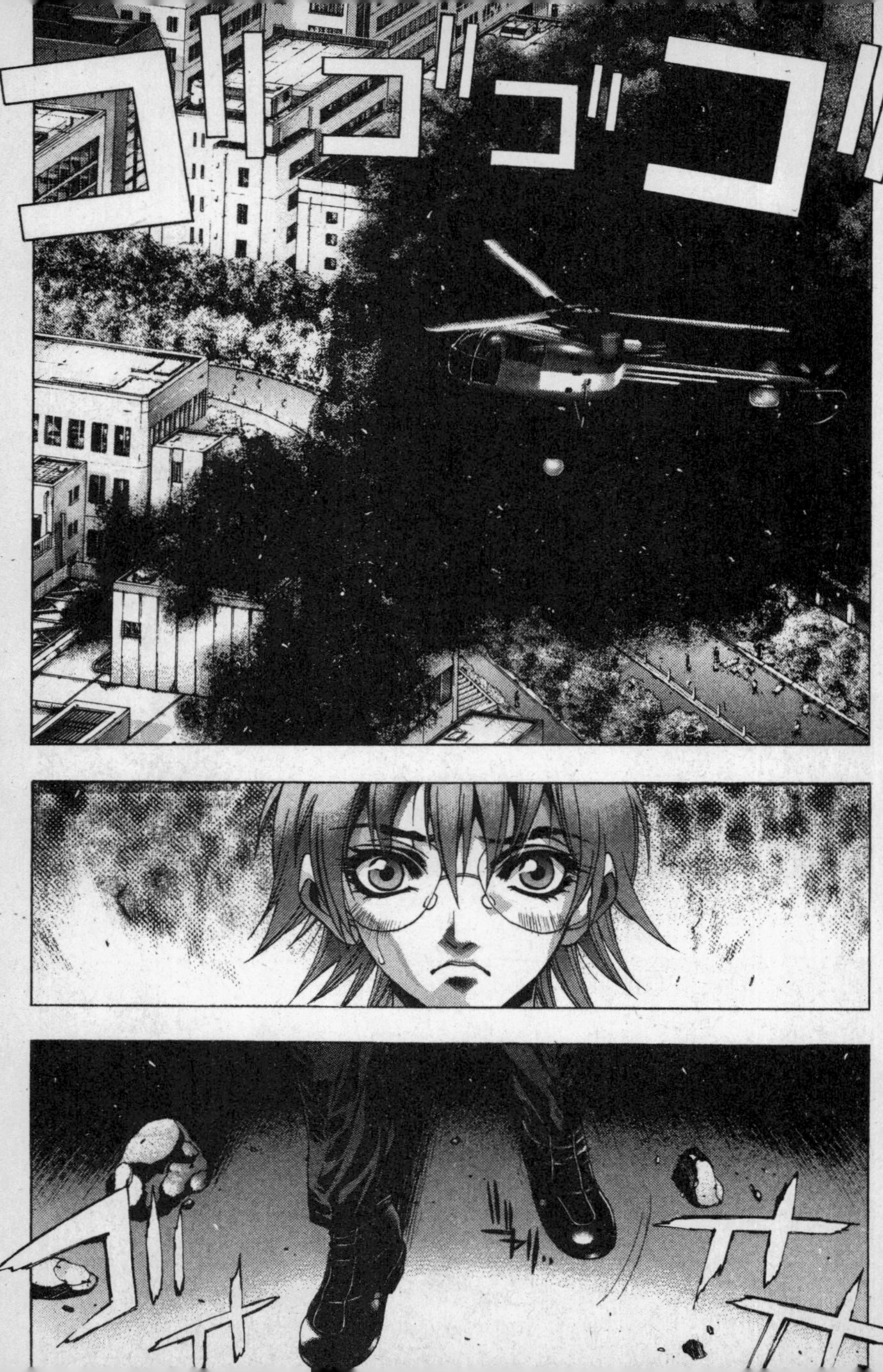
ゴゴゴゴ

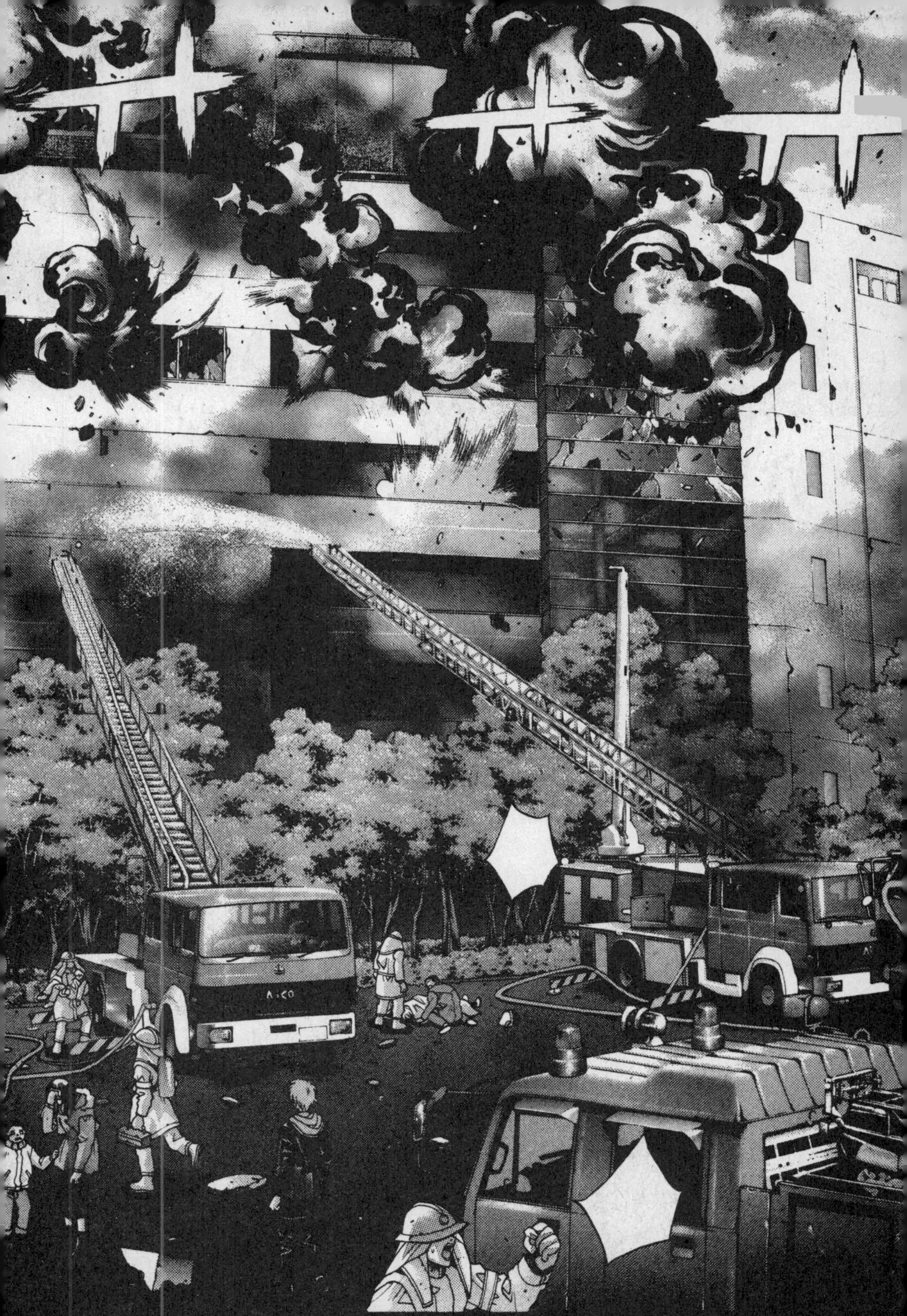

Chapter 24: The Predecessor Woman

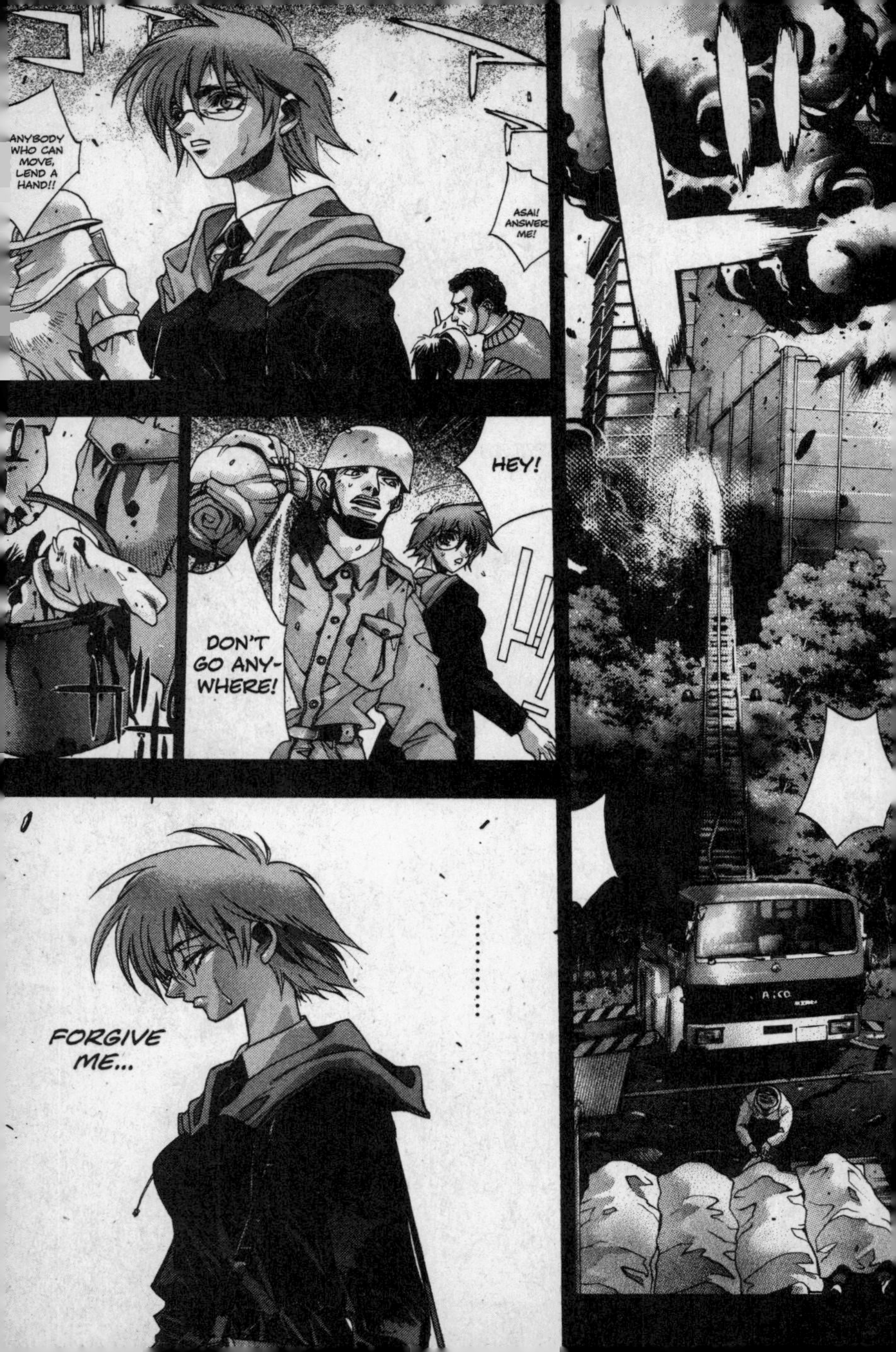
ASAI! ANSWER ME!
ANYBODY WHO CAN MOVE, LEND A HAND!!
HEY!
DON'T GO ANY-WHERE!
......
FORGIVE ME...

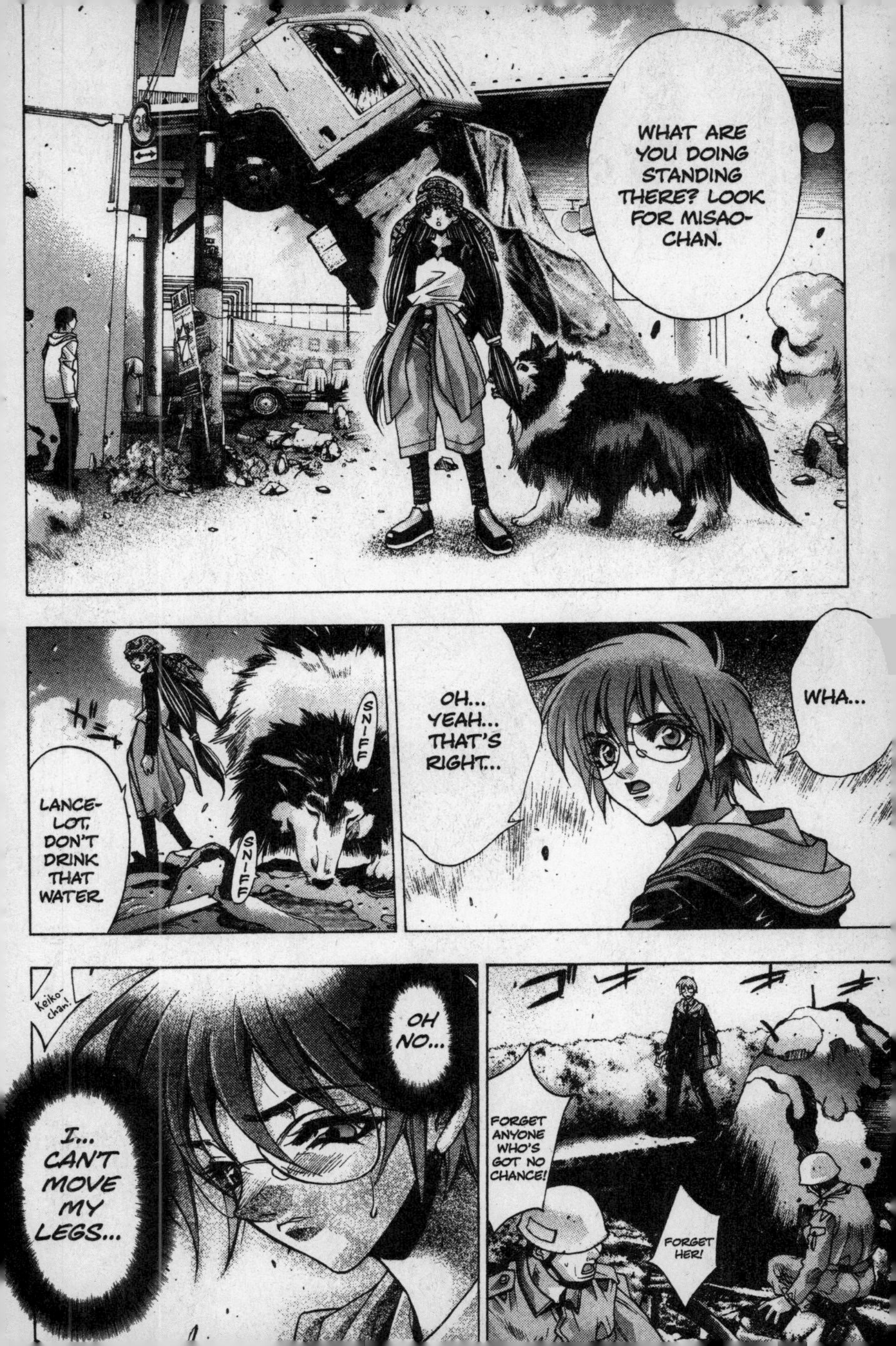
WHAT ARE YOU DOING STANDING THERE? LOOK FOR MISAO-CHAN.
WHA...
OH... YEAH... THAT'S RIGHT...
SNIFF
SNIFF
LANCE-LOT, DON'T DRINK THAT WATER
FORGET ANYONE WHO'S GOT NO CHANCE!
FORGET HER!
OH NO...
Keiko-chan!
I... CAN'T MOVE MY LEGS...

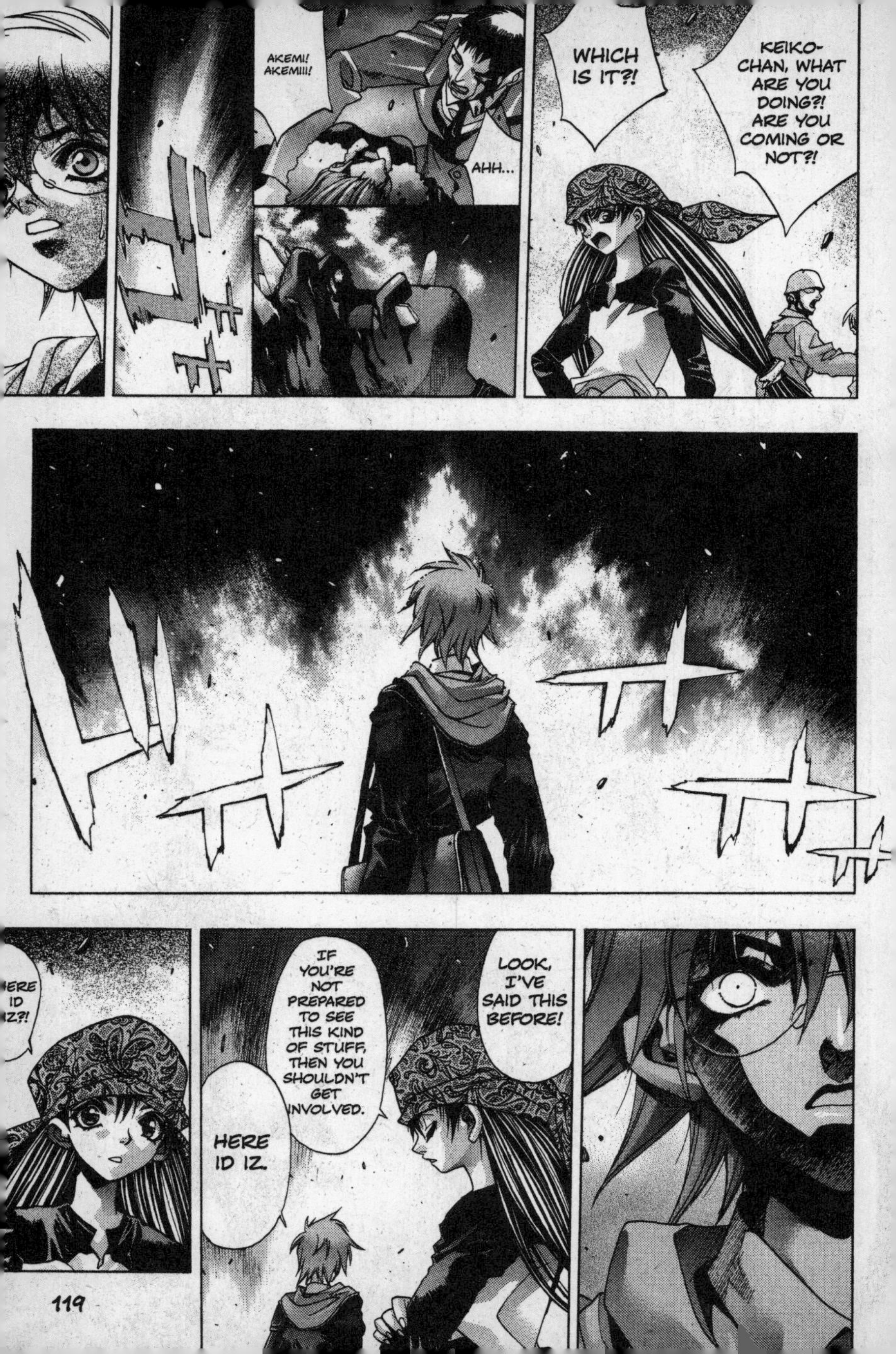
KEIKO-CHAN, WHAT ARE YOU DOING?! ARE YOU COMING OR NOT?!
WHICH IS IT?!
AKEMI! AKEMIII!
AHH...
LOOK, I'VE SAID THIS BEFORE!
IF YOU'RE NOT PREPARED TO SEE THIS KIND OF STUFF, THEN YOU SHOULDN'T GET INVOLVED.
HERE ID IZ.

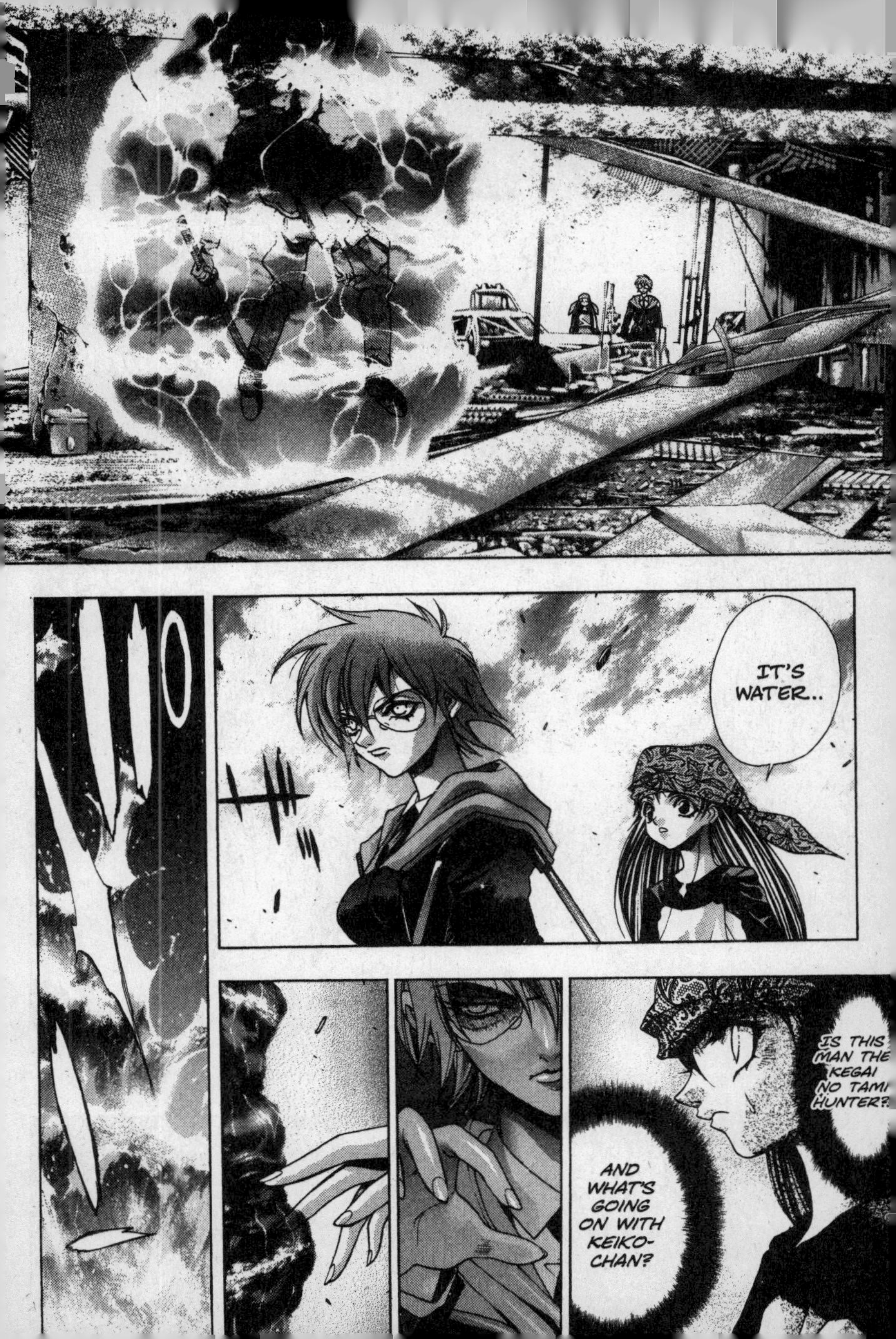
IT'S WATER...
IS THIS MAN THE KEGAI NO TAMI HUNTER?
AND WHAT'S GOING ON WITH KEIKO-CHAN?

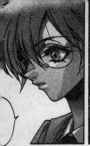
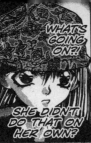WHAT'S GOING ON?!

SHE DIDN'T DO THAT ON HER OWN?

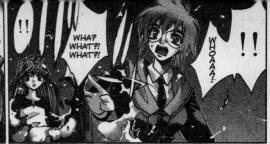!! WHA? WHAT?! WHAT?!

WHOAAA!

!!

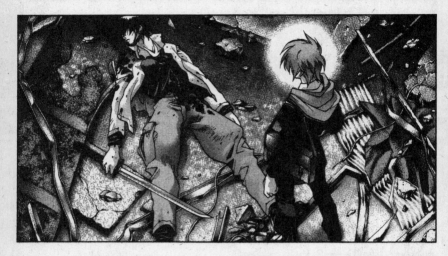

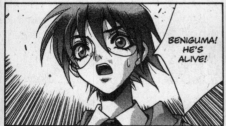BENIGUMA! HE'S ALIVE!

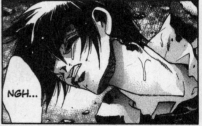NGH...

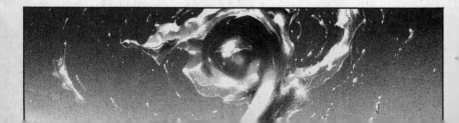

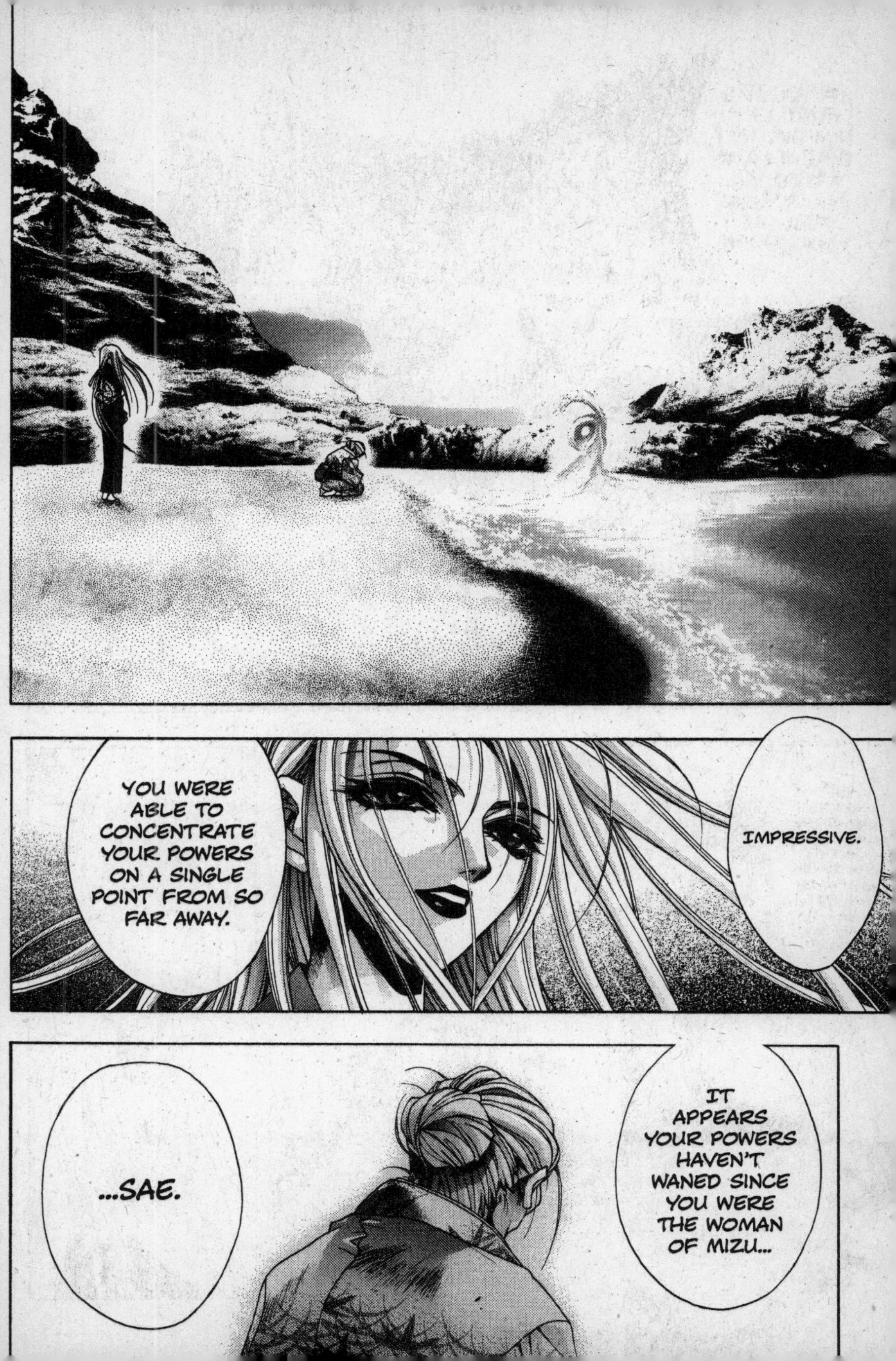
IMPRESSIVE.
YOU WERE ABLE TO CONCENTRATE YOUR POWERS ON A SINGLE POINT FROM SO FAR AWAY.
IT APPEARS YOUR POWERS HAVEN'T WANED SINCE YOU WERE THE WOMAN OF MIZU...
...SAE.

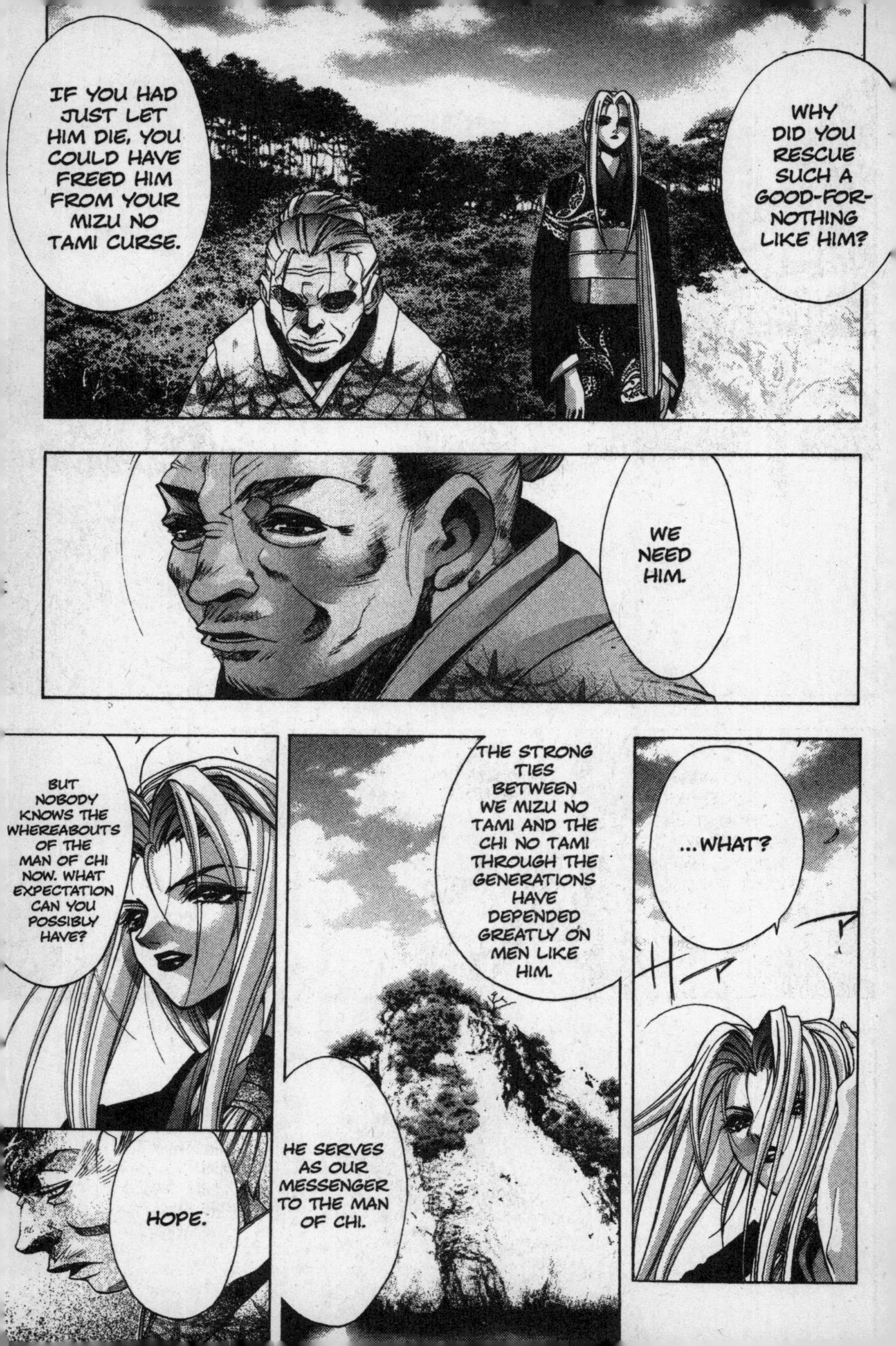
WHY DID YOU RESCUE SUCH A GOOD-FOR-NOTHING LIKE HIM?
IF YOU HAD JUST LET HIM DIE, YOU COULD HAVE FREED HIM FROM YOUR MIZU NO TAMI CURSE.
WE NEED HIM.
...WHAT?
THE STRONG TIES BETWEEN WE MIZU NO TAMI AND THE CHI NO TAMI THROUGH THE GENERATIONS HAVE DEPENDED GREATLY ON MEN LIKE HIM.
HE SERVES AS OUR MESSENGER TO THE MAN OF CHI.
BUT NOBODY KNOWS THE WHEREABOUTS OF THE MAN OF CHI NOW. WHAT EXPECTATION CAN YOU POSSIBLY HAVE?
HOPE.

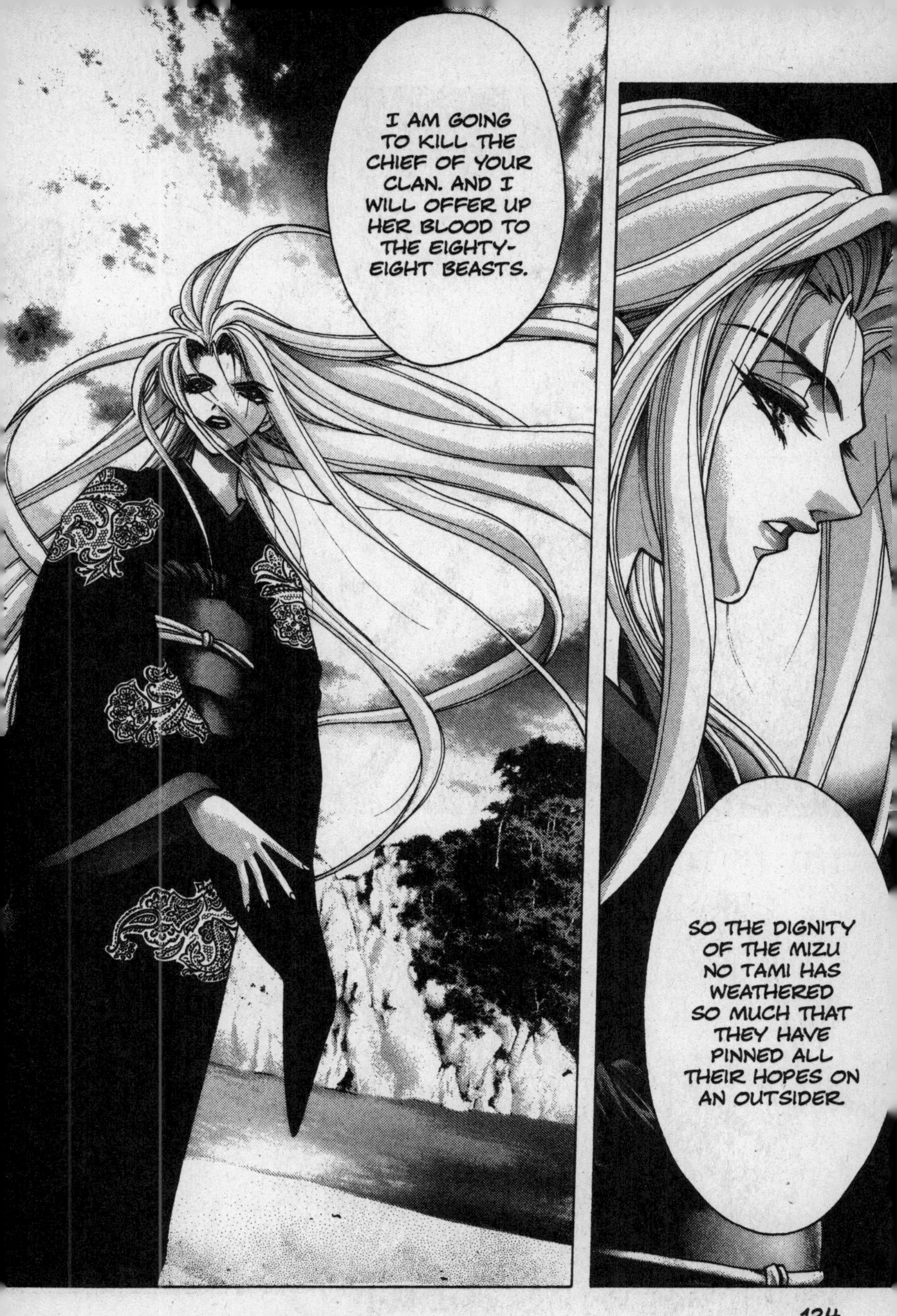
SO THE DIGNITY OF THE MIZU NO TAMI HAS WEATHERED SO MUCH THAT THEY HAVE PINNED ALL THEIR HOPES ON AN OUTSIDER
I AM GOING TO KILL THE CHIEF OF YOUR CLAN. AND I WILL OFFER UP HER BLOOD TO THE EIGHTY-EIGHT BEASTS.

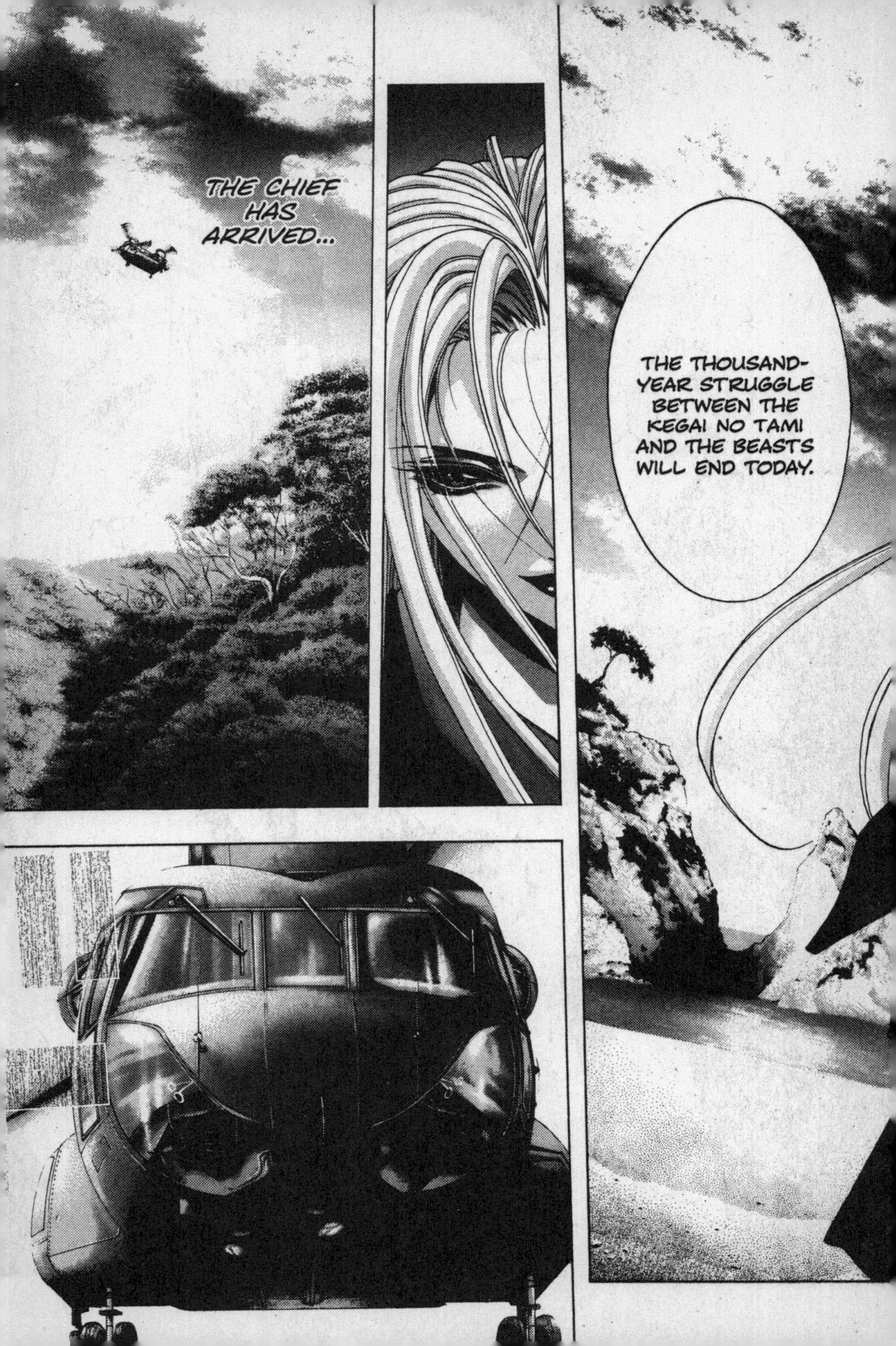
THE THOUSAND-YEAR STRUGGLE BETWEEN THE KEGAI NO TAMI AND THE BEASTS WILL END TODAY.
THE CHIEF HAS ARRIVED...

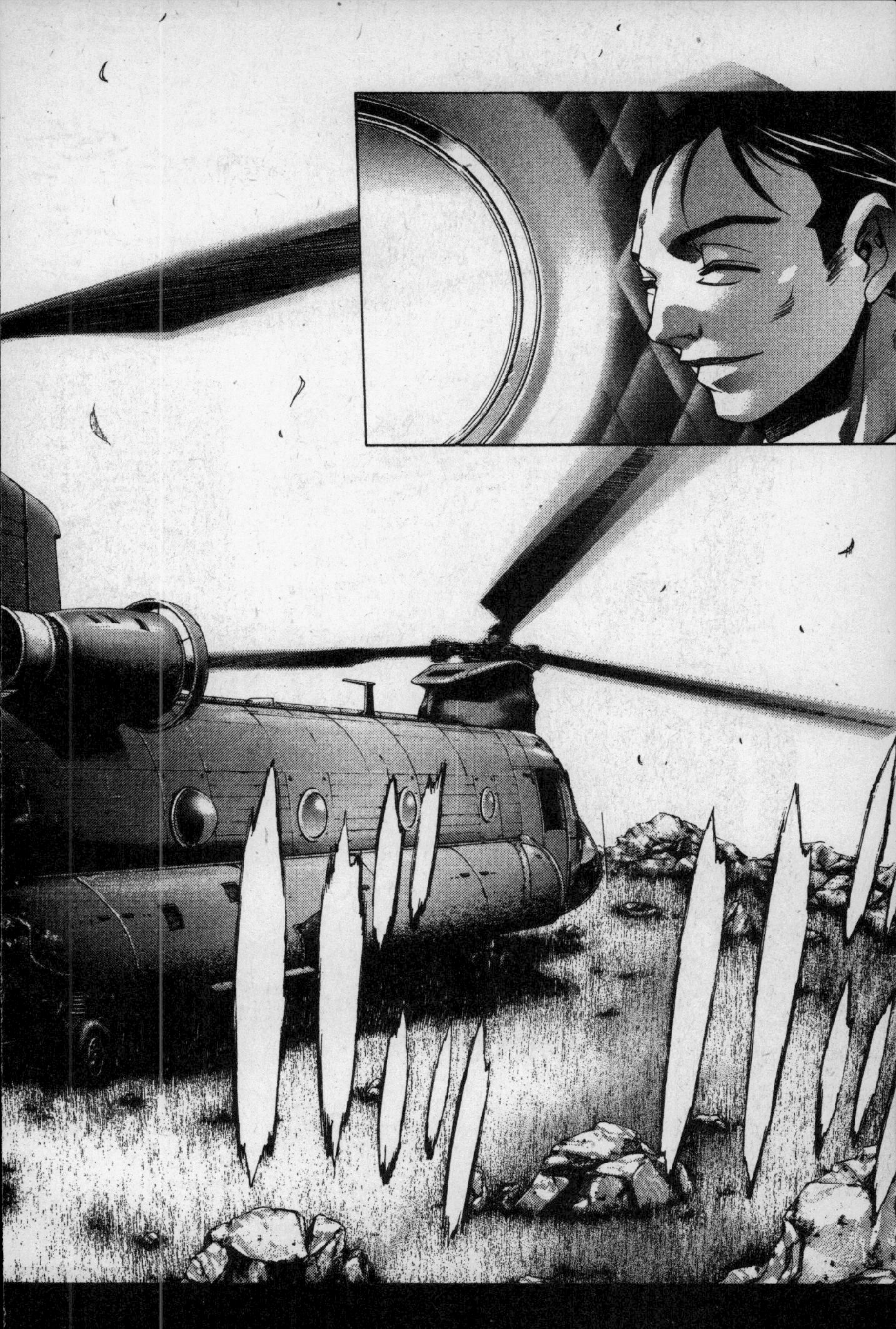

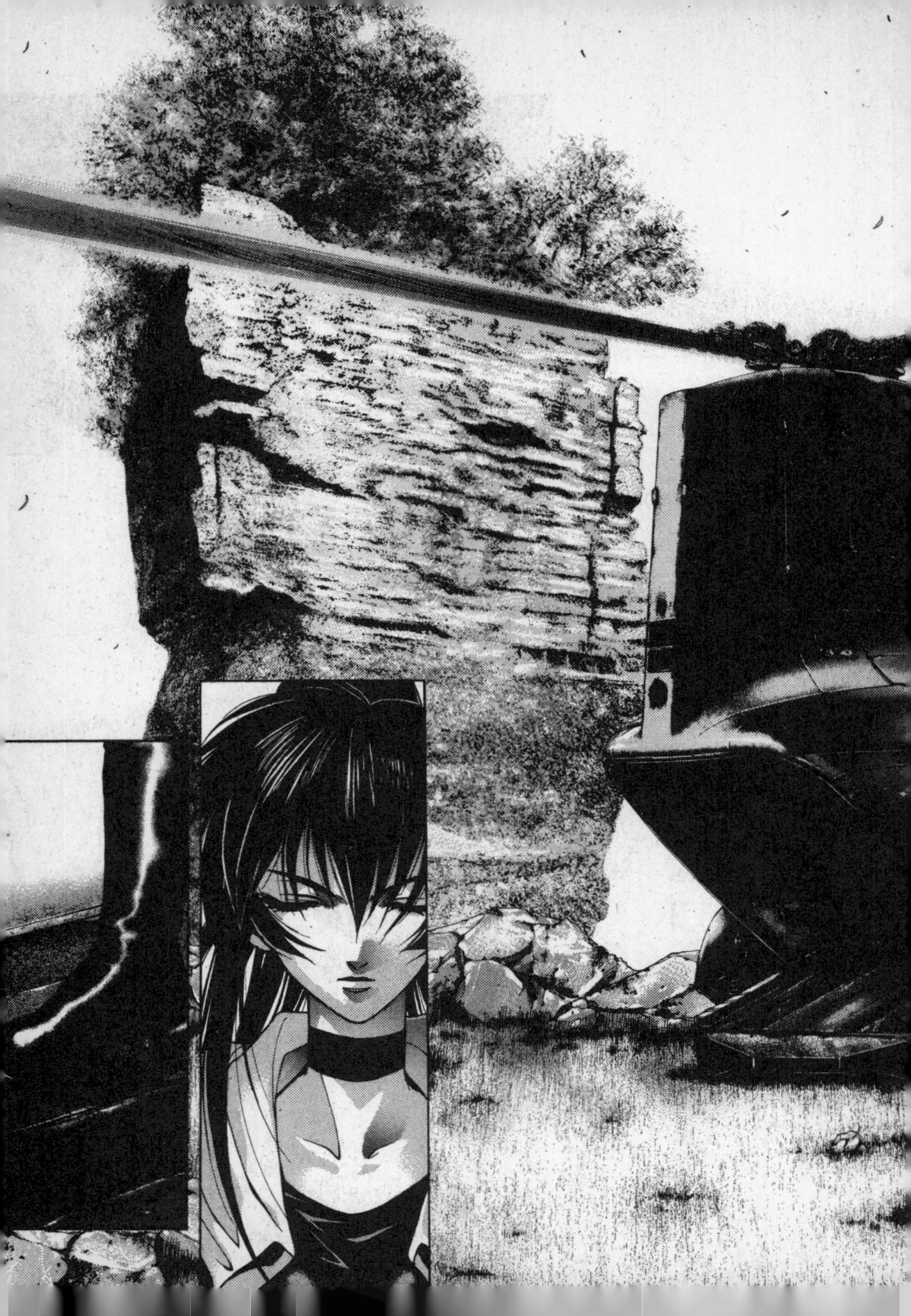

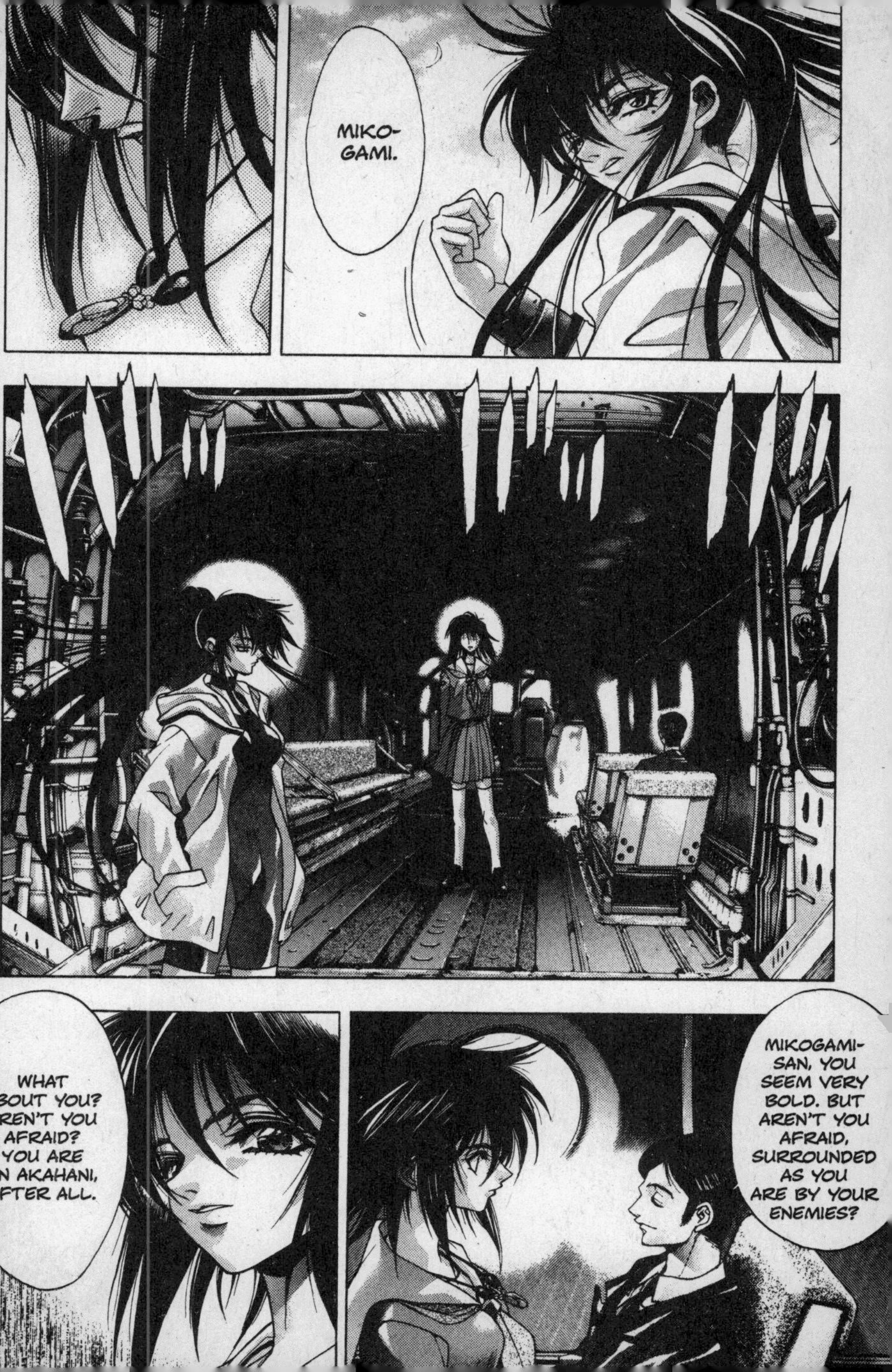
MIKO-GAMI.
MIKOGAMI-SAN, YOU SEEM VERY BOLD. BUT AREN'T YOU AFRAID, SURROUNDED AS YOU ARE BY YOUR ENEMIES?
WHAT ABOUT YOU? AREN'T YOU AFRAID? YOU ARE AN AKAHANI, AFTER ALL.

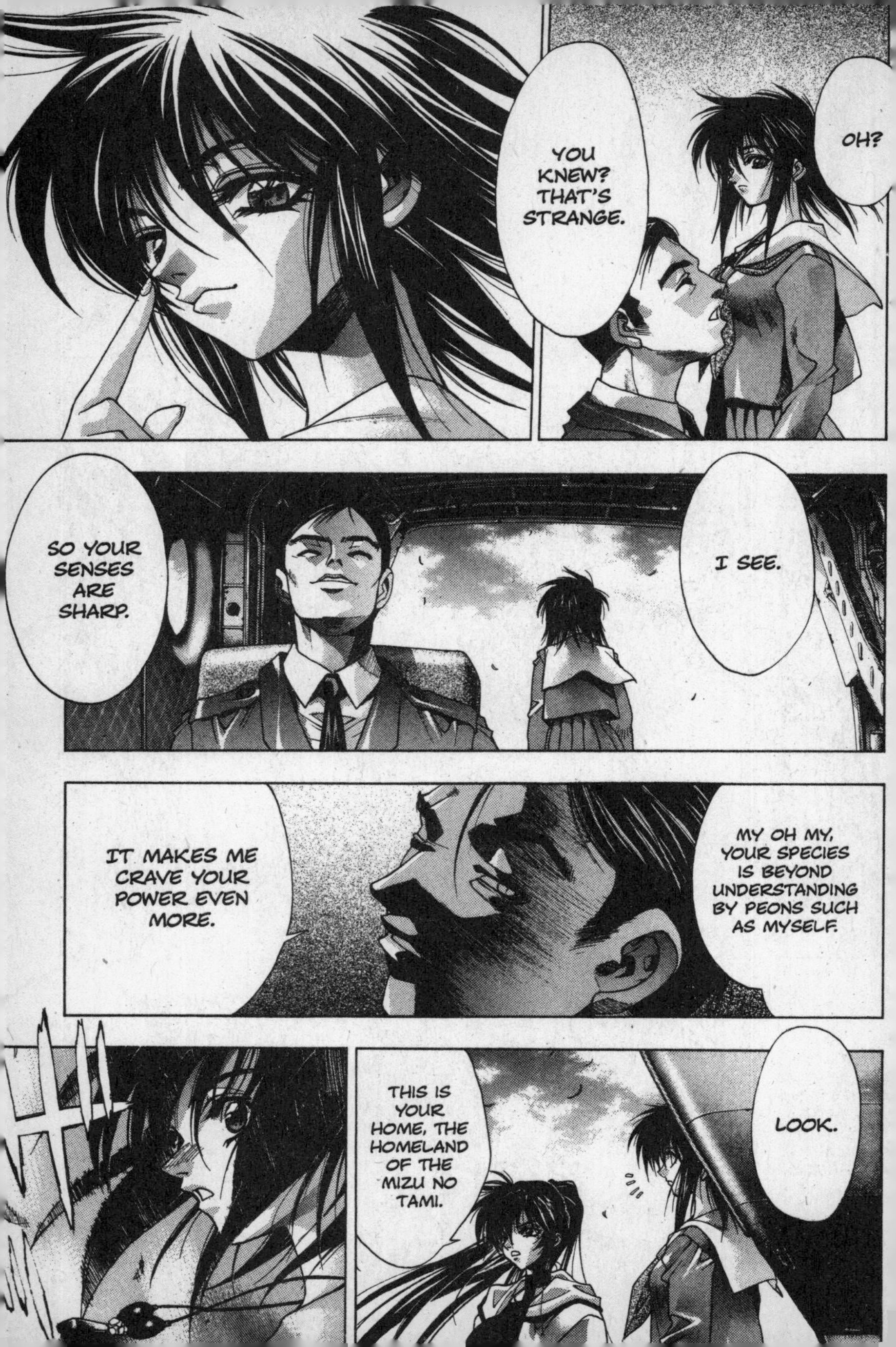
OH?
YOU KNEW? THAT'S STRANGE.
I SEE.
SO YOUR SENSES ARE SHARP.
MY OH MY, YOUR SPECIES IS BEYOND UNDERSTANDING BY PEONS SUCH AS MYSELF.
IT MAKES ME CRAVE YOUR POWER EVEN MORE.
LOOK.
THIS IS YOUR HOME, THE HOMELAND OF THE MIZU NO TAMI.

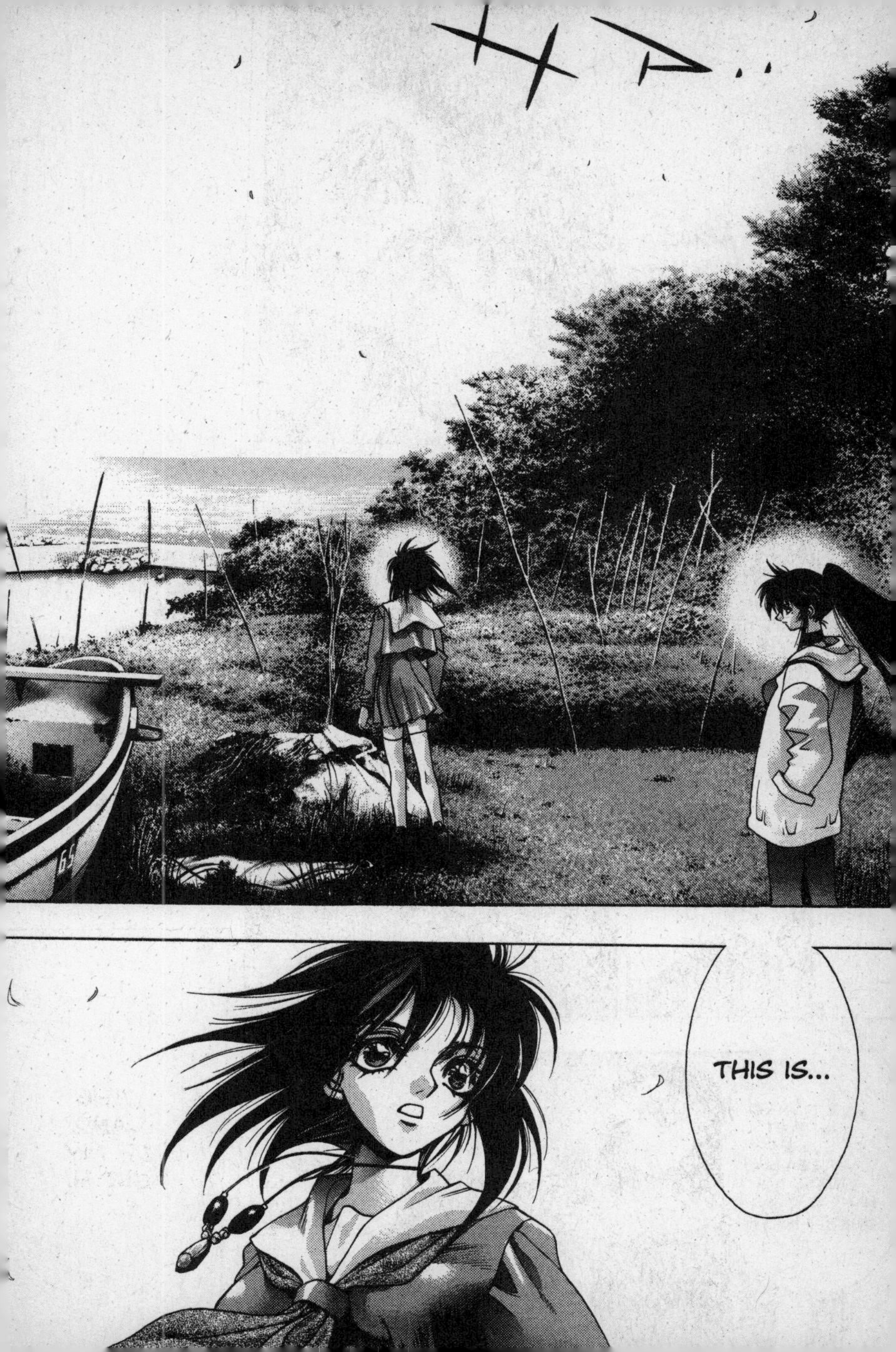
THIS IS...

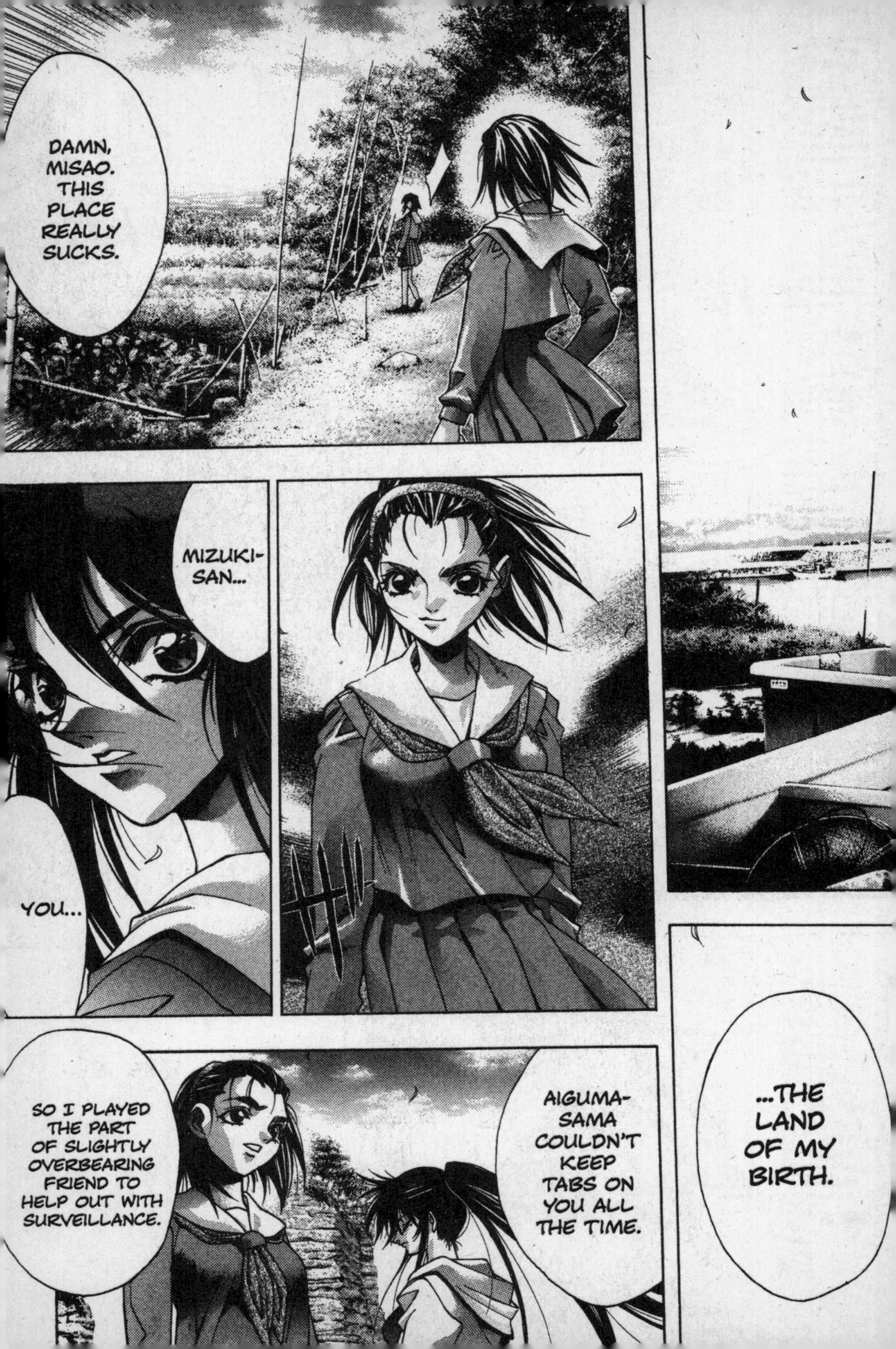
DAMN, MISAO. THIS PLACE REALLY SUCKS.
...THE LAND OF MY BIRTH.
MIZUKI-SAN...
YOU...
AIGUMA-SAMA COULDN'T KEEP TABS ON YOU ALL THE TIME.
SO I PLAYED THE PART OF SLIGHTLY OVERBEARING FRIEND TO HELP OUT WITH SURVEILLANCE.

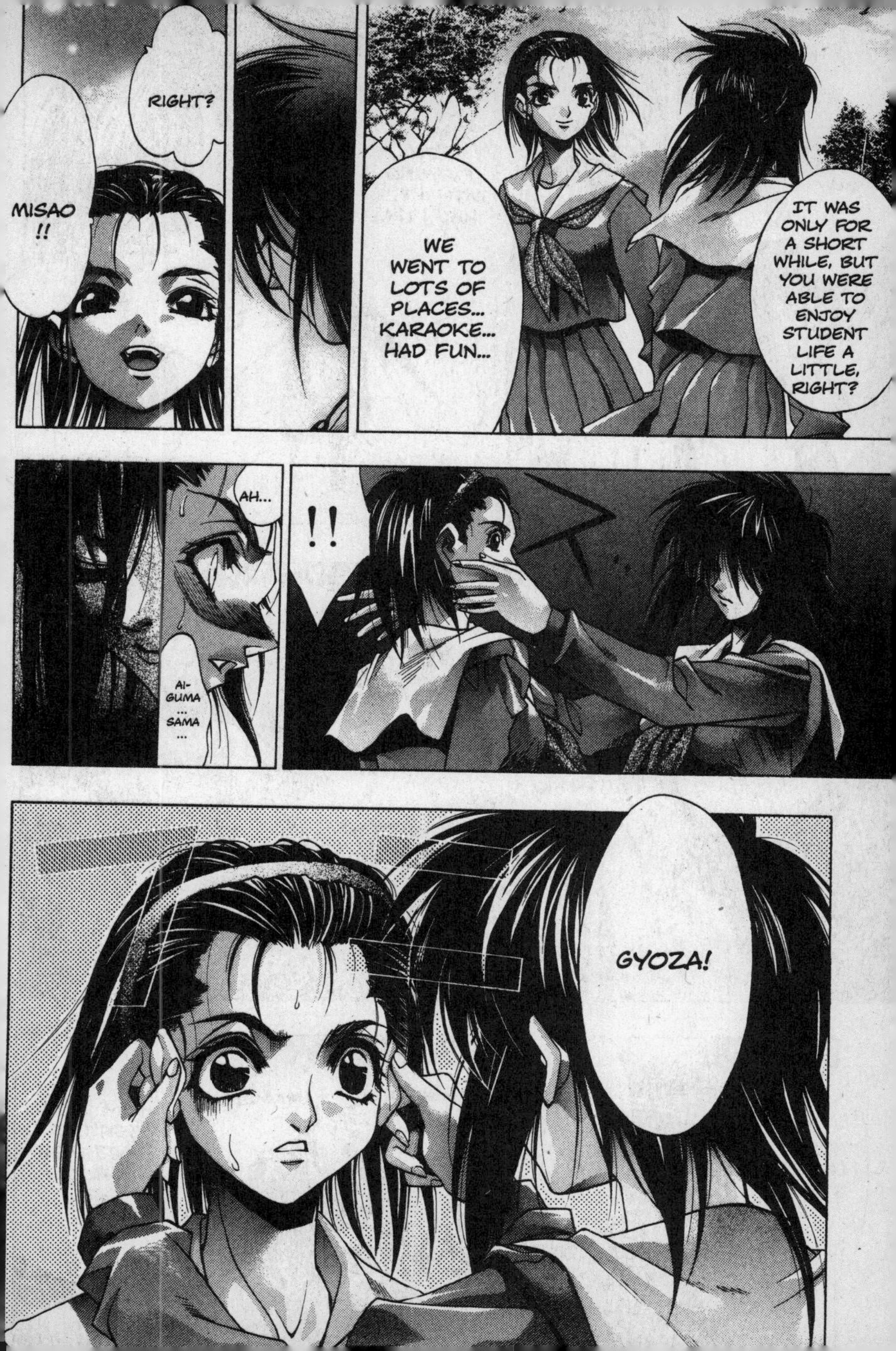
IT WAS ONLY FOR A SHORT WHILE, BUT YOU WERE ABLE TO ENJOY STUDENT LIFE A LITTLE, RIGHT?
WE WENT TO LOTS OF PLACES... KARAOKE... HAD FUN...
RIGHT?
MISAO !!
!!
AH...
AI-GUMA ... SAMA ...
GYOZA!

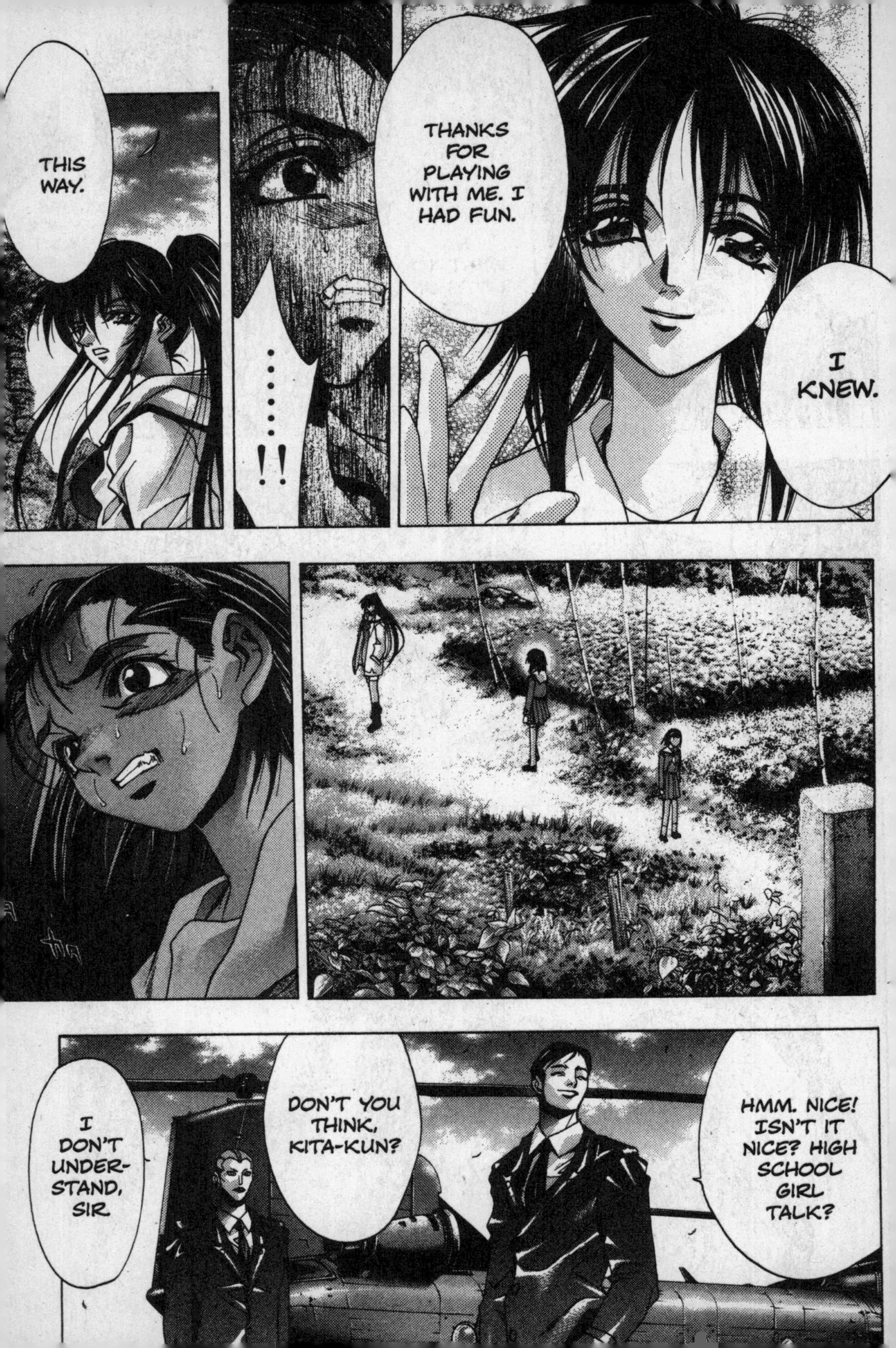
I KNEW.
THANKS FOR PLAYING WITH ME. I HAD FUN.
......!!
THIS WAY.
HMM. NICE! ISN'T IT NICE? HIGH SCHOOL GIRL TALK?
DON'T YOU THINK, KITA-KUN?
I DON'T UNDER-STAND, SIR.

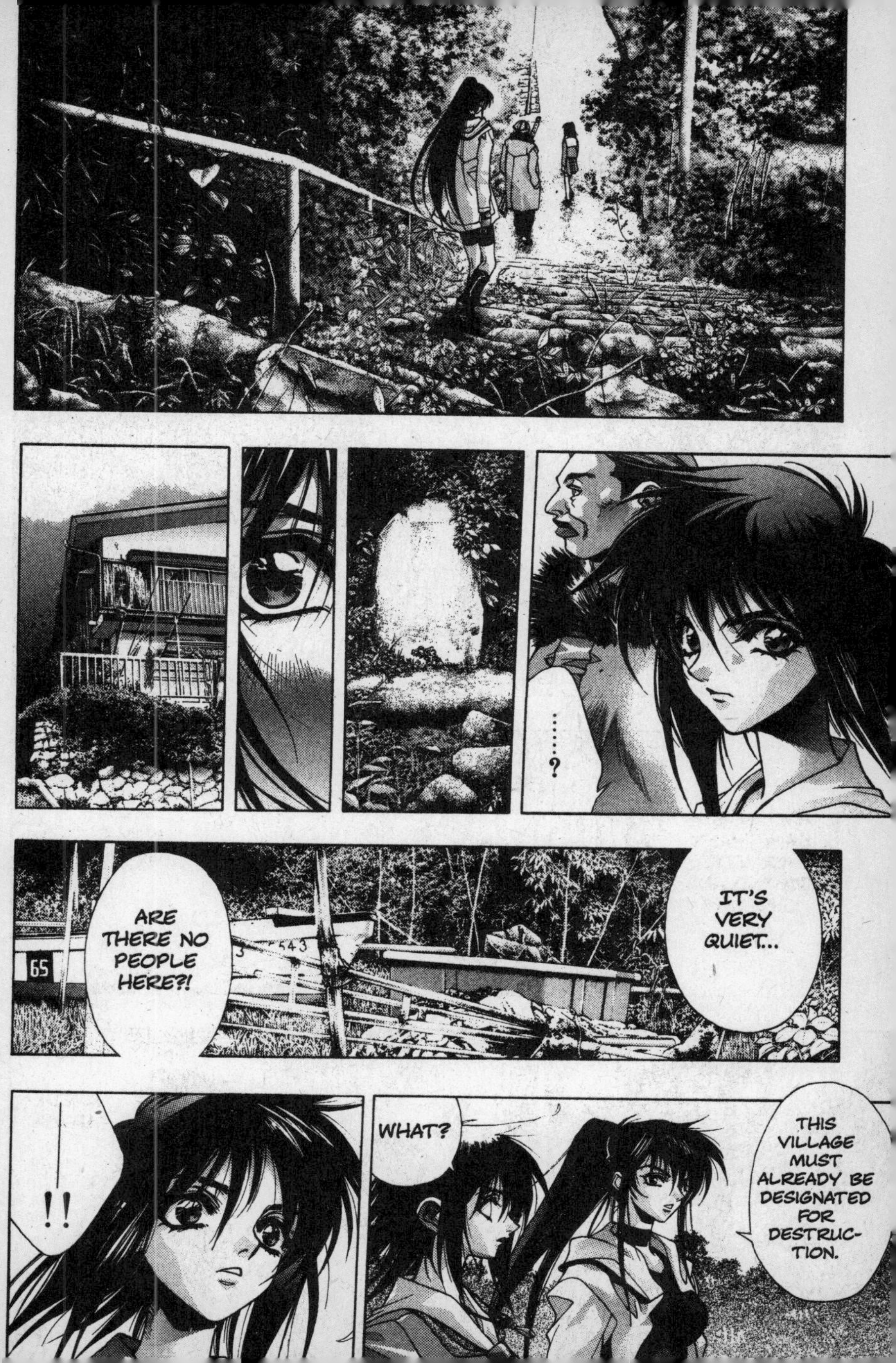
......?
IT'S VERY QUIET...
ARE THERE NO PEOPLE HERE?!
THIS VILLAGE MUST ALREADY BE DESIGNATED FOR DESTRUCTION.
WHAT?
!!

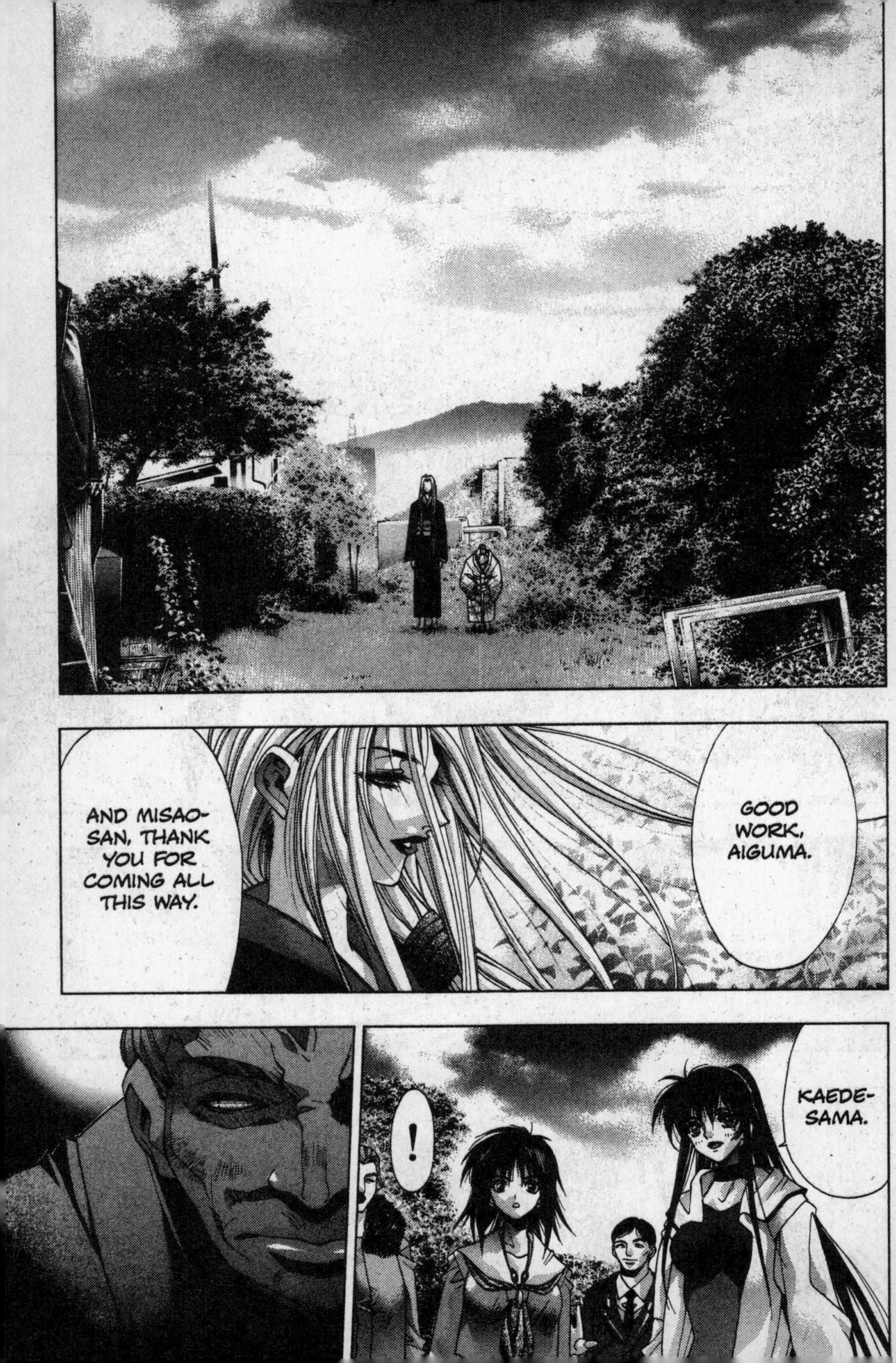
GOOD WORK, AIGUMA.
AND MISAO-SAN, THANK YOU FOR COMING ALL THIS WAY.
KAEDE-SAMA.
!

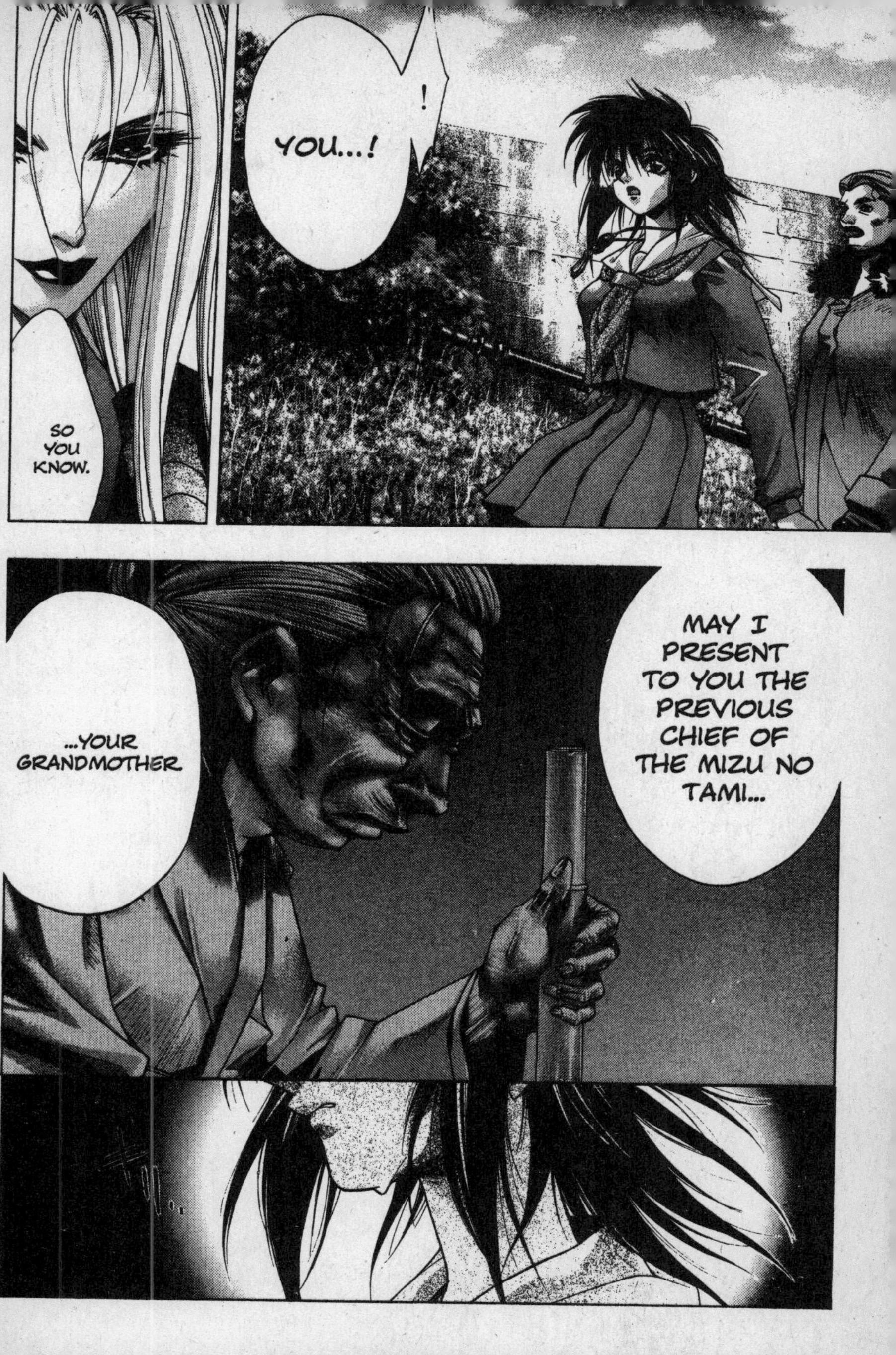
!
YOU...!
SO YOU KNOW.
MAY I PRESENT TO YOU THE PREVIOUS CHIEF OF THE MIZU NO TAMI...
...YOUR GRANDMOTHER

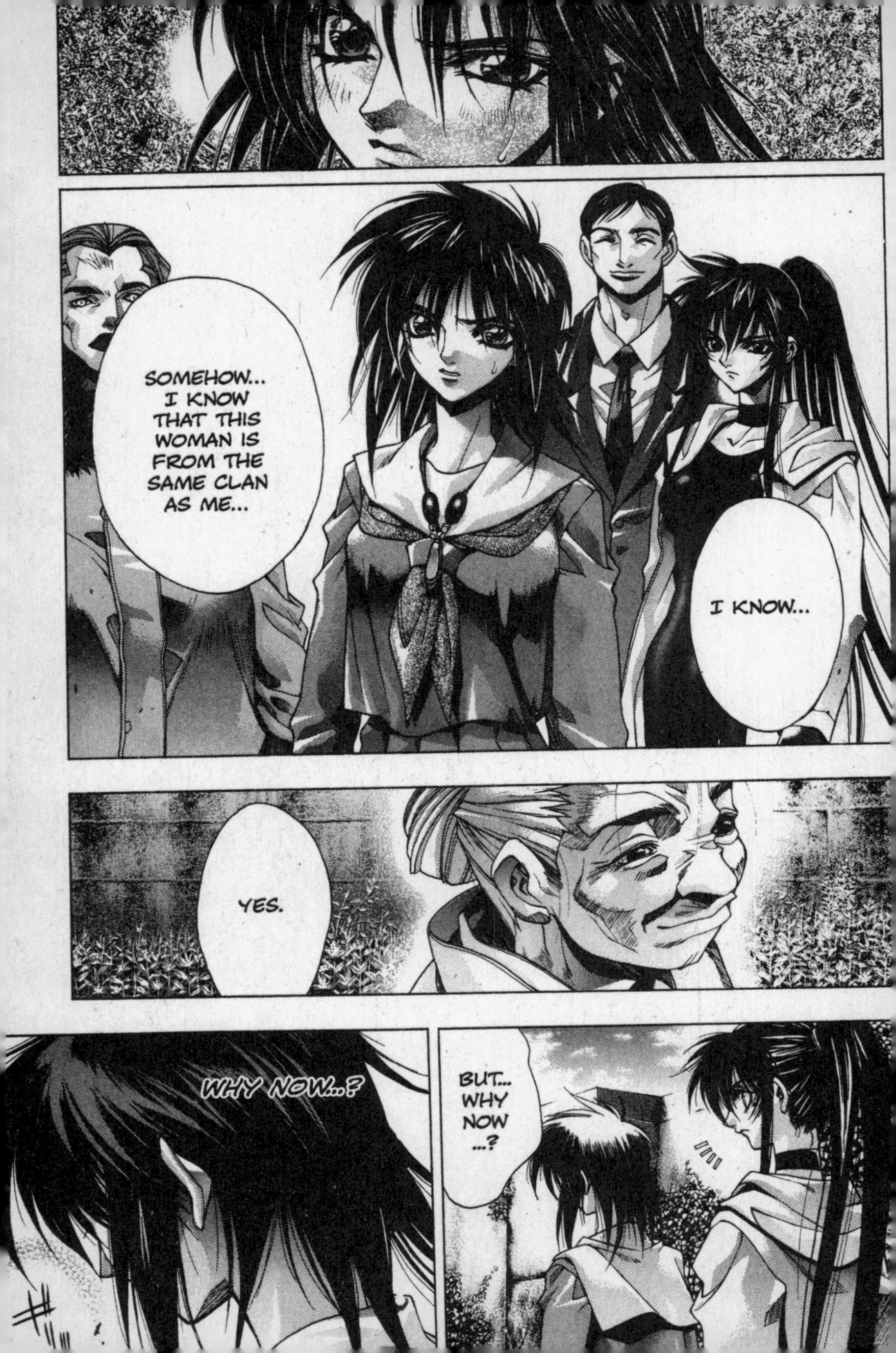

SOMEHOW... I KNOW THAT THIS WOMAN IS FROM THE SAME CLAN AS ME...
I KNOW...
YES.
BUT... WHY NOW ...?
WHY NOW...?

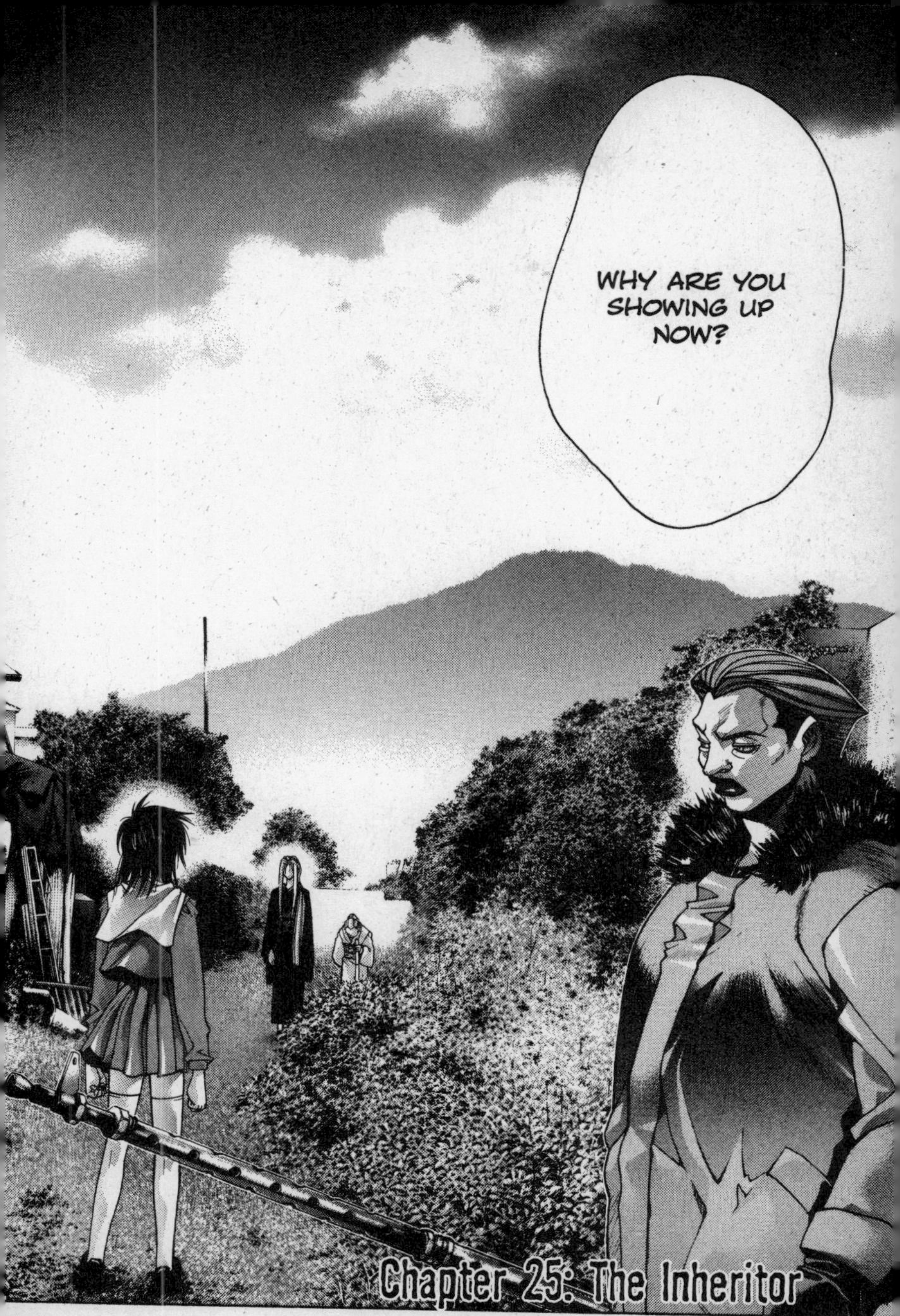
WHY ARE YOU SHOWING UP NOW?
Chapter 25: The Inheritor

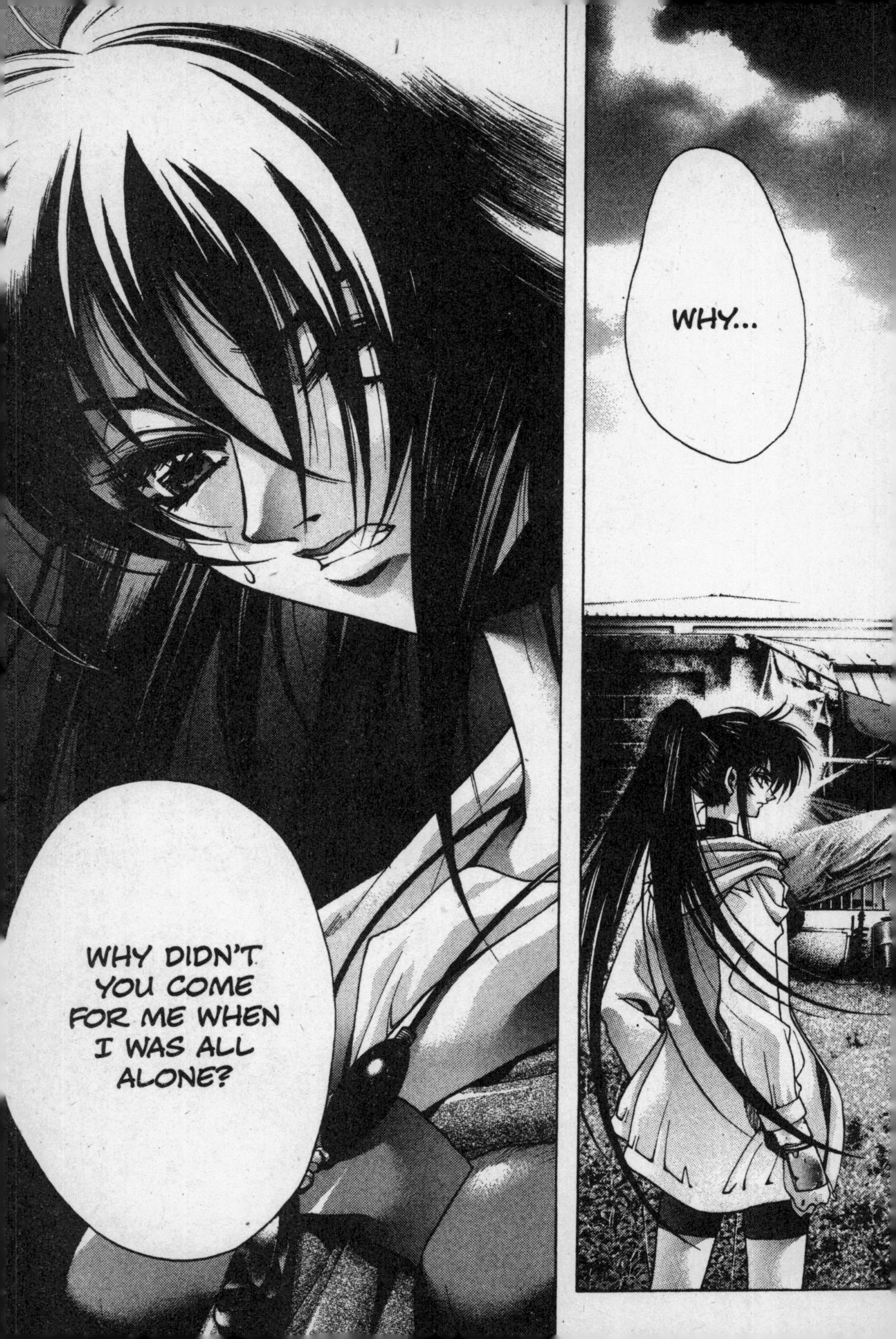
WHY...
WHY DIDN'T YOU COME FOR ME WHEN I WAS ALL ALONE?

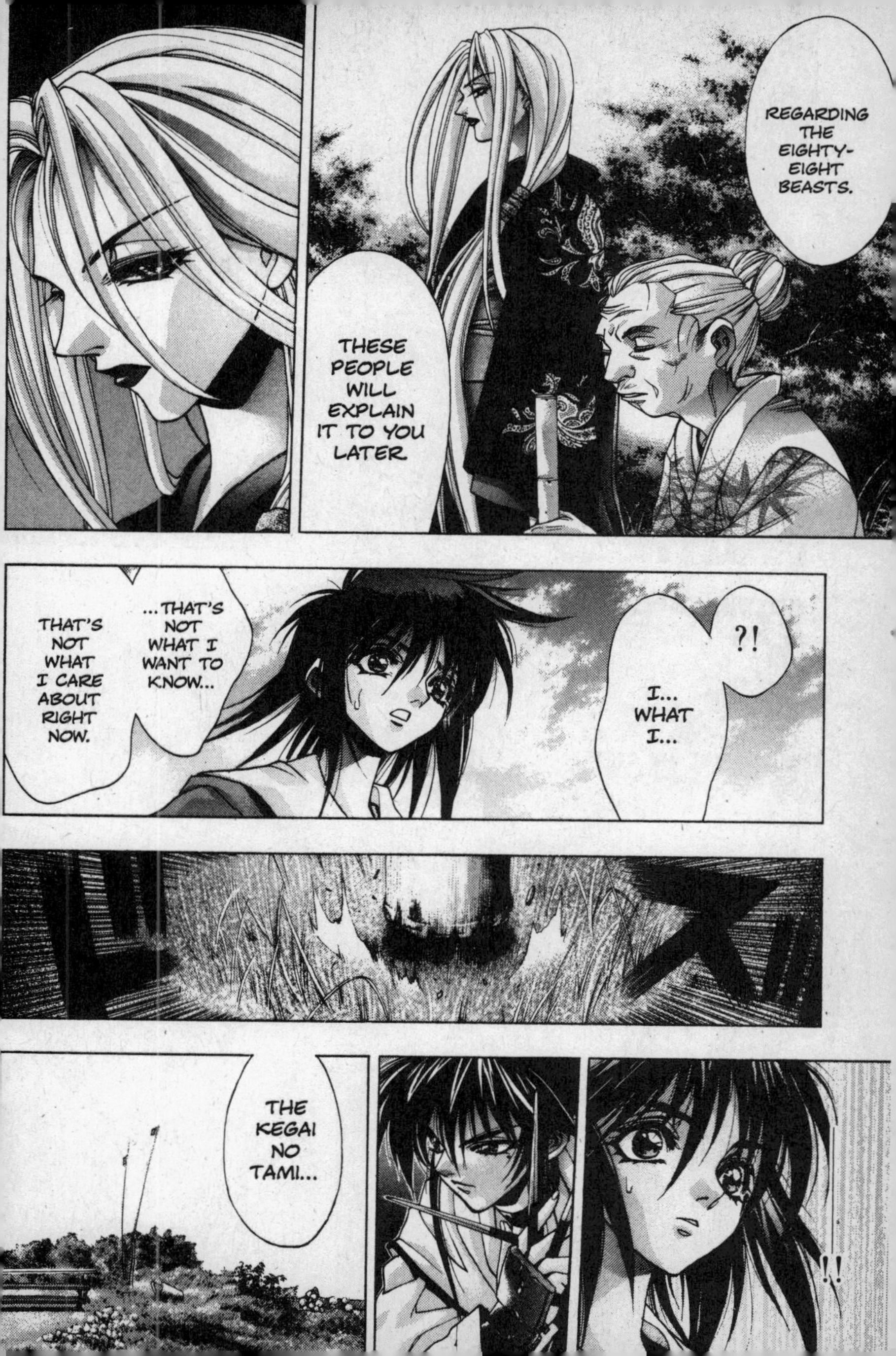
REGARDING THE EIGHTY-EIGHT BEASTS.
THESE PEOPLE WILL EXPLAIN IT TO YOU LATER.
?!
I... WHAT I...
...THAT'S NOT WHAT I WANT TO KNOW...
THAT'S NOT WHAT I CARE ABOUT RIGHT NOW.
!!
THE KEGAI NO TAMI...

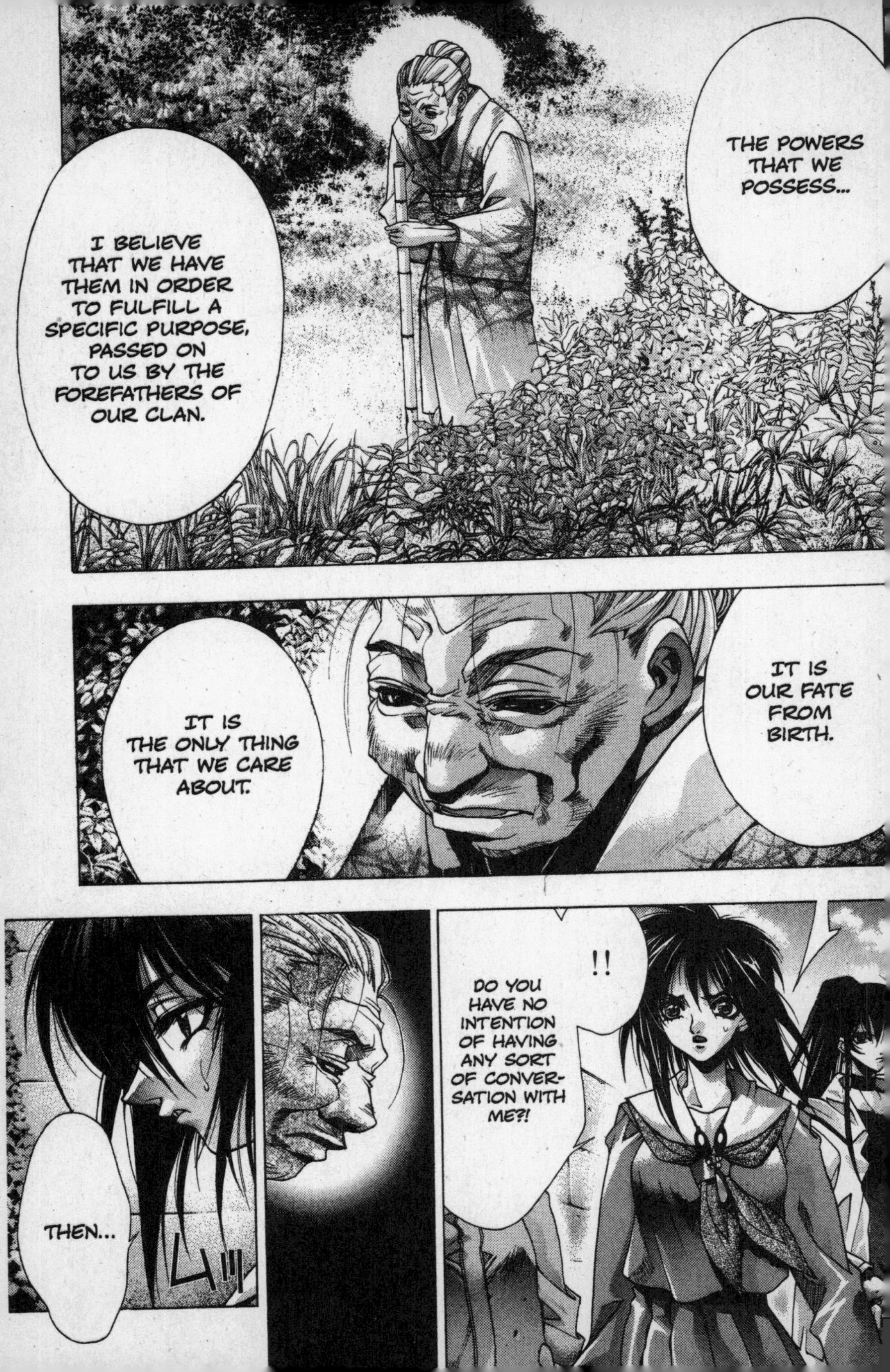
THE POWERS THAT WE POSSESS...
I BELIEVE THAT WE HAVE THEM IN ORDER TO FULFILL A SPECIFIC PURPOSE, PASSED ON TO US BY THE FOREFATHERS OF OUR CLAN.
IT IS OUR FATE FROM BIRTH.
IT IS THE ONLY THING THAT WE CARE ABOUT.
DO YOU HAVE NO INTENTION OF HAVING ANY SORT OF CONVER-SATION WITH ME?!
!!
THEN...
ムッ

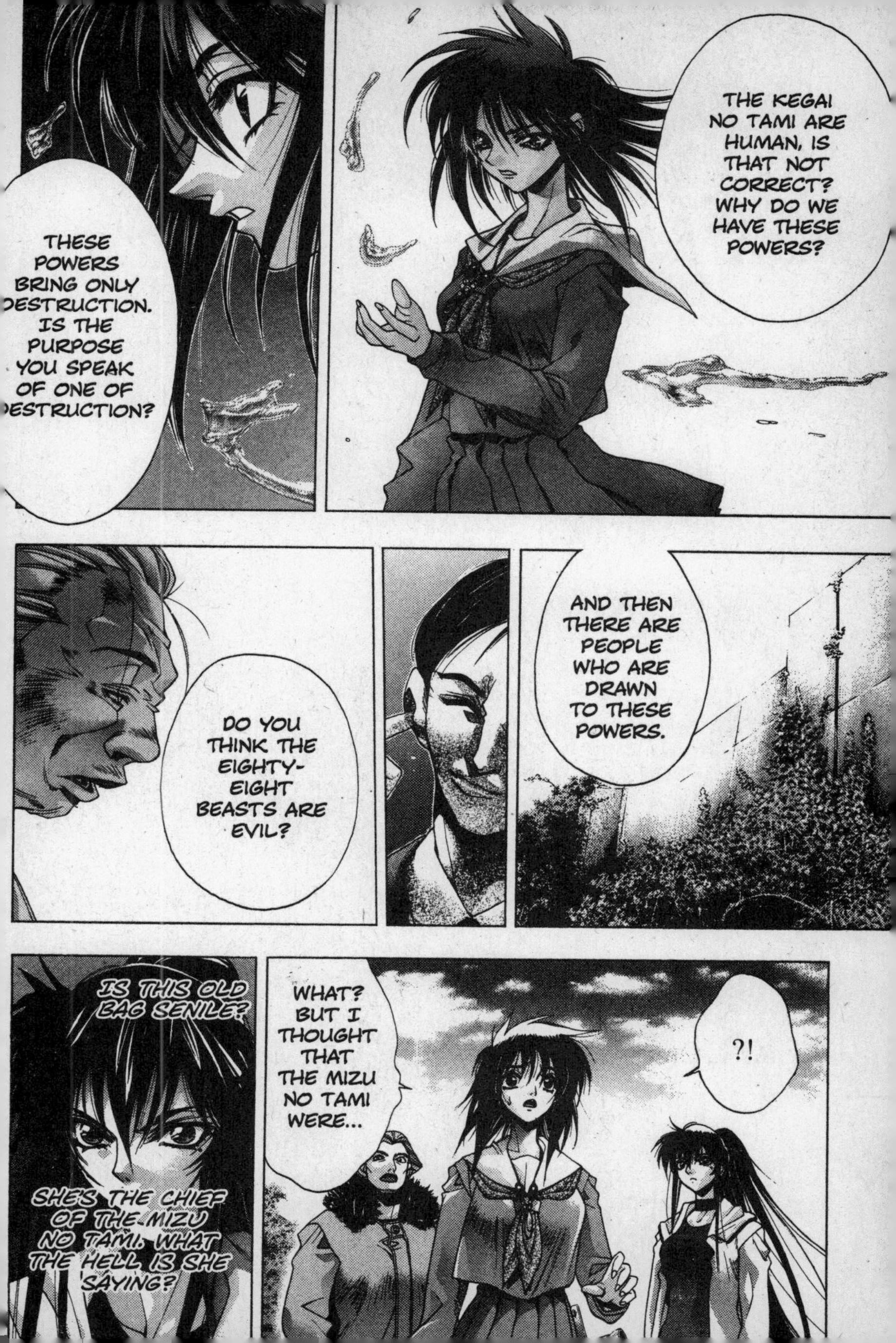
THE KEGAI NO TAMI ARE HUMAN, IS THAT NOT CORRECT? WHY DO WE HAVE THESE POWERS?
THESE POWERS BRING ONLY DESTRUCTION. IS THE PURPOSE YOU SPEAK OF ONE OF DESTRUCTION?
AND THEN THERE ARE PEOPLE WHO ARE DRAWN TO THESE POWERS.
DO YOU THINK THE EIGHTY-EIGHT BEASTS ARE EVIL?
?!
WHAT? BUT I THOUGHT THAT THE MIZU NO TAMI WERE...
IS THIS OLD BAG SENILE?
SHE'S THE CHIEF OF THE MIZU NO TAMI. WHAT THE HELL IS SHE SAYING?

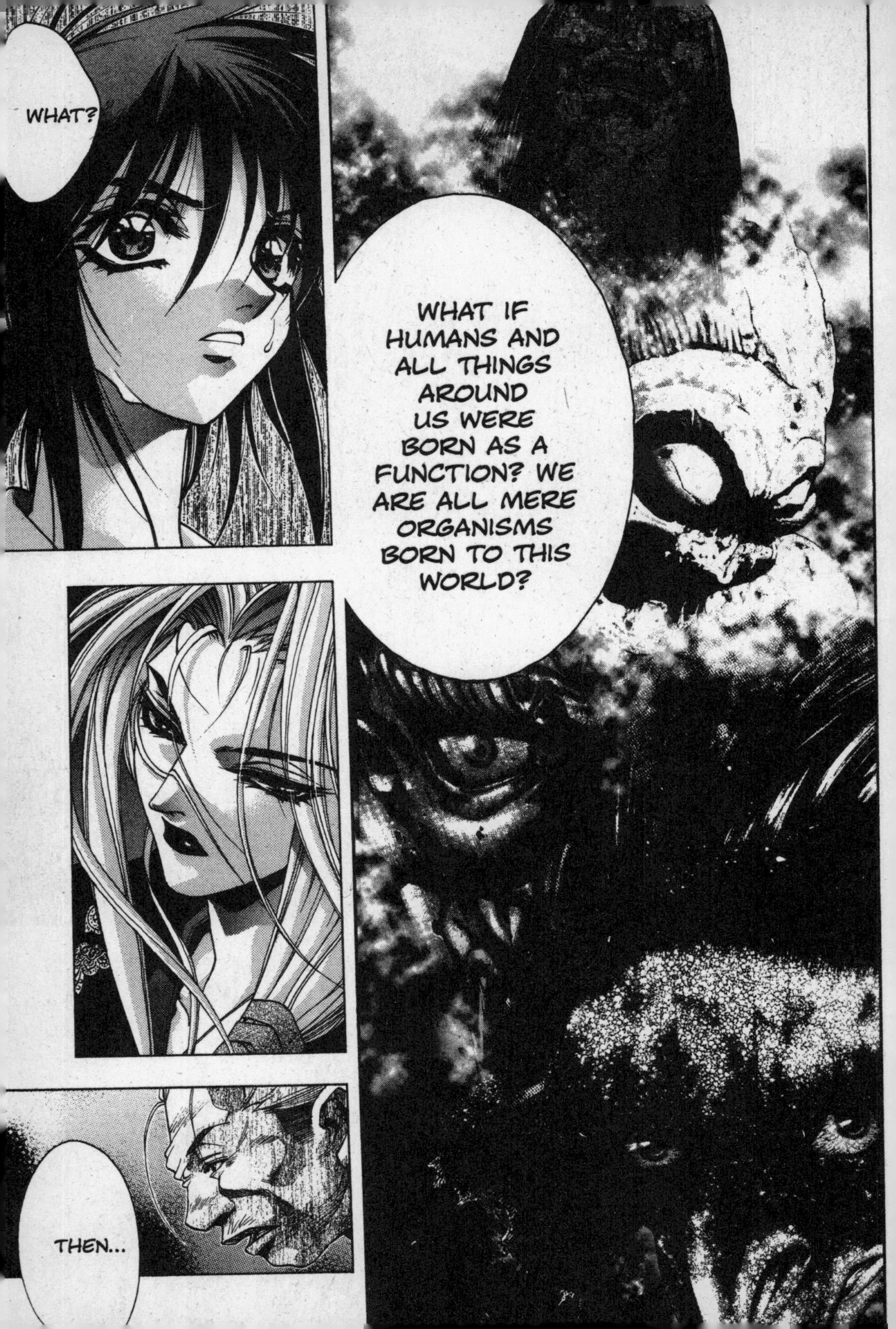
WHAT IF HUMANS AND ALL THINGS AROUND US WERE BORN AS A FUNCTION? WE ARE ALL MERE ORGANISMS BORN TO THIS WORLD?
WHAT?
THEN...

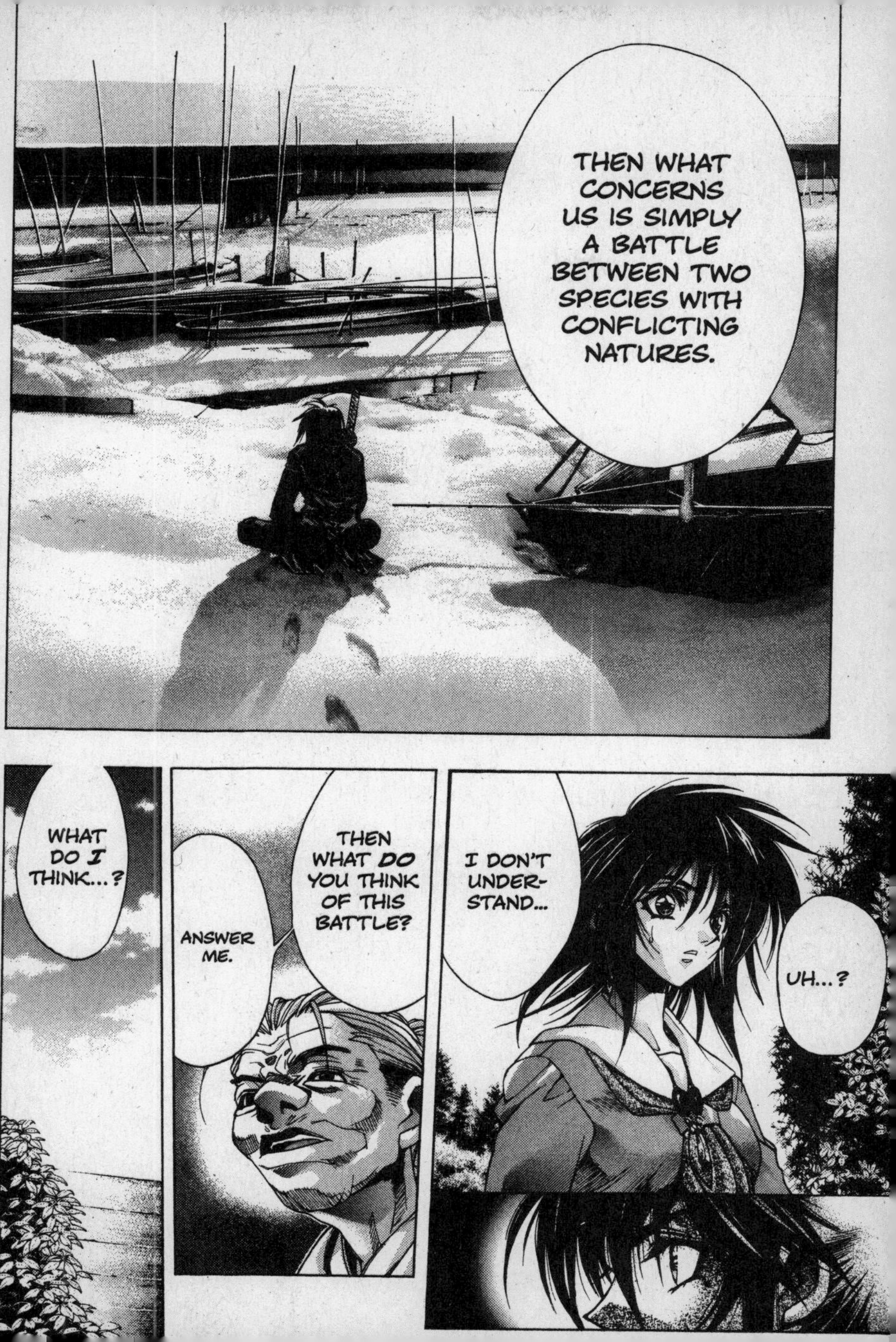
THEN WHAT CONCERNS US IS SIMPLY A BATTLE BETWEEN TWO SPECIES WITH CONFLICTING NATURES.
UH...?
I DON'T UNDER-STAND...
THEN WHAT *DO* YOU THINK OF THIS BATTLE?
ANSWER ME.
WHAT DO *I* THINK...?

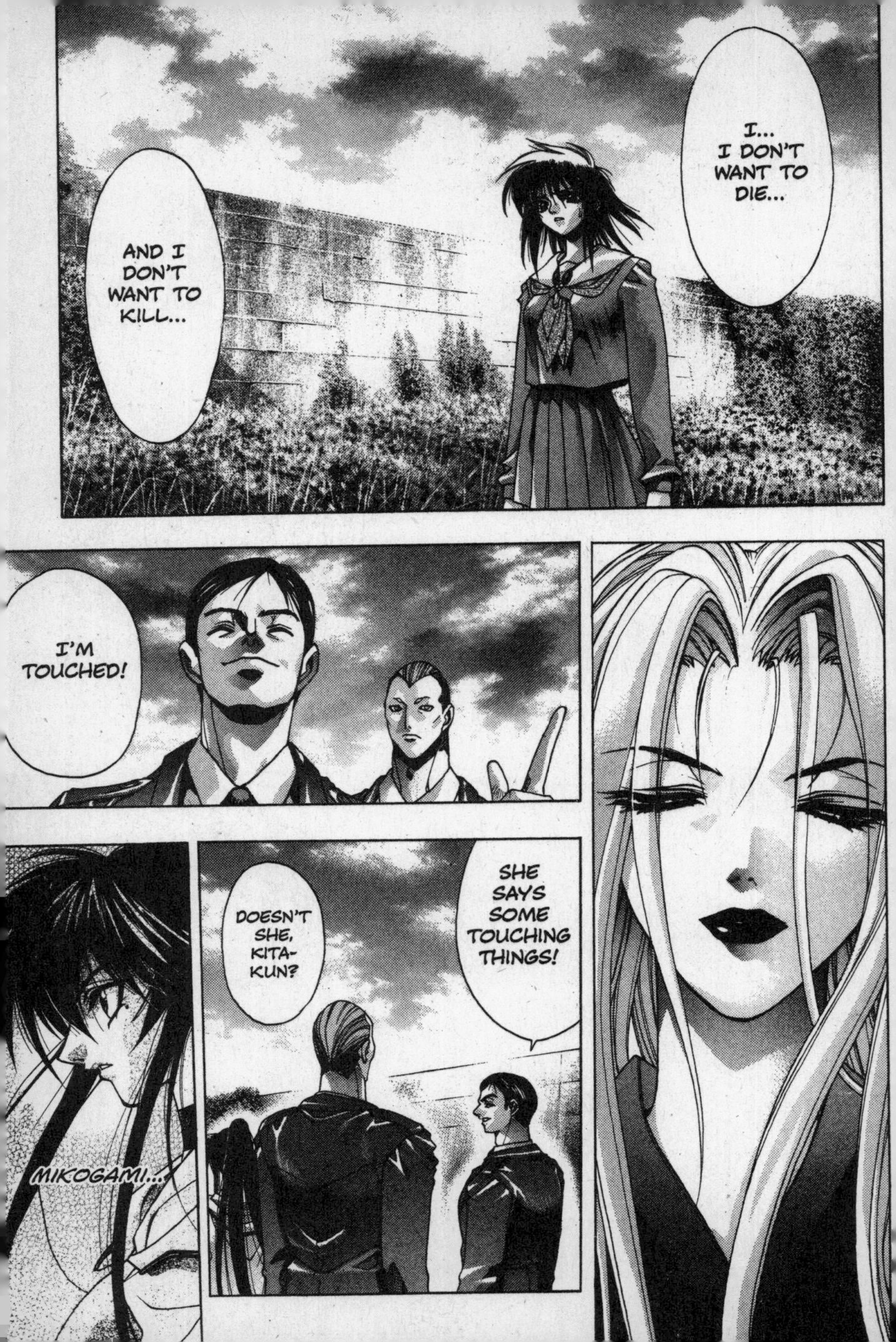
I... I DON'T WANT TO DIE...
AND I DON'T WANT TO KILL...
I'M TOUCHED!
SHE SAYS SOME TOUCHING THINGS!
DOESN'T SHE, KITA-KUN?
MIKOGAMI...

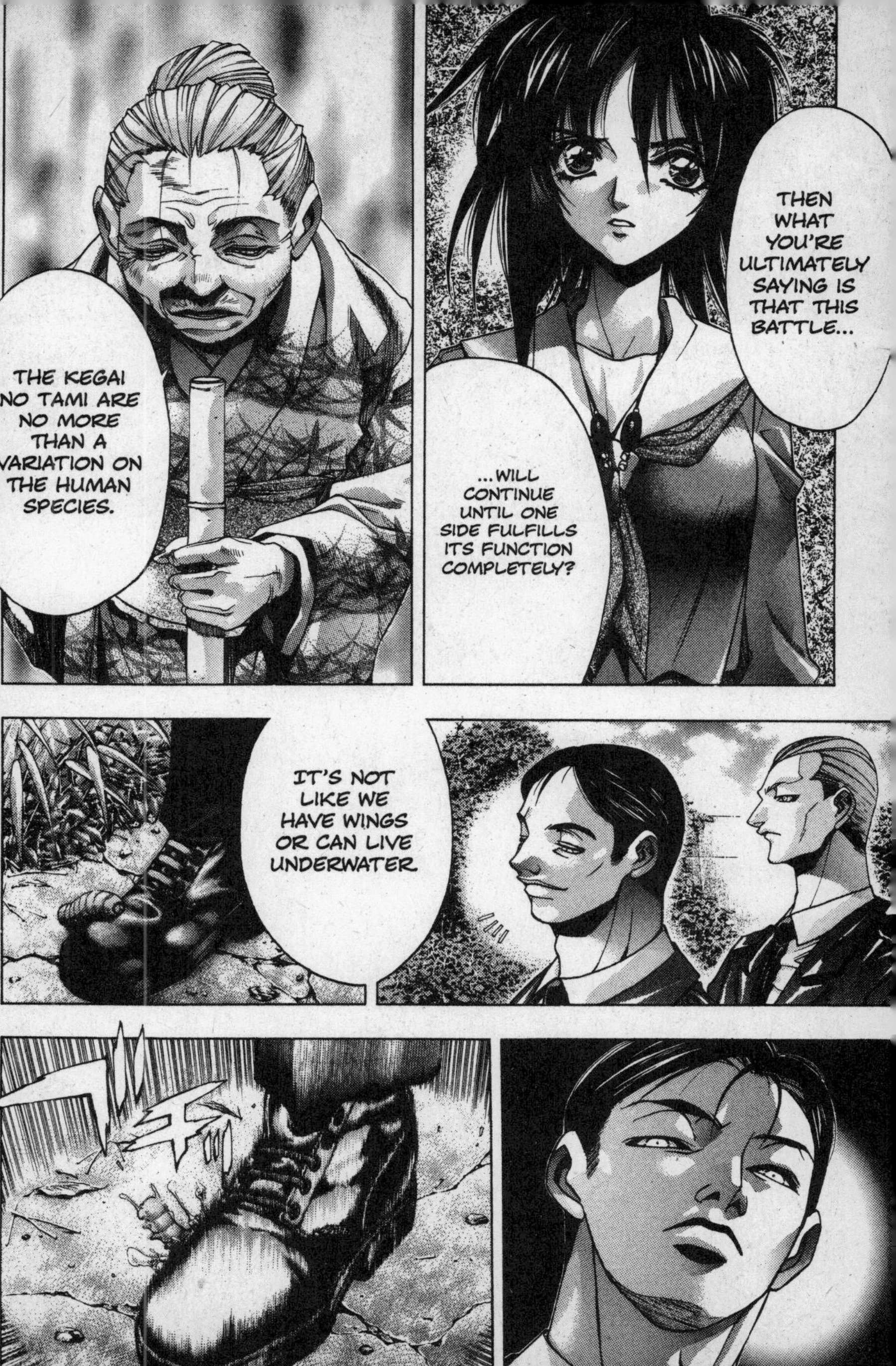
THEN WHAT YOU'RE ULTIMATELY SAYING IS THAT THIS BATTLE...
...WILL CONTINUE UNTIL ONE SIDE FULFILLS ITS FUNCTION COMPLETELY?
THE KEGAI NO TAMI ARE NO MORE THAN A VARIATION ON THE HUMAN SPECIES.
IT'S NOT LIKE WE HAVE WINGS OR CAN LIVE UNDERWATER

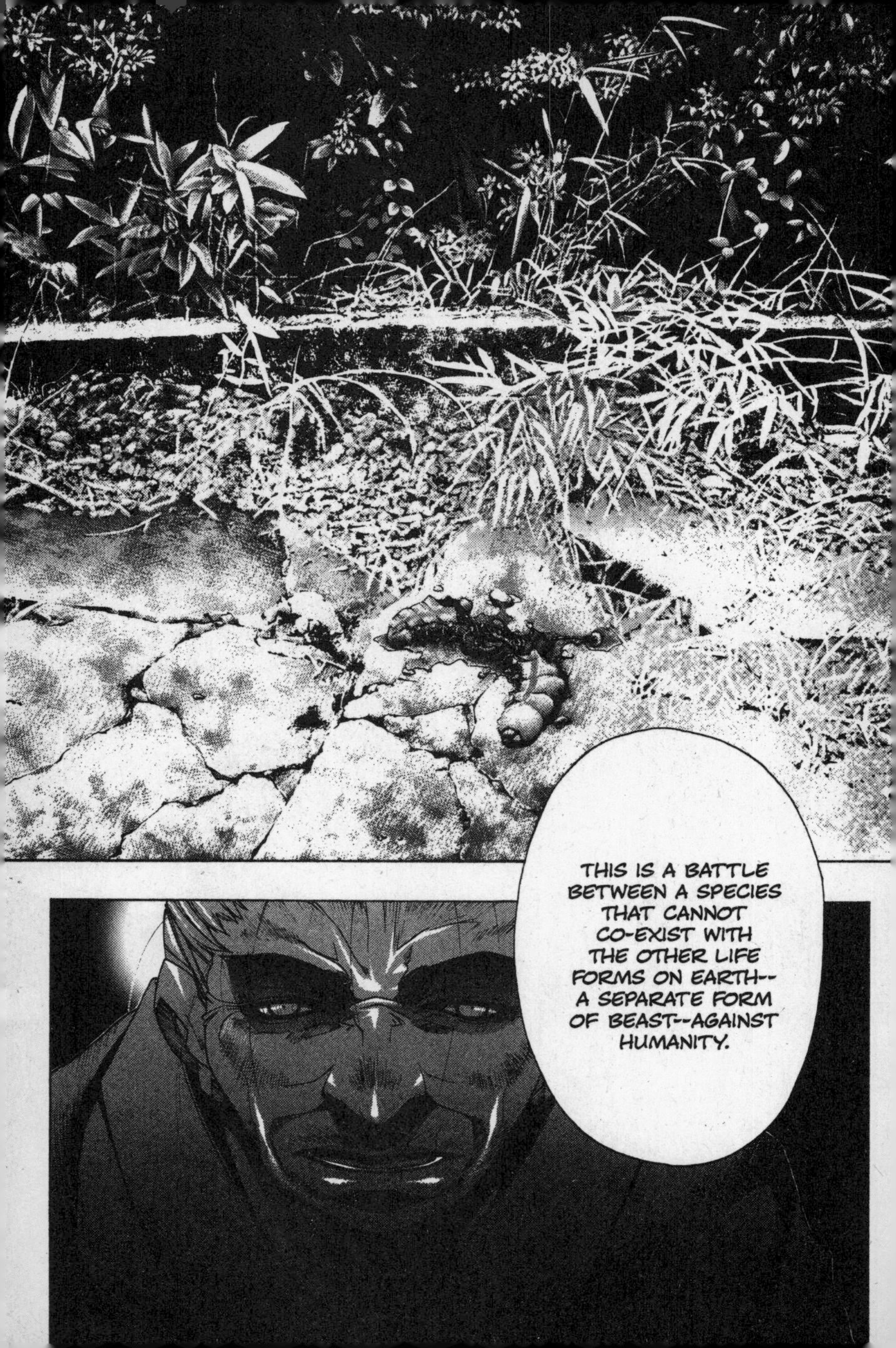
THIS IS A BATTLE BETWEEN A SPECIES THAT CANNOT CO-EXIST WITH THE OTHER LIFE FORMS ON EARTH-- A SEPARATE FORM OF BEAST--AGAINST HUMANITY.

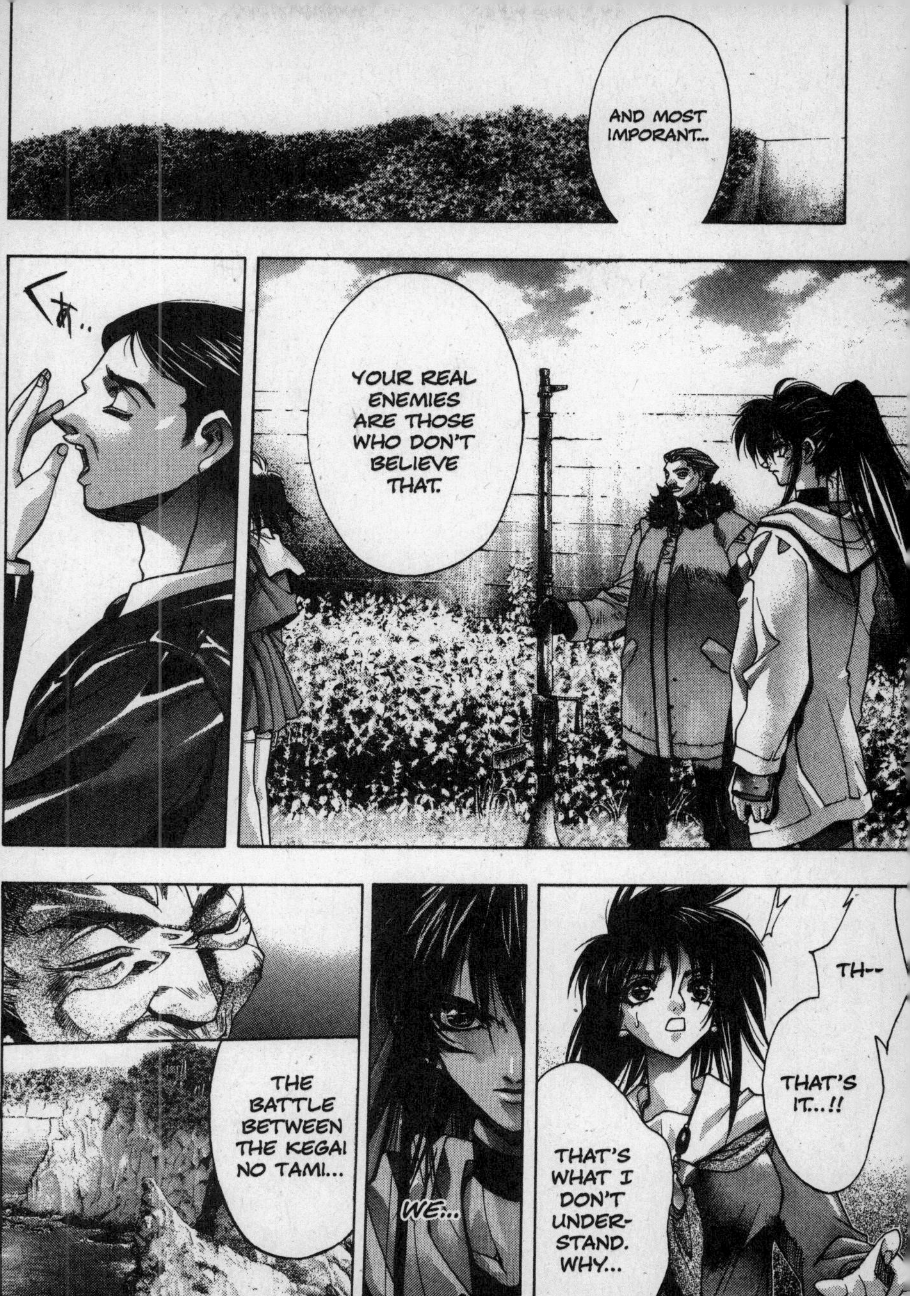
AND MOST IMPORANT...
YOUR REAL ENEMIES ARE THOSE WHO DON'T BELIEVE THAT.
くあ..
TH--
THAT'S IT...!!
THAT'S WHAT I DON'T UNDER-STAND. WHY...
WE...
THE BATTLE BETWEEN THE KEGAI NO TAMI...

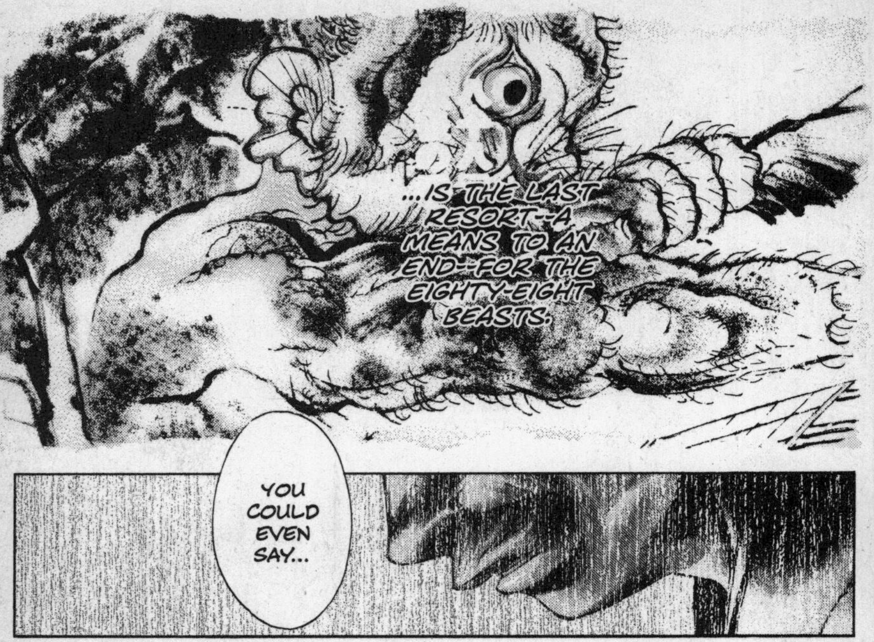
...IS THE LAST RESORT--A MEANS TO AN END--FOR THE EIGHTY-EIGHT BEASTS.
YOU COULD EVEN SAY...
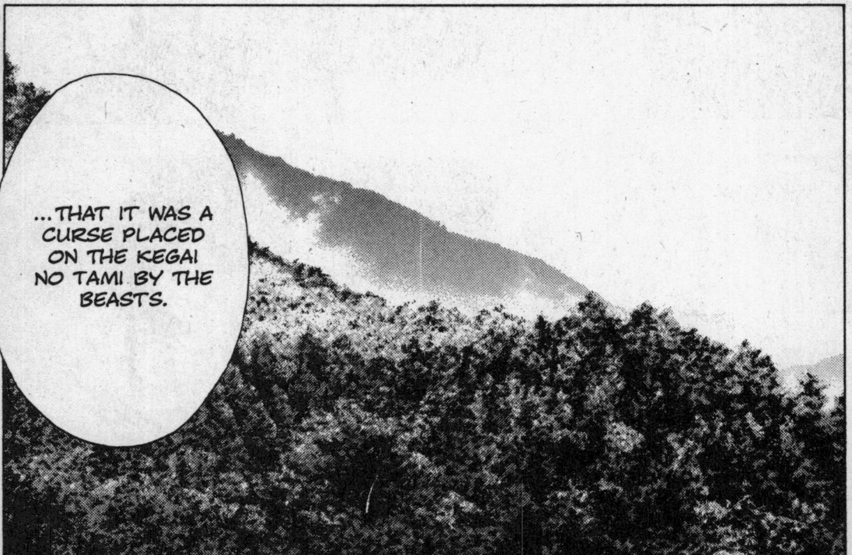
...THAT IT WAS A CURSE PLACED ON THE KEGAI NO TAMI BY THE BEASTS.

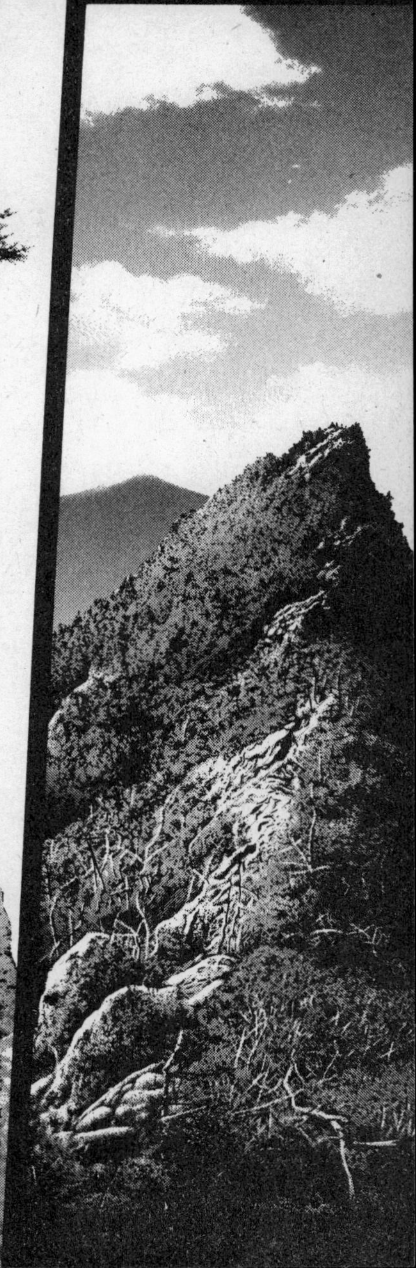
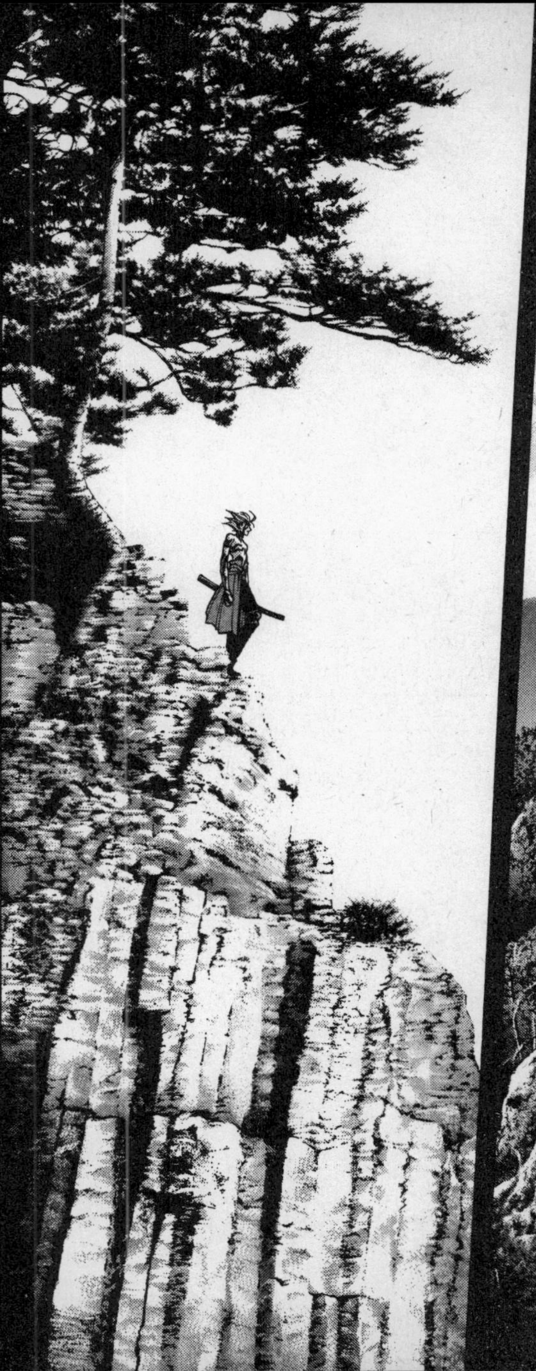

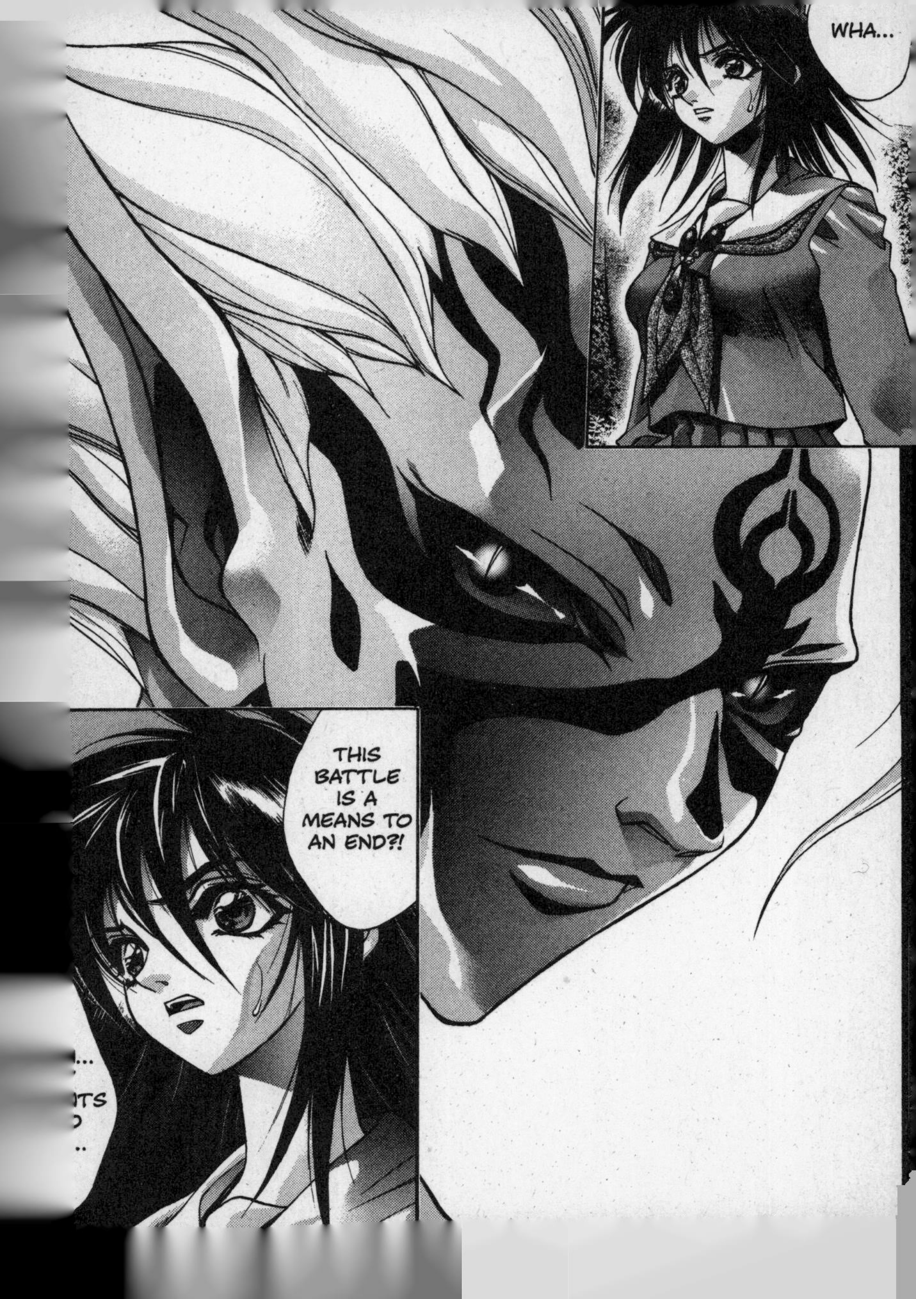
WHA...
THIS BATTLE IS A MEANS TO AN END?!

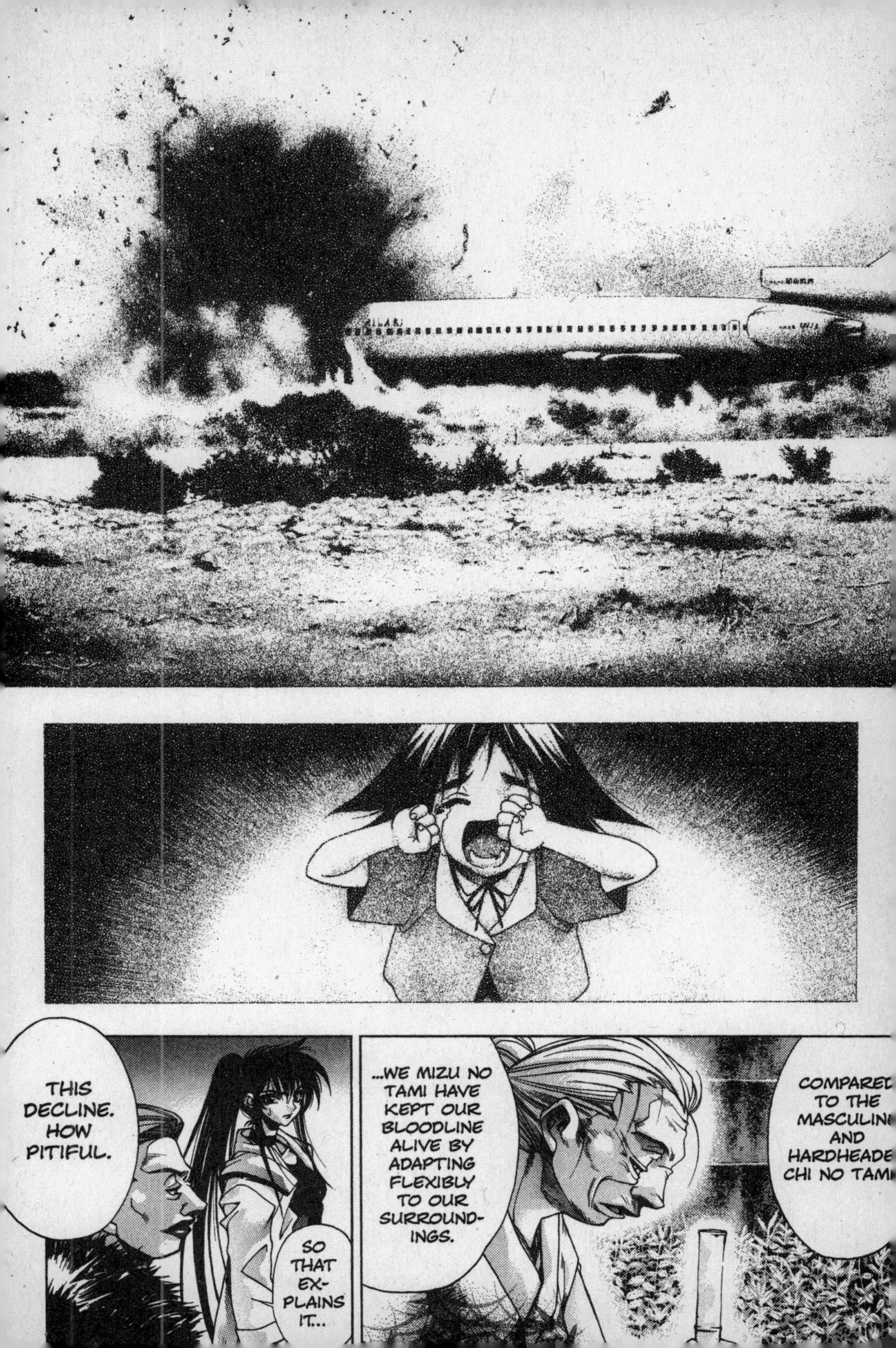
COMPARED TO THE MASCULIN AND HARDHEADE CHI NO TAM
...WE MIZU NO TAMI HAVE KEPT OUR BLOODLINE ALIVE BY ADAPTING FLEXIBLY TO OUR SURROUND-INGS.
THIS DECLINE. HOW PITIFUL.
SO THAT EX-PLAINS IT...

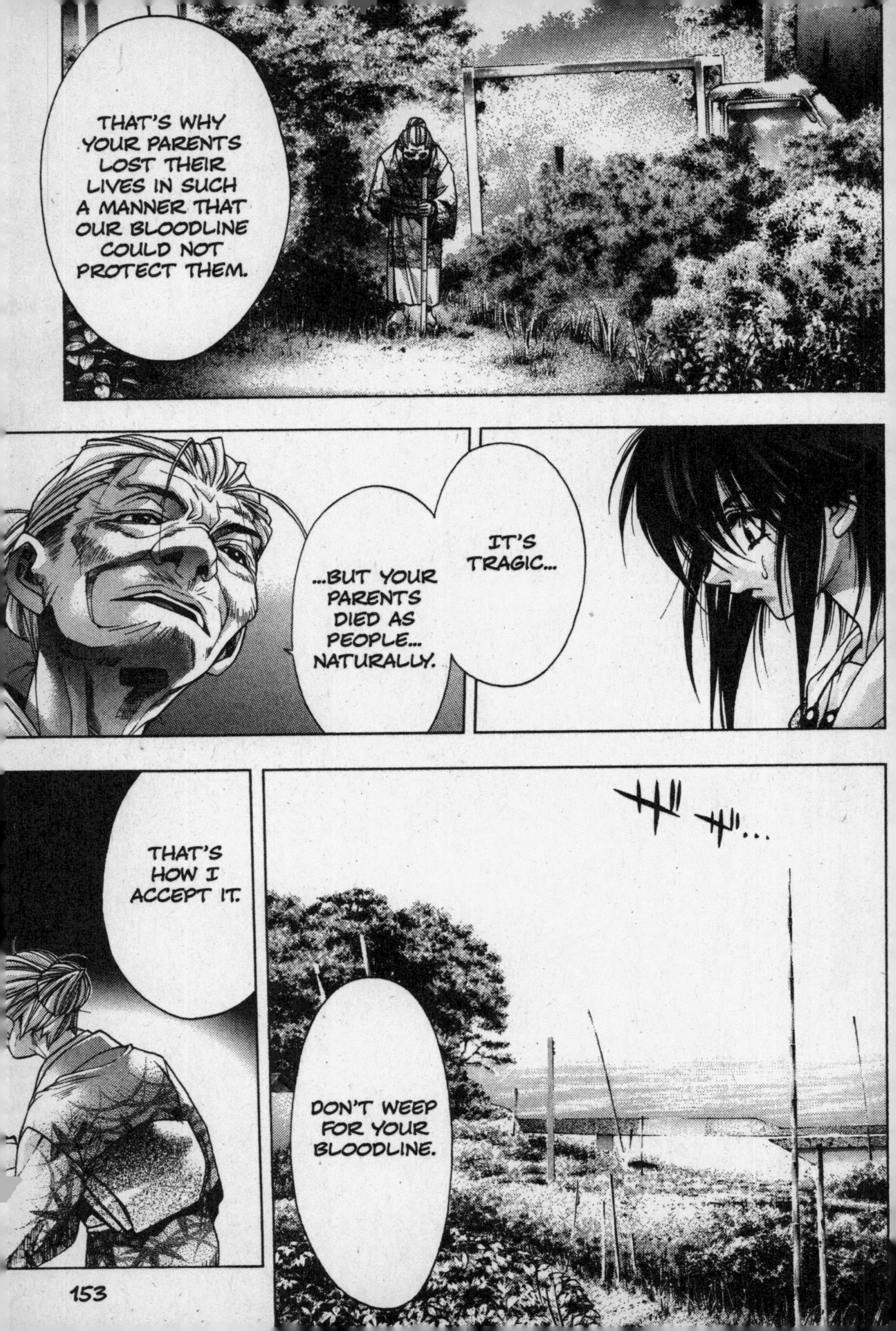
THAT'S WHY YOUR PARENTS LOST THEIR LIVES IN SUCH A MANNER THAT OUR BLOODLINE COULD NOT PROTECT THEM.
IT'S TRAGIC...
...BUT YOUR PARENTS DIED AS PEOPLE... NATURALLY.
ザッ ザッ...
DON'T WEEP FOR YOUR BLOODLINE.
THAT'S HOW I ACCEPT IT.

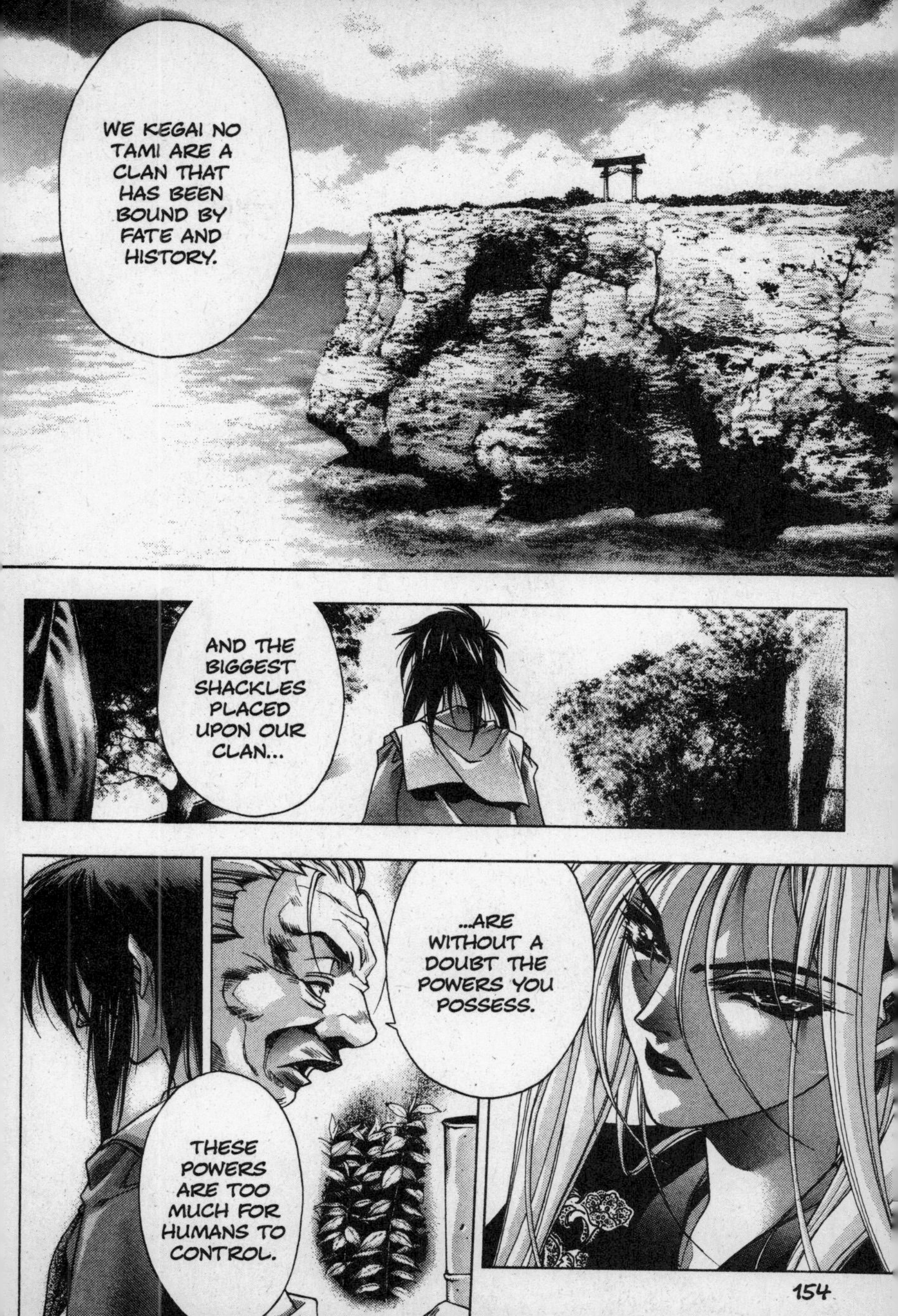
WE KEGAI NO TAMI ARE A CLAN THAT HAS BEEN BOUND BY FATE AND HISTORY.
AND THE BIGGEST SHACKLES PLACED UPON OUR CLAN...
...ARE WITHOUT A DOUBT THE POWERS YOU POSSESS.
THESE POWERS ARE TOO MUCH FOR HUMANS TO CONTROL.

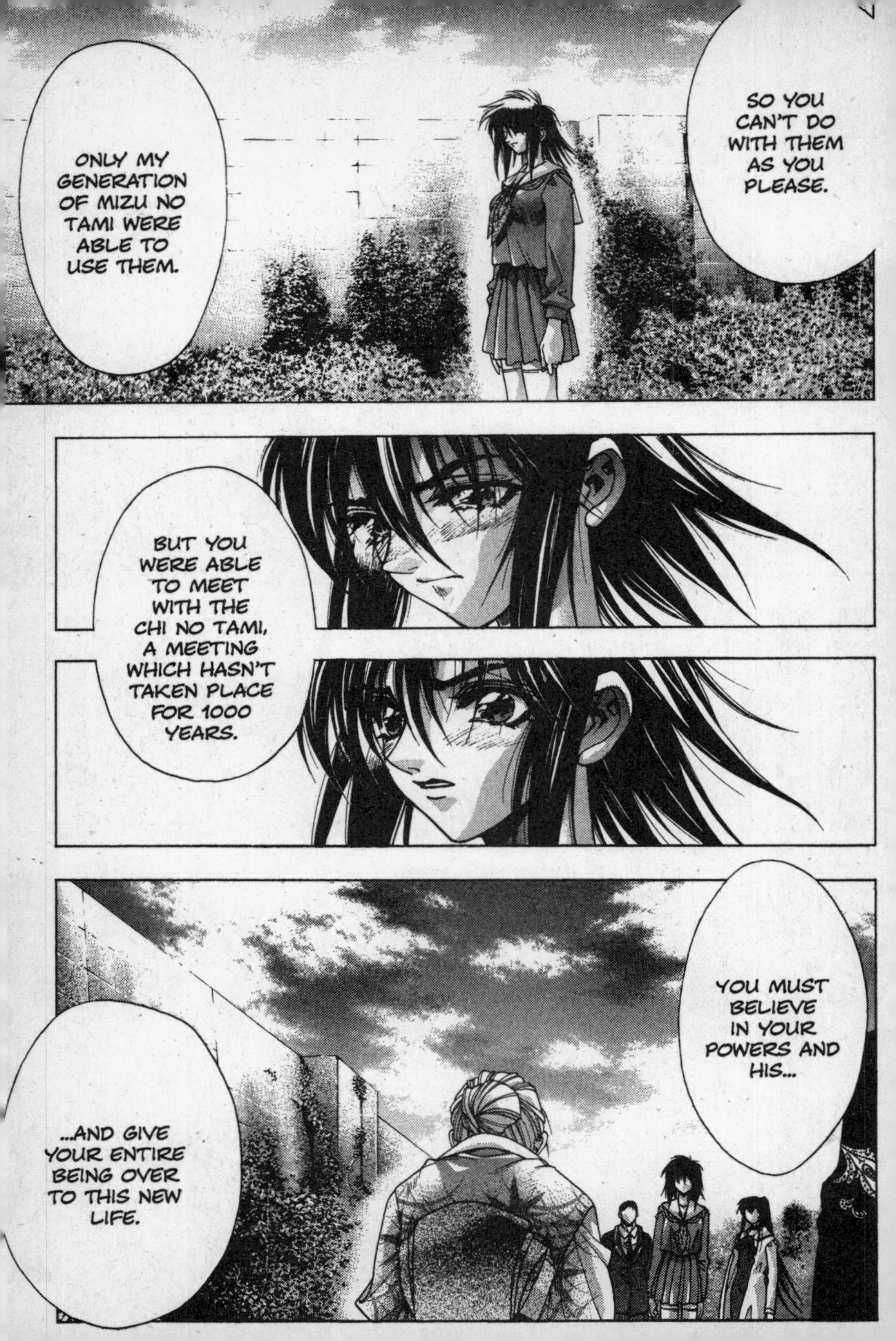
SO YOU CAN'T DO WITH THEM AS YOU PLEASE.
ONLY MY GENERATION OF MIZU NO TAMI WERE ABLE TO USE THEM.
BUT YOU WERE ABLE TO MEET WITH THE CHI NO TAMI, A MEETING WHICH HASN'T TAKEN PLACE FOR 1000 YEARS.
YOU MUST BELIEVE IN YOUR POWERS AND HIS...
...AND GIVE YOUR ENTIRE BEING OVER TO THIS NEW LIFE.

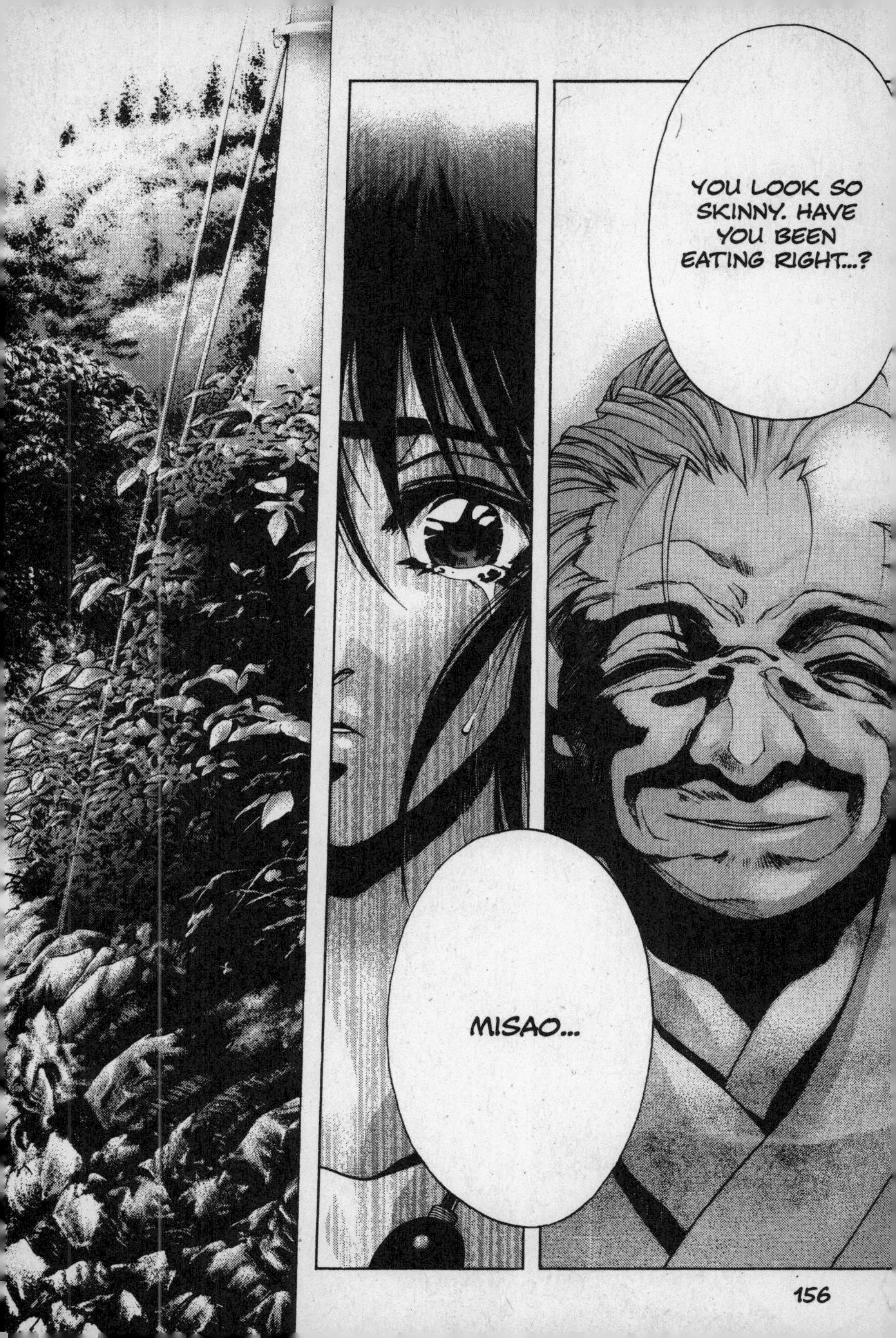
YOU LOOK SO SKINNY. HAVE YOU BEEN EATING RIGHT...?
MISAO...

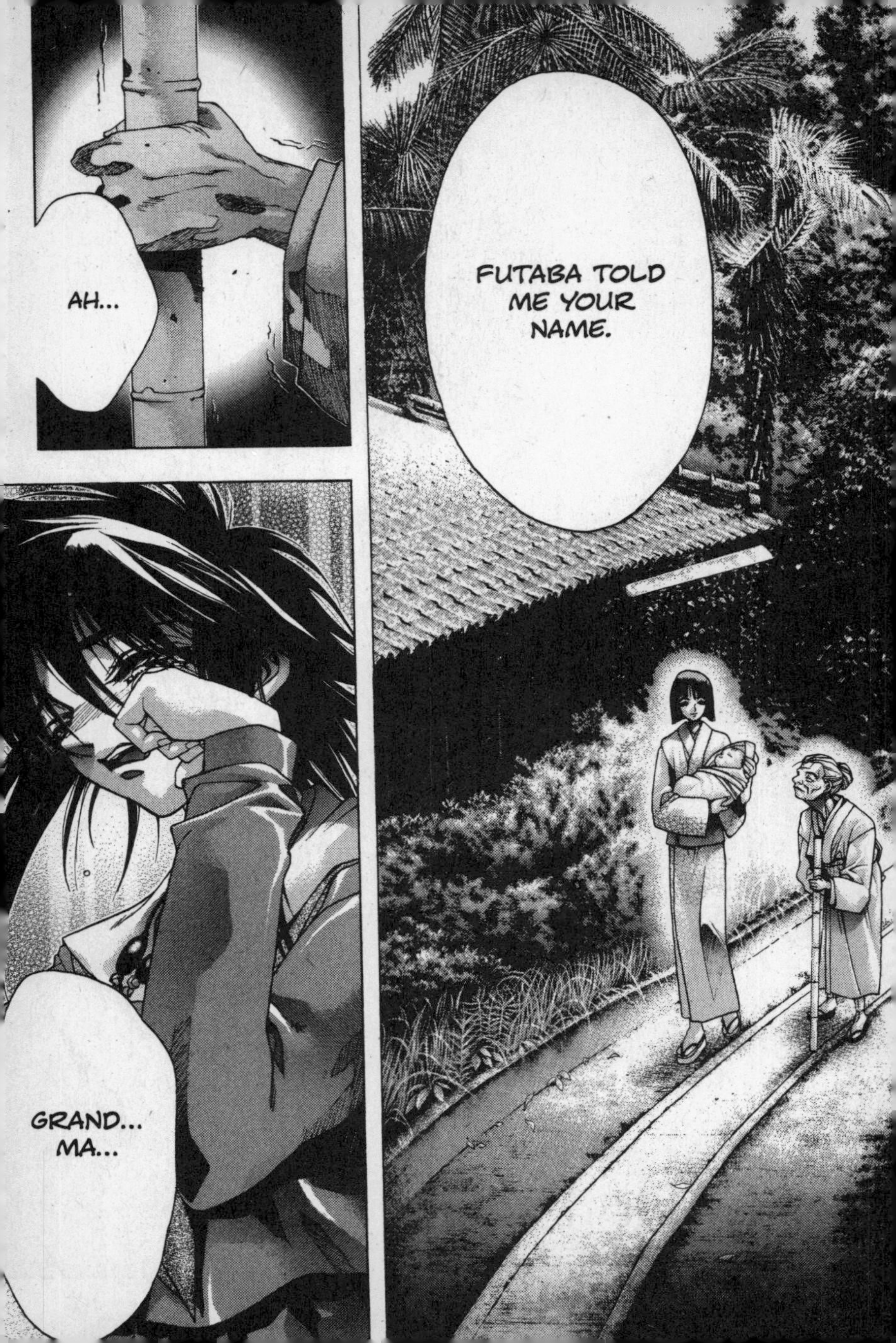
FUTABA TOLD ME YOUR NAME.
AH...
GRAND... MA...

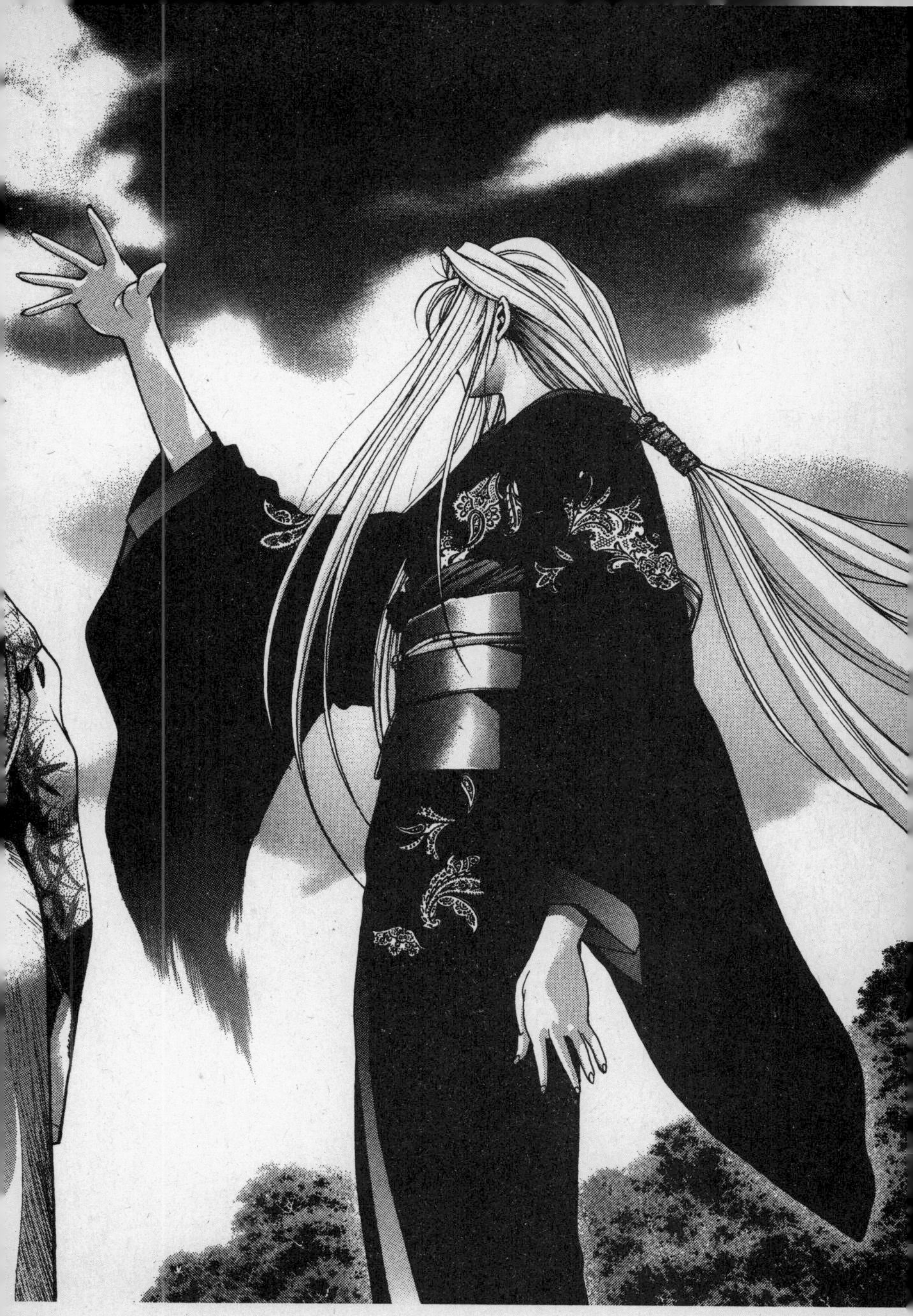

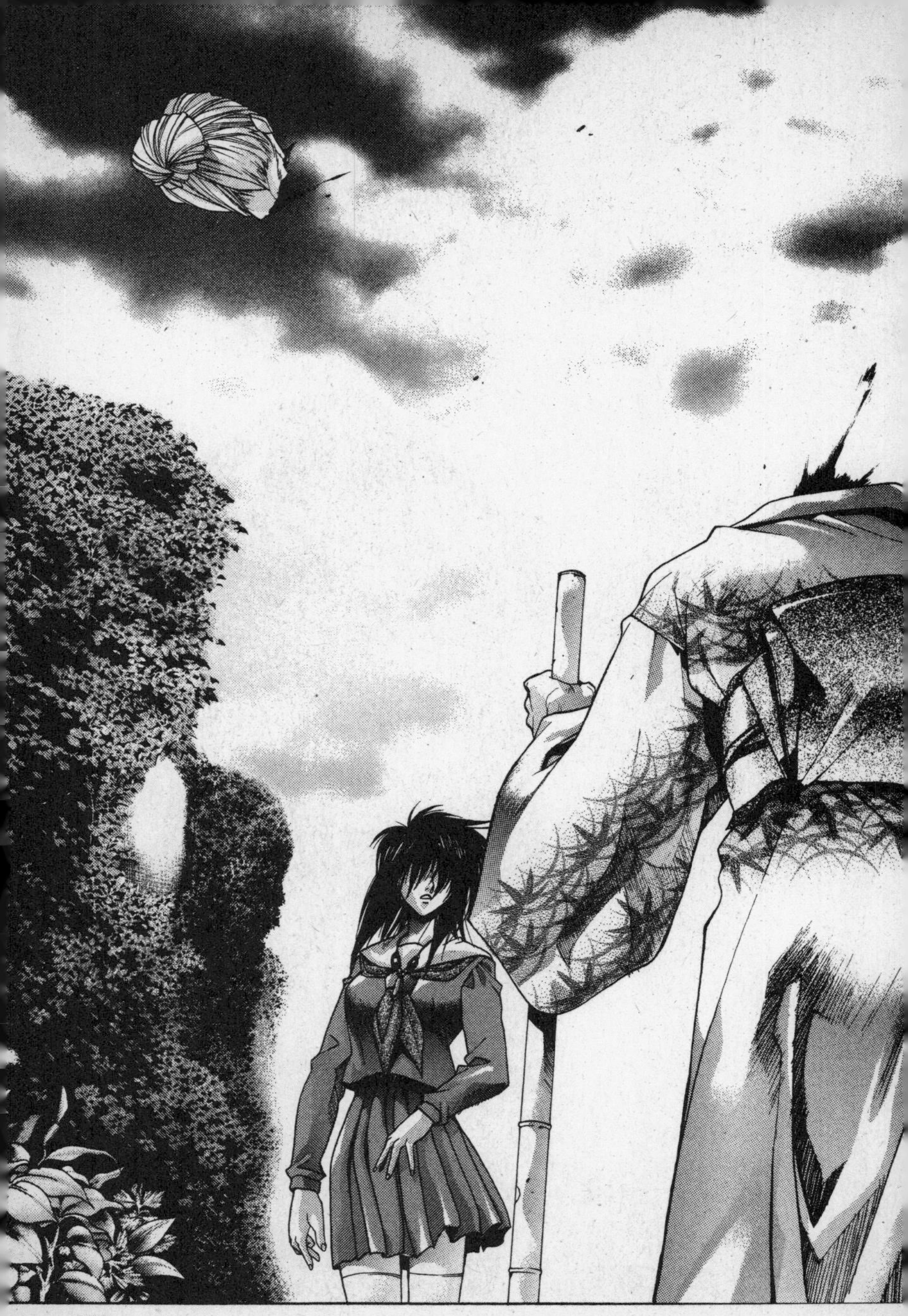

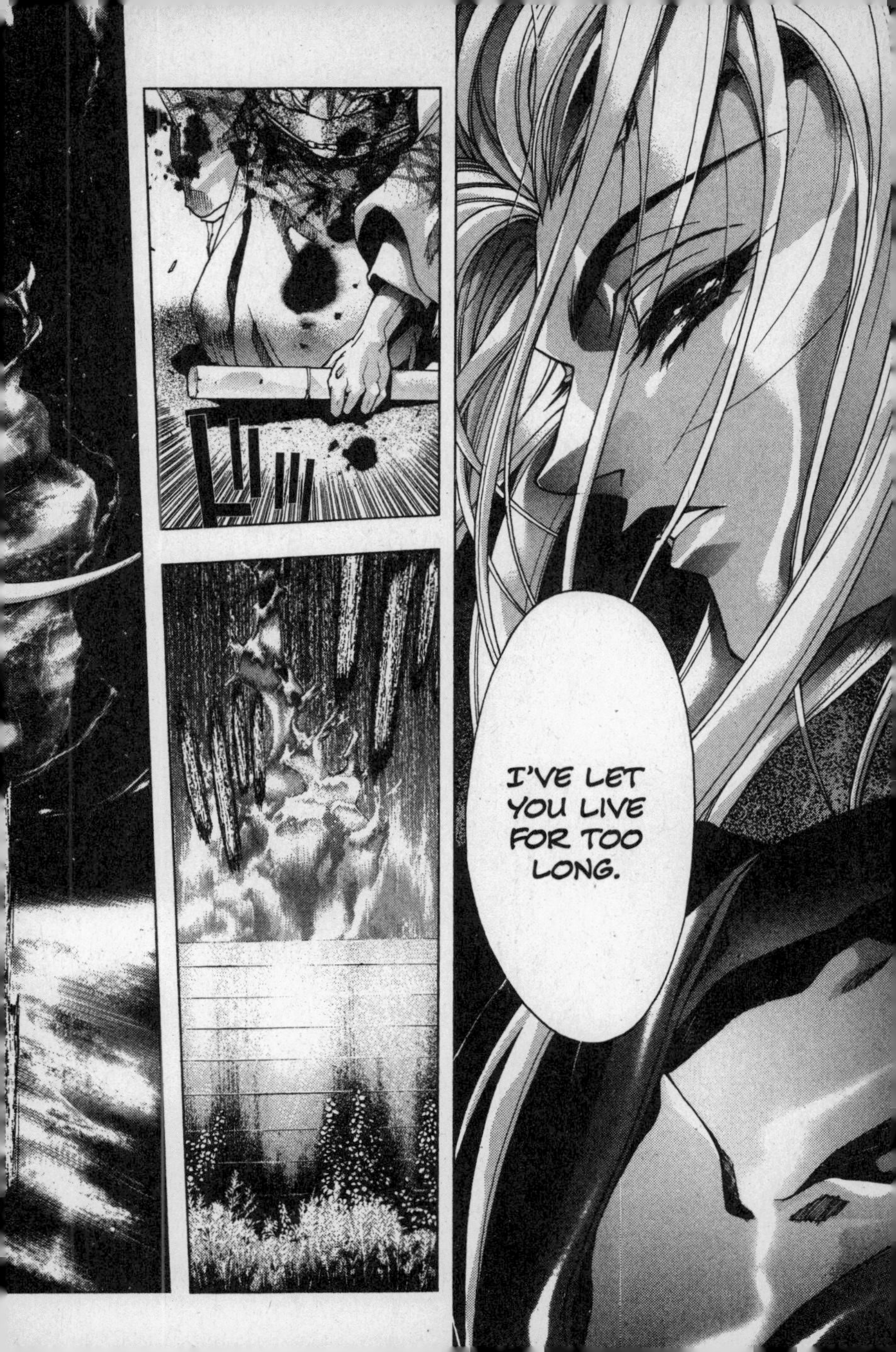
I'VE LET YOU LIVE FOR TOO LONG.

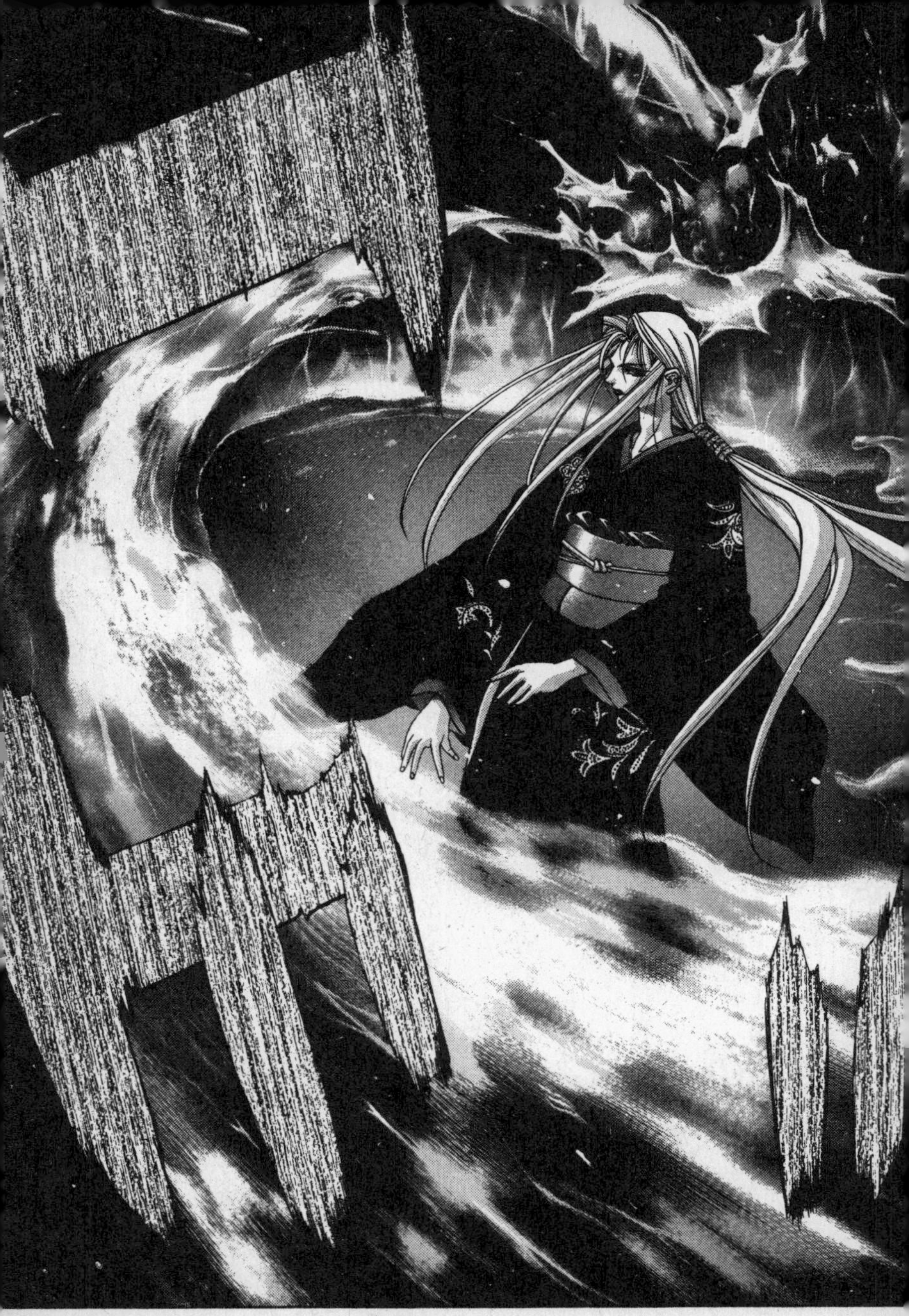

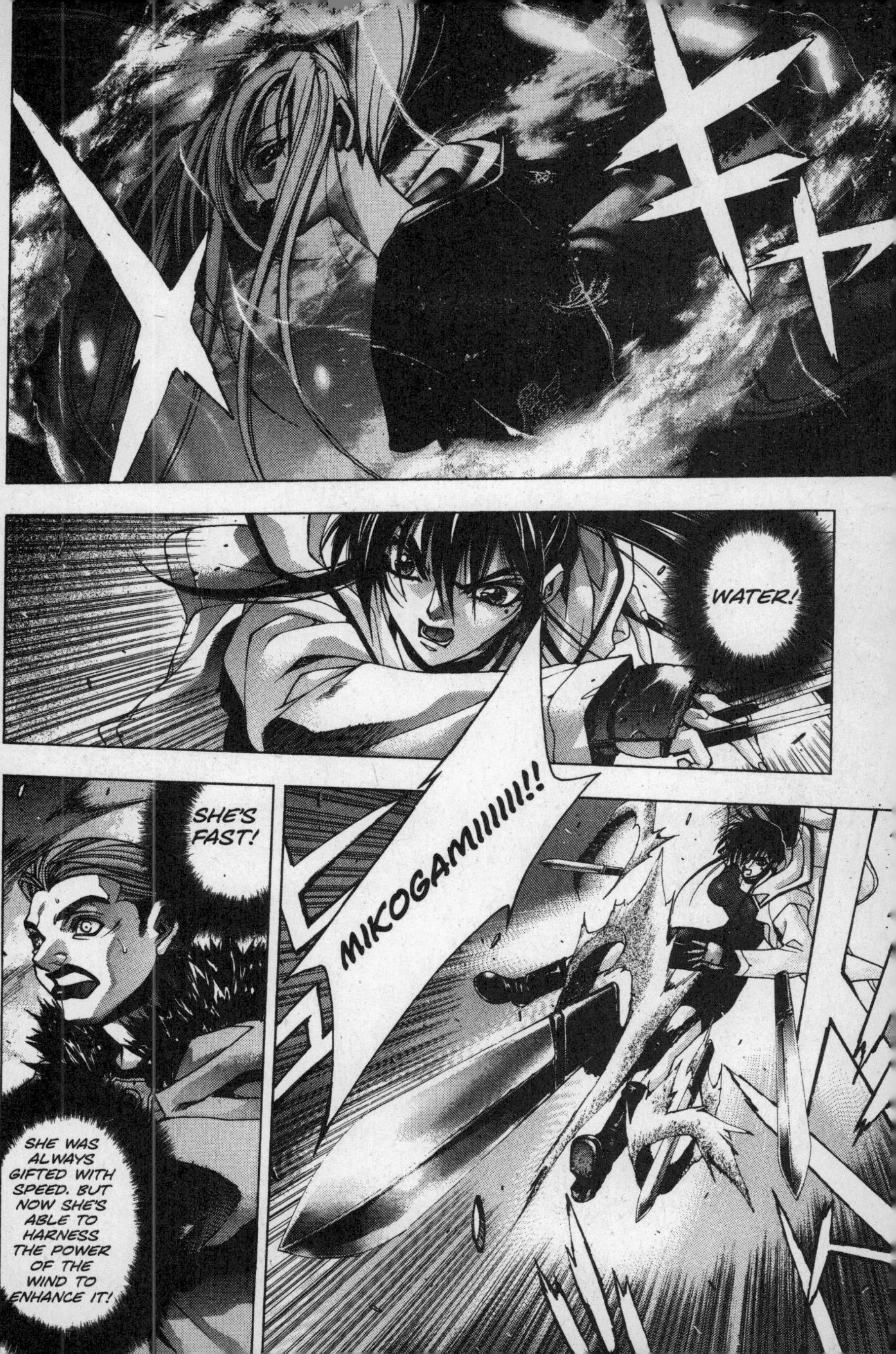
WATER!
MIKOGAMIIIIIII!!
SHE'S FAST!
SHE WAS ALWAYS GIFTED WITH SPEED. BUT NOW SHE'S ABLE TO HARNESS THE POWER OF THE WIND TO ENHANCE IT!

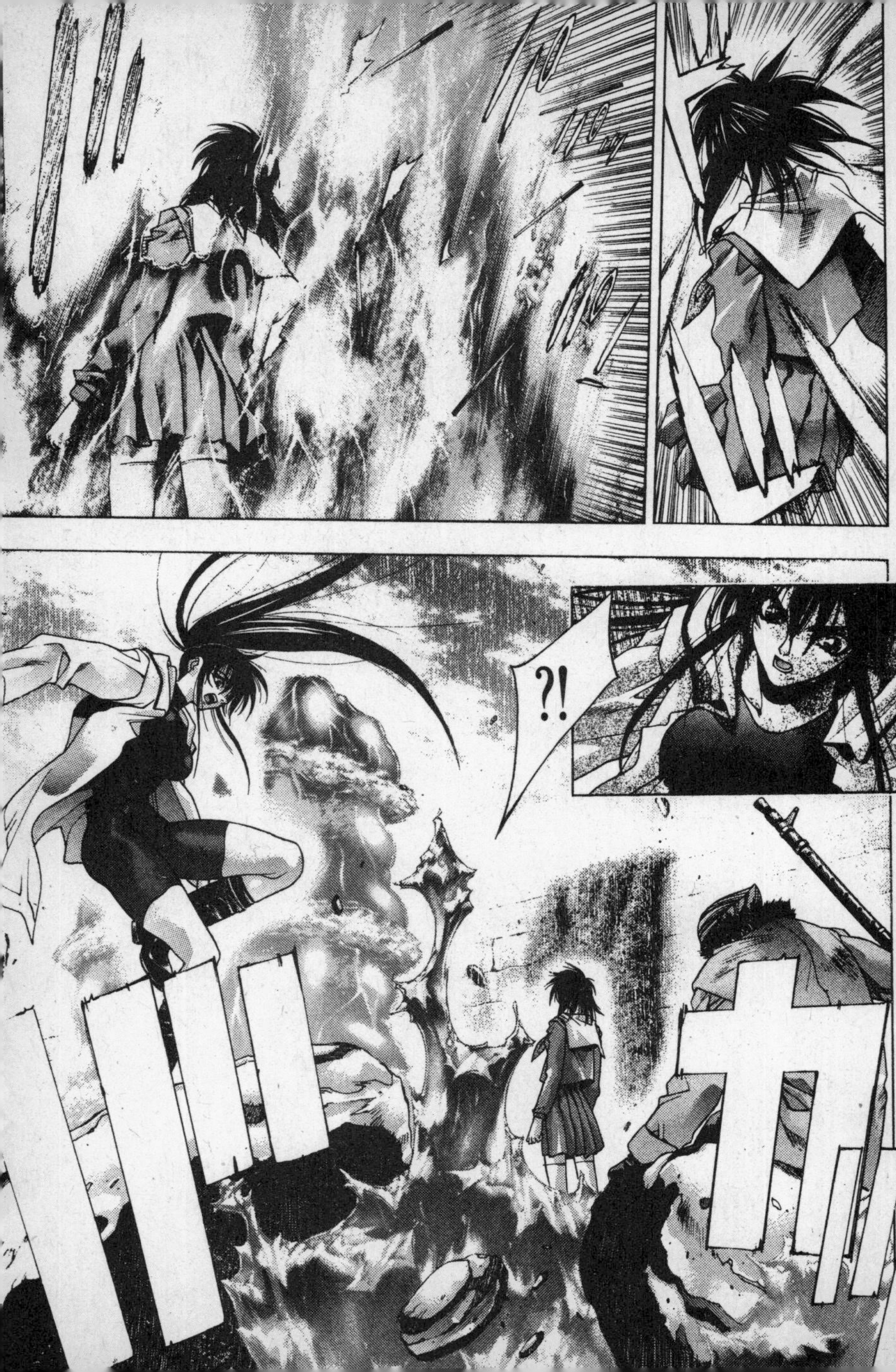
?!

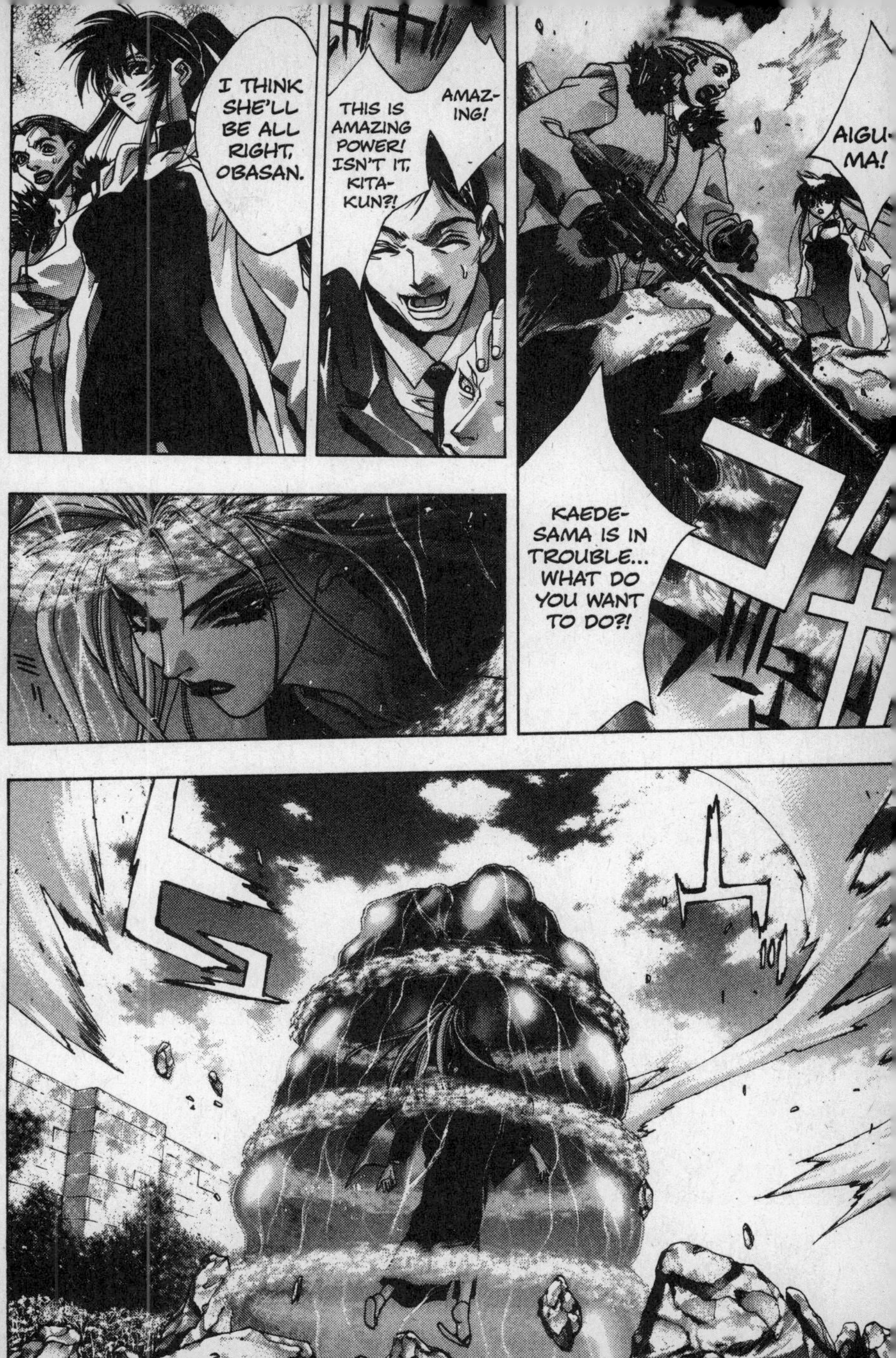
AIGU-MA!
KAEDE-SAMA IS IN TROUBLE... WHAT DO YOU WANT TO DO?!
AMAZ-ING!
THIS IS AMAZING POWER! ISN'T IT, KITA-KUN?!
I THINK SHE'LL BE ALL RIGHT, OBASAN.

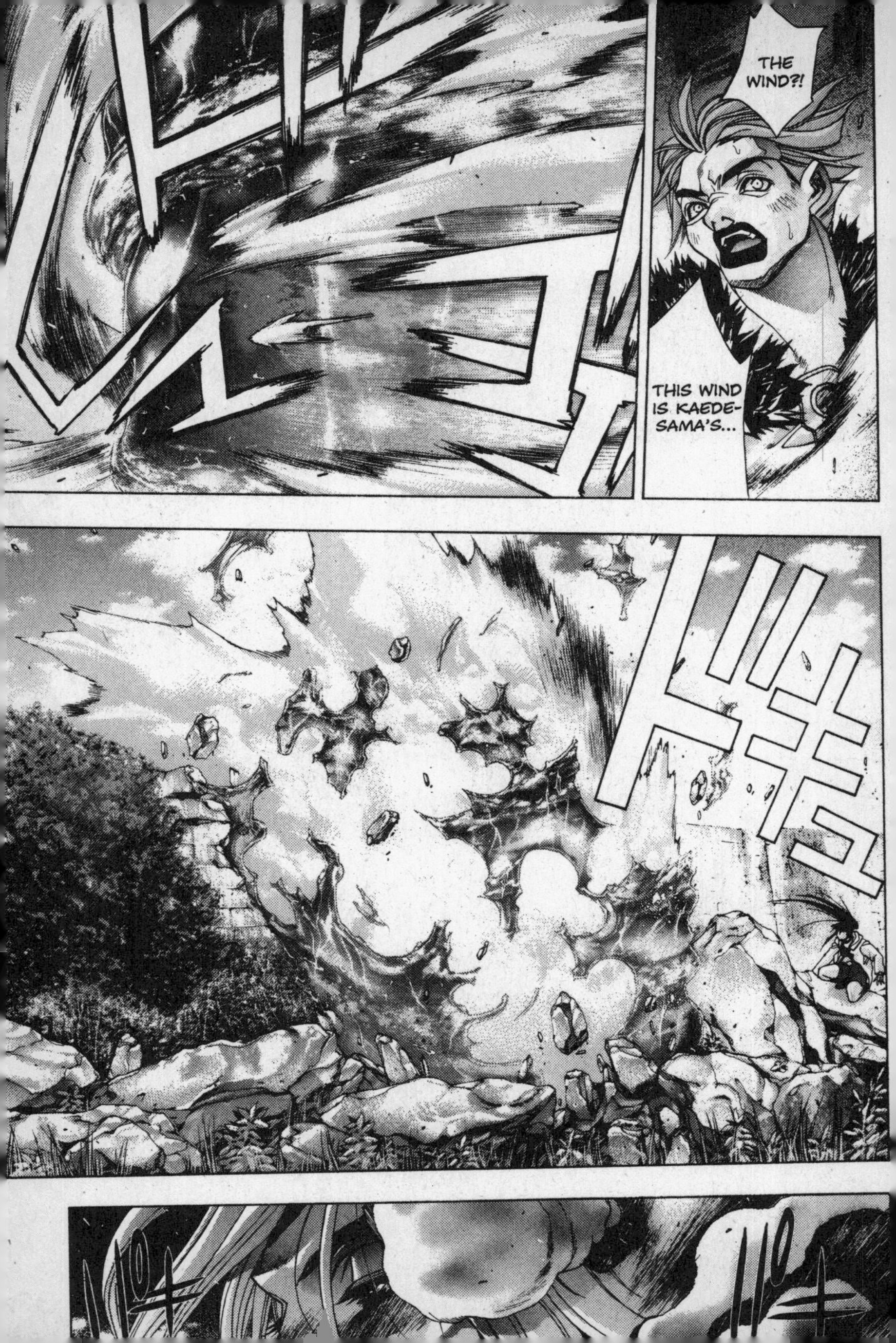
THE WIND?!
THIS WIND IS KAEDE-SAMA'S...

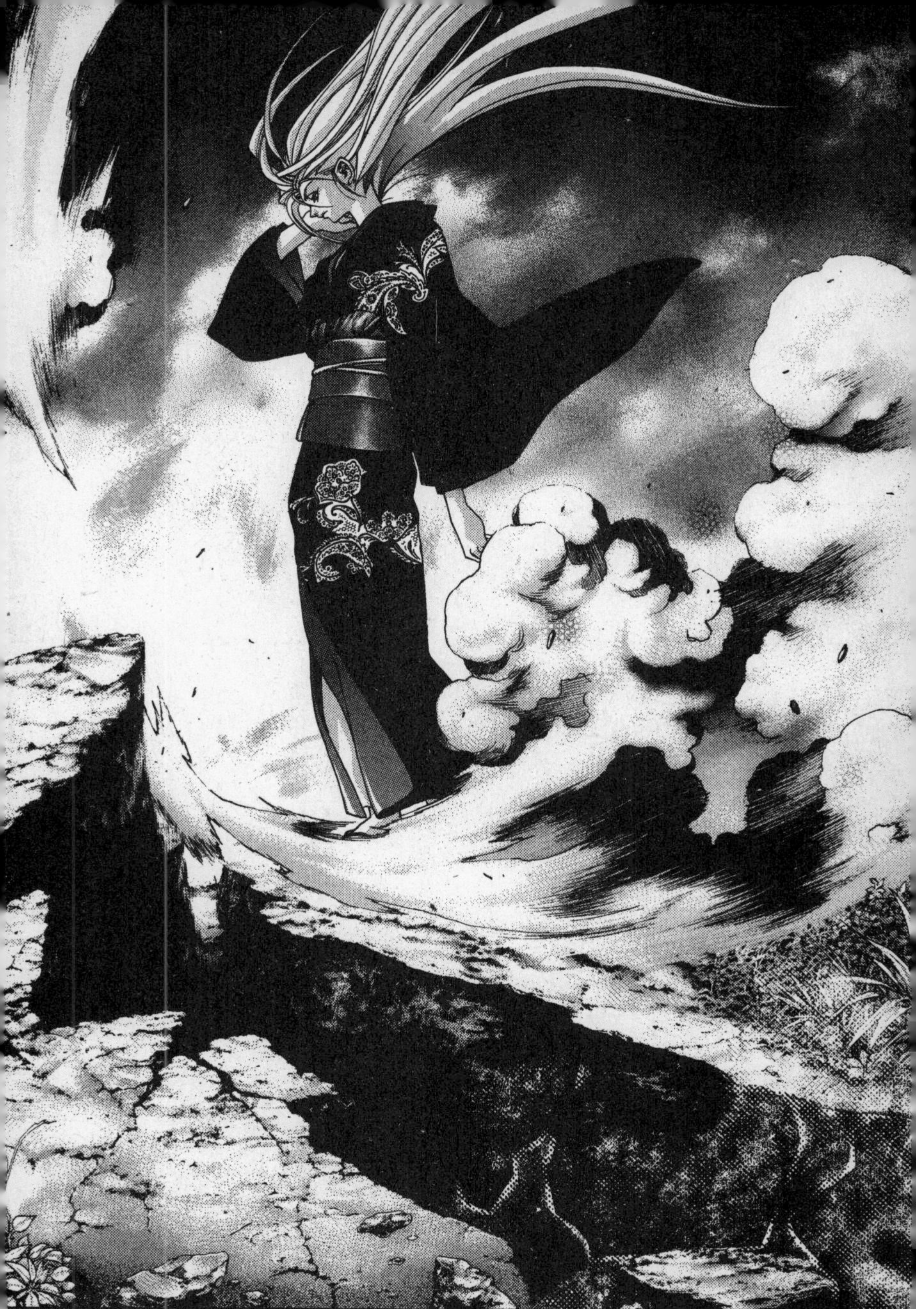

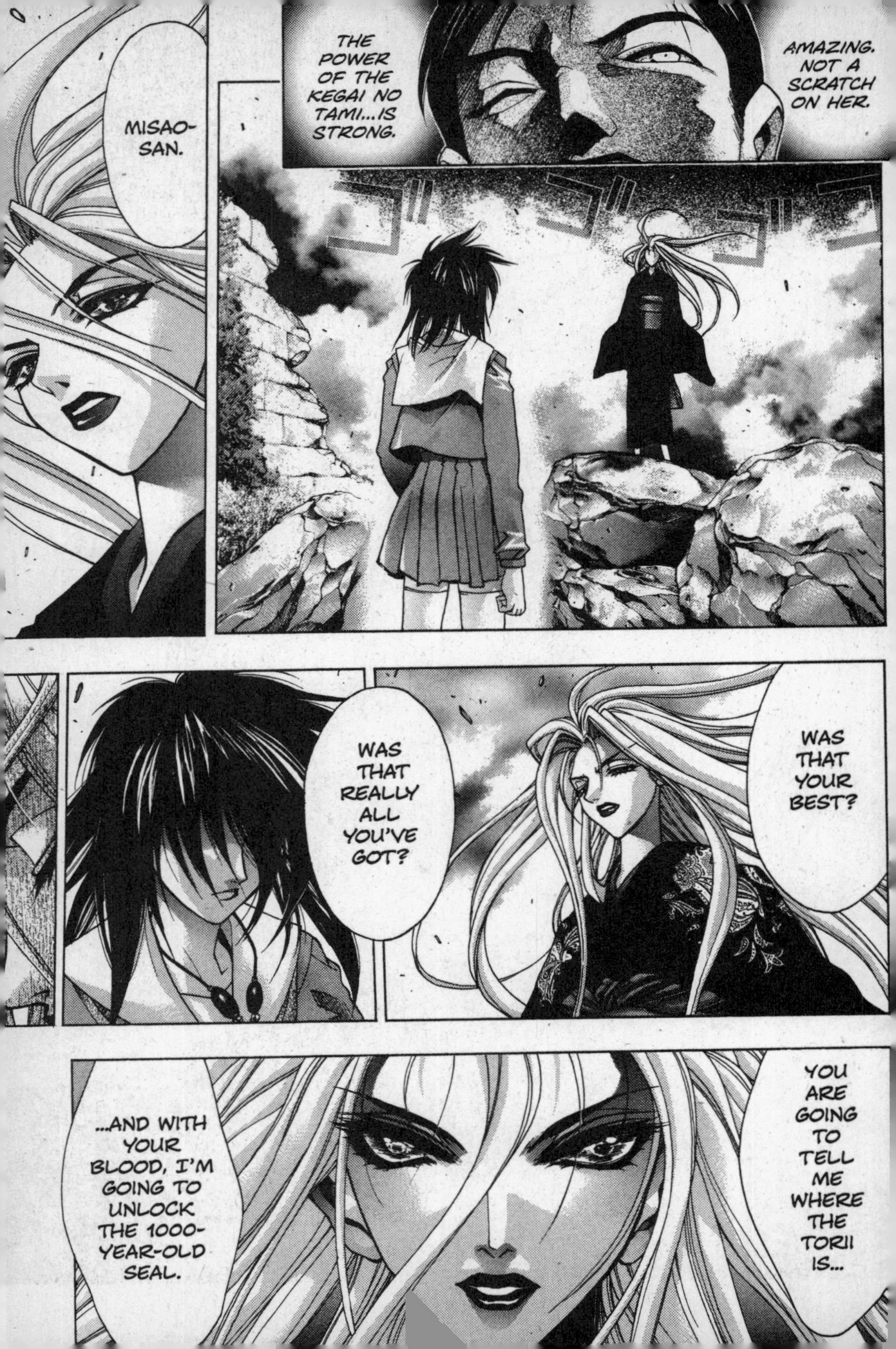
AMAZING. NOT A SCRATCH ON HER.
THE POWER OF THE KEGAI NO TAMI...IS STRONG.
MISAO-SAN.
WAS THAT YOUR BEST?
WAS THAT REALLY ALL YOU'VE GOT?
YOU ARE GOING TO TELL ME WHERE THE TORII IS...
...AND WITH YOUR BLOOD, I'M GOING TO UNLOCK THE 1000-YEAR-OLD SEAL.

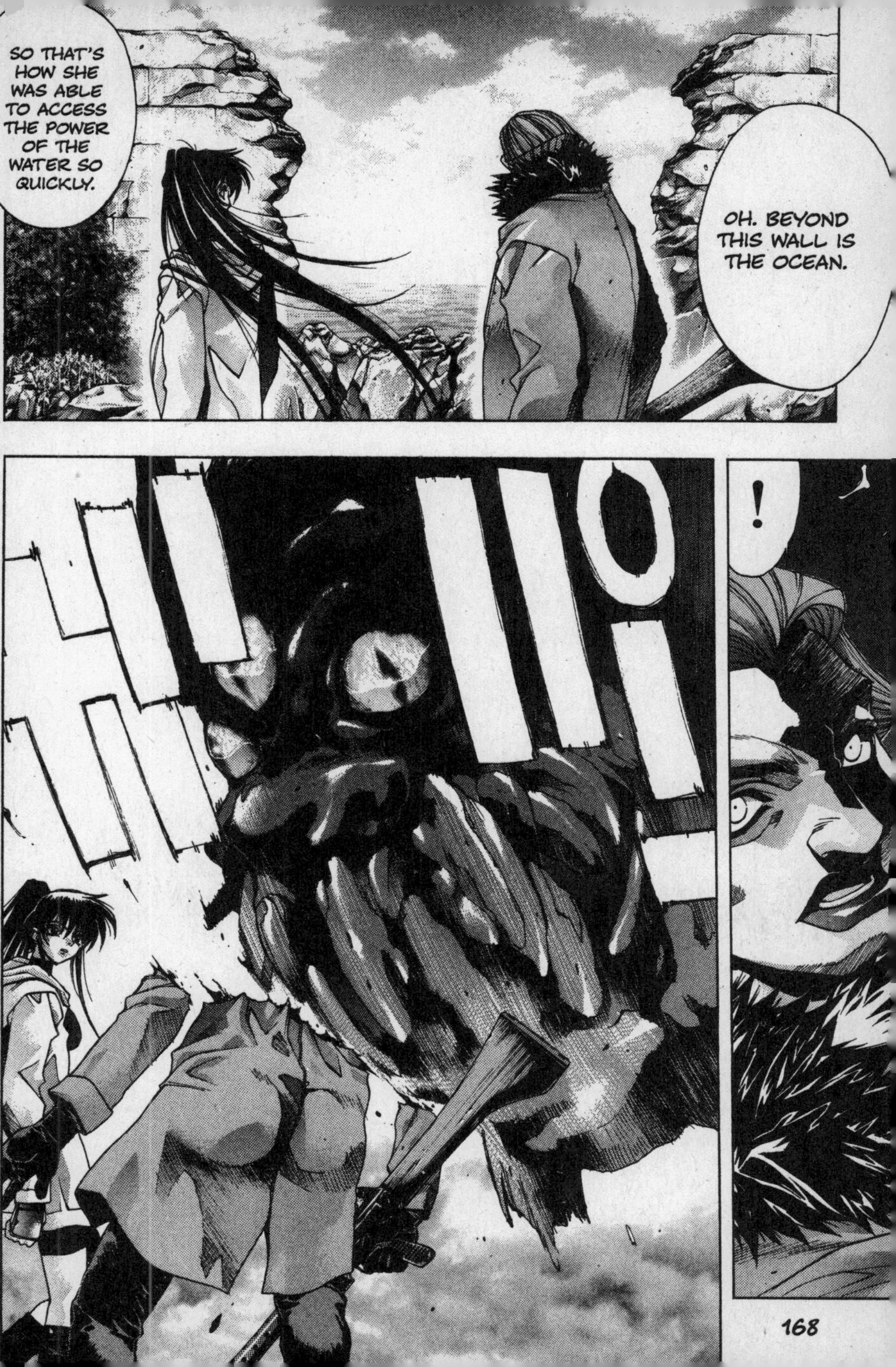
OH. BEYOND THIS WALL IS THE OCEAN.
SO THAT'S HOW SHE WAS ABLE TO ACCESS THE POWER OF THE WATER SO QUICKLY.
!

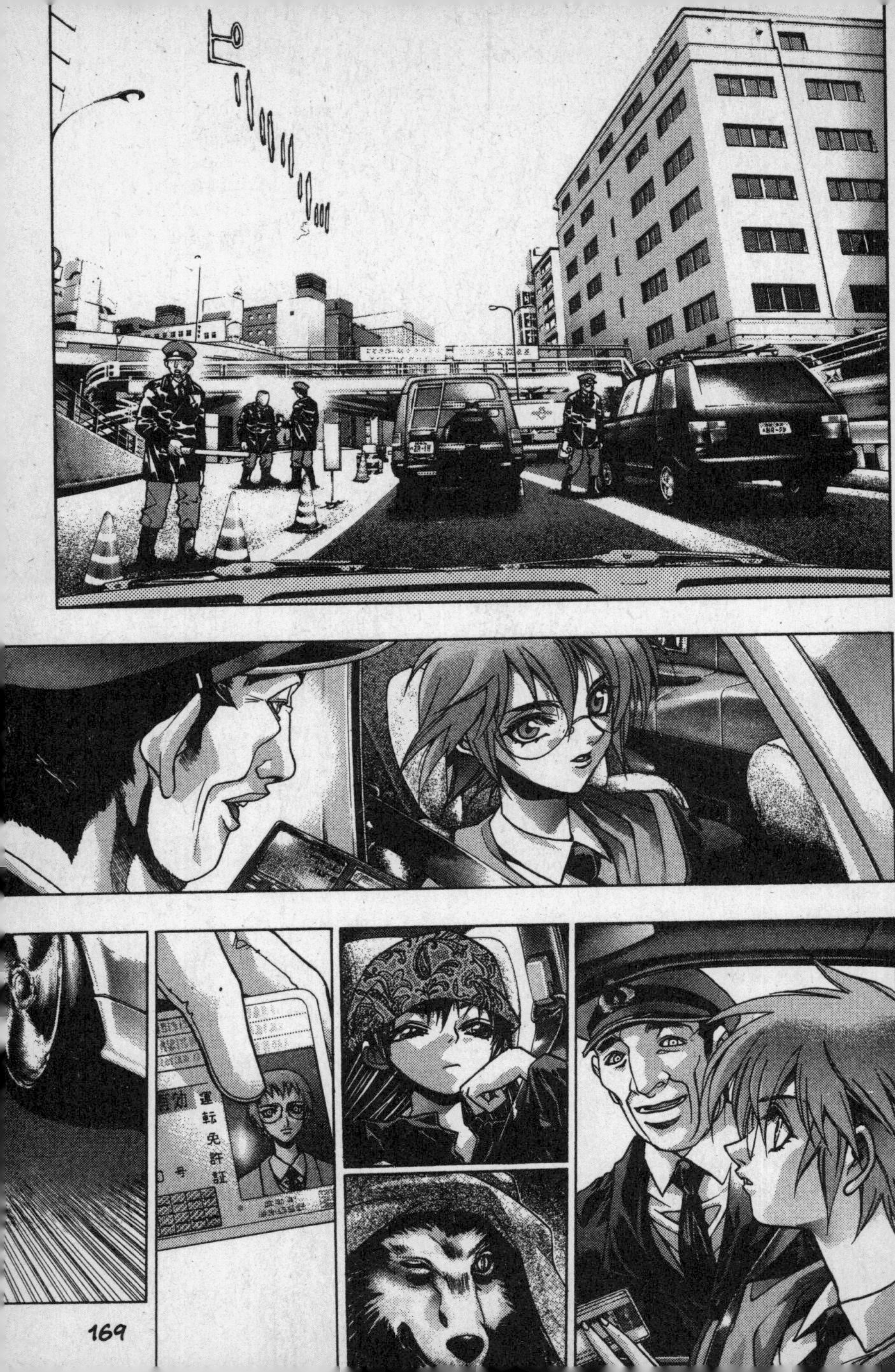
ピー
有効
運転免許証

Chapter 26: To Greater Power

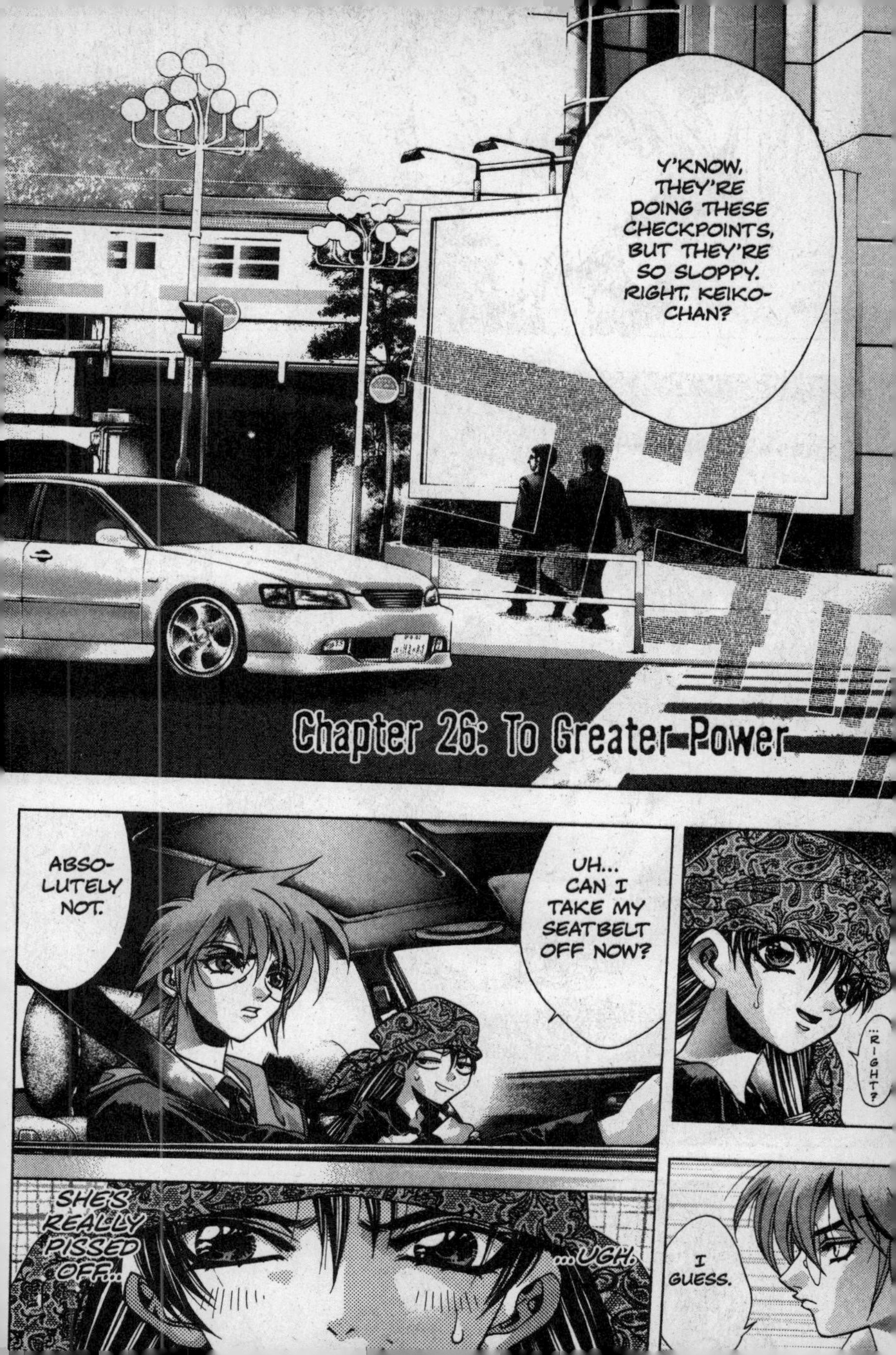
Y'KNOW, THEY'RE DOING THESE CHECKPOINTS, BUT THEY'RE SO SLOPPY. RIGHT, KEIKO-CHAN?
...RIGHT?
UH... CAN I TAKE MY SEATBELT OFF NOW?
ABSO-LUTELY NOT.
I GUESS.
SHE'S REALLY PISSED OFF...
...UGH.

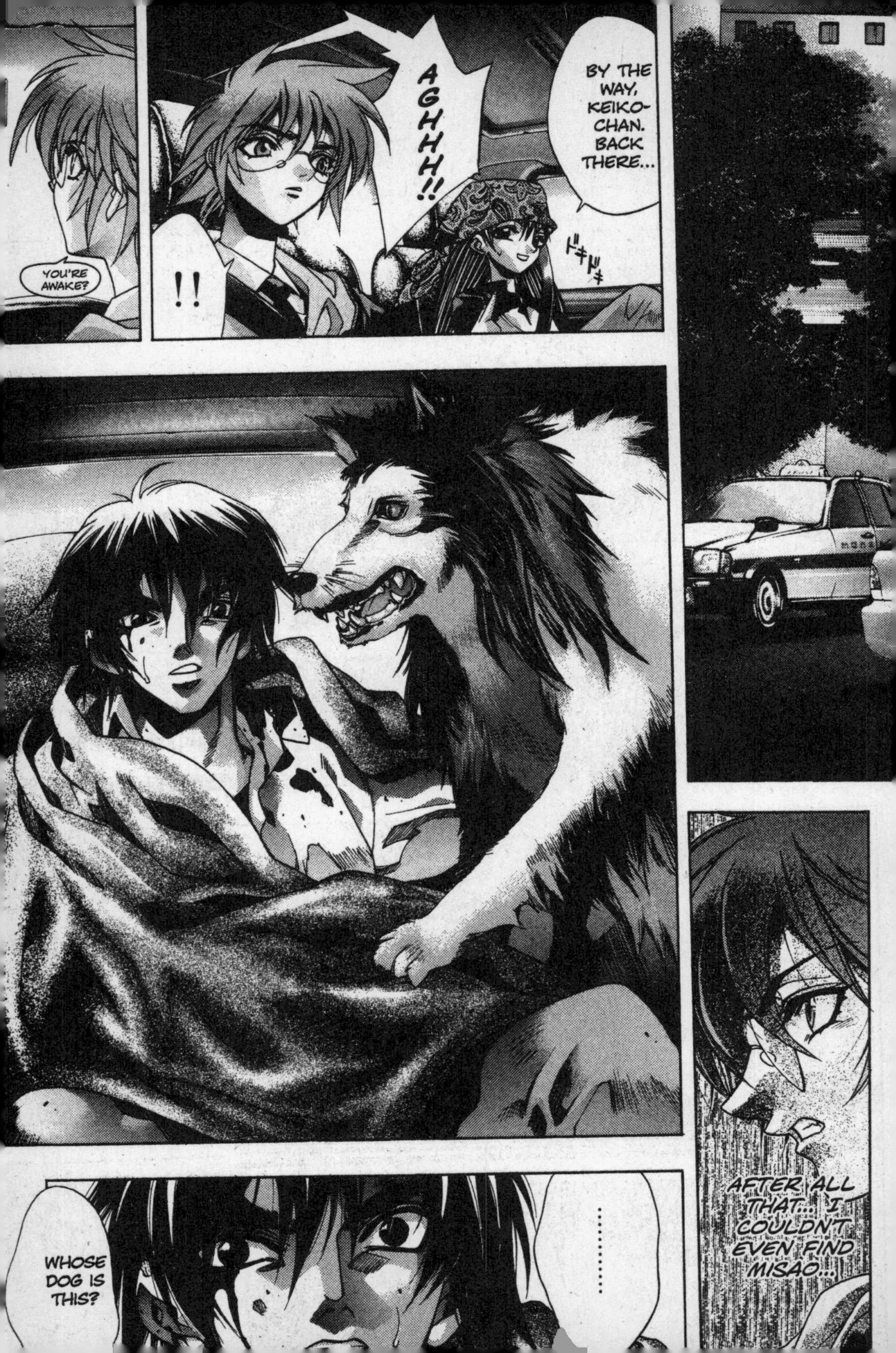
BY THE WAY, KEIKO-CHAN. BACK THERE...
AGHHHH!!
ドキドキ
!!
YOU'RE AWAKE?
AFTER ALL THAT... I COULDN'T EVEN FIND MISAO...
......
WHOSE DOG IS THIS?

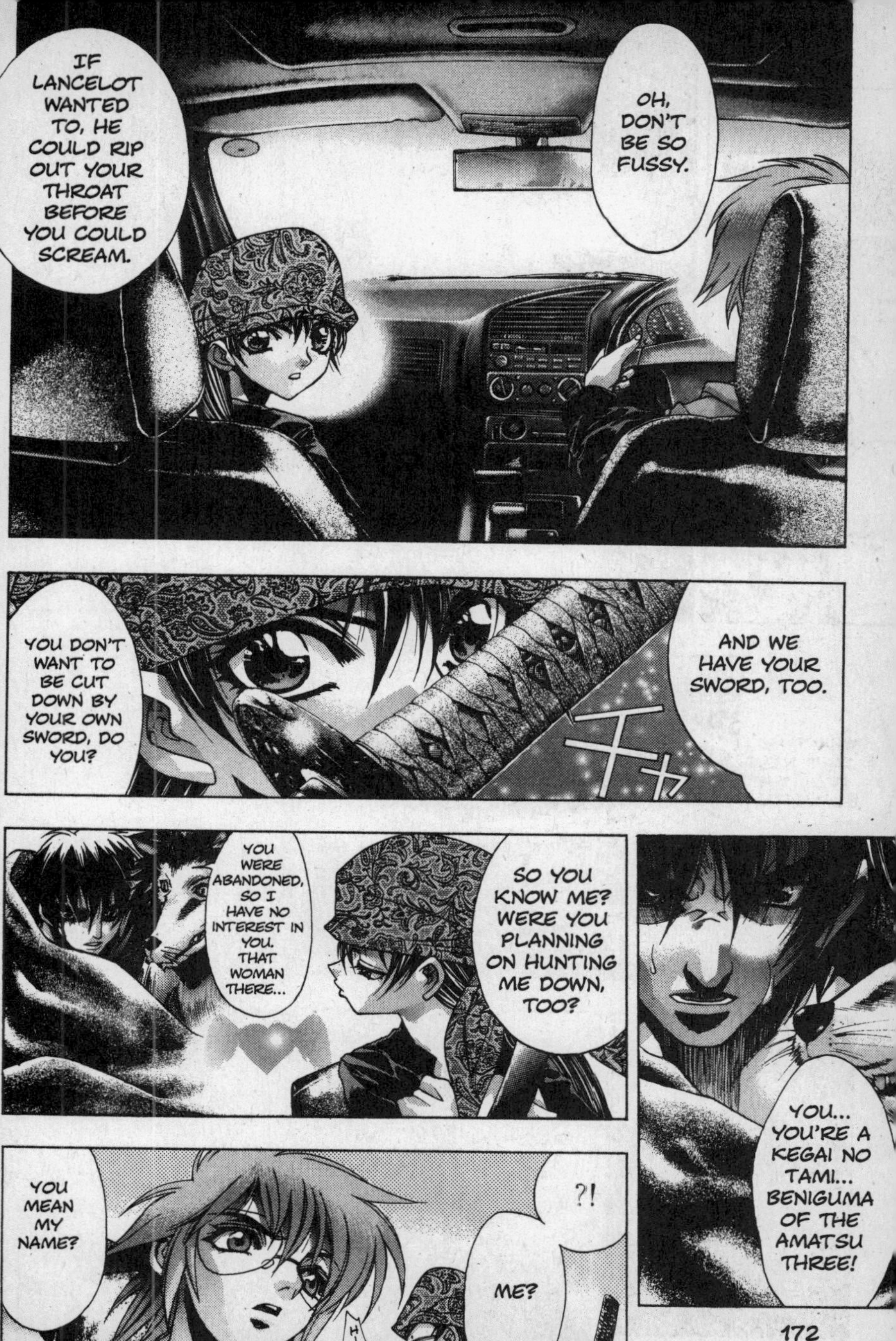
OH, DON'T BE SO FUSSY.
IF LANCELOT WANTED TO, HE COULD RIP OUT YOUR THROAT BEFORE YOU COULD SCREAM.
AND WE HAVE YOUR SWORD, TOO.
YOU DON'T WANT TO BE CUT DOWN BY YOUR OWN SWORD, DO YOU?
YOU... YOU'RE A KEGAI NO TAMI... BENIGUMA OF THE AMATSU THREE!
SO YOU KNOW ME? WERE YOU PLANNING ON HUNTING ME DOWN, TOO?
YOU WERE ABANDONED, SO I HAVE NO INTEREST IN YOU. THAT WOMAN THERE...
?!
ME?
YOU MEAN MY NAME?
HISS

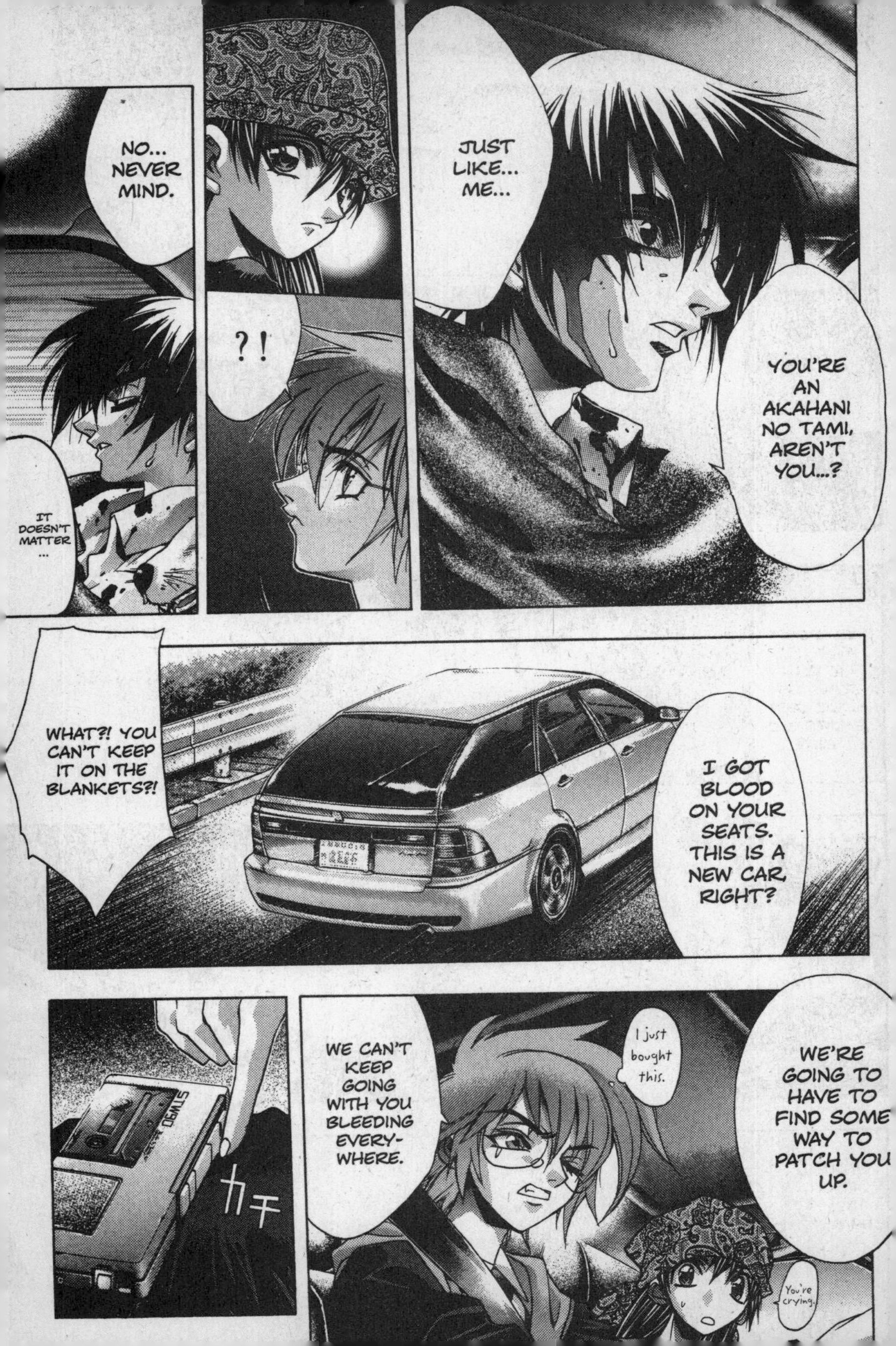
JUST LIKE... ME...
YOU'RE AN AKAHANI NO TAMI, AREN'T YOU...?
NO... NEVER MIND.
?!
IT DOESN'T MATTER ...
I GOT BLOOD ON YOUR SEATS. THIS IS A NEW CAR, RIGHT?
WHAT?! YOU CAN'T KEEP IT ON THE BLANKETS?!
WE'RE GOING TO HAVE TO FIND SOME WAY TO PATCH YOU UP.
I just bought this.
WE CAN'T KEEP GOING WITH YOU BLEEDING EVERY-WHERE.
You're crying.
カチ

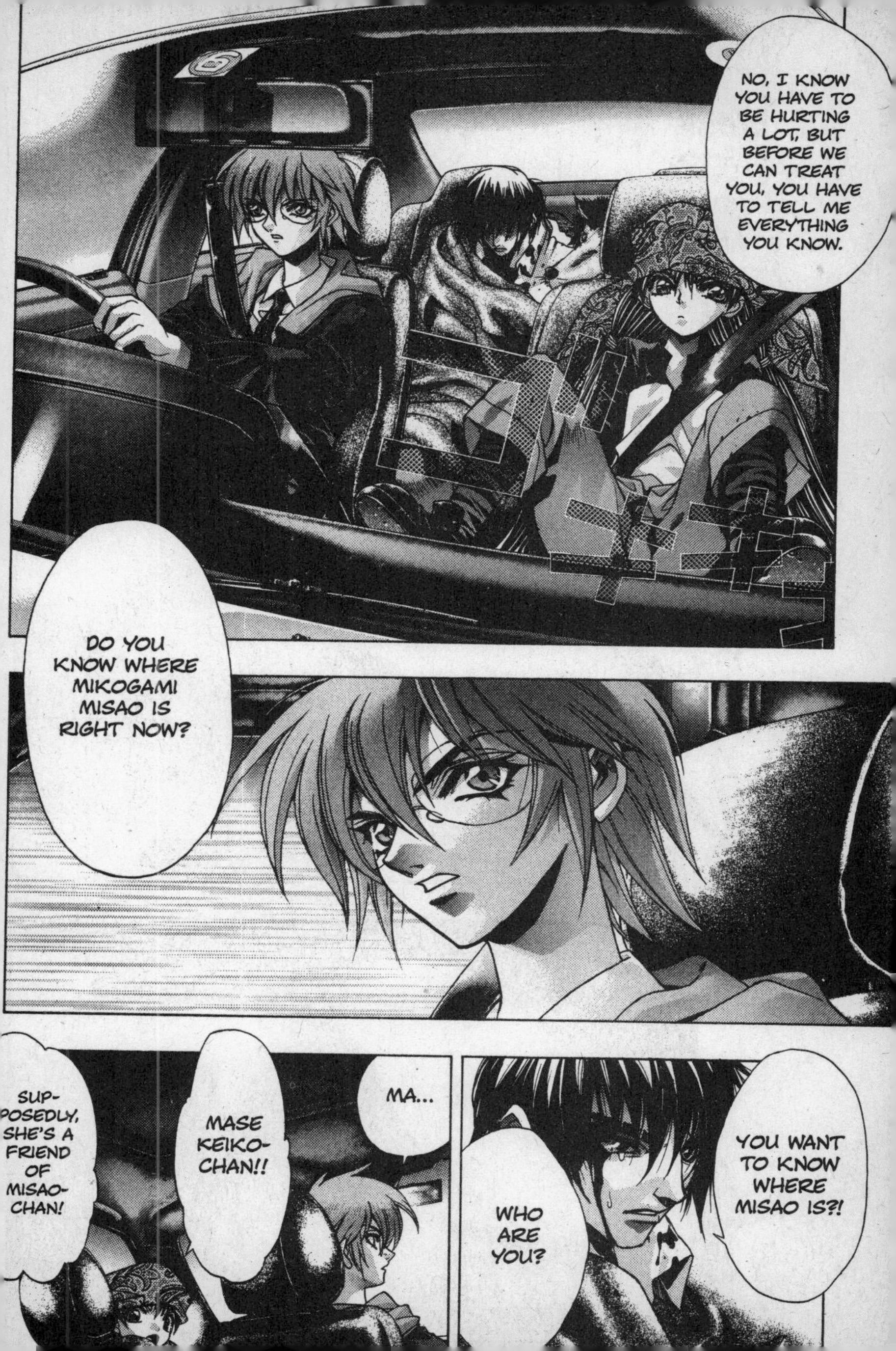

NO, I KNOW YOU HAVE TO BE HURTING A LOT, BUT BEFORE WE CAN TREAT YOU, YOU HAVE TO TELL ME EVERYTHING YOU KNOW.
DO YOU KNOW WHERE MIKOGAMI MISAO IS RIGHT NOW?
YOU WANT TO KNOW WHERE MISAO IS?!
WHO ARE YOU?
MA...
MASE KEIKO-CHAN!!
SUP-POSEDLY, SHE'S A FRIEND OF MISAO-CHAN!

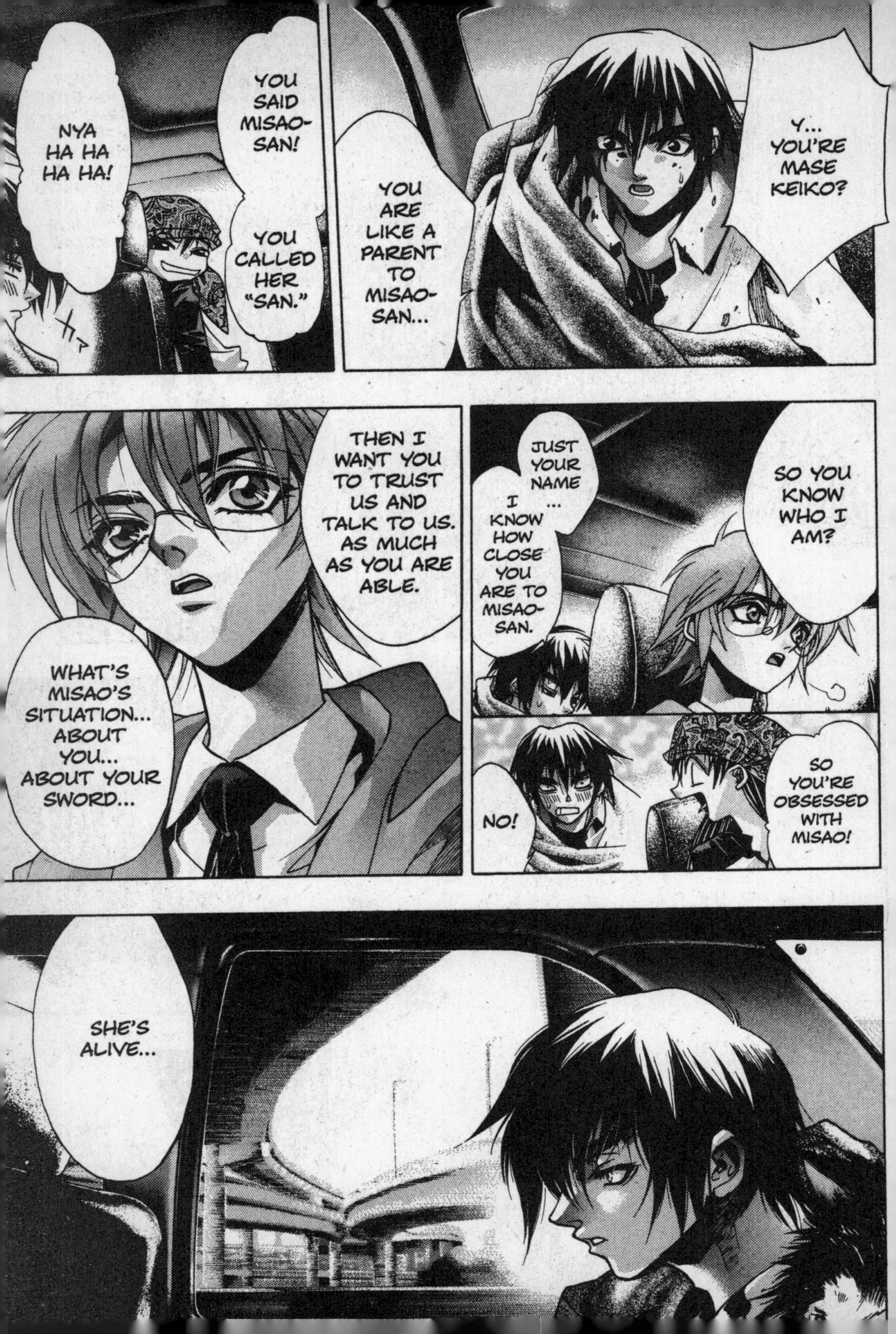
Y... YOU'RE MASE KEIKO?
YOU ARE LIKE A PARENT TO MISAO-SAN...
YOU SAID MISAO-SAN!
YOU CALLED HER "SAN."
NYA HA HA HA HA!
SO YOU KNOW WHO I AM?
JUST YOUR NAME... I KNOW HOW CLOSE YOU ARE TO MISAO-SAN.
SO YOU'RE OBSESSED WITH MISAO!
NO!
THEN I WANT YOU TO TRUST US AND TALK TO US. AS MUCH AS YOU ARE ABLE.
WHAT'S MISAO'S SITUATION... ABOUT YOU... ABOUT YOUR SWORD...
SHE'S ALIVE...

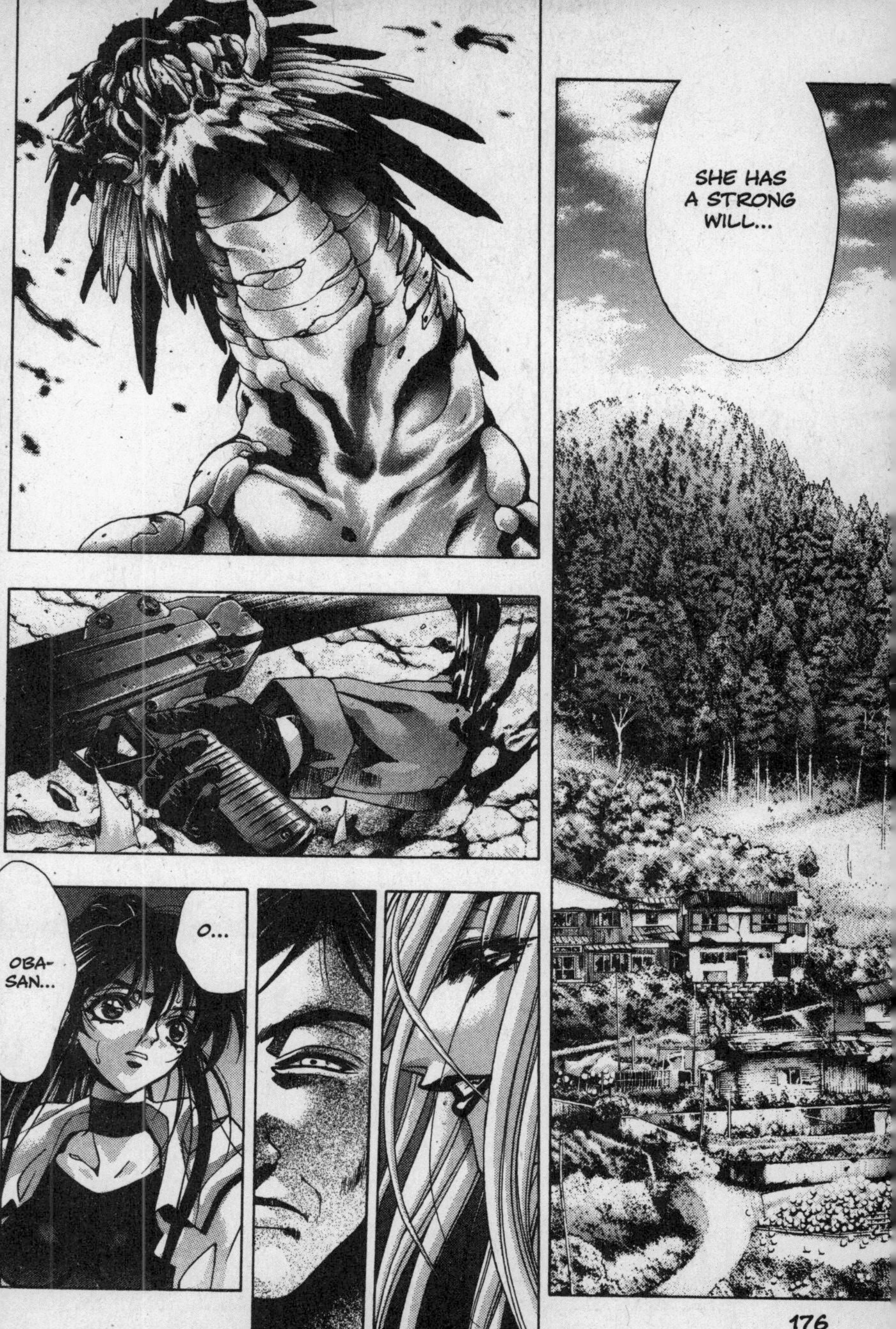
SHE HAS A STRONG WILL...
O...
OBA-SAN...

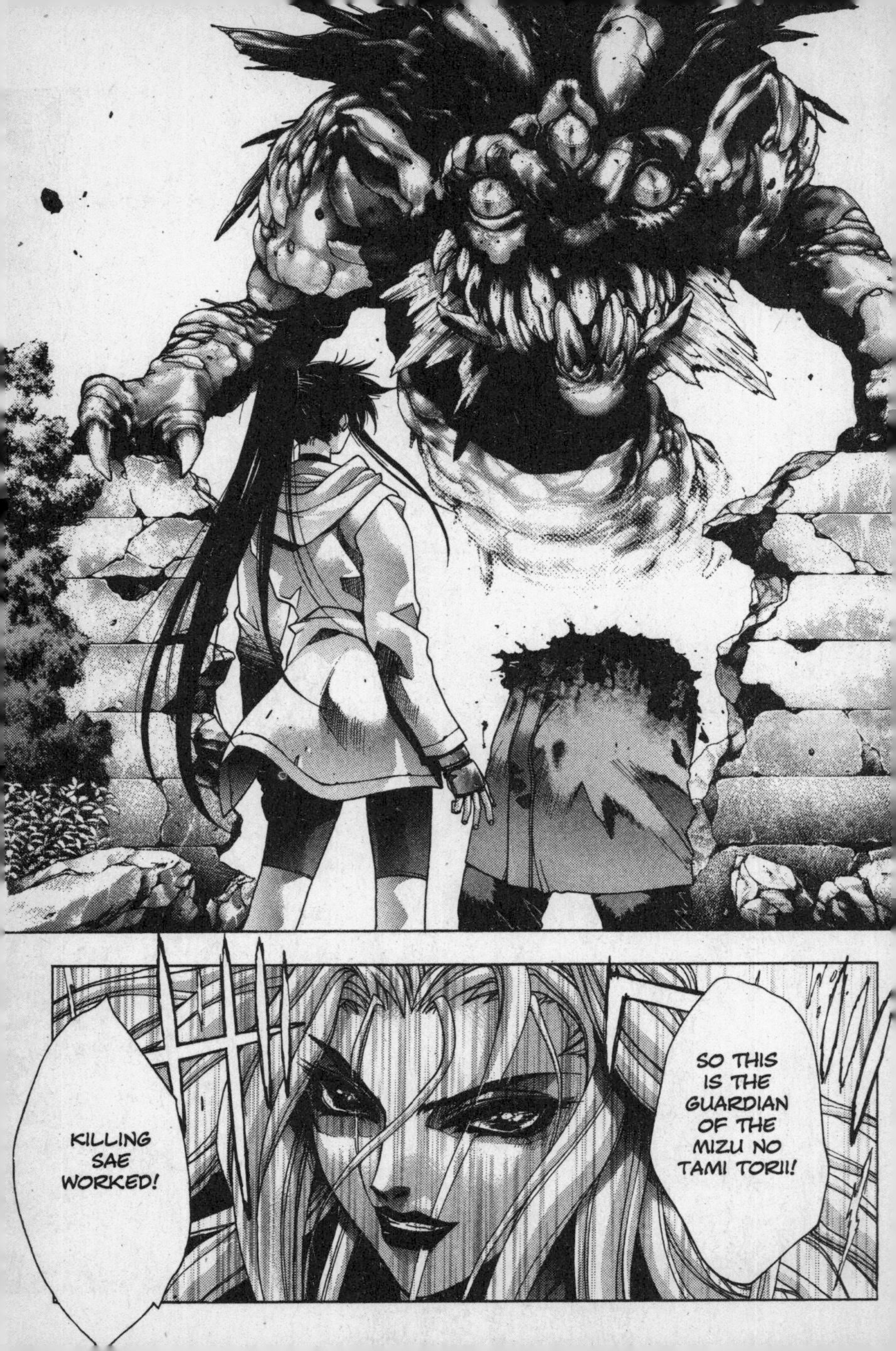
SO THIS IS THE GUARDIAN OF THE MIZU NO TAMI TORII!
KILLING SAE WORKED!

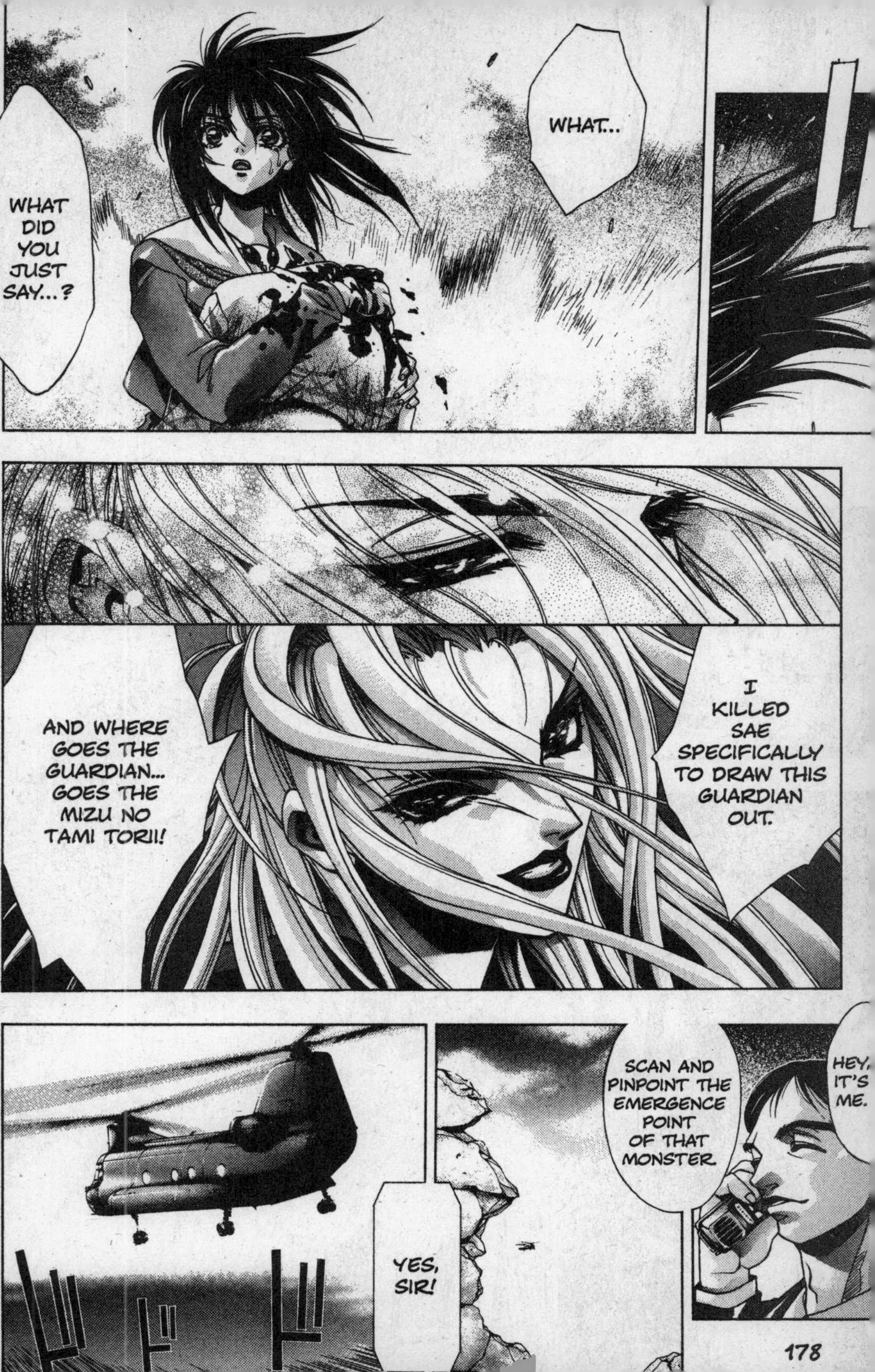
WHAT...
WHAT DID YOU JUST SAY...?
I KILLED SAE SPECIFICALLY TO DRAW THIS GUARDIAN OUT.
AND WHERE GOES THE GUARDIAN... GOES THE MIZU NO TAMI TORII!
HEY, IT'S ME.
SCAN AND PINPOINT THE EMERGENCE POINT OF THAT MONSTER.
YES, SIR!

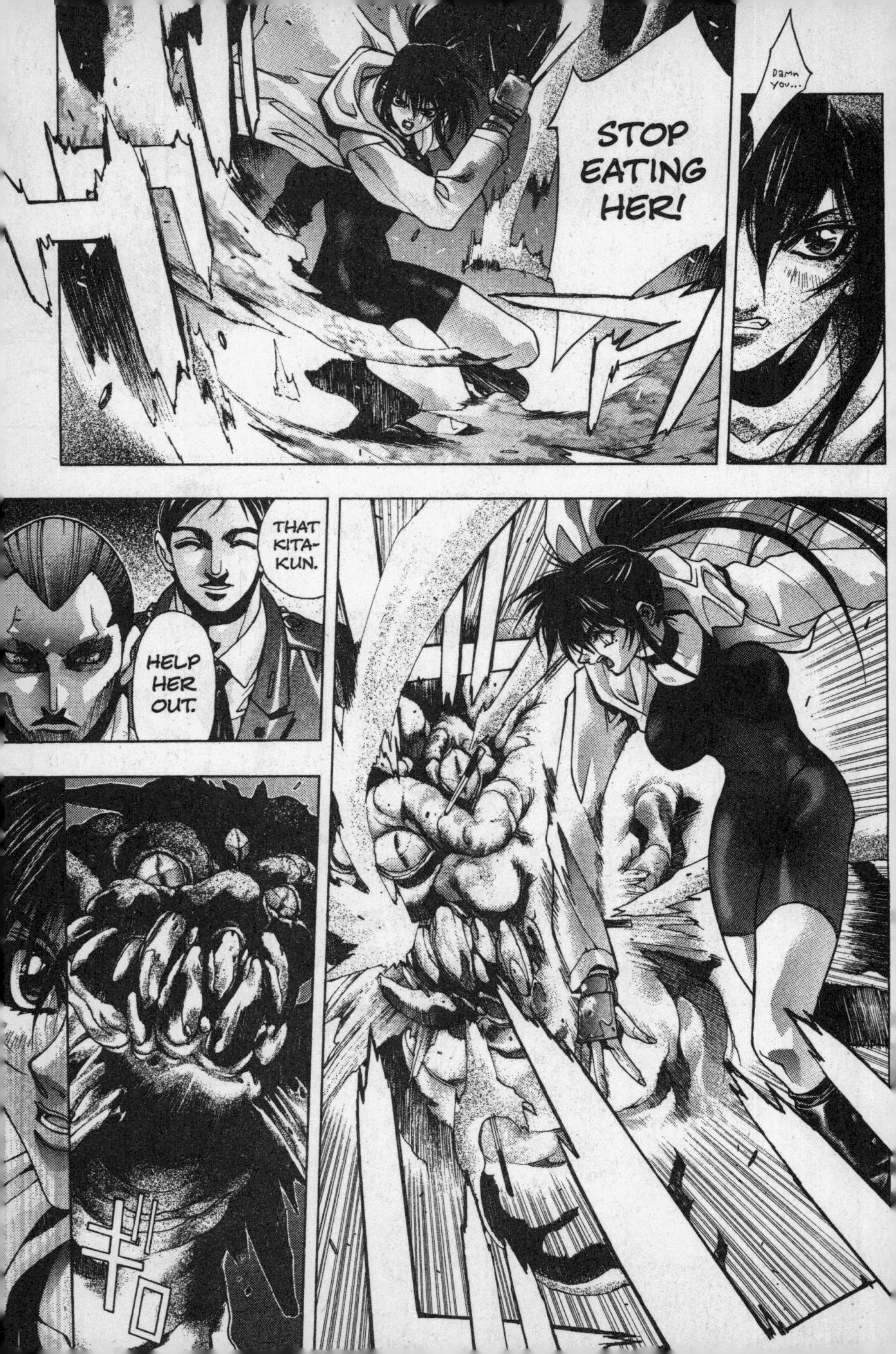
Damn you...
STOP EATING HER!
THAT KITA-KUN.
HELP HER OUT.
ギロ

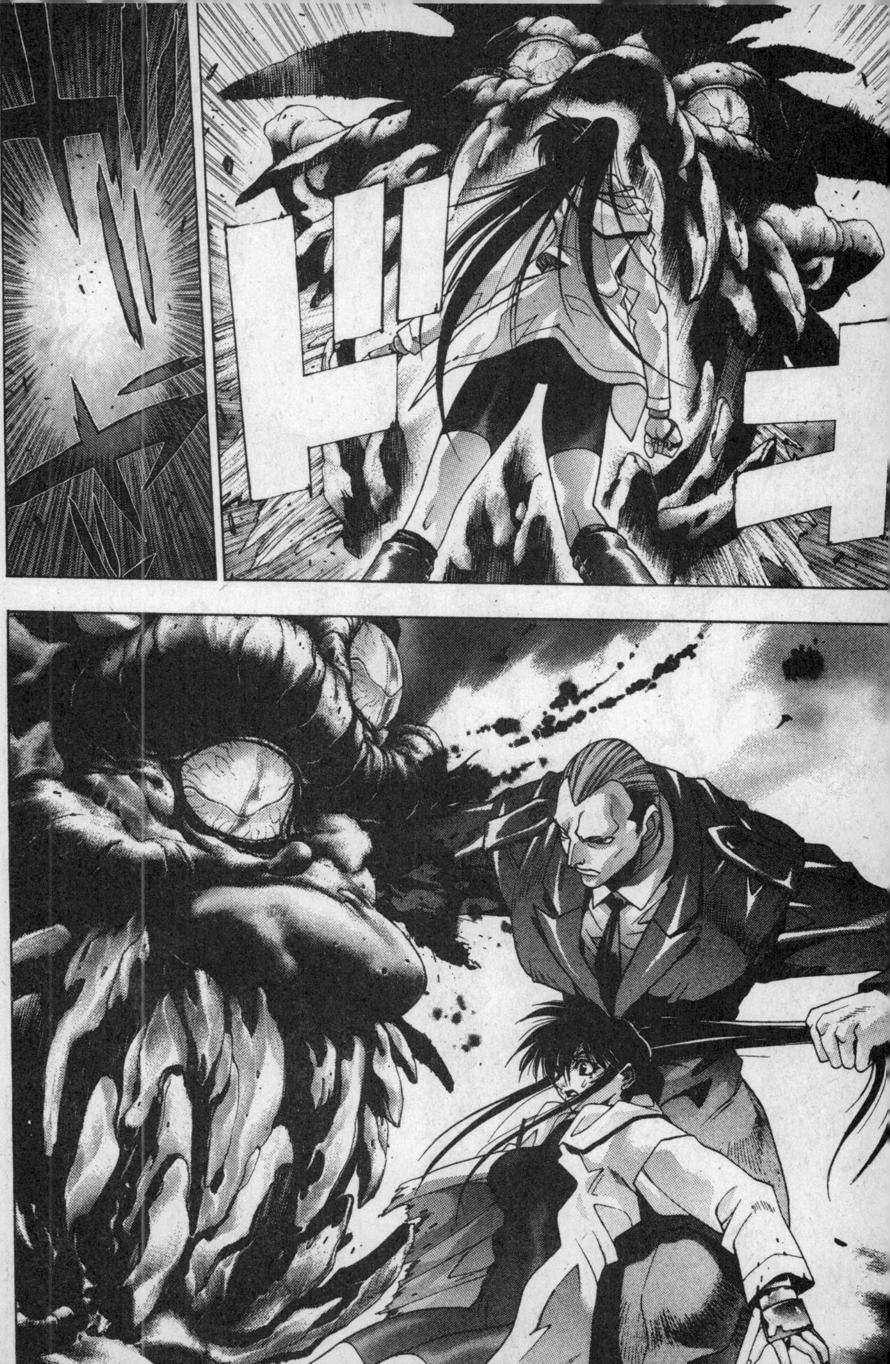

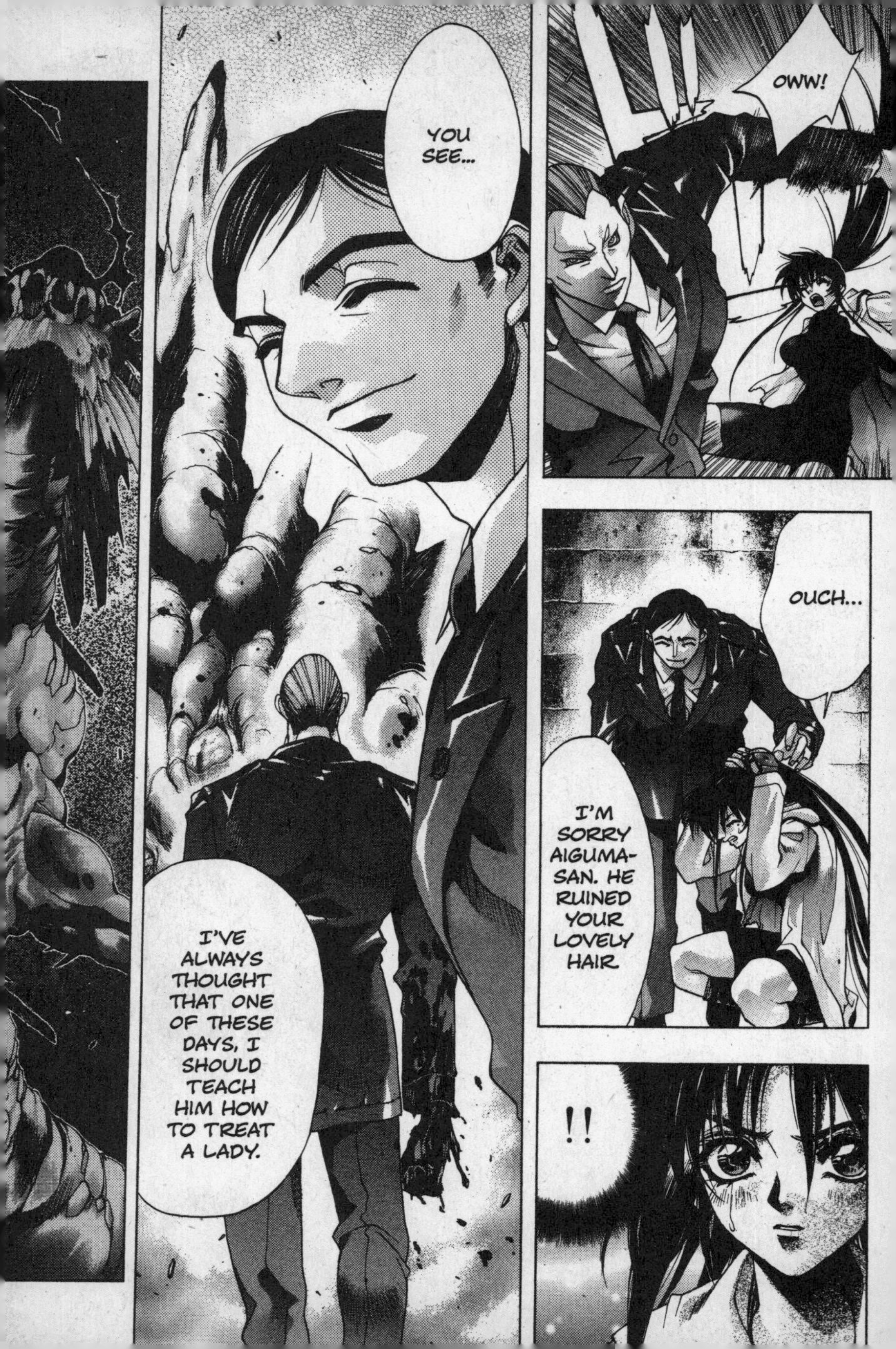
OWW!
OUCH...
I'M SORRY AIGUMA-SAN. HE RUINED YOUR LOVELY HAIR
!!
YOU SEE...
I'VE ALWAYS THOUGHT THAT ONE OF THESE DAYS, I SHOULD TEACH HIM HOW TO TREAT A LADY.

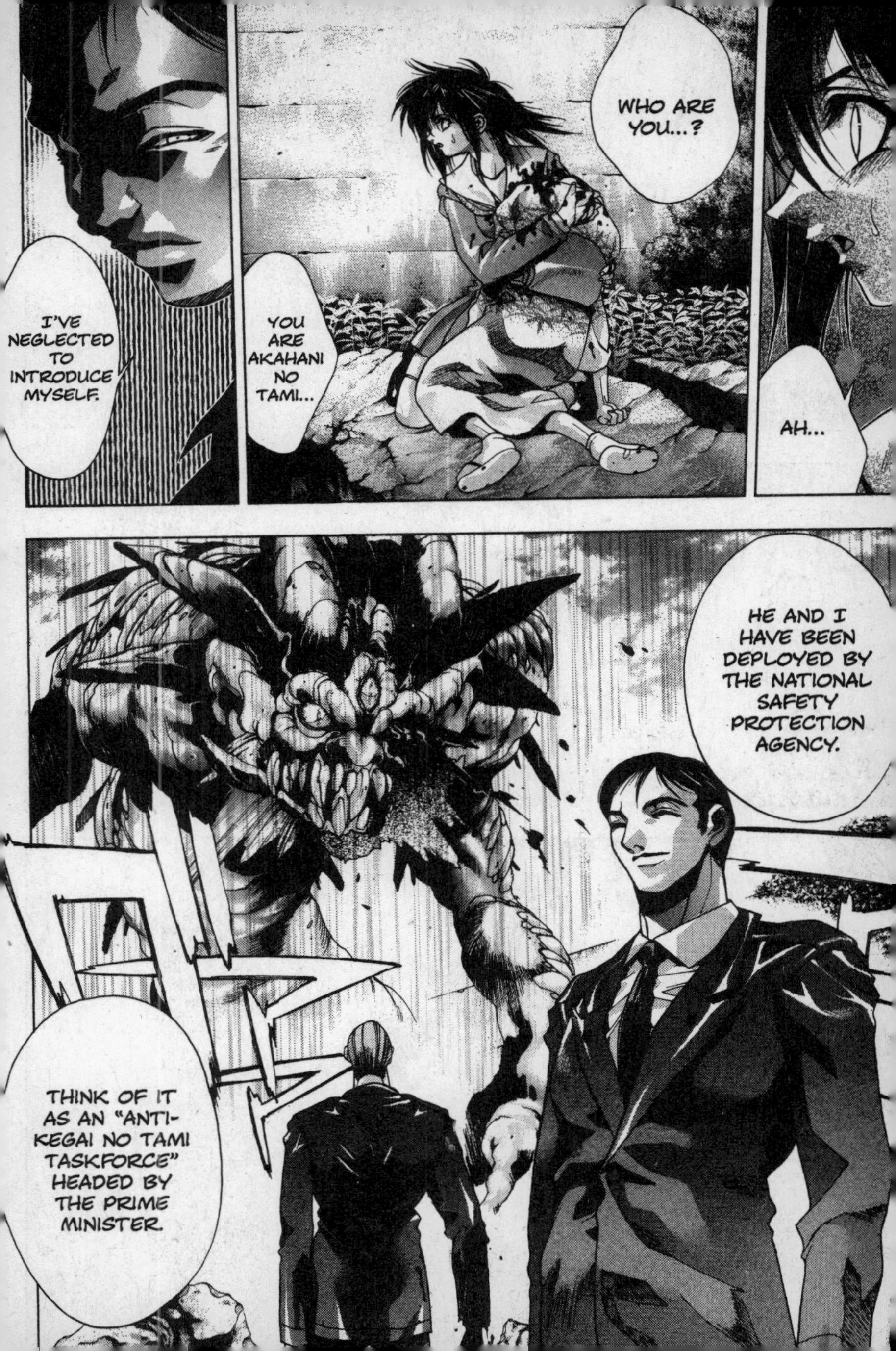
AH...
WHO ARE YOU...?
YOU ARE AKAHANI NO TAMI...
I'VE NEGLECTED TO INTRODUCE MYSELF.
HE AND I HAVE BEEN DEPLOYED BY THE NATIONAL SAFETY PROTECTION AGENCY.
THINK OF IT AS AN "ANTI-KEGAI NO TAMI TASKFORCE" HEADED BY THE PRIME MINISTER.

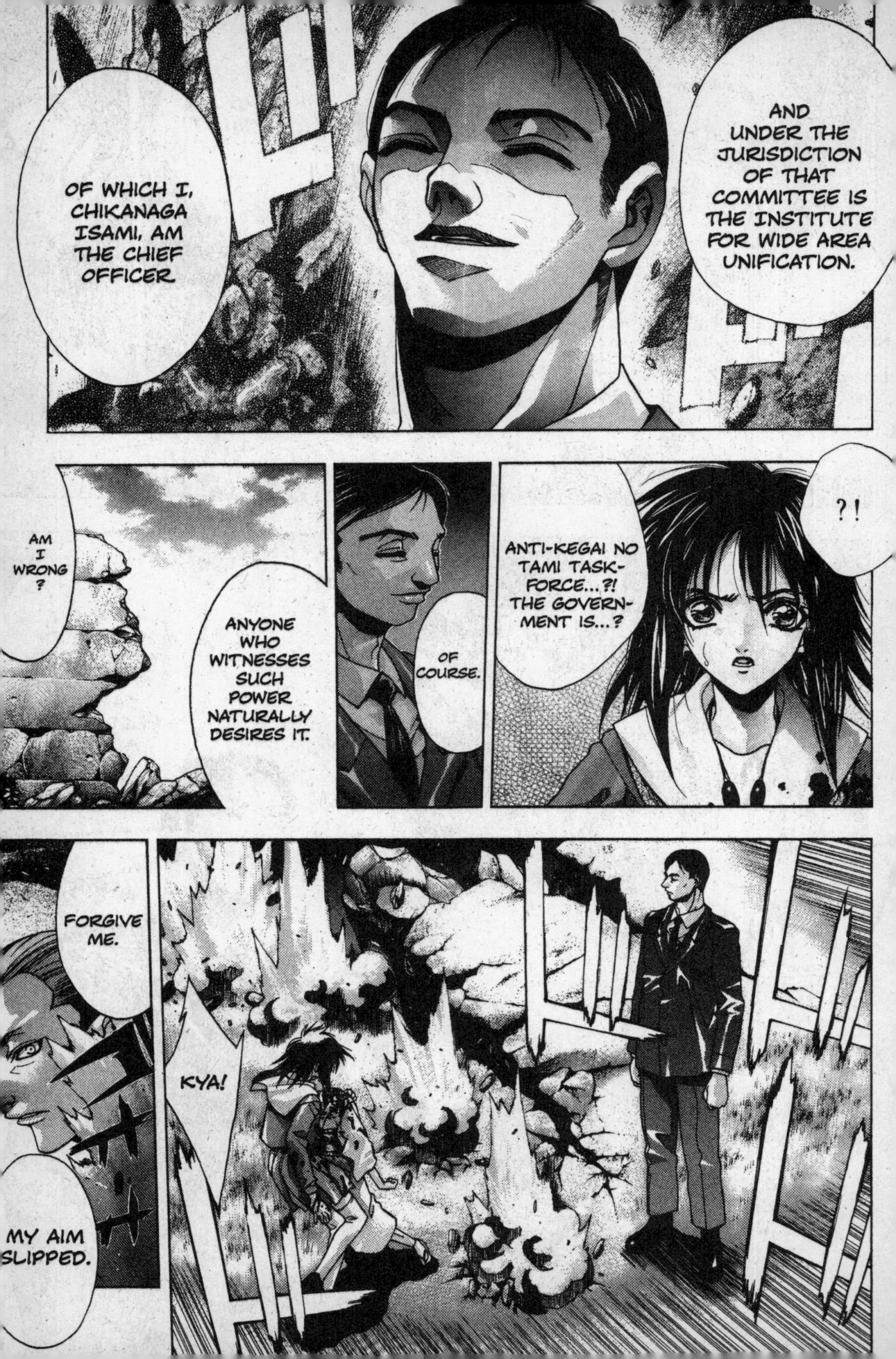
AND UNDER THE JURISDICTION OF THAT COMMITTEE IS THE INSTITUTE FOR WIDE AREA UNIFICATION.
OF WHICH I, CHIKANAGA ISAMI, AM THE CHIEF OFFICER
?!
ANTI-KEGAI NO TAMI TASK-FORCE...?! THE GOVERNMENT IS...?
OF COURSE.
ANYONE WHO WITNESSES SUCH POWER NATURALLY DESIRES IT.
AM I WRONG?
KYA!
FORGIVE ME.
MY AIM SLIPPED.

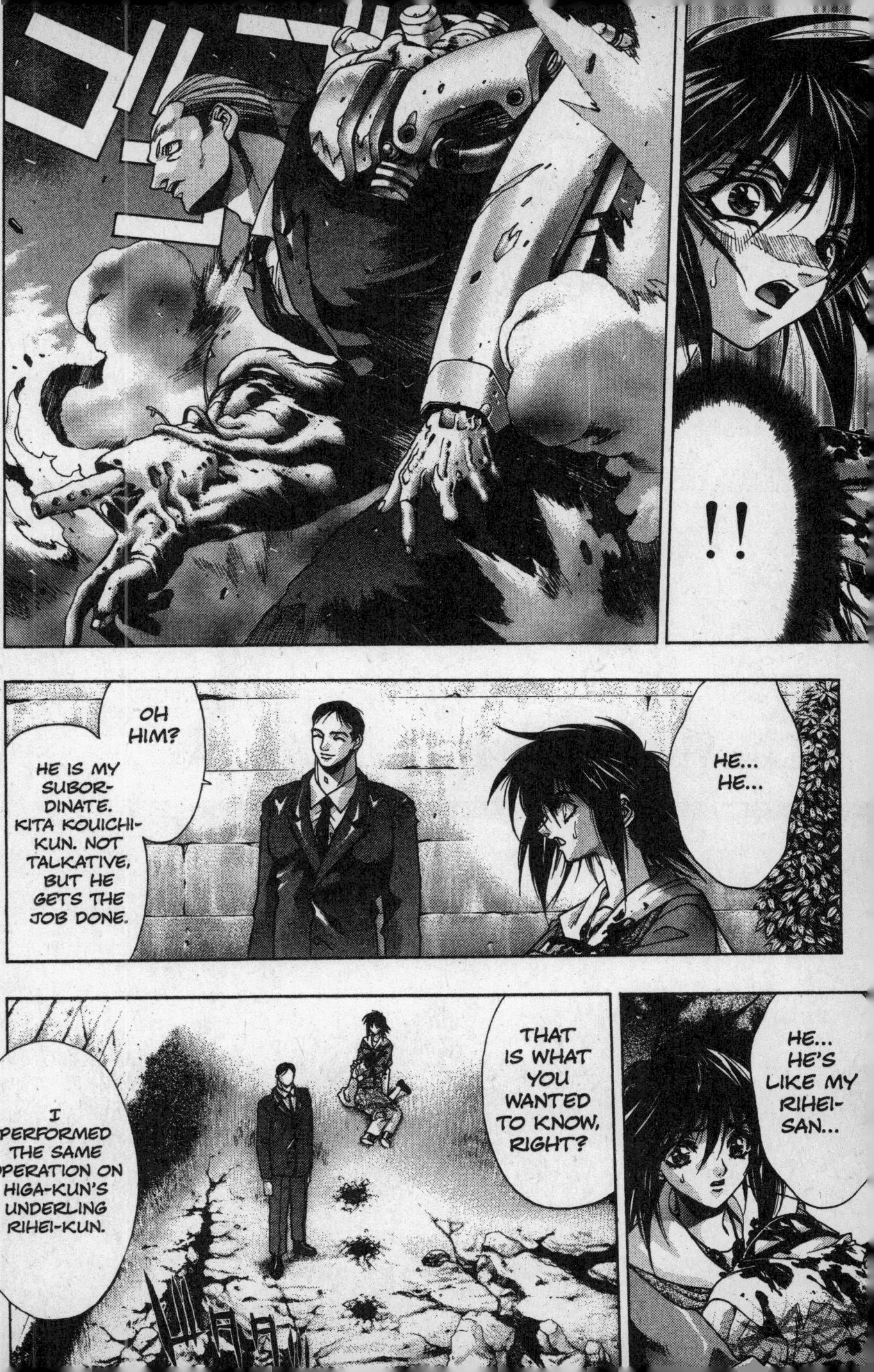
!!
HE... HE...
OH HIM?
HE IS MY SUBOR-DINATE. KITA KOUICHI-KUN. NOT TALKATIVE, BUT HE GETS THE JOB DONE.
HE... HE'S LIKE MY RIHEI-SAN...
THAT IS WHAT YOU WANTED TO KNOW, RIGHT?
I PERFORMED THE SAME OPERATION ON HIGA-KUN'S UNDERLING RIHEI-KUN.

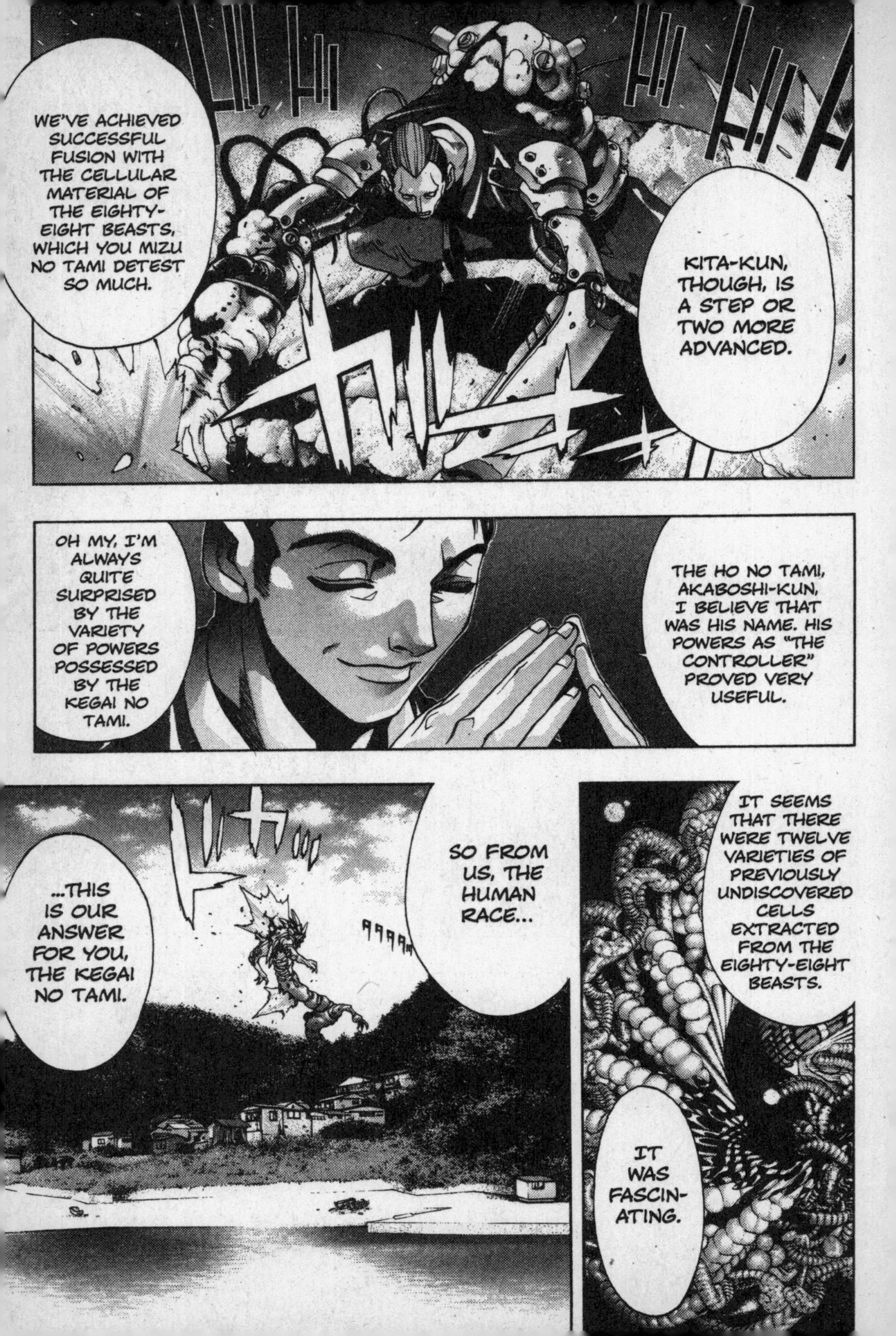
WE'VE ACHIEVED SUCCESSFUL FUSION WITH THE CELLULAR MATERIAL OF THE EIGHTY-EIGHT BEASTS, WHICH YOU MIZU NO TAMI DETEST SO MUCH.
KITA-KUN, THOUGH, IS A STEP OR TWO MORE ADVANCED.
THE HO NO TAMI, AKABOSHI-KUN, I BELIEVE THAT WAS HIS NAME. HIS POWERS AS "THE CONTROLLER" PROVED VERY USEFUL.
OH MY, I'M ALWAYS QUITE SURPRISED BY THE VARIETY OF POWERS POSSESSED BY THE KEGAI NO TAMI.
IT SEEMS THAT THERE WERE TWELVE VARIETIES OF PREVIOUSLY UNDISCOVERED CELLS EXTRACTED FROM THE EIGHTY-EIGHT BEASTS.
IT WAS FASCINATING.
SO FROM US, THE HUMAN RACE...
...THIS IS OUR ANSWER FOR YOU, THE KEGAI NO TAMI.

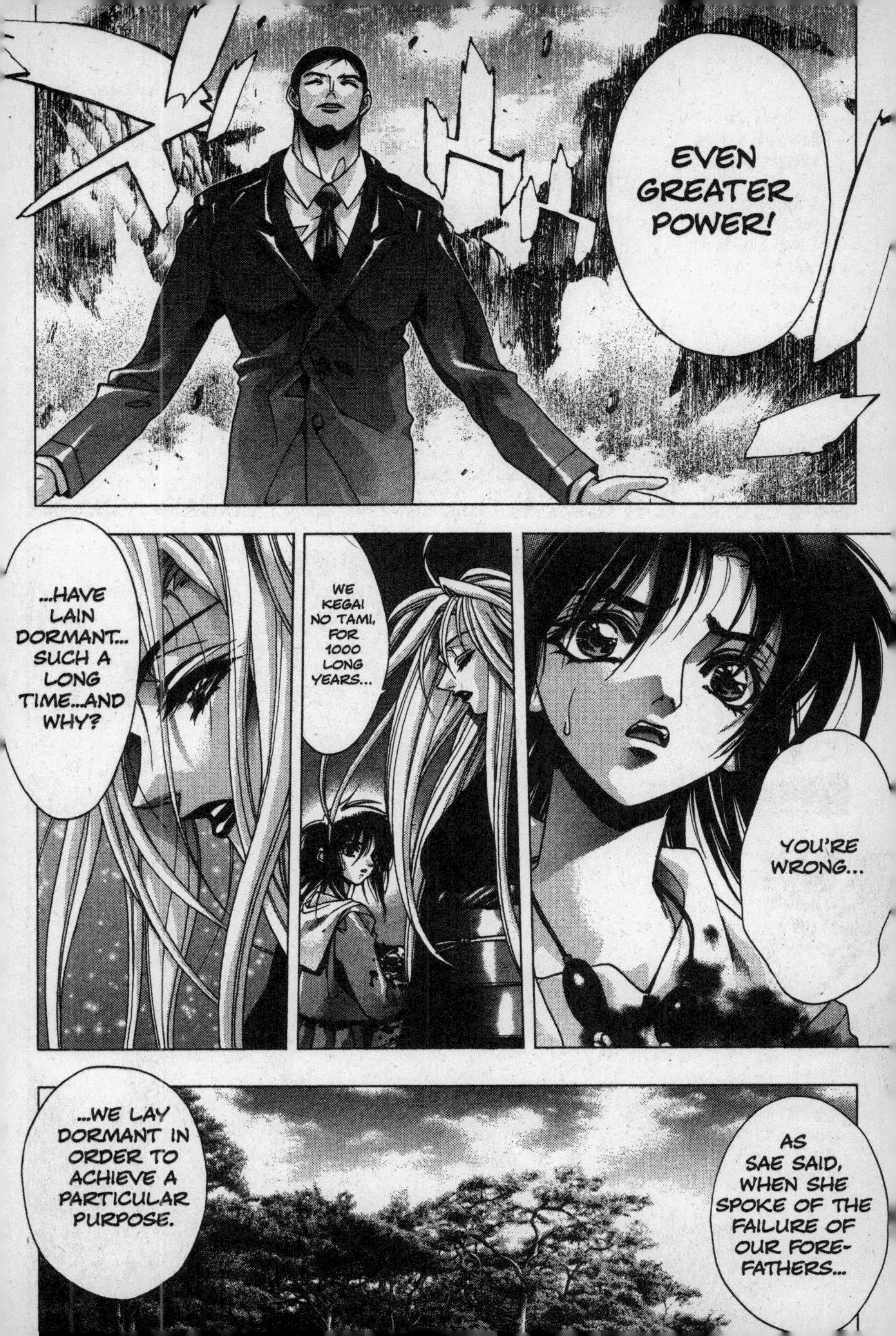
EVEN GREATER POWER!
YOU'RE WRONG...
WE KEGAI NO TAMI, FOR 1000 LONG YEARS...
...HAVE LAIN DORMANT... SUCH A LONG TIME...AND WHY?
AS SAE SAID, WHEN SHE SPOKE OF THE FAILURE OF OUR FORE-FATHERS...
...WE LAY DORMANT IN ORDER TO ACHIEVE A PARTICULAR PURPOSE.

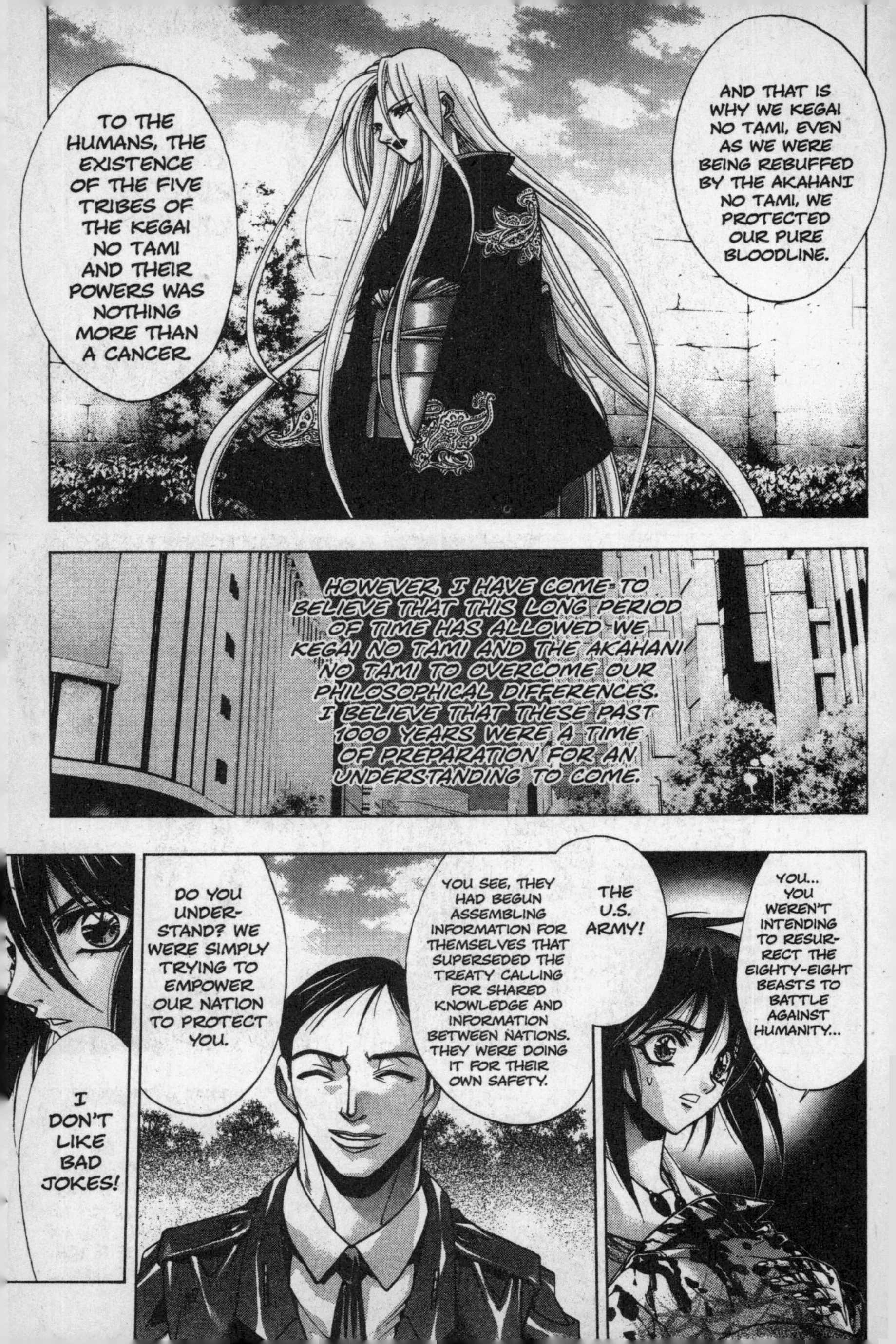
TO THE HUMANS, THE EXISTENCE OF THE FIVE TRIBES OF THE KEGAI NO TAMI AND THEIR POWERS WAS NOTHING MORE THAN A CANCER.
AND THAT IS WHY WE KEGAI NO TAMI, EVEN AS WE WERE BEING REBUFFED BY THE AKAHANI NO TAMI, WE PROTECTED OUR PURE BLOODLINE.
HOWEVER, I HAVE COME TO BELIEVE THAT THIS LONG PERIOD OF TIME HAS ALLOWED WE KEGAI NO TAMI AND THE AKAHANI NO TAMI TO OVERCOME OUR PHILOSOPHICAL DIFFERENCES. I BELIEVE THAT THESE PAST 1000 YEARS WERE A TIME OF PREPARATION FOR AN UNDERSTANDING TO COME.
YOU... YOU WEREN'T INTENDING TO RESURRECT THE EIGHTY-EIGHT BEASTS TO BATTLE AGAINST HUMANITY...
THE U.S. ARMY!
YOU SEE, THEY HAD BEGUN ASSEMBLING INFORMATION FOR THEMSELVES THAT SUPERSEDED THE TREATY CALLING FOR SHARED KNOWLEDGE AND INFORMATION BETWEEN NATIONS. THEY WERE DOING IT FOR THEIR OWN SAFETY.
DO YOU UNDERSTAND? WE WERE SIMPLY TRYING TO EMPOWER OUR NATION TO PROTECT YOU.
I DON'T LIKE BAD JOKES!

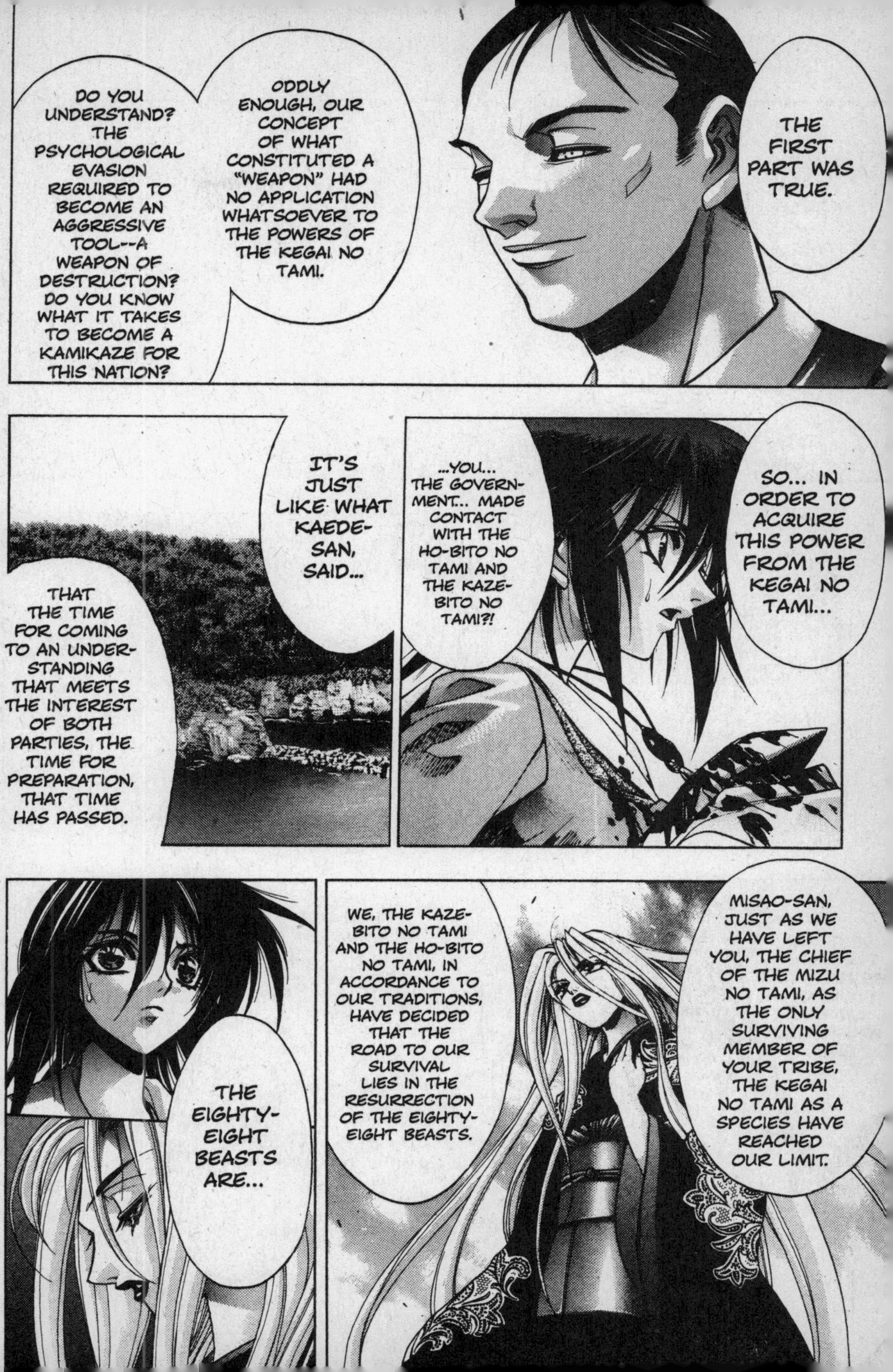
THE FIRST PART WAS TRUE.
ODDLY ENOUGH, OUR CONCEPT OF WHAT CONSTITUTED A "WEAPON" HAD NO APPLICATION WHATSOEVER TO THE POWERS OF THE KEGAI NO TAMI.
DO YOU UNDERSTAND? THE PSYCHOLOGICAL EVASION REQUIRED TO BECOME AN AGGRESSIVE TOOL--A WEAPON OF DESTRUCTION? DO YOU KNOW WHAT IT TAKES TO BECOME A KAMIKAZE FOR THIS NATION?
SO... IN ORDER TO ACQUIRE THIS POWER FROM THE KEGAI NO TAMI...
...YOU... THE GOVERNMENT... MADE CONTACT WITH THE HO-BITO NO TAMI AND THE KAZE-BITO NO TAMI?!
IT'S JUST LIKE WHAT KAEDE-SAN, SAID...
THAT THE TIME FOR COMING TO AN UNDERSTANDING THAT MEETS THE INTEREST OF BOTH PARTIES, THE TIME FOR PREPARATION, THAT TIME HAS PASSED.
MISAO-SAN, JUST AS WE HAVE LEFT YOU, THE CHIEF OF THE MIZU NO TAMI, AS THE ONLY SURVIVING MEMBER OF YOUR TRIBE, THE KEGAI NO TAMI AS A SPECIES HAVE REACHED OUR LIMIT.
WE, THE KAZE-BITO NO TAMI AND THE HO-BITO NO TAMI, IN ACCORDANCE TO OUR TRADITIONS, HAVE DECIDED THAT THE ROAD TO OUR SURVIVAL LIES IN THE RESURRECTION OF THE EIGHTY-EIGHT BEASTS.
THE EIGHTY-EIGHT BEASTS ARE...

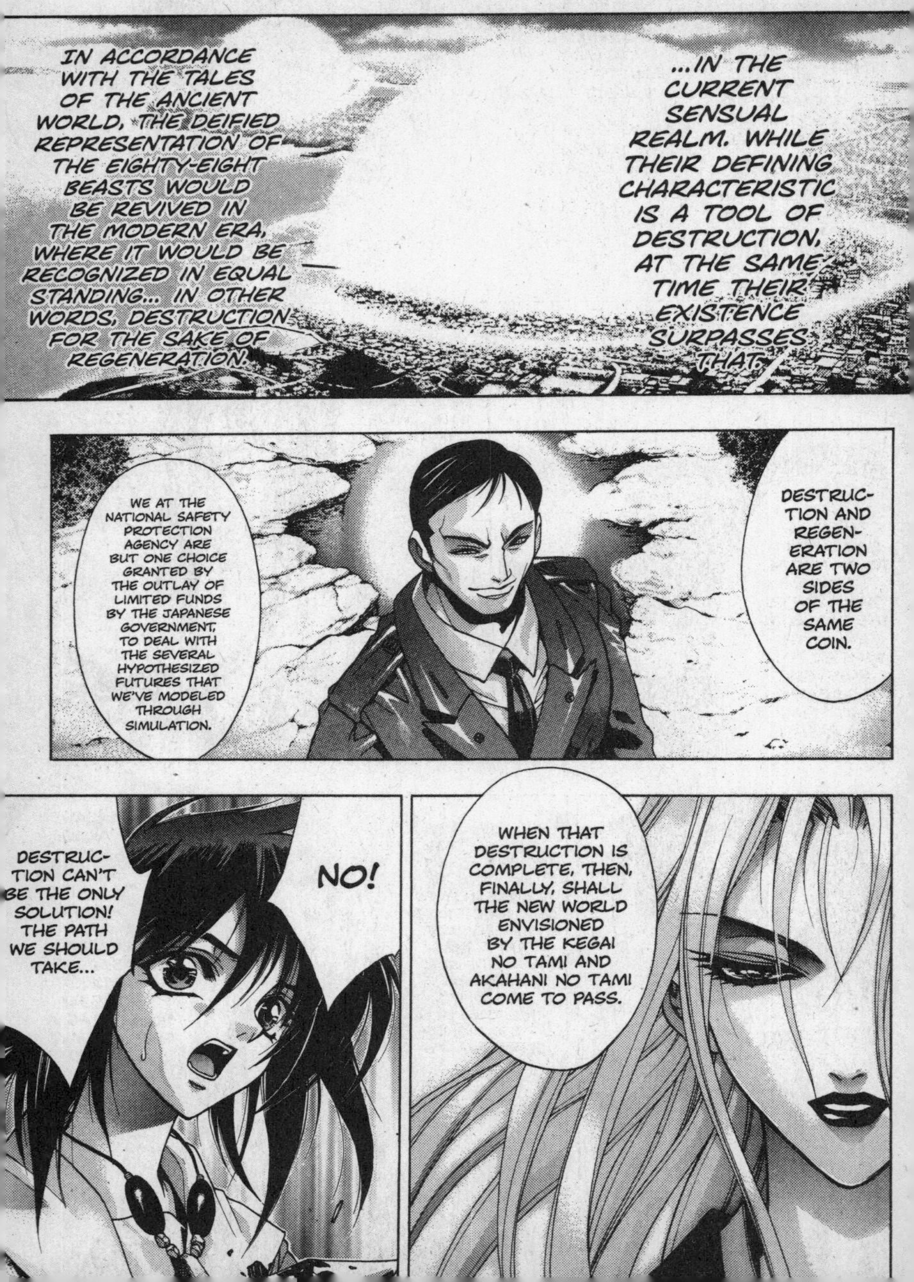
IN ACCORDANCE WITH THE TALES OF THE ANCIENT WORLD, THE DEIFIED REPRESENTATION OF THE EIGHTY-EIGHT BEASTS WOULD BE REVIVED IN THE MODERN ERA, WHERE IT WOULD BE RECOGNIZED IN EQUAL STANDING... IN OTHER WORDS, DESTRUCTION FOR THE SAKE OF REGENERATION.
...IN THE CURRENT SENSUAL REALM. WHILE THEIR DEFINING CHARACTERISTIC IS A TOOL OF DESTRUCTION, AT THE SAME TIME THEIR EXISTENCE SURPASSES THAT.
DESTRUCTION AND REGENERATION ARE TWO SIDES OF THE SAME COIN.
WE AT THE NATIONAL SAFETY PROTECTION AGENCY ARE BUT ONE CHOICE GRANTED BY THE OUTLAY OF LIMITED FUNDS BY THE JAPANESE GOVERNMENT, TO DEAL WITH THE SEVERAL HYPOTHESIZED FUTURES THAT WE'VE MODELED THROUGH SIMULATION.
WHEN THAT DESTRUCTION IS COMPLETE, THEN, FINALLY, SHALL THE NEW WORLD ENVISIONED BY THE KEGAI NO TAMI AND AKAHANI NO TAMI COME TO PASS.
NO!
DESTRUCTION CAN'T BE THE ONLY SOLUTION! THE PATH WE SHOULD TAKE...

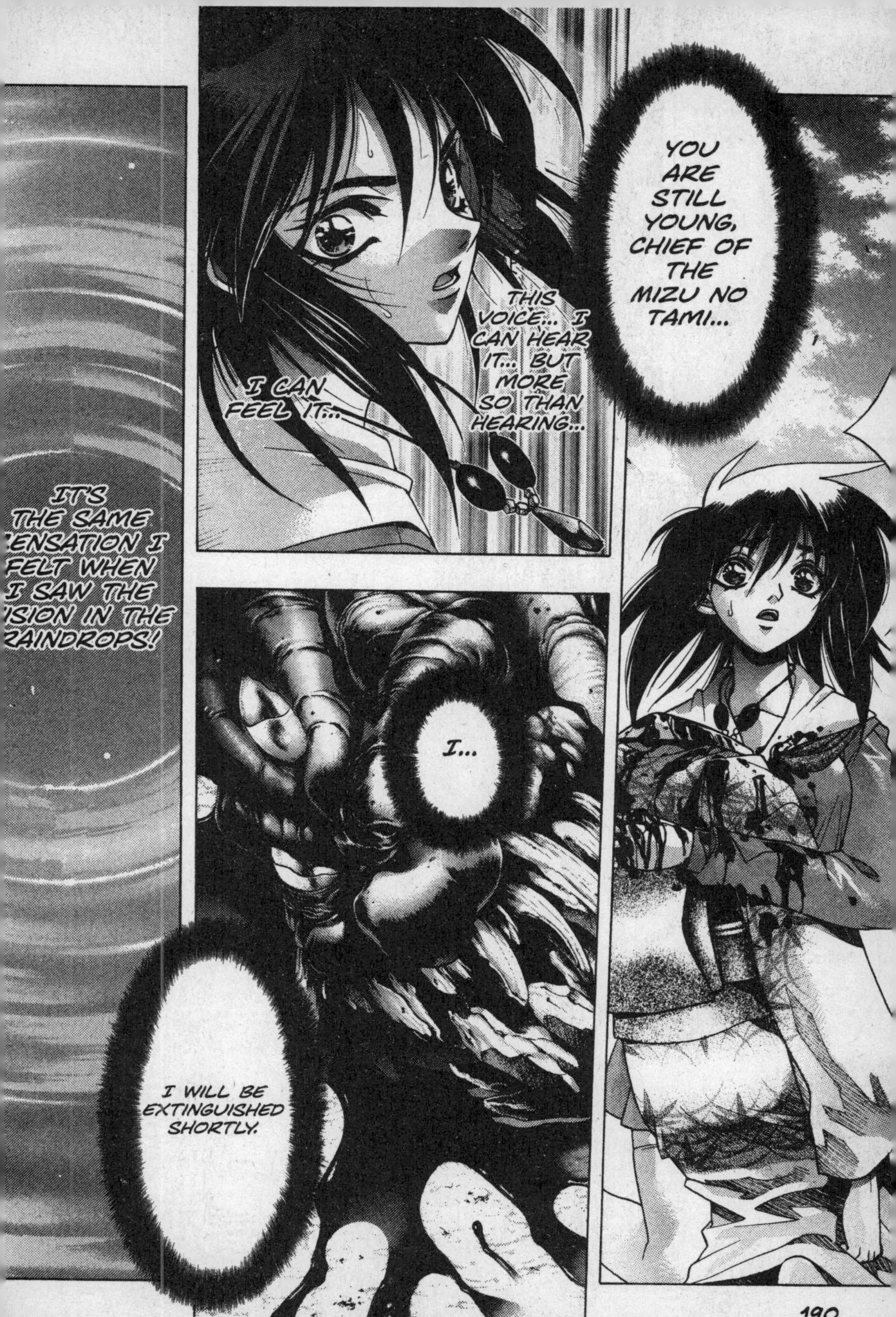
YOU ARE STILL YOUNG, CHIEF OF THE MIZU NO TAMI...
THIS VOICE... I CAN HEAR IT... BUT MORE SO THAN HEARING...
I CAN FEEL IT...
I...
I WILL BE EXTINGUISHED SHORTLY.
IT'S THE SAME ENSATION I FELT WHEN I SAW THE ISION IN THE RAINDROPS!

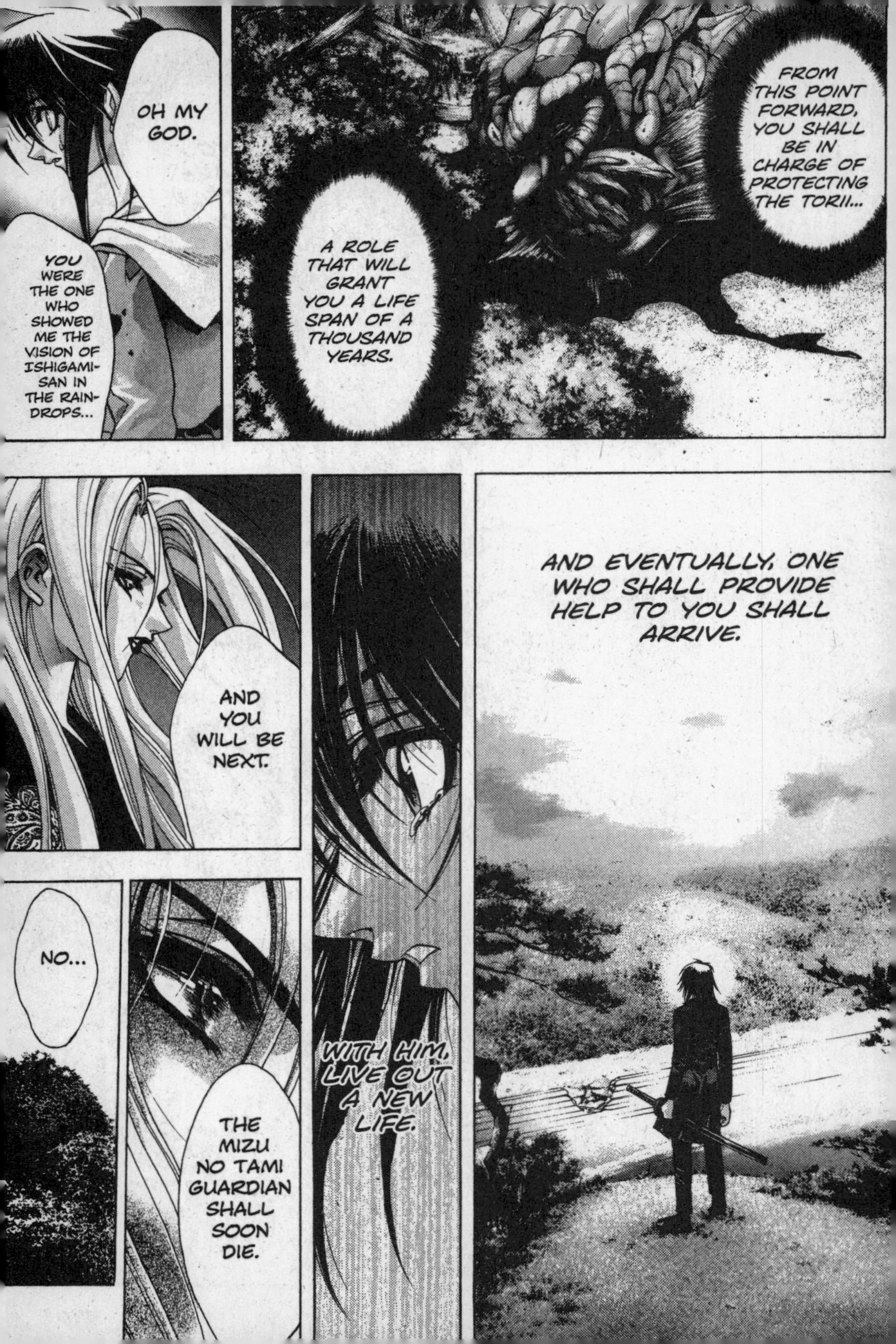
FROM THIS POINT FORWARD, YOU SHALL BE IN CHARGE OF PROTECTING THE TORII...
A ROLE THAT WILL GRANT YOU A LIFE SPAN OF A THOUSAND YEARS.
OH MY GOD.
YOU WERE THE ONE WHO SHOWED ME THE VISION OF ISHIGAMI-SAN IN THE RAIN-DROPS...
AND EVENTUALLY, ONE WHO SHALL PROVIDE HELP TO YOU SHALL ARRIVE.
WITH HIM, LIVE OUT A NEW LIFE.
AND YOU WILL BE NEXT.
THE MIZU NO TAMI GUARDIAN SHALL SOON DIE.
NO...

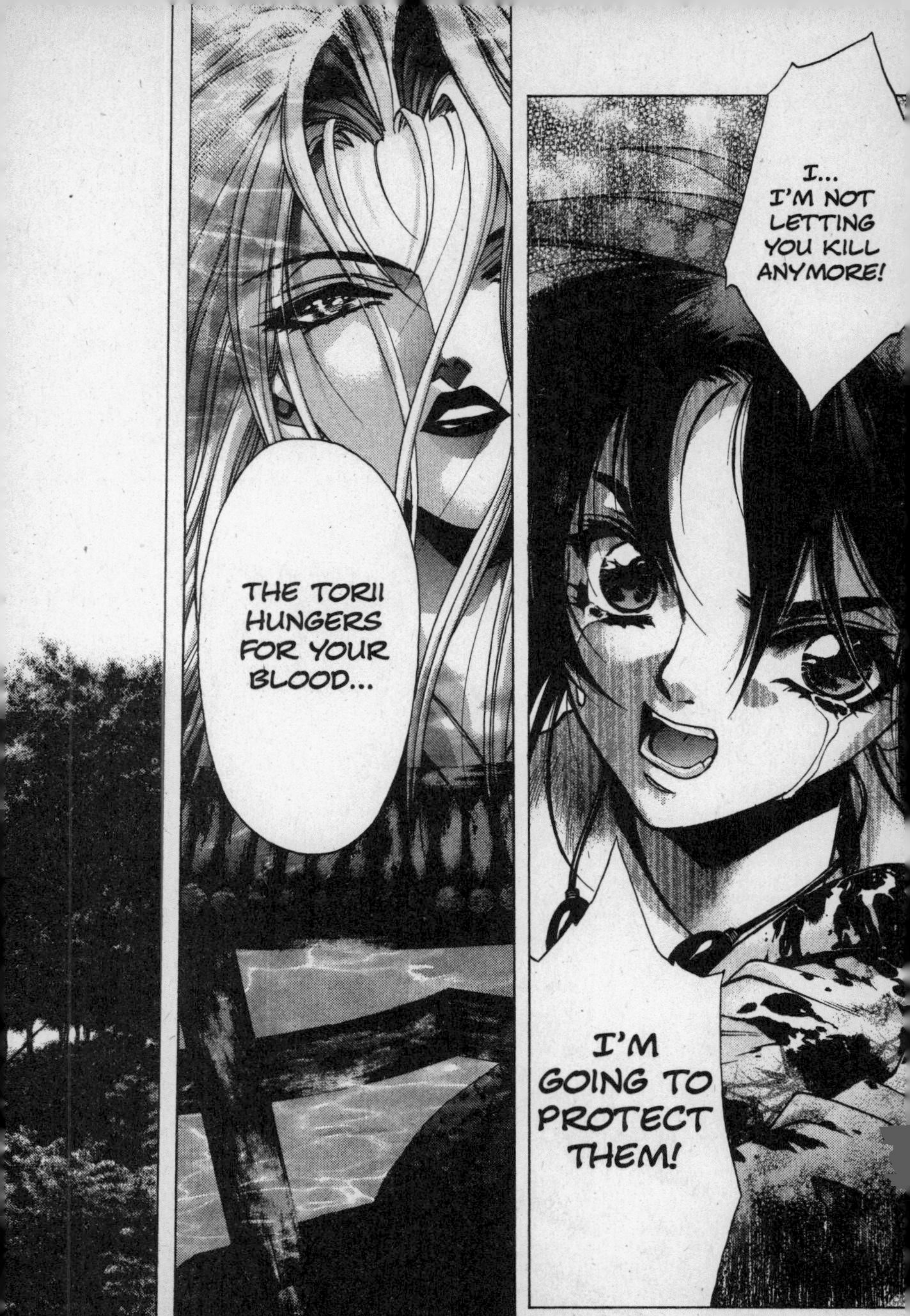
I... I'M NOT LETTING YOU KILL ANYMORE!
I'M GOING TO PROTECT THEM!
THE TORII HUNGERS FOR YOUR BLOOD...

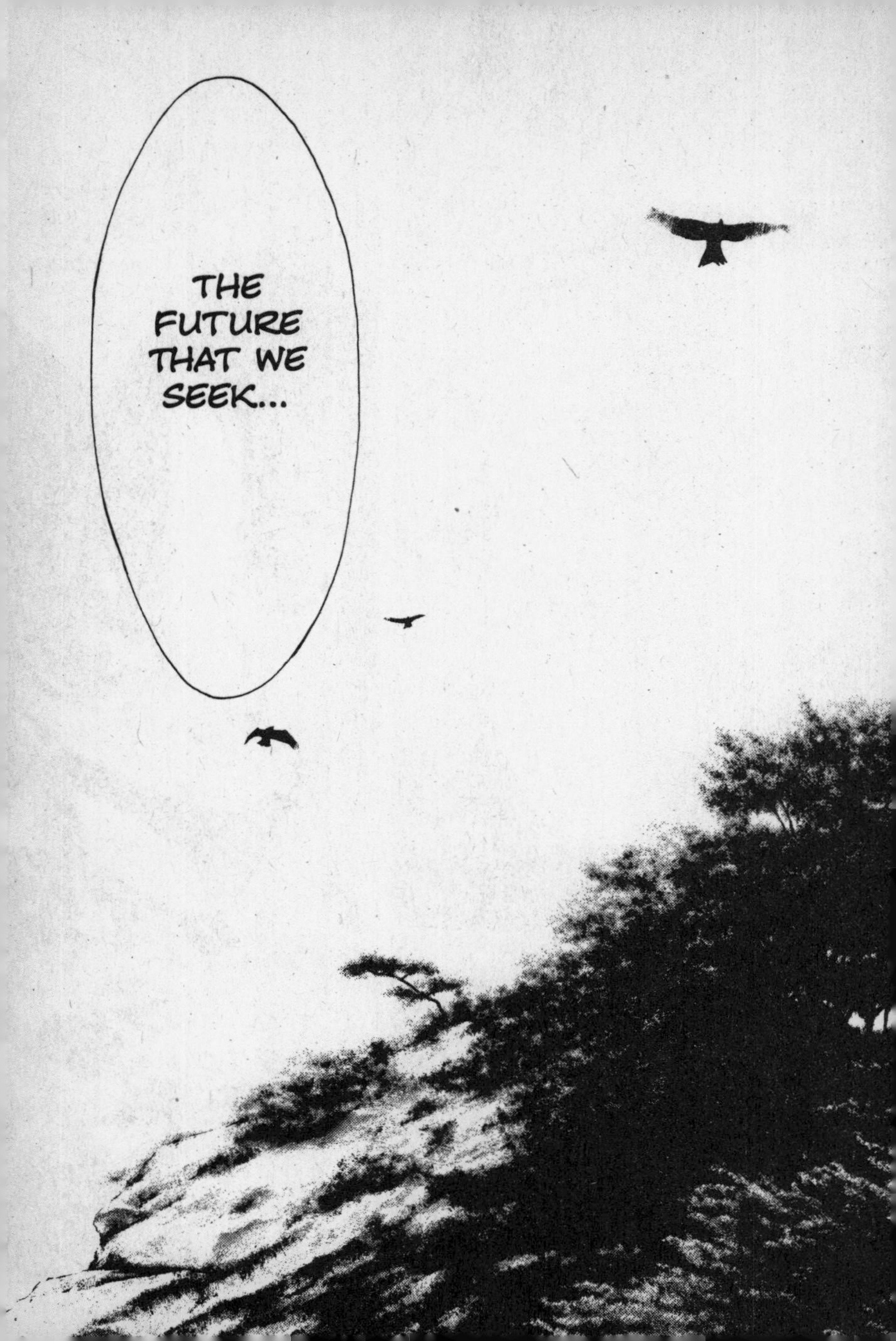
THE FUTURE THAT WE SEEK...

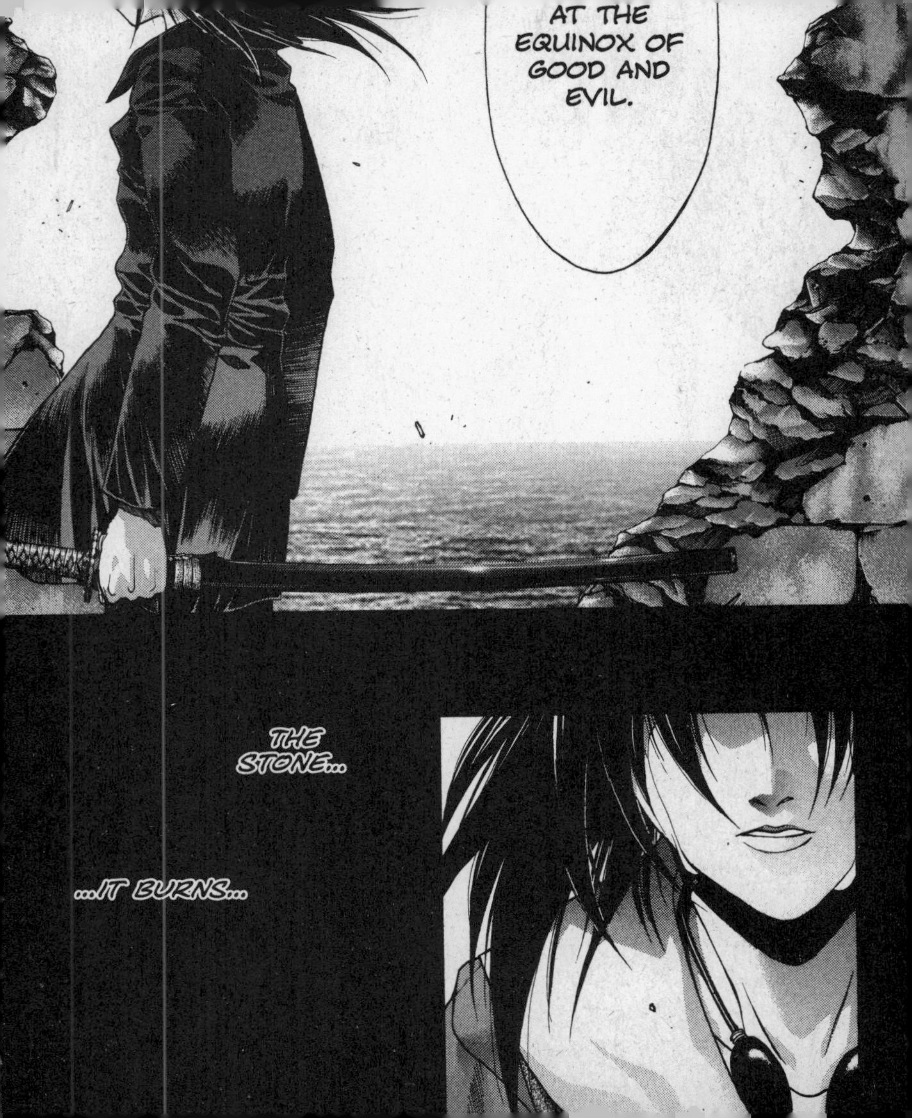
AT THE EQUINOX OF GOOD AND EVIL.
THE STONE...
...IT BURNS...

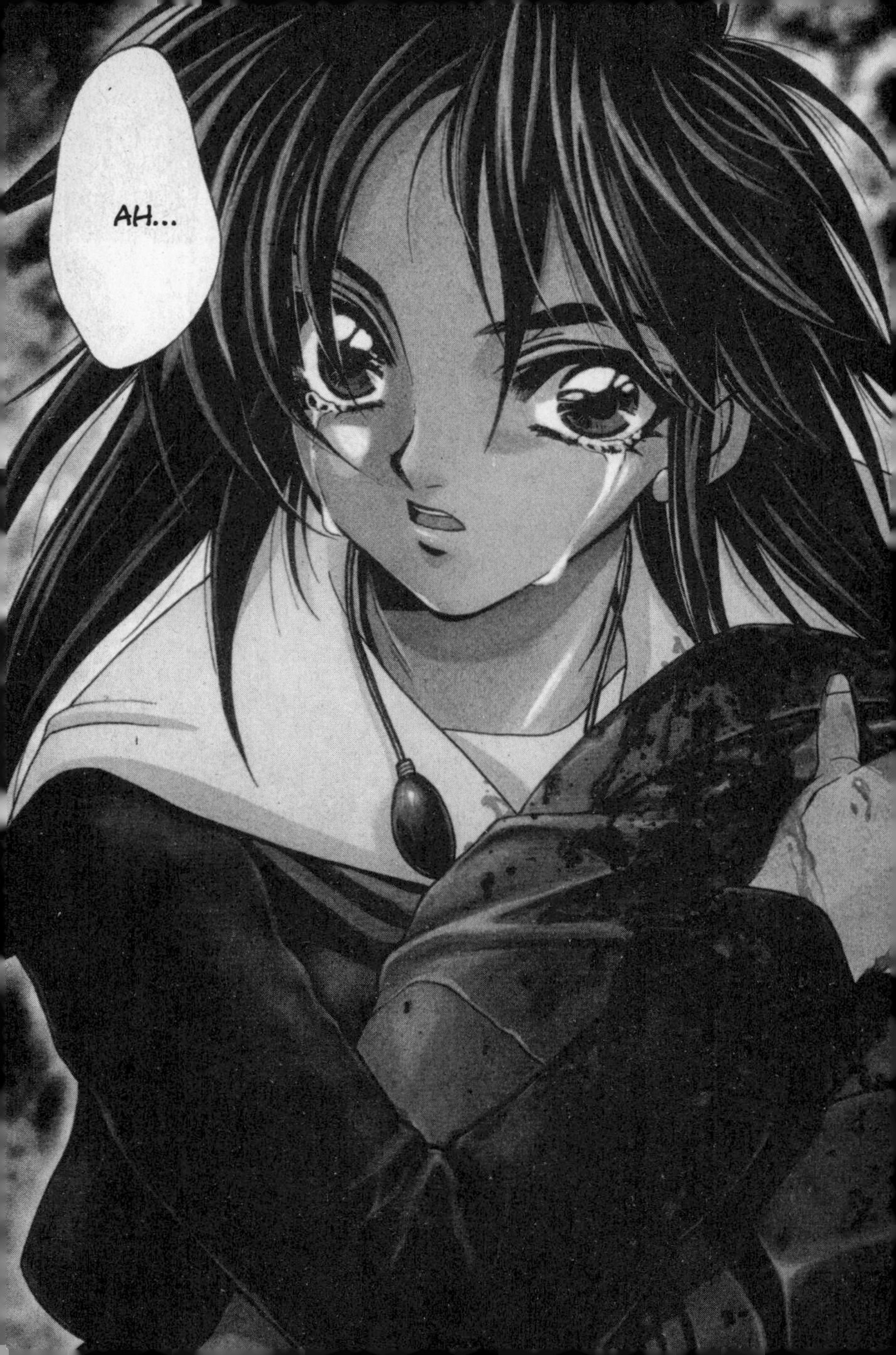
AH...

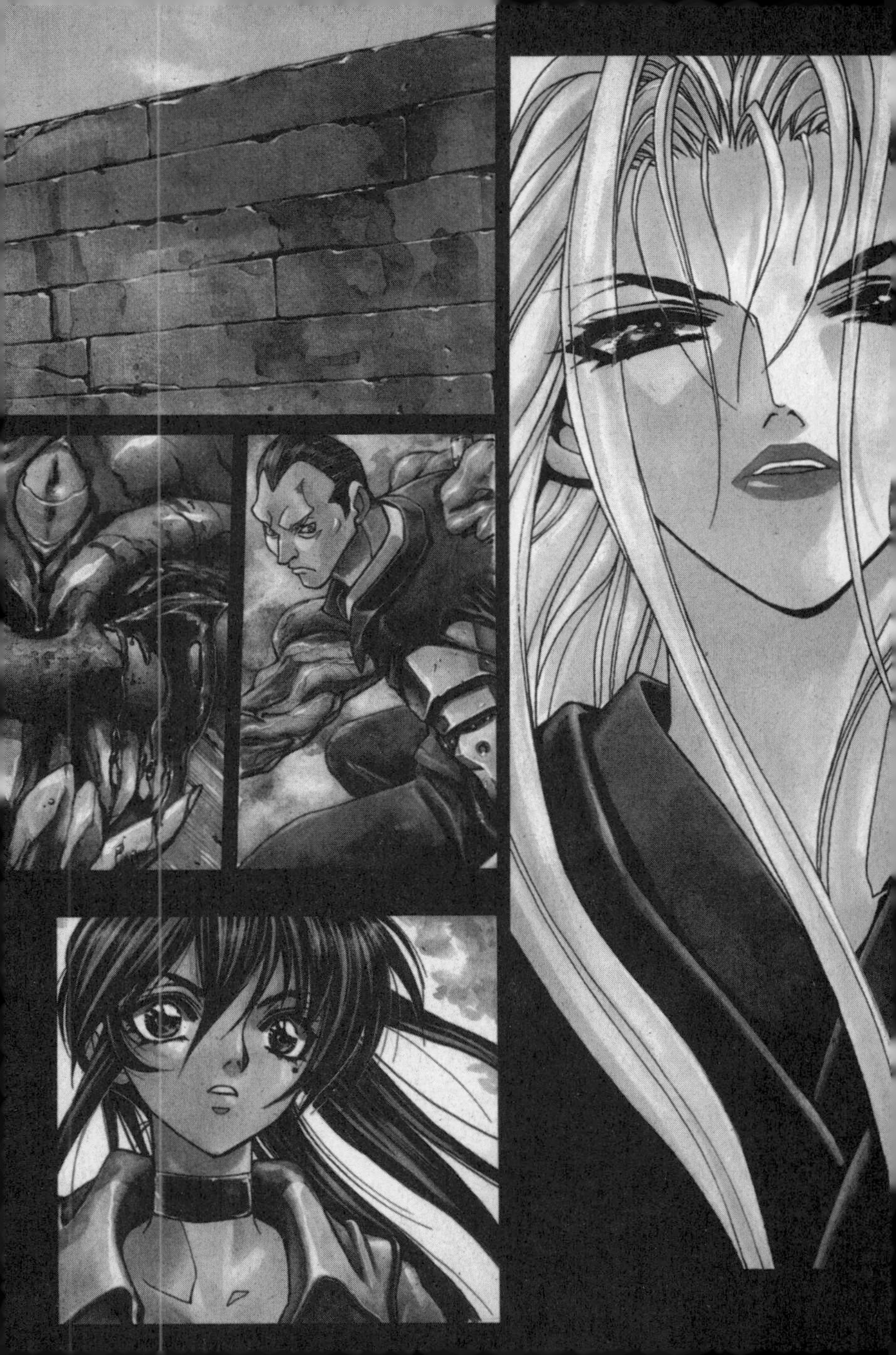

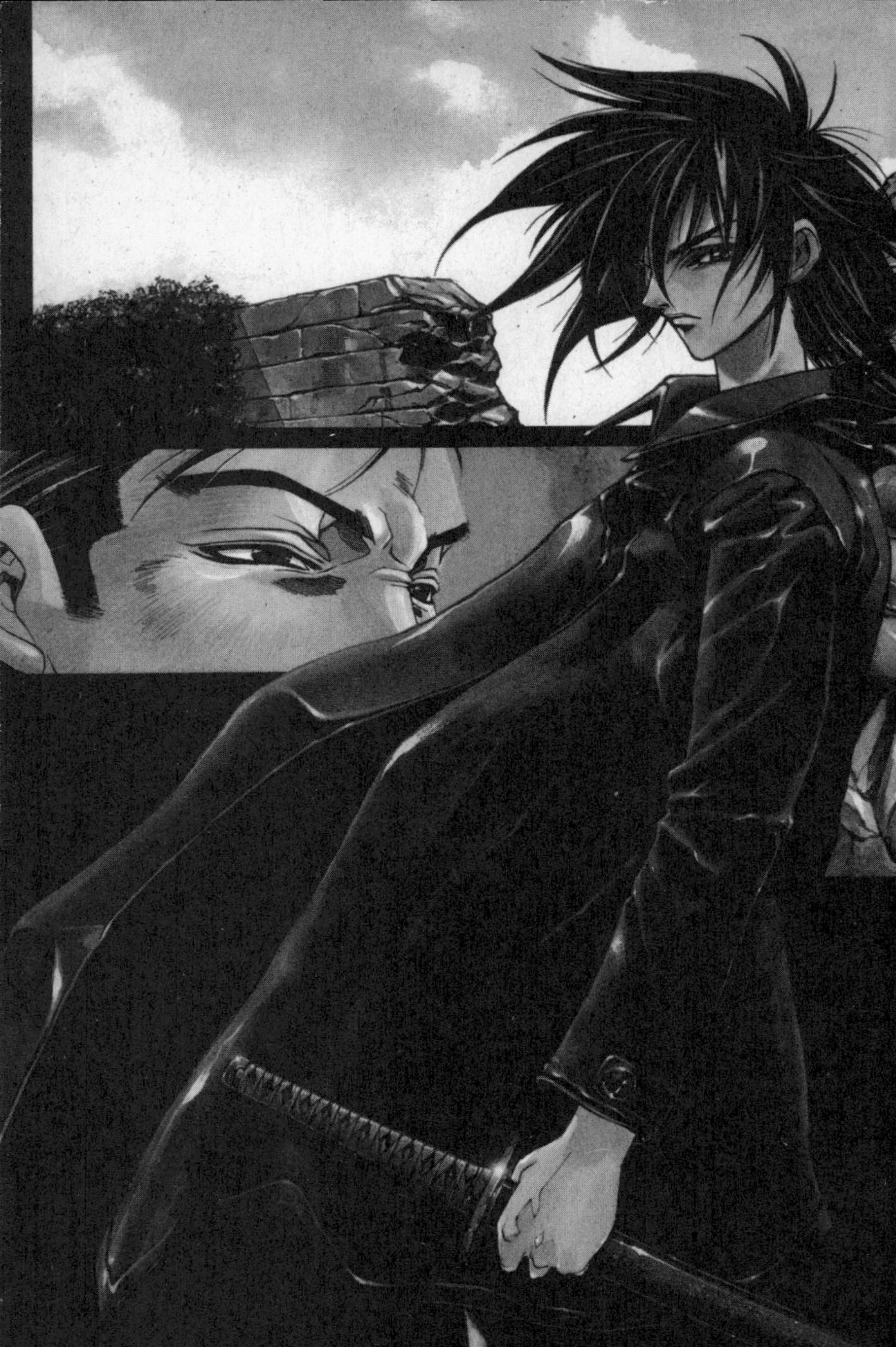

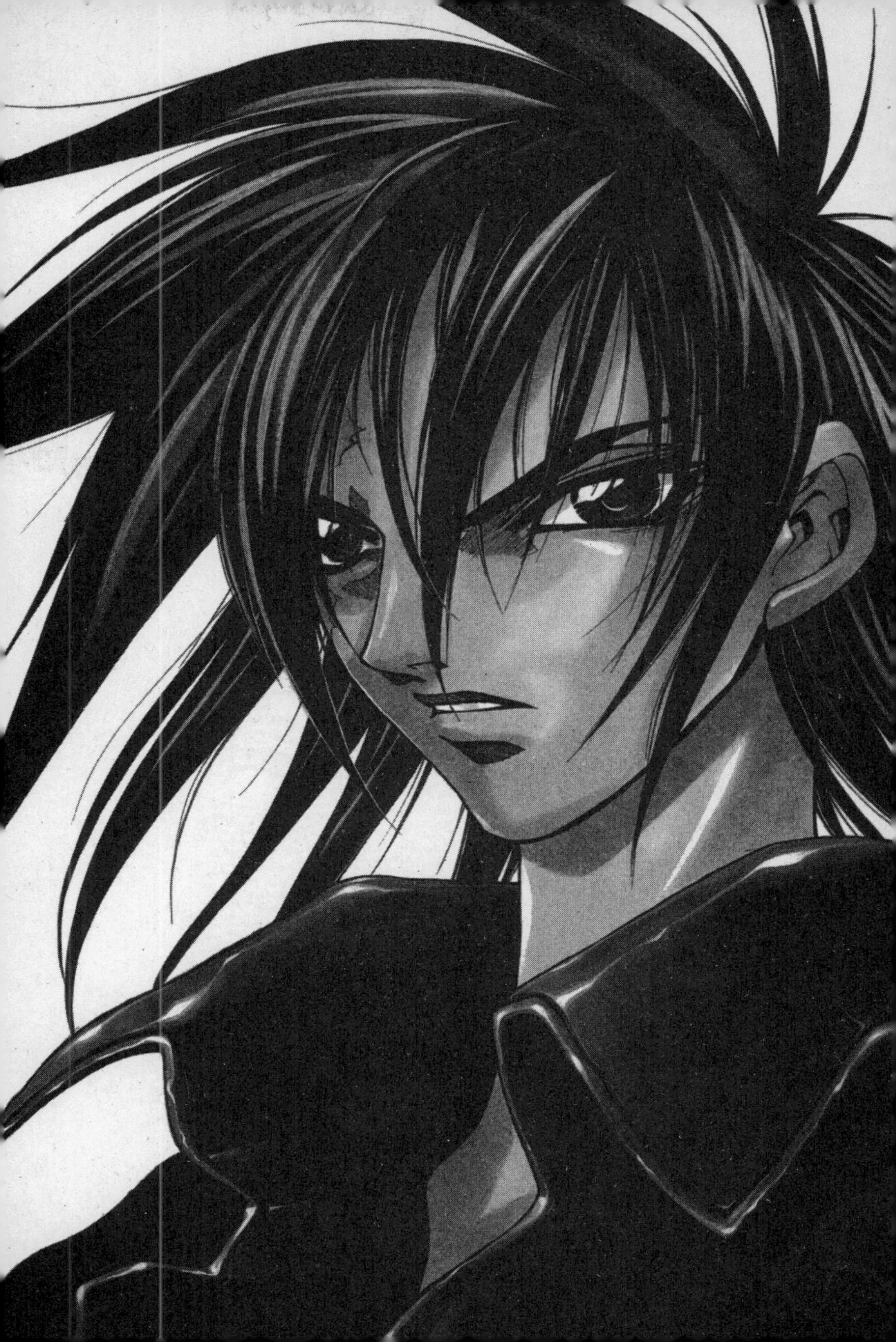

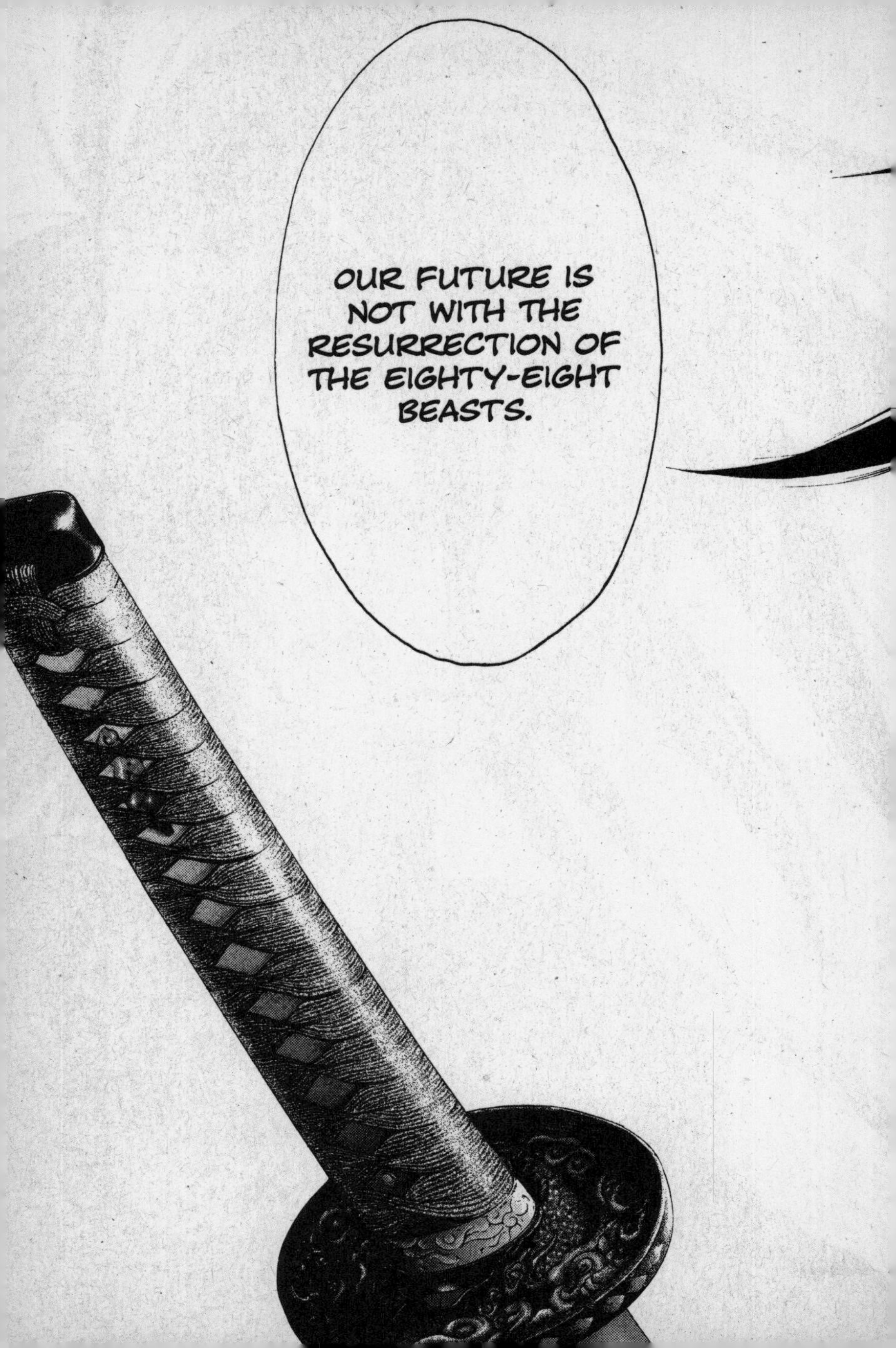
OUR FUTURE IS NOT WITH THE RESURRECTION OF THE EIGHTY-EIGHT BEASTS.

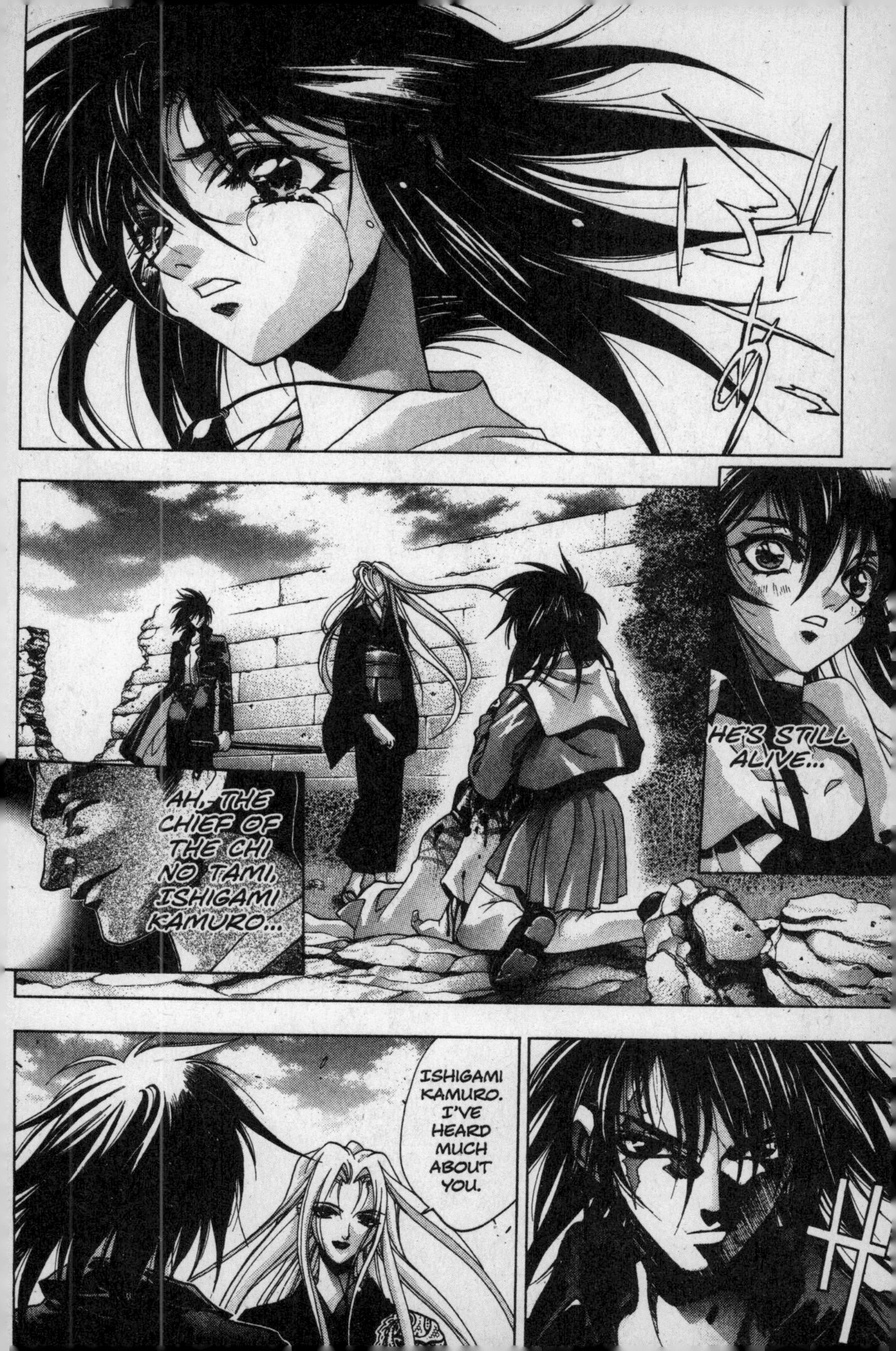
HE'S STILL ALIVE...
AH, THE CHIEF OF THE CHI NO TAMI, ISHIGAMI KAMURO...
ISHIGAMI KAMURO. I'VE HEARD MUCH ABOUT YOU.

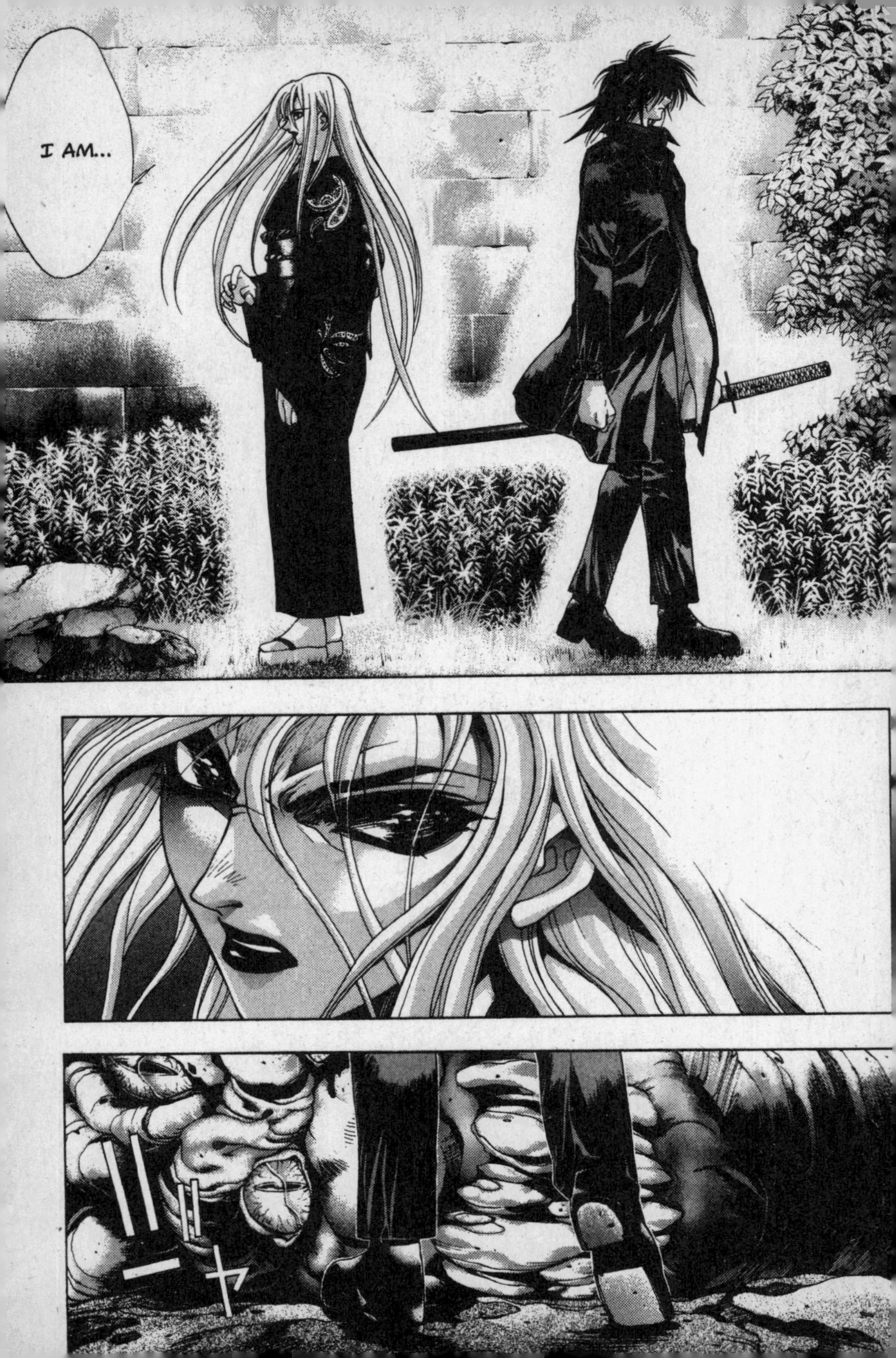
I AM...

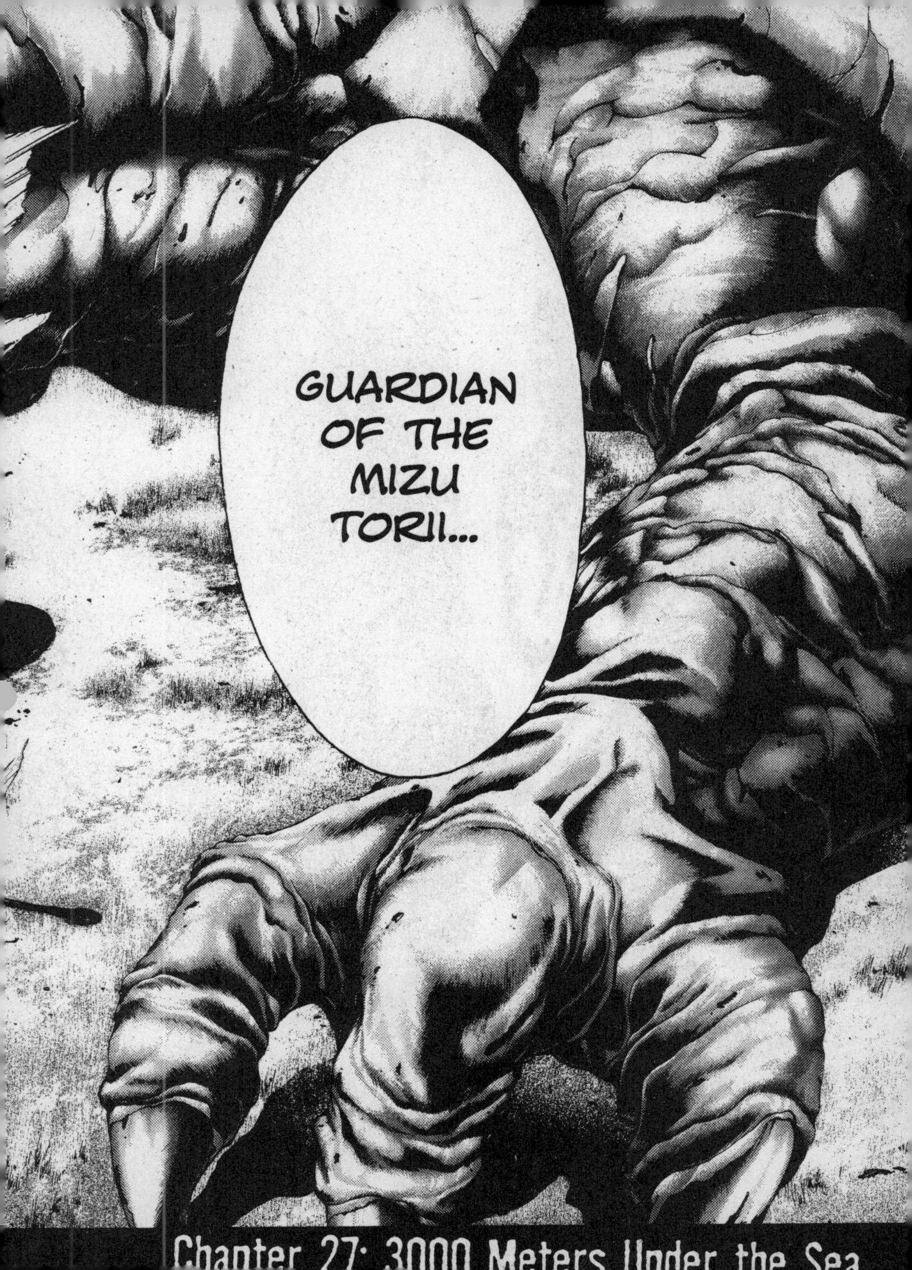
GUARDIAN OF THE MIZU TORII...

Chapter 27: 3000 Meters Under the Sea

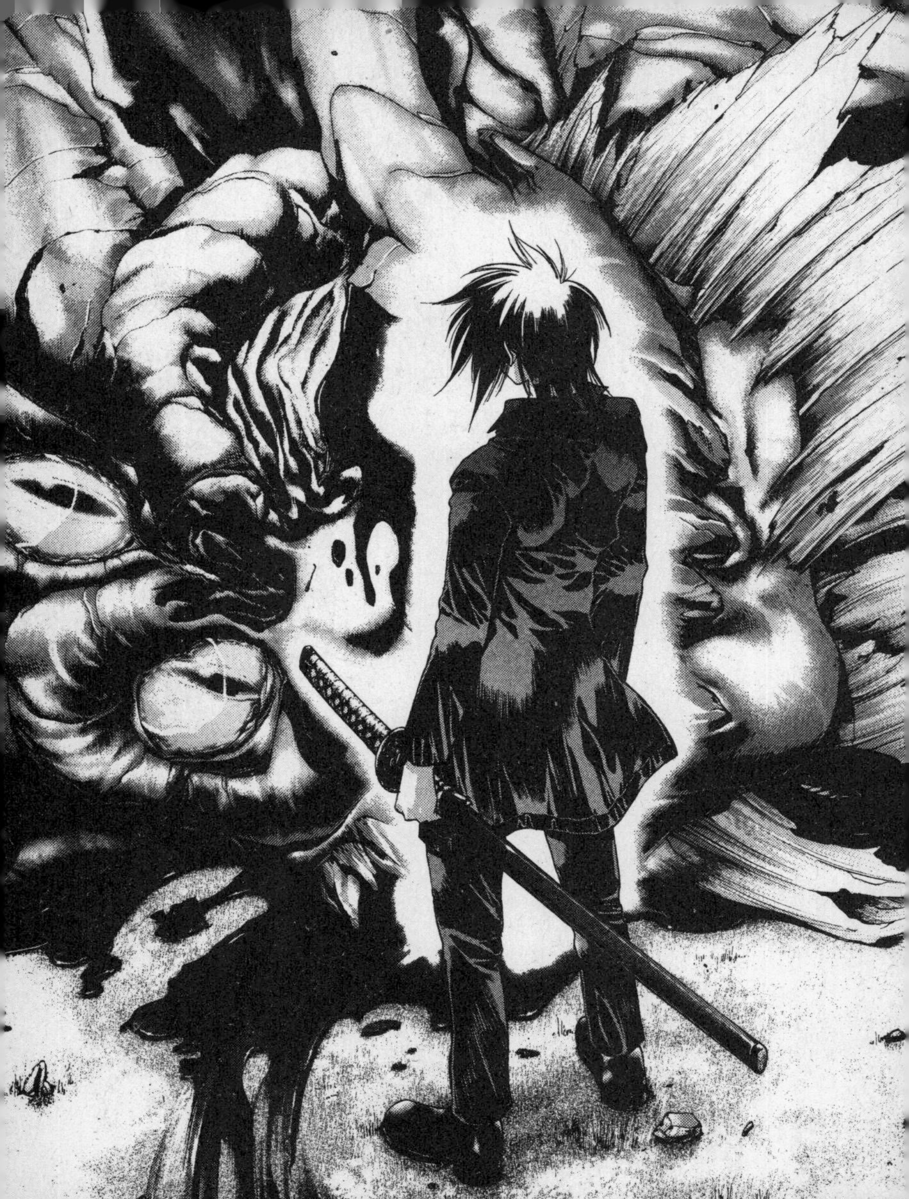

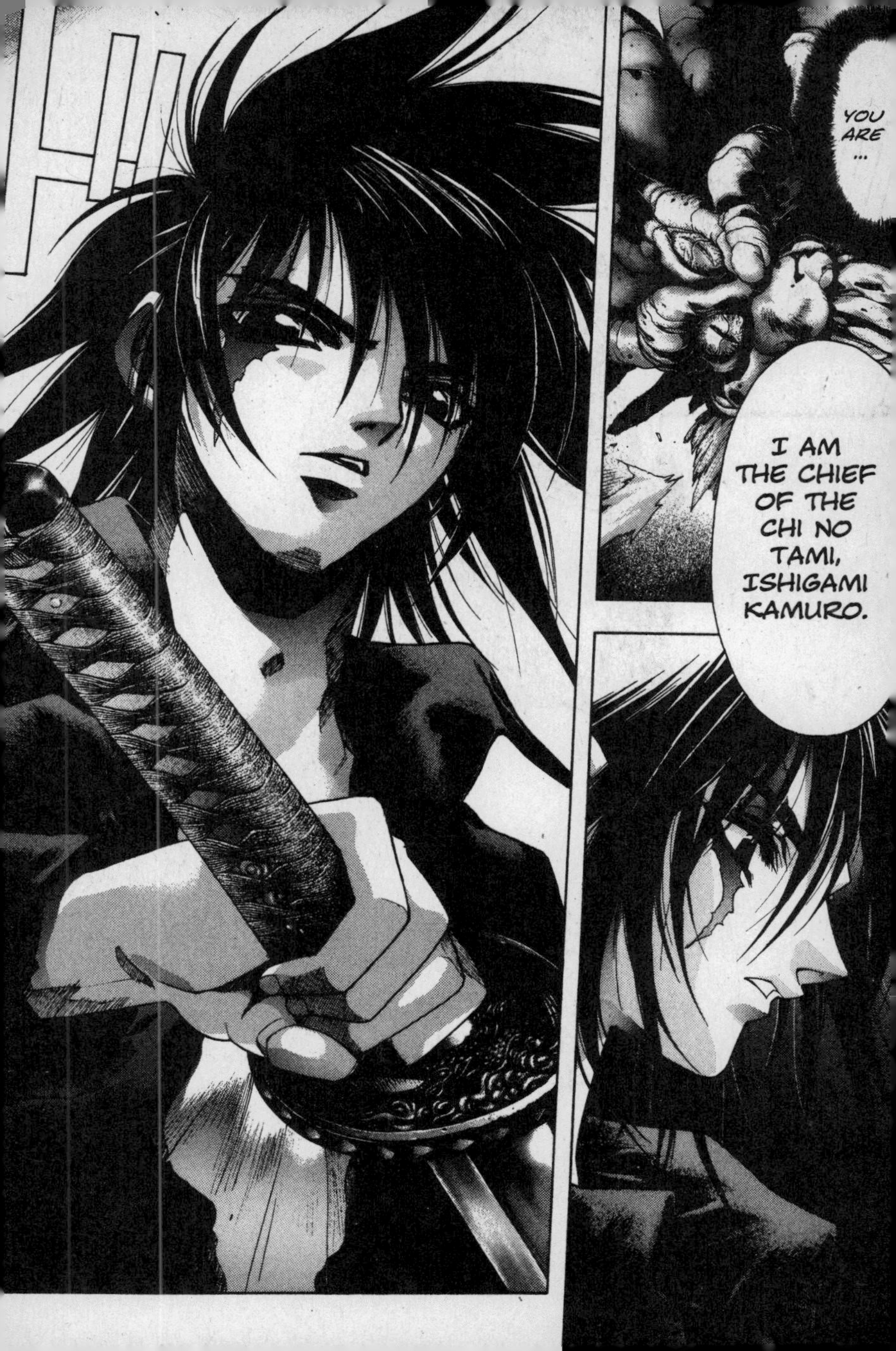
YOU ARE ...
I AM THE CHIEF OF THE CHI NO TAMI, ISHIGAMI KAMURO.

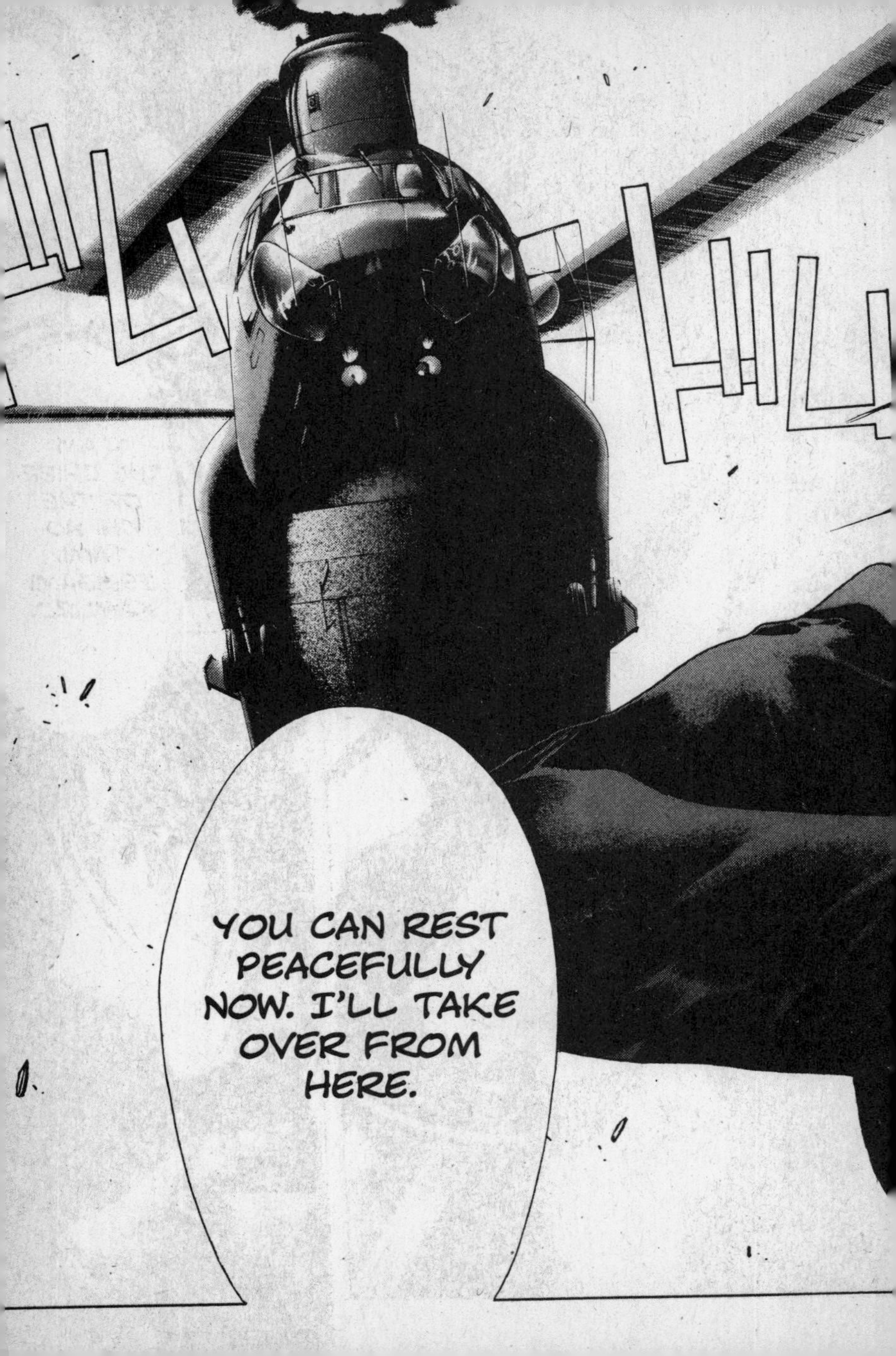
YOU CAN REST PEACEFULLY NOW. I'LL TAKE OVER FROM HERE.

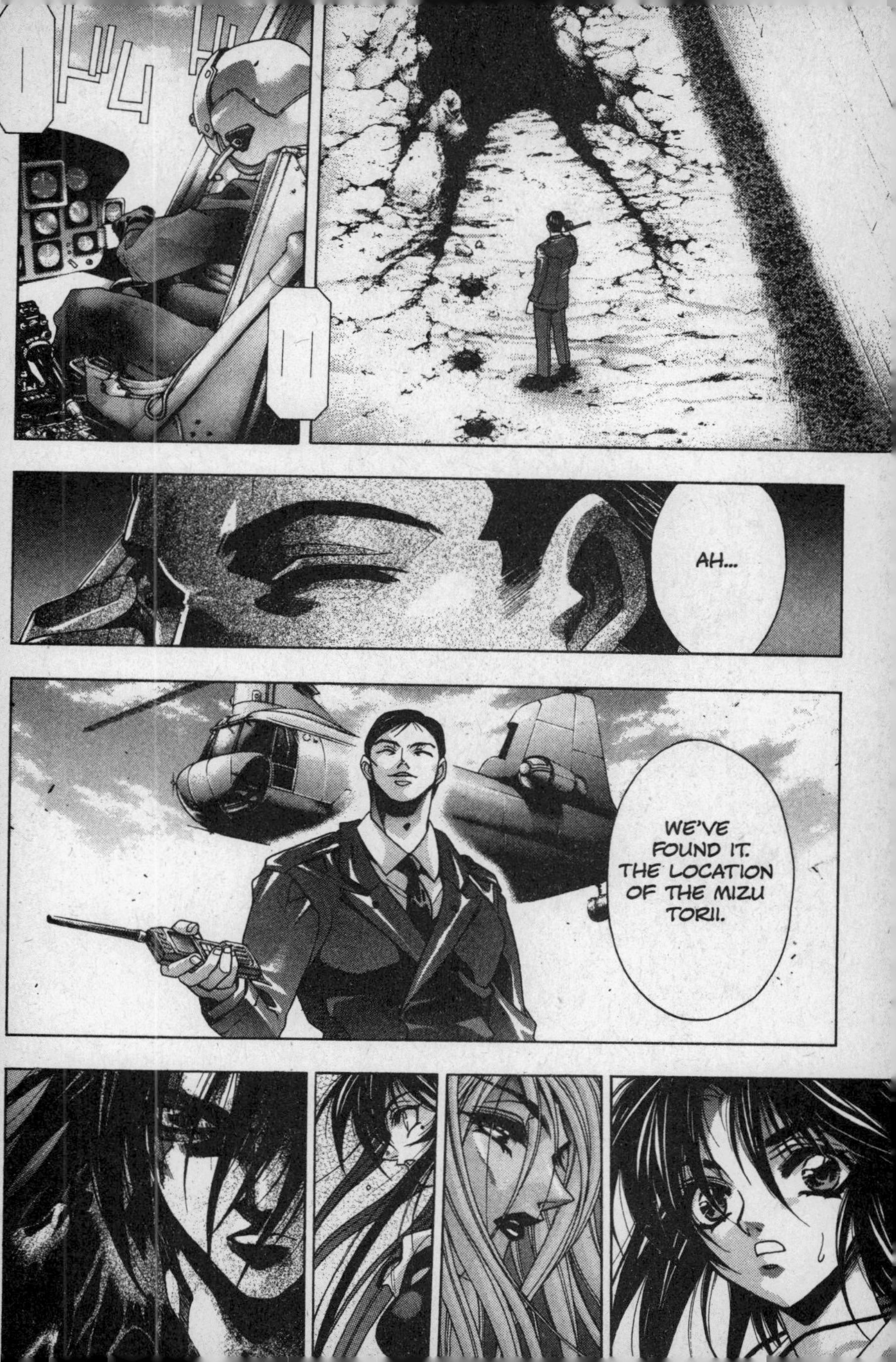
AH...
WE'VE FOUND IT. THE LOCATION OF THE MIZU TORII.

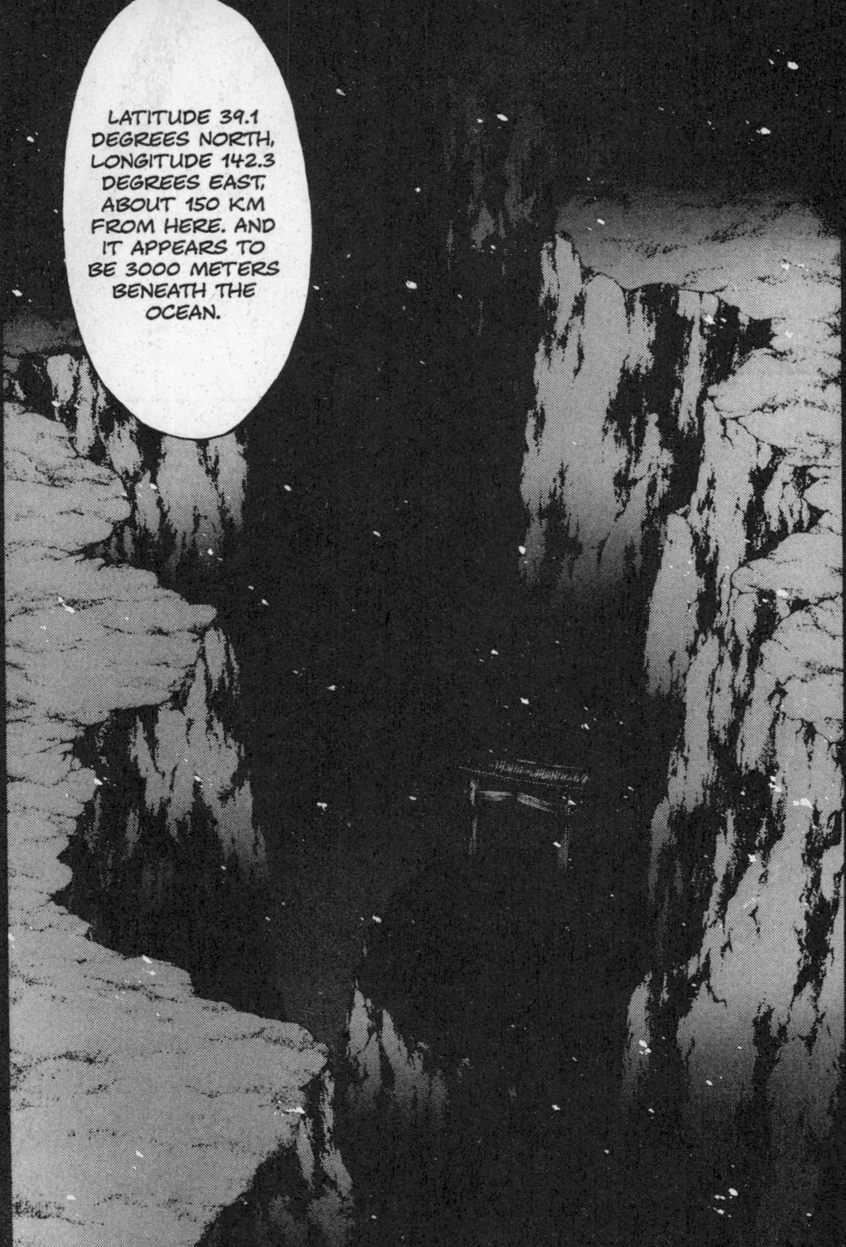
LATITUDE 39.1 DEGREES NORTH, LONGITUDE 142.3 DEGREES EAST, ABOUT 150 KM FROM HERE. AND IT APPEARS TO BE 3000 METERS BENEATH THE OCEAN.

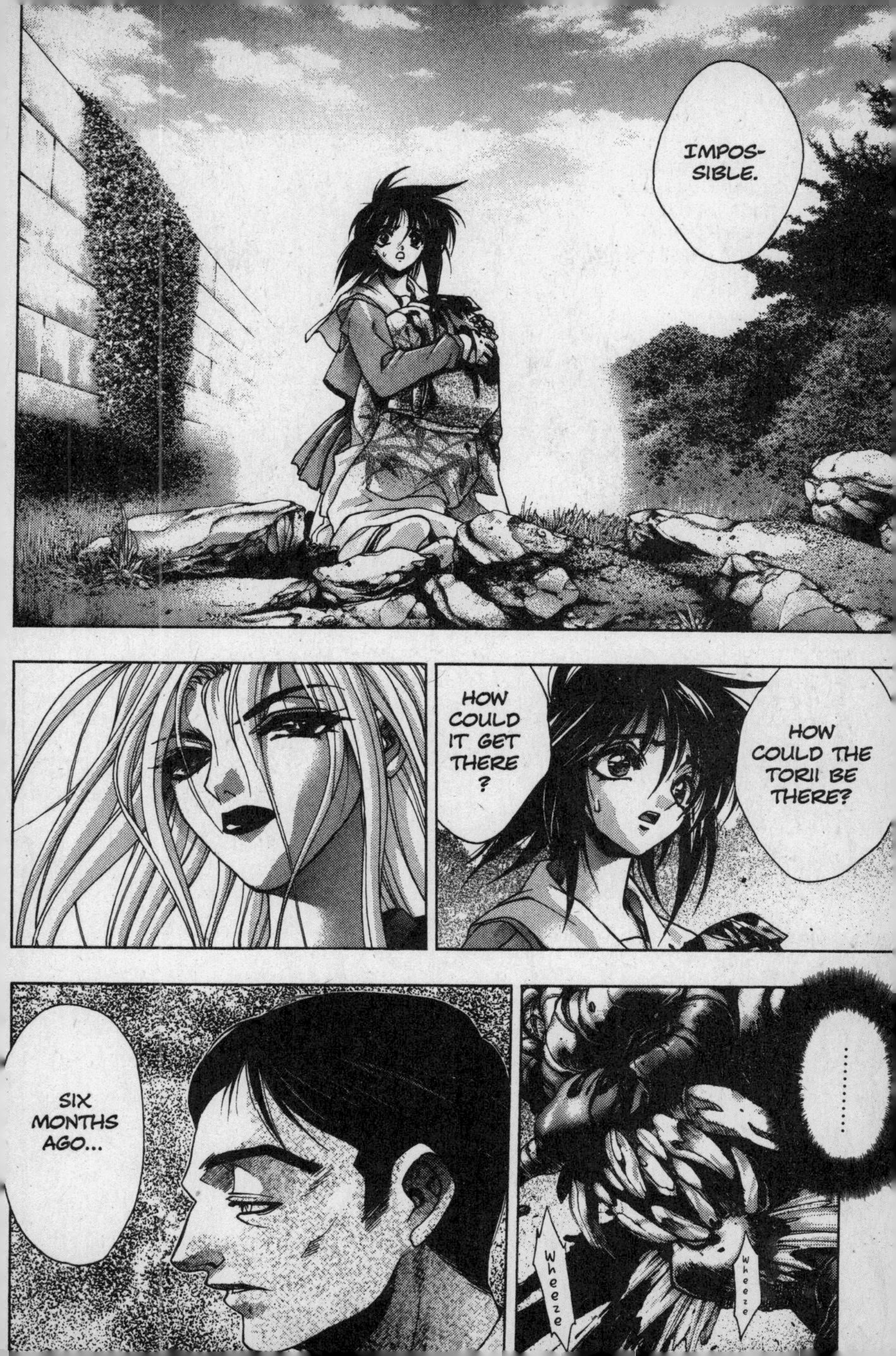
IMPOS-SIBLE.
HOW COULD THE TORII BE THERE?
HOW COULD IT GET THERE?
......
Wheeze
Wheeze
SIX MONTHS AGO...

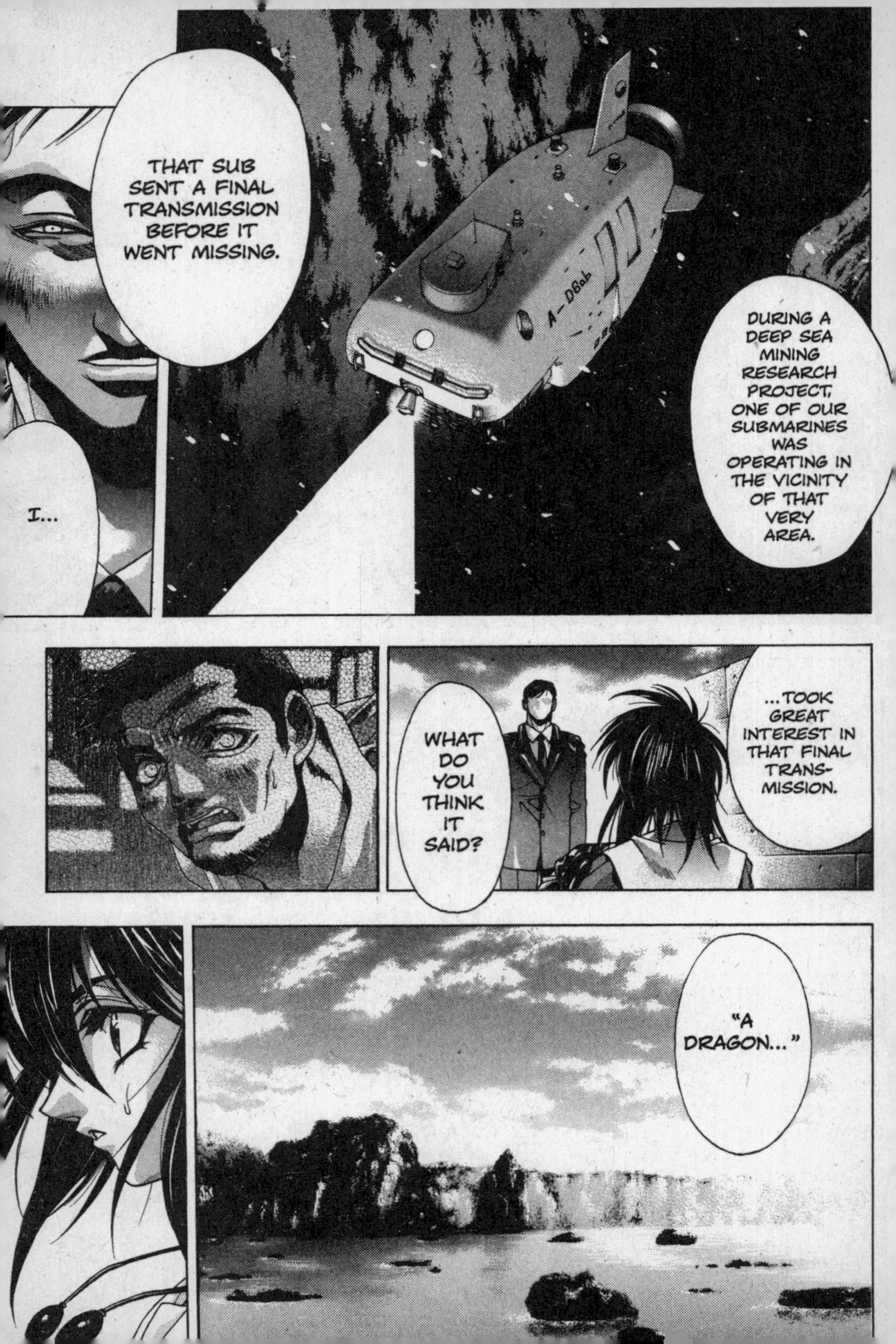
DURING A DEEP SEA MINING RESEARCH PROJECT, ONE OF OUR SUBMARINES WAS OPERATING IN THE VICINITY OF THAT VERY AREA.
THAT SUB SENT A FINAL TRANSMISSION BEFORE IT WENT MISSING.
I...
...TOOK GREAT INTEREST IN THAT FINAL TRANS-MISSION.
WHAT DO YOU THINK IT SAID?
"A DRAGON..."

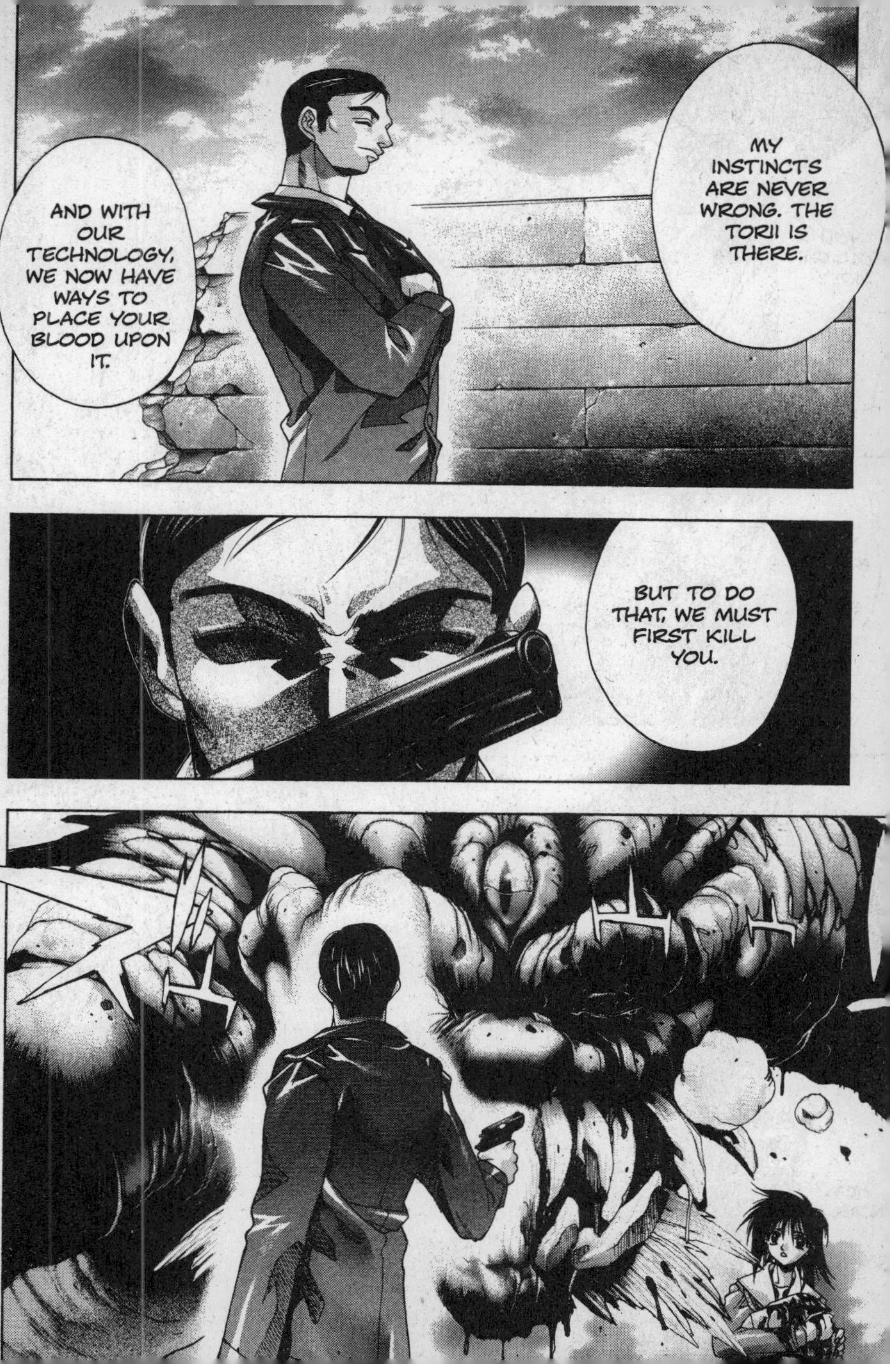
MY INSTINCTS ARE NEVER WRONG. THE TORII IS THERE.
AND WITH OUR TECHNOLOGY, WE NOW HAVE WAYS TO PLACE YOUR BLOOD UPON IT.
BUT TO DO THAT, WE MUST FIRST KILL YOU.

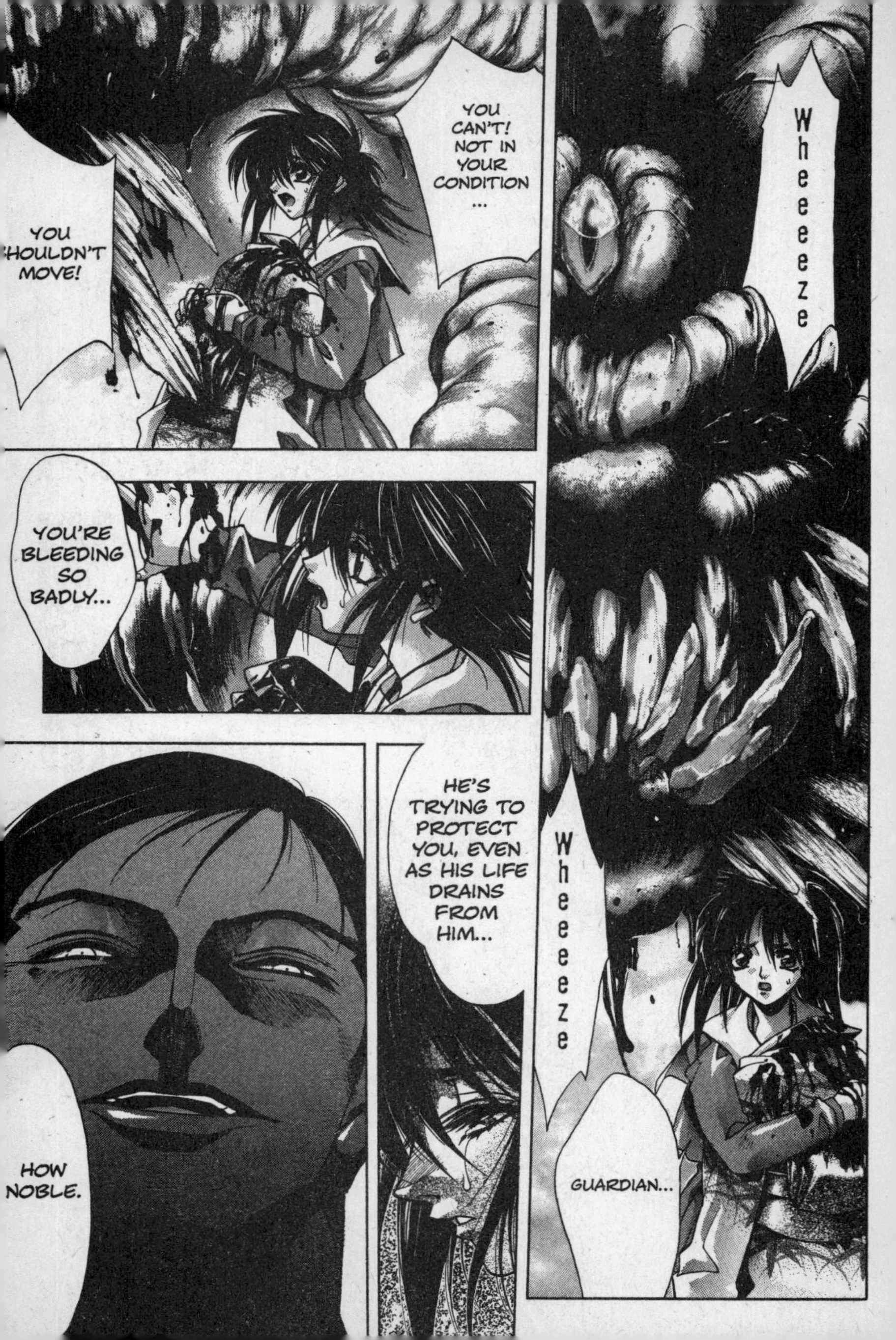
Wheeeze
Wheeeze
GUARDIAN...
YOU CAN'T! NOT IN YOUR CONDITION ...
YOU SHOULDN'T MOVE!
YOU'RE BLEEDING SO BADLY...
HE'S TRYING TO PROTECT YOU, EVEN AS HIS LIFE DRAINS FROM HIM...
HOW NOBLE.

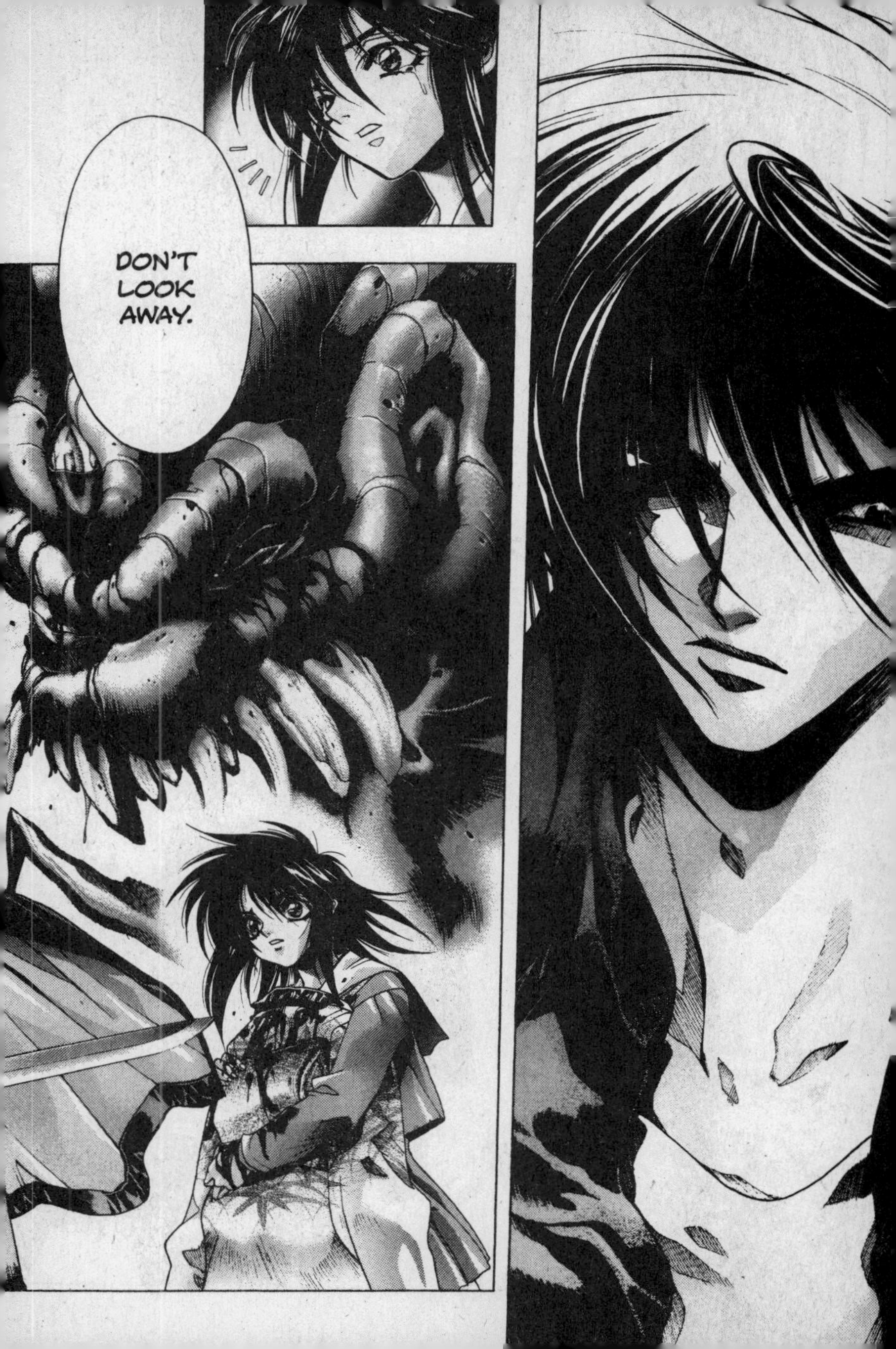
DON'T LOOK AWAY.

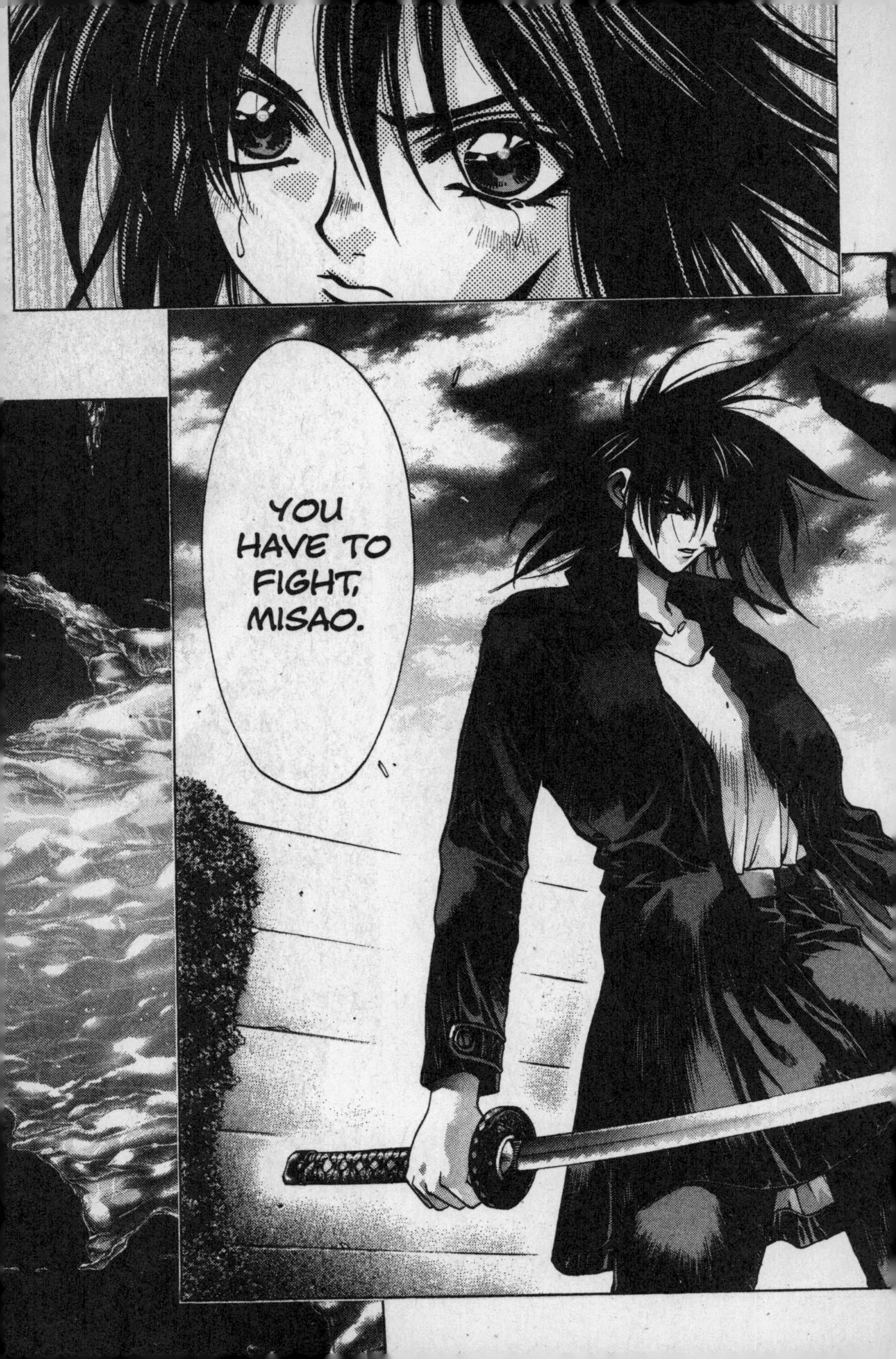
YOU HAVE TO FIGHT, MISAO.

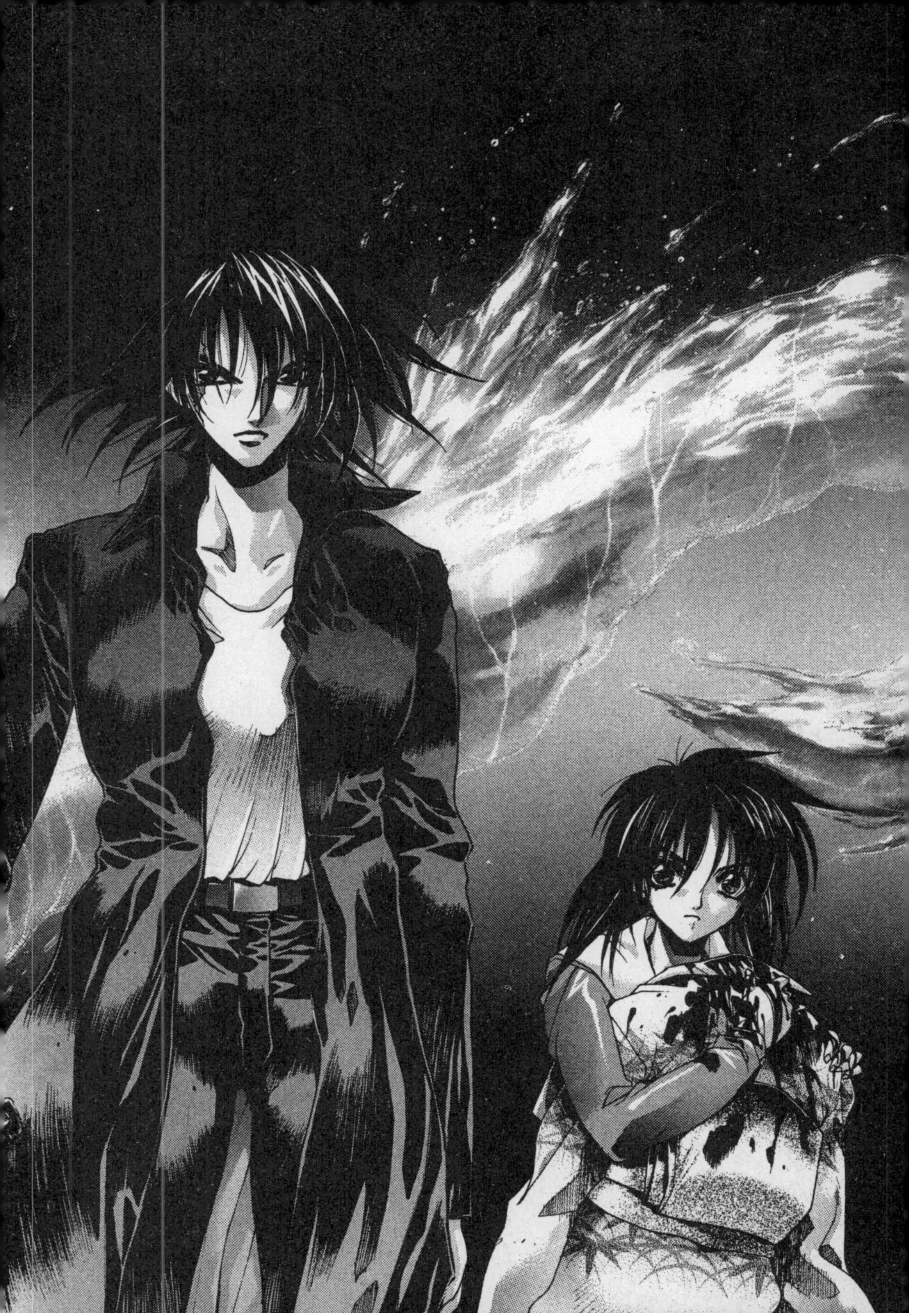

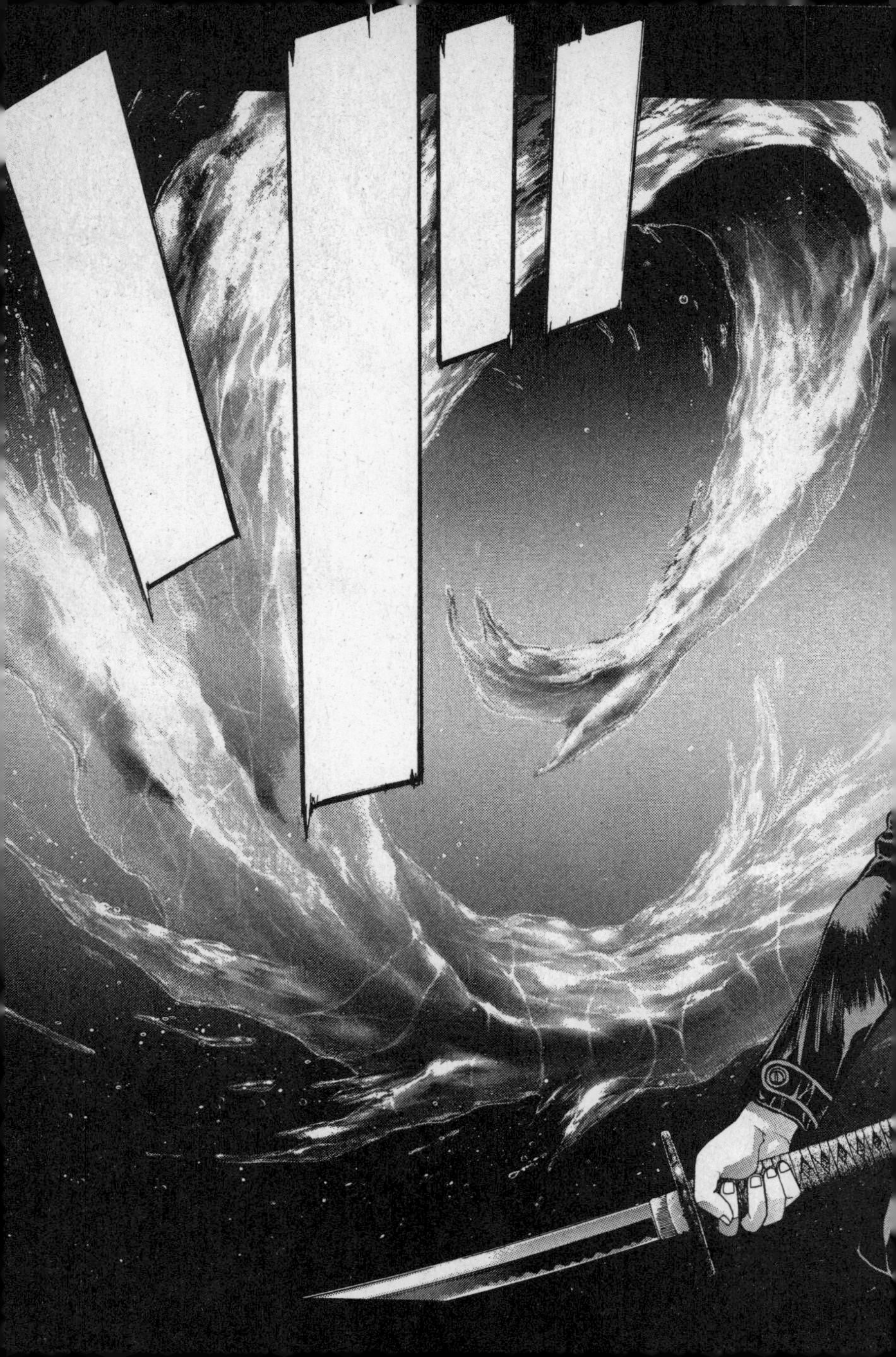

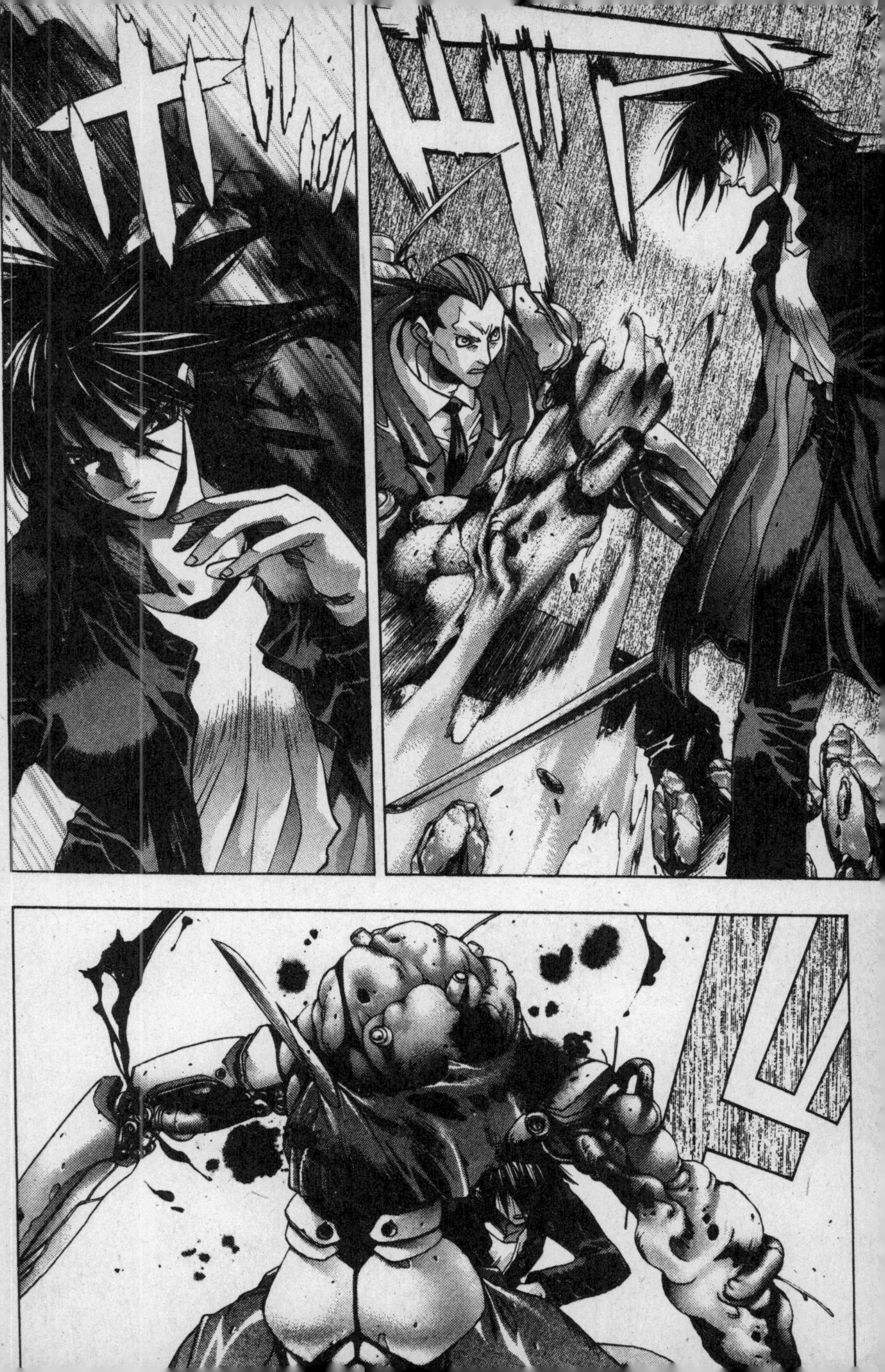

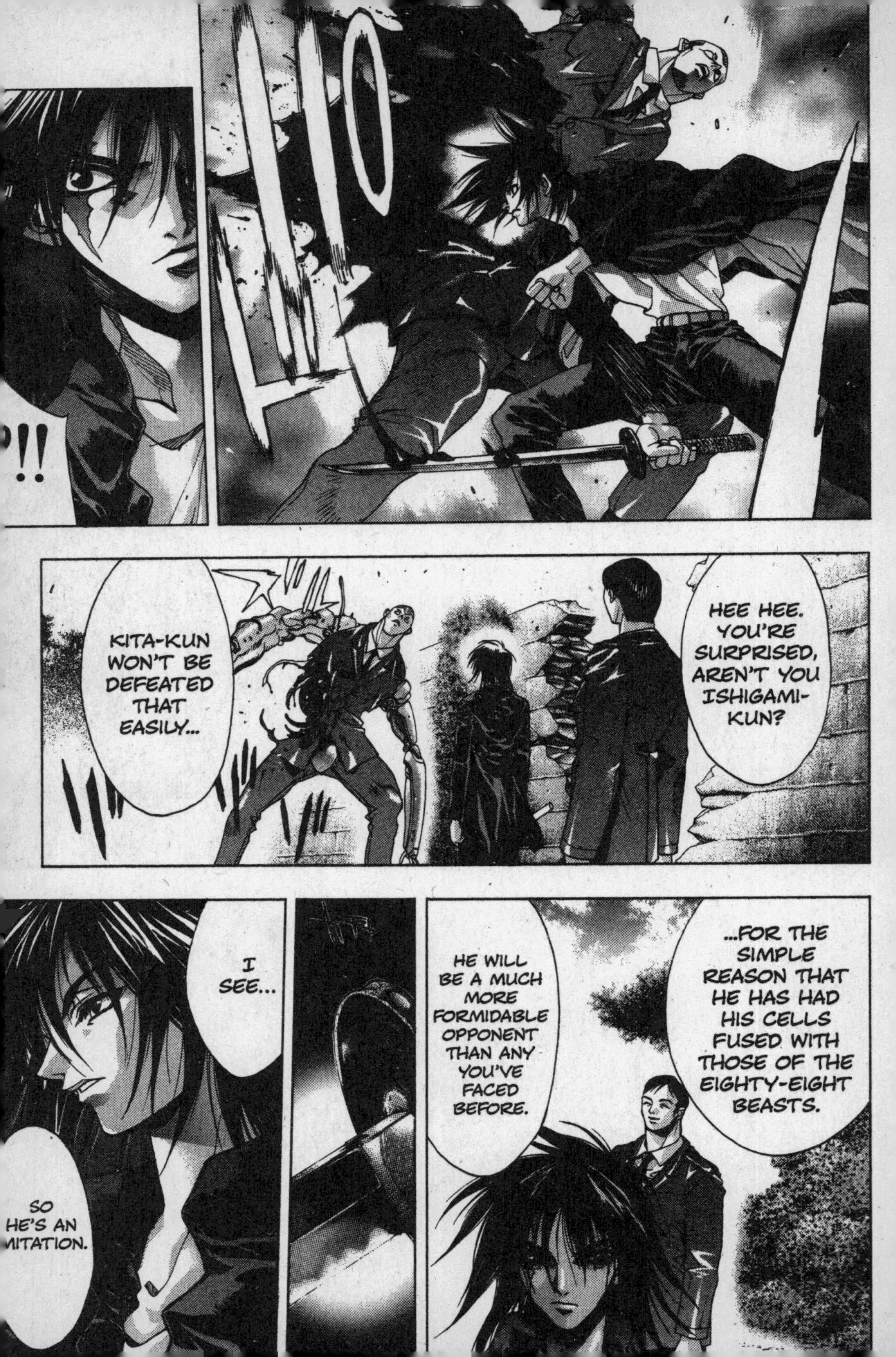
!!
HEE HEE. YOU'RE SURPRISED, AREN'T YOU ISHIGAMI-KUN?
KITA-KUN WON'T BE DEFEATED THAT EASILY...
...FOR THE SIMPLE REASON THAT HE HAS HAD HIS CELLS FUSED WITH THOSE OF THE EIGHTY-EIGHT BEASTS.
HE WILL BE A MUCH MORE FORMIDABLE OPPONENT THAN ANY YOU'VE FACED BEFORE.
I SEE...
SO HE'S AN MITATION.

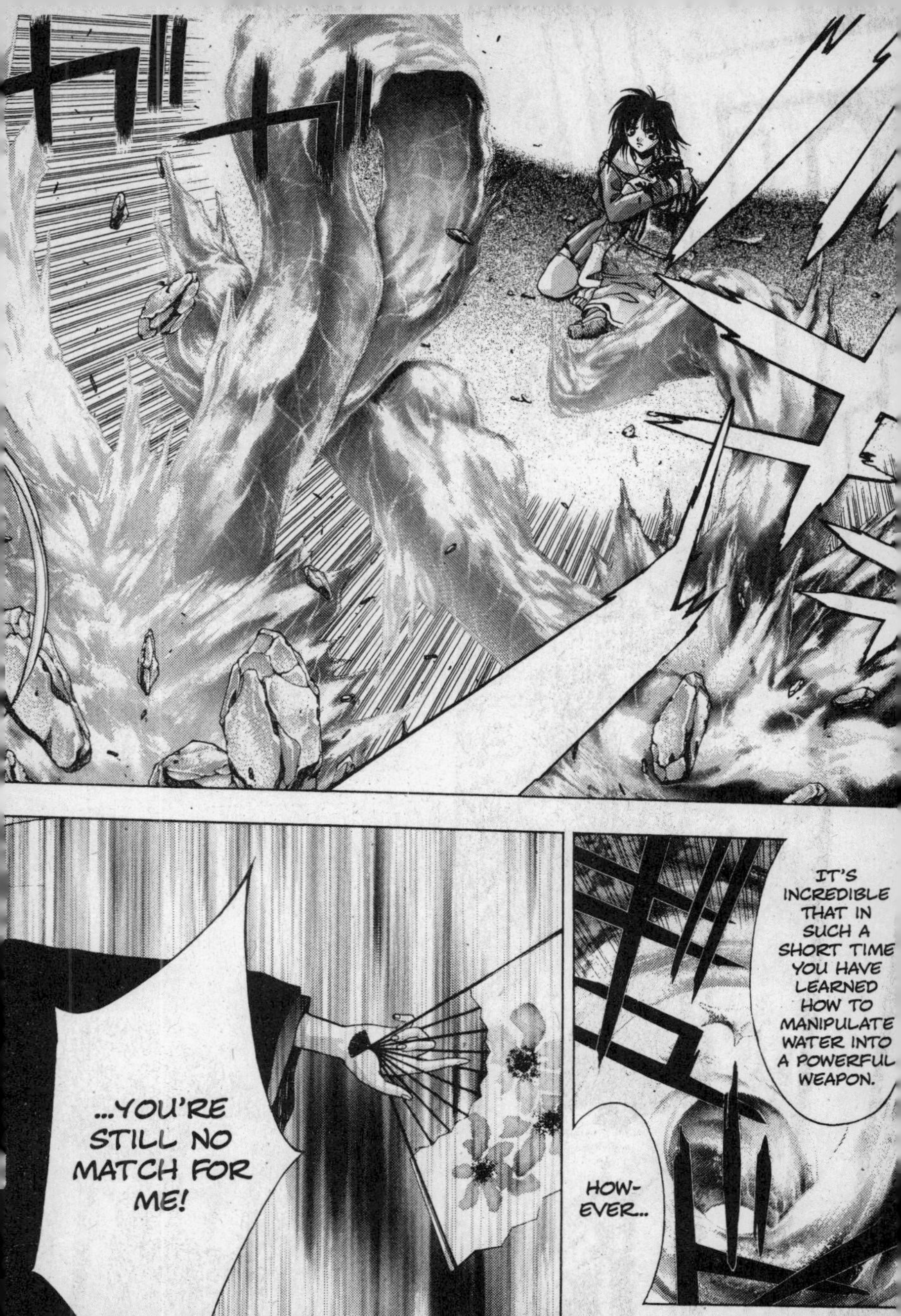
IT'S INCREDIBLE THAT IN SUCH A SHORT TIME YOU HAVE LEARNED HOW TO MANIPULATE WATER INTO A POWERFUL WEAPON.
HOW-EVER...
...YOU'RE STILL NO MATCH FOR ME!

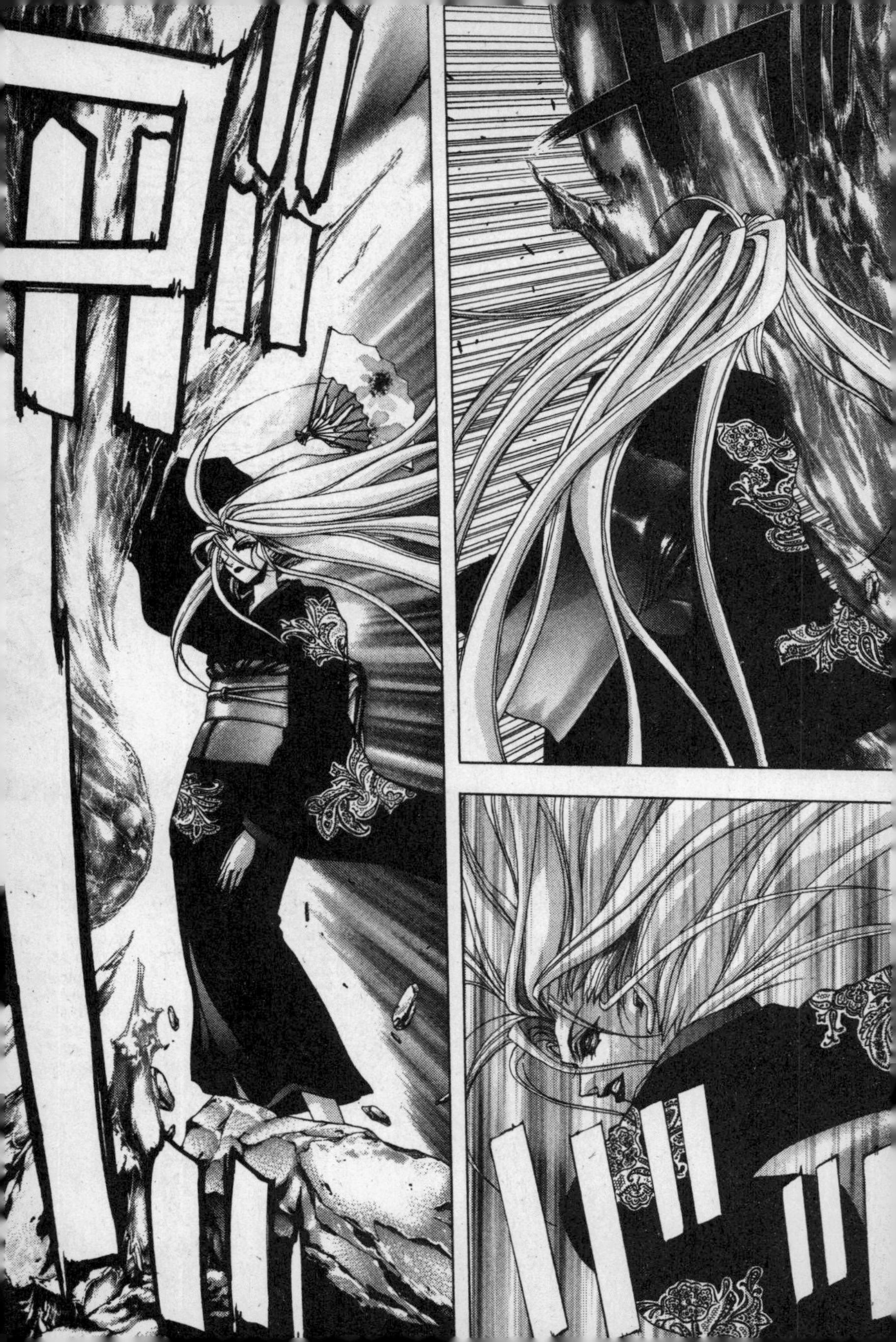

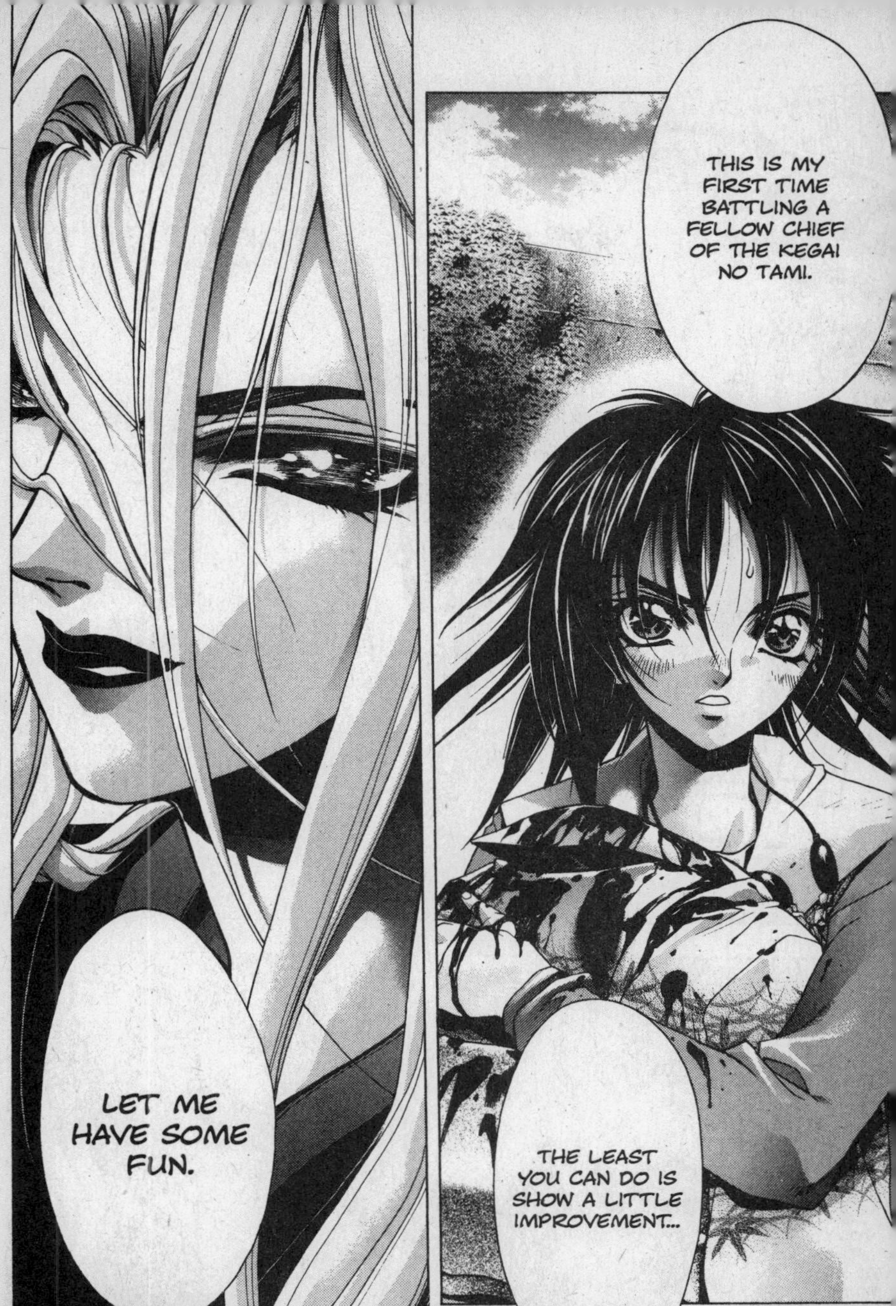
THIS IS MY FIRST TIME BATTLING A FELLOW CHIEF OF THE KEGAI NO TAMI.
THE LEAST YOU CAN DO IS SHOW A LITTLE IMPROVEMENT...
LET ME HAVE SOME FUN.

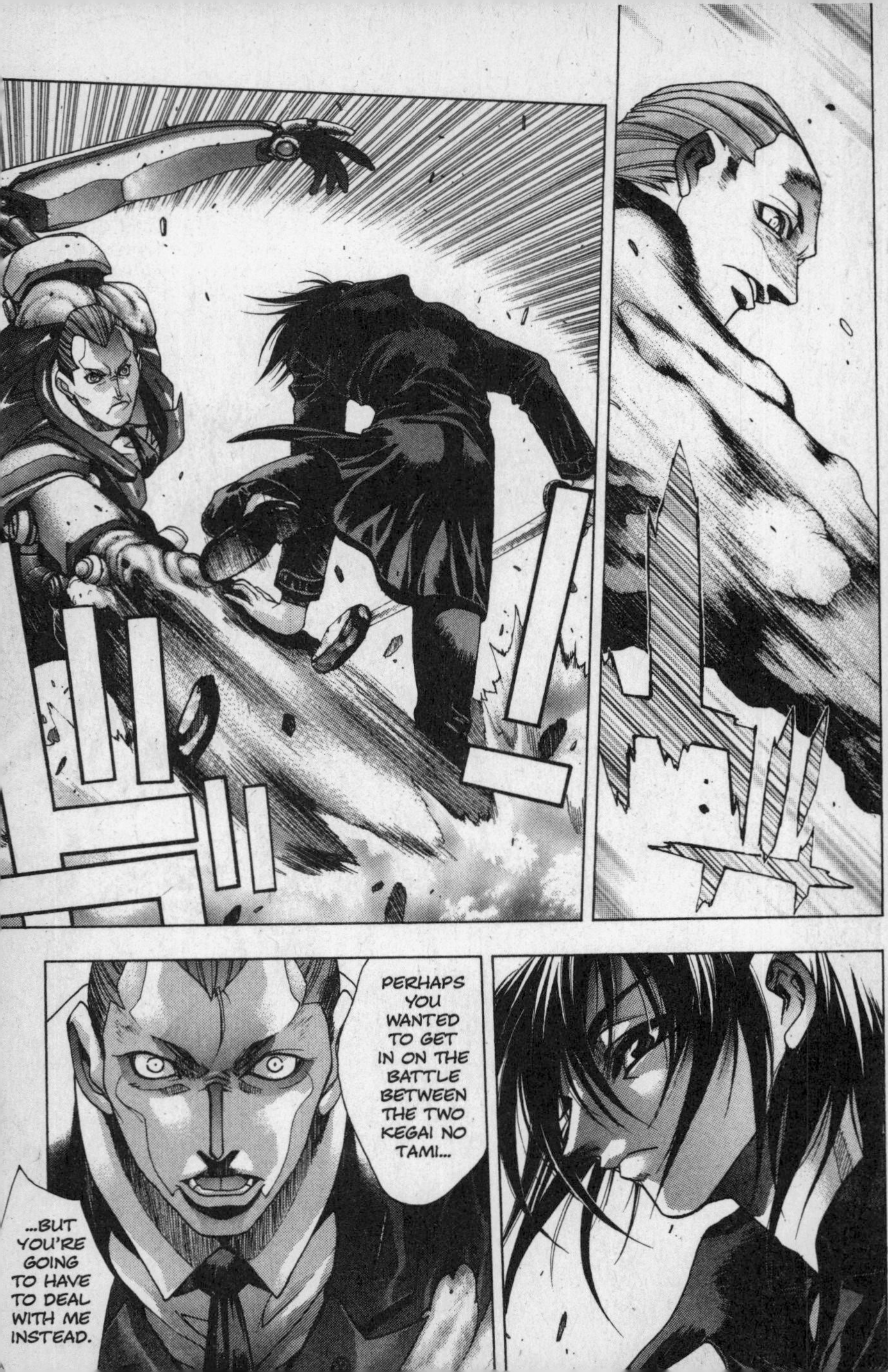
PERHAPS YOU WANTED TO GET IN ON THE BATTLE BETWEEN THE TWO KEGAI NO TAMI...
...BUT YOU'RE GOING TO HAVE TO DEAL WITH ME INSTEAD.

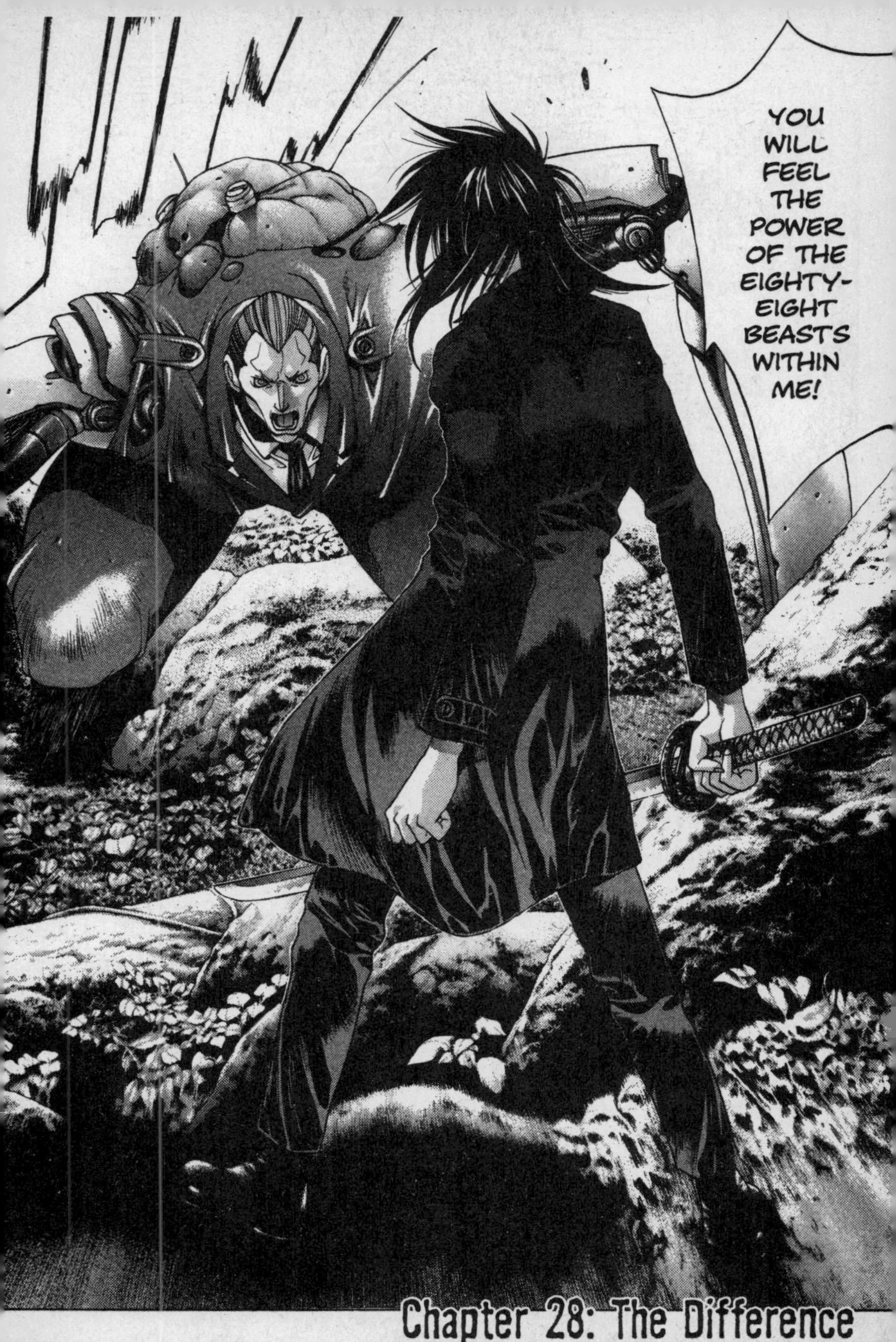
YOU WILL FEEL THE POWER OF THE EIGHTY-EIGHT BEASTS WITHIN ME!

Chapter 28: The Difference

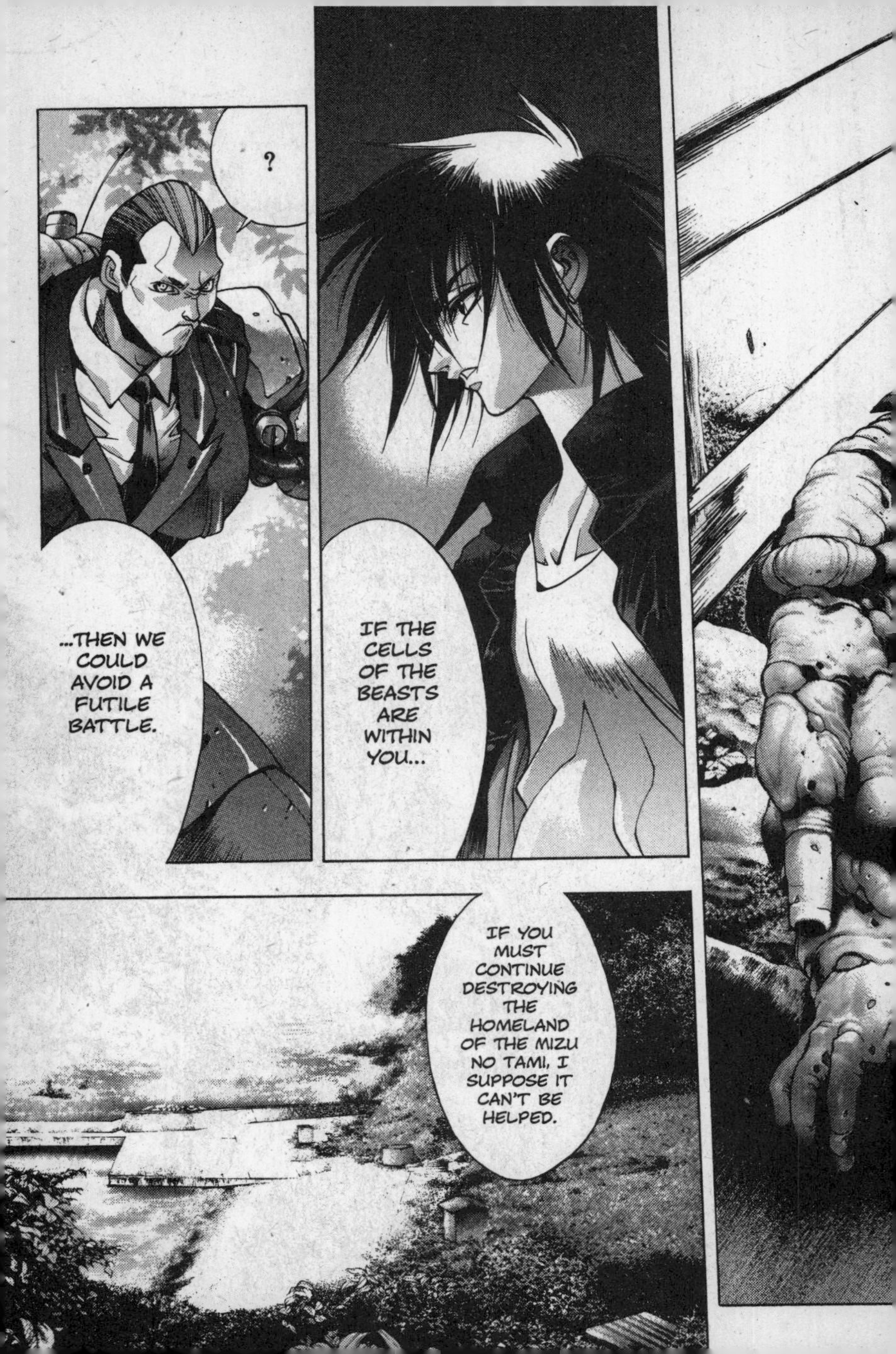
IF THE CELLS OF THE BEASTS ARE WITHIN YOU...
?
...THEN WE COULD AVOID A FUTILE BATTLE.
IF YOU MUST CONTINUE DESTROYING THE HOMELAND OF THE MIZU NO TAMI, I SUPPOSE IT CAN'T BE HELPED.

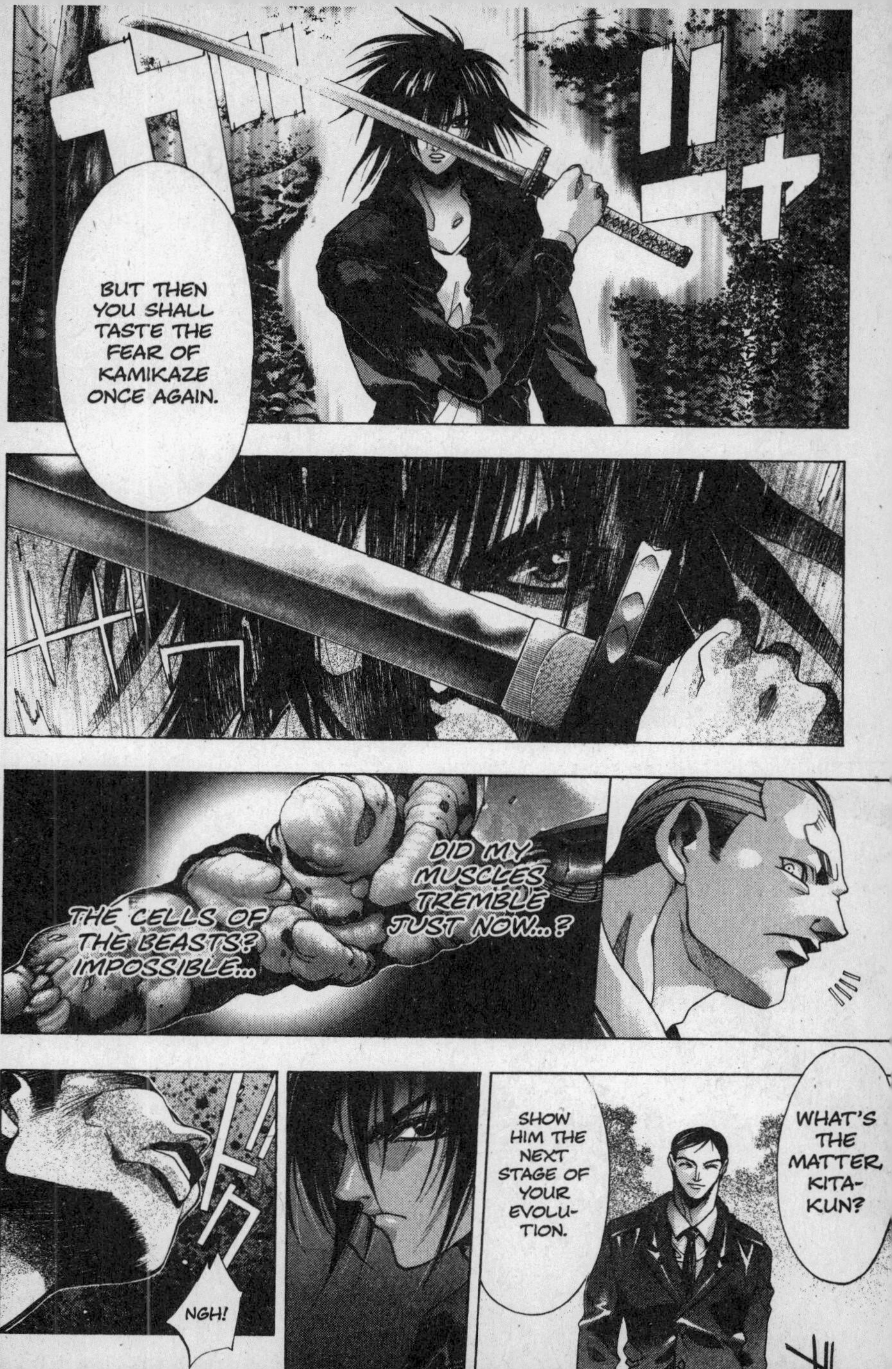
BUT THEN YOU SHALL TASTE THE FEAR OF KAMIKAZE ONCE AGAIN.
DID MY MUSCLES TREMBLE JUST NOW...?
THE CELLS OF THE BEASTS? IMPOSSIBLE...
WHAT'S THE MATTER, KITA-KUN?
SHOW HIM THE NEXT STAGE OF YOUR EVOLU-TION.
NGH!

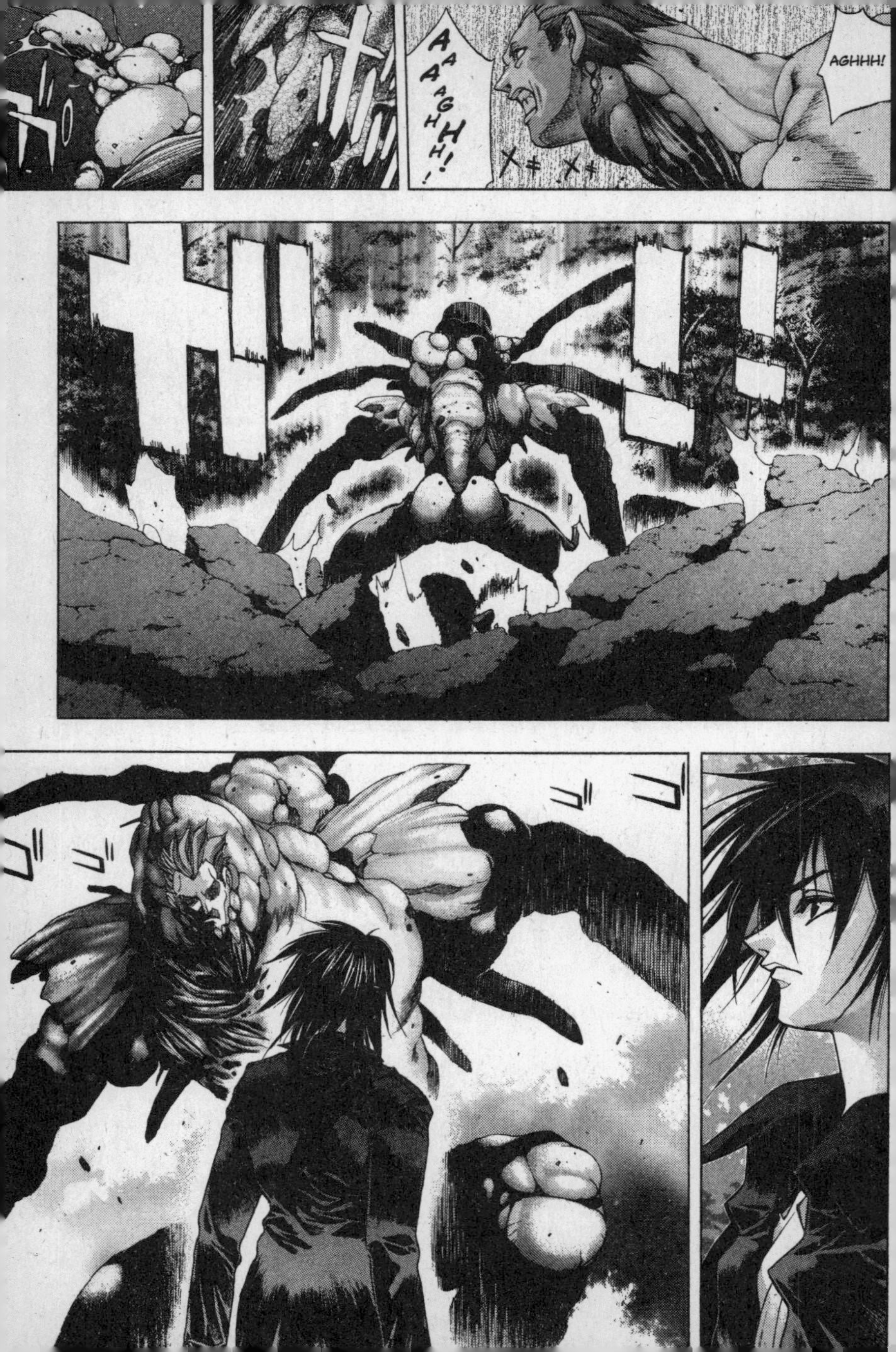
AGHHH!
AAAAGHHHH!!

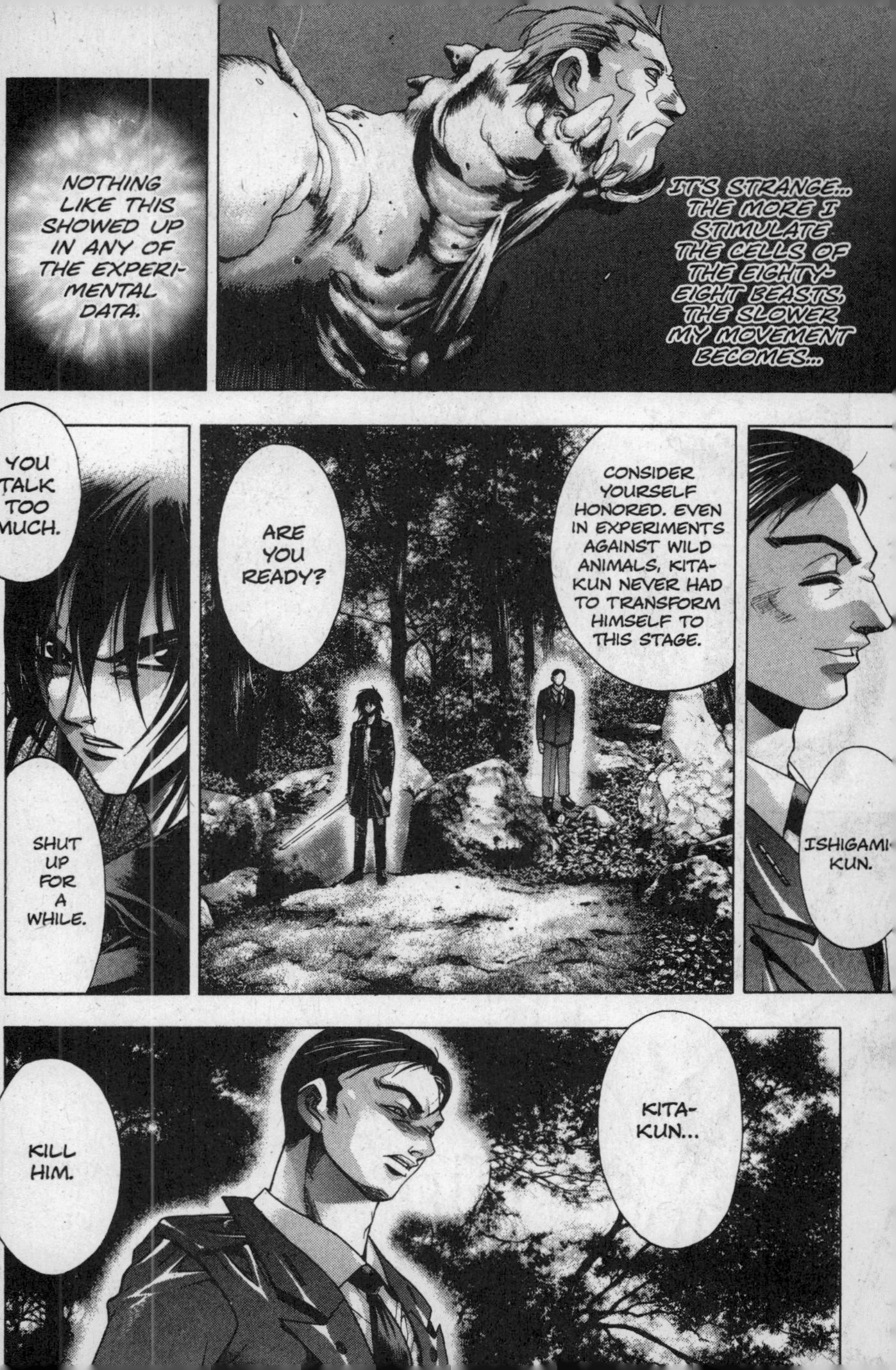
IT'S STRANGE... THE MORE I STIMULATE THE CELLS OF THE EIGHTY-EIGHT BEASTS, THE SLOWER MY MOVEMENT BECOMES...
NOTHING LIKE THIS SHOWED UP IN ANY OF THE EXPERIMENTAL DATA.
ISHIGAMI-KUN.
CONSIDER YOURSELF HONORED. EVEN IN EXPERIMENTS AGAINST WILD ANIMALS, KITA-KUN NEVER HAD TO TRANSFORM HIMSELF TO THIS STAGE.
ARE YOU READY?
YOU TALK TOO MUCH.
SHUT UP FOR A WHILE.
KITA-KUN...
KILL HIM.

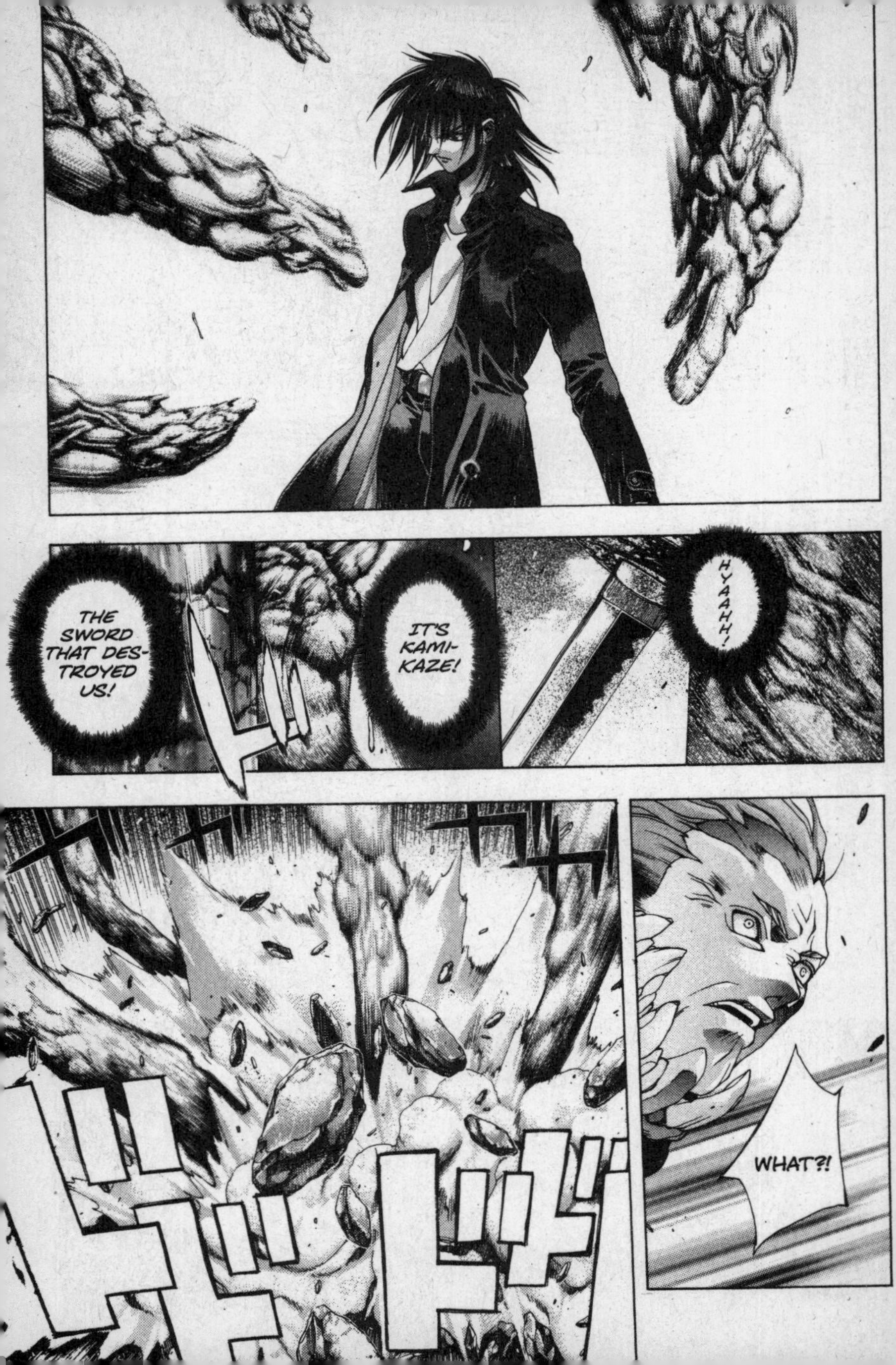
HYAAHH!
IT'S KAMI-KAZE!
THE SWORD THAT DES-TROYED US!
WHAT?!

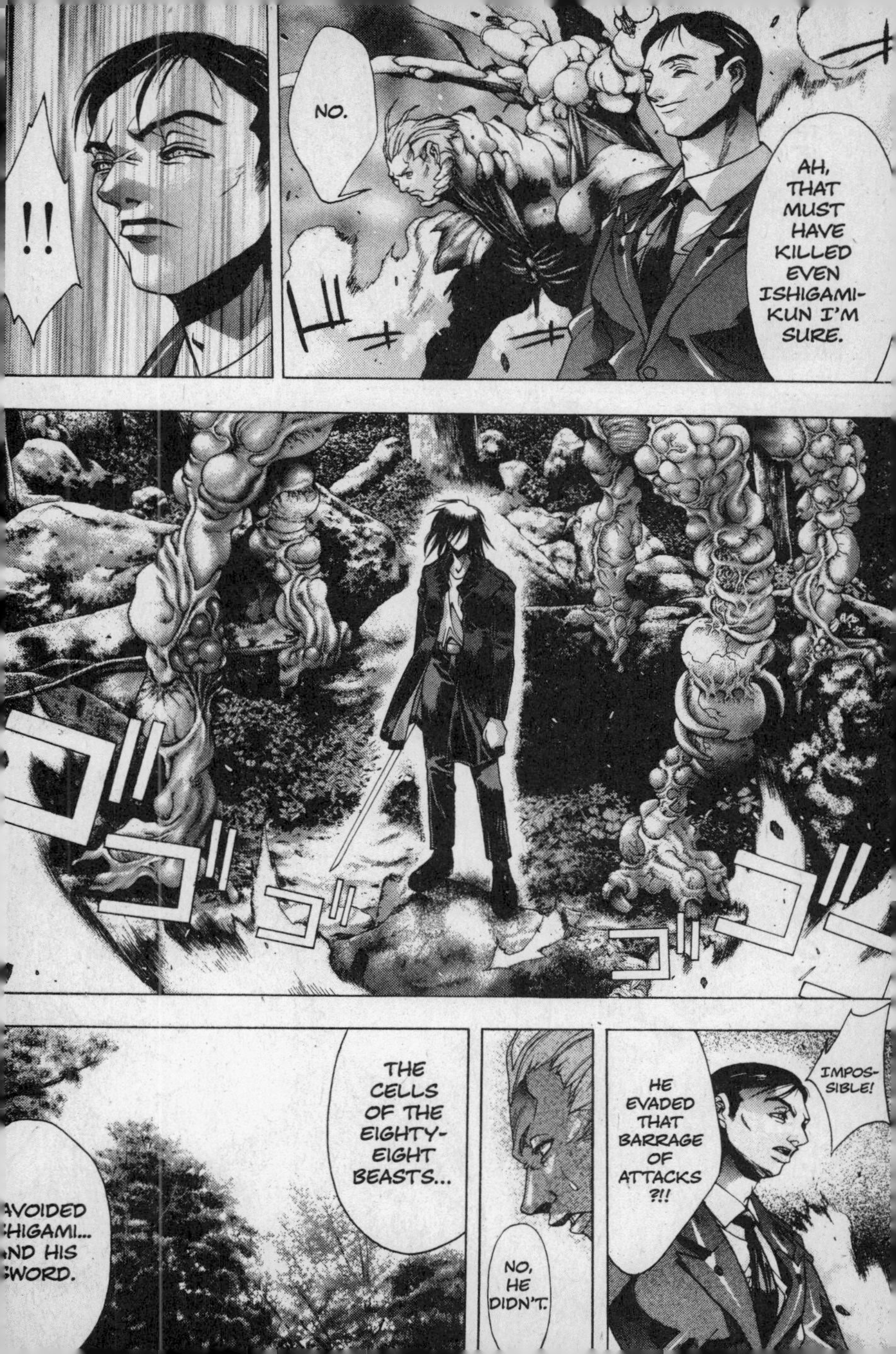
AH, THAT MUST HAVE KILLED EVEN ISHIGAMI-KUN I'M SURE.
NO.
!!
IMPOS-SIBLE!
HE EVADED THAT BARRAGE OF ATTACKS ?!!
NO, HE DIDN'T.
THE CELLS OF THE EIGHTY-EIGHT BEASTS...
AVOIDED
HIGAMI...
ND HIS
WORD.

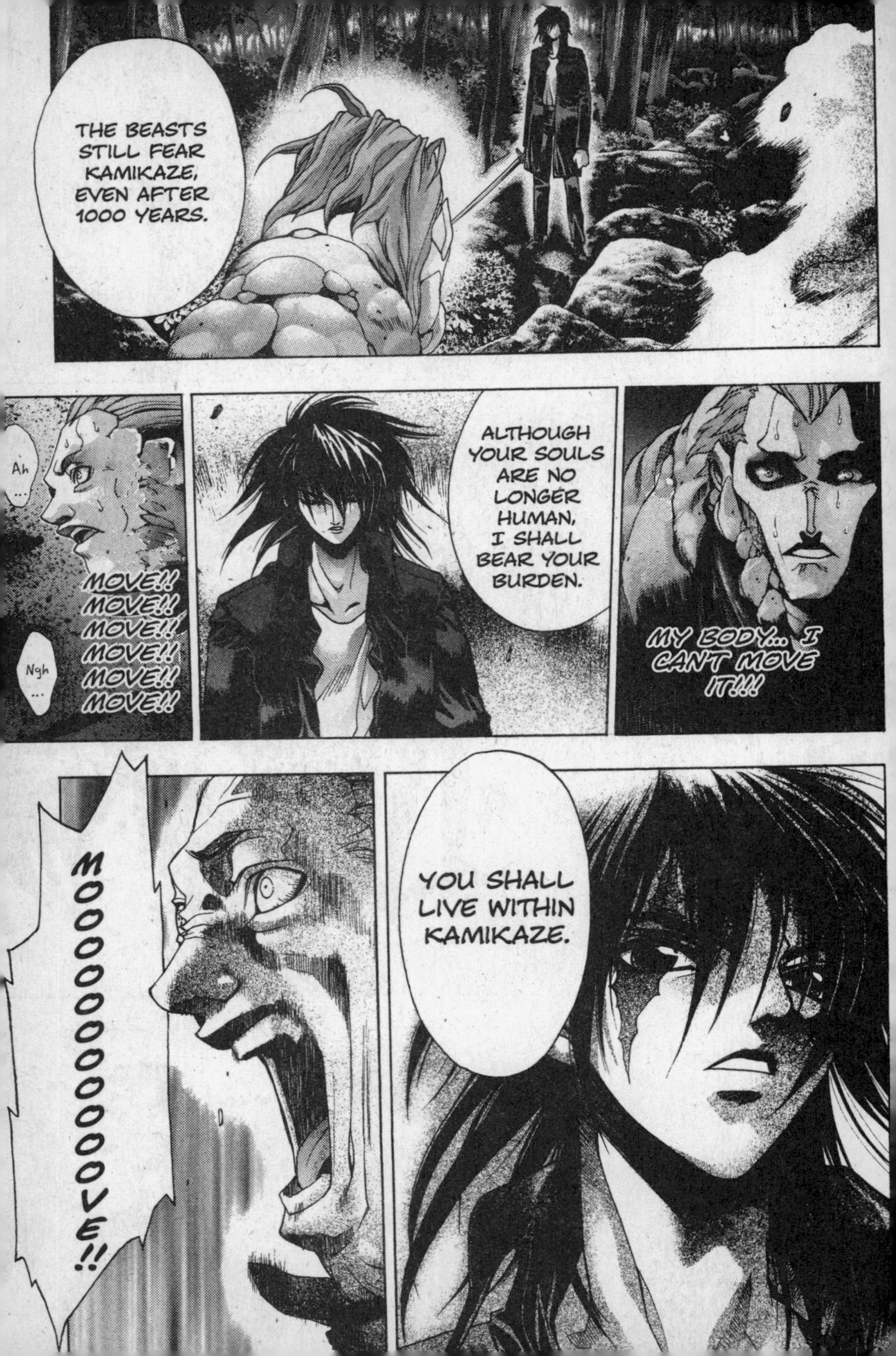
THE BEASTS STILL FEAR KAMIKAZE, EVEN AFTER 1000 YEARS.
MY BODY... I CAN'T MOVE IT!!!
ALTHOUGH YOUR SOULS ARE NO LONGER HUMAN, I SHALL BEAR YOUR BURDEN.
Ah ...
MOVE!! MOVE!! MOVE!! MOVE!! MOVE!! MOVE!!
Ngh ...
YOU SHALL LIVE WITHIN KAMIKAZE.
MOOOOOOOOOOOVE!!

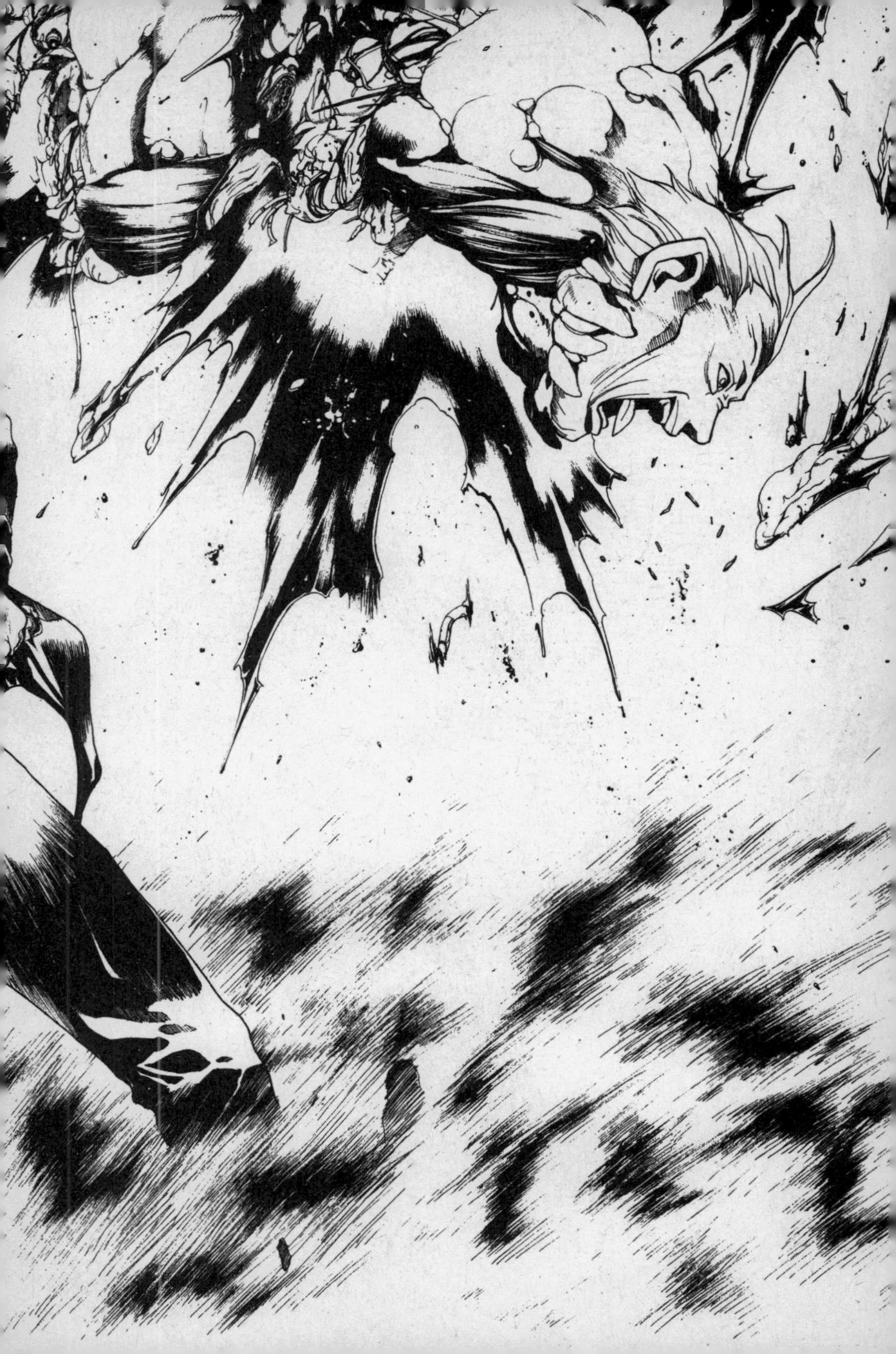

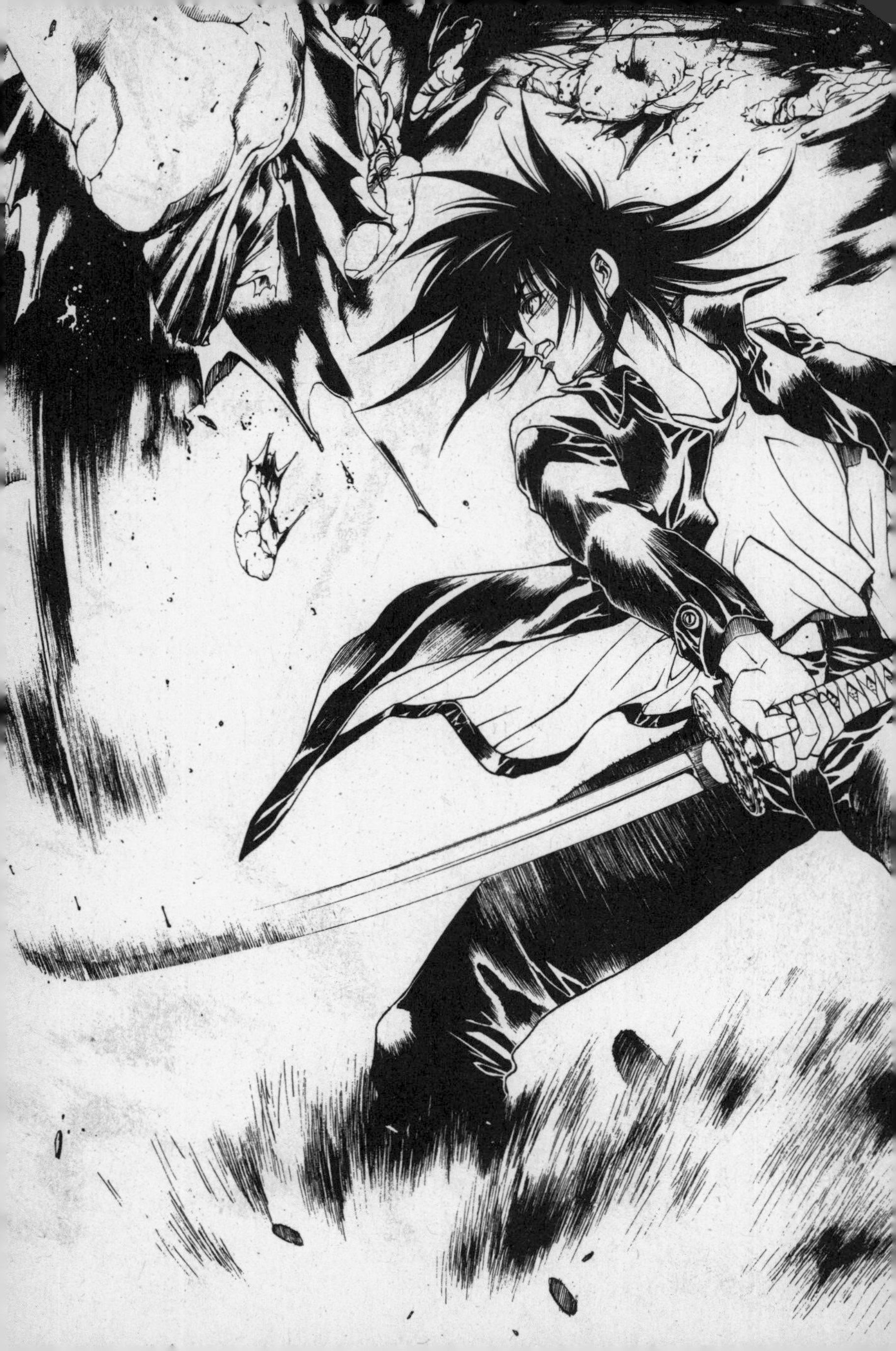

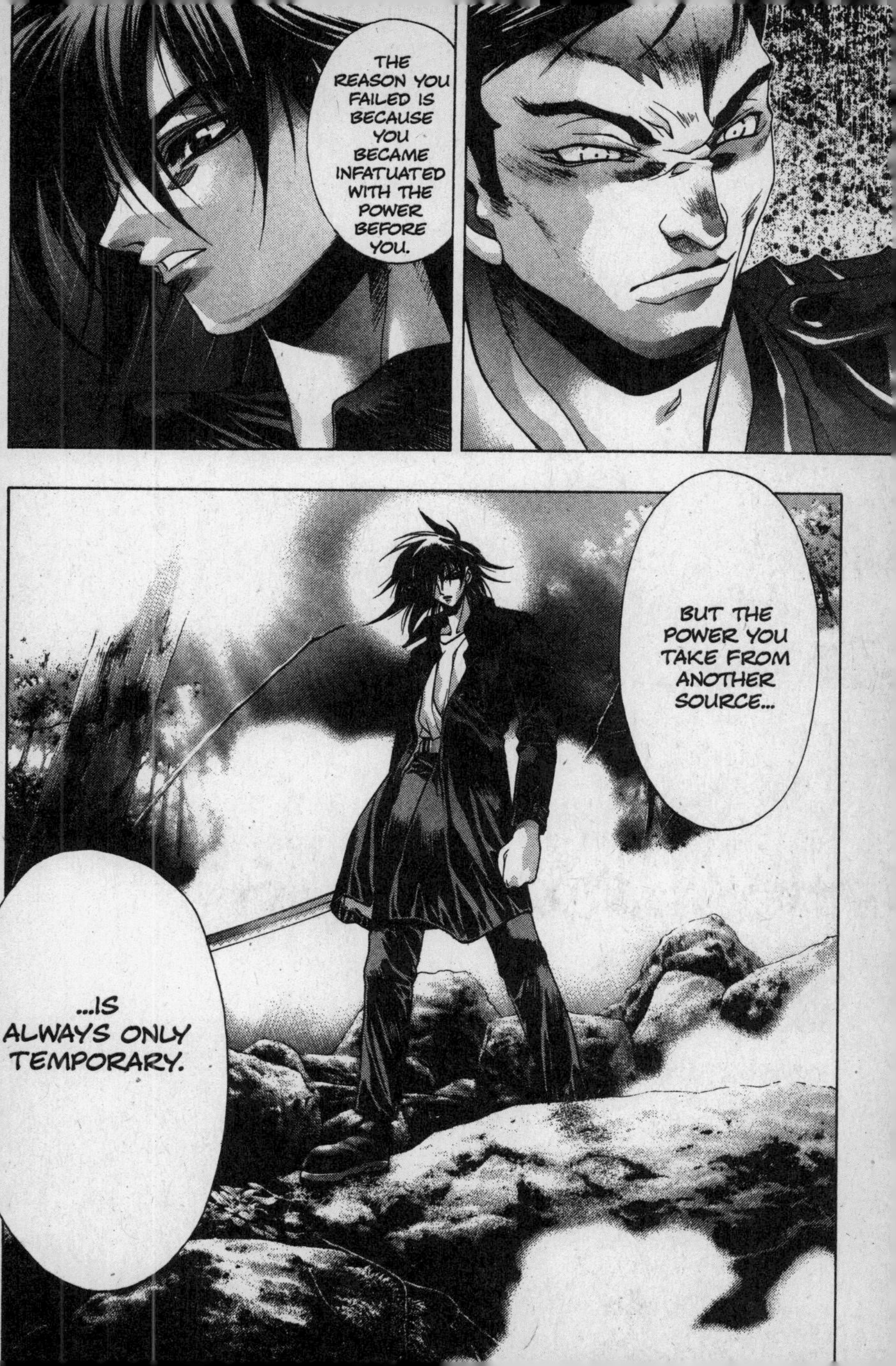
THE REASON YOU FAILED IS BECAUSE YOU BECAME INFATUATED WITH THE POWER BEFORE YOU.
BUT THE POWER YOU TAKE FROM ANOTHER SOURCE...
...IS ALWAYS ONLY TEMPORARY.

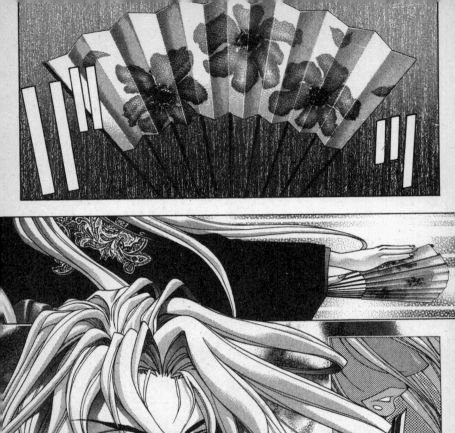
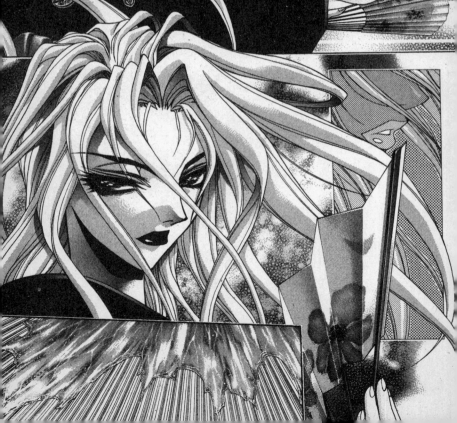

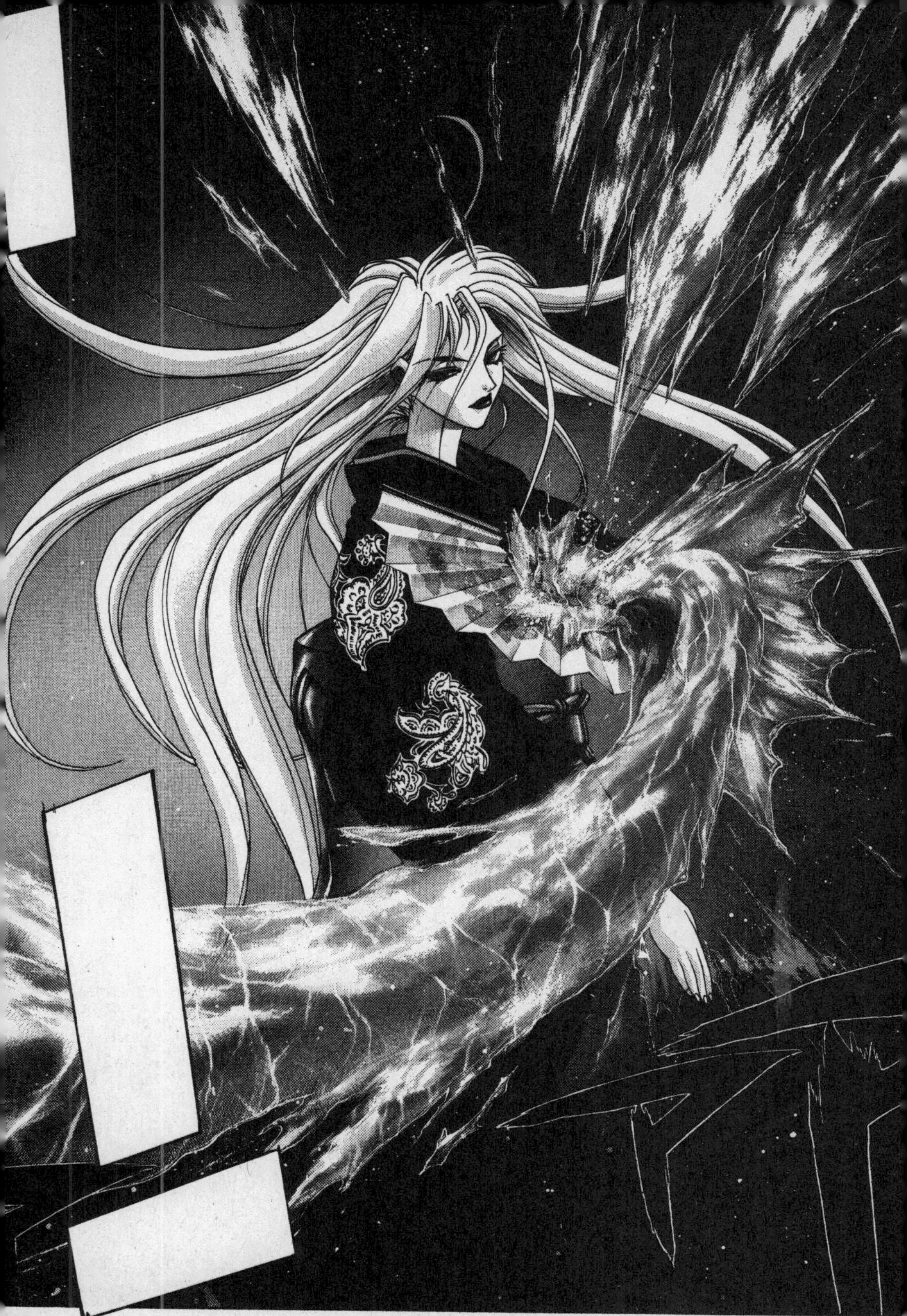

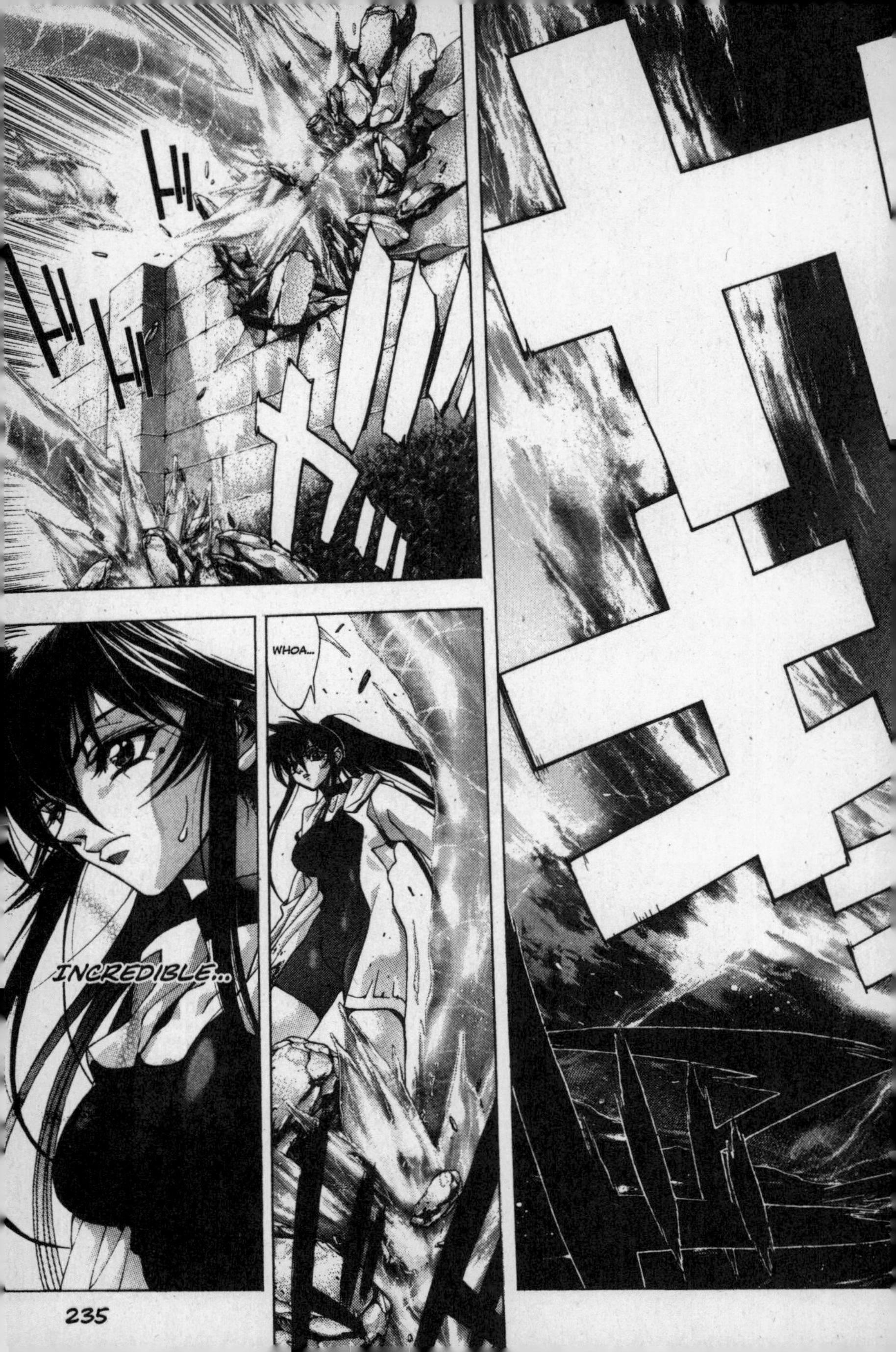
WHOA...
INCREDIBLE...

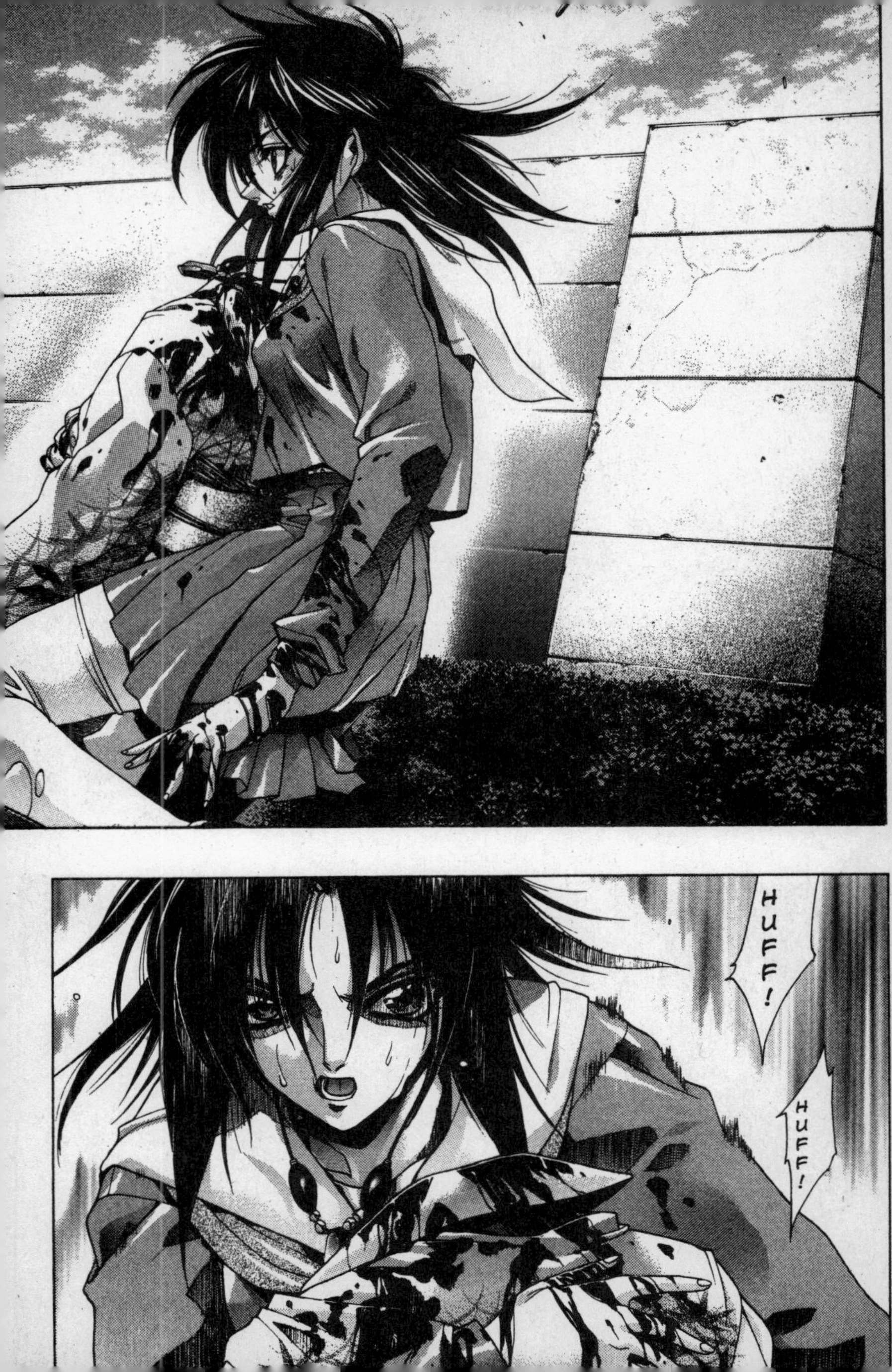
HUFF!
HUFF!

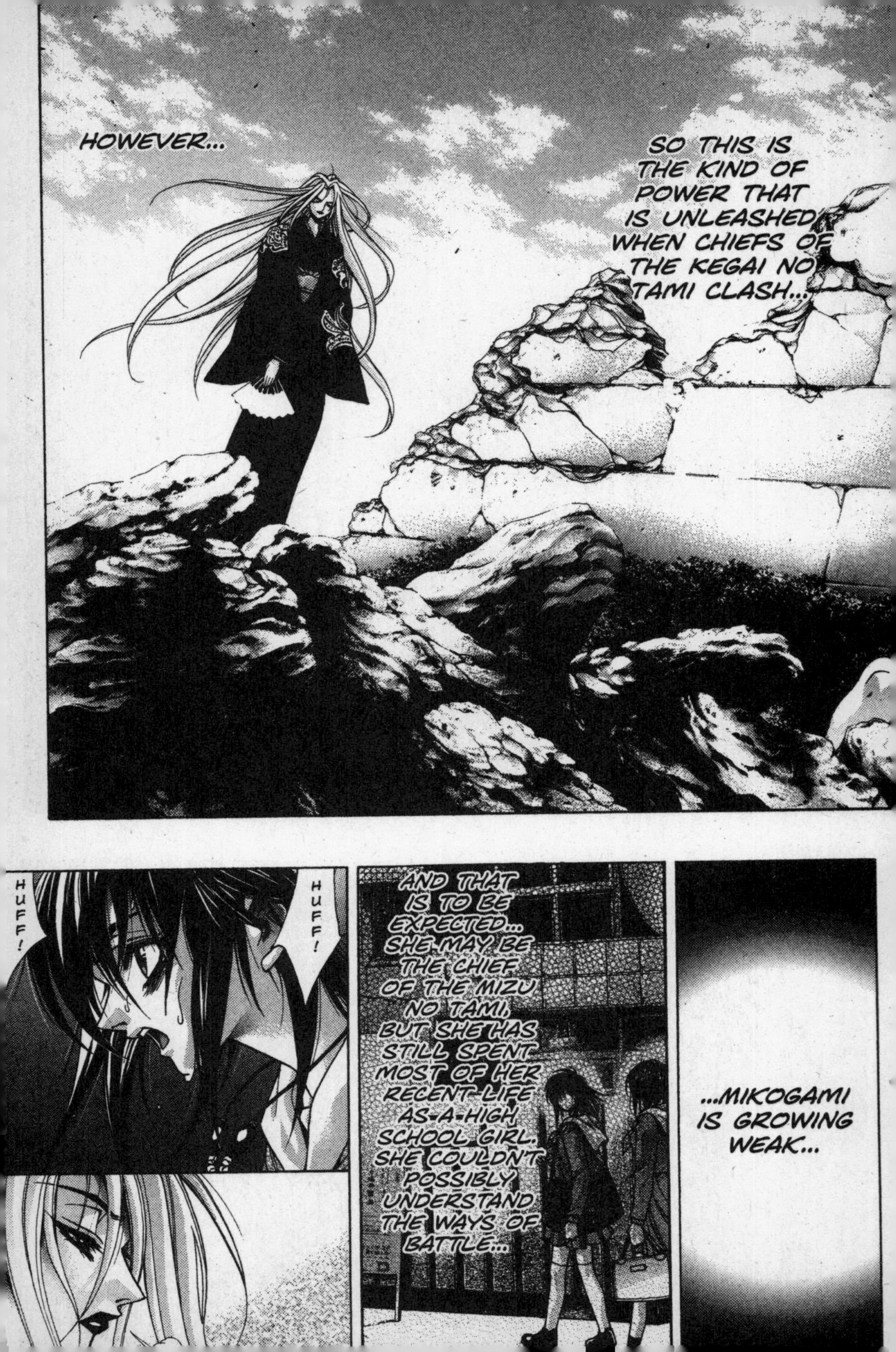
SO THIS IS THE KIND OF POWER THAT IS UNLEASHED WHEN CHIEFS OF THE KEGAI NO TAMI CLASH...
HOWEVER...
...MIKOGAMI IS GROWING WEAK...
AND THAT IS TO BE EXPECTED... SHE MAY BE THE CHIEF OF THE MIZU NO TAMI, BUT SHE HAS STILL SPENT MOST OF HER RECENT LIFE AS A HIGH SCHOOL GIRL. SHE COULDN'T POSSIBLY UNDERSTAND THE WAYS OF BATTLE...
HUFF!
HUFF!

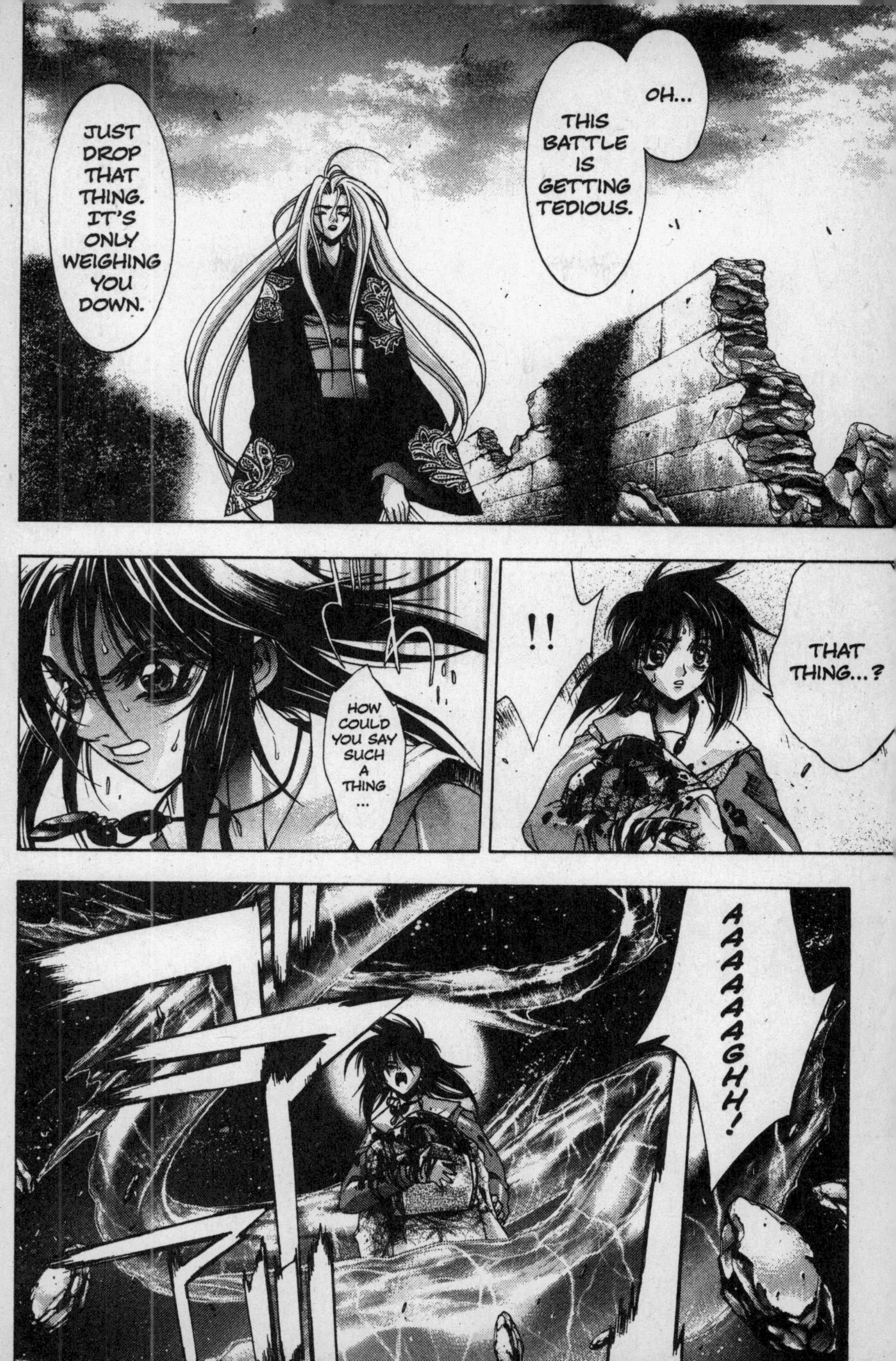
OH...
THIS BATTLE IS GETTING TEDIOUS.
JUST DROP THAT THING. IT'S ONLY WEIGHING YOU DOWN.
THAT THING...?
!!
HOW COULD YOU SAY SUCH A THING...
AAAAAAGHH!

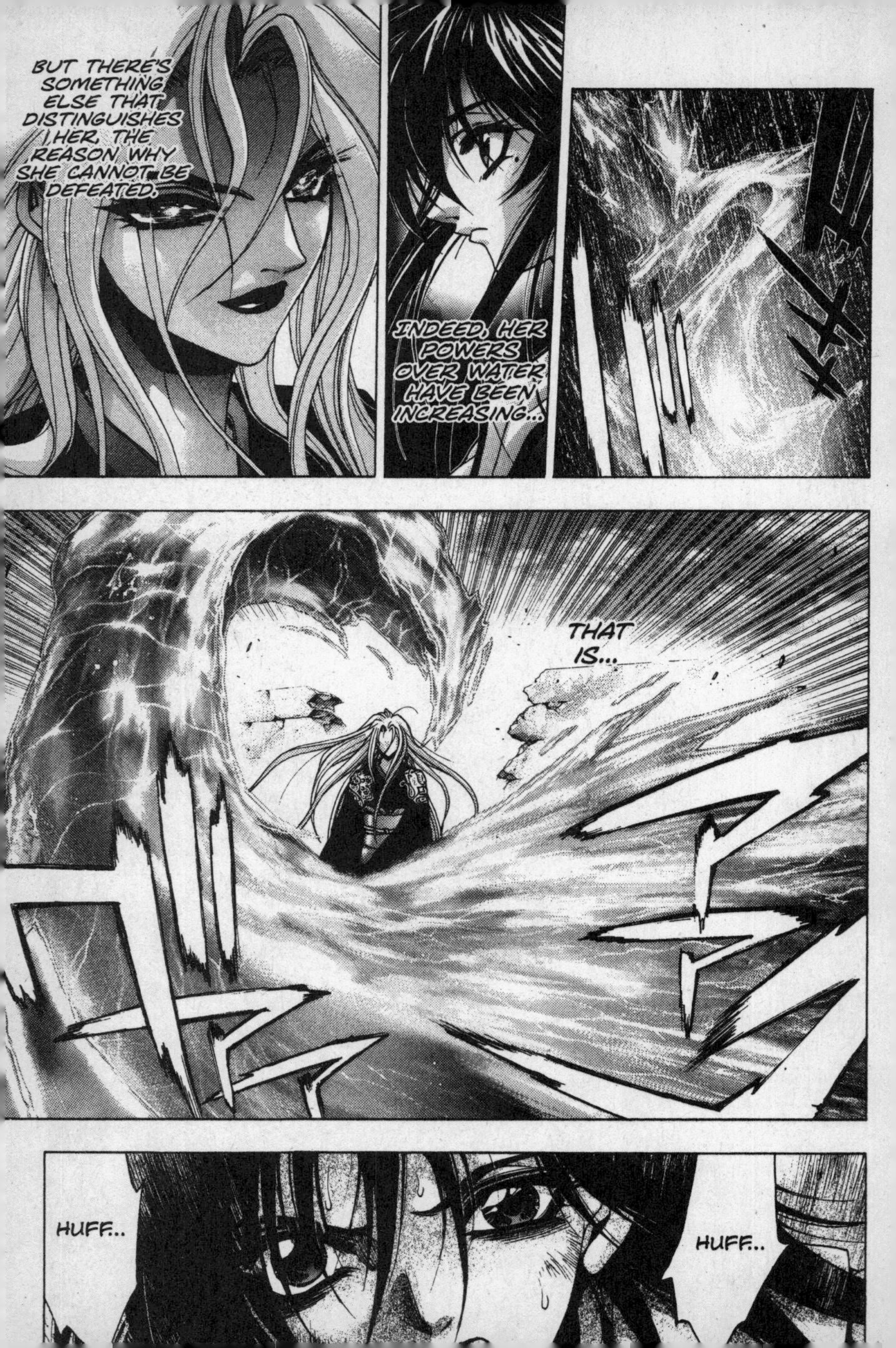
INDEED, HER POWERS OVER WATER HAVE BEEN INCREASING...
BUT THERE'S SOMETHING ELSE THAT DISTINGUISHES HER, THE REASON WHY SHE CANNOT BE DEFEATED.
THAT IS...
HUFF...
HUFF...

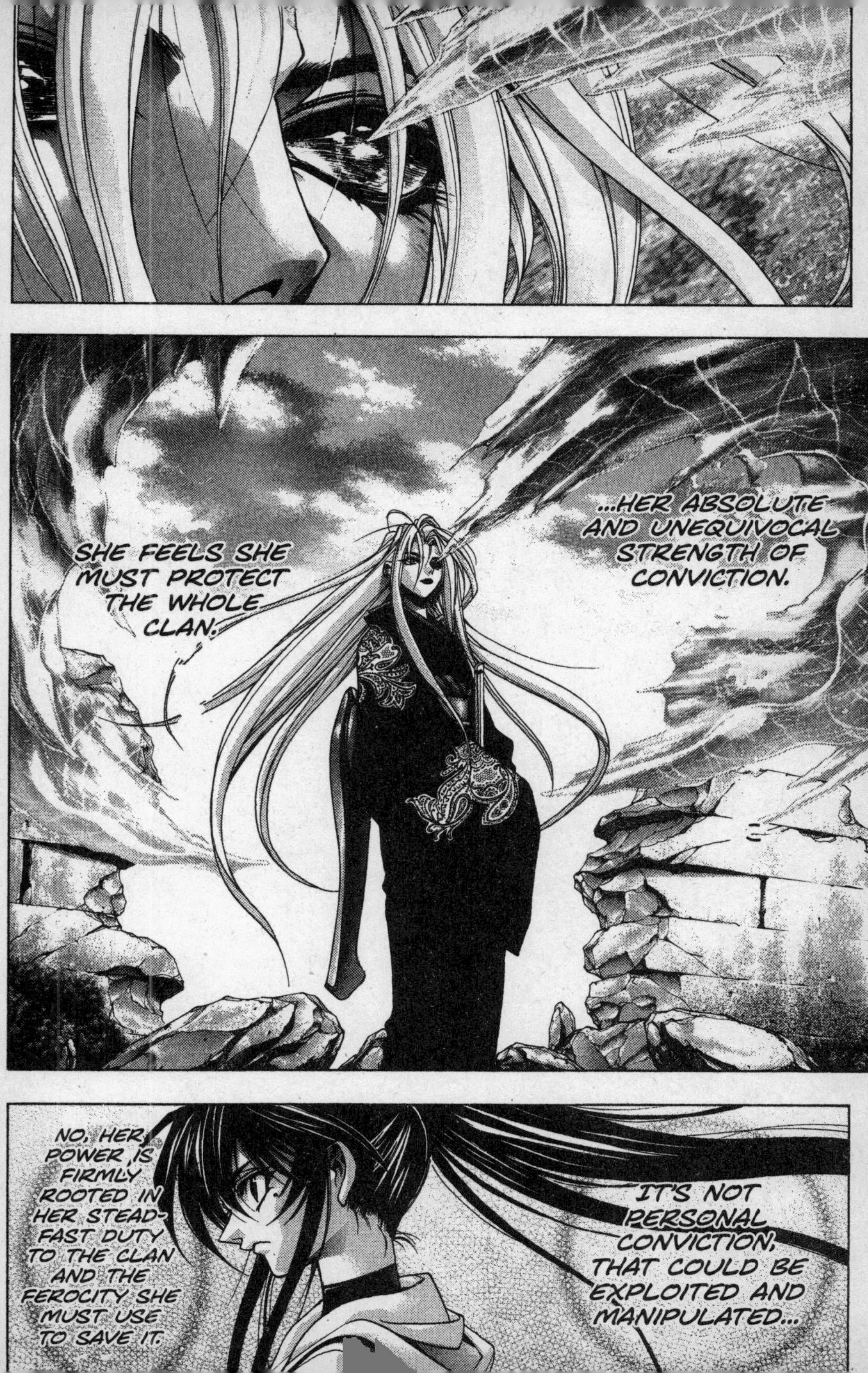
...HER ABSOLUTE AND UNEQUIVOCAL STRENGTH OF CONVICTION.
SHE FEELS SHE MUST PROTECT THE WHOLE CLAN.
IT'S NOT PERSONAL CONVICTION, THAT COULD BE EXPLOITED AND MANIPULATED...
NO, HER POWER IS FIRMLY ROOTED IN HER STEAD-FAST DUTY TO THE CLAN AND THE FEROCITY SHE MUST USE TO SAVE IT.

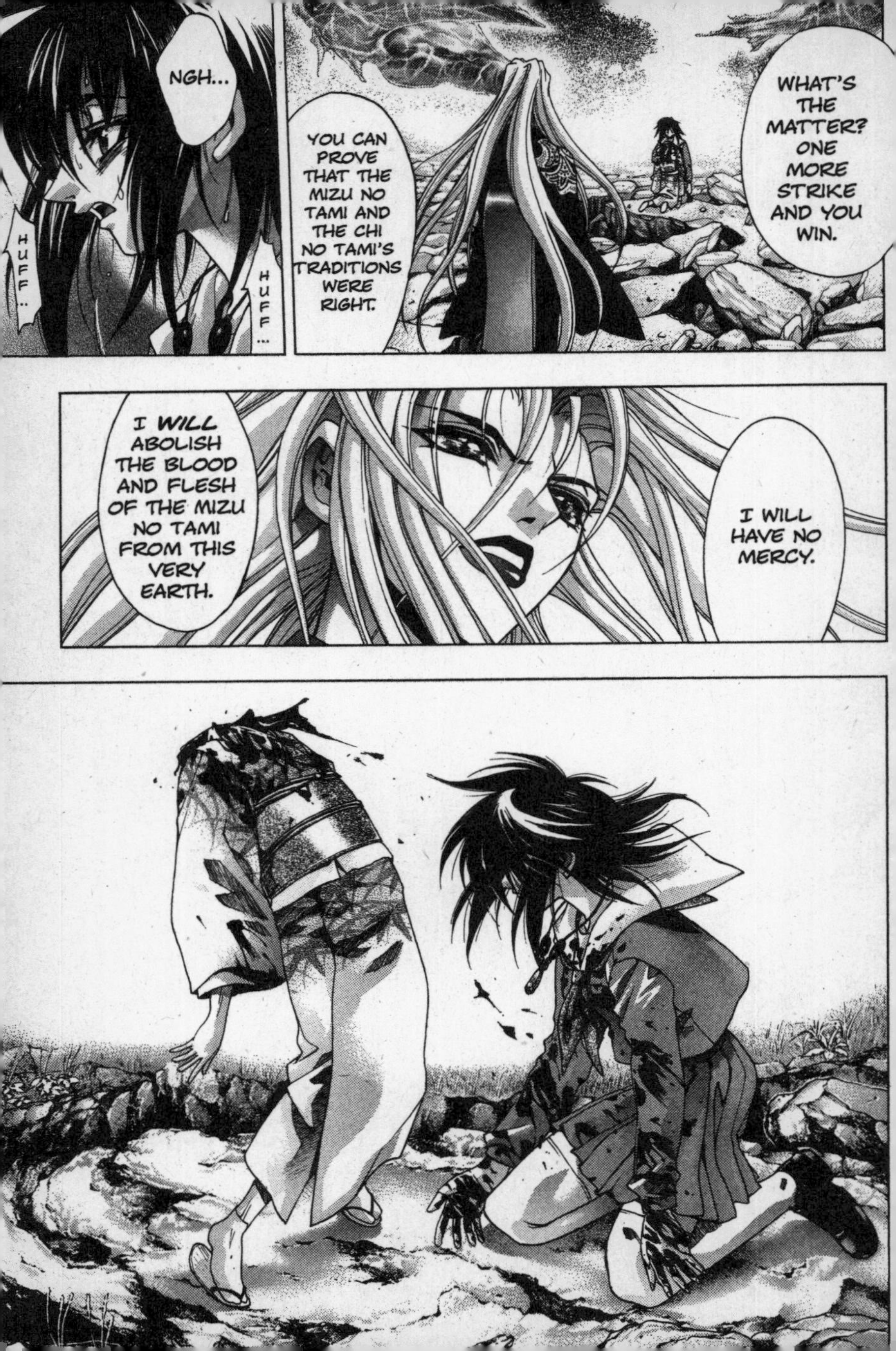
WHAT'S THE MATTER? ONE MORE STRIKE AND YOU WIN.
YOU CAN PROVE THAT THE MIZU NO TAMI AND THE CHI NO TAMI'S TRADITIONS WERE RIGHT.
NGH...
HUFF...
HUFF...
I WILL HAVE NO MERCY.
I WILL ABOLISH THE BLOOD AND FLESH OF THE MIZU NO TAMI FROM THIS VERY EARTH.

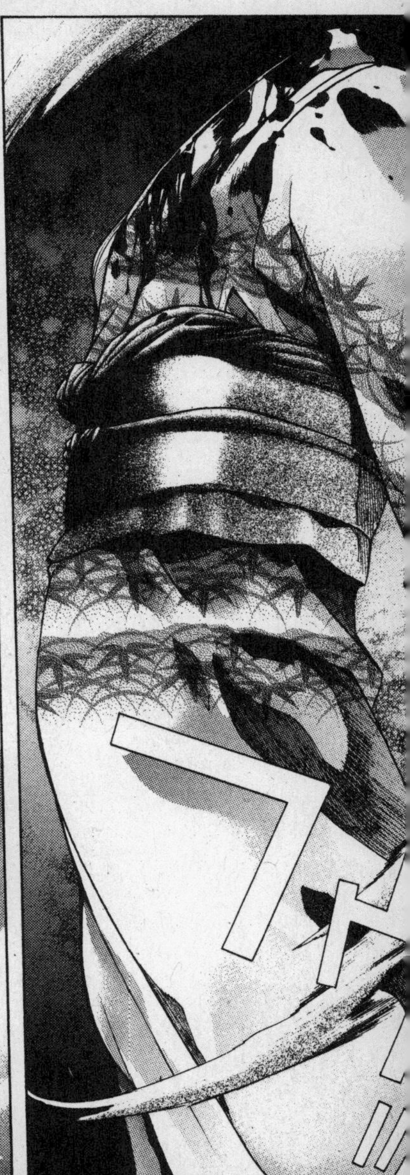
フ
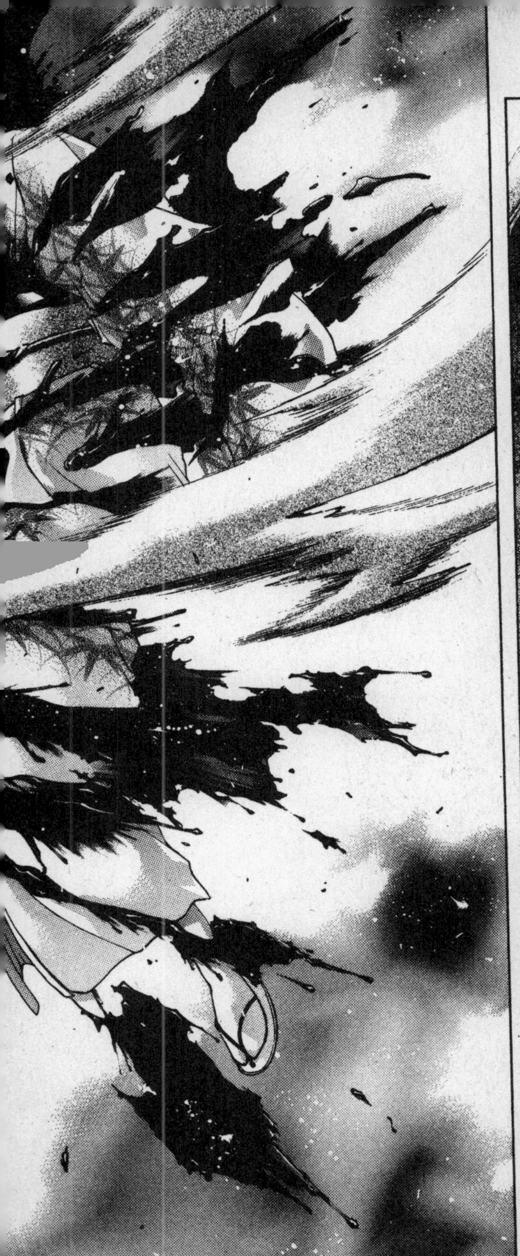

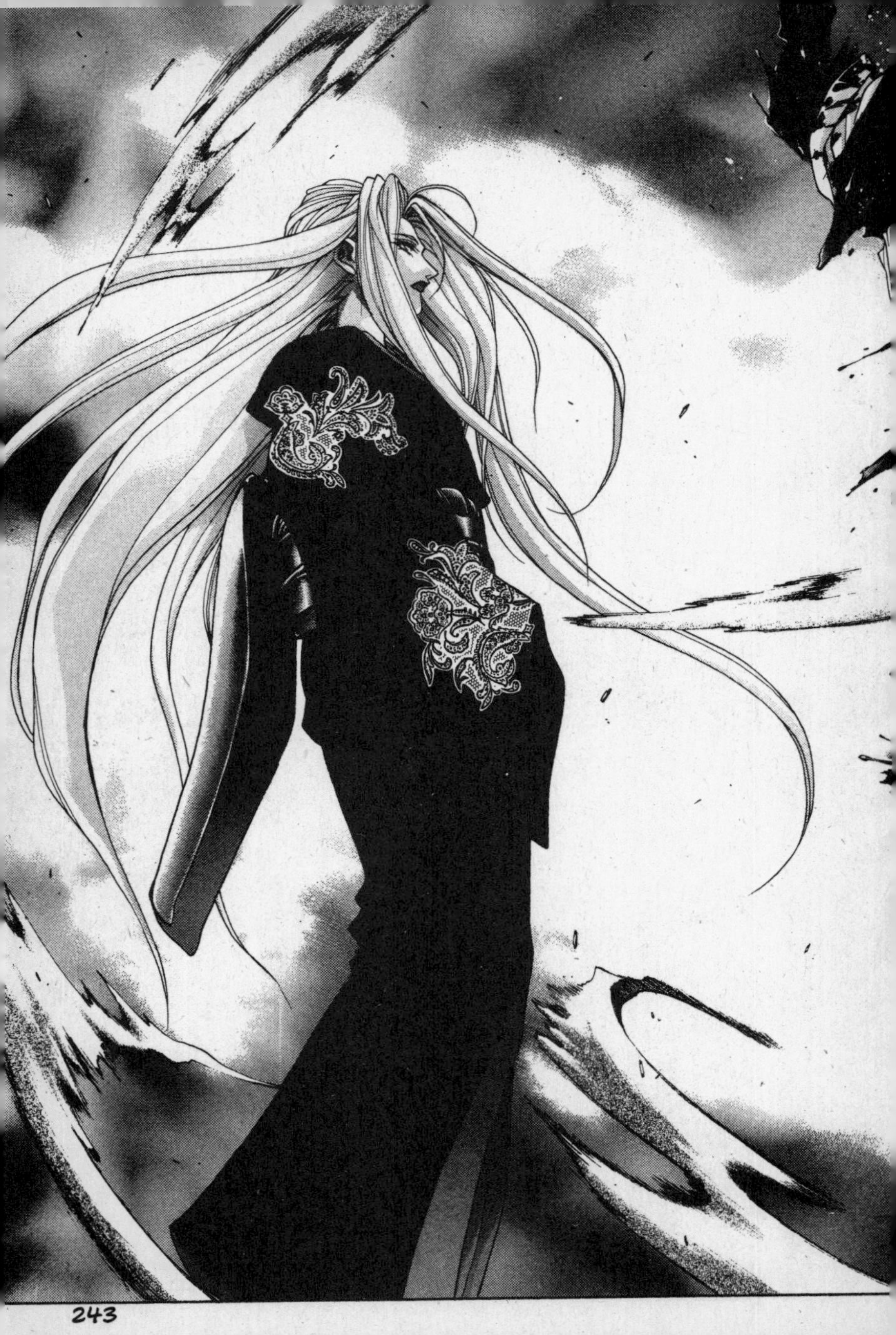

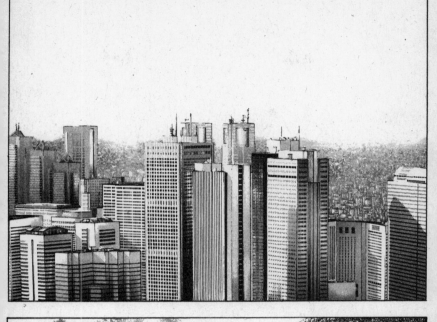

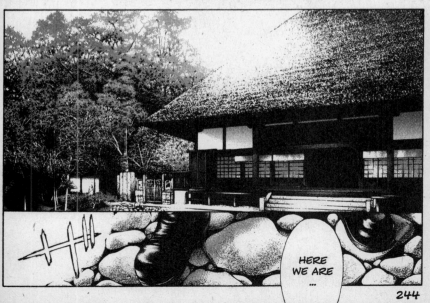

HERE
WE ARE
...

244

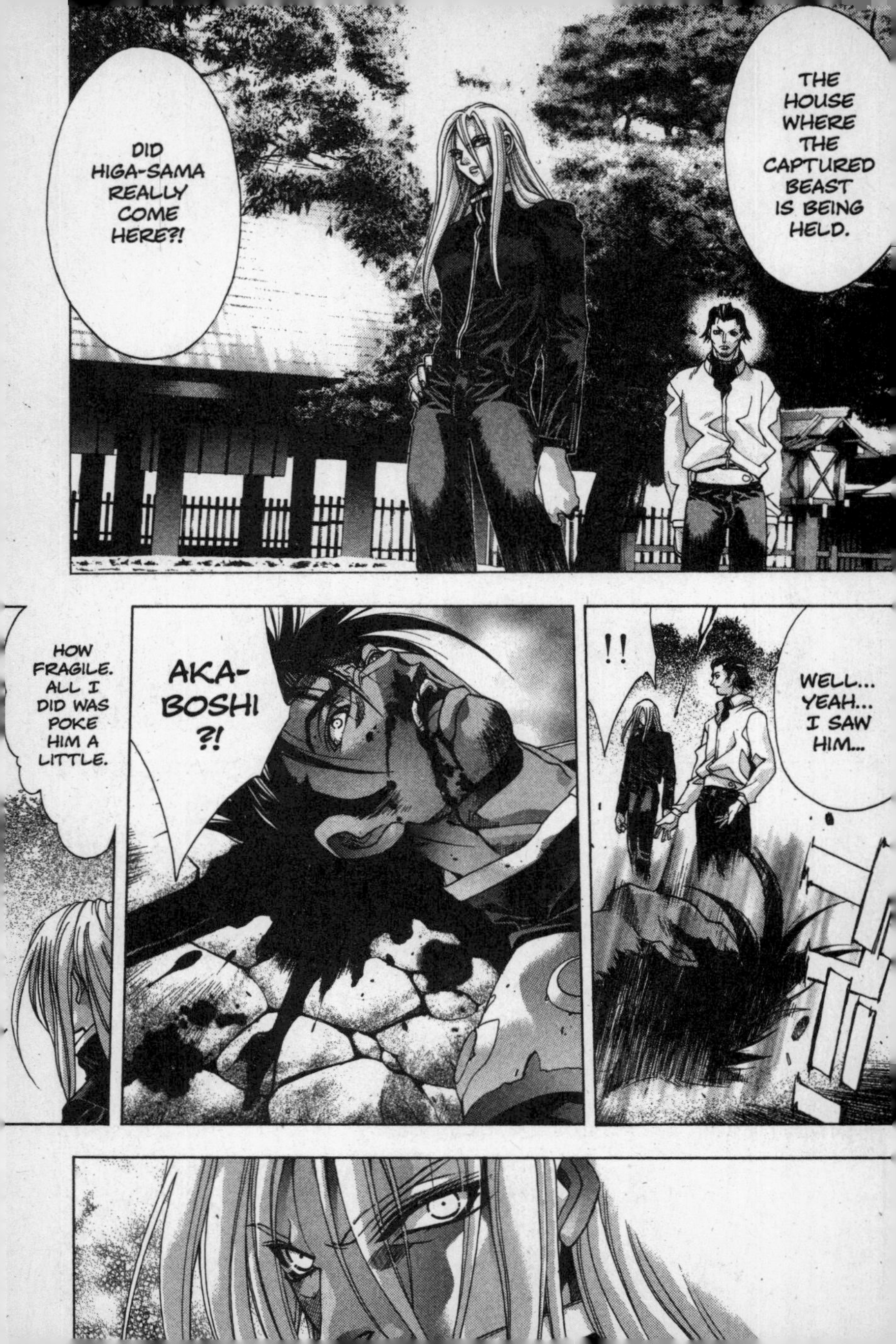
THE HOUSE WHERE THE CAPTURED BEAST IS BEING HELD.
DID HIGA-SAMA REALLY COME HERE?!
WELL... YEAH... I SAW HIM...
!!
AKA-BOSHI ?!
HOW FRAGILE. ALL I DID WAS POKE HIM A LITTLE.

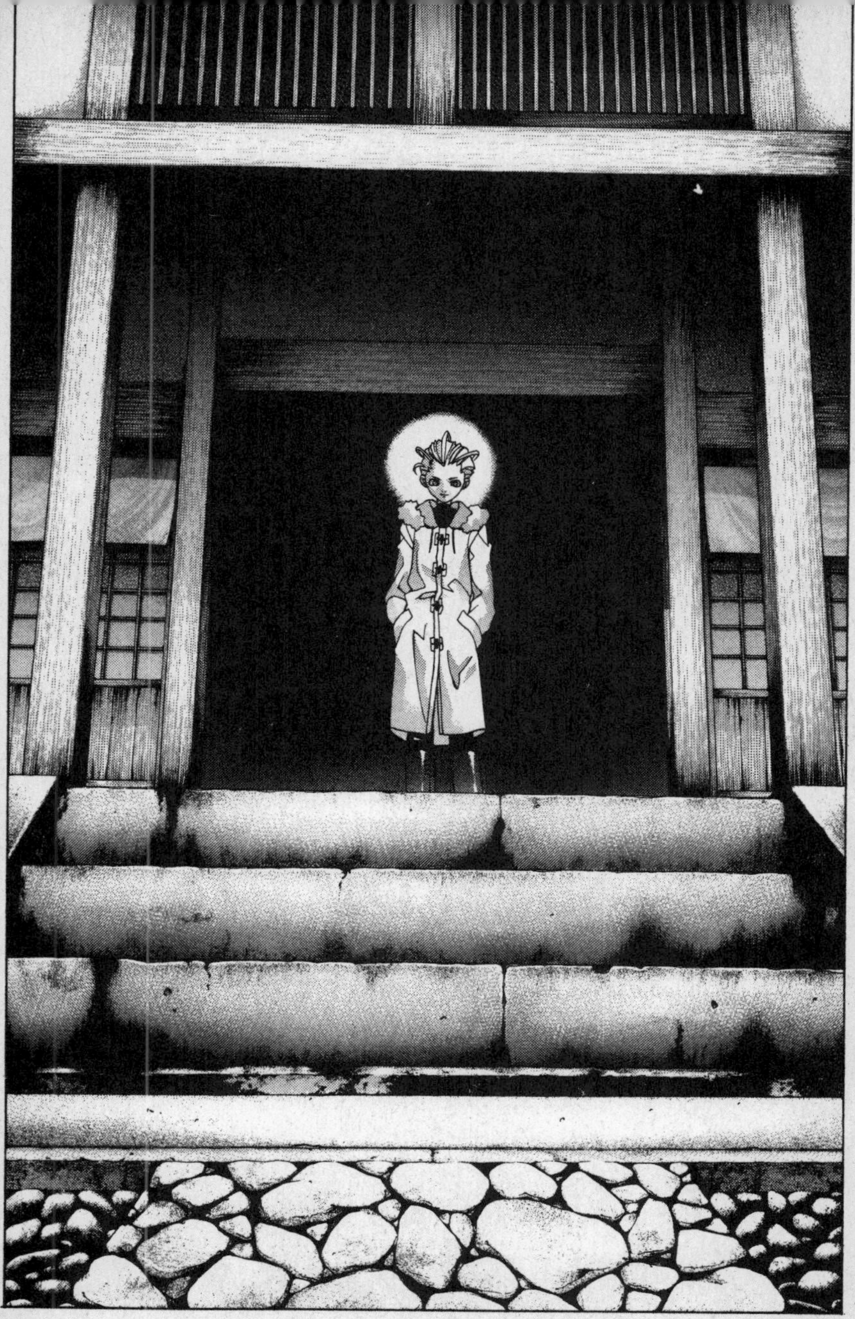

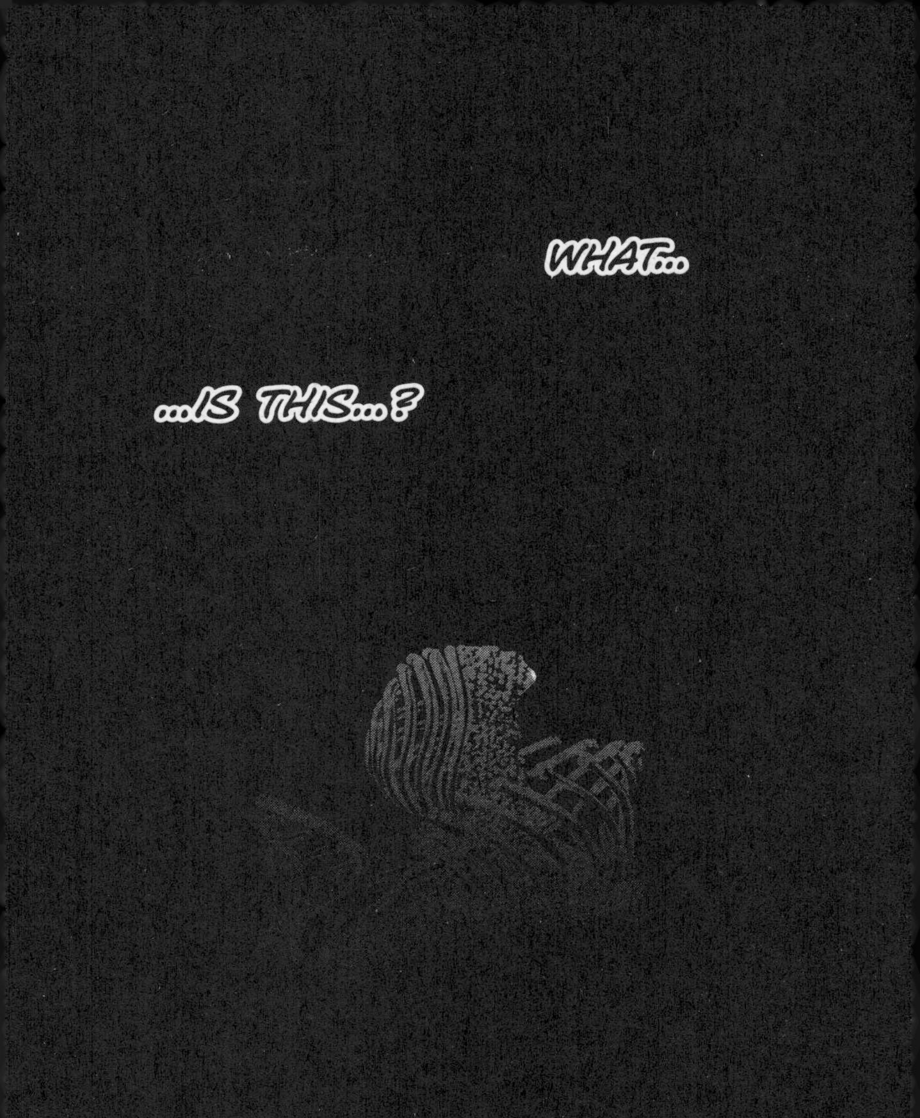
WHAT...
...IS THIS...?

Chapter 29: A Long Day

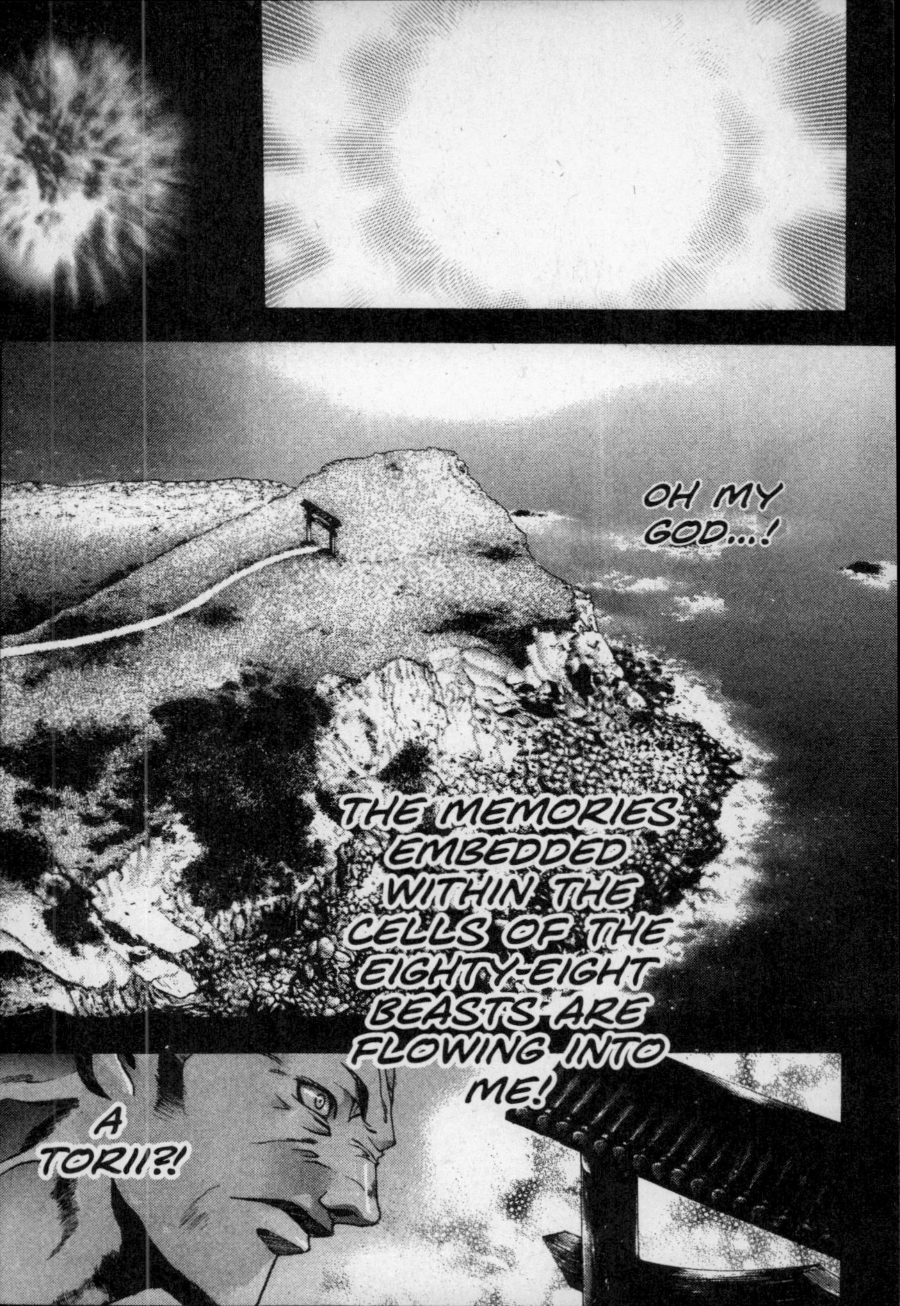
OH MY GOD...!
THE MEMORIES EMBEDDED WITHIN THE CELLS OF THE EIGHTY-EIGHT BEASTS ARE FLOWING INTO ME!
A TORII?!

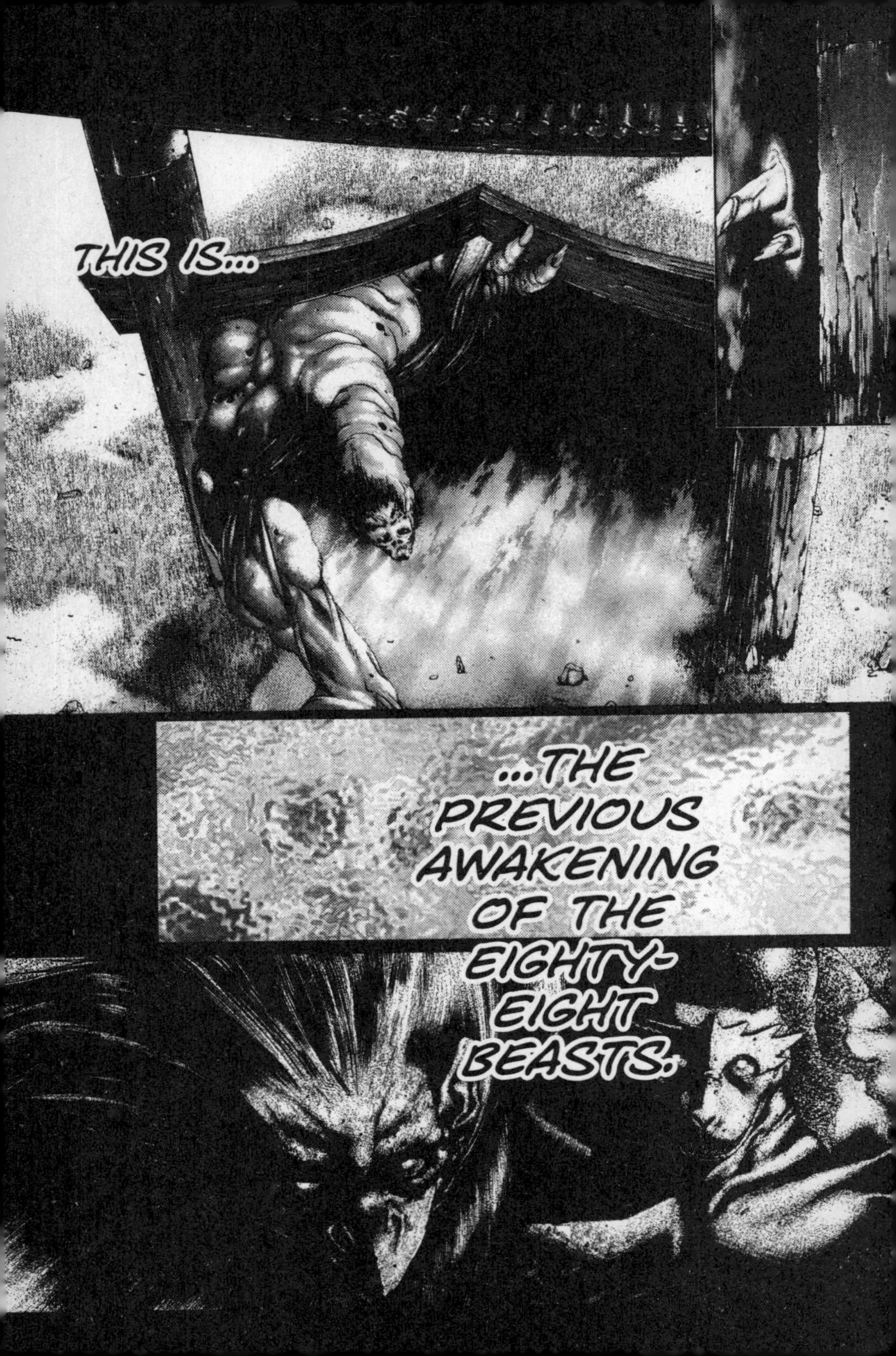
THIS IS...
...THE PREVIOUS AWAKENING OF THE EIGHTY-EIGHT BEASTS.

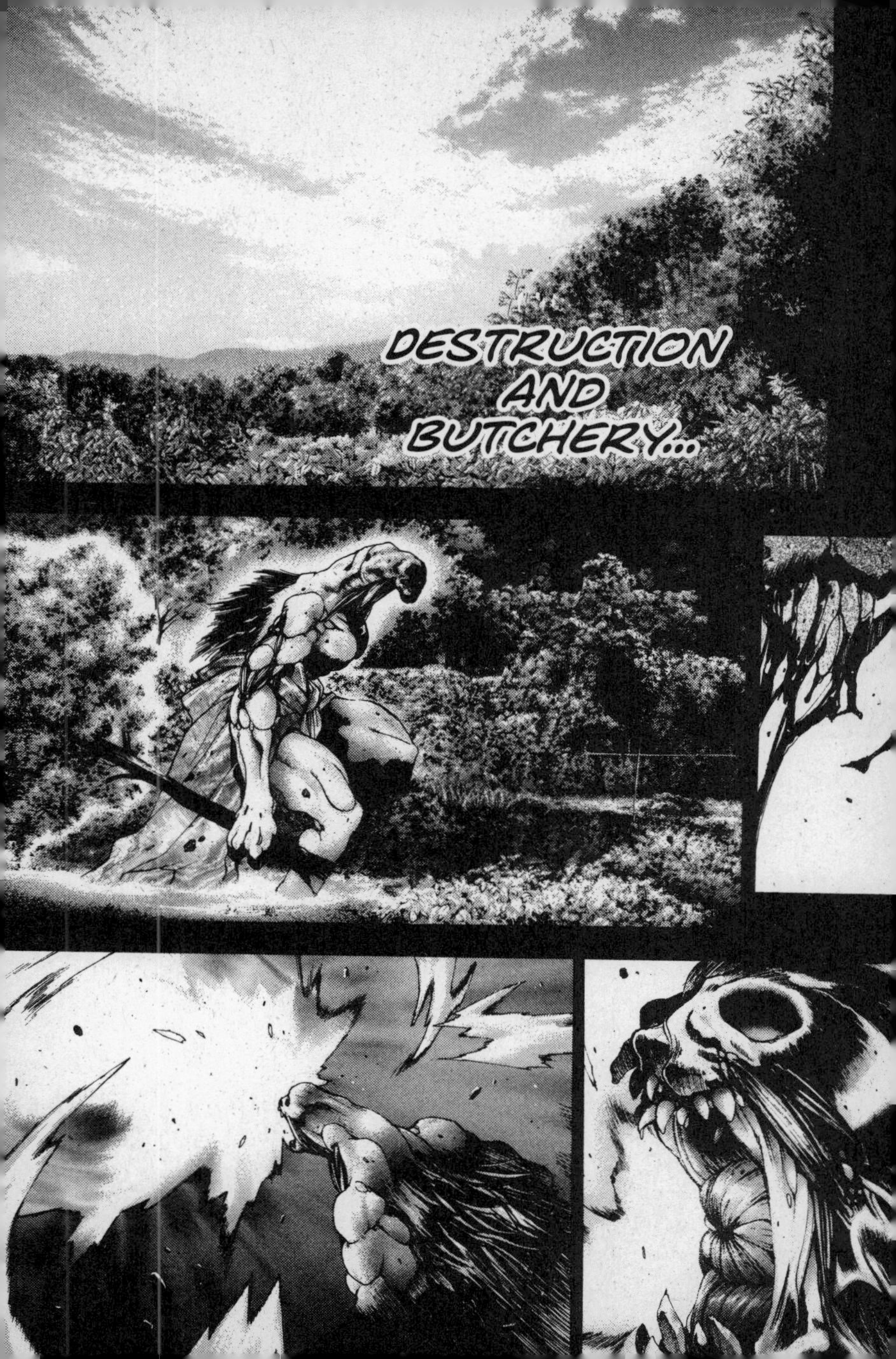
DESTRUCTION AND BUTCHERY...

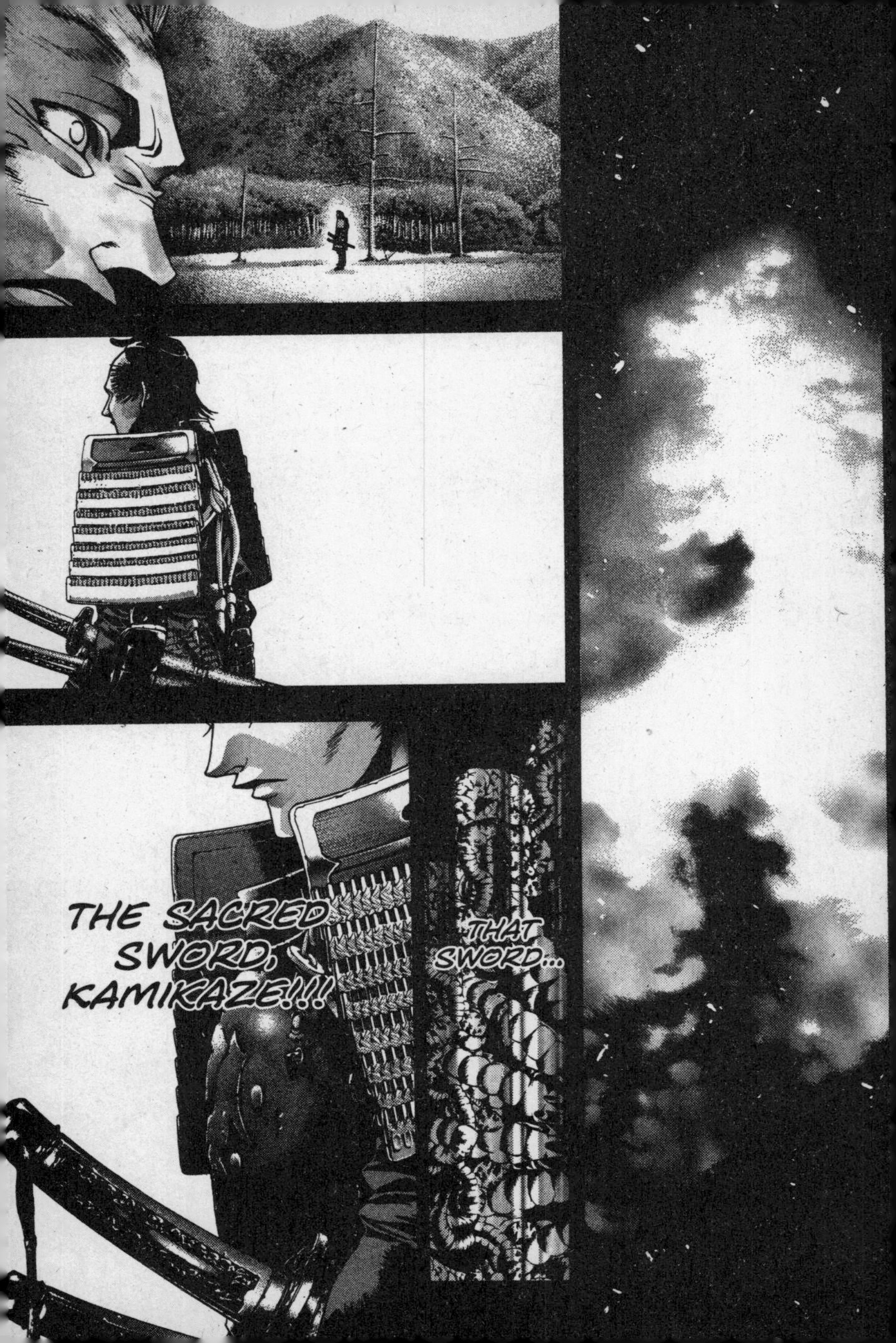
THAT SWORD...
THE SACRED SWORD, KAMIKAZE!!!

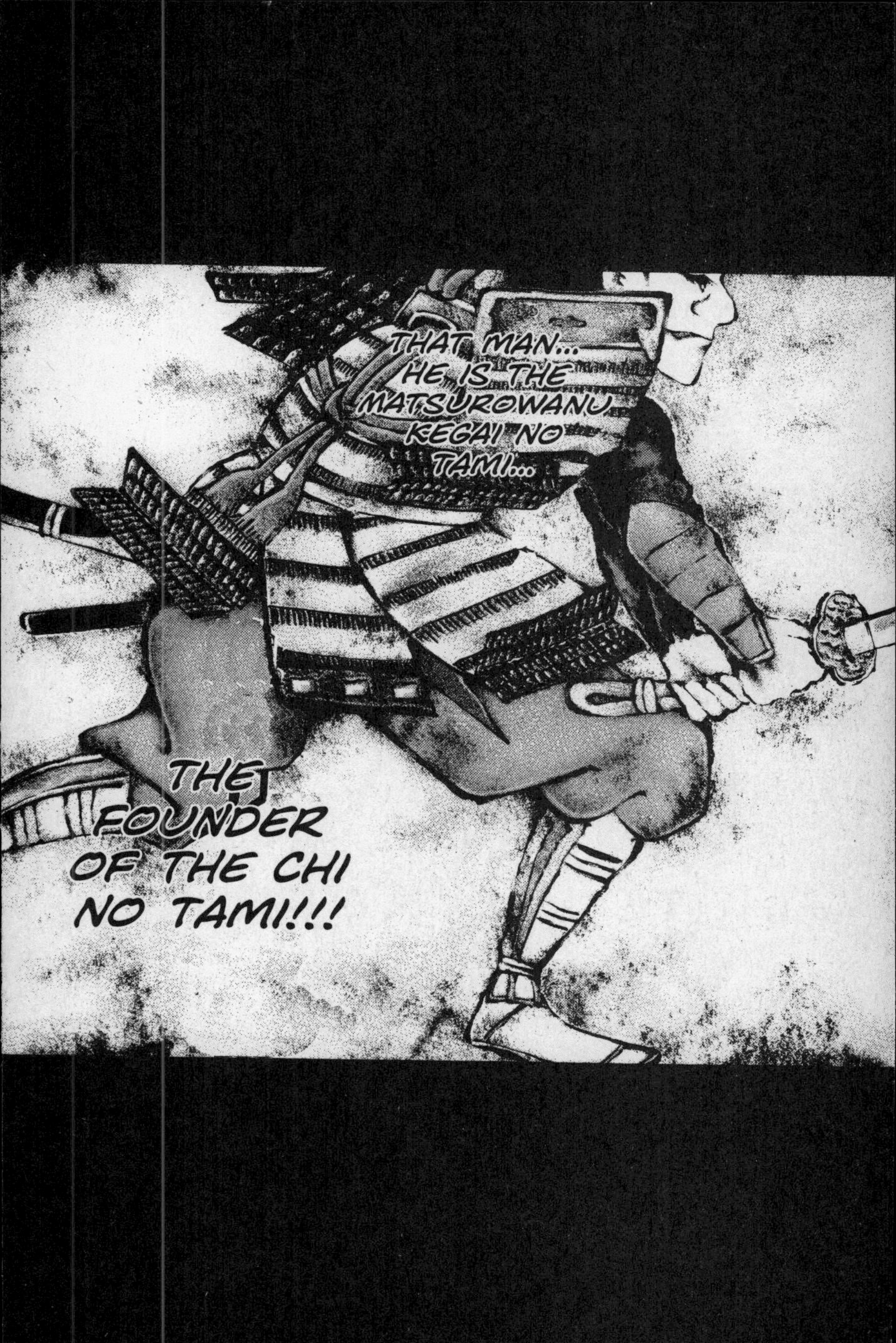
THAT MAN... HE IS THE MATSUROWANU KEGAI NO TAMI...
THE FOUNDER OF THE CHI NO TAMI!!!

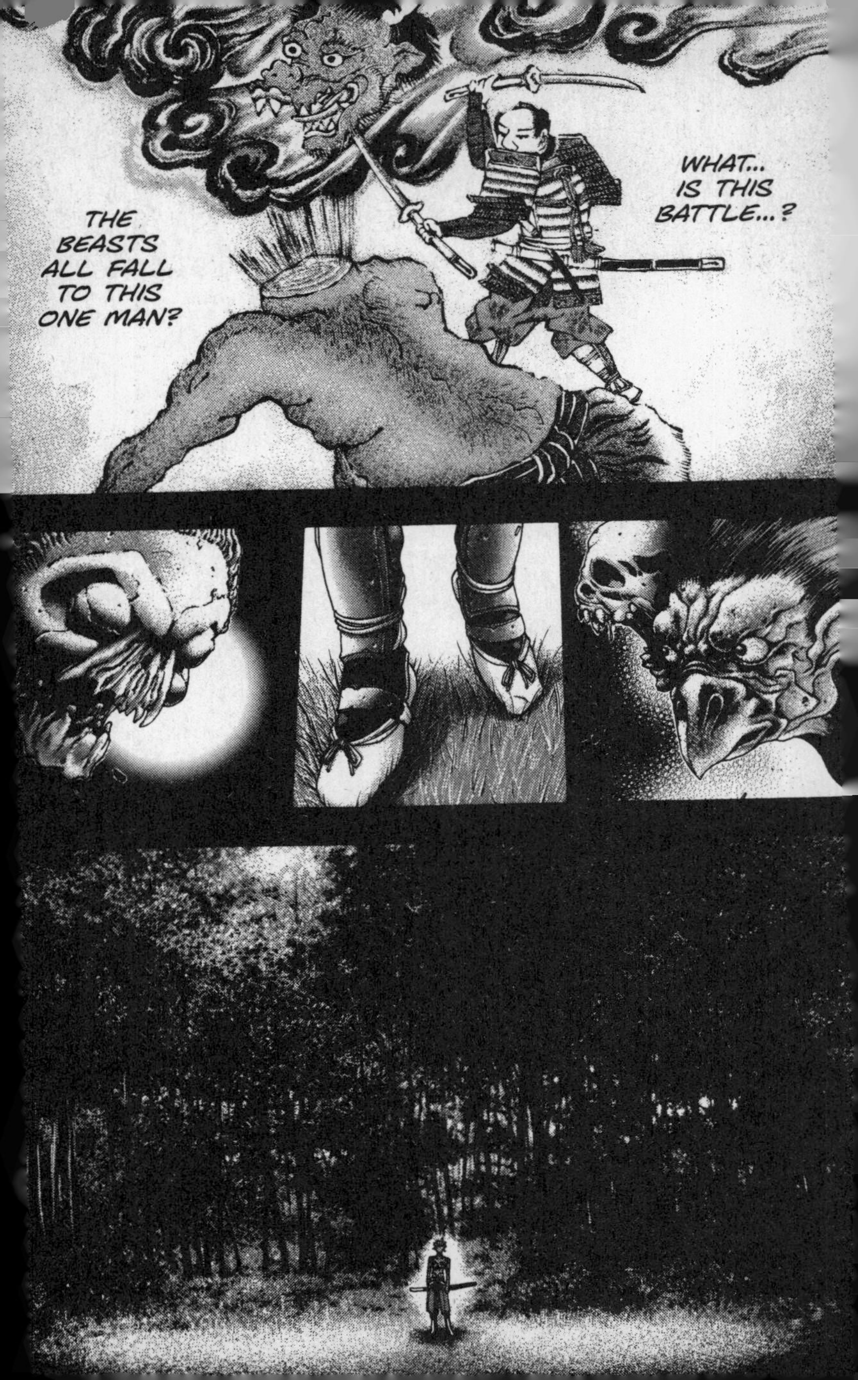
WHAT... IS THIS BATTLE...?
THE BEASTS ALL FALL TO THIS ONE MAN?

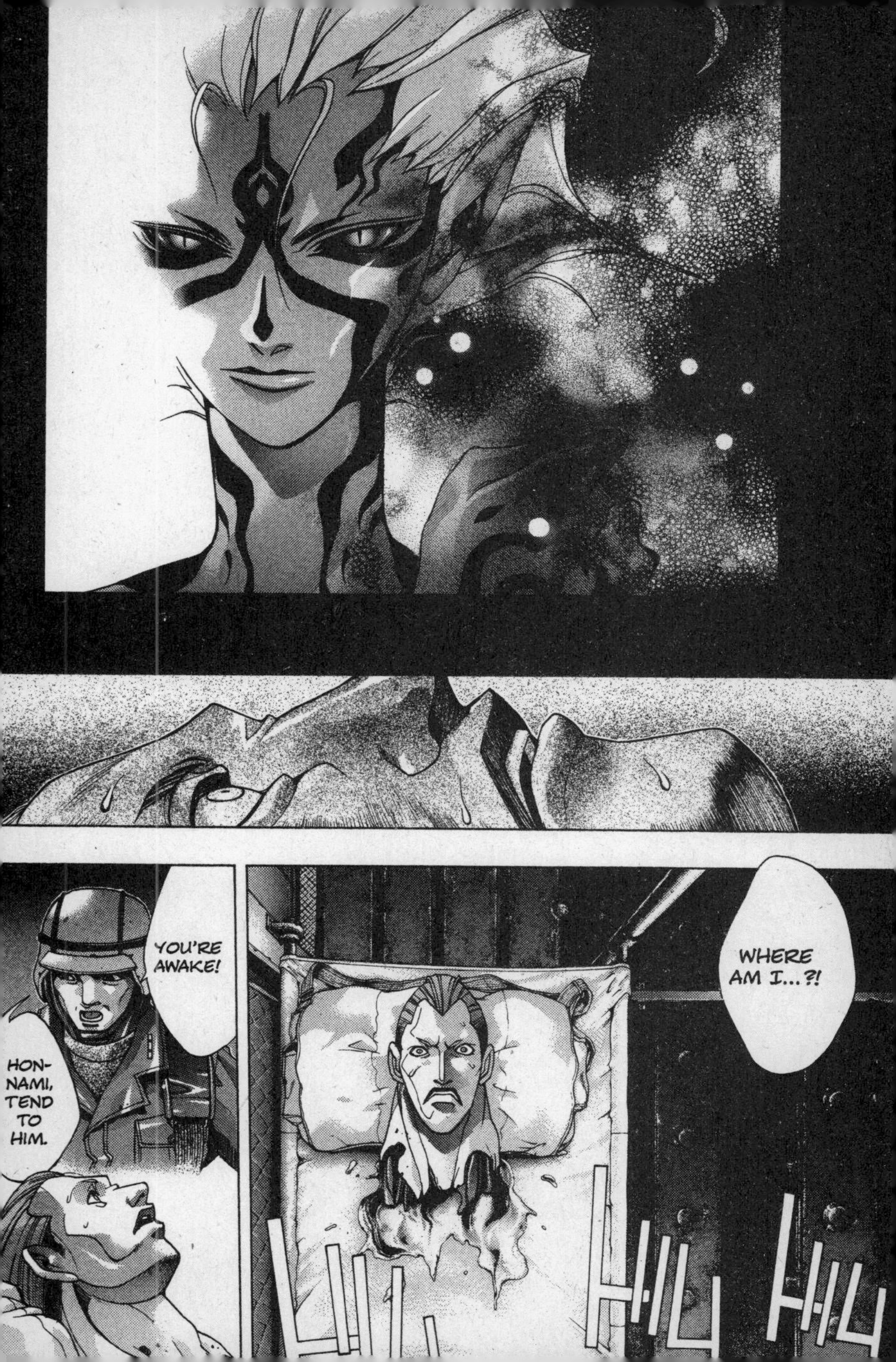
WHERE AM I...?!
YOU'RE AWAKE!
HON-NAMI, TEND TO HIM.

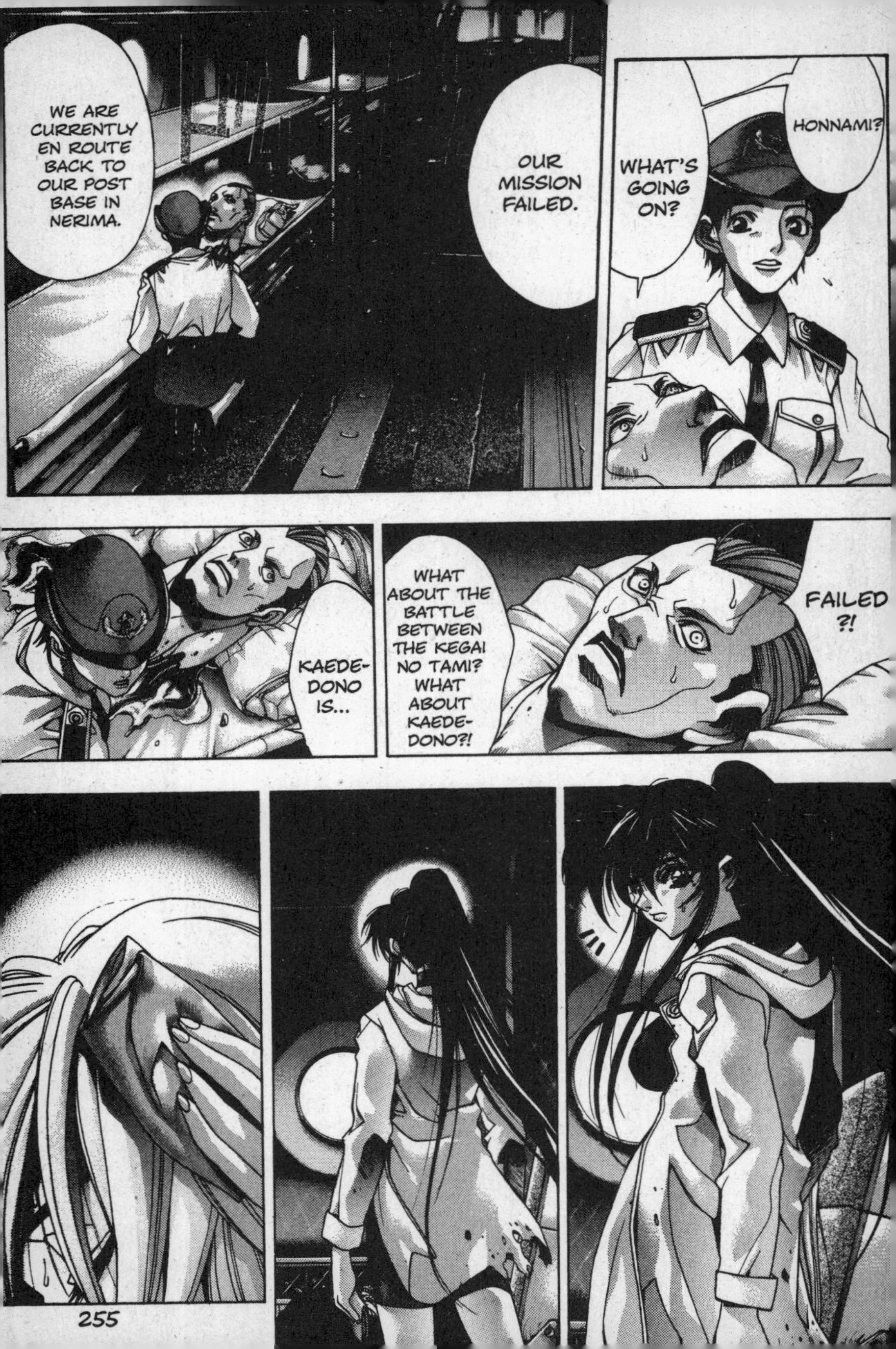
HONNAMI?
WHAT'S GOING ON?
OUR MISSION FAILED.
WE ARE CURRENTLY EN ROUTE BACK TO OUR POST BASE IN NERIMA.
FAILED ?!
WHAT ABOUT THE BATTLE BETWEEN THE KEGAI NO TAMI? WHAT ABOUT KAEDE-DONO?!
KAEDE-DONO IS...

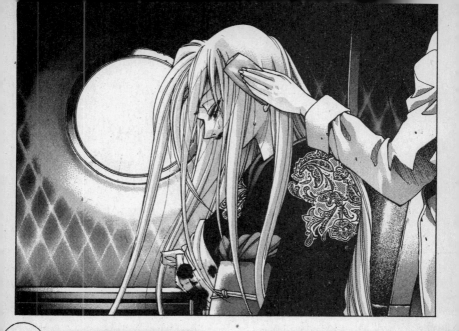

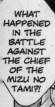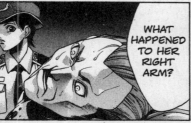 WHAT HAPPENED IN THE BATTLE AGAINST THE CHIEF OF THE MIZU NO TAMI?!

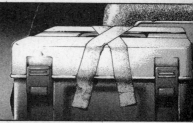 WHAT HAPPENED TO HER RIGHT ARM?

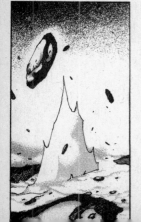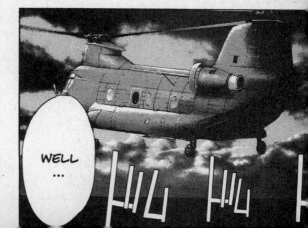 WELL ...

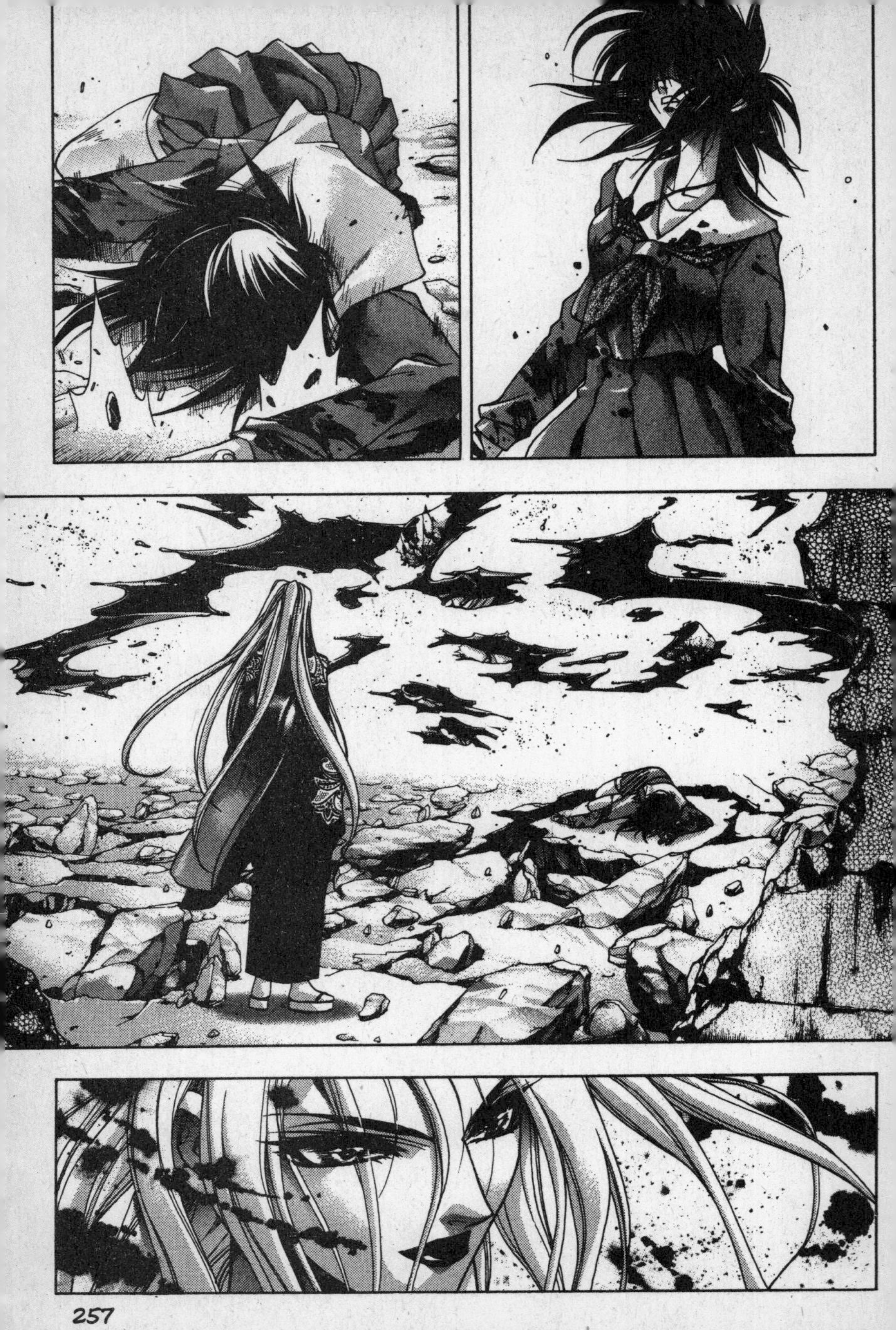

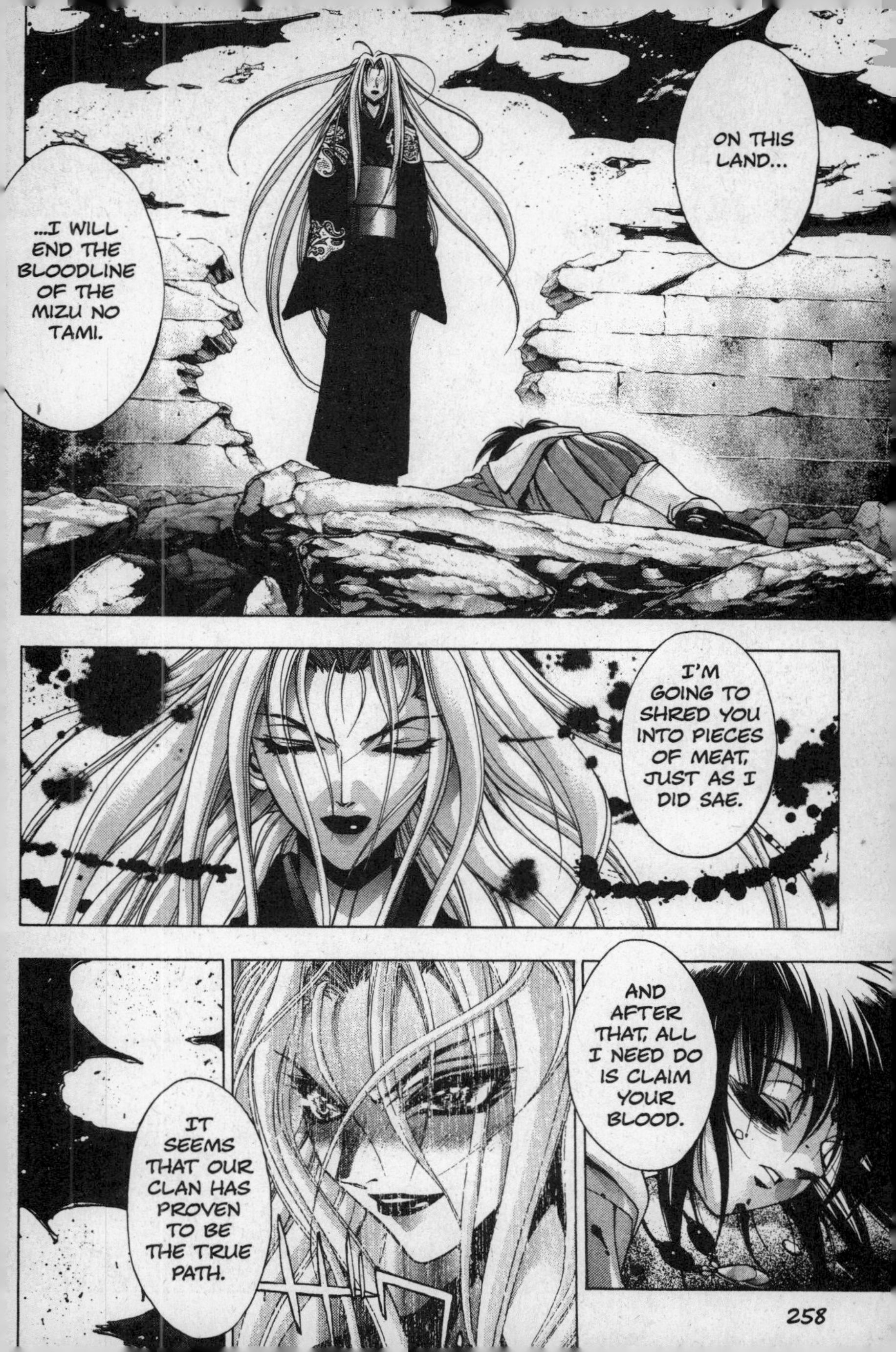
ON THIS LAND...
...I WILL END THE BLOODLINE OF THE MIZU NO TAMI.
I'M GOING TO SHRED YOU INTO PIECES OF MEAT, JUST AS I DID SAE.
AND AFTER THAT, ALL I NEED DO IS CLAIM YOUR BLOOD.
IT SEEMS THAT OUR CLAN HAS PROVEN TO BE THE TRUE PATH.

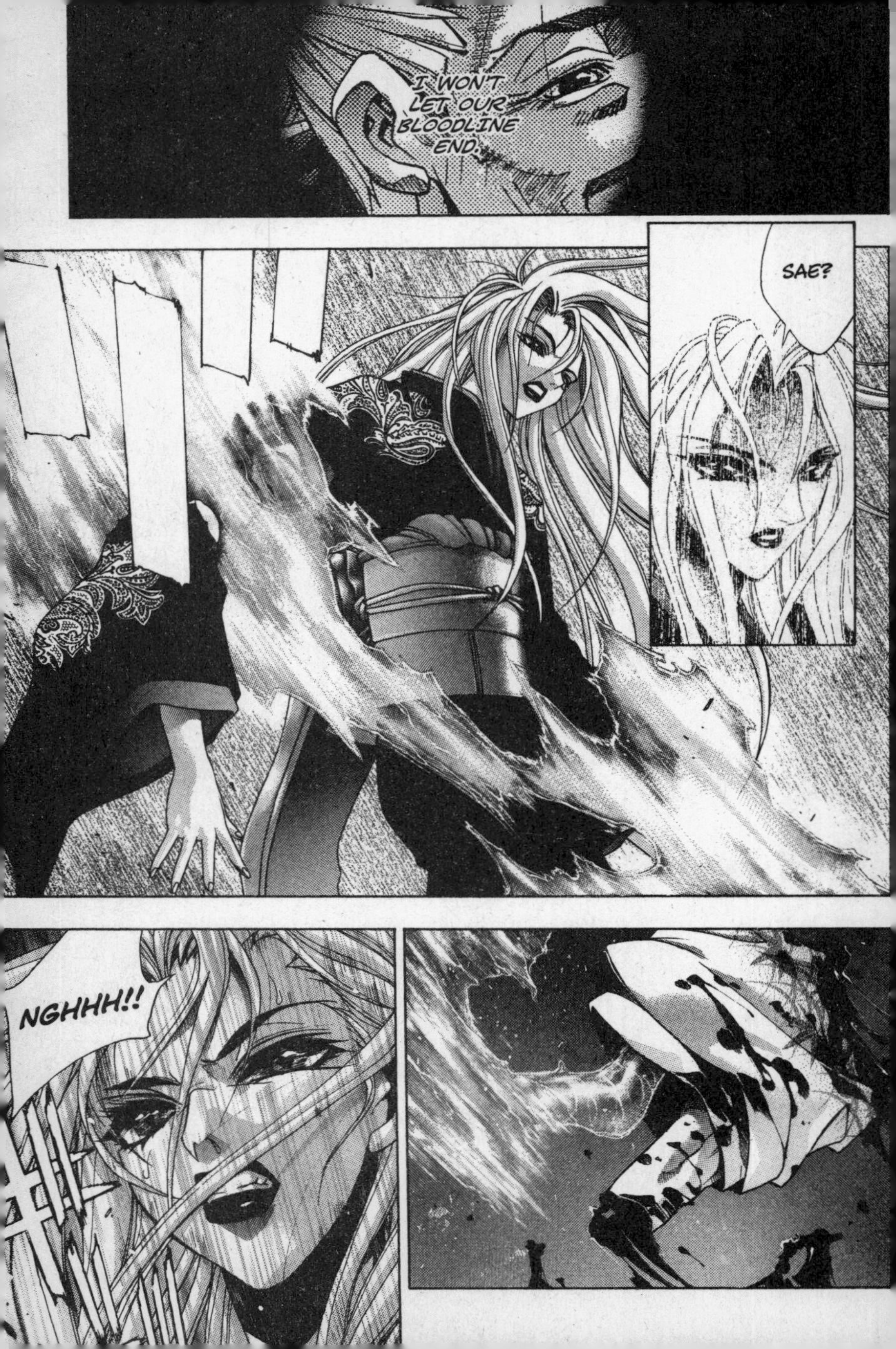
I WON'T LET OUR BLOODLINE END.
SAE?
NGHHH!!

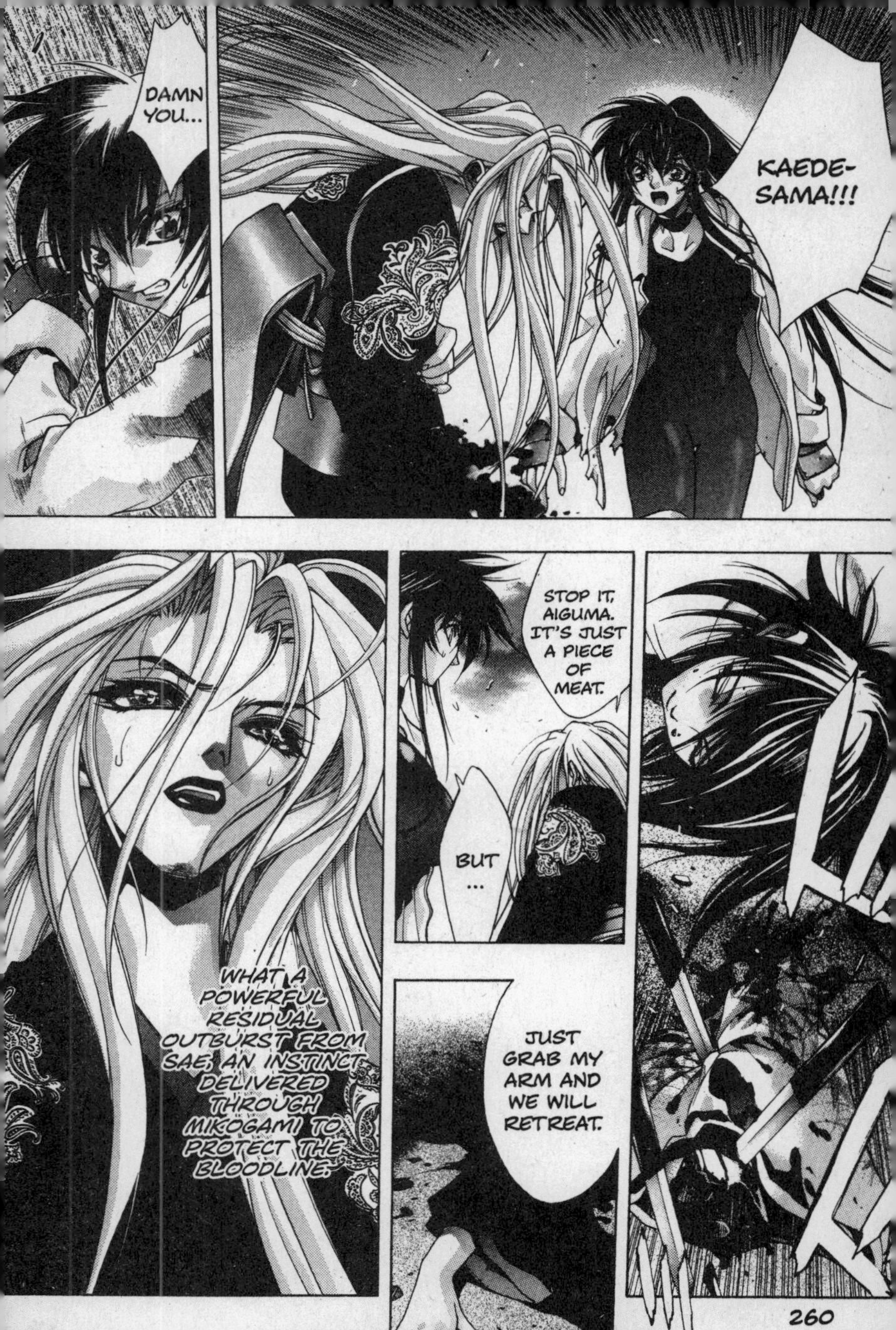
KAEDE-SAMA!!!
DAMN YOU...
STOP IT, AIGUMA. IT'S JUST A PIECE OF MEAT.
BUT ...
JUST GRAB MY ARM AND WE WILL RETREAT.
WHAT A POWERFUL RESIDUAL OUTBURST FROM SAE, AN INSTINCT DELIVERED THROUGH MIKOGAMI TO PROTECT THE BLOODLINE.

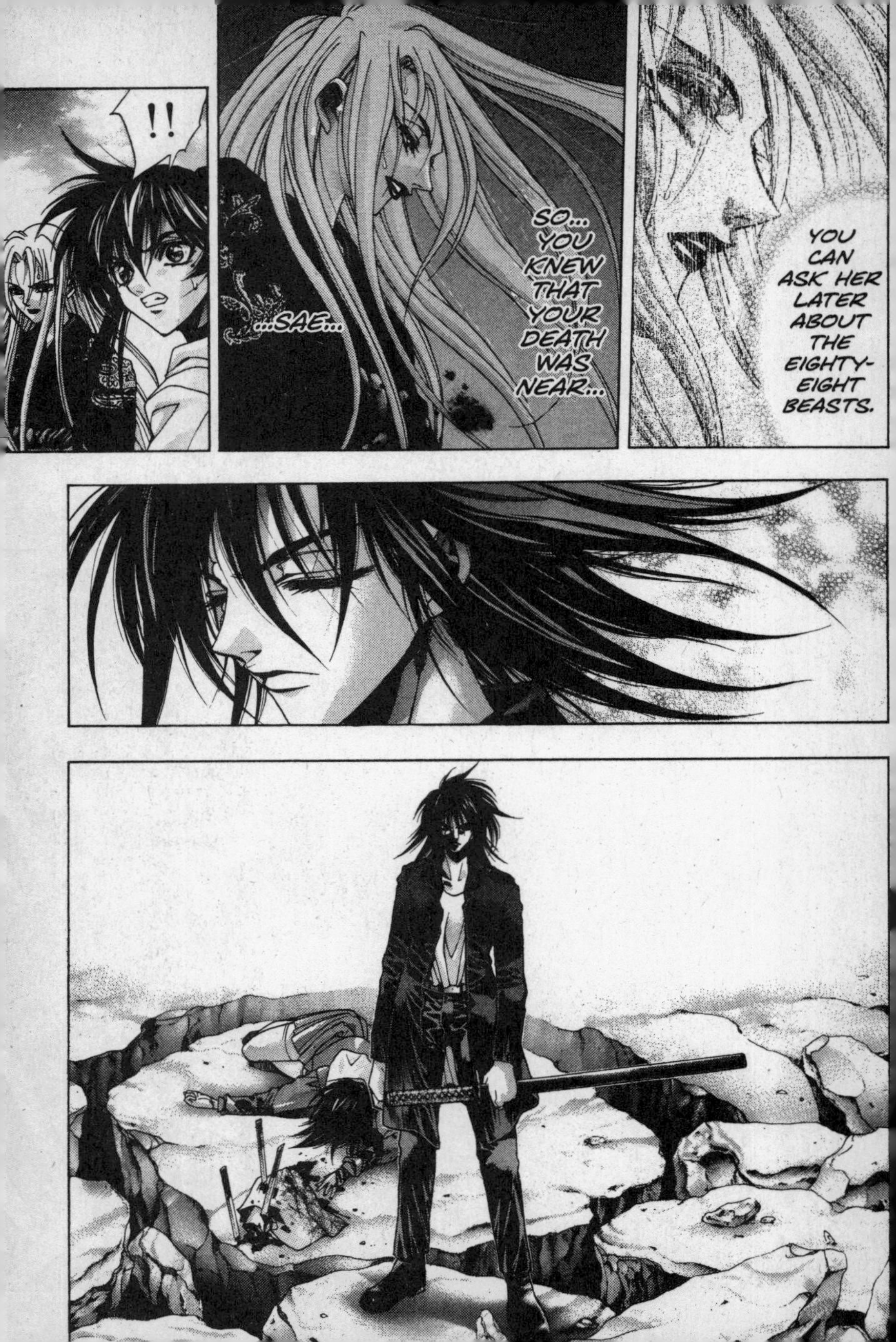
YOU CAN ASK HER LATER ABOUT THE EIGHTY-EIGHT BEASTS.
SO... YOU KNEW THAT YOUR DEATH WAS NEAR...
...SAE...
!!

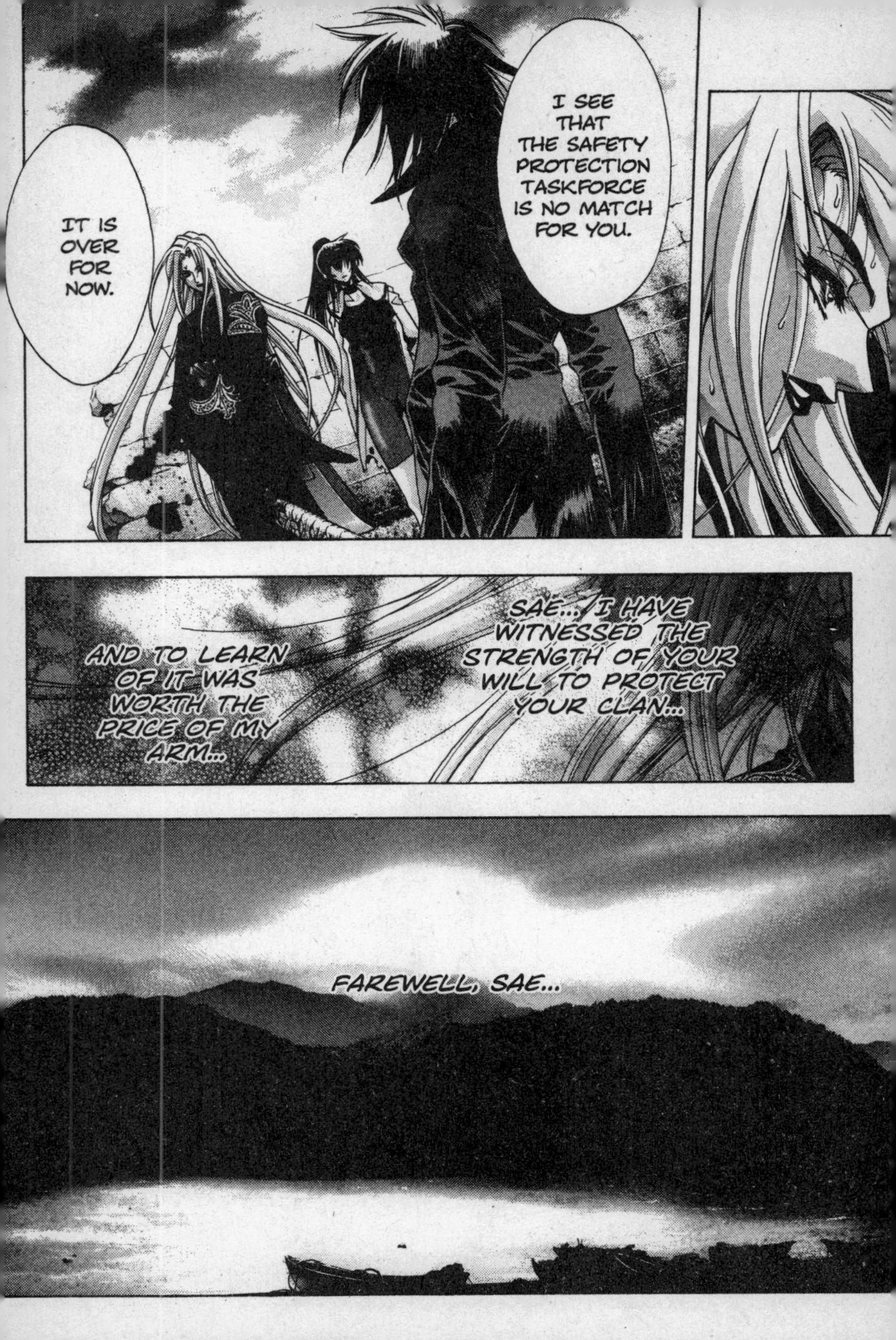
I SEE THAT THE SAFETY PROTECTION TASKFORCE IS NO MATCH FOR YOU.
IT IS OVER FOR NOW.
SAE... I HAVE WITNESSED THE STRENGTH OF YOUR WILL TO PROTECT YOUR CLAN...
AND TO LEARN OF IT WAS WORTH THE PRICE OF MY ARM...
FAREWELL, SAE...

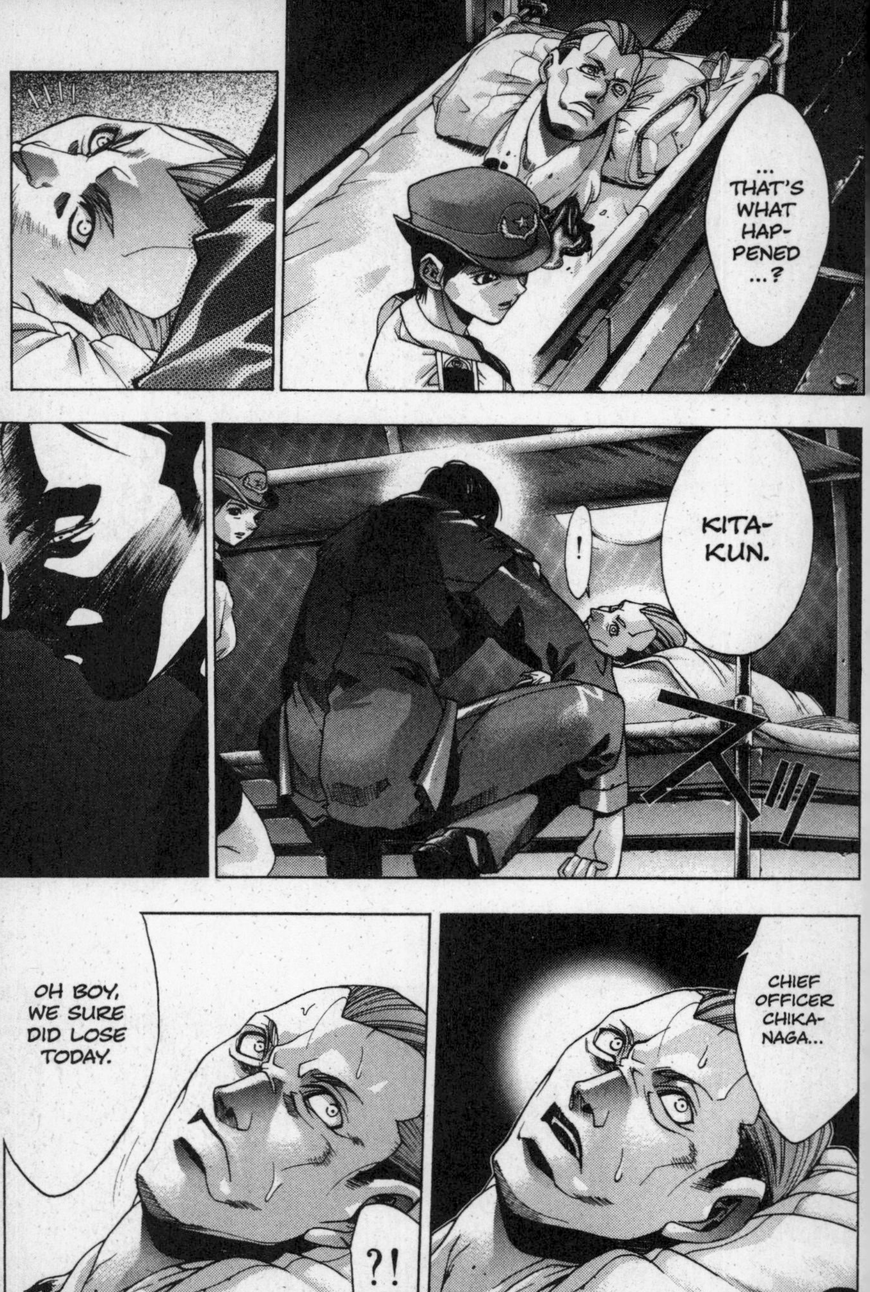

... THAT'S WHAT HAP-PENED ...?
KITA-KUN.
!
CHIEF OFFICER CHIKA-NAGA...
OH BOY, WE SURE DID LOSE TODAY.
?!

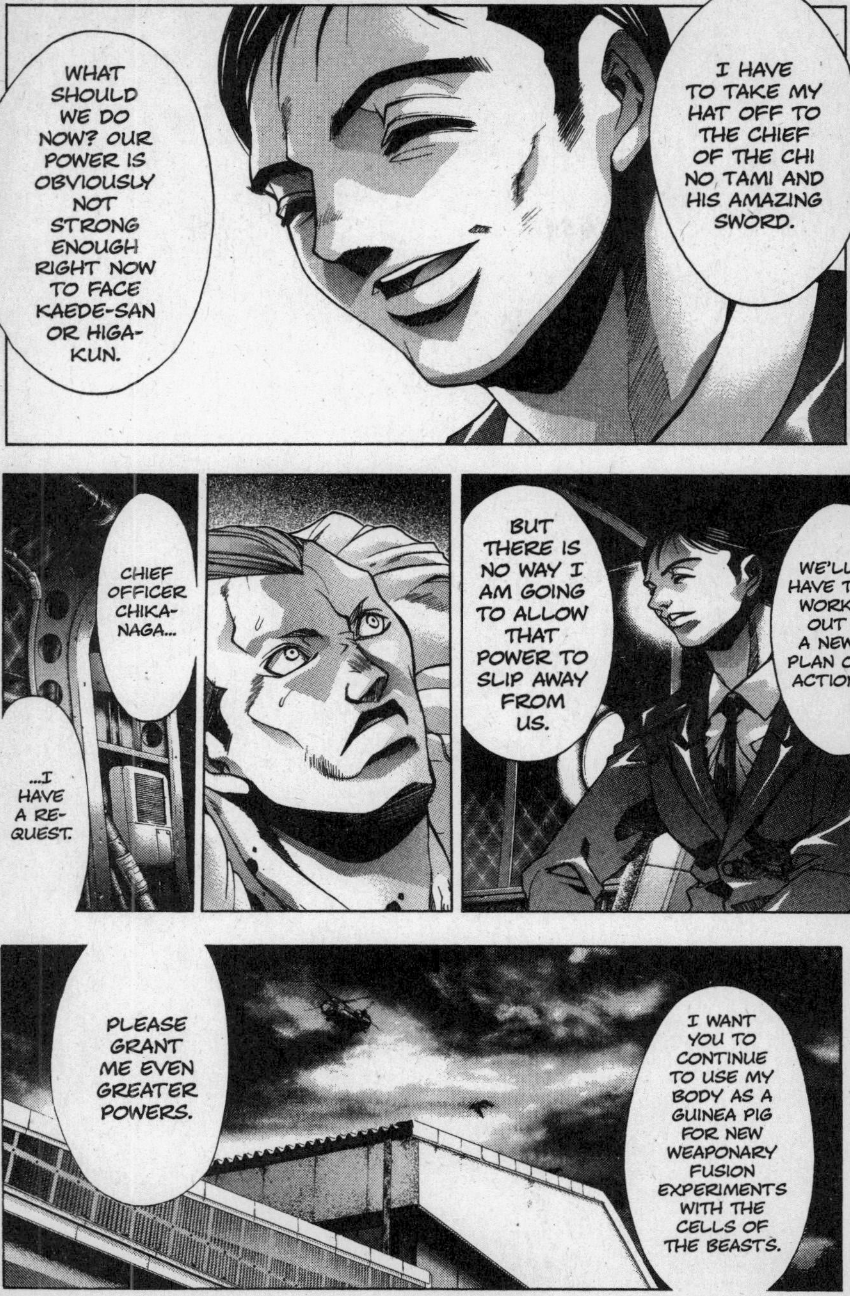
I HAVE TO TAKE MY HAT OFF TO THE CHIEF OF THE CHI NO TAMI AND HIS AMAZING SWORD.
WHAT SHOULD WE DO NOW? OUR POWER IS OBVIOUSLY NOT STRONG ENOUGH RIGHT NOW TO FACE KAEDE-SAN OR HIGA-KUN.
WE'LL HAVE TO WORK OUT A NEW PLAN OF ACTION.
BUT THERE IS NO WAY I AM GOING TO ALLOW THAT POWER TO SLIP AWAY FROM US.
CHIEF OFFICER CHIKA-NAGA...
...I HAVE A RE-QUEST.
PLEASE GRANT ME EVEN GREATER POWERS.
I WANT YOU TO CONTINUE TO USE MY BODY AS A GUINEA PIG FOR NEW WEAPONARY FUSION EXPERIMENTS WITH THE CELLS OF THE BEASTS.

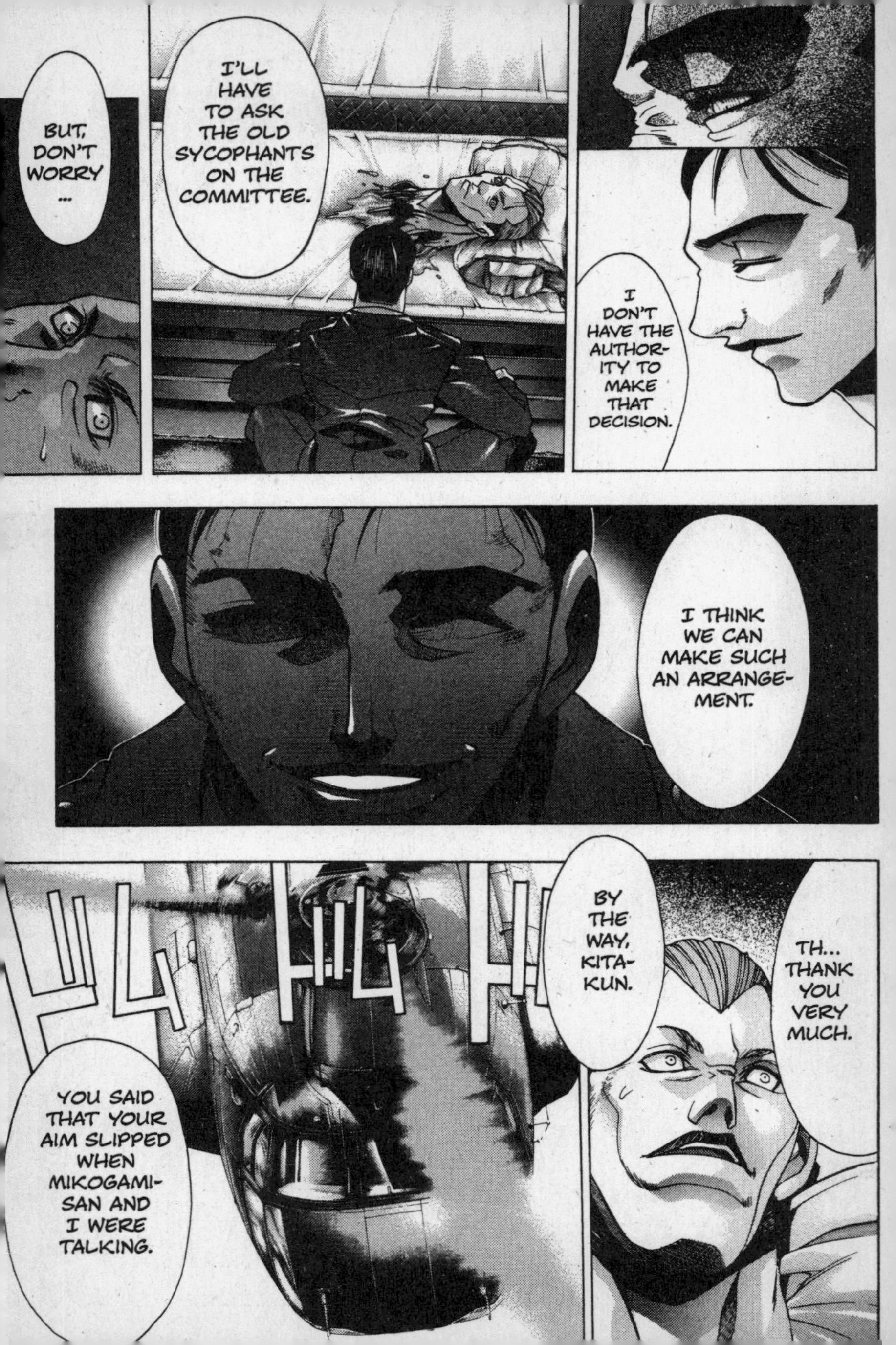
I DON'T HAVE THE AUTHORITY TO MAKE THAT DECISION.
I'LL HAVE TO ASK THE OLD SYCOPHANTS ON THE COMMITTEE.
BUT, DON'T WORRY ...
I THINK WE CAN MAKE SUCH AN ARRANGEMENT.
TH... THANK YOU VERY MUCH.
BY THE WAY, KITA-KUN.
YOU SAID THAT YOUR AIM SLIPPED WHEN MIKOGAMI-SAN AND I WERE TALKING.

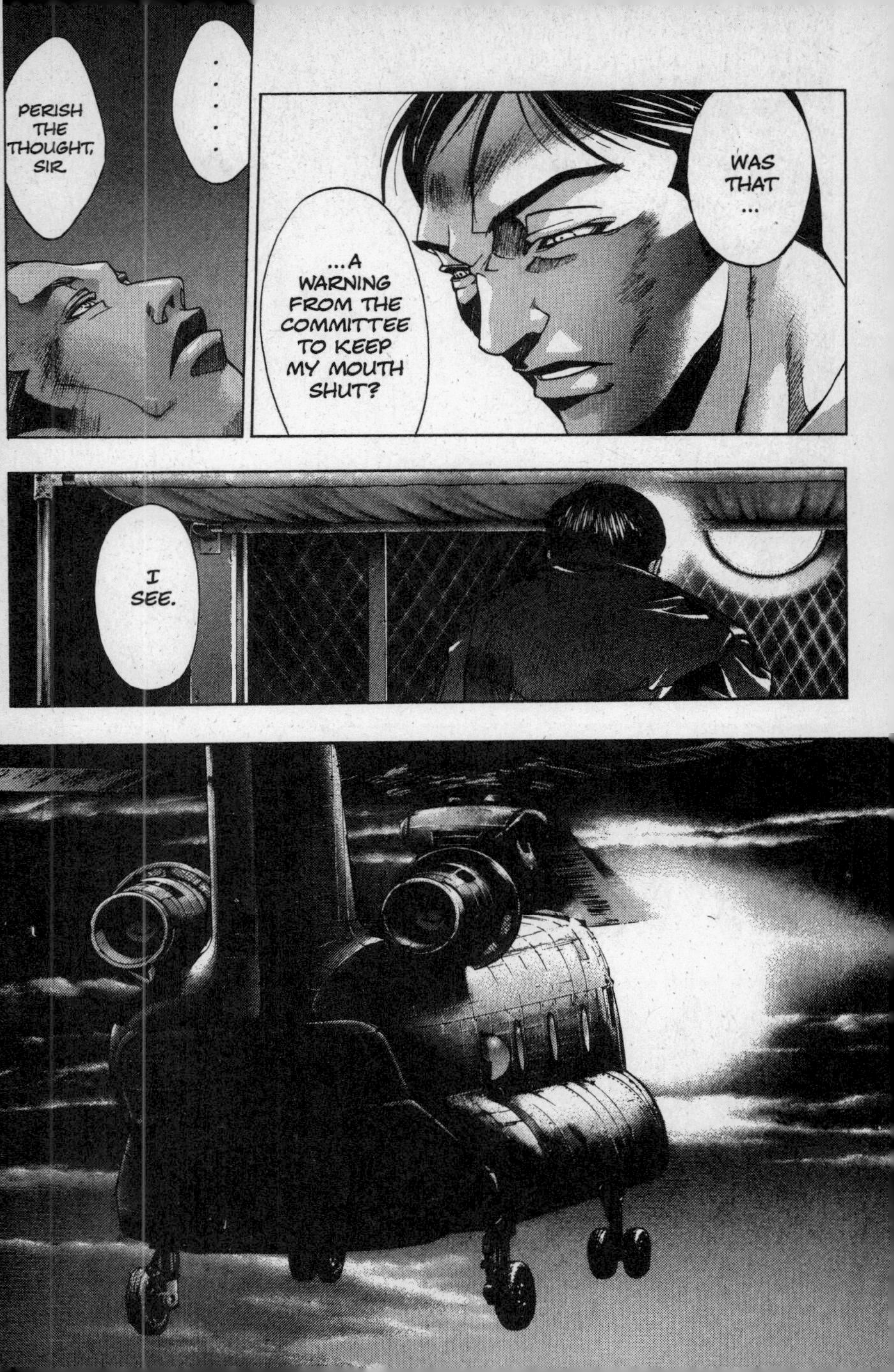
WAS THAT ...
...A WARNING FROM THE COMMITTEE TO KEEP MY MOUTH SHUT?
.....
PERISH THE THOUGHT, SIR
I SEE.

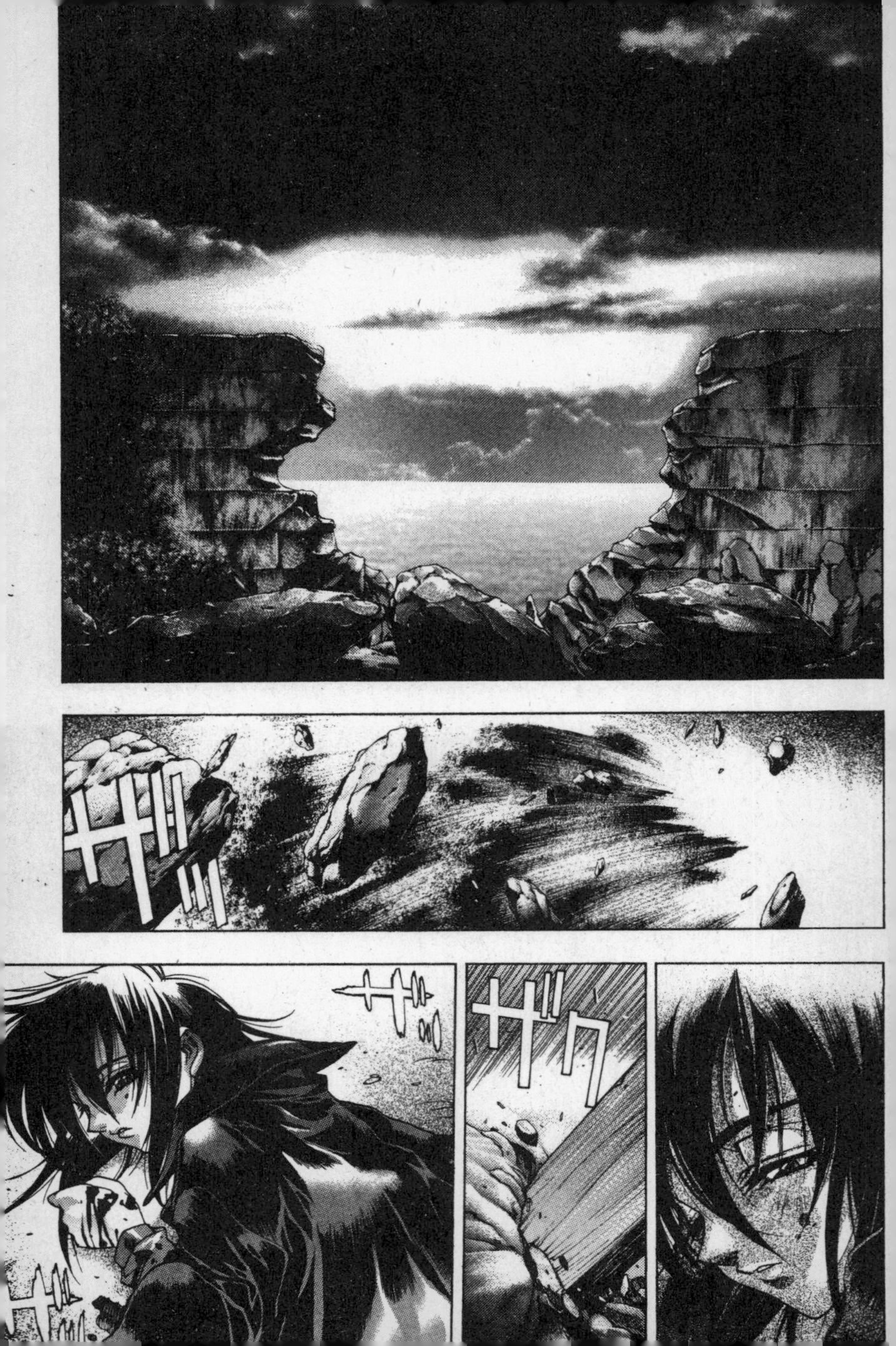
ザク

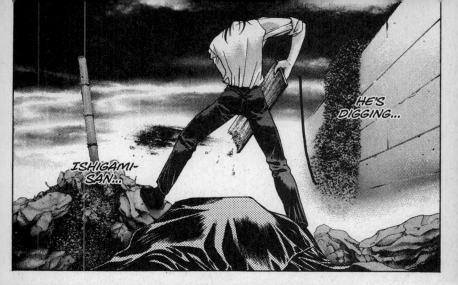

HE'S DIGGING...

ISHIGAMI-SAN...

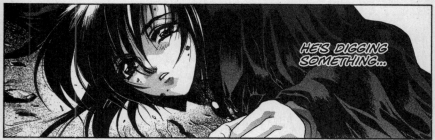

HE'S DIGGING SOMETHING...

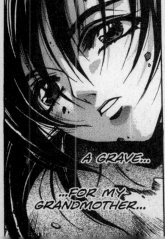

A GRAVE...

...FOR MY GRANDMOTHER...

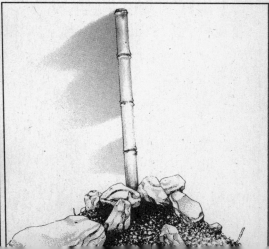

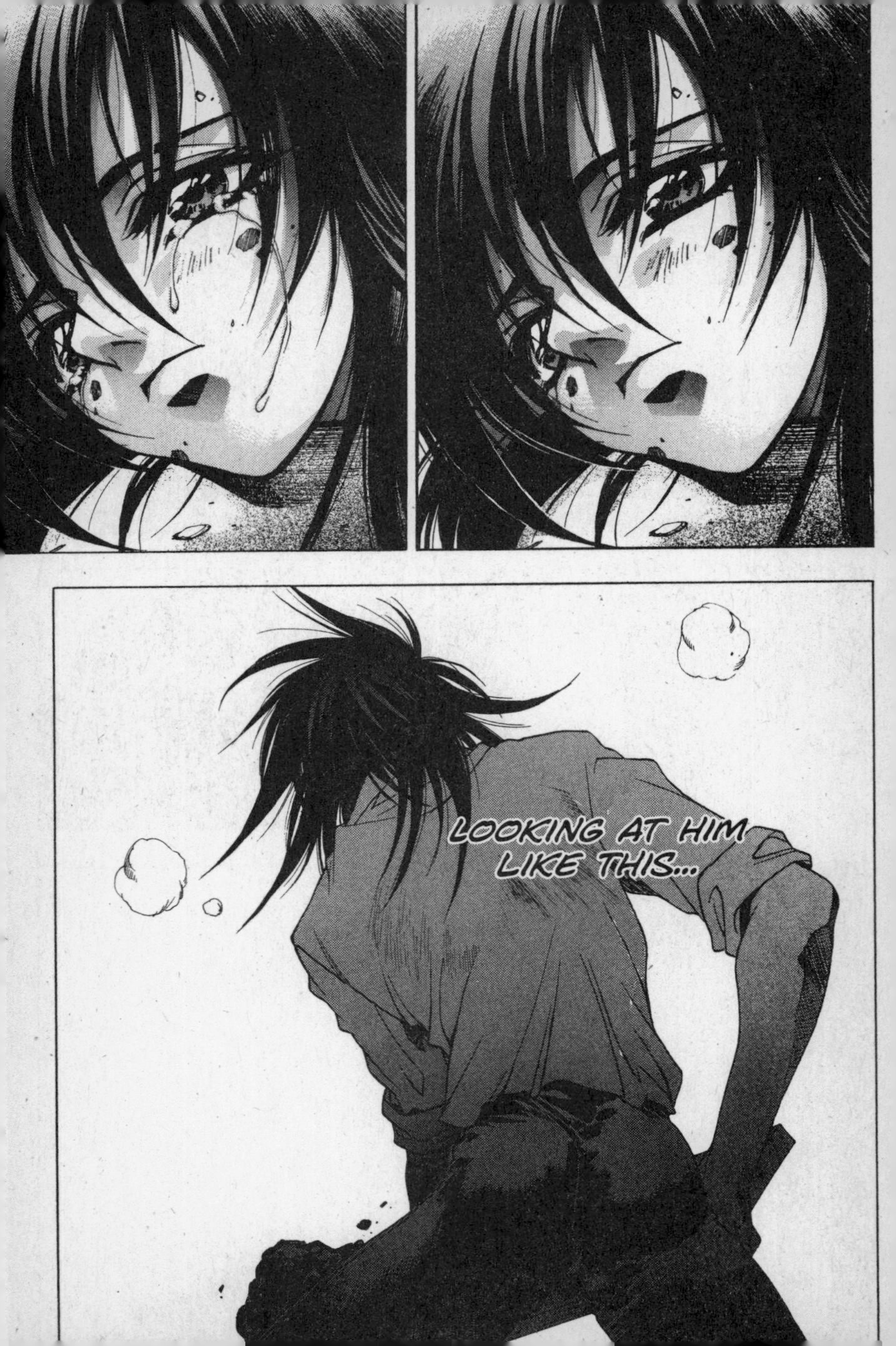
LOOKING AT HIM LIKE THIS...

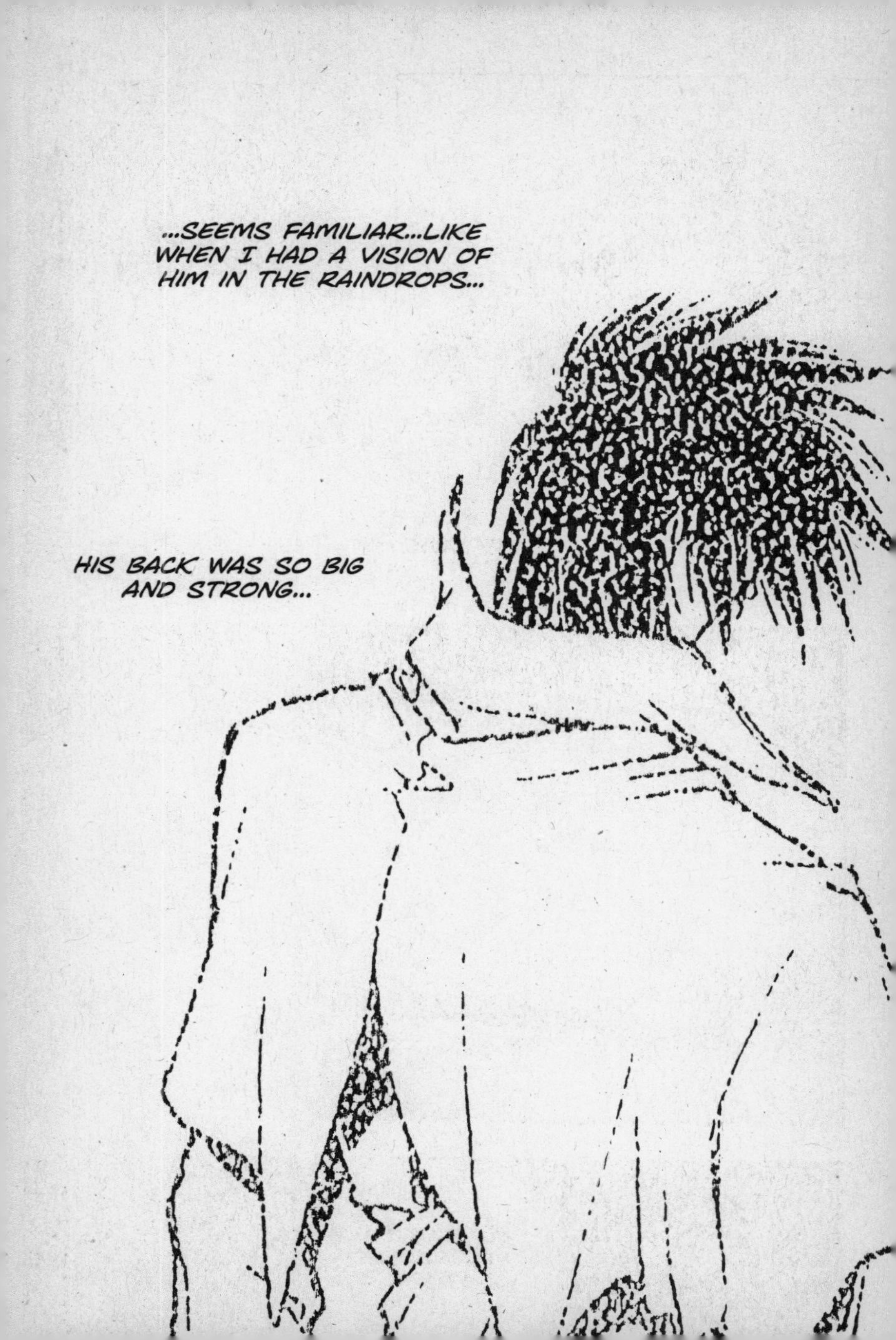
...SEEMS FAMILIAR...LIKE WHEN I HAD A VISION OF HIM IN THE RAINDROPS...
HIS BACK WAS SO BIG AND STRONG...

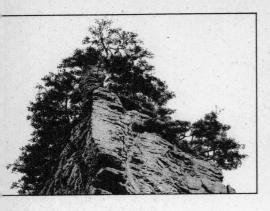

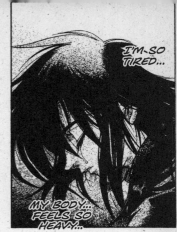

I'M SO TIRED...

MY BODY... FEELS SO HEAVY...

TODAY WAS SUCH A LONG DAY...

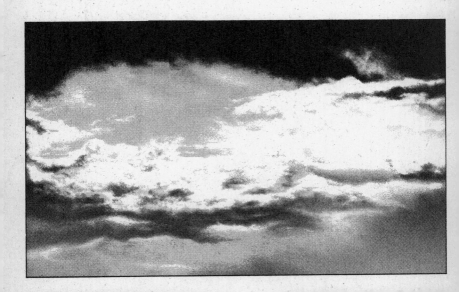

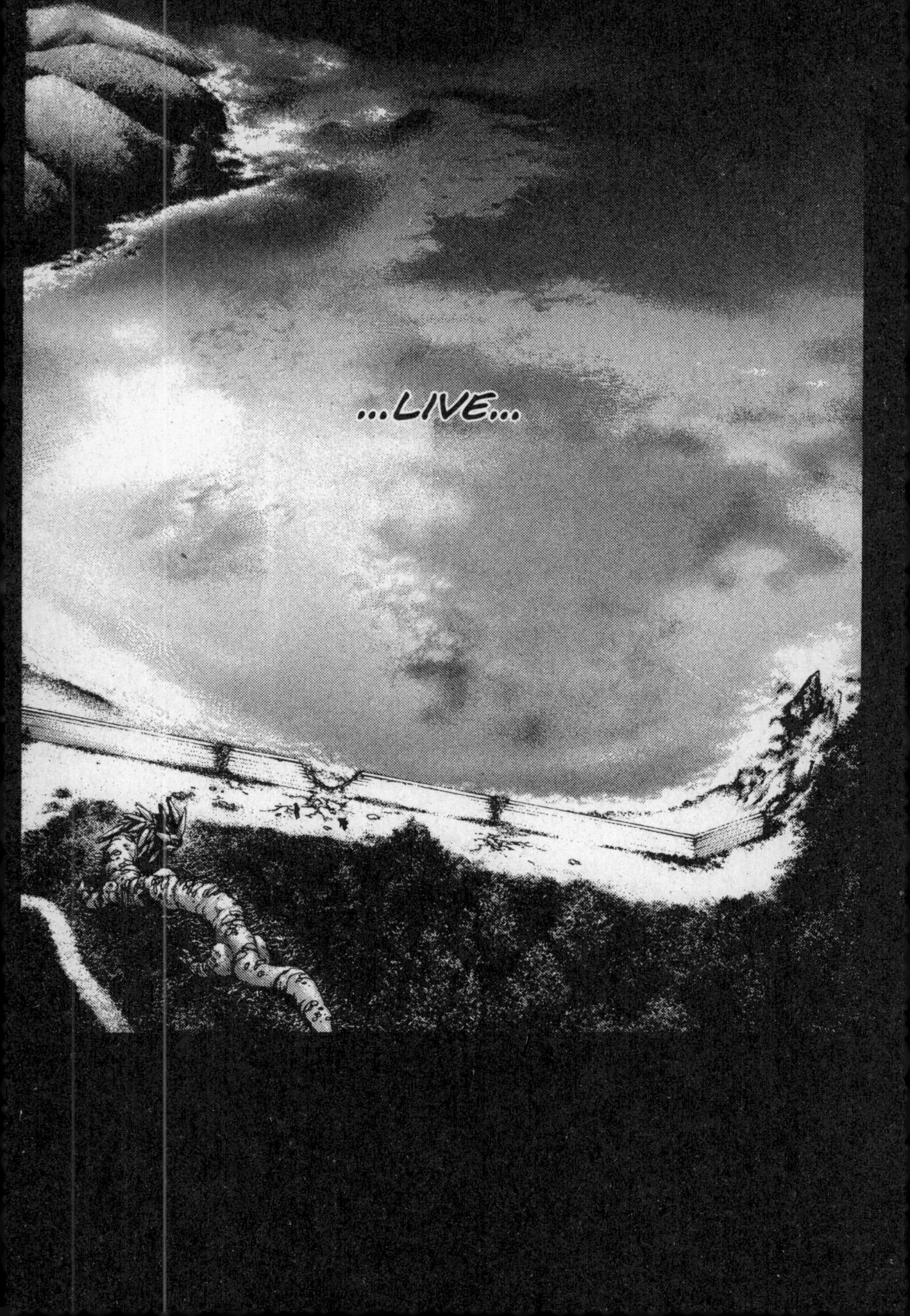
...LIVE...

To be continued in VOLUME 4

In the next VOLUME of

KAMI·KAZE ™

Once divided, our heroes are rejoined and new battles unfold. Beniguma reunites with Misao, surprised by the newfound strength she seems to possess, only to come across Kamuro locked in combat with a hot-headed Aida. Together, the group journeys to the Hani no Tami village—Kamuro's birthplace. There Kamuro will confront demons of the inner sort as he faces the graves of his murdered people. But it is a necessary struggle, for he must make peace with his past if he is to have any hope of defeating what lies ahead in his future.

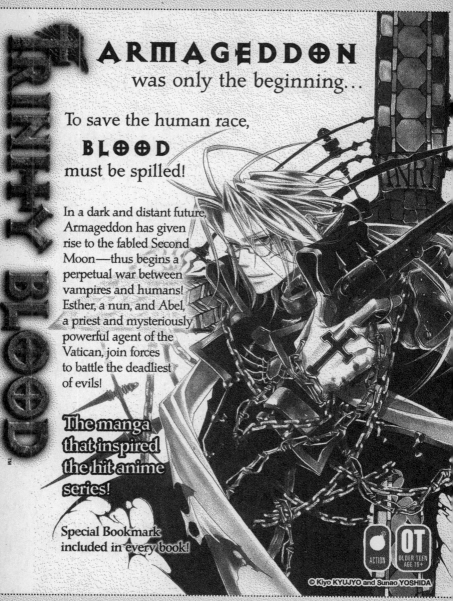

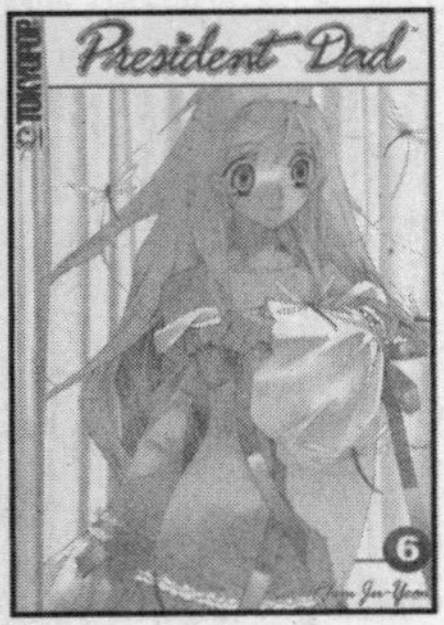
President Dad
TOKYOPOP
6

COMEDY

TEEN AGE 13+

PRESIDENT DAD

BY JU-YEON RHIM

In spite of the kind of dorky title, this book is tremendously fun and stylish. The mix of romance and truly bizarre comedy won me over in a heartbeat. When young Ami's father becomes the new president of South Korea, suddenly she is forced into a limelight that she never looked for and isn't particularly excited about. She's got your typical teenage crushes on pop idols (and a mysterious boy from her past who may be a North Korean spy! Who'd have thought there'd be global politics thrown into a shojo series?!), and more than her fair share of crazy relatives, but now she's also got a super-tough bodyguard who can disguise himself as anyone you can possibly imagine, and the eyes of the nation are upon her! This underrated manhwa totally deserves a second look!

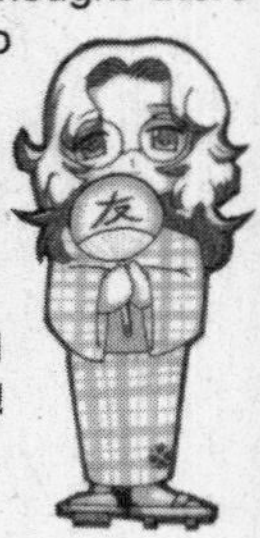

~Lillian Diaz-Pryzbyl, Editor

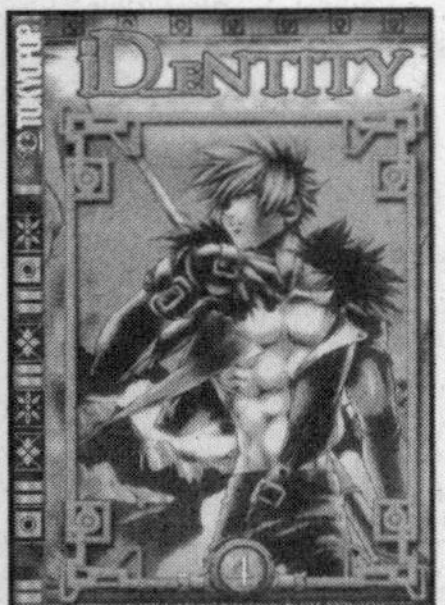
iDENTITY
TOKYOPOP
4

ACTION

TEEN AGE 13+

ID_ENTITY

BY HEE-JOON SON AND YOUN-KYUNG KIM

As a fan of online gaming, I've really been enjoying *iD_eNTITY.* Packed with action, intrigue and loads of laughs, *iD_eNTITY* is a raucous romp through a virtual world that's obviously written and illustrated by fellow gamers. Hee-Joon Son and Youn-Kyung Kim utilize gaming's terms and conventions while keeping the story simple and entertaining enough for noobs (a glossary of gaming terms is included in the back). Anyone else out there who has already absorbed *.hack* and is looking for a new gaming adventure to go on would do well to start here.

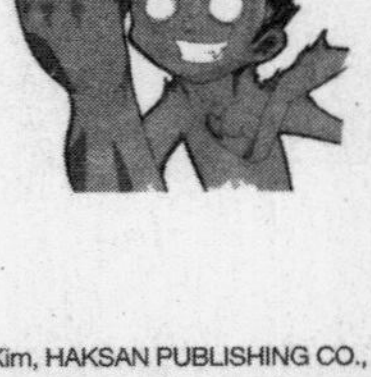

~Tim Beedle, Editor

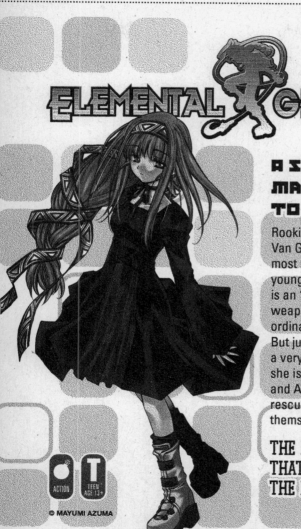

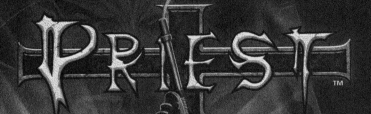

STOP!

This is the back of the
You wouldn't want to spoil a great ending

This book is printed "manga-style," in the authentic Japanese right-to-left format. Since none of the artwork has been flipped or altered, readers get to experience the story just as the creator intended. You've been asking for it, so TOKYOPOP® delivered: authentic, hot-off-the-press, and far more fun!

DIRECTIONS

If this is your first time reading manga-style, here's a quick guide to help you understand how it works.

It's easy... just start in the top right panel and follow the numbers. Have fun, and look for more 100% authentic manga from TOKYOPOP®!

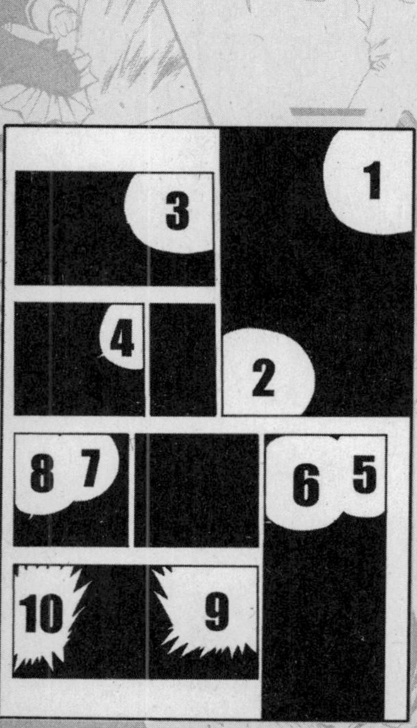
1
2
3
4
5
6
7
8
9
10

THE MANGA REVOLUTION · LEADING · 漫画革命 · LEADING · THE MANGA REVOLUTION

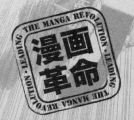